Defending Young People

in the criminal justice system

SECOND EDITION

Mark Ashford is a solicitor with Taylor Nichol, a legal aid practice in north London, where he specialises in representing young people. He regularly trains both lawyers and social workers on the youth justice system as well as speaking on subjects related to youth crime.

Alex Chard is a social work consultant at Youth Crime Training and Consultancy Services which provides management and consultancy to local authorities regarding their services to young offenders. He also trains lawyers, magistrates and social workers.

The Legal Action Group is a national, independent charity which campaigns for equal access to justice for all members of society. Legal Action Group:
- provides support to the practice of lawyers and advisers
- inspires developments in that practice
- campaigns for improvements in the law and the administration of justice
- stimulates debate on how services should be delivered.

Defending Young People

in the criminal justice system

SECOND EDITION

Mark Ashford, SOLICITOR
and
Alex Chard, SOCIAL WORK CONSULTANT

 Legal Action Group
2000

This edition published in Great Britain 2000
by LAG Education and Service Trust Limited
242 Pentonville Road, London N1 9UN

First edition printed 1997

Legal Action Group
242 Pentonville Road
London N1 9UN

British Library Cataloguing in Publication Data
A CIP catalogue record for this book is available from the British Library

ISBN 0 905099 92 3

Typeset by RefineCatch Ltd, Bungay, Suffolk
Printed in Great Britain by Bell & Bain Ltd, Glasgow

Preface

The first edition of Defending Young People was published less than a month after the Labour Party came to power in 1997. Since then, there has been a torrent of policy initiatives, two major pieces of legislation, the creation of the Youth Justice Board of England and Wales and multi-agency youth offending teams. As a result of these changes, the need for well-informed and committed defence lawyers has never been greater.

This edition has been substantially revised and expanded to include all changes introduced by recent legislation. We have also established an Internet website at *www.youthjustice.co.uk* which gives access to relevant official guidance and related youth justice information. Access to this website is free.

As with the first edition, we cannot claim the credit for all the ideas contained in this book. We do, however, have to accept responsibility for any mistakes.

We have endeavoured to state the law in England and Wales as at 1 January 2000. Since then, while the book was being produced, amendments and implementation dates have been introduced by the Youth Justice and Criminal Evidence Act 1999. Wherever possible these have been added or noted in the text. At the last moment we have also added the Practice Direction on trial of children and young persons in the Crown Court at appendix 9 although it was not possible to refer to it in the text.

Mark Ashford
Alex Chard

March 2000

Preface to first edition

This book has been written during a period when the pendulum of political debate and media rhetoric with regard to young offenders has swung towards blame, punishment and vilification. The rhetoric ignores the fact that these young offenders are children. In our experience, almost without exception, those who appear in the youth court suffer poverty, neglect and abuse. Many of their parents lead chaotic, desperate lives, ground down by poverty and lack of opportunity. As both of the main political parties compete to be 'tough on crime', we are deeply concerned that many of the most vulnerable children in our society will pay the price. We can only hope that this book will help defence advocates to redress the balance.

We cannot claim credit for all the ideas contained in this book. Particular thanks are due to Helen Johnston for writing the early versions of Chapter 2, 'The relevance of age', Chapter 6, 'Parental involvement' and Chapter 11, 'The trial process'. Inevitably, we have also been informed by discussions and debate with colleagues, prosecutors, court clerks and magistrates. We would also like to express our thanks to all those, too numerous to mention individually, who have read and commented on parts of the text, as well as the staff of the Legal Action Group who have waited patiently for the text to be delivered. Finally, this book is dedicated to all those young people with whom we have worked. Because of them we have learned much about the law, through them we have learned much about life.

We have endeavoured to state the law in England and Wales as at 1 February 1997.

Mark Ashford
Alex Chard

April 1997

In loving memory of Basil Ashford

Contents

Table of cases

Table of statutes

Table of statutory instruments

Table of other legislation

List of tables

The youth justice system

Introduction

1.1   The youth justice system is the system of criminal justice insofar as it relates to children and young people.[1] In recent years the system has come under considerable criticism for its management deficiencies as well as its perceived failure to tackle youth offending. In 1996 the Audit Commission carried out a comprehensive survey of the youth justice system.[2] Their report identified a lack of co-ordination among the various agencies involved in the system which resulted in inefficient working practices and enormous delays. The Commission went on to make recommendations for significant change. Many of the recommendations for changes in the management of the system were introduced in the Crime and Disorder Act 1998.

1.2   The Labour government has published a White Paper: *No More Excuses – A New Approach to Tackling Youth Crime In England and Wales* (Cm 3809). In the preface the Home Secretary, Jack Straw, explains his assessment of the faults of the existing criminal justice system as it affects children and young persons:

> An excuse culture has developed within the youth justice system. It excuses itself for its inefficiency, and too often excuses the young offenders before it, implying that they cannot help their behaviour because of their social circumstances. Rarely are they confronted with their behaviour and helped to take more personal responsibility for their actions. The system allows them to go on wrecking their own lives as well as disrupting their families and communities.

In response to these perceived faults substantial reforms have been instituted. The White Paper states that the reform programme aims to provide:

– a clear strategy to prevent offending and re-offending;
– that offenders, and their parents, face up to their offending behaviour and take responsibility for it;
– earlier and more effective intervention when young people first offend;
– faster, more efficient procedures from arrest to sentence; and
– partnership between all youth justice agencies to deliver a better, faster system.

To effect these changes there has been a complete overhaul of the management structure of the agencies involved in the youth justice

---

1   Crime and Disorder Act 1998 s42(1).
2   *Misspent Youth* (Audit Commission, 1996).

system. The Youth Justice Board has been established to ensure national co-ordination and at the local level the various agencies are now required to work together to establish multi-agency teams called youth offending teams which will provide relevant services to the courts and young offenders.

Youth Justice Board for England and Wales

1.3 The Youth Justice Board was established on 30 September 1998 by the Crime and Disorder Act 1998 s41. The Board is a non-departmental public body, sponsored by the Home Office, and accountable to the Home Secretary. The Board consists of between ten and 12 members appointed by the Home Secretary, including people who have extensive recent experience of the youth justice system.

1.4 The functions of the Board include:

- monitoring the operation of the youth justice system and the provision of youth justice services;
- advising the Home Secretary on this and the setting of national standards for the provision of youth justice services and custodial accommodation;
- advising on how the principal aim of the youth justice system might most effectively be pursued; and
- identifying and promoting, and making grants for the development of, good practice in the operation of the youth justice system and the preventing of youth offending.[3]

In order to perform its function of monitoring the operation of the youth justice system, the Board has powers to require local authorities, police authorities, probation committees and health authorities to provide information.[4]

1.5 The government has decided in principle to extend this role to include the commissioning and purchasing of secure facilities for juveniles on remand and under sentence. This is likely to mean that the Board will also take over from the Home Office the responsibility for allocating juvenile prisoners within the secure estate. The Board is anticipated to assume this role in April 2000.[5]

3 Crime and Disorder Act 1998 s41(5).
4 Ibid, s41(5)(d).
5 Youth Justice Board for England and Wales *Corporate Plan 1999–2000 to 2001–02.*

Provision of youth justice services

1.6   Youth justice services are defined as:

- appropriate adult services;
- assessment and intervention work in support of a final warning;
- bail support;
- the placement in local authority accommodation of children and young people remanded or committed to such accommodation;
- reports and other information required by the courts;
- providing responsible officers in relation to parenting orders, child safety orders, reparation and action plan orders;
- supervision of children and young persons under supervision orders and detention and training orders;
- supervision of young persons under probation orders, community service orders or combination orders; and
- post-release supervision of children and young persons released from custody;[6]
- the implementation of referral orders under the Youth Justice and Criminal Evidence Act 1999.

1.7   By Crime and Disorder Act 1998 s38(1) every local authority with responsibility for education and social services has a duty to secure that, to such an extent as is appropriate for their area, all the youth justice services listed above are available in their area. A duty to co-operate with the local authority in the discharge of this obligation is placed on:

- every chief officer of police or police authority any part of whose area lies within the local authority's area;
- every probation committee or health authority any part of whose area lies within the local authority's area.[7]

1.8   Local authorities have been under statutory duties to provide most of the youth justice services listed above for some time. It should be noted, however, that for the first time there is now an express duty to provide an appropriate adult service as well as a duty to provide bail support services.

1.9   The Crime and Disorder Act 1998 s38 is currently only in force in certain pilot areas.[8] It is expected that it will be in force nationally in April 2000.

6   Ibid, s38(4) as amended by Youth Justice and Criminal Evidence Act 1999 Sch 4 para 28.
7   Ibid, s38(2).
8   For the pilot areas, see Appendix 8.

Youth offending teams

1.10   Every local authority with responsibility for education and social services is under a duty to establish for its area one or more youth offending teams.[9] It is possible for neighbouring local authorities to establish a joint youth offending team.[10] A duty is placed on the relevant police service, probation committee and health authority to co-operate in the discharge of the local authority's duty to establish youth offending teams.[11]

1.11   A youth offending team must consist of at least one of each of the following:

- a probation officer;
- a social worker of a local authority social services department;
- a police officer;
- a person nominated by a health authority; and
- a person nominated by the chief education officer.[12]

1.12   The first youth offending teams were established in pilot areas on 30 September 1998.[13] It is intended that youth offending teams will be established in all local authority areas by April 2000.

Youth justice plans

1.13   Following consultation with the relevant police service, probation committee and health authority every local authority with responsibility for education and social services must formulate and implement an annual youth justice plan. The plan must detail:

- how youth justice services are to be provided and funded;
- how the youth offending team is to be composed and funded, how it is to operate and what functions it is to carry out.

Youth justice plans must be submitted to the Youth Justice Board each year and published as directed by the Secretary of State.[14]

---

9 Ibid, s39(1).
10 Ibid, s39(2).
11 Ibid, s39(3).
12 Ibid, s39(5).
13 For the pilot areas see Appendix 8.
14 Ibid, s40(4). The Youth Justice Board has indicated that the first youth justice plans will be required by December 1999 (see *Corporate Plan 1999–2000 to 2001–02*).

Sources of law

1.14   The law and guiding principles applicable to the youth justice system may be found in both domestic law and in international standards.

Domestic law

1.15   Despite the existence of a specialist criminal court to deal with defendants under the age of 18, the law relating to children and young persons is not to be found solely in one statute. Instead relevant statutory provisions are scattered through a series of statutes spanning more than 60 years. It is perhaps inevitable that the relevant law is not wholly consistent in content or purpose.

1.16   Even following the major reforms of the management of the youth justice system introduced by the Crime and Disorder Act 1998, it is still best to think of the law relating to children and young persons in the criminal justice system as an adaptation of the rules applying to adults. The main pieces of legislation which alter those rules are the Children and Young Persons Acts of 1933, 1963 and 1969, although important procedural rules are also contained in the Magistrates' Courts Act 1980. In relation to sentencing practice, the framework established by the Criminal Justice Act 1991 applies, with modifications, to children and young persons. The possible sentences which may be imposed upon a child or young person are contained in seven different statutes (soon to be eight, upon implementation of the Youth Justice and Criminal Evidence Act 1999).[15]

1.17   As well as having a good working knowledge of the procedural rules, the defence lawyer must be familiar with the Children Act 1989. This Act creates the legal framework for the role of the state in the care of children and as such is of great significance when working with children or young persons in trouble with the law. The Act also imposes certain specific obligations upon local authorities which relate to the criminal justice system.

---

15   In the opinion of the authors there is much to be said for a consolidating statute which would contain all statutory provisions relating to the youth justice system.

International standards

European Convention on Human Rights (1951)

1.18 The European Convention for the Protection of Human Rights and Fundamental Freedoms (1950) (Cmd 8969) was adopted by the member states of the Council of Europe in 1950. It was ratified by the United Kingdom in 1951. It is usually referred to as the European Convention on Human Rights. With implementation of the Human Rights Act 1998 (due in October 2000) it will be unlawful for any public authority, including a court, to act in a manner which is incompatible with a Convention right. Even in the case of primary legislation every court will have to strive to interpret the statute to ensure compatibility with Convention rights. If this proves impossible the higher courts (High Court, Court of Appeal and House of Lords) will be able to issue declarations of incompatibility which could lead to early amendment of the relevant legislation. Once the 1998 Act is implemented, the Convention is bound to assume ever greater importance in the youth justice system.

1.19 Relevant principles applicable to the youth justice system are:

- article 3: protection from inhuman and degrading treatment;
- article 5: guarantee of the right to liberty and the security of the person;
- article 6: guarantee of due process (fair trial, impartial and independent tribunal, etc); and
- article 8: right to privacy and family life.

1.20 The Convention does not deal with the rights of children and young persons expressly but the European Commission on Human Rights has made it clear that in relation to the criminal justice system, the due process guarantees of article 6 apply with equal force to juveniles as they do to adults. The youth justice system was considered by the Commission in the case of *Nortier v Netherlands*.[16] It was confirmed that due process protection cannot be sacrificed in the name of welfare or rehabilitation:

> Juveniles facing criminal charges are as fully entitled as adults to benefit from all the Convention requirements for a fair trial. Great care must always be taken to ensure that this entitlement is not diluted by considerations of rehabilitation or reform. These are

16 (1993) 17 EHRR 273.

considerations which should be in addition to all the procedural predictions available. Fair trial and proper proof of guilt are absolute conditions precedent.[17]

1.21   As well as being entitled to the full protection of due process, it was also suggested that children and young persons should receive extra protection as a result of their youth:

> [M]inors are as entitled to the same protection of their fundamental rights as adults . . . but the developing state of their personality – and consequently their limited social responsibility – should be taken into account in applying article 6 of the Convention.[18]

1.22   An extensive body of case law has been developed by the European Court of Human Rights which interprets the rights contained in the Convention. There is not space in this book to cover this jurisprudence, and accordingly the reader is referred to one of the specialist textbooks.[19]

UN Convention on the Rights of the Child (1989)

1.23   Although not part of domestic law, it is relevant, when considering the welfare of the child or young person, to note that the United Kingdom is a signatory to the United Nations Convention on the Rights of the Child (1989). Accordingly, government departments are obliged to ensure that relevant legislation and practice in the criminal justice system conforms to the principles set out in the Convention. To this end, the *National Standards for the Supervision of Offenders in the Community* (published jointly by the Home Office, Department of Health and the Welsh Office) make specific reference to its principles.

1.24   The following articles are relevant to the youth justice system:

– article 3: the best interests of the child to be the primary consideration in any proceedings before a court of law;
– article 12: the right of a child to express views in all matters affecting the child;
– article 37(b): the deprivation of liberty through detention shall be used as a measure of last resort and for the shortest appropriate period of time;

17 Ibid, per Judge Walsh at p290.
18 Ibid, per Judge Morenilla at p291.
19 Eg, Starmer, K *European Human Rights Law* (LAG, 1999).

- article 40(1): a youth justice system should treat a child in a manner consistent with his/her age and the desirability of promoting the child's reintegration and the child's assuming a constructive role in society;
- article 40(2): specific guarantees of due process in the youth justice system.[20]

1.25 Although not directly enforceable before domestic courts, the standards established in the Convention are being increasingly accepted as relevant to decisions regarding the rights of children and young persons under the European Convention on Human Rights.[21]

Other international standards

1.26 The United Nations has adopted detailed standards for children and young persons involved in the youth justice system. These are contained in:

- the UN Standard Minimum Rules for the Administration of Juvenile Justice (1985) ('the Beijing Rules');
- the UN Rules for the Protection of Juveniles Deprived of their Liberty (1990) ('the Havana Rules'); and
- the UN Guidelines for the Administration of Juvenile Delinquency (1990) ('the Riyadh Guidelines').[21A]

Although these provisions are not binding on the United Kingdom, they form part of the international standards that would be relevant to considering a human rights question relating to a child or young person.

Principles of the youth justice system

1.27 Domestic law establishes five principles which are relevant to the youth justice system. These are:

- preventing offending by children and young persons;

20 These articles are reproduced in Appendix 3. For a detailed discussion of their scope see van Bueren, G *The International Law on the Rights of the Child* (Nijhoff, 1998) Chapters 7 and 8.
21 See, for example, *Costello-Roberts v UK* (1995) 19 EHRR 112; *A v UK* [1995] FLR 959 and *V v UK* (judgment delivered 16 December 1999, application number 24888/94).
21A The Beijing Rules are reproduced in Appendix 3. The Havana Rules and the Riyadh Guidelines may be viewed at www.youthjustice.co.uk/bookshelf.

– having regard to the welfare of children and young persons;
– avoiding delay;
– proportionality in sentencing; and
– the prevention of discrimination.

Although not specifically referred to in any statute, there is also increasing emphasis on the principles of restorative justice.

Preventing offending

1.28   The Crime and Disorder Act 1998 s37 provides:

1)   The principal aim of the youth justice system shall be to prevent offending by children and young persons.

2)   In addition to any other duty to which they are subject, it shall be the duty of all persons and bodies carrying out functions in relation to the youth justice system to have regard to that aim.

The section came into force on 30 September 1998 throughout England and Wales.

1.29   The government has issued guidance on the implementation of s37 (*Youth Justice: the statutory principal aim of preventing offending by children and young people*). The need for a principal aim is explained as follows:

The new statutory aim of preventing offending . . . provides a new guiding principle to which all agencies and individuals can relate their work and responsibilities. There has been conflict within the youth justice system between the interests of the victim and the public and the interests of the child or young person who has offended or is alleged to have offended. There has been conflict between promoting the welfare of the child or young person and taking firm action to deal with his or her offending behaviour. These conflicts have affected the operation of the youth justice system . . . An effective youth justice system must ensure that justice is delivered for *all* concerned and that the best interests of *all* are served. There must be consideration, by all agencies and individuals, of the welfare of the child or young person: this is required by the UN Convention on the Rights of the Child to which the UK is a signatory. But there must also be a balance between the interests of the child or young person who has offended and the interests of the victim, or potential victim.[22]

---

22   Home Office framework document, *Youth justice: the statutory principal aim of preventing offending by children and young people*, para 1.

1.30   The guidance suggests that this aim may be achieved by the following objectives:

1) the swift administration of justice so that every young person accused of breaking the law has the matter resolved without delay;

2) confronting young offenders with the consequences of their offending, for themselves and their families, victims and the community;

3) intervention which tackles the particular factors (personal, family, social, educational or health) that puts the young person at risk of offending and which strengthens 'protective factors';

4) punishment proportionate to the seriousness and persistency of the offending behaviour;

5) encouraging reparation by young offenders for victims; and

6) reinforcing parental responsibility.

To enable comprehensive assessment of the need for intervention in a young offender's life the Youth Justice Board, in partnership with Oxford University, is developing the ASSET assessment profile. The profile is intended to identify the risk factors and the protective factors that exist, thereby helping to determine what work needs to be done to prevent further offending. It is also expected that the youth offending team will update the ASSET assessment every time there is a new contact with a young offender.

1.31   The Home Office guidance also emphasises the importance of developing strategies which will have a long-term effect upon the behaviour of the child or young person who has contact with the youth justice system:

> Achieving the aim of preventing offending children and young people means that interventions following a police final warning or as part of a sentence should seek to prevent offending beyond the formal response as well as during it. The objective should be to re-integrate the young person into the community. This means planning ahead; maintaining links with the community where a young person is serving a custodial sentence; putting in place longer term action to tackle education, employment, health issues or homelessness; and encouraging young people to become involved in sporting or other constructive leisure activities which can provide structure and support for young people beyond their sentence or final warning intervention.[23]

23 Ibid, para 18.3.

The role the defence lawyer has to play in relation to this statutory aim is considered in Chapter 2.

Welfare of the child or young person

1.32   The Children and Young Persons Act 1933 s44 provides:

> Every court in dealing with a child or young person who is brought before it, either as an offender or otherwise, shall have regard to the welfare of the child or young person, and shall in proper cases take steps for removing him from undesirable surroundings, and for securing that proper provision is made for his education and training.

1.33   There is no statutory definition of 'welfare', nor has the concept received any judicial attention. Individual courts have been left to apply the principle as seems appropriate in the circumstances. When considering s44, a court must interpret it in the context of subsequent legislation. For example, the court is required in proper cases to take steps to remove a child or young person from undesirable surroundings. Many courts may wish to interpret this as meaning removal from the care of parents who are not deemed to be appropriate carers. Such a decision could run counter to the philosophy of the Children Act 1989 which is based on the belief that children are best looked after within the family while aiming to protect children both from the harm which can arise from failures or abuse within the family and from the harm which can be caused by unwarranted intervention in their family life.[24] Perhaps even more significantly, the Criminal Justice Act 1991 established a statutory framework for sentencing offenders which emphasises proportionality and protection of the public. It is difficult to reconcile these sentencing principles with that of the welfare of the child or young person.

1.34   A court dealing with a child or young person must, therefore, balance competing factors before reaching a decision. In such circumstances s44 only requires the court to 'have regard' to the welfare of the child or young person. The weight given to the principle in practice will depend on the seriousness of the offence and the stage of the proceedings.

24   Department of Health, *The Children Act 1989 Guidance and Regulations* (HMSO, 1991), Introduction.

Scope

1.35 The youth court, with its near exclusive remit to deal with children and young persons, will usually have a particular ethos which gives prominence to the welfare principle. This will be reinforced by the special training justices on the youth court panel receive. It is, however, important to note that the principle applies in 'every court', a fact often overlooked by adult magistrates' courts and the Crown Court. The defence lawyer may have to ensure that these courts have regard to the principle.

1.36   It should be noted that the duty imposed by s44 applies not only to the defendant but to any child or young person brought before it as a witness. It has been held that the court can only have regard to the welfare of a witness who is a child or young person when that person appears before the court to testify.[25] It would seem, therefore, that only the welfare of the defendant can be taken into account until that stage.

Parental involvement

1.37 All courts have a power to require the attendance of parents or guardians at hearings. In cases where the child or young person is estranged from the parent, the defence lawyer may wish to raise the welfare of the child or young person as an opposing factor to the presumption that a parent should attend. Similarly, when the court is considering imposing a financial penalty upon a parent, the defence lawyer may wish to draw to the court's attention the effect that the consequent loss of income will have upon a family reliant on welfare benefits or a low wage. If the family will have to forgo basics, this will clearly have an impact upon the young offender's welfare.

Bail and remands

1.38 The welfare of a child or young person is referred to in the Bail Act 1976 but only as a ground for refusing bail. Instead the Act establishes the importance of preventing further offences, ensuring the defendant's attendance at court and avoiding interference with the administration of justice. With such concerns prominent in the bail decision-making process it may be difficult to ensure the court

25 *R v Highbury Corner Magistrates' Court ex p Deering* (1996) 161 JP 138; [1997] 1 FLR 683; [1997] Crim LR 59, QBD.

considers the defendant's welfare. Nevertheless, the defence lawyer should draw to the court's attention the consequences of any bail conditions which, for example, prevent parental contact or interfere with schooling. If a custodial remand is contemplated, s/he will also want to highlight any concerns about the ability of the young person to cope in a remand centre or prison.

Background

1.39 Any court will only be able to have proper regard of the welfare of the child or young person if it has available to it sufficient information regarding the background of the defendant. Accordingly, social services and education departments are under an obligation to provide background information to the court.[26] Where such information is not available youth courts are required to consider the desirability of adjourning the proceedings to allow the necessary enquiries to be made.[27] Furthermore, the occasions when any court may dispense with a pre-sentence report before sentencing a child or young person are particularly limited.[28]

Sentencing

1.40 It has already been noted that it is difficult to reconcile the welfare principle with the conflicting principle of proportionality and protection of the public contained in the Criminal Justice Act 1991. The practical implications of this are explored in more detail in Chapter 13.

Other agencies

1.41 Section 44 only applies to the courts, nevertheless the Crown Prosecution Service has indicated that it will have regard to the welfare principle when deciding whether it is in the public interest to prosecute a child or young person.[29]

---

26 Children and Young Persons Act 1969 s9.
27 Magistrates' Courts (Children and Young Persons) Rules 1992 SI No 2071 r10(2)(c).
28 Criminal Justice Act 1991 ss3 and 7.
29 *Code for Crown Prosecutors* (1994) available from the Crown Prosecution Service, Information Branch, 50 Ludgate Hill, London EC4M 7EX. See also Chapter 6.

Avoiding delay

1.42   In family proceedings involving children there is a statutory presumption that delay is prejudicial to the welfare of the child.[30] No such statutory presumption exists in relation to the youth justice system. Nevertheless, there is strong official encouragement for an assumption that it is desirable that any case involving a child or young person should be dealt with expeditiously:

> Speedy procedure avoid the uncertainty and stress of a long wait for trial for the child or young person accused of an offence and for the victim of the alleged offence; minimise the risks of offending while awaiting trial; ensure that, if found guilty, the sentence is meaningful and understood by the young person as a consequence of his or her behaviour; and ensure that early action can be taken to help prevent further offending. Dealing with cases quickly, so that action can be taken to prevent further offending if the young person is found guilty, is particularly important where the child or young person has a history of offending or is alleged to have committed several offences.[31]

1.43   In order to reduce delay, the Labour government has resorted to the following:

- targets to ensure a more efficient management of cases;
- encouraging the establishment of fast track schemes for some young offenders; and
- the introduction of statutory time limits.

Efficient management of cases

1.44   Following the election of a Labour government in May 1997 there has been a much greater emphasis on the efficient management of the youth justice system. One of the key aims has been to reduce the time that it takes to deal with a young offender from arrest to sentence. During 1997 all agencies were encouraged to do everything possible to reduce delays (Lord Chancellor's letter dated 21 May 1997 addressed to youth court chairmen and an inter-departmental circular dated 15 October 1997). As well as encouraging inter-agency working, this guidance suggested that courts should:

- scrutinise the need for adjournments;
- consider whether reports are needed before sentencing;

---

30   Children Act 1989 s1(2).
31   Home Office framework document, *Youth Justice: the statutory principal aim of preventing offending by children and young persons*, para 11.1.

- sentence for offences before the court without waiting for other matters to be disposed of.

Fast tracking

1.45   An election pledge of the Labour government was to ensure that those young offenders who offend frequently (commonly referred to as persistent young offenders) should be processed through the youth justice system more quickly than other defendants. The Youth Justice Board aims to ensure that all courts have fast track schemes for persistent young offenders by March 2000.[32]

1.46   The Home Office has adopted the following definition for a persistent young offender:

> A child or young person sentenced by any court on three or more separate occasions for one or more recordable offence, and within three years of the last sentencing occasion is subsequently arrested or has an information laid against him/her for a further recordable offence.

1.47   Where a child or young person satisfies this definition the joint Home Office/Lord Chancellor's circular *Measuring performance to reduce delays on the youth justice system* (issued 15 September 1998) gives the following guidelines on the length of time each stage of the youth justice process should take in a straightforward case:

Cases dealt with in youth court		*Cases committed to Crown Court*	
Arrest to charge	2 days	Arrest to charge	2 days
Charge to first appearance	7 days	Charge to first appearance	7 days
First appearance to start of trial	28 days	First appearance to committal for trial	28 days
Verdict to sentence	14 days	Committal to PDH	14 days
		PDH to start of Crown Court trial	28 days
		Verdict to sentence	14 days

---

32   Youth Justice Board, *Corporate Plan 1999/2000 to 2001/02*, para 14.

Statutory time limits

1.48 The Crime and Disorder Act 1998 ss43 to 45 introduce statutory time limits for all stages of the criminal justice process from arrest to sentence. These sections are being piloted from 1 November 1999.[33] Full implementation is not expected until the autumn of 2001.

Proportionality

1.49 The Criminal Justice Act 1991 establishes the sentencing principle that punishment must be proportionate to the seriousness of the offence(s) before the court. This principle applies to both the choice of sentence and also the length of that sentence.[34] When sentencing a young offender, the question of proportionality is the first consideration, but preventing offending and the welfare of the child or young person are important in deciding which type of sentence to impose.

Non-discrimination

1.50 The Criminal Justice Act 1991 s95(1) provides:

> The Secretary of State shall in each year publish such information as he considers expedient for the purpose of –
>
> . . .
>
> (b) facilitating the performance by such persons of their duty to avoid discrimination against any persons on the grounds of race or sex or any other improper ground.

1.51 Recent government guidance has emphasised the importance of the principle within the youth justice system:

> In delivering all [the objectives of the youth justice system], and in all other work with children and young people in the youth justice system, agencies and individuals must carry out their responsibilities fairly and without discrimination on grounds of race, sex or any other irrelevant factor. Section 95 of the Criminal Justice Act 1991 makes clear the responsibility of all those in the administration of justice to avoid unfair discrimination.[35]

---

33 For pilot areas see Appendix 8.
34 Criminal Justice Act 1991 ss1 and 2.
35 Home Office framework document, *Youth justice: the statutory principal aim of preventing offending by children and young people*, para 12.

CHAPTER 2

The defence lawyer

For complete chapter contents, see overleaf

2.1   Introduction

2.3   Professional and ethical issues

2.4   General duties owed to a client in criminal proceedings

2.5   Who is the client?

2.8   Confidentiality

2.10   Withholding information from a young client

2.12   Involvement of parents or guardians

2.16   Representing a young client

2.17   Taking instructions

*Explaining the role of the defence lawyer • Understanding legal
rights • Understanding legal procedure • Obtaining factual
instructions • Making decisions*

2.26   Working within the youth justice system

2.26   A role in preventing offending

2.29   Giving meaning to the welfare principle

2.30   Office management

2.32   Getting to know local services

*Youth justice services • Social services children and families
provision • Education provision*

2.36   Legal aid

2.36   In the police station

2.41   Advice and assistance

2.43   Criminal legal aid

*Interests of justice • Financial means • Appropriate contributor • Applicant
not living at home • Parent/guardian refuses to co-operate with
application • Parent/guardian refuses to pay contribution • Compulsory
grant of legal aid*

2.57   Access to Justice Act 1999 (*not in force*)

Introduction

> Work in the [youth] court has traditionally been seen as the 'kids' stuff' of the legal profession. This must be challenged. It will not be done by merely providing the facilities for more legal representation. However, the presence of a representative can be a precursor to providing justice. The legal profession must become as concerned with the substance of [youth] justice as with its form if it wishes to be more than a passive participant in the rhetoric of due process. (Allison Morris, *Legal representation and justice*, in Morris and Giller (eds) *Providing criminal justice for children.* Edward Arnold, 1983.)

2.1 Advocacy on behalf of young clients is a specialist area, undervalued by many criminal defence lawyers. As a result of this attitude representation in the youth court is often delegated to the most junior lawyers. In practice the youth of the client, the frequent chaos of their lives and the complexity of the procedural rules applicable to children and young persons make this an extremely challenging area of defence practice. As well as a detailed knowledge of the law applicable to children and young persons, the defence lawyer needs:

- an ability to communicate effectively with the young client;
- a knowledge of the role of the various agencies involved in the youth justice process as well as an ability to interact effectively with those agencies on behalf of the young client;
- knowledge of other local services relevant to the young client; and
- an advocacy style appropriate to the more informal environment of the youth court.

2.2 This chapter considers some of the professional challenges that may arise when representing children and young persons. It also offers some practical guidance on working with a young client.

Professional and ethical issues

2.3 Very little attention has been paid to the professional or ethical implications of representing a child or young person in the criminal justice system. There is no guidance in statute or procedural rules, as found in family proceedings, nor is there specific guidance from any professional body.[1] What follows is an attempt to consider the issues

---

1 See, for example, the guidance issued to solicitors acting for children in family proceedings: *Guide to Good Practice for Solicitors Acting for Children* (Family Law Solicitors Association, 4th edn, 1997).

which may arise and to offer practical solutions. If there is ever any doubt, the defence solicitor is advised to consult the Professional Ethics Division at the Law Society (or, in the case of a barrister, the Bar Council).

General duties owed to a client in criminal proceedings

2.4   *The Guide to the Professional Conduct of Solicitors* (Law Society Publishing, 8th edn, 1999) para 21.20 states that the criminal defence solicitor is under a duty to ensure that the prosecution discharges the onus placed upon it to prove the guilt of the accused and to say on behalf of the client what the client should properly say for him/herself if the client possessed the requisite skill and knowledge. A similar duty is imposed on barristers. A solicitor must not discriminate on grounds of race, sex or sexual orientation, and must not discriminate unfairly or unreasonably on the ground of disability, in his/her dealings with clients.[1A]

Who is the client?

2.5   Unlike civil proceedings, where a person under the age of 18 is presumed incapable of looking after his/her own affairs, a child or young person may be prosecuted in his/her own name and no adult will be appointed to act as a guardian ad litem. This will apply to any child who has attained the age of ten, the current age of criminal responsibility.

2.6   In family proceedings the lawyer is expected to determine whether the young client is competent to give instructions. If the minor is considered competent, s/he should be represented in accordance with those instructions; if s/he is not considered to be so, the lawyer should act in the child's best interests.[2] This notion sits uneasily with the criminal defence lawyer's duty towards a client. It is the opinion of the authors that a defence lawyer should always act on the instructions of the young defendant. A rare exception would be where s/he is clearly incapable of giving any instructions, in which case serious consideration should be given to arguing that the accused is not fit to plead.[3]

1A   Solicitors' Anti-Discrimination Rules 1995 (see *The Guide to the Professional Conduct of Solicitors* (Law Society Publishing, 8th edn, 1999)).
2   Family Proceedings Courts (Children Act 1989) Rules 1991 (SI No 1395) r12(1).
3   See para 4.3.

2.7 In addition to the general duties owed to a client, it may be helpful to quote two of the general principles given in guidance by the Solicitors Family Law Association to solicitors acting for children in family proceedings:

> The lawyer should retain a professional and objective relationship with the client and not allow his/her own emotional response to either the child or any issue in the case interfere with that professional relationship.

> A child [or young person] as client should always be given the same respect afforded to an adult as client.[4]

Confidentiality

2.8 A duty of confidentiality is owed by a lawyer to a child or young person in the same way as it is owed to adult clients. It is important to explain to a child or young person how this duty of confidentiality works in practice. The concept should be explained at the first meeting in terms appropriate for the age and understanding of the client. It should be expressly stated that it applies in relation to parents or other carers.

2.9 There is perhaps one limited exception to this duty of confidentiality owed to a young client. *The Guide to the Professional Conduct of Solicitors* (Law Society Publishing, 8th edn, 1999) annex 16A states that where there is a substantial fear that the young client may be in danger of abuse the solicitor may have to consider whether to breach his/her client's confidence. The defence lawyer should first attempt to persuade the client to reveal the abuse. If this is not possible the lawyer will be required to make a judgement regarding the level of the client's maturity.[5] If the client is considered to be a mature child the duty of confidentiality is absolute unless the lawyer knows or strongly suspects that younger siblings are being abused or where the child is in fear of his/her life or of serious injury. If the child is not considered to be mature, the lawyer should consider disclosing the information to the child's parents or, if appropriate, a third party such as the social services department. If the client's confidence is breached, the solicitor should advise the client that s/he has a right to instruct another solicitor.

---

4   *Guide to Good Practice for Solicitors Acting for Children*, see n1.
5   See *Gillick v West Norfolk and Wisbech Area Health Authority and DHSS* [1986] AC 112, HL.

Withholding information from a young client

2.10   *The Guide to the Professional Conduct of Solicitors* (Law Society Publishing, 8th edn, 1999) para 16.06 states that a solicitor is usually under a duty to pass on to the client and use all information which is material to the client's case regardless of the source of the information. Accordingly s/he should not agree to accept information on the basis that it will not be disclosed to the client. However, a solicitor may have to consider withholding information where the imparting to the client of the information received by the solicitor could be harmful to the client because it will affect the client's mental or physical condition. The example given is where a medical report received by the solicitor discloses that the client has a terminal illness.

2.11   When representing children or young persons there may be rare cases when it may also be appropriate to withhold information concerning a third party such as a parent.

Involvement of parents or guardians

2.12   The parent may wish to play a role in the process of taking instructions. When acting for a child or young person, the defence lawyer is under a duty to take instructions from the young client and not from any adult on his/her behalf. This applies even if the adult is the young client's parent. This may cause difficulties where the child is very young or where the parent believes that s/he has the right to make decisions on the child's behalf. The defence lawyer should explain the role of the solicitor to the parent and child or young person at the outset, including confirmation of the duty to take instructions from the child or young person and to act on those instructions.

2.13   It is perfectly proper for the defence lawyer to see the child or young person in the absence of the parent to take instructions. This should be done, where possible, with the agreement of all parties as the exclusion of an aggrieved parent from an interview may be problematic, especially if the client gives instructions which the parent believes are against the interests of the child or young person. Where a parent does object to a private interview, matters may be resolved by taking instructions from the child or young person in the presence of the parent but ensuring that there is ample opportunity for him/her to talk privately with the lawyer and to speak freely. In any event, should the wishes or instructions of the child or young person conflict with the opinions of the parent, it is the young client's instructions which must prevail.

2.14   The defence lawyer should always ensure that any parent (or guardian) who attends a police station or court with the child or young person understands what will happen and what may be expected of them. In the case of a parent who does not speak English, this could involve asking the police or the court to arrange for an interpreter to be present.

2.15   When at court, it may be necessary to remind the court that the lawyer's professional duties are solely owed to the young defendant. This is particularly important when the court is considering exercising its power to hold the parent responsible for any financial penalty or to impose a bindover or parenting order. Courts frequently invite submissions from the defence lawyer on behalf of the parent. If it is apparent that any such submissions would involve supplying the court with information detrimental to the interests of the defendant, the lawyer should decline to do so. It is advisable to canvass the possibility of this happening with the parent before the hearing. The parent should be advised to seek the advice of the court duty solicitor.

Representing a young client

2.16   It is important to establish a rapport with a child or young person. For most young people the only adults outside the family they have dealt with are figures of authority such as their teachers. With some individuals the defence lawyer will have to expend considerable effort in establishing a relationship.

Taking instructions

2.17   When taking instructions it will be important to make allowances for the limitations of maturity and understanding of any particular child or young person. Legal jargon should be avoided and the defence lawyer should ensure that matters of fact and law are clearly and simply explained so that the child or young person is able to make informed decisions and give proper instructions.

2.18   The fact that the client is likely still to be developing cognitive skills and moral understanding means that the defence lawyer needs to be particularly alert to any problems that could arise. As it is impossible to predict a young person's cognitive development simply by reference to his/her age, it becomes more important than with an adult client for the defence lawyer to obtain background information regarding the young client. This could include any statement of special educational need.

Explaining the role of the defence lawyer

2.19   A defence lawyer should never assume that a young client understands the role of a lawyer. There may be considerable confusion among young clients about the role of the lawyer and even whether the lawyer is on the young person's side. A salutary example for lawyers may be taken from the following:

> In a Canadian project . . . 22 children who were legally represented [in juvenile court] were asked 'who was on your side in court?' Only seven mentioned their lawyer; four referred to the judge. Only six children thought their lawyer helped them in court and only four thought their lawyer was the best person to whom to tell their story. Some children did not even realise they had a lawyer and, where they did realise it, some did not think that he had been there to assist them.[6]

Furthermore, research indicates that young clients also have difficulty distinguishing between the function of the defence lawyer and the authority of the court.[7]

2.20   As a minimum, the lawyer should explain or confirm the young client's understanding of a lawyer's:

– duty to protect the client's legal interests;
– duty to act on the client's instructions; and
– duty of confidentiality.

Understanding legal rights

2.21   The concept of a legal right as an entitlement belonging to the child or young person may not be fully understood. Research in the United States into young people's understanding of their rights to remain silent and to have a lawyer (the so-called Miranda rights), suggests that it is only around the age of 13 or 14 that a young suspect develops the capacity to think of a right as 'belonging' to them. A research study funded by the United States government revealed that even with older juveniles there is often a failure to understand the meaning of a 'right'.

---

6   Quoted by Allison Morris 'Legal Representation and Justice', in A Morris and H Giller (eds) *Providing Criminal Justice for Children* (Edward Arnold, 1983).
7   Grisso, T 'Juvenile Competency to Stand Trial: Questions in an Era of Punitive Reform', *Criminal Justice* 12(3) Fall 1997, available at www.youthjustice.co.uk.

Even at ages 14 to 16, only about one-fourth of delinquent youth, as compared to about one-half of adult offenders, described a 'right' in a way that connotes an entitlement. Thus, when asked what is meant when police said, 'You do not have to make a statement and have the right to remain silent', many youths indicated a conditional view of legal rights, such as 'You can be silent unless you are told to talk,' or 'You have to be quiet unless you are spoken to.' Even though youths may develop the capacity for understanding rights early in adolescence, it often takes additional time and life experiences before their capacity influences their actual understanding.[8]

2.22 In the light of such research findings the defence lawyer clearly must take extra care to explain legal rights and how they can be exercised. Practical advice on explaining the right of silence to a young client is given at para 5.132. It will also be important when considering whether admissions should be excluded. The lawyer may wish to obtain expert evidence from a forensic psychologist as to the understanding of the caution and the understanding that a right to legal advice and representation existed and could be exercised.

Understanding legal procedure

2.23 The defence lawyer needs to ensure that even the most basic elements of court procedure are explained fully to the young client. It may be helpful to draw a basic diagram showing the layout of the courtroom and marking on it the positions of the respective professionals. While doing this, their roles can be explained. If it is possible to do so, the lawyer could also show the courtroom to the young client and any parent before the court starts sitting.

Obtaining factual instructions

2.24 The ability to recall an incident is a skill that develops significantly through adolescence. The young client may therefore have difficulty giving a logical and coherent account of an incident which lead to his/her arrest. The defence lawyer will need to be prepared to spend much longer taking factual instructions.

---

8 See note 6; see also Grisso T, 'Juveniles' Capacity to Waive Miranda Rights: An Empirical Analysis', 68 Calif L Rev 134 (1980).

Making decisions

2.25   Young clients may find it particularly difficult to make decisions relating to their case. This may be because they have problems understanding the options and their consequences or simply because they do not have the intellectual and emotional maturity to face a complex problem with no easy solution.[8A] The defence lawyer must ensure that the various options are explained clearly and that the possible consequences of each decision are also set out fully. The young client may wish to involve other adults such as parents or other carers in the decision-making process. Subject to concerns regarding confidentiality this should not be a problem, provided that the defence lawyer is alert to the risk of such adults making the decision on behalf of the young client. With some young clients there is a similar risk that the child or young person wants to pass responsibility for the decision-making to the lawyer.

Working within the youth justice system

A role in preventing offending?

2.26   As discussed above, the professional obligation of the defence lawyer is to protect the legal interests of the defendant. This will involve putting the prosecution to proof and presenting to the court all favourable information relevant to mitigation. The defence lawyer has no professional obligation to do otherwise.

2.27   How can a defence lawyer help to prevent offending whilst still fulfilling his/her professional obligations to his/her client? The government view, as expressed in its guidance *Youth justice: The statutory principal aim of preventing offending by children and young people*, is that the lawyer can further the aim by doing the following:

- acting quickly and efficiently to reduce delay;
- ensuring that the decisions of the court are understood by the young client and any parent or guardian;
- encouraging parents or guardians to attend court; and
- giving an opportunity for the defendant to participate in youth court proceedings.

8A   If this proves to be a significant problem, the question of whether the young client is able to participate effectively in his/her own defence should be considered. See para 3.26.

2.28   This list focuses on the court process itself. The defence lawyer has an equally important role to ensure that the young client receives services from statutory and voluntary agencies to help remove factors which mean there is a risk of further offending. This broader advocacy role could involve ensuring:

- social services provide support to the client's family where needed;[9]
- appropriate education provision is provided;[10] and
- welfare benefits advice is given or a referral to a specialist agency is made.[11]

Giving meaning to the welfare principle

2.29   In an increasingly punitive justice system which emphasises children and young persons taking responsibility for their wrongdoing, the challenge for the defence lawyer is to ensure that the welfare principle is given real meaning in practice.

Office management

2.30   For the defence lawyer to be able to prepare cases quickly and efficiently, maximum use will need to be made of case management systems in the office so that all cases for a client in both courts and police stations can be co-ordinated. In particular, with the introduction of fast tracking, priority will need to be given to the preparation of cases for clients treated as persistent young offenders.

2.31   The criteria established by the Legal Aid Board for its youth court block contract pilots require each firm to designate lawyers to conduct youth court advocacy. Such designated lawyers should have relevant training and regular access to information regarding changes in law and procedure which affect the youth court. Freelance solicitors and barristers instructed to appear in the youth court will be expected to have similar experience and training.

---

9   See the local authority's duty to provide services to a child in need under the Children Act 1989 s17 – see para 4.30.

10 For detailed treatment of educational law see Ford, Hughes and Ruebain, *Education Law and Practice* (LAG, 1999). If referral to a specialist education lawyer is necessary contact the Advisory Centre for Education – see Appendix 7 for contact details.

11 Welfare benefits provision for 16- and 17-year-olds involves complex rules; see Carolyn George et al, *Welfare Benefits Handbook 1999/2000* (CPAG, 1999).

Getting to know local services

2.32 To operate effectively in the youth court the defence lawyer needs to be familiar with the services provided in the local area for young people.

Youth justice services

2.33 The defence lawyer should obtain a copy of the youth justice plans for all local authorities covered by his/her local courts. S/he would also be well advised to familiarise him/herself with local diversion, bail support or community sentence programmes. Many such projects will have publicity material and some will organise open days for criminal justice professionals or the general public. Being familiar with local projects will allow the defence lawyer to explain to his/her client how the projects work as well as being able to explain their operation to a court.

Social services children and families provision

2.34 Although not directly involved in the criminal justice process, the services provided by the social services department to children and families are of considerable importance. The defence lawyer should obtain the children services plan produced by all the local authorities covered by his/her local courts.

Education provision

2.35 Research reveals that a significant proportion of young defendants have truanted from school or have been excluded from mainstream education. The defence lawyer can expect therefore to deal with many defendants who have had contact with the education welfare service and who have attended special schools or pupil referral units. The defence lawyer would again be well advised to become familiar with local provision.

Legal aid

In the police station

2.36 Article 6(3)(c) of the European Convention on Human Rights establishes the right of every person charged with a criminal offence to legal assistance at public expense when the interests of justice require it.[11A] This right is of particular importance for children and young persons as they are unlikely to have the financial means to pay a lawyer privately. In England and Wales publicly funded legal representation is currently provided under the Legal Aid Act 1988. This will be replaced by a right to representation provided by the Criminal Defence Service under the Access to Justice Act 1999.

2.37 Legal aid in the police station is provided under the Legal Advice and Assistance Regulations 1989 (SI No 340 as amended). It is not means-tested.[12] Legal advice and assistance is available to any person who:

- is arrested and held in custody in a police station or other premises;
- is being interviewed in connection with a serious service offence; or
- is a volunteer.[13]

2.38 A volunteer is defined as 'a person who, for the purposes of assisting with an investigation, attends voluntarily at a police station or any other place where a constable is present'.[14] This definition arguably includes a child or young person who is interviewed by a police officer either at home or on school premises.

2.39 A solicitor may accept an application for advice and assistance from a child or young person under the age of 16 if s/he falls into one of the categories listed above and the solicitor is satisfied that the application cannot reasonably be made by a parent or guardian or other person in whose care the child or young person is.[15] In practice this would usually allow taking initial instructions direct from the detained client.

2.40 A solicitor may also accept an application from the parent/ guardian or carer on behalf of a person under the age of 16. It is also arguable that an appropriate adult is entitled to apply for advice and assistance from a solicitor as the adult would satisfy the definition of a volunteer discussed above.

Advice and assistance

2.41 Initial advice and assistance in relation to any matter of English law may be provided under the Legal Advice and Assistance Regulations

11A A similar right is recognised by article 40(2)(b)(iii) of the United Nations Convention on the Rights of the Child.
12 Legal Advice and Assistance Regulations 1989 reg 6(4).
13 Ibid, reg 6(1).
14 Ibid, reg 3.
15 Ibid, reg 14(2).

1989 (SI No 340 as amended). This is means-tested on the basis of the applicant's income and savings.

2.42   A solicitor may accept an application directly from a young person aged 16 or 17. In the case of a person under the age of 16, reg 14 would usually prohibit the solicitor accepting an application directly from the young client without the prior authority of the Legal Aid Board. However, it would seem that the exception in reg 14(2A) applies which would allow this to be done. Regulation 14(2A) permits a solicitor to accept an application from a client under the age of 16 for advice and assistance in relation to proceedings in which the client is entitled to bring, prosecute or defend without a next friend or guardian ad litem. This is clearly the case when a child or young person is faced with criminal proceedings.

Criminal legal aid

2.43   Legal aid for representation before a criminal court is available under the Legal Aid in Criminal and Care Proceedings (General) Regulations 1989 (SI No 344 as amended). The application for legal aid is submitted to the relevant magistrates' court and a decision is made on the following criteria:

– whether it is in the interests of justice for the defendant to be legally represented; and
– whether the applicant's means make him/her financially eligible.

Interests of justice

2.44   The criteria for deciding whether it is in the interests of justice to grant legal aid are the same for a child or young person as for an adult.[16] The Legal Aid Act 1988 s22(2) provides that the factors to be taken into account when deciding whether to grant legal aid shall include the following:

– the offence is such that if proved it is likely that the court would impose a sentence which would deprive the accused of his/her

---

16   Refusal to grant legal aid to a defendant aged 16 who wishes to challenge whether a police officer has acted in the execution of his/her duty is irrational, because the expertise required to cross-examine police witnesses and find, select and proof defence witnesses is beyond that of a defendant aged 16: *R v Scunthorpe Justices ex p S (a minor)* (1998) *Times*, 5 March, QBD.

liberty, or lead to loss of his/her livelihood or serious damage to his/her reputation;

- the determination of the case may involve consideration of a substantial question of law;
- the accused may be unable to understand the proceedings or to state his/her own case because of inadequate knowledge of English, mental disorder or other mental or physical disability;
- the nature of the defence is such as to involve the tracing and interviewing of witnesses or expert cross-examination of a witness for the prosecution;
- it is in the interests of someone other than the accused that the accused be represented.

It should be noted that this list is not exhaustive.

2.44A   When completing a legal aid application form on behalf of a child or young person, the defence lawyer will always wish to draw the court's attention to the age of the defendant. The youth of the accused will usually mean that a court is more likely to grant legal aid.

2.45   In normal circumstances legal aid would be granted in favour of the firm of solicitors nominated by the applicant. Where there are co-defendants the court may allocate another solicitor who already represents another defendant unless there is a conflict of interest. If no such conflict exists it may still be in the interests of justice for a child or young person to be represented by the solicitors of his/her choice, if the firm is already dealing with other outstanding cases or if the young client has developed a good relationship with a particular solicitor.

Financial means

2.46   In the case of a 16- or 17-year-old, the application will be assessed on the financial means of the defendant. The young defendant should therefore complete the financial means form detailing his/her own financial resources.

2.47   In the case of a defendant under the age of 16,[17] Legal Aid in Criminal and Care Proceedings (General) Regulations 1989 reg 23(3)

---

17 An applicant who attains the age of 16 after the date on which an application for legal aid is made but before the making of legal aid order shall be treated as not having attained that age: Legal Aid in Criminal and Care Proceedings (General) Regulations 1989 reg 5.

states that a proper officer (the justices' clerk in a magistrates' court) may require either the applicant or an appropriate contributor, or both, to submit a statement of means and documentary proof.

Appropriate contributor

2.48   An appropriate contributor is defined as:

- the defendant's father (or any person who has been adjudged to be his/her father) or his/her mother; or
- the defendant's guardian.[18]

'Guardian' for the purposes of the regulation has the meaning assigned by the Child Care Act 1980 s87, namely 'a person appointed by deed or will or by order of a court of competent jurisdiction to be the guardian of the child'.[19] This definition would not include step-parents, relatives acting as carers, foster parents or employees of local authorities.

2.49   The court will usually wish to process a legal aid application for a defendant under the age of 16 on the basis of the parent's income. This may cause practical problems if the client is not living at home or if the parent refuses to complete the form or fails to provide the requisite documentary evidence.

Applicant not living at home

2.50   Most applicants under the age of 16 who do not live with their parents, will be looked after by a local authority. In such circumstances it is arguable that any parent is not an appropriate contributor. As the local authority does not satisfy the definition of a guardian, the legal aid application should be processed on the basis of the financial means of the applicant only.

Parent/guardian refuses to co-operate with application

2.51   Where the applicant lives with his/her parent(s) but they refuse to co-operate with the application, the defence lawyer will be left with no option but to submit the legal aid application forms completed solely by the child or young person.

---

18   Ibid, reg 3.
19   Ibid.

2.52   Regulation 23(3) clearly gives the court the power to process the application solely on the basis of the financial means of the child or young person. In a covering letter the defence lawyer should set out the reasons why a financial means form completed by the parent or guardian has not been submitted. The court should then be asked to process the application on the basis of the means of the child or young person. In view of the statutory duty to consider the welfare of the child or young person it will usually be in the interests of justice for the young defendant to be legally represented.[19A]

Parent/guardian refuses to pay contribution

2.53   If legal aid contributions are not paid, the court may send a notice to the 'legally assisted person' requiring him/her to pay the sums due within seven days or to explain why the contributions may not be paid.[20] If the contributions are not brought up to date, the court may revoke the legal aid certificate, having considered any representations received.[21]

2.54   The legally assisted person is always the defendant, even in the case of a defendant under the age of 16, yet s/he has no control over the payment of contributions. If notice is received that parental contributions are in arrears the defence lawyer should attempt to establish the reasons. If the parent will not make further contributions, representations should be made to the court that it would not be in the interests of the child or young person to be without legal representation during the proceedings and therefore the power to revoke the certificate should not be exercised. It is also possible to ask the court to review its decision as to who should be the appropriate contributor.

2.55   In some contexts the question of whether the young defendant has failed or refused to apply for legal aid will be important, for example, as a preliminary to remanding a 15- or 16-year-old into custody. Where a parent has failed to co-operate with a legal aid application, it may be necessary to argue that this should not be construed as a failure or refusal by the child or young person.

19A See also article 6(3)(c) of the ECHR – para 2.36.
20   Legal Aid in Criminal and Care Proceedings (General) Regulations 1989, reg 36(1).
21   Ibid, reg 36(3).

Compulsory grant of legal aid

2.56   Subject to financial means, legal aid must be granted in the following circumstances:

- when a defendant is charged with murder; [22]
- when a defendant is remanded in custody or to local authority accommodation[23] and he may be again so remanded; [24]
- where the defendant has been remanded in custody or to local authority accommodation[25] for the preparation of reports prior to sentencing;[26] and
- where a court is considering imposing a custodial sentence upon a child or young person.[27]

Access to Justice Act 1999 (*not in force*)

2.57   When Part I of the Act is in force, the Legal Aid Board will be replaced by the Criminal Defence Service, a part of the Legal Services Commission. The Criminal Defence Service will contract with firms of solicitors to provide advice and assistance to people being investigated for criminal offences as well as representation at court. The right to representation at court will still depend on similar criteria to those set out in para 2.44, but there will be no means-testing. Consideration is also being given to the possibility of separate contracts for the provision of representation before the youth court. If this is introduced, the Criminal Defence Service will expect firms seeking contracts to demonstrate a particular expertise in representing children and young people.

---

22   Legal Aid Act 1988 s21(3)(a)
23   Ibid, by virtue of s23(11).
24   Ibid, s21(3)(c).
25   Ibid, s21(11).
26   Ibid, s23(3)(d).
27   Criminal Justice Act 1982 s3(1).

CHAPTER 3

The relevance of age

For complete chapter contents, see overleaf

Introduction

3.1 Age is of fundamental relevance in criminal proceedings. It determines whether a person will be held criminally responsible, it may influence the decision whether to prosecute and it also determines where and in what manner the accused may be tried and sentenced.

3.2 As age has such relevance it is important for the defence lawyer to note the age of his/her client at the earliest opportunity. A note should also be made of the client's age at the time of the alleged offence and whether a birthday is imminent. This information may be crucial to the tactics used to defend the client.

Terminology

3.3 Various terms are used to describe persons of particular ages. Unfortunately the relevant statutes do not use the terms consistently. The following terms are used.

Child

3.4 'Child' is defined as a person aged between 10 and 13 inclusive.[1] However, it should be noted that for the purposes of the Children Act 1989 the term refers to a person under the age of 18.[2]

Young person

3.5 In general, defined as a person who has attained the age of 14 and is under the age of 18.[3] However, it should be noted that for the purposes of the Children and Young Persons Act 1969 s23 (remand to local authority accommodation) and the Police and Criminal Evidence Act 1984, the term refers to persons who are under the age of 17.[4]

---

1   Children and Young Persons Act 1933 s107(1).
2   Children Act 1989 s105(1).
3   Children and Young Persons Act 1933 s107(1).
4   Children and Young Persons Act 1969 s23(12) and Police and Criminal Evidence Act 1984 s37(15).

Juvenile

3.6   In the context of the police station a juvenile is defined as a person under the age of 17.[5] To confuse matters the term is also used in the Magistrates' Courts Act 1980 s29 to mean a person under the age of 18.

Young offender

3.7   This term has no statutory definition but it used in sentencing law to refer to offenders under the age of 21 to whom the sentence of imprisonment is not available.

Terminology in the book

3.8   No generic term exists which covers the full age range of 10 years to 17 years – the jurisdiction of the youth court. Some lawyers, particularly when in the magistrates' court, refer loosely to the defendant being a 'youth'. However, this term has no legal status. Because of the word's negative connotations the authors have decided not to adopt it as a generic term. Instead it has been decided to use the following terms:

- child: ages 10–13 years
- young person: ages 14–17 years; and
- juvenile: ages 10–16 years (in the context of the police station and bail hearings only).

Determining age

3.9   A person attains a particular age at the commencement of the relevant anniversary of his/her birth.[6]

3.10   When a child or young person is first brought before a court, the justices must establish his/her age. The Children and Young Persons Act 1933 s99(1) provides:

> Where a person ... is brought before any court otherwise than for the purpose of giving evidence, and it appears to the court that he is a child or young person, the court shall make due enquiry as to the age

---

5   Police and Criminal Evidence Act 1984 s37(15) and PACE Code C, 1.5.
6   Family Law Reform Act 1969 s9.

of that person, and for that purpose shall take such evidence as may be forthcoming at the hearing of the case.

In normal circumstances the court will accept the date of birth given to it by the child or young person. There will be occasions where the defendant has previously lied about his/her age, and the prosecution do not accept the details now given to the court. In such circumstances the court will usually ask a parent or other adult relative to confirm the defendant's date of birth. In extreme cases the court may require the production of a birth certificate. Alternatively a parent may be called to give evidence. In any event the court must make a determination of the defendant's age at the hearing based on the available evidence.

Effect of discovering the defendant's true age later

3.11 The Children and Young Persons Act 1933 s99(1) provides:

> ... [A]n order or judgement of the court shall not be invalidated by any subsequent proof that the age of that person has not been correctly stated to the court, and the age presumed or declared by the court to be the age of the person so brought before it shall, for the purposes of this Act, be deemed to be the true age of that person.

3.12 This provision applies to the determination of age in relation to the following:

- jurisdiction of youth court (s46);
- parental liability for financial orders (s55);
- s53(2) detention; and
- detention during Her Majesty's pleasure (s53(1)).

3.13 By virtue of the Children and Young Persons Act 1969 s70(3) the above provision also applies to the 1969 Act and therefore applies to the following:

- remand to local authority accommodation (s23);
- supervision orders (ss11–19).

3.14 Section 99(1) would not seem to cover a mistake in determining the age of an offender for the purposes of other sentences passed by a court. The consequences of such a mistake have been considered by the Court of Appeal in the case of *R v Brown*[7] where a 20-year-old was sentenced to a term of imprisonment because the judge mistakenly

7 (1989) 11 Cr App R (S) 263, CA.

believed him to be 21 years old. On appeal it was argued that the sentence had to be quashed because the Criminal Justice Act 1982 s1(1) prohibited the passing of a sentence of imprisonment upon an offender under the age of 21. The argument was rejected by reference to s1(6) of the Act which required the sentencing court to determine the offender's age 'as that which appears to the court after considering any available evidence'. The Court held that all the evidence before the judge on the day of sentence indicated that the offender was 21 years old. The sentence of imprisonment was consequently not invalidated. This decision may be contrasted with the case of *R v Harris*,[8] where a sentence of imprisonment was later quashed because although the judge believed that the offender had attained the age of 21, the police antecedent form gave his correct age of 20 years. Distinguishing the case of *Brown*, the Court ruled that, as the sentencing judge had before him evidence showing the true age, s 1(6) could not be invoked to save the sentence.

3.15   Similar statutory provisions apply to the following sentences:

- conditional discharge: Powers of Criminal Courts Act 1973 s1B(10);
- probation order: Powers of Criminal Courts Act 1973 s2(1);
- combination and curfew orders: Criminal Justice Act 1991 s99(2);
- secure training order: Criminal Justice and Public Order Act 1994 s1(9); and
- action plan, reparation, parenting, drug treatment and testing and detention and training orders: Crime and Disorder Act 1998 s117(3).

It is likely that the same principle would be held to apply to these sentences too.

Age and criminal responsibility

3.16   A person's age may be significant to the question of criminal responsibility. The law predetermines the assessment of criminal responsibility according to age.

8   (1990) 12 Cr App R (S) 318, CA.

Under ten years

3.17 It is conclusively presumed that persons under the age of 10 cannot be guilty of any offence.[9] The age of 10 is therefore usually referred to as the age of criminal responsibility.

3.18 In practical terms the presumption means that the police may not arrest a person known to be under that age and they also may not be prosecuted. It follows that a person who causes a person under the age of 10 to commit a criminal act is a principal and not a secondary party to the offence. The child is treated as an innocent agent. A further consequence of the presumption is illustrated by the case of *Walters v Lunt*[10] where the parents of a seven-year-old child were held to be not guilty of dishonestly receiving a bicycle from their child even though they knew that it was stolen. As the child could not steal, the court ruled that in law it was not stolen.

3.19 Children under the age of 10, who come to the attention of the police for behaviour which would constitute a criminal offence if the child had been over 10, may be the subject of an application for a child safety order. Such an application is made by the relevant local authority to the family proceedings court.[11]

Children aged 10 to 13 years

3.20 The irrebuttable presumption that a boy aged under 14 was physically incapable of committing rape was abolished by the Sexual Offences Act 1993 s1.

3.21 The common law presumed that children under the age of 14 are incapable of committing crime. This presumption (often referred to as doli incapax) has been abolished for any offence committed on or after 30 September 1998. As the defence lawyer will still deal with offences that pre-date abolition of the doctrine, a summary of the extensive case law is given here.

3.22 To rebut the presumption of doli incapax, the prosecution must prove:

- that the child defendant did the act(s) charged; and
- when doing the act(s) s/he knew it was a seriously wrong act as distinct from an act of mere naughtiness or childish mischief.

---

9 Children and Young Persons Act 1933 s50:
10 [1951] 2 All ER 645.
11 Crime and Disorder Act 1998 ss11–13. See Chapters 24 and 25.

3.23   The criminal standard of proof applies. The fact that the child has attained the age of 14 by the time of the trial is irrelevant; so is the fact that s/he realises that the act was seriously wrong after being arrested.

3.24   The presumption was considered in detail by the House of Lords in *C (a Minor) v DPP*.[12] In deciding that it remained a part of the common law, Lord Lowry surveyed the existing case law. The relevant points may be summarised as follows:

1) The evidence to prove guilty knowledge cannot be the mere proving of the offence charged however horrifying or obviously wrong that act may be.

2) The older the child is and the more obviously wrong the act, the easier it will be to prove guilty knowledge.

3) The surrounding circumstances are relevant and what the defendant said or did before or after the act may go to prove guilty mind.[13]

4) Running away is usually equivocal – it can as easily follow a naughty act as a wicked one.

5) In order to obtain evidence to rebut the presumption, apart from anything said or done, the prosecution has to rely on interviewing the suspect, having him psychiatrically examined or adducing the evidence of someone who knows him/her well, eg a teacher.

6) Failure to mention relevant facts which could result in an inference under the Criminal Justice and Public Order Act 1994 s34 is not relevant to the rebuttal of the presumption.

7) Previous convictions (and cautions) cannot be adduced merely to rebut the presumption.[14]

Young persons

3.25   Once a person has attained the age of 14 the law makes no concessions regarding criminal responsibility even if there is clear evidence that the young person is immature for his/her age. Nevertheless, the age of the accused will still be relevant in certain trials, where, for

---

12 [1995] 2 Cr App R 1.
13 For subsequent consideration of what constitutes 'surrounding circumstances' see *T v DPP* [1997] Crim LR 127, QBD; *A v DPP* [1997] 1 Cr App R 27, [1997] Crim LR 125, QBD; and *R v Shaw*, CA, unreported.
14 Details of a previous incident dealt with by way of the school disciplinary procedure may, however, be admissible: *Graham v DPP* (1998) 162 JP 62, QBD.

example, the court must consider the issue of specific intent or duress.[15]

Ability to participate effectively in the trial process

3.26 Article 6 of the European Convention on Human Rights guarantees to all defendants the right to a fair hearing. Until recently there has been virtually no judicial consideration of when a young defendant might be too young to have such a fair hearing. This is likely to change following the European Court of Human Rights decision in *V v UK*.[16] This case concerned two applicants convicted of murder at the age of 11. The court did not consider that setting the age of criminal responsibility at the age of 10 years was in itself a breach of the Convention. It did, however, declare that:

> Article 6, read as a whole, guarantees the right of an accused to participate effectively in his trial ... [para 85] [I]t is essential that a child charged with an offence is dealt with in a manner which takes full account of his age, level of maturity and intellectual and emotional capacities, and that steps are taken to promote his ability to understand and participate in the proceedings. [para 86]

Having considered extensive psychiatric evidence the court concluded that, given the applicants' immaturity and disturbed emotional state, they had not been able to give factual instructions to their lawyers nor had they been able to follow the trial proceedings. It was held, therefore, that the applicants had been denied a fair hearing in breach of article 6.

3.26A In the light of this decision, the defence lawyer must be alert to the possibility that his/her client may be unable to participate effectively in the trial process. This is particularly important when the client:

- is under the age of 14; or
- has learning problems or a history of absence from school.

Where doubts exist the defence lawyer should consider obtaining a psychological assessment of his/her client. Before any expert is instructed the defence lawyer should obtain as much information as possible regarding his/her young client's general development

---

15 See para 3.33 onwards.
16 Judgment delivered on 16 December 1999 (Application no 24888/94); see also (1999) *Times*, 17 December.

and educational attainment (including any statement of special educational need). This background information should be sent to a forensic psychologist with experience of assessing adolescents.

3.27   The psychologist should be asked to:

- assess the client's intelligence;
- identify any developmental or cognitive deficits; and
- assess how any deficits are likely to affect the client's ability to:

   a) understand the charges and the possible consequences of guilty and not guilty pleas;
   b) make rational decisions relevant to the legal process;
   c) remember relevant facts;
   d) communicate in a coherent manner;
   e) understand testimony in court; and
   f) behave appropriately in the courtroom.[17]

Where any concerns are not significant, consideration should be given to seeking modifications of the trial procedure (see para 12.11). However, where significant concerns are raised by the psychologist's report, the defence lawyer may have to consider raising the question of fitness to plead.

Fitness to plead

3.28   The test of whether a defendant is fit to plead was set out by Alderson B in *R v Pritchard*[18] over 150 years ago and is now 'firmly embodied in our law'.[19] In deciding whether the defendant is fit to plead, the court should consider:

> Whether he is of sufficient intellect to comprehend the course of proceedings on the trial, so as to make a proper defence – to know that he might challenge [any jurors] to whom he may object – and to comprehend the details of the evidence ... if you think that there is no certain mode of communicating the details of the trial to the prisoner, so that he can clearly understand them, and be able properly to make his defence to the charge; you ought to find that he is not of sane mind. It is not enough, that he may have a general capacity of communicating on ordinary matters.

17   This checklist is based on US research into the competence of juvenile defendants to stand trial – see Grisso, T *Forensic Analysis of Juveniles* (Professional Resource Press, 1998).
18   (1836) 7 C&P 303.
19   Lord Parker CJ in *R v Podola* [1960] 1 QB 325, CA.

Despite Alderson B's reference to finding the accused 'not of sane mind', a defendant may be unfit to plead even if not legally insane.[20] It is submitted that fitness to plead should encompass an inability to participate in the trial process because of immaturity.

Burden of proof

3.29 If the issue is raised by the defence the burden of proof must be discharged by the defendant on a balance of probabilities.[21]

Summary trial

3.30 If it is contended that a young defendant is unfit to plead because s/he is unable to understand the proceedings, this should be dealt with as a preliminary issue in the trial. The expert evidence will be considered by the justices. If they reject the submission, then the trial of the substantive issue can proceed; if they accept that the defendant is unfit to plead, s/he should be acquitted.

Trial on indictment

3.31 In the Crown Court there is a special procedure for considering the question of fitness to plead giverned by the Criminal Procedure (Insanity) Act 1964. A jury is empanelled to determine whether the defendant is fit to plead. If, after hearing evidence, that jury decides that the defendant is fit to plead, a second jury will be empanelled to decide on the defendant's guilt.

3.32 If the written or oral evidence of two or more registered medical practitioners (at least one of whom is registered under the Mental Health Act 1983 s12) leads the first jury to conclude that the defendant is not fit to plead, the same jury shall proceed to determine whether the defendant did the act or made the omission charged against him/her. If the jury concludes that the defendant committed the act, the disposals available to the judge are as follows:

- an admission order to such hospital as the Secretary of State specifies;
- a guardianship order;

20 *R v Governor of Stafford Prison ex p Emery* [1909] 2 KB 81 (a case involving a deaf defendant who was unable to read, write or communicate with sign language).
21 *R v Robertson* [1968] 1 WLR 1767, CA.

- a supervision and treatment order; or
- an absolute discharge.

In the case of a child or young person deemed too young to stand trial, only the final option would seem appropriate.

Age and the criminal law

3.33　The criminal law makes few concessions to the youth of an accused. This may produce very harsh results, especially after the abolition of the presumption of doli incapax.

3.34　The law imposes a particularly exacting standard upon a child or young person when considering his/her understanding of the consequences of his/her actions. The standard is not so exacting in relation to the potential availability of legal defences.

Recklessness

3.35　The test for recklessness in relation to offences under the Criminal Damage Act 1971 is set out in *R v Caldwell*.[23] An accused is reckless as to whether any property would be damaged or destroyed if:

- s/he does an act which in fact creates an obvious risk that property would be destroyed or damaged; and
- when s/he does the act s/he either has not given any thought to the possibility of there being any such risk or has recognised that there was some risk involved and has nonetheless gone on to do it.

In his judgment Lord Diplock held that the question whether there was an obvious risk could only be answered by considering whether any ordinary prudent person would have realised there was a risk of serious harmful consequences. In subsequent cases this objective test, using the yardstick of the ordinary prudent adult person, has been applied against children and young persons, even if with some reluctance.

3.36　In *Elliott v C (a Minor)*[24] the defendant, a girl with learning disabilities who had just attained the age of 14 years, went into a garden shed during the night. She poured spirit onto the floor and set it alight. When the flames flared out of control she left the shed, which

23　[1982] AC 341, HL.
24　[1983] 1 WLR 939, QBD.

was completely destroyed. She was charged with arson. At trial the justices found that she had given no thought to the possibility of a risk that property would be destroyed. They reached this decision by taking into account among other factors her age and intelligence. The information was dismissed. The prosecution appealed by way of case stated and the Divisional Court allowed the appeal. It was held that the justices had erred in law by taking into account the age of the accused when considering whether the risk of damage was an obvious one. This decision has been reaffirmed by the Court of Appeal in *Stephen Malcolm v R*.[25] The defendant, aged 15 years, was charged with arson with intent to endanger life. In interview with the police he admitted throwing a home-made petrol bomb at the wall of a house. He explained that he thought the petrol would go out after it had burned for only a few minutes. He and his friends had not intended to cause any injury to the occupants of the house, their intention was merely to frighten them. He said he did not realise at the time that if the petrol bomb had gone through a window it might have killed the occupant. He had only realised this when he was interviewed by the police. Ackner LJ held that the fact that this particular 15-year-old did not spot an obvious risk was immaterial and his conviction was upheld.

3.37 Psychological evidence is not admissible to establish that a particular defendant would not have been able to identify a risk obvious to the reasonably prudent person.[26]

3.38 A different test for recklessness applies to offences under the Offences Against the Person Act 1861 which require malice. The test was defined in *R v Cunningham*[27] where it was held that the accused must have realised that there was a risk of injury being caused. In *W (a Minor) v DPP*[28] a young person was charged with malicious wounding after he fired an air rifle at his friend. The justices found that he had not foreseen that any harm would come to the victim but, nevertheless, they convicted him. The conviction was quashed by the Divisional Court.

25 (1984) 79 Cr App R 334.
26 *R v Coles* [1994] Crim LR 820, CA.
27 [1957] 2 QB 396.
28 (1983) 78 Cr App R 1, QBD.

Duress

3.39 When a person commits a criminal offence under the threat of violence from another s/he may be able to rely on the excuse of duress. The threat involved must be of death or grievous bodily harm. The fact that the defendant took the threat seriously is not enough if a person of reasonable firmness *sharing the characteristics of the defendant* would not have given way to the threats.[29] It has been held that the youth of the accused is a relevant characteristic, which should be taken into account when considering the reasonableness of the behaviour.[30]

3.40 Even with the subjective element in the test for duress, there will still be many occasions when children or young persons committed crimes out of a fear of others. The fear may be understandable in the light of the accused's age but not be sufficient to constitute duress. In such circumstances the defence lawyer should consider making representations to the Crown Prosecution Service regarding discontinuance, arguing that the prosecution is not in the public interest.[31]

Self-defence

3.41 To have available a defence of self-defence the accused must have used reasonable force. The test as to whether the degree of force used was reasonable has both an objective and subjective element. According to Ormrod LJ in *R v Shannon*[32] the court or jury will have to apply two tests:

> . . . an objective test, that is what is reasonable judged from the viewpoint of an outsider looking at the situation quite dispassionately, and 'the subjective test', that is the viewpoint of the accused himself with the intellectual capabilities of which he may be possessed and with all the emotional strains and stresses to which at the moment he may be subjected.

The second subjective element would allow the court to take into account the youth of a defendant.

---

29 *R v Howe* [1987] AC 417, HL.
30 *R v Hudson* [1971] 2 QB 202, CA.
31 See para 6.42.
32 (1980) 71 Cr App R 192.

Provocation

3.42 Provocation is a defence to a charge of murder only. It has been defined as some act, or series of acts, done by the dead person to the accused which would cause in any reasonable person, and actually causes in the accused, a sudden and temporary loss of control, rendering the accused so subject to passion as to make him/her for the moment not the master of his/her mind.[33] In *R v Camplin*[34] Lord Diplock stated that 'to require old heads upon young shoulders is inconsistent with the law's compassion to human infirmity'. It was held that the age of the accused at the time of the killing was a relevant characteristic to be taken into account by the jury.

Changing age during the proceedings

Age at time of offence

3.43 The age of the offender at the time of the offence has a procedural significance in relation to the following sentences:

- secure training order (offender must have attained the age of 12 by date of offence); and
- detention during Her Majesty's pleasure (offender must be aged under 18 at the time of the offence).

As the age on the date of offence generally has little procedural significance, there will be occasions when the court will have much greater powers by the time the offender comes before the court. The relevance of this fact to the court's decision making has been considered in a series of recent Court of Appeal decisions (*R v Cuddington*,[35] *R v Divisi*[36] and *R v Dashwood*[37]) which all involved the dilemma of how to sentence an adult for sexual offences committed a number of years earlier when the offender was a young person. In each of the cases the court had to consider whether it was relevant that at the time of the commission of the offences there were severe limitations on the length of a custodial sentence which could be imposed upon a young person. In *Cuddington*, Potter J

---

33 *R v Duffy* [1949] 1 All ER 932.
34 [1978] AC 707, HL.
35 [1994] Crim LR 698.
36 [1994] Crim LR 699.
37 (1995) 16 Cr App R (S) 733.

considered that the fact that if the offences had been prosecuted at the time would have meant that a maximum penalty of 12 months detention would have been available was a powerful factor to be taken into account. In *Dashwood*, Lord Taylor CJ agreed with this proposition but added that it was not the sole and determinative factor. The court would also have to consider all the circumstances of the case including the way in which the accused conducted his/her defence.

3.44   Adapting these principles to the more usual situation in the youth court, the defence lawyer would wish to draw the court's attention to the following:

- the age of the offender at the time of the offence;
- the length of time since the offence;
- whether any delays in bringing the case to court may be attributed to the police or Crown Prosecution Service;[38] and
- changes in the lifestyle and circumstances of the child or young person since the offence.

Attaining the age of 18 years

3.45   Attaining the age of 18 after arrest for an offence may affect the jurisdiction of the youth court to hear the case. The Children and Young Persons Act 1963 s29(1) provides:

> Where proceedings in respect of a young person are begun for an offence and he attains the age of eighteen before the conclusion of the proceedings, the court may deal with the case and make any order which it could have made if he had not attained that age.

This section allows the youth court to continue dealing with a young person who has appeared before it and subsequently attains the age of 18. It does not remove the accused's right to elect jury trial in the case of an indictable offence where s/he has attained the age of 18 prior to the court considering mode of trial.[39]

3.46   Section 29(1) will also allow a sentencing court to pass a sentence such as a supervision order where otherwise the offender would be too old.

---

38 See also below, 'Deliberate delays' at para 3.51.
39 See Chapter 9.

Relevant age for sentencing

3.47   The rule for determining the relevant age depends upon whether the court is sentencing the offender for the offence for the first time or is sentencing him/her after the breach of an earlier sentence.

Original sentence

3.48   The relevant age is the offender's age on the date of conviction. This is the date of the finding of guilt (ie, when the offender enters a guilty plea or is found guilty).[40] This principle has been confirmed in relation to the power to commit for sentence under the Magistrates' Courts Act 1980 s37[41] as well as the sentences of detention in a young offender institution[42] and s53(2) detention.[43] There seems no reason why the same rule would not apply to other sentences.

Re-sentencing following discharge/revocation/breach

3.49   The relevant age is the offender's age on the date when he was originally convicted for the following:

- attendance centre order;[44]
- reparation order;[45]
- action plan order;[46]
- supervision order (imposed on or after 30 September 1998).[47]

3.50   The relevant age is the offender's age on the date when the existing order is revoked or discharged for each of the following:

- probation order;[48]
- community service order;[49]
- combination order;[50]
- curfew order;[51]

---

40   *R v T (a juvenile)* [1979] Crim LR 588.
41   *R v Starkey* (1993) 15 Cr App R (S) 576, [1994] Crim LR 380, CA.
42   R v Danga (1992) 13 Cr App R (S) 408, CA.
43   *R v Robinson* (1992) 14 Cr App R (S) 448, CA.
44   Criminal Justice Act 1982 s19; *R v Wyre Magistrates' Court ex p Boardman* (1987) 9 Cr App R (S) 214.
45   Crime and Disorder Act 1998 Sch 5 para 3.
46   Ibid.
47   Children and Young Persons Act 1969 s15(3) and (5) as amended by Crime and Disorder Act 1998 s72.
48   Criminal Justice Act 1991 Sch 2 paras 3 and 4.
49   Ibid.
50   Ibid but cf, *R v McDonagh* [1995] Crim LR 512, CA.
51   Ibid.

- drug treatment and testing order;[52]
- supervision order made before 30 September 1998 (if supervised person has attained the age of 18 or the order was made as a direct alternative to custody).[53]

In the case of a conditional discharge which has been breached, the relevant age would seem to be the offender's age at the date when s/he is convicted of the subsequent offence.[54]

Deliberate delays

3.51 There will be occasions when the police or a court will be tempted to delay taking action to await the next birthday of a child or young person so that greater powers may be available to the court. This should be challenged by the defence lawyer.

Delays by the police

3.52 Where it may be demonstrated that the police deliberately delayed in charging a child or young person to await the attainment of a certain age, the question of abuse of process may fall to be determined by the court. This question was considered by the Divisional Court in *R v Rotherham Justices ex p Brough*.[55] The defendant had been 16 years old when he was arrested for 'glassing' another youth. The police referred the file to the Crown Prosecution Service for advice. He was eventually summonsed for the offence of wounding with intent to appear after his 17th birthday (which at the time would have meant that he had to go to the adult magistrates' court). It later transpired that the police had been advised to ensure that the defendant's first appearance was after he had attained the age of 17. When this was discovered it was argued that the prosecution was an abuse of process as it was a deliberate manipulation of the situation to suit the prosecution. The magistrates held there was no abuse of process and proceeded to commit the defendant to stand trial. An application for judicial review to quash the committal was rejected. The Divisional Court ruled that the prosecution had manipulated the date of first

---

52 Ibid.
53 Children and Young Persons Act 1969 s15(3)(b) and (4) before implementation of Crime and Disorder Act 1998 s72.
54 Powers of Criminal Courts Act 1973 s1B.
55 [1991] Crim LR 522.

appearance in an unacceptable way but that it could not be said that any element of mala fides could be attributed to this action. It was considered that no great harm had been done to the defendant. Although it was accepted that the defendant had been deprived of the 'protective jurisdiction' of the juvenile court (as it then was), the court noted that the delay was of just under a week and that in any event a juvenile court would almost certainly have adjudged committal for trial to have been appropriate for the offence in question. Moreover, if he were convicted the court had no doubt that the trial judge would take account of the defendant's age at the time of the offence and the circumstances of the committal.

3.53   While the decision reached in this particular case is not surprising, it does arguably leave open the possibility of a successful abuse of process argument in other situations.

Delay by the court

3.54   It has been held in *Arthur v Stringer*[56] that the power to adjourn for sentence must be exercised judicially and would not be so exercised if done solely for the purpose of allowing the offender to attain the minimum age for a certain sentence. By analogy it is argued that it would be improper to adjourn before taking pleas solely to ensure that the defendant has attained the minimum age for a sentence the court wishes to impose.

56   (1986) 84 Cr App R 361; [1987] Crim LR 563; 151 JP 97, QBD.

CHAPTER 4

The Children Act

For complete chapter contents, see overleaf

Introduction

4.1 In a text dealing with the criminal justice system, it may be surprising to see a chapter devoted to the major piece of child care legislation. It is the authors' strong belief that a thorough understanding of the Children Act is necessary to represent a child or young person in the criminal courts.

Objectives of the Children Act

4.2 The Children Act not only codifies the law relating to both the private and public law on the care of children, but also introduces new principles and practice. Principles relevant to children who appear before the criminal courts include:

- the overriding purpose is to promote and safeguard the welfare of children;
- children are best looked after within the family with both parents playing a full part without recourse to legal proceedings;
- where parents are unable to care for a child properly any help should be provided, if possible, on a voluntary basis with the local authority working in partnership with the parents;
- while caring for a child, a local authority must promote contact with the child's parents;
- in caring for a child, a local authority must take into account a child's racial origin and cultural and linguistic background; and
- children should be protected both from the harm which can arise from failures or abuse within the family and from the harm which can be caused by unwarranted intervention in their family life.

Glossary

4.3 This glossary is designed to provide an explanation of the most important terms that may not be familiar to a criminal defence lawyer. It is not intended that the discussion which follows be comprehensive and for more detailed analysis the reader is referred to specialist legal textbooks.[1]

---

1 The standard reference work is *Clarke, Hall and Morrison on Children* (Butterworths, loose-leaf).

Advice and assistance

4.4   Any person under the age of 21 who has been looked after by a local authority for a period of more than 24 hours at any time since attaining the age of 16 is entitled to advice and assistance. This service must be provided by the authority in whose area the young person is, rather than the authority who previously looked after him/her.[2]

4.5   There is considerable variation in the way that local authorities arrange their services. In some local authorities the service is provided through a specialist leaving care team; in others the service is provided through the fieldwork teams. The range of provision includes nomination to housing departments or housing associations, grants to cover such things as rent deposits and basic furnishings as well as practical advice and support.

Child

4.6   Defined as a person under the age of 18.[3]

Care order

4.7   Children are made the subject of care orders under s31(1) following family proceedings. Upon the making of the order the local authority acquires parental responsibility.[4] The local authority is under a duty to accommodate and maintain any child for whom a care order is held.[5] The authority may also determine the extent to which a parent or guardian may meet the parental responsibility to the child.[6]

Education supervision order

4.8   This order is made in a family proceedings court on the application of a local education authority. It may only be made if the court is satisfied that a child of compulsory school age is not being properly educated.[7] Before applying for the order the education authority must

---

2   Children Act 1989 s24(1) and (2). See also *R v Lambeth LBC ex p Cadell* [1998] 1 FLR 253; [1998] 2 FCR 6.
3   Ibid, s105(1).
4   Ibid, s31(3)(a).
5   Ibid, s23(1).
6   Ibid, s31(3)(b).
7   Ibid, s36(1) and (3).

consult with the local services department. The order cannot be made in relation to a child in care.[8]

4.9 The supervisor will be an education social worker or welfare officer whose duty is to advise, assist and befriend, and give directions to the child and parents to secure proper education of the child.[9] Failure to comply with such directions is an offence.[10]

4.10 An education supervision order is distinct from an education requirement attached to a supervision order under the Children and Young Persons Act 1969 s12C. Such an additional requirement cannot be imposed while an education supervision order is in force.

Emergency protection order

4.11 An emergency protection order is initially limited to eight days and is made by a court to ensure the safety of a child where there is reasonable cause to believe the child would otherwise suffer significant harm if not moved to (or kept in) accommodation provided by the applicant (usually a local authority).[11] While an emergency protection order is in force it gives the applicant parental responsibility.[12]

Independent visitor

4.12 A local authority must appoint an independent visitor for a child they are looking after if it appears that:

- communication between the child and his/her parent or any other person with parental responsibility has been infrequent; or
- s/he has not visited or been visited by (or lived with) any such person during the preceding 12 months; and in either case
- it would be in the child's best interests to appoint such a visitor.[13]

An independent visitor has the duty of visiting, advising and befriending the child.[14]

8 Ibid, s36(6).
9 Ibid, Sch 3 Part III para 12.
10 Ibid, Sch 3 Part III para 18.
11 Ibid, s44.
12 Ibid, s44(4)(c) and (5)(b).
13 Ibid, Sch 2 Part II para 17(1).
14 Ibid, Sch 2 Part II para 17(2).

Local authority accommodation

4.13 Local authorities are under a duty to provide accommodation to a child in the following circumstances:

- there is no person who has parental responsibility;
- the child is lost or abandoned;
- the person caring for the child is prevented from providing him/her with suitable accommodation and care.[15]

4.14 In the case of children who have attained the age of 16, local authorities must also accommodate a child whose welfare the authority considers will be seriously prejudiced if they do not provide him/her with accommodation.[16] There is furthermore a discretion to provide accommodation in a community home for a child if it is considered that this would safeguard or promote the child's welfare.[17]

4.15 When meeting its obligation to provide accommodation the authority may:

- place him/her with a parent, relative or foster parent;
- place him/her in a residential home;
- place him/her in a Youth Treatment Centre (run by the Department of Health); or
- make such other arrangements as seem appropriate to the authority (subject to regulations issued by the Secretary of State).[18]

Looked after child

4.16 A 'looked after' child is any child who is in care or who has been provided with local authority accommodation for a continuous period of 24 hours.[19]

Parental responsibility

4.17 'Parental responsibility' is defined as 'all the rights, duties, powers, responsibilities and authority which, by law, a parent has in relation to a child and his property'.[20] Where parents are married at the time of

15 Ibid, s20(1).
16 Ibid, s20(3).
17 Ibid, s20(5).
18 Ibid, s23(2).
19 Ibid, s22(1) and (2).
20 Ibid, s3(1).

the child's birth, both have parental responsibility automatically; otherwise the mother alone has it. A father who does not have parental responsibility may acquire it by making a parental responsibility agreement with the mother or by applying to a court for an order.[21] People, other than parents, may only acquire parental responsibility by the private appointment of a guardian or by order of a court.

4.18   A local authority only acquires parental responsibility as the result of the making of one of the following orders:

- a care order;[22] and
- an emergency protection order.[23]

Note that parental responsibility is not acquired when the court makes a supervision order under s31 in favour of a local authority.

4.19   The issue of who holds parental responsibility is relevant in criminal proceedings because it determines who may be ordered to pay any financial penalty.[24]

Police protection

4.20   Where a constable has reasonable cause to believe that a child would otherwise be likely to suffer significant harm, s/he may:

- remove the child to suitable accommodation and keep him/her there; or
- take such steps as are reasonable to ensure that the child's removal from any hospital, or other place, in which s/he is then being accommodated is prevented.[25]

4.21   As soon as practicable after taking the child into police protection, the constable is required to:

- inform the local authority in whose area the child was found of the steps which have been, and are proposed to be, taken with respect to the child and the reasons for taking them;
- give details to the authority within whose area the child is ordinarily resident of the place at which the child is being accommodated;
- inform the child (if s/he appears capable of understanding) of the steps taken and those steps proposed;

21 Ibid, s4(1).
22 Ibid, s33(3).
23 Ibid, s44(4)(c).
24 See Chapter 7.
25 Children Act 1989 s46(1).

- secure that the case is inquired into by an officer designated for the purpose; and
- secure the child's transfer to local authority accommodation if s/he is not already in police protection in such accommodation.[26]

4.22   Once the child is in police protection, the constable must take such steps as are reasonably practicable to notify the child's parents or other carer.[27] The designated officer is under a duty to complete an investigation into the welfare of the child, and on completing the investigation s/he must release the child from police protection unless s/he considers that there is reasonable cause for believing that the child would be likely to suffer significant harm if released.[28]

Reviews and care plans

4.23   It is the duty of a local authority looking after any child:

- to safeguard and promote his/her welfare; and
- to make such use of services available for children cared for by their own parents as appears to the authority reasonable in the child's case.[29]

4.24   To fulfil this obligation local authorities must draw up a care plan for any child who is being looked after. In formulating this plan, the local authority must, so far as is reasonably practicable, ascertain the wishes and feelings of :

- the child;
- his/her parents;
- any person who is not a parent but who has parental responsibility; and
- any other person whose wishes and feelings are considered to be relevant.[30]

Due consideration should be given to the views expressed by any of the above as well as to the child's religious persuasion, racial origin and cultural and linguistic background.[31]

4.25   The care plan should be reviewed within a month of the child

---

26   Ibid, s46(3).
27   Ibid, s46(4).
28   Ibid, s46(5).
29   Ibid, s22(3).
30   Ibid, s22(4).
31   Ibid, s22(5).

being looked after. There should then be a further review after three months and thereafter within six months.[32]

Significant harm

4.26 When construing the meaning of serious harm, the following definitions are to be used:

- – 'harm' means ill-treatment or the impairment of health or development;
- – 'development' means physical, intellectual, emotional, social or behavioural development;
- – 'health' means physical or mental health;
- – 'ill-treatment' includes sexual abuse and forms of abuse which are not physical.[33]

4.27 Where the question of whether harm suffered by a child is significant turns on the child's health or development, his/her health or development shall be compared with that which could be reasonably expected of a similar child.[34]

Supervision order

4.28 A child may be made the subject of a supervision order under s31(1)(b) following family proceedings. The local authority does not acquire parental responsibility when such an order is made.

4.29 While a supervision order is in force it shall be the duty of the supervisor to advise, assist and befriend the supervised person and to take such steps as are reasonably necessary to give effect to the order.[35] There is no criminal sanction if the child does not comply with any directions. In such circumstances the supervisor may only apply to the court for variation or discharge of the order.

32 Review of Childrens' Cases Regulations 1991 SI No 895 reg 3.
33 Children Act 1989 ss31(9) and 105(1).
34 Ibid, ss31(10) and 105(1).
35 Ibid, s35(1).

Making the Children Act work for defendants before the courts

Young offenders as children in need

4.30   By the Children Act 1989 s17(1) it is the general duty of every local authority to provide an appropriate range and level of services:

– to safeguard and promote the welfare of children within their area who are in need; and
– so far as is consistent with that duty, to promote the upbringing of such children by their families.

4.31   A child in defined as being in need if:

– s/he is unlikely to achieve or maintain, or have the opportunity of achieving or maintaining a reasonable standard of health or development without the provision for him/her of services by the local authority; or
– his/her health or development is likely to be significantly impaired, or further impaired, without the provision of local authority services; or
– s/he is disabled.[36]

4.32   Every local authority is required to take reasonable steps to identify the extent to which there are children in need within their area.[37] Information regarding their services must be provided and steps must be taken to ensure that those who might benefit receive information about services.[38]

4.33   The extent to which local authorities give consideration to young offenders and their families within their child care planning and in service provision varies enormously. The provision of services to young offenders is usually through the youth justice (or youth offending) team. The extent to which the needs of young offenders are recognised and met by other departments of the local authority will depend on local variations in service structure. Although clearly a very needy group, young offenders compete with other groups for scarce resources – money spent on a young offender is money which cannot be spent on child protection or a family centre.

4.34   The obligations under s17(1) may be invoked to seek:

36 Ibid, s17(10).
37 Ibid, Sch 2 Part I para 1.
38 Ibid, Sch 2 Part I para 2.

- financial support for a family;
- respite care for children in the family;
- outreach workers to be allocated to the family to work with the child or young person; and
- the provision of resources to supplement any bail support.

Where any request for help under this section is meeting resistance, the defence lawyer may wish to remind the local authority of its duty to reduce the need for criminal proceedings[39] and to encourage children not to commit crime.[40]

Provision of accommodation

4.35 The fact that a defendant does not have a fixed address is likely to lead to a refusal of bail. Faced with a homeless young person the defence lawyer will need to ensure that the local authority meets its obligations under s20.[41]

4.36 If the social services department does not immediately accept that the young persons' welfare will be seriously prejudiced, the defence lawyer will need to take detailed instruction regarding the young person's background in order to demonstrate the risk of serious prejudice. Relevant factors could include:

- no access to welfare benefits;
- problems continuing with education or training without stable accommodation;
- history of physical, sexual or emotional abuse;
- alcohol, drug or substance abuse;
- risk of prostitution;
- offending a direct result of lack of stable accommodation; and
- risk of custodial remand if accommodation not provided.

It is important to establish whether the young person has previously been a looked after child at any time since attaining the age of 16. If this is the case, the local authority has a specific duty to provide advice and assistance.[42]

4.37 If the local authority has agreed to provide accommodation to a homeless defendant, the court can either bail to a particular address

---

39 Children Act 1989 Sch 2 Part I para 7(a)(ii).
40 Ibid, Sch 2 Part I para 7(b).
41 See paras 4.13–4.15.
42 Children Act 1989 s24(2) and see para 4.4.

or bail with a condition to reside as directed by the relevant local authority.[43]

4.38   If it proves impossible to persuade a local authority to provide accommodation for a 16-year-old under either s20(3) or s20(5), the defence lawyer could invite the court to refuse bail for his/her own welfare. Upon a remand to local authority accommodation under the Children and Young Persons Act 1969 s23(1) the designated local authority would then have a statutory obligation to receive the child and provide accommodation.[44]

Duty to accommodate detained and remanded children

4.39   Every local authority is under a duty to receive, and provide accommodation for, children:

   - transferred from police detention under the Police and Criminal Evidence Act 1984 s38(6); and
   - remanded to local authority accommodation under the Children and Young Persons Act 1969 s23(1).[45]

Children in police detention

4.40   There are no criteria for selecting the local authority which should receive and provide accommodation for a detained child. The obligation would seem to fall upon whichever local authority the custody officer contacts.[46] In practice this will usually be the local authority in whose area the police station is situated, unless another authority has already been involved, perhaps by the provision of an appropriate adult.

4.41   This lack of a definition may cause problems where a child has been arrested in another local authority area to the area where s/he lives or, in the case of children of travellers, where there may be no clear connection with any authority. If two or more authorities disagree about responsibility for providing accommodation, the authority in whose area the child is currently detained should be reminded that they are permitted to recover the costs of providing the accommodation from the local authority where the child is ordinarily resi-

---

43   See Chapter 10.
44   See para 4.42.
45   Children Act 1989 s21(2).
46   Ibid, s21(2)(b).

dent.[47] In determining where a child is 'ordinarily resident', any period spent in any of the following should be disregarded:

- a residential school;
- any place where the child has lived pursuant to the requirements of a supervision order; or
- any place where the child has been provided with accommodation by or on behalf of a local authority.[48]

Remanded children

4.42   The duty to receive the child and provide accommodation falls upon the authority specified by the court as the designated local authority. In the case of a defendant already being looked after by a local authority, it shall be that authority. In all other cases it may be either:

- the authority in whose area it appears to the court that the defendant resides; or
- the authority in whose area the offence or one of the offences was committed.[49]

4.43   The type of accommodation chosen by the local authority is completely in their discretion; however, the Department of Health has given the following guidance:

> While a remand to 'local authority accommodation' continues to leave the authority with discretion about the most appropriate placement for the juvenile on remand, full account should be taken of the fact that:
> (a) The court has already been required to consider why the juvenile should not be bailed and allowed to return home, and has determined that this would not be appropriate;
> (b) The local authority has a responsibility to ensure that the juvenile is produced in court at the date, place and time specified, and to take all reasonable steps to protect the public from the risk of the juvenile committing further offences during the remand period. (The nature of the steps required to protect the public will depend on the juvenile concerned and on the alleged offence.)[50]

4.44   Where there is a risk that the court will be considering a custodial remand, it is important for the defence lawyer to ensure that the local

---

47   Ibid, s29(8).
48   Ibid, s105(6).
49   Children and Young Persons Act 1969 s23(2).
50   *The Children Act 1989 Guidance and Regulations* (HMSO, 1991), Vol 1, Court Orders, para 6.37.

authority is prepared to allocate sufficient resources to the placement to satisfy the court that the public will be adequately protected from serious harm. It should be noted that the local authority may exercise any of its powers under the Children Act with respect to a 'looked after' child if it considers it necessary for the purpose of protecting members of the public from serious injury.[51] This power may be exercised even when not consistent with promoting the welfare of the child. The Secretary of State for Health may direct the local authority to exercise its powers in order to protect the public.[52]

4.45   Even where a child has been remanded into custody, the designated local authority should keep the question of alternative local authority accommodation under active review:

> On each occasion that a juvenile is returned to the court for the remand to be reviewed, careful consideration should be given to advising the court whether alternative arrangements might be considered. For example, where a juvenile has been remanded to a penal establishment [under section 23(5)], the court may be willing to consider a remand to local authority accommodation if they are presented with a clear statement of how the juvenile would be accommodated within the care system in such a way that the public would be protected from the risk of further offending and that he would be produced in court when required.[53]

4.46   A defendant remanded to local authority accommodation is a looked after child for the purposes of the Act. The local authority, therefore, has the same obligations to him/her that apply to any other looked after child. This means that the authority must establish a care plan and review that plan regularly. The Department of Health accept that it has the same obligations as with any other looked after child:

> [I]n considering how they exercise their general powers in relation to [remanded children] under section 22, local authorities may have regard to the need to protect members of the public from serious injury (section 22(6)). Because of the transitory nature of the status of remanded alleged juvenile offenders it is not practicable to make long-term plans for such children, but interim contingency plans might be formulated to take account of the sentencing options available to the court if convicted.[54]

51   Children Act 1989 s22(6).
52   Ibid, s22(7) and (8).
53   *The Children Act 1989 Guidance and Regulations* (see n50), para 6.39.
54   Ibid, para 6.36.

Even an interim plan could be extremely useful when presenting mitigation to the sentencing court and it is important to ensure that such planning does in fact take place.

Duty to investigate alleged abuse against children

4.47   Where a local authority has reasonable cause to suspect that a child who lives, or is found, in their area is suffering or is likely to suffer significant harm, the authority shall make or cause to be made, such enquiries as it considers necessary to enable it to decide whether it should take any action to safeguard or promote the child's welfare.[55]

4.48   This duty has apparently been used by at least two local authorities to investigate alleged abuse against juvenile prisoners in prisons, remand centres or young offender institutions in their areas. The existence of such an investigation would be a powerful factor in any subsequent bail application.

Remedies

4.49   When the defence lawyer wishes to secure particular local authority services for his/her client during the course of criminal proceedings, time will usually be of the essence. The quickest way to resolve any problem will always be to negotiate with the social services department. If necessary, attempts may have to be made to contact senior management. If such representations are not successful, the following may have to be considered.

Complaints procedure

4.50   Every local authority must establish a procedure for considering representations and complaints by (or on behalf of) a child regarding the provision of services under Part III of the Act.[56] Part III covers the duties to provide services to children in need as well as the duties to provide accommodation and the use of secure accommodation

---

55   Children Act 1989 s47.
56   Children Act 1989 s26(3).

orders.[57] This complaints procedure should be advertised by the authority.[58]

4.51　　The procedure should ensure that at least one person who is not a member of the local authority takes part in the consideration of any representations or complaints and any discussions which are held by the authority about the action (if any) to be taken in relation to the child.[59] The authority is required to provide a written response within 28 days of receiving the complaint.[60]

Judicial review

4.52　Judicial review is a discretionary remedy. It is a general principle that relief will not generally be granted unless all other remedies have been exhausted. The complaints procedure is designed to be the main remedy for persons aggrieved by the services (or lack of them) provided by a local authority. As a result the Divisional Court will be reluctant to entertain an application for judicial review.[61] It has, however, demonstrated that it will interfere where it can be demonstrated that the local authority has failed to have regard to the recommendations of a complaints panel.[62] Where the services of the local authority are required urgently and the complaints procedure is therefore not an effective remedy, it is arguable that an application for judicial review might be possible immediately without the need for making a complaint. This might be the case where the authority's refusal to provide a service has resulted in the child's remand in custody.

Default powers of the Secretary of State

4.53　If the Secretary of State for Health is satisfied that any local authority has failed without reasonable excuse to comply with any duty imposed on them by the Children Act, s/he may make an order declaring that authority to be in default with respect to that duty.[63] An

---

57　Complaints regarding other local authority services and decisions may be made under the Local Authority Social Services Act 1970 s7B.

58　Children Act 1989 s26(8).

59　Ibid, s26(4).

60　Representations Procedure (Children) Regulations 1991 SI No 894 reg 6(1).

61　See, for example, *R v Birmingham City Council ex p A (a Minor)* (1997) *Times*, February 19, FD.

62　See *Re T (Accommodation by local authority)* [1995] 1 FLR 159 and *R v Avon County Council ex p M (a Minor)* [1994] 2 FCR 259.

63　Children Act 1989 s84(1).

order may be issued giving such directions as appear necessary to ensure that the duty is complied with.[64] These directions are enforceable by the Secretary of State by means of an application for judicial review to the Divisional Court.[65]

4.54   There seems to be little evidence that this power is being used. It is not clear whether it would be an effective remedy where a local authority has refused to allocate resources in a particular case or whether its main use is where an authority does not have a service envisaged under the Act.[66]

---

64   Ibid, s84(3).
65   Ibid, s84(4).
66   For example, in *R v Barnet LBC ex p B* [1994] 1 FLR 592 where it was alleged that the authority had no day-care service.

CHAPTER 5

Police powers

For complete chapter contents, see overleaf

Stop and search powers

5.1 By the Police and Criminal Evidence Act 1984 s1 a police constable in a public place may search any person or motor vehicle for stolen or prohibited articles. The constable must have reasonable grounds to believe that s/he will find such an article as a result of the search.

5.2 A prohibited article is an offensive weapon or bladed article or an article made or adapted for use in the course of or in connection with an offence of burglary, theft, taking without consent or obtaining property by deception.[1]

5.3 A separate power to stop and search for controlled drugs also exists under the Misuse of Drugs Act 1971 s23.

5.4 'Public place' is defined as:

- any place to which at the time of the proposed search the public or any section of the public has access, on payment or otherwise as of right or by virtue of express or implied permission; or
- any other place to which people have ready access at the time of the proposed search but which is not a dwelling.[2]

5.5 If the person whom the constable intends to search is in a garden or yard occupied with or used for the purposes of a dwelling or on other land so occupied and used, a constable may not search that person unless the constable has reasonable grounds for believing:

- that the person does not reside in the dwelling; and
- that s/he is not in the place in question with the express or implied permission of a person who resides in the dwelling.[3]

5.6 A police officer may seek to search a member of the public with their co-operation. This is a potential way to circumvent the safeguards of the Act and the Home Office have issued a circular regarding the stop and search powers which states:

> In any situation where a constable exercises a power of search under this Act, the co-operation of the citizen should not be taken as implying consent, and the exercise of the power should be noted in the appropriate record. Whilst it is legitimate to invite co-operation from the public in circumstances where there is no power to require it, the subject of a voluntary search must properly understand the

---

1 Police and Criminal Evidence Act 1984 s1(7) and (8).
2 Ibid, s1(1).
3 Ibid, s1(4).

position and not be left with the impression that a power is being exercised.[4]

Juveniles are deemed to be persons who are incapable of giving informed consent and they should not be subject to a voluntary search.[5]

5.7   A person who has been searched is entitled to a copy of the national search record if s/he applies to the police station where the officer is based within 12 months of the search.[6]

Power of arrest

5.8   The same police powers of arrest exist for children and young persons as exist for adult suspects. In addition there are some powers specific to children and young persons.

Arrest under warrant

5.9   A police constable may arrest a child or young person against whom a court has issued an arrest warrant. This will usually be after the child or young person has failed to attend a court hearing, although it is possible to initiate court proceedings by means of a warrant. The court may endorse the warrant as with or without bail.

5.10   When arrested on warrant a juvenile must not be released unless his/her parent or guardian enters into a recognisance for such amount as the custody officer at the police station where s/he is detained considers will secure the juvenile's attendance at the hearing of the charge. Any recognisance entered into may, if the custody officer thinks fit, be conditioned for the attendance of the parent or guardian at the hearing in addition to the juvenile.[7]

Arrestable offences

5.11   The Police and Criminal Evidence Act 1984 s24 gives a power of summary arrest (ie arrest without warrant) to a police officer who:

– has reasonable grounds for believing that a person is guilty of an arrestable offence;

---

4   Home Office Circular 88/1985, *The Police and Criminal Evidence Act 1984.*
5   Code A Note for Guidance 1E.
6   Code A para 2.6.
7   Children and Young Persons Act 1969 s29(1).

- has reasonable grounds for believing that a person is about to commit an arrestable offence.

5.12   An arrestable offence is defined as follows:

- an offence for which the penalty is fixed by law;
- an offence for which a person aged 21 or over may be sentenced to imprisonment for a term of five years;
- certain specific offences which do not satisfy the above criterion including: going equipped for stealing, taking a conveyance without consent and aggravated vehicle taking.[8]

General arrest conditions

5.13   Under the Police and Criminal Evidence Act 1984 s25 a constable may arrest a person where the constable has reasonable grounds for believing that the person has committed or attempted to commit an offence (other than an arrestable one), where one of the general arrest conditions apply.

5.14   The general arrest conditions are as follows:

- the name and address of the suspect is unknown to, and cannot be readily ascertained by, the constable;
- the constable has reasonable grounds for doubting whether a name furnished by the suspect as his/her name is the real name;
- the suspect has failed to furnish a satisfactory address for service or the constable has reasonable grounds for doubting whether the address furnished by the suspect is a satisfactory address for service;
- the constable has reasonable grounds for believing arrest is necessary to prevent the suspect:
  - i)   causing physical harm to him/herself or any other person
  - ii)   suffering physical injury
  - iii)   causing loss or damage to property
  - iv)   committing an offence against public decency
  - v)   causing an unlawful obstruction of the highway;
- the constable has reasonable grounds for believing that arrest is necessary to protect a child or other vulnerable person from the suspect.

8   For a full list see Police and Criminal Evidence Act 1984 s24(2).

Relevance of age

5.15   There is no statutory restriction on the exercise of a power of arrest in relation to a child or young person. In practice most police forces will make very few concessions to the youth of a suspect when exercising the power of arrest.

Suspects under 10 years of age

5.16   Such suspects are under the age of criminal responsibility and as such are conclusively deemed to be incapable of committing a criminal offence.[9] A police officer will not, therefore, be able to arrest a child who is known to be under the age of 10 as there will be no power of arrest derived from the suspicion that a criminal offence has been committed.[10]

5.17   A constable may have a power to detain a child under the age of 10 if s/he is considered to be in breach of a local child curfew order or a truant from school in a designated area. For both of these powers see Chapter 25.

Arresting juveniles at their place of education

5.18   The Codes of Practice give the following guidance:

> It is preferable that a juvenile is not arrested at his place of education unless this is unavoidable. Where a juvenile is arrested at his place of education, the principal or his nominee must be informed.[11]

Wards of court

5.19   A police officer may arrest a ward of court suspected of a criminal offence without seeking the leave of the High Court. The guardian ad litem should be informed of the arrest as soon as practicable.[12] It is the duty of those having care of the ward to inform the court at the earliest practical opportunity of what has taken place.[13]

---

9   Children and Young Persons Act 1933 s50.
10   A police officer faced with such a situation may wish to exercise the power to take a child into police protection under the Children Act 1989 s46.
11   Code C Note for Guidance 11C.
12   *Practice Direction* [1988] 2 All ER 1015.
13   *Re R, re G (minors)* [1981] 2 All ER 193, QBD.

Authorising detention

Initial authorisation

5.20   A custody officer may authorise the detention of a suspect at a police station. The custody officer must first determine if there is sufficient evidence to charge the suspect for the offence for which s/he has been arrested. If the custody officer considers there is not sufficient evidence the suspect *must* be released on bail or without bail, unless the custody officer has reasonable grounds for believing that the suspect's detention without being charged is *necessary*:

- to secure or preserve evidence relating to an offence for which s/he is under arrest;
- to obtain such evidence by questioning him/her.[14]

Detention reviews

5.21   A detention review must be conducted by a police officer of the rank of at least inspector:

- not later than six hours after detention is first authorised;
- not later than nine hours after the first review; and
- at nine-hourly intervals thereafter.[15]

5.22   The review officer must be a police officer of at least the rank of inspector who is not involved in the investigation of the offence. To authorise further detention the review officer must be satisfied that there are still grounds for the detention of the suspect. S/he has to be satisfied, therefore, that detention is necessary:

- to charge the suspect;
- to secure or preserve evidence; or
- to obtain evidence by questioning the suspect.

Extension of custody time limits

5.23   In general, no suspect may be detained without charge for more than 24 hours from the time of arrival at the police station.[16] This time limit applies equally to juveniles. It may only be extended as follows in the case of serious arrestable offences:

14 Police and Criminal Evidence Act 1984 s37(1).
15 Ibid, s40.
16 Ibid, s41.

- up to 36 hours on the authority of an officer of at least the rank of superintendent;
- beyond 36 hours and up to 96 hours with a warrant of further detention issued by a magistrates' court.

Serious arrestable offence

5.24   The Police and Criminal Evidence Act 1984 s116 lists a number of offences as always being serious. These include:

- treason;
- murder;
- manslaughter;
- rape;
- kidnapping;
- incest with a girl under the age of 13;
- buggery with a person under the age of 16;
- indecent assault which constitutes an act of indecency;
- causing explosion likely to endanger life or property;
- sexual intercourse with a girl under the age of 13;
- possession of a firearm with intent to injure;
- use of firearms to resist arrest;
- carrying firearms with criminal intent;
- hostage taking;
- hijacking;
- torture;
- causing death by dangerous driving;
- causing death by careless driving when under the influence of drink or drugs;
- any offence mentioned in s1(3)(a)–(f) of the Drug Trafficking Act 1994;
- possession of indecent photographs or pseudo-photographs of children;
- publication of obscene matter.

5.25   Any other arrestable offence is serious only if its commission has led to or is intended to lead to any of the following consequences:

- serious harm to the security of the State or to public order;
- serious interference to with the administration of justice or with the investigation of offences or a particular offence;
- the death of any person;
- serious injury to any person;

- substantial financial gain to any person;
- serious financial loss to any person.

Extension by superintendent

5.26 Before the expiry of the initial 24-hour detention period, a police officer of the rank of at least superintendent may authorise further detention up to a maximum of 36 hours.[17] This may only be done if s/he has reasonable grounds for believing:

- the offence for which the suspect is under arrest is a serious arrestable offence;
- the detention of the suspect without charge is necessary to secure or preserve evidence relating to an offence for which s/he is under arrest or to obtain such evidence by questioning him/her; and
- the investigation is being conducted diligently and expeditiously.[18]

Before authorising such detention the officer must give the suspect, any appropriate adult and his/her solicitor, if available at the time of the review, the opportunity to make representations.[19] The suspect should be informed of the grounds for his/her continued detention and they should be recorded in the custody record.[20]

Warrants of further detention

5.27 A magistrate's court, on an application on oath made by a police constable and supported by an information, may issue a warrant of further detention if the court is satisfied that there are reasonable grounds for believing:

- the detention without charge of the suspect is necessary to secure or preserve evidence relating to an offence for which s/he is under arrest or to obtain such evidence by questioning him/her;
- an offence for which s/he is under arrest is a serious arrestable offence; and
- the investigation is being conducted diligently and expeditiously.[21]

The court may issue a warrant authorising further detention for up to 36 hours. Further applications may be made but detention may not

17 Ibid, s42.
18 Ibid, s43.
19 Ibid, s42(6) and Code C para 15.1.
20 Ibid, para 15.6.
21 Police and Criminal Evidence Act 1984 s43.

be authorised for more than a total of 96 hours. The suspect has the right to be represented legally at the hearing.

5.28   In the case of a child or young person it would seem that an adult magistrates' court bench may still hear the application as such warrants of further detention are not matters specifically assigned to the youth court under the Children and Young Persons Act 1933 s46.[22]

A juvenile

5.29   A juvenile is a person who has not attained the age of 17. For the purposes of the Codes of Practice:

> If any person appears to be under the age of 17 then he shall be treated as a juvenile for the purposes of this code in the absence of clear evidence to the contrary.[23]

The police are, therefore, required to treat a suspect as a juvenile if his/her physical appearance suggests that s/he is under the age of 17 and they have no clear evidence to the contrary. Equally, if the suspect lies about his/her age and s/he looks mature enough to be 17 years old the police are entitled to treat the suspect as an adult. Obviously as soon as the error is discovered the police must treat the suspect as a juvenile.

5.30   A juvenile is considered as a vulnerable suspect by the Codes of Practice, and consequently a number of protective measures have been imposed to protect the juvenile suspect. None of these protective measures apply to 17-year-old suspects.

Duty to notify

5.31   When a juvenile arrives at the police station, the custody officer has a duty to notify various persons of the arrest.

Person responsible for a juvenile's welfare

5.32   The custody officer shall take such steps as are practicable to ascertain the identity of the person responsible for his/her welfare.[24] This may be:

22 See para 9.1.
23 Code C para 1.5.
24 Children and Young Persons Act 1933 s34(2).

– the juvenile's parent or guardian;[25] or

– any other person who has for the time being assumed responsibility for his/her welfare.[26]

5.33   If it is practicable to ascertain the identity of a person responsible for the juvenile's welfare that person shall be informed unless it is not practicable to do so:

– that the juvenile has been arrested;

– why s/he has been arrested; and

– where s/he is being detained.[27]

If it is practicable to contact a person responsible for the welfare of the juvenile, the above information shall be given. The obligation exists whether or not the juvenile wishes to inform anyone of his/her arrest and cannot be delayed for any reason.

5.34   If the juvenile is in the care of the local authority or voluntary organisation but is living with his/her parents or other adults responsible for his/her welfare, the police should normally notify that person as well as the care organisation, unless the person is suspected of involvement in the offence. Even if a juvenile in care is not living with his/her parent, consideration should be given to informing them as well.[28]

Subject to a supervision order

5.35   In the case of a juvenile who is known to be subject to a supervision order as defined in the Children and Young Persons Act 1969 s11 (ie, an order imposed in criminal proceedings only), reasonable steps must also be taken to notify the person supervising him/her.[29]

The rights of a person detained

5.36   A person in police custody has three rights:

– to have a person informed of his/her arrest;

25 'Guardian' includes a local authority if the child is in care: Police and Criminal Evidence Act 1984 s118.

26 Children and Young Persons Act 1933 s34(5).

27 Ibid, s34(3).

28 Code C Note for Guidance 3C.

29 Children and Young Persons Act 1933 s34(7); see also Code C para 3.8.

- to obtain legal advice; and
- to consult a copy of the Codes of Practice.

The custody officer is obliged to inform the prisoner of these rights when a person is brought to the police station under arrest or when a volunteer is arrested at the police station. The prisoner should also be informed that these rights are continuing and may be exercised at any time while under arrest. A written copy of the rights should be handed to the prisoner.

5.37   In the case of a juvenile, the rights must be confirmed at some point in the presence of the appropriate adult. In normal circumstances the appropriate adult will not be present when the juvenile is brought into the police station. The custody officer should inform the juvenile of his/her rights and allow him/her to exercise any of them immediately without waiting for an appropriate adult to be contacted.[30] However, when the appropriate adult attends the station the juvenile should be informed of his/her rights again in the presence of the appropriate adult. If an appropriate adult attends the station with the juvenile the rights will be read in the presence of the appropriate adult.

Right to inform another of arrest

5.38   A suspect under arrest and held in a police station or other premises, may have one friend or relative or other person who is known to him/ her or who is likely to take an interest in his/her welfare informed of the arrest. This right may be exercised as soon as is practicable.[31] If the person nominated to be informed cannot be contacted, the suspect may choose up to two alternatives. If they cannot be contacted the person in charge of detention or the person in charge of the investigation has discretion to allow further attempts until the information has been conveyed.[32]

5.39   It may only be delayed in the case of a serious arrestable offence and on the authority of an officer of at least the rank of superintendent. This officer may only authorise delay if s/he has reasonable grounds for believing that telling the named person of the arrest will:

- lead to interference with or harm to evidence connected with a

---

30   Code C Note for Guidance 3G.
31   Police and Criminal Evidence Act 1984 56(1).
32   Code C para 5.1.

serious arrestable offence or interference with or physical injury to other persons; or

- lead to the alerting of other persons suspected of having committed such an offence but not yet arrested for it; or
- will hinder the recovery of any property obtained as a result of such an offence.[33]

5.40   The delay may only be authorised for a maximum of 36 hours. The duty to inform the parent or guardian of a juvenile's arrest is unaffected by this power. In any event the custody officer must make arrangements for an appropriate adult to attend the police station.

5.41   In addition to the right to have someone informed of the arrest, a detained person shall be supplied with writing materials on request and allowed to speak on the telephone for a reasonable time to one person. This right may only be delayed or denied by an officer of the rank of inspector or above:

- if the person is detained in relation to an arrestable offence; and
- the officer considers that the sending of a letter or the making of a telephone call will lead to any of the consequences listed above at para 5.39.[34]

Legal advice

5.42   A person arrested and held in custody in a police station or other premises shall be entitled, if s/he so requests, to consult a solicitor privately at any time.[35] If s/he makes such a request it should be recorded in the custody record and s/he should be permitted to consult with the solicitor as soon as is practicable.

5.43   A suspect may nominate a solicitor of his/her choice. If the suspect does not know of a solicitor, s/he may ask to speak to the duty solicitor. If the suspect does not want to consult the duty solicitor s/he should be provided with a list of solicitors willing to provide advice. All legal advice in the police station is free of charge.

5.44   This right may only be delayed in the case of a serious arrestable offence on the authority of a police officer of at least the rank of superintendent who has reasonable grounds for believing that the

---

33 Police and Criminal Evidence Act 1984 s56(5). Note the right may also be delayed in drug trafficking cases where notification will hinder the recovery of the proceeds of trafficking: s56(5A).

34 Code C para 5.6.

35 Police and Criminal Evidence Act 1984 s58(1).

exercise of the right to legal advice at the time when the suspect wishes to exercise it will:

- lead to interference with or harm to evidence connected with a serious arrestable offence or interference with or physical injury to other persons; or
- lead to the alerting of other persons suspected of having committed such an offence but not yet arrested for it; or
- hinder the recovery of any property obtained as a result of such an offence.[36]

Access to a solicitor may only be delayed for a maximum of 36 hours.[37] The superintendent may only authorise delay in access to a specific solicitor if s/he has reasonable grounds for believing that the specific solicitor will, inadvertently or otherwise, pass on a message from the detained person or act in some other way which will lead to any of the three results listed above. In such circumstances the officer should offer the detained person access to the duty solicitor scheme.[38]

5.45   The duty to inform the parent or guardian of a juvenile's arrest is unaffected by this power. In any event the custody officer must make arrangements for an appropriate adult to attend the police station.

The appropriate adult

The role of the appropriate adult

5.46   The custody officer is required to inform the appropriate adult that his/her role is to assist the juvenile and to advise him/her.[39] In addition the appropriate adult must be present while the juvenile:

- is informed of his/her rights by the custody officer (Code C para 3.11);
- is strip searched (Code C Annex A para 11(c));
- is required to submit to an intimate search (Code C Annex A para 5);
- is interviewed (Code C para 11.14);
- is charged (Code C para 16.3); or
- takes part in any identification procedure (Code D para 1.14).

36   Ibid, s58(8).
37   Ibid, s58(5).
38   Code C Annex B Note for Guidance B4; see also *R v Samuels* (1987) 87 Cr App R 232, CA.
39   Code C para 3.12.

Who may act?

5.47 The codes of practice give the police the following guidance as to who to select as the appropriate adult (Code C para 1.7):

> In this code 'the appropriate adult' means:
> (a) in the case of a juvenile:
>   (i)   his parent or guardian (or, if he is in care, the care authority or voluntary organisation. The term 'in care' is used in this code to cover all cases in which a juvenile is 'looked after' by a local authority under the terms of the Children Act 1989);
>   (ii) a social worker;
>   (iii) failing either of the above, another responsible adult aged 18 or over who is not a police officer or employed by the police.

The codes of practice can be seen to establish a clear order of preference. The police should therefore attempt to arrange for a parent/guardian or social worker to act before approaching any other responsible adult. A solicitor acting in a professional capacity or a lay visitor should never act as the appropriate adult.[40]

5.48 In general only one person should be designated to act as the appropriate adult, but there may be occasions when it would be proper for more than one adult to be present in the interview, for example when both parents wish to perform the role.[41]

Parent or guardian

5.49 In the vast majority of cases it will be the parent or guardian who attends the police station to act as the appropriate adult. There are, however, occasions when it is unsuitable for the parent/guardian to act in this capacity.

Estrangement from the juvenile

5.50 The codes of practice give the following guidance:

> If the parent of a juvenile is estranged from the juvenile, he should not be asked to act as the appropriate adult if the juvenile expressly and specifically objects to his presence.[42]

In many cases where the juvenile is estranged from his/her parent(s),

---

40 Code C, Note for Guidance 1F.
41 *H and M v DPP* [1998] Crim LR 653, QBD.
42 Code C Note for Guidance 1C; see also *DPP v Blake* [1989] 1 WLR 432, CA.

the question of objecting to the police's choice of appropriate adult will not arise, as the parent will refuse to attend the police station. If the parent has attended the issue of estrangement will call for professional judgement. There will often be a tense relationship between a parent and his/her child in the police station. However, if the relationship is noticeably worse than this the defence lawyer should consider whether the parent should be excluded from acting as the appropriate adult. This will obviously be a difficult decision for the juvenile to make as it may provoke further repercussions after the juvenile's release from custody, nevertheless, the defence lawyer should always tactfully enquire in a private consultation in the absence of the appropriate adult whether the parent's presence at the police station will be a problem for the juvenile. If it will be, the juvenile should be advised of his/her right to object to the parent's presence.

Physical disability or mental disorder/disability

5.51   If the parent has a disability which would affect his/her ability to fulfil the role of an appropriate adult, they are likely to be unsuitable to act as the appropriate adult.

Physical disability

5.52   A parent who has a disability for which special provision is made in the codes of practice is probably not a suitable person to act as an appropriate adult. This would include a person who is blind or deaf. However, if the police arranged for a sign interpreter for a deaf parent, it would seem that the role could be performed effectively.

Mental disorder/disability

5.53   A parent who would require an appropriate adult him/herself is clearly not an appropriate adult and if the mental condition of the parent becomes apparent to the police or the lawyer then another adult should be sought.

5.54   The courts have had to consider on a number of occasions whether to exclude evidence obtained from a juvenile in the presence of a mentally disordered parent. It has been held that the test as to whether a particular adult may fulfil the role is an objective one. An interview may be excluded if the court is satisfied that a parent's intelligence was too low to perform the role adequately, even if the police were unaware of the parent's condition and there was no suggestion of impropriety.[43] However, an interview will not be excluded if the court is satisfied that the parent was able to fulfil the role.[44]

Unable to speak English

5.55 If the parent or guardian cannot communicate in English s/he will not be able to safeguard the juvenile's interests. In certain cases the police may be willing to arrange for an interpreter to attend to translate for the parent. Although cumbersome, this would allow the parent to fulfil the role effectively.

Suspected of involvement in the crime

5.56 Where a parent or guardian has been arrested or is suspected of being involved in the offence, there is likely to be a conflict of interest between the juvenile and the adult which means that the parent or guardian is not an impartial adult suitable to act as the appropriate adult. In any event the police would usually object to the parent acting in such circumstances.

Parent is the complainant or witness

5.57 The codes of practice give the following guidance:

> A person, including a parent or guardian, should not be an appropriate adult if he is suspected of involvement in the offence in question, is the victim, is a witness, [or] is involved in the investigation . . .[45]

Received an admission from the juvenile

5.58 The codes of practice give the following guidance:

> A person, including a parent or guardian, should not be an appropriate adult if he . . . has received admissions prior to attending to act as the appropriate adult.[46]

---

43 *R v Morse* [1991] Crim LR 195, Wisbech Crown Court.
44 *R v W* [1994] Crim LR 130, CA.
45 Code C, Note for guidance 1C.
46 Ibid.

Social worker

5.59 This could include a generic social worker, a specialist youth justice social worker, a residential care worker or a member of an emergency out-of-hours team. Inevitably the level of experience and familiarity with police stations will vary enormously.

5.60 In certain circumstances in may be inappropriate for certain individuals from a social services department to act as the appropriate adult. Such circumstances would include:

– when s/he is the complainant or a witness to the offence;
– when s/he has received an admission of guilt from the juvenile.

Complainant or witness to the offence

5.61 As with parents (see above) the codes prohibit a person acting as the appropriate adult in such circumstances. This most frequently arises when an incident occurs in a children's home and a member of staff calls the police who subsequently arrest the juvenile. In those circumstances the juvenile will inevitably see all members of the staff at the home as being against him/her. In such circumstances it is advisable that someone other than a care worker is asked to act as the appropriate adult. In practice this may have to be the local authority's duty social worker.

Received admissions of guilt

5.62 It should be noted that the person is only barred from acting if the admission was received before the person took on the role of the appropriate adult. However, when an admission to a social worker, particularly a residential care worker, results in the police being informed, it is again advisable that a person wholly unconnected with the children's home should be asked to act as the appropriate adult as there is a significant danger that the juvenile will not regard the care worker as impartial.

Another responsible person

5.63 In the experience of the authors this has included other members of the family, friends, priests of various religious denominations, volunteers from local authority schemes, local shopkeepers, the Salvation Army, and even members of the public passing the police station.

5.64 The codes require that the responsible person must be an adult over the age of 18 who is not a police officer or employed by the police (presumably in any capacity). It may also be suggested that there should be a sufficient age gap between the responsible person and the juvenile so that the adult is able to exercise some degree of authority over the juvenile.[47]

Elder brother or sister

5.65 Older siblings may often be very effective appropriate adults as they are well known to the juvenile and are not so likely to wish to punish the juvenile for being arrested. However, the police may seek to object to the suitability of a sibling especially if s/he is recognised by a police officer as having been arrested on a number of occasions in the past. No such objection is usually raised to a parent who is known to have a criminal record. It is submitted that if there is a sufficient gap between the ages of the sibling and the juvenile, the lawyer should seek to dissuade the custody officer from objecting, rather than extend further the juvenile's detention.

Teacher

5.66 There will be occasions when a teacher is asked to act as the appropriate adult especially if an interview is to take place at school. The codes of practice state that a teacher should not act as the appropriate adult at an interview at school if the juvenile is suspected of an offence against the educational establishment.[48] By extension it is submitted that a teacher is not a suitable adult if the alleged offence relates to the juvenile's school or a member of the school staff called in the police. In such circumstances the teacher cannot be seen as impartial by the juvenile.

Rights of the appropriate adult

5.67 The appropriate adult may do the following while performing the role:
- read the custody record as soon as practicable after arrival at the police station (Code C para 2.4);
- consult with the juvenile in private at any time (Code C para 3.12);
- instruct a solicitor at any time on behalf of the juvenile *or* instruct

---

47 *Palmer v R* (1991) September *Legal Action* 21, CC.
48 Code C para 11.15.

a solicitor to advise him/her while performing the role of appropriate adult (Code C para 3.13).

Confidentiality

5.68   The presence of the appropriate adult in the police station can cause problems in relation to the disclosure of information. This could arise after s/he has received information directly from the juvenile or by being present during a consultation between the juvenile and the defence lawyer.

Disclosure of information

5.69   There is no specific duty of confidentiality imposed upon a person acting as an appropriate adult. As a consequence, the defence lawyer should be alert at all times to the danger of disclosure. A parent or guardian may be confused and upset to learn of their child's arrest and s/he may volunteer information or disclose it if approached by a police officer. A social worker will subscribe to the general principle that information received from a client should not be disclosed. There are, however, exceptions to this and disclosure may take place if the social worker considers that the juvenile suspect presents a danger to another person or the public in general.[48A] Even if the particular social worker at the station does not wish to disclose information, s/he may be directed to do so by a line manager.

5.70   As a result of concerns regarding disclosure the Criminal Law Committee of the Law Society has issued guidance to solicitors.[49] This advises that a solicitor should give initial advice to the juvenile suspect in the absence of the appropriate adult. In this initial consultation the juvenile should be advised of the danger of disclosure. The advice continues that the question of whether the appropriate adult's presence is desirable or not during any further consultation can then be considered in consultation with the appropriate adult, taking into account any risk of disclosure and the wishes of the juvenile who may find reassurance in the presence of an appropriate adult whom s/he knows. In addition many social services departments have issued guidance to their staff. This usually advises a social worker acting as appropriate adult to see the juvenile on his/her own and to explain both the role of the appropriate adult and that it is not possible to

48A   The Department of Health has issued guidance to social services departments, which contemplates disclosure in such circumstances: see LAC(88)17.
49   (1993) LS Gaz 19 May.

guarantee that any information would remain confidential. It is the opinion of the authors that such a procedure would be good practice.

Admissibility of information disclosed by an appropriate adult

5.71　There is a real risk that information received by an appropriate adult from a juvenile suspect may be admitted as evidence. In *R v Marcus Brown*[49A] a 16-year-old was arrested on suspicion of attempted murder. He was interviewed in the presence of a solicitor and a social worker from the local youth justice team. This social worker was also the appellant's supervising officer for a current supervision order. No admissions were made during the interview. After the interview the appellant was left alone for a short while with the social worker. During a *voir dire* at the trial the judge accepted that the social worker had initiated a conversation in which she indicated that she thought that the appellant knew what had happened. The appellant replied by indicating that he had been involved in the serious assault. It was further accepted that the appellant had responded to the social worker's comment because he did not think that his reply would be disclosed. It was argued at his appeal against conviction that the trial judge should have excluded the conversation with the social worker under PACE s76 or s78. Buxton LJ held that the trial judge had reasonably admitted the conversation into evidence.

5.72　The position would seem to be slightly different where the appropriate adult overhears a privileged conversation between the juvenile and his/her lawyer. In such circumstances it would seem that no direct reference may be made to the conversation in any subsequent trial. This situation is arguably comparable to the situation where privileged information falls into the hands of the opposing party. In *R v Tompkins*[50] a note written by the defendant was passed to his trial advocate. The note later came into the possession of the prosecutor. During his testimony the defendant contradicted the contents of the note. The prosecutor was subsequently allowed to cross-examine the defendant on the basis of the contents in the note but not to make direct reference to it. This approach was upheld by the Court of Appeal.

49A　Unreported, 98/7320/Y2, (1999) 21 May.
50　(1977) 67 Cr App R 18, CA.

Searches

Search of the person

Upon arrest

5.73   A police constable may search an arrested person:

- in any case where the person has been arrested at a place other than a police station, if the constable has reasonable grounds for believing that the arrested person may present a danger to himself or others;
- to search for anything which the arrested person might use to escape from lawful custody; or
- to search for anything which might be evidence to an offence.[51]

The power to search for articles to assist escape or for evidence only exists to the extent that it is reasonably required for the purpose of discovering any such thing or any such evidence. The power does not authorise a constable to require a person to remove any of his/her clothing in public other than an outer coat, jacket or gloves, but does authorise a search of a person's mouth.

5.74   In practical terms this power of search will normally involve no more than the arrested person being required to empty his/her pockets and to be subject to a body rub down. The search may take place at the point of arrest or on arrival at the police station. In the case of a juvenile, the presence of an appropriate adult is not required.

Power of seizure

5.75   On searching a person a police constable may seize and retain anything which the constable has reasonable grounds for believing:

- the suspect might use to cause physical injury to him/herself or to another;
- the suspect might use to assist him/her to escape from lawful custody; or
- is evidence of an offence or has been obtained in the consequence of the commission of an offence.[52]

Items subject to legal privilege may not be seized or retained under this power.

---

51   Police and Criminal Evidence Act 1984 s32(1).
52   Ibid, s32(8) and (9).

Strip search

5.76 A strip search is defined as 'a search involving the removal of more than outer clothing.'[53] The following guidance is given for the use of strip searches:

> A strip search may take place only if it is considered necessary to remove an article which a person would not be allowed to keep, and the officer reasonably considers that the person might have concealed such an article. Strip searches shall not routinely be carried out where there is no reason to consider that articles have been concealed.[54]

The police officer carrying out a strip search must be of the same sex as the person searched. The search must take place in an area where the person being searched cannot be seen by anyone who does not need to be present, nor by a member of the opposite sex (except an appropriate adult who has been specifically requested by the person being searched). Except in cases of urgency, where there is a risk of serious harm to the person detained or to others, wherever a strip search involves exposure of intimate parts of the body, there must be at least two people present other than the person being searched.[55]

5.77 Except in cases of urgency (ie, where there is a risk of serious harm to the person detained or to others) a juvenile should only be strip searched in the presence of an appropriate adult. The presence of the appropriate adult may only be dispensed with if the juvenile signifies in the presence of the appropriate adult that s/he prefers the search to be done in his/her absence and the appropriate adult agrees. A record must be made of the juvenile's decision and this record should be signed by the appropriate adult.[56]

5.78 The search shall be conducted with proper regard to the sensitivity and vulnerability of the person in these circumstances and every reasonable effort shall be made to secure the person's co-operation and minimise embarrassment. People who are searched should not normally be required to have all their clothes removed at the same time. The Codes of Practice suggest that a man should be allowed to put on his shirt before removing his trousers and a woman should be allowed to put on her blouse and upper garments before further clothing is removed. Where necessary to assist the search, the person

---

53 Code C Annex B para 9.
54 Code C Annex A para 10.
55 Code C Annex A para 11.
56 Ibid.

may be required to hold his/her arms in the air or to stand with his/her legs apart and to bend forward so that a visual examination may be made of the genital and anal areas provided that no physical contact is made with any body orifice.[57]

Intimate search

5.79   This is defined by the Codes of Practice as follows:

> An 'intimate search' is a search which consists of the physical examination of a person's body orifices other than the mouth.[58]

5.80   An intimate search may only be authorised by a police officer of at least the rank of superintendent who has reasonable grounds for believing:

- that an article which could cause physical injury to a detained person or others at the police station has been concealed; or
- that the person has concealed a Class A drug which s/he intended to supply to another or export; and
- in either case, an intimate search is the only practicable means of removing it.[59]

An intimate search may not be authorised to search for evidence.

5.81   An intimate search may only be carried out by a registered medical practitioner or registered nurse, unless an officer of at least the rank of superintendent considers that it is not practicable and the search is for an article which could cause physical injury.[60] The intimate search must take place at a hospital, doctor's surgery or other medical premises unless it is a search for an article likely to cause injury in which case the search may be carried out in a police station.[61]

5.82   An intimate search for an article likely to cause injury which is carried out by a police officer must be carried out by an officer of the same sex as the suspect. Subject to the requirement for an appropriate adult, no person of the opposite sex who is not a medical practitioner or nurse shall be present, nor shall anyone whose presence is unnecessary. A minimum of two people, other than the person being

---

57   Ibid.
58   Code C, Annex A, para 1.
59   Police and Criminal Evidence Act 1984 s55(1).
60   Ibid, s55(5).
61   Ibid, s55.

searched, must be present during the search. The search shall be conducted with proper regard to the sensitivity and vulnerability of the person in these circumstances.[62]

5.83 An intimate search of a juvenile must be carried out in the presence of an appropriate adult of the same sex (unless the juvenile specifically requests the presence of a particular adult of the opposite sex who is readily available). The search may take place in the absence of the appropriate adult only if the juvenile signifies in the presence of the appropriate adult that s/he prefers the search to be done in his/her absence and the appropriate adult agrees. A record shall be made of the juvenile's decision and signed by the appropriate adult.[63]

Search of premises

5.84 Having arrested a person a police officer may enter and search:

- the premises where the suspect is arrested or where s/he was immediately before arrest (Police and Criminal Evidence Act 1984 s32); and
- any premises controlled by the suspect (Police and Criminal Evidence Act 1984 s18).

Section 32 search

5.85 A police constable has a power to enter and search any premises in which a suspect was when arrested or immediately before s/he was arrested for evidence relating to the offence for which s/he has been arrested.[64]

5.86 This power only extends to a search which is reasonably required for the purpose of discovering any such thing or any such evidence.[65]

Section 18 search

5.87 A police constable may enter and search any premises occupied or controlled by a person who is under arrest for an arrestable offence, if the constable has reasonable grounds for suspecting that there is on the premises evidence other than items subject to legal privilege that relates to that offence or to some other arrestable offence which is connected with or similar to that offence.

---

62 Code C, Annex A, para 6.
63 Ibid, para 5.
64 Police and Criminal Evidence Act 1984 s32(2)(b).
65 Ibid, s32(3).

5.88   The power to search is only a power to search to the extent that is reasonably required for the purpose of discovering such evidence. A constable may seize and retain anything which s/he reasonably believes may be evidence relating to the offence for which the suspect is under arrest or some other arrestable offence connected with or similar to that offence.[66]

Premises occupied or controlled by the suspect

5.89   This will usually be the place where the young suspect is living. It is not clear in the case of a young suspect living in the parental home whether the power to search extends to the whole property or only to the part of the property which the young suspect has control of, for example his/her bedroom.

Authorisation

5.90   A s18 search should only be carried out with the written authority of a police officer of at least the rank of inspector unless the search is carried out before the suspect is taken to the police station and his/her presence is necessary for the effective investigation of the offence.[67]

Conditions of detention

5.91   The Codes of Practice provide detailed guidance as to how the police should treat a suspect while in custody.

Cell

5.92   As far as practicable only one prisoner should be held in a cell at any one time.[68] The cells should be adequately heated, cleaned and ventilated. They must also be adequately lit.[69] Blankets, mattresses, pillows and other bedding should be provided and should be of a reasonable standard and in a clean and sanitary condition.[70] Access to toilet and washing facilities must be provided.[71]

66   Ibid, s18(2).
67   Ibid, s18(4) and (5).
68   Code C, para 8.1.
69   Code C, para 8.2.
70   Code C, para 8.3.
71   Code C, para 8.4.

5.93   A juvenile should not be placed in a police cell unless no other secure accommodation is available and the custody officer considers that it is not practicable to supervise him/her if s/he is not placed in a cell or the custody officer considers that a cell provides more comfortable accommodation than other secure accommodation in the police station. If a juvenile is placed in a cell, the reason must be recorded on the custody record. A juvenile must never be placed in a cell with a detained adult.[72]

5.94   Some police stations have detention rooms where juveniles will normally be detained. From the inside the difference between a detention room and a cell is not immediately obvious. While the appropriate adult is at the station it may be possible to persuade the custody officer to allow the juvenile to sit with the appropriate adult in an interview or other room in the custody area.

Supervision

5.95   People detained shall be visited every hour, and those who are drunk, at least every half hour.[73] Whenever possible juveniles and other people at risk should receive visits more regularly than every hour.[74]

Food

5.96   At least two light meals and one main meal shall be offered on any period of 24 hours. Drinks should be provided at meal times and upon reasonable request between meal times. As far as practicable, meals provided shall offer a varied diet and meet any special dietary needs or religious beliefs that the person may have. A detained person may also have meals supplied by his/her family or friends at their expense.[75]

Clothing

5.97   If it is necessary to remove a person's clothes for the purposes of investigation, for hygiene or health reasons or for cleaning, replacement clothing of a reasonable standard of comfort and cleanliness

---

72 Code C, para 8.8.
73 Code C, para 8.10.
74 Code C, note 8A.
75 Code C, para 8.6.

shall be provided. A person may not be interviewed unless adequate clothing has been offered to him/her.[76]

5.99   The alternative clothing the police normally offer is a paper suit and plimsolls. There is no reason why alternative clothing may not be brought from the suspect's home.

Medical

5.100   Every police station has a GP or rota of GPs who attend to meet the medical needs of prisoners and also to examine injuries with a view to gathering evidence. This GP may be referred to as the police doctor, the divisional surgeon or the forensic medical examiner (FME).

5.101   The custody officer must immediately call the police surgeon if a person brought to a police station or already detained there:

- appears to be suffering from physical illness or a mental disorder;
- is injured;
- fails to respond normally to questions or conversation (other than through drunkenness alone); or
- otherwise appears to need medical attention.[77]

The above requirement does not apply to minor ailments or injuries which do not need attention. However, all such ailments or injuries must be recorded in the custody record and any doubt must be resolved in favour of calling the police surgeon.[78]

5.102   If a detained person requests a medical examination the police surgeon must be called as soon as practicable. S/he may in addition be examined by a medical practitioner of his/her own choice at his/her own expense.[79]

Reasonable force

5.103   Reasonable force may be used if necessary for the following purposes:

- to secure compliance with reasonable instructions, including instructions given in pursuance of the provisions of a code of practice; or

76 Code C, para 8.5.
77 Code C, para 9.2.
78 Code C, Note for Guidance 9A.
79 Code C, para 9.4.

— to prevent escape, injury, damage to property or the destruction of evidence.[80]

No additional restraints shall be used within a locked cell unless absolutely necessary, and then only suitable handcuffs.

The police interview

Definition

5.104   Code C, para 11.1A of the Codes of Practice defines an interview as follows:

> An interview is the questioning of a person regarding his involvement or suspected involvement on a criminal offence or offences which, by virtue of paragraph 10.1 of Code C, is required to be carried out under caution.

Paragraph 10.1 states:

> A person whom there are grounds to suspect of an offence must be cautioned before any questions about it (or further questions if it is his answers to previous questions which provide the grounds for suspicion) are put to him regarding his involvement or suspected involvement in that offence if his answers or his silence (i.e. failure or refusal to answer a question or to answer satisfactorily) may be given in evidence to a court in a prosecution.

It is clear that the term 'interview' is not restricted to a formal taped interview in the police station.

Caution

5.105   The caution should be in the following terms:

> You do not have to say anything. But it may harm your defence if you do not mention when questioned something which you later rely on in court. Anything you do say may be given in evidence.[81]

Minor deviations from this wording do not constitute a breach of the requirement that a caution must be administered before questioning a suspect provided that the sense of the caution is preserved.

---

80   Code C, para 8.9.
81   Code C, para 10.4.

5.106 If a juvenile is cautioned in the absence of the appropriate adult, the caution must be repeated in the adult's presence.[82]

Interview records

5.107 By Code C, para 11.5 an accurate record must be made of each interview with a person suspected of an offence, whether or not the interview takes place at a police station. The record must state the place of the interview, the time it begins and ends, the time the record was made (if different), any breaks in the interview and the names of all those present. The record must be made during the course of the interview, unless in the investigating officer's view this would not be practicable or would interfere with the conduct of the interview. If the interview record is not made during the course of the interview it must be made as soon as practicable after its completion.

Verification by suspect

5.108 Unless it is impracticable, the person interviewed shall be given the opportunity to read the interview record and to sign it as correct or to indicate the respects in which s/he considers it inaccurate.[83] If the suspect agrees to sign the interview record, s/he should be asked to endorse the record with words such as 'I agree that this is a correct record of what was said.'[84]

Verification by appropriate adult or solicitor

5.109 If the appropriate adult or the suspect's solicitor is present during the interview, s/he should also be given an opportunity to read and sign the interview record.[85]

Interviewing a juvenile at their place of education

5.110 The Codes of Practice give the following guidance:

> Juveniles may only be interviewed at their places of education in exceptional circumstances and then only where the principal or his nominee agrees. Every effort should be made to notify both the parent(s) or other person responsible for the juvenile's welfare and the appropriate adult (if this a different person) that the police want to

82 Code C, para 10.6.
83 Code C, para 11.10.
84 Code C, Note for Guidance 11D.
85 Code C, para 11.11.

interview the juvenile and reasonable time should be allowed to enable the appropriate adult to be present at the interview. Where awaiting the appropriate adult would cause unreasonable delay and unless the interviewee is suspected of an offence against the educational establishment, the principal or his nominee can act as the appropriate adult for the purposes of the interview.

Presence of the appropriate adult

5.111 A juvenile must not be interviewed by the police in the absence of an appropriate adult.[86] There are two exceptions to this rule:

- if an urgent interview is necessary before the juvenile arrives at the police station; or
- if an urgent interview is necessary at a police station.

Prior to arrival at the police station

5.112 Following a decision to arrest, the suspect should not be interviewed about the offence except at a police station unless the consequent delay would be likely:

- to lead to interference with or harm to evidence connected with an offence or interference with or physical harm to other people; or
- to lead to the alerting of other people suspected of having committed an offence but not yet arrested for it; or
- to hinder the recovery of property obtained in consequence of the commission of an offence.[87]

Interviewing in any of these circumstances must cease once the relevant risk has been averted or the necessary questions have been put in order to attempt to avert the risk.[88]

At the police station

5.113 An officer of the rank of superintendent or above may authorise that a juvenile be interviewed in the absence of an appropriate adult if s/he considers that delay will lead to:

- interference with or harm to evidence connected with an offence; or

---

86 Code C, para 11.14.
87 Code C, para 11.1.
88 Code C, para 11.1.

– interference with or physical harm to other people.[89]

Such authority should only be given in exceptional cases of need.[90] Questioning must not continue once sufficient information to avert the immediate risk has been obtained.[91] A record shall be made of the grounds for any decision to interview a juvenile in such circumstances.[92-93]

Admissibility of an interview conducted in the absence of the appropriate adult

5.114   The admissibility of such an interview with a juvenile is considered in Chapter 12.

Right to silence

5.115   The provisions of the Criminal Justice and Public Order Act 1994 notwithstanding, a suspect may still refuse to answer questions put to him/her by a police officer. To that extent the right to silence may be considered to have been preserved. However, the right has been curtailed in a significant respect in that a court may be invited to draw adverse inference from a suspect's failure to answer questions.

5.116   The relevant provisions are set out in s34 and ss36 and 37 of the Criminal Justice and Public Order Act 1994. When a suspect who is interviewed after arrest fails to answer certain questions, or to answer them satisfactorily, after due warning, a court or jury may draw such inference as appears proper under the following provisions.

Section 34

5.117   At any time before s/he was charged with the offence, when questioned under caution by a constable trying to discover whether or by whom the offence was committed, the suspect failed to mention any fact relied on in his/her defence in those proceedings.

Section 36

5.118   Having been arrested by a constable or officer of Customs and Excise, on his/her person, in or on his/her clothing or footwear or otherwise

---

89 Code C, Annex C, para 1.
90 Code C, Annex C, Note for Guidance C1.
91 Code C, Annex C, para 2.
92–93 Code C, Annex C, para 3.

in his/her possession or in any place in which s/he is at the time of his/her arrest, there is any object or mark on any such object and the suspect fails to or refuses to account for the objects, marks or substances found.

Section 37

5.119 The suspect is arrested by a constable or officer of Customs and Excise and s/he was found by the arresting officer at a place at or about the time the offence for which s/he was arrested is alleged to have been committed and the suspect fails to or refuses to account for his/her presence at that place.

Special warnings

5.120 No inference may be drawn under ss36 and 37 unless the interviewing officer gives the suspect a 'special warning'. The interviewing officer must tell the suspect in ordinary language:

- what offence s/he is investigating;
- what fact s/he is asking the suspect to account for;
- that s/he believes this fact may be due to the suspect's taking part in the commission of the offence in question;
- that a court may draw a proper inference if the suspect fails or refuses to account for the fact about which s/he is being questioned; and
- that a record is being made of the interview and that it may be given in evidence if s/he is brought to trial.[94]

Advising a young suspect

Attending the police station

5.121 By reason of their age alone suspects under the age of 18 are vulnerable. Some lawyers consider attendance not to be important either because it is a petty offence which will have no serious consequences for the young suspect or the suspect is a regular client and 'knows what to do'. In the first category, there is still a need for advice and assistance because the person is likely to be unfamiliar with police procedures and susceptible to pressure, and may not have very effective support from the appropriate adult. In the case of regular young

---

94 Code C, paras 10.5A and 10.5B.

suspects the attendance of a lawyer is still important as the young person's familiarity with police custody may lead them to underestimate the seriousness of the situation.

Establishing a rapport with a young suspect

5.122   Children and many adolescents have little experience of dealing with adults outside the immediate family, except for professionals such as teachers, who may not be seen as being on the young person's side. Frequent offenders, in particular, may have very negative experiences of dealing with adults and may be extremely suspicious of an adult stranger even if s/he is supposedly there to help.

5.123   If the lawyer is to represent a young suspect effectively s/he should make every effort to establish a rapport with him/her. Spending some time at the beginning of the consultation to break the ice usually pays dividends. Care should be taken too to grade the language used so that it is comprehensible to the young suspect.

Appropriate adults

5.124   Although intended as a safeguard for juveniles, it is all too common that the presence of the appropriate adult, particularly if s/he is the parent of the juvenile, can undermine the other legal protections for the young suspect. It is very difficult for a lawyer to step between a parent and their child at a very stressful time and try to ensure that the parent's anger at the juvenile's perceived wrongdoing does not affect the juvenile's legal rights. Although the lawyer must at all times keep in mind that the juvenile is the client, it is vital that every effort is made to win over a parent acting as the appropriate adult.

5.125   Because of concerns regarding confidentiality, the defence lawyer should always see the juvenile initially in the absence of the appropriate adult.[95] Parents acting as appropriate adults will often object to this and it is common for custody officers to disapprove too. The lawyer should explain to the appropriate adult that s/he is required to have such a consultation by professional rules and s/he should refer the custody officer to Code C, Note for Guidance 1EE which states:

> A person should always be given an opportunity, when an appropriate adult is called to the police station, to consult privately with a solicitor in the absence of the appropriate adult if they wish to do so.

95 See para 5.70.

5.126   In this initial consultation the lawyer should introduce him/ herself and establish whether there will be any problems with the appropriate adult who has been called to the station. The juvenile should also be given the option of having the appropriate adult present during the rest of the consultation or of continuing the consultation in private with the lawyer. In any event it should be explained to the juvenile that the lawyer has a duty of confidentiality to his/her client which may not extend to anything overheard by the appropriate adult and therefore if the juvenile wishes something to remain confidential s/he should discuss it with the lawyer when they are alone.

5.127   Once the danger of disclosure has been explained to the juvenile, the defence lawyer should discuss with the juvenile whether s/he wants the appropriate adult to be present for the rest of the consultation. It may be preferable to delay inviting the adult to join the consultation until any discussion about the allegation has been completed. This does need to be balanced against the age of the juvenile and any reassurance to be derived from having a familiar adult present. In any event, it is wise to make a point of speaking to the appropriate adult after any consultation both to explain what decisions have been made regarding the conduct of the interview and to ensure that the adult understands his/her role in the interview.

Explaining the elements of the offence

5.128   Having explained the allegation to the young suspect and described the evidence the police have, it is important that it is made clear to him/her what are the legal elements of the offence alleged. Young people may not have reached a level of understanding to distinguish between criminal offences and behaviour contrary to parental or school rules.

5.129   Frequently, young suspects will be worried about what their parents may say. Even if the young suspect has not committed a criminal offence, s/he may fear retribution from parents because s/he broke a parental curfew, went to an area of town prohibited by parents or was arrested with another young person of whom his/her parents disapprove. If necessary the lawyer should try to speak to the parent and ensure that any disciplining for such infractions should be postponed until after the juvenile's release.

Explaining police procedures

5.130   Explaining what will happen next and giving some idea of the time scale will both take away the sense of uncertainty and in most cases reassure the young suspect that s/he will be released shortly. The popular television programme *The Bill* will often provide an easy way to explain basic police procedures.

5.131   Warning suspects that the police may seize trainers or wish to take fingerprints or DNA samples also removes the shock of being told bluntly by the custody officer that such procedures will take place.

Advising on the exercise of the right to silence

5.132   When explaining about the right to silence, it is important that the lawyer explains that a police interview is a unique type of conversation for which the normal social conventions do not apply. The young suspect may need to be reassured that s/he will not be accused of being rude if s/he refuses to answer police questions. It may be helpful to specifically state that the interview is not the same as would be expected if a parent or teacher were questioning the young person when rule breaking is suspected.

5.133   When considering whether to advise that the right to silence should be exercised Cape, in *Defending Suspects in the Police Station* (3rd edn, LAG, 1999) identifies the following criteria:

- knowledge of the police case;
- apparent strength of the police evidence;
- admissibility of the police evidence;
- prior comments and/or 'significant silences' of the client;
- likely fairness of the interview;
- apparent intelligence of the client;
- apparent mental condition of the client;
- strength of the client's defence;
- any reason for early statement of the client's defence;
- specific reasons for remaining silent (eg, to protect others);
- possible advantages of early admission of the offence(s); and
- whether a statement at charge would be more appropriate.

All of these criteria are equally valid when dealing with a young suspect. It is proposed only to highlight considerations which are of particular relevance to young suspects.

Youth of suspect

5.134 Interviewing a child or young person is not necessarily unfair but the extreme youth of the suspect makes the chance of unfairness much more likely. If a lawyer is concerned that a young suspect does not have the maturity to cope with a police interview then the exercise of the right to silence should be considered for that reason alone.

Preparing for the interview

5.135 If the right to silence is to be exercised, the young suspect will need as much support as possible before the interview and during the interview. One easy way to boost the young suspect's confidence is to practice the interview. The lawyer should take the role of the police officer and should both ask the anticipated questions and include likely strategies the police may employ to induce a suspect to talk. In the context of young suspects these could include:

- asking seemingly innocent questions about school or leisure interests;
- inviting the parent acting as appropriate adult to express his/her disapproval of the juvenile's alleged conduct;
- informing the suspect that friends have already admitted the offence and have implicated the suspect; and
- emphasising the potential for a court to draw adverse inference from the exercise of the right to silence.

Practising an interview with an appropriate adult present also has the advantage of giving him/her the opportunity to see how an interview is conducted and this may help to reassure the adult who has never been in a police custody area before.

Possibility of a caution (or reprimand or warning)

5.136 The police are much more likely to caution a juvenile than older offenders. Before the police may caution an offender there must be a clear admission of guilt and many police officers would expect that admission to be in the taped interview. If a police officer has indicated that a caution is likely if the young suspect admits the offence in interview this is something which should be explained to the client.

The conduct of the interview

5.137   The Codes of Practice give the following general advice:

> It is important to bear in mind that, although juveniles ... are often capable of providing reliable evidence, they may, without knowing or wishing to do so, be particularly prone in certain circumstances to provide information which is unreliable, misleading or self-incriminating. Special care should therefore always be exercised in questioning such a person and the appropriate adult should be involved, if there is any doubt about a person's age, mental state or capacity. Because of the risk of unreliable evidence it is also important to obtain corroboration of any facts admitted whenever possible.[96]

Role of the appropriate adult

5.138   The interviewing officer is required to advise the appropriate adult at the start of the interview that:

- s/he is not expected simply to act as an observer; and
- the purpose of his/her presence is:
  - (i)   to advise the juvenile being questioned;
  - (ii)   to observe whether the interview is being conducted properly and fairly; and
  - (iii) to facilitate communication with the juvenile being interviewed.[97]

Failure to give this notice to the appropriate adult is a breach of the Codes of Practice. Whether it is a substantial breach requiring the exclusion of the interview depends on the circumstances of each individual case.[97A]

Role of the lawyer

5.139   Cape, *Defending Suspects in the Police Station* (3rd edn, LAG, 1999), summarises the objectives of the lawyer in the interview as follows:

- ensuring that the suspect does his/her best in the interview whether or not s/he is answering questions;
- keeping an accurate record of the interview;
- ensuring the police act fairly and in accordance with PACE and the Codes of Practice; and
- protecting the suspect from unnecessary pressure and distress.

96   Code C, Note for Guidance 11B.
97   Code C, para 11.16.
97A   *H and M v DPP* [1998] Crim LR 653, QBD.

Ensuring the young suspect does his/her best

5.140 Building up a rapport in the private consultation and preparing thoroughly for the interview will go a long way to ensuring that the young suspect performs to his/her best in the interview. Most importantly it will ensure that s/he has confidence in his/her lawyer and it will prove much more difficult for the police to undermine that confidence.

5.141 The lawyer should also be aware of the physical conditions in the interview room. The Codes of Practice require that as far as practicable the interview room should be adequately heated, lit and ventilated.[98] The lawyer should pay attention to the seating arrangements and ensure that the young suspect has somebody sitting next to them who will provide moral support. In normal circumstances this will be the appropriate adult in the case of a juvenile; however, if the current relationship appears frosty, the lawyer should consider sitting next to the juvenile. In any event the lawyer should sit in a position which is visible to the young suspect and preferably where eye contact is possible.

Ensuring the police act fairly

5.142 If the lawyer has advised the young suspect to answer police questions in the interview, the questioning should be monitored with particular attention paid to the complexity of the language and the use of such ploys as multiple questions, leading questions and hypothetical questions, especially regarding intent.

5.143 It is also important that the lawyer monitors the use made of any admissions claimed to have come from friends of the young suspect. It is wise in every case where young suspects are arrested together to explain before the interview that admissions of a co-suspect are generally inadmissible as evidence against them.

5.144 The lawyer must also be vigilant for any signs that a young suspect may be susceptible to any veiled threat by the police which may not be immediately obvious. A young suspect being interviewed in the absence of parents may be desperate for his/her parents not to find out about the arrest and any mention by the police of telling the parents if the matter is not resolved in the interview could induce a false confession. Even seemingly bizarre considerations may affect a young suspect's willingness to confess, for example the police making it clear that in the absence of a confession a young suspect's trainers will have to be seized for forensic analysis.

98 Code C, para 12.4.

Protecting the young suspect from pressure or distress

5.145   A lawyer must always ensure that the interview is not conducted in an oppressive manner. In the case of a young suspect s/he must be particularly sensitive to factors which may put undue pressure on the interviewee. The officers raising their voices or demanding that a young suspect looks at them when they are talking can put enormous pressure on someone so young and also reinforces associations with parental disciplining. Similar considerations apply to an officer rebuking a young suspect for smiling or giggling out of nervousness.

5.146   It is also very easy to demoralise a juvenile whose parents have not attended the police station to act as appropriate adults by suggesting that the juvenile has been deserted by the parents.

Tape recording

5.147   Most interviews carried out in a police station should be tape recorded.[99] The standard police interview room has a double tape recorder. Blank tapes should be opened in the presence of the suspect.[100] At the start of the interview the interviewing officers will introduce themselves and ask all other people to introduce themselves.

5.148   At the end of the interview one of the two tapes will be selected by the suspect and sealed in his/her presence. Both the suspect and any appropriate adult will be asked to sign the seal.[101] If the suspect is charged s/he has a right to a copy of the interview tape as soon as practicable.[102]

Methods of identification

Consent

5.149   When considering identification procedures the Police and Criminal Evidence Act 1984 s65 states that references to 'appropriate consent' shall be construed as follows:

- in relation to a person who has attained the age of 17 years, the consent of that person;

---

99   Code E, para 3.1.
100   Code E, para 4.1.
101   Code E, para 4.15.
102   Code E, para 4.16.

- in relation to a person who has not attained that age but has attained the age of 14 years, the consent of that person and his parent or guardian; and
- in relation to a person who has not attained the age of 14 years, the consent of his/her parent or guardian.

It should be noted that the Act only refers to the consent of the parent or guardian not the consent of the appropriate adult. It therefore follows that an appropriate adult who is not a parent or guardian cannot give valid consent.

Fingerprints

5.150　In certain circumstances as specified by the Police and Criminal Evidence Act 1984 s61 a suspect's fingerprints may be taken. If fingerprints may be taken without consent reasonable force may be used to take them.[103]

Before charge

5.151　A suspect's fingerprints may be taken before charge:

- by consent; or
- without consent, if authorised by a police officer of at least the rank of superintendent who has reasonable grounds for suspecting that the suspect has been involved in a criminal offence and that the taking of the fingerprints will tend to confirm or disprove his/her involvement in that offence.[104]

Consent to the taking of a person's fingerprints must be in writing if it is given at a time when s/he is at a police station.[105]

After charge

5.152　A suspect's fingerprints may be taken without consent if:

- s/he is charged with a recordable offence;
- s/he is informed that s/he will be reported for such an offence; and
- s/he has not had his/her fingerprints taken in the course of the investigation of the offence by the police.[106]

103　Code D, para 3.2.
104　Police and Criminal Evidence Act 1984 s61(4).
105　Ibid, s61(2).
106　Ibid, s61(3)(b).

Photographs

5.153   The photograph of a person who has been arrested may be taken at a police station only:

- with his written consent;
- if s/he is arrested at the same time as other people, and a photograph is necessary to establish who was arrested, at what time and at what place;
- if s/he has been charged with, or reported for a recordable offence and has not yet been released or brought before a court;
- if s/he is convicted of such an offence and his/her photograph has not already been taken earlier in the investigation; or
- if an officer of at least the rank of superintendent authorises it, having reasonable grounds for suspecting the involvement of the person in a criminal offence and where there is identification evidence in relation to that offence.[107]

Force may not be used to take a photograph.[108]

Samples

Intimate

5.154   An intimate sample means:

- a sample of blood, semen or any other tissue fluid, urine or pubic hair;
- a dental impression;
- a swab taken from a person's body orifice other than the mouth.[109]

5.155   An intimate sample may only be taken from a person in police detention if:

- a police officer of at least the rank of superintendent authorises it; and
- the appropriate consent is given.[110]

5.156   Authorisation may only be given if the officer has reasonable grounds for:

---

107   Code D, paras 4.1 and 4.2
108   Code D, para 4.3.
109   Police and Criminal Evidence Act 1984 s65.
110   Ibid, s62(1).

- suspecting the involvement of the person from whom the sample is to be taken in a recordable offence; and
- believing that the sample will tend to confirm or disprove his/her involvement.[111]

Refusal of consent

5.157 Where the appropriate consent to the taking of an intimate sample from a person was refused without good cause, a court may draw such adverse inferences from the refusal as appear proper.[112]

5.158 It is questionable whether it is proper to draw an adverse inference when the appropriate consent is not given because of the non-cooperation of the parent or guardian of a juvenile.

Procedure

5.159 After the authority of an officer of the rank of superintendent or above has been obtained, the suspect must be informed that authorisation has been given and the grounds for giving it.[113] The suspect must be asked whether s/he consents to the taking of the intimate sample. The suspect must be warned that an adverse inference may be drawn from the refusal to consent to a sample being taken. This information and any request for consent must take place in the presence of the appropriate adult. The appropriate consent must be in writing.[114]

5.160 Except for a sample of urine, intimate samples or dental impressions may only be taken by a registered medical or dental practitioner as appropriate. Where clothing needs to be removed in circumstances likely to cause embarrassment to the suspect, no person of the opposite sex who is not a medical practitioner or nurse shall be present, unless the presence of an appropriate adult of the opposite sex is specifically requested and is readily available.[115]

5.161 In the case of a juvenile an appropriate adult must be present during the taking of an intimate sample involving the removal of clothing in embarrassing circumstances unless the juvenile signifies in the presence of the appropriate adult that s/he prefers that the adult is not present and the adult agrees.[116]

---

111   Ibid, s62(2).
112   Ibid, s62(10).
113   Ibid, s62(5).
114   Code D, para 5.2.
115   Code D, para 5.12.
116   Ibid.

Non-intimate

5.162 A non-intimate sample means:
- a sample of hair other than pubic hair;
- a sample taken from a nail or from under a nail;
- a swab taken from any part of a person's body including the mouth but not any other body orifice;
- saliva;
- a footprint or a similar impression of any part of a person's body other than a part of his/her hand.[117]

Non-intimate samples may be taken both before and after charge.

Before charge

5.163 A non-intimate sample may be taken from a person in police custody if:
- s/he consents; or
- an officer of at least the rank of superintendent authorises it to be taken without the appropriate consent.[118]

5.164 Authorisation may only be given if the officer has reasonable grounds for:
- suspecting the involvement of the person from whom the sample is to be taken in a recordable offence; and
- for believing that the sample will tend to confirm or disprove the suspect's involvement.[119]

After charge

5.165 A non-intimate sample may be taken without consent when s/he is charged with a recordable offence or is informed that s/he will be reported for such an offence.[120]

Procedure

5.166 Where a non-intimate sample is to be taken, the suspect must be informed that authorisation has been given and the grounds for giving it.[121] Where clothing needs to be removed in circumstances likely

---

117 Police and Criminal Evidence Act 1984 s65.
118 Ibid, s63(3).
119 Ibid, s63(4).
120 Ibid, s63(3A).
121 Ibid, s63(6).

to cause embarrassment to the suspect, no person of the opposite sex who is not a medical practitioner or nurse shall be present, unless the presence of an appropriate adult of the opposite sex is specifically requested and is readily available.[122]

5.167 In the case of a juvenile an appropriate adult must be present during the taking of an intimate sample involving the removal of clothing in embarrassing circumstances unless the juvenile signifies in the presence of the appropriate adult that s/he prefers that the adult is not present and the adult agrees.[123]

Identification by witnesses

5.168 If the identity of the perpetrator of a crime is in doubt, the police have a number of ways of seeking identification evidence. If the identity of the suspect is not known, the police may seek a street identification or an identification by photographs. If the suspect's identity is known the police have the following options:

- identification parade;
- group identification;
- video identification; or
- confrontation.

Identification parade

5.169 Whenever a suspect disputes an identification, an identification parade shall be held if the suspect consents unless the suspect's unusual appearance makes a parade impracticable. A parade may also be held if the officer in charge of the investigation considers that it would be helpful and the suspect consents.[124]

5.170 A parade may take place in a normal room or a special identification suite with a two-way mirror. A suspect must be given a reasonable opportunity to have a solicitor or friend present.[125] In the case of a juvenile the parade must take place in the presence of an appropriate adult.[126]

5.171 The parade shall consist of at least eight volunteers who so far as is possible resemble the suspect in age, height, general appearance

---

122 Code D, para 5.12.
123 Ibid.
124 Code C, paras 2.3 and 2.4.
125 Code D, Annex A, para 1.
126 Code D, para 1.14.

and position in life. In normal circumstances only one suspect may stand on a parade at any one time. However, if there are two suspects of roughly similar appearance, they may be paraded together but in that case there must be at least 12 volunteers.[127]

5.172   The suspect may choose his/her place in the line-up and if there are more than one witness s/he may change position between witnesses. Witnesses must view the parade one at a time. A colour photograph or a video film of the parade shall be taken.[128]

Video identification

5.173   A video consisting of clips of the suspect and at least eight volunteers will be compiled for viewing by any witnesses. The volunteers should resemble the suspect in age, height, general appearance and position in life.[129] The suspect and other people shall as far as possible be filmed in the same positions or carrying out the same activity and under identical conditions.[130]

5.174   The suspect and his/her solicitor, friend or appropriate adult must be given a reasonable opportunity to see the complete film before it is shown to witnesses. If there is a reasonable objection to the video film or any of its participants, steps shall be taken to remove the grounds for objection.[131]

5.175   The suspect or any lawyer must be given reasonable notification of the time and place that it is intended to conduct a video identification in order that a representative may attend on behalf of the suspect. For obvious reasons the suspect may not attend the showing.[132]

Group identification

5.176   A group identification should take place in a place where other people are either passing by or waiting around informally, in groups such that the suspect is able to join them and be capable of being seen by the witness at the same time as others in the group.[133] They are usually held at train, bus or underground stations or in busy shopping areas. In selecting the venue the identification officer must reasonably expect that over the period the witness observes the group,

127   Code D, Annex A, para 9.
128   Code D, Annex A, para 19.
129   Code D, Annex B, para 3.
130   Code D, Annex B, para 4.
131   Code D, Annex B, para 7.
132   Code D, Annex B, para 8.
133   Code D, Annex E, para 3.

s/he will be able to see from time to time a number of other members of the public who are broadly similar to the suspect.[134]

5.177 With a young suspect it is particularly important to consider whether a busy place will have many young people at the time of the parade. For example, a commuter station at the rush hour will be crowded but it is unlikely to have many teenagers walking around.

5.178 A group identification may be carried out with the suspect's consent or covertly (if it is practicable for the police to do so).[135] If it is carried out by consent, the suspect must be given a reasonable opportunity to have a solicitor or friend present.[136] In the case of a juvenile the identification must take place in the presence of an appropriate adult.

Confrontation

5.179 Confrontations may take place without the suspect's consent but must not take place unless none of the identification procedures are practicable.[137] Confrontations should normally take place in a police station.[138]

5.180 The confrontation should take place in the presence of the suspect's solicitor or friend unless this would cause unreasonable delay. In any event, in the case of a juvenile, an appropriate adult must be present. The suspect must be confronted independently by each witness, who shall be asked, 'Is this the person?'.[139]

Bail prior to charge

5.181 The custody officer is required to determine whether there is sufficient evidence to charge.[140] If there is clearly not enough evidence at that stage and no more evidence can be collected immediately s/he must:

---

134 Code D, Annex E, para 5.
135 Code D, paras 2.7 and 2.8 and Annex E, para 2.
136 Code D, Annex E, para 13.
137 Code D, para 2.13.
138 Code D, Annex C, para 4.
139 Code D, Annex C, para 3.
140 Police and Criminal Evidence Act 1984 s37(1).

- release the suspect without requiring him/her to return (no further action)[141]; or
- release the suspect on bail with a duty to surrender to the police station at a specified time while further enquiries are made.[142]

5.182   During the period of bail, essential witness statements will be taken or investigations into the suspect's explanation of events. In some police forces a juvenile will be bailed to return for a consideration of whether a charge will follow.[143]

5.183   The custody officer has no power to impose any bail conditions on a suspect prior to charge. If the suspect fails to answer his/her bail s/he commits an offence under the Bail Act 1976. In addition the police have a power of arrest for anyone who has failed to return to the police station having been granted bail.[144]

5.184   On occasions a custody officer may refuse to release a juvenile prior to charge until s/he can be bailed 'into the care of an appropriate adult'. There is no such requirement in the Codes of Practice. The defence lawyer should query this stance: either the custody officer is authorising the continued detention of the juvenile under s37 or s/he is keeping the juvenile in police protection under the Children Act 1989 s46.[145] If the custody officer claims to be using the first power, the defence lawyer may argue that further detention is unlawful unless the detention is necessary for the investigation of the offence. If no further progress can made in the investigation at that stage, the juvenile should be released with or without bail. If the second power is relied upon, the defence lawyer should establish what significant harm the juvenile is thought likely to suffer if released in the absence of an appropriate adult. If a juvenile remains in police protection, the custody officer should also observe the detailed procedure contained in the Children Act.[146]

141   Ibid, s37(2).
142   Ibid, s47(2).
143   With the increased emphasis on avoiding delay in the youth justice system, this practice is becoming less common.
144   Police and Criminal Evidence Act 1984, s46A as inserted by Criminal Justice and Public Order Act 1994 s29.
145   See paras 4.20–4.22.
146   Ibid.

Possible disposals

5.185　The fact that there appears to be sufficient evidence for a successful prosecution does not mean that court proceedings will automatically follow. The police may also take no further action or decide to divert the young offender from the court system. The possible diversionary disposals are a caution or (in the pilot areas) a reprimand or warning. These disposals are considered in Chapter 6. The defence lawyer at the police station will need to explain these disposals both to the young client and his/her parent or guardian.

Charge

5.186　A suspect must be charged as soon as the custody officer is aware that there is sufficient evidence.[147] The charge must be read out to the suspect by the custody officer and a written copy of the charge must be handed to the suspect. If the suspect is a juvenile, the charging process must take place in the presence of the appropriate adult and the written notice of the charge should be handed to the adult.[148]

5.187　　A record must be made of anything said upon charge.[149] A court may draw an inference from the fact that a suspect does not mention when charged a fact, which in the circumstances existing at the time s/he could reasonably have been expected to mention, and which s/he subsequently relies upon in his/her defence.[150]

Choice of court

5.188　In general a child or young person will appear before a youth court.[151] Custody officers sometimes overlook this rule, particularly with 17-year-olds, therefore it is advisable for the defence lawyer to check that the correct court has been chosen. If a child or young person has been refused bail and either kept in police custody or transferred to local authority accommodation, s/he must be produced at the next

---

147　Police and Criminal Evidence Act 1984 s37(1).
148　Code C, para 16.3.
149　Code C, para 16.7.
150　Criminal Justice and Public Order Act 1984 s34.
151　Children and Young Persons Act 1933 s46(1). For the various exceptions to this rule see paras 9.5–9.11.

available court sitting.[152] If no youth court is due to sit the next day, special arrangements may be made to convene a youth bench or, more frequently, the accused will be sent to the adult court.[153]

Bail after charge

5.189   Following charge an accused shall be released by the custody officer (subject to the Criminal Justice and Public Order Act 1994 s25[154]) unless:

– his/her name or address cannot be ascertained or the custody officer has reasonable grounds for doubting whether a name or address furnished by him/her as his/her name or address is his/her real name or address;

– the custody officer has reasonable grounds for believing that the person arrested will fail to appear in court to answer bail;

– (in the case of a person arrested for an imprisonable offence) the custody officer has reasonable grounds for believing that the detention of the person is necessary to prevent him from committing an offence;

– (in the case of a person arrested for a non-imprisonable offence) the custody officer has reasonable grounds for believing that the detention of the person is necessary to prevent him from causing physical injury to any other person or from causing loss or damage to property;

– the custody officer has reasonable grounds for believing that the detention of the person is necessary to prevent him from interfering with the administration of justice or with the investigation of offences or a particular offence;

– the custody officer has reasonable grounds for believing that the detention of the person is necessary for his own protection;

– in the case of a juvenile, the custody officer has reasonable grounds for believing that s/he ought to be detained in his/her own interests.[155]

There is no definition of a juvenile's 'own interests' but the fact that it exists as a separate grounds for detention must mean that it has a wider meaning than the juvenile's physical safety which would

---

152 Police and Criminal Evidence Act 1984 s47(2).
153 Children and Young Persons Act s46(2).
154 See para 10.7.
155 Police and Criminal Evidence Act 1984 s38(1).

be covered by the penultimate exception. It has been invoked by custody officers who are concerned about the juvenile's health or moral well-being, for example when the juvenile is known to be a drug addict or to be involved in prostitution. It should be noted that even if bail has been refused in the juvenile's interests, there will still be an obligation to transfer to local authority accommodation.[156]

Conditional bail

5.190   The custody officer has the power to impose conditions on bail granted after charge.[157] The accused has a right to unconditional bail unless the custody officer is satisfied that conditions are necessary for the purposes of preventing the accused from:

- failing to surrender;
- committing an offence while on bail;
- interfering with witnesses;
- otherwise obstructing the course of justice whether in relation to him/herself or any other person.[158]

The custody officer may impose any condition available to a court,[159] except a condition of residence in a probation hostel.[160] There seems no reason in principle why a social services department could not offer a bail support package for a child or young person in serious risk of being refused bail by a custody officer. In practice this is extremely rare. Application may be made to a custody officer or a court for variation of the bail conditions.[161]

Narey hearings

5.191   Where a custody officer grants bail after charge, s/he shall appoint for the first court appearance:

- a date which is not later than the first sitting of the court after s/he is charged with an offence; or

---

156   See para 5.194.
157   Police and Criminal Evidence Act 1984 s47(1A).
158   Bail Act 1976 s3A(5).
159   The practical considerations of bail conditions imposed upon children and young persons are considered in detail in Chapter 10.
160   Bail Act 1976 s3A(2).
161   Ibid, s3A(4) and Magistrates' Courts Act 1980 s43A. See para 10.197.

- where s/he is informed by the clerk to the justices for the relevant petty sessions area that the appearance cannot be accommodated until a later date, that later date.[162]

In the case of children and young persons this will usually mean the next sitting of the youth court.

Statutory time limit (pilot areas only)

5.192   The Prosecution of Offences Act 1985 ss22, 22A and 22B (as amended by the Crime and Disorder Act 1998 ss43–45) impose a statutory time limit. The Prosecution of Offences (Youth Courts Time Limits) Regulations 1999 SI No 2743 have been introduced. They only have effect from 1 November 1999 in pilot areas.[163] An offender aged under 18 arrested in a pilot area for an offence must be charged and appear before a court within 36 calendar days of his/her arrest.[164] If the time limit would otherwise expire on a Saturday, Sunday, Christmas Day, Good Friday or any other bank holiday, it shall be treated as expiring on the first preceding day that is not one of these days.[165]

5.193   If the time limit expires before the young suspect is charged with an offence, s/he shall not be charged unless further evidence relating to the offence is obtained.[166] If the time limit expires after charge but before the first court appearance, the court shall stay the proceedings.[167] There is provision for the police or the prosecution to apply to a court for an extension of this time limit (for which see Chapter 8).[168]

Transfer to local authority accommodation

Duty to transfer

5.194   In the case of a juvenile refused bail under the Police and Criminal Evidence Act 1984 s38(1), the custody officer shall secure that the detained juvenile is moved to local authority accommodation unless:

162   Police and Criminal Evidence Act s47(3A) as inserted by the Crime and Disorder Act 1998 s46.
163   See Appendix 8 for pilot areas.
164   Prosecution of Offences (Youth Courts Time Limits) Regulations 1999 reg 5.
165   Ibid, reg 1(5).
166   Prosecution of Offences Act 1985 s22A(4).
167   Ibid, s22A(5).
168   Ibid, s22A(3).

- it is impracticable for the custody officer to do so; or
- in the case of a juvenile aged 12 to 16, no secure accommodation is available and keeping him/her in other local authority accommodation would not be adequate to protect the public from serious harm from him/her.[169]

After charge

5.195 The duty to transfer applies when the custody officer has refused bail under s38(1), that is 'where a person arrested for an offence otherwise than under a warrant endorsed for bail is charged with an offence'. There is therefore no obligation upon the custody officer to secure a juvenile's move to local authority accommodation in the following circumstances:

- when a juvenile is arrested on a court warrant not backed for bail; or
- when a juvenile is arrested for breach of bail conditions under the Bail Act 1976 s7 or for breach of remand conditions under the Children and Young Persons Act 1969 s23A.

Local authority accommodation

5.196 This is defined as 'accommodation provided by or on behalf of a local authority (within the meaning of the Children Act 1989)'.[170] The choice of accommodation remains in the discretion of the local authority. It could include a placement back with parents, a remand foster placement, a residential children's home or secure accommodation. When exercising this discretion, the Department of Health advises local authorities 'to have regard to the fact that the police custody officer has not ordered the juvenile's release from police detention, either on bail or without bail'.[171]

Secure accommodation

5.197 'Secure accommodation' means accommodation provided for the purpose of restricting liberty.[172] Upon receiving a child or young person from police detention the local authority may only place him/her in secure accommodation if it appears that any accommodation

---

169   Police and Criminal Evidence Act 1984 s38(6).
170   Ibid s38(6A); see also para 4.15.
171   *The Children Act 1989 Guidance and Regulations* (HMSO, 1991), Vol 1, Court Orders, para 6.40.
172   Police and Criminal Evidence Act 1984 s38(6A).

other than that provided for the purpose of restricting liberty is inappropriate because:

1) the child is likely to abscond from such other accommodation; or
2) the child is likely to injure himself or other people if he is kept in any such other accommodation.[173]

The local authority may only keep a child or young person in secure accommodation without the authority of a court for a maximum of 72 hours.[174]

Custody officer to produce certificate

5.198   If a juvenile is not transferred to local authority accommodation the custody officer must certify which exception applied. If no transfer took place because it was impracticable to do so, the certificate should specify the circumstances which resulted in this.[175]

5.199   The certificate signed by the custody officer must be produced to the court before which the juvenile is first brought.[176] In the experience of the authors the contents of the certificate are never considered in any court hearing.

Exceptions to the duty to transfer

Transfer is impracticable

5.200   It is suggested that this should be interpreted narrowly, applying only if it is physically impossible to secure a move to local authority accommodation. This interpretation is supported by Home Office Circular No 78/1992 *Criminal Justice Act 1991: Detention etc. of Juveniles* which states:

> The circumstances in which a transfer would be impracticable are those, and only those, in which it is physically impossible to place the juvenile in local authority accommodation. These might include extreme weather conditions (eg, floods or blizzards), or the impossibility of contacting the local authority.

5.201   A wider definition of 'impracticable' was contemplated by the Divisional Court in *R v Chief Constable of Cambridgeshire ex p Michel.*[177]

173 Children (Secure Accommodation) Regulations 1991 SI No 1505 reg 6.
174 Ibid, reg 10.
175 Police and Criminal Evidence Act 1984 s38(6).
176 Ibid, s38(7).
177 (1990) 91 Cr App R 325; [1991] Crim LR 382, QBD.

Here it was held that it would be impracticable to transfer to local authority accommodation if no secure accommodation was available and in the custody officer's opinion secure accommodation is the only type of accommodation suitable to avoid the consequences which led to the decision to refuse bail. This decision would seem to have been overruled by the Criminal Justice Act 1991 which created the separate exception of protection of the public.[178] This point is made clear by the Codes of Practice:

> . . . neither a juvenile's behaviour nor the nature of the offence with which he is charged provides grounds for the custody officer to decide that it is impracticable to seek to arrange for his transfer to the care of the local authority. Similarly, the lack of secure local authority accommodation shall not make it impracticable for the custody officer to transfer him. The availability of secure accommodation is only a factor in relation to a juvenile aged 12 or over when the local authority accommodation would not be adequate to protect the public from serious harm from the juvenile. The obligation to transfer a juvenile to local authority accommodation applies as much to a juvenile charged during the daytime as it does to a juvenile to be held overnight . . . [179]

Protection of public from serious harm

5.202 This exception applies to both males and females. It should also be noted that the minimum age is lower than the minimum for a custodial remand by a court. This means that a juvenile can be kept in police detention in circumstances where a court would have no power to remand in custody after the first court appearance.

5.203 The custody officer must first determine whether the juvenile presents a risk of serious harm to the public. Only if a risk of serious harm is identified can the custody officer refuse to transfer to local authority accommodation.

5.204 'Serious harm' is defined as follows:

> . . . any reference, in relation to an arrested juvenile charged with a violent or sexual offence,[180] to protecting the public from serious harm from him shall be construed as a reference to protecting members of the public from death or serious personal injury, whether physical or

---

178 This view is endorsed by Home Office Circular No 78/1992.
179 Code C, Note for Guidance 16B.
180 Violent and sexual offences have the same meanings as in the Criminal Justice Act 1991 s31. See paras 10.77 and 10.81.

psychological, occasioned by further such offences committed by him.[181]

5.205   There is no statutory definition of serious harm in relation to other offences. The Home Office Circular 78/1992 does, however, offer the following guidance:

> 'Serious harm' is not defined in relation to other offences. However, the definition for sexual or violent offences suggests the gravity of the harm to which the public would have to be exposed from a juvenile charged with any other offence before the test is likely to be satisfied.

Negotiating a transfer

5.206   Having a juvenile produced from local authority accommodation rather than police detention can have a significant impact upon the choice of remand placement made by the court before which the juvenile is first produced. The fact that the juvenile has been accommodated overnight by the local authority and produced at court can demonstrate to the court that s/he can be successfully supervised in the community.

Complaints[182]

5.207   A complaint regarding police conduct may be made by any member of the public including suspects. A complaint made by a juvenile must be considered in just the same way as a complaint made by an adult and it is not necessary for the complaint to be made with the permission of a parent or guardian.

5.208   When a complaint is made it is the duty of the police to record it. The Codes of Practice give the following guidance when a complaint is made while in police custody:

> If a complaint is made by or on behalf of a detained person about his treatment since his arrest, or it comes to the notice of any officer that he may have been treated improperly, a report must be made as soon as practicable to an officer of the rank of inspector or above who is not connected with the investigation. If the matter concerns a possible assault or the possibility of the unnecessary or unreasonable use of

---

181   Police and Criminal Evidence Act 1984 s38(6A).
182   For more detailed information about complaints and civil actions, see Harrison and Cragg *Police Misconduct: Legal Remedies* (LAG, 3rd edn, 1996).

force then the police surgeon must also be called as soon as practicable.[183]

It is usual for the duty inspector to take brief details of the complaint and then to pass the complaint onto the relevant complaints unit who will later contact the complainant to take a full statement and identify any potential witnesses to the incident.

5.209 A complaint may be dealt with by way of a formal investigation or informal resolution.

Informal resolution

5.210 Informal resolution can involve an explanation of the behaviour or an apology given by the officer complained of. A record of the complaint and its informal resolution should be made and the complainant has a right to receive a copy if a request is made within three months of the resolution.

5.211 A complaint may only be resolved informally if the complainant consents and the investigating officer is satisfied that even if proved the conduct would not justify criminal or disciplinary proceedings.

Formal investigation

5.212 If the complaint is not suitable for informal investigation then an officer must be appointed to investigate the complaint. An investigation will take place and the investigating officer must prepare a report. The possible outcomes are as follows:

– the complaint is held to be unsubstantiated;
– the complaint is not investigated because dispensation is obtained not to investigate (usually on the grounds that the complainant has failed to co-operate); or
– the complaint is upheld and disciplinary and/or criminal proceedings follow.

Police Complaints Authority

5.213 This is an independent body set up under the Police and Criminal Evidence Act 1984 to supervise the investigation of complaints against the police. All complaints involving the death of a person or serious injury must be referred to the Authority. It is also possible for other complaints to be referred to the Authority.

183 Code C, para 9.1.

Diversion

Introduction

6.1   There is a widely held belief that children and young persons should be kept out of the criminal justice system wherever possible. This has its basis in the desire to avoid children and young persons suffering from the stigma of a criminal conviction as well as an acceptance that offending is a feature of the adolescence of many people and that maturity will bring a natural end to such behaviour.

6.2   Both the major agencies involved in the detection and prosecution of offenders have an important role to play in diverting children and young persons from the criminal courts. The police have always been able to exercise their discretion when deciding whether to charge a suspect. For its part, the Crown Prosecution Service may choose to discontinue criminal proceedings where it is considered not in the public interest to proceed with the prosecution. When taking this decision the prosecutor will have regard to the welfare of the child or young person pursuant to the Children and Young Persons Act 1933 s44(1).[1] In addition, the social services department has a role to play both in the decision-making process and by providing resources to avoid the need for criminal prosecutions.[2]

6.3   Diversion has been demonstrated to work for the vast majority of young offenders. In one official survey it was revealed that only 11 per cent of 10- to 14-year-olds and 16 per cent of 14- to 16-year-olds who had been cautioned were convicted of a 'standard list'[3] offence within two years.[4]

6.4   The defence lawyer has a role to play too by ensuring that the issue of diversion is considered at each stage of the proceedings and that any relevant information about the young offender and any change of circumstances are brought to the attention of the prosecutor.

---

1   See para 1.41.
2   Children Act 1989 Sch 2 Part I para 7(a)(ii).
3   'Standard list' offences include all indictable offences and some summary-only offences, eg, assaulting a police officer and motor vehicle interference.
4   Home Office Statistical Bulletin 20/92 (Government Statistical Service, 1992).

Cautioning

6.5 Cautioning offenders is not subject to any statutory guidelines. Instead the practice is governed by Home Office Circular 18/1994 and National Standards for the Cautioning of Offenders.

6.6 The purpose of a caution is:

 – to deal quickly and simply with less serious offenders;
 – to divert them from unnecessary appearance in the criminal courts; and
 – to reduce the chances of their re-offending.

6.7 In some areas of the country diversion schemes for children and young persons have been developed. These are often referred to as 'cautioning plus'. In such schemes support is offered to the child or young person who is accepting the caution. This may include:

 – voluntary involvement in intermediate treatment or reparation schemes;
 – contact with education welfare officers;
 – referral to youth work projects; and
 – befriending by adult volunteers.

6.8 Nationally the majority of young people coming to police attention are cautioned, but significant differences in outcomes for young people according to police area can be seen.[5] In Surrey 81 per cent of 14- to 18-year-old males are cautioned, the highest proportion in England or Wales. Conversely, Durham has the lowest rate at 37 per cent. Females are more likely to be cautioned than males: nationally 61 per cent of 14- to 18-year-old males are cautioned whereas the figure for females aged 14 to 18 is 81 per cent. Age is also a factor: 87 per cent of males aged 10 to 14 are cautioned, while for females the figure is 97 per cent. Evidence also suggests that black suspects are less likely to be cautioned.[6]

Procedural requirements

6.9 The following conditions must be met before a caution can be administered:

---

5 Home Office *Criminal Statistics England and Wales 1994* (HMSO, 1995).
6 *Juvenile Cautioning and Ethnic Monitoring* (Commission for Racial Equality, 1989).

- there must be *evidence of the offender's guilt* sufficient to give a realistic prospect of conviction;
- the offender must *admit the offence*; and
- the offender (or, in the case of a juvenile, his/her parents or guardian) must understand the significance of the caution and give *informed consent* to being cautioned.

Evidence of the offender's guilt

6.10   The evidential test is whether there is sufficient evidence to provide a realistic prospect of a conviction. This is the same test as the custody officer should use to decide whether there is sufficient evidence to charge and the same test employed by the Crown Prosecution Service.

Admit the offence

6.11   A caution may not be administered unless there is a clear admission of guilt. The National Standards for Cautioning give the following guidance:

> A caution will not be appropriate where a person does not make a clear and reliable admission of the offence (for example, if intent is denied or there are doubts about his mental health or intellectual capacity).

There should be an admission to the offence before formal consideration is given to proceeding by way of a caution.[7] This admission does not have to be during a formal taped interview.[8]

Informed consent

6.12   This criterion raises two issues:

- who can give consent to the caution being administered?
- when can consent be described as 'informed'?

Who can give consent?

6.13   A 17-year-old may give consent for a caution to be administered to him/her. In the case of a juvenile, the National Standards seem to

---

7   *R v Commissioner of the Metropolitan Police ex p Thompson* [1997] 1 WLR 1519, QBD.
8   *R v Chief Constable of Lancashire ex p Atkinson*, unreported, CO/3775/96, 5.2.98 Kennedy LJ.

require that consent is given only by the parent or guardian. It should be noted that no reference is made to the appropriate adult's consent being sufficient.

6.14   Consent is only informed if given in full knowledge of the implications of a caution. The National Guidelines require the following information to be given:

- that a record of the caution will be kept;
- that the fact of a previous caution may influence the decision whether or not to prosecute if the person should offend again; and
- that it may be cited in court if the person is subsequently found guilty of an offence.

Public interest considerations

6.15   The police have a discretion whether or not to caution an offender even where the above criteria are satisfied.[9] The Home Office Circular 18/1994 does not give detailed guidance as to when a caution would be appropriate but it suggests that the proper use of discretion is a matter of common sense. In each case the police should consider:

- whether the circumstances are such that the caution is likely to be effective; and
- whether the caution is appropriate to the offence.

6.16   When considering these two questions the Circular and the National Standards for Cautioning give specific guidance on the following factors:

- the seriousness of the offence;
- any presumption against prosecuting;
- the offender's record;
- the offender's attitude; and
- the views of the victim.

Seriousness of the offence

6.17   The Home Office Circular 18/1994 strongly discourages the use of cautions for serious offences:

---

9   *R v Chief Constable of Kent and Crown Prosecution Service ex p GL (a Minor)* (1991) 93 Cr App R 416; [1991] Crim LR 841, QBD.

> Cautions should never be used for the most serious indictable only offences such as [attempted murder and rape], and only in exceptional circumstances (one example might be a child taking another's pocket money by force, which in law is robbery) for other indictable-only offences, regardless of the age or previous record of the offender.

6.18   For other offences it may still be the case that the offence is too serious to allow consideration of a caution. Home Office Circular 18/1994 suggests the following (non-exhaustive) list of factors:

- the nature and extent of the harm or loss resulting from the offences, relative to the victim's age and means;
- whether the offence was racially motivated;
- whether it involved a breach of trust;
- whether the offence was carried out in a systematic and organised way.

Presumption against prosecuting

6.19   In the past, Home Office guidance has encouraged police forces to use cautions particularly in relation to juveniles. In Home Office Circular 18/1994 the idea of cautioning certain vulnerable groups is accepted but young offenders are not included in that category. Indeed, the guidance seems to be at pains to emphasise that young offenders are not to be treated more leniently simply because of their age:

> [T]he presumption in favour of diverting juveniles from the courts [does not] mean that they should automatically be cautioned, as opposed to prosecuted, simply because they are juveniles.[10]

Offender's record

6.20   The Home Office Circular 18/1994 states that more than one caution should not be considered except where:

- the subsequent offence is trivial; or
- where there has been a sufficient lapse of time since the first caution to suggest that it had some effect.

Offender's attitude

6.21   The National Standards for Cautioning require police officers to consider the offender's attitude to the offence and in particular:

10 Home Office Circular 18/1994 para 4.

- the wilfulness with which the offence was committed; and
- the offender's subsequent attitude.

The National Standards suggest that a practical demonstration of regret (eg, apologising to the victim and/or offering to put matters right as far as possible) may support a decision to caution.

Views of the victim

6.22 The National Standards for Cautioning state that it is desirable that before a caution is administered the victim is contacted to establish:

- his/her views about the offence;
- the nature and extent of any harm or loss, and their significance relative to the victim's circumstances;
- whether the offender has made any form of reparation or paid compensation.

Procedure for administering a caution

6.23 As cautions may be cited in court, it is important that they are administered in such a way that their significance is understood. As already mentioned, the police are under a duty to explain the significance of a caution before consent is sought. The caution should normally be administered by an officer in uniform of at least the rank of inspector. The caution should be administered personally and wherever practicable at a police station. A juvenile may only be cautioned in the presence of an appropriate adult (this need not be a parent or guardian).

Challenging a caution

6.24 A caution administered in clear breach of the guidelines issued by the Home Office may be challenged by way of a judicial review of the decision to administer a caution. The Divisional Court is only likely to quash the caution if the breach of the guidelines means that the caution is fatally flawed.[11] Cautions have been quashed when there

---

11 *R v Commissioner of Police for the Metropolis ex p P (a Minor)* (1995) 160 JP 367, QBD.

was no admission to the offence[12] or where the admission was obtained as a result of an unlawful inducement.[13]

Reprimands and warnings (pilot areas only)

6.25   The Crime and Disorder Act 1998 introduces for the first time a statutory framework for diverting offenders from the criminal courts. This framework only applies to offenders under the age of 18.

6.26   A first offence may result in a reprimand, warning or prosecution. A warning rather than a reprimand will be given where the first offence is considered too serious to justify a reprimand. Following a reprimand a subsequent offence may only be dealt with by a warning or charge. Any further offence will normally lead to a prosecution; however, a second warning may be administered but only where the offence is not serious and more than two years have passed since the first warning was given. No person may receive more than two warnings.[14]

6.27   Reprimands and warnings have only been introduced in pilot areas. National implementation is expected in June 2000. No caution may be given to a child or young person wherever reprimands and warnings are in force.[15]

Pre-conditions

6.28   Before a reprimand or warning may be administered there must be:
- sufficient evidence of the offence to provide a realistic prospect of a conviction; and
- an admission of guilt by the child or young person.[16]

The police must also be satisfied that it would not be in the public interest for the offender to be prosecuted. A reprimand or warning may never be administered to a child or young person who has already been convicted of an offence.[17]

6.29   There is no requirement that either the child or young person or

12   Ibid.
13   *R v Commissioner of the Metropolitan Police ex p Thompson* [1997] 1 WLR 1519, QBD.
14   Crime and Disorder Act 1998 s65(2)–(4).
15   Ibid, s65(8).
16   Crime and Disorder Act 1998 s65(1).
17   Ibid.

his/her parent or guardian consents to the administering of the reprimand or warning. The only recourse would be to apply for judicial review to quash the reprimand or warning if the pre-conditions outlined above had not been satisfied.[18]

Procedure

6.30   A reprimand or warning must be administered at a police station. If the offender is under the age of 17, it must be administered in the presence of an appropriate adult.[19]

6.31   An appropriate adult is defined as:

1) the juvenile offender's parent or guardian or, if s/he is in the care of a local authority or voluntary organisation, a person representing that authority or organisation;
2) a social worker of a local authority social services department;
3) if no person falling within paragraph (1) or (2) above is available, any responsible person aged 18 or over who is not a police officer or a person employed by the police.[20]

The constable administering the reprimand or warning must explain its effect (see below).

Effect of a reprimand

6.32   The reprimand will be recorded by the police. It may be cited in subsequent criminal proceedings in the same circumstances as a conviction may be cited.[21]

Effect of a warning

6.33   When a child or young person is given a warning s/he shall be referred to a youth offending team as soon as practicable.[22] The youth offending team must carry out an assessment of the offender and unless it considers it inappropriate to do so, it shall arrange for the young offender to participate in a rehabilitation programme.[23]

6.34   The warning will be recorded by the police. It may be cited in

18 Compare the case-law developed regarding cautioning; see para 6.24.
19 Crime and Disorder Act 1998, s65(5).
20 Ibid, s65(7).
21 Ibid, s66(5)(a).
22 Ibid, s66(1).
23 Ibid, s66(2).

subsequent criminal proceedings in the same circumstances as a conviction may be cited.[24]

6.35   If a person is convicted of an offence within two years of receiving a warning, the sentencing court may not conditionally discharge him/her, unless it is of the opinion that there are exceptional circumstances which justify its doing so.[25] There is no such restriction upon a court imposing an absolute discharge.

Rehabilitation programme

6.36   The purpose of a rehabilitation programme is to rehabilitate participants and to prevent them from re-offending.[26] It may include short-term counselling or group work, reparation to victims, supervised youth activities or work to improve school attendance.

6.37   If a young offender fails to participate in the rehabilitation programme s/he cannot be prosecuted, but a report on his/her failure to participate in the programme may be cited in criminal proceedings in the same circumstances as a conviction.[27] The decision whether there has been non-compliance rests with the youth offending team not a court. It should be noted that the legislation does not incorporate any requirement to assess the reasonableness of any alleged non-compliance.

Transitional arrangements

6.38   Any caution given to a child or young person before the introduction of reprimands and warnings shall be treated as a reprimand. Any second or subsequent caution shall be treated as a warning.[28]

6.39   Following the introduction of reprimands and warnings, there will be young offenders in court who will have previous cautions deemed to be warnings. Such offenders will not have participated in a rehabilitation programme. This fact should be brought to the attention of the sentencing court.

---

24   Ibid, s66(5)(b).
25   Ibid, s66(4).
26   Ibid, s66(6).
27   Ibid, s66(5)(c).
28   Ibid, Sch 9 para 5.

Prosecution

6.40 In normal circumstances the decision to prosecute is taken solely by the police. In some cases the police will seek the advice of the Crown Prosecution Service before charge, usually where there is some doubt concerning the sufficiency of evidence or where the case is sensitive.

6.41 Once an accused person has been charged by the police, responsibility for the prosecution passes to the Crown Prosecution Service.[29] If it is not thought proper to continue with the prosecution, notice of discontinuance may be served upon the court and the defendant.[30]

6.42 The conduct of a prosecution is governed by the *Code for Crown Prosecutors* issued under the Prosecution of Offences Act 1985 s10.[31] To continue with a prosecution brought by the police, a prosecutor must be satisfied that:

 – there is sufficient admissible evidence to secure a conviction; and
 – it is in the public interest.

Public interest

6.43 Even if the prosecutor is satisfied that there is sufficient evidence to secure a conviction it does not automatically follow that the prosecution will proceed. The *Code for Crown Prosecutors* paras 6.4 and 6.5 require the prosecutor to weigh up the various factors for and against a prosecution. These factors are set out in Table 1 on pp148 and 149.

6.44 In the past the code made specific reference to the youth of a defendant being a reason to consider discontinuance. The 1994 version of the code requires Crown Prosecutors to consider the interests of a child or young person when deciding whether to prosecute; however, it states that the decision not to prosecute should not be based solely on the defendant's age.[32]

Making representations to the Crown Prosecution Service

6.45 It is always open to the defence lawyer to make representations to the Crown Prosecution Service regarding the decision to proceed with a

---

29 Prosecution of Offences Act 1985 s3(2).
30 Ibid, s17.
31 See Chapter 1 n29.
32 *Code for Crown Prosecutors* (1994) para 6.8.

prosecution. In many circumstances the prosecutor has very little personal information regarding a child or young person and therefore any review of the prosecution on public policy grounds can only be on a very limited basis. By supplying more extensive information the defence lawyer may be able to influence the decision.

Mitigating the rigours of the criminal law

6.46 Where the criminal law makes limited concessions to the youth of the offender, it may be possible to persuade the prosecutor to discontinue proceedings on the basis that a prosecution would be harsh. This could happen, for example, where a young person committed an offence under pressure from another but where the threats do not amount to the defence of duress.

Intervention by social services more appropriate

6.47 Where the arrest and charge has resulted in the intervention of the social services department, the defence lawyer may wish to draw this to the attention of the Crown Prosecution Service. The work of the department may remove any underlying cause of the offending and it may be possible to argue that court proceedings are no longer in the public interest.

Applying the principle of diversion to 17-year-olds

6.48 Despite the inclusion of 17-year-olds in the age range of the youth court, many police forces do not include suspects of that age in their review procedures prior to charge and consequently there is a much lower incidence of cautioning. The defence lawyer may therefore have a role in challenging the decision to prosecute 17-year-old defendants by encouraging a more thorough review by the prosecutor and, if appropriate, submitting formal representations.

Discontinuing outstanding cases

6.49 Where a frequent offender has received a substantial sentence there will often be a number of outstanding cases awaiting disposal. The defence lawyer may be able to persuade the relevant prosecutor to discontinue these cases. Written representations should be made to the reviewing lawyer.

Judicial review of the decision to prosecute

6.50   In exceptional circumstances it may be possible to apply for judicial review of the decision by the Crown Prosecution Service to continue with the prosecution of a child or young person where it could be shown that the decision was contrary to the stated policy on cautioning juveniles.[33]

---

33   *R v Chief Constable of Kent and Crown Prosecution Service ex p GL (a Minor)* (1991) 93 Cr App R 416; [1991] Crim LR 841, QBD.

Table 1: Decision to prosecute – public interest criteria

Factors in favour of prosecution

- a conviction is likely to result in a significant sentence;
- a weapon was used or violence was threatened during the commission of the offence;
- the offence was committed against a person serving the public (eg, a police or prison officer, or a nurse);
- the defendant was in a position of trust;
- the evidence shows that the defendant was a ringleader or an organiser of the offence;
- there is evidence that the offence was premeditated;
- there is evidence that the offence was carried out by a group;
- the victim of the offence was vulnerable, has been put in considerable fear or suffered personal attack, damage or disturbance;
- the offence was motivated by any form of discrimination against the victim's ethnic or national origin, sex, religious beliefs, political views or sexual preference;
- there is a marked difference between the actual or mental ages of the defendant and the victim, or there is an element of corruption;
- the defendant's previous convictions or cautions are relevant to the present offence;
- the defendant is alleged to have committed the offence while under an order of the court;
- there are grounds for believing that the offence is likely to be continued or repeated, for example, by a history of recurring conduct; or
- the offence, although not serious in itself, is widespread in the area where it was committed.

Factors against prosecution

- the court is likely to impose a very small or nominal penalty;
- the offence was committed as a result of a genuine mistake or misunderstanding (these factors must be balanced against the seriousness of the offence);
- the loss or harm can be described as minor and was the result of a single incident, particularly if it was caused by a misjudgment;
- there has been a long delay between the offence taking place and the date of the trial, unless:
  - the offence is serious;
  - the delay has been caused in part by the defendant;
  - the offence has only recently come to light; or
  - the complexity of the offence has meant that there has been a long investigation;
- a prosecution is likely to have a very bad effect on the victim's physical or mental health, always bearing in mind the seriousness of the offence;
- the defendant is elderly, is or was at the time of the offence suffering from significant mental or physical ill health, unless the offence is serious or there is a real possibility that it may be repeated;
- the defendant has put right the loss or harm that was caused (but defendants must not avoid prosecution simply because they can pay compensation);
- details may be made public that could harm sources of information, international relations or national security.

CHAPTER 7

Parental involvement

For complete chapter contents, see overleaf

Introduction

7.1   Under the Criminal Justice Act 1991 the concept of parental involvement was justified in terms of parents taking responsibility for criminal offences committed by their children. The scheme of the Act was
explained in Home Office Circular 30/1992 *Criminal Justice Act 1991:
Young People and the Youth Court,* para 32:

> The Government believes that parents must be involved when the
> children under 16 come to court in criminal proceedings. It will often
> be right for the parents of 16 and 17 olds to be involved. Most
> parents take their responsibilities seriously, but the purpose of the
> 1991 Act is to ensure that all parents do so.
>
> Under the Act . . . courts have a duty, subject to exceptions, to involve
> the parents of children and young people under 16. The Act gives
> courts a power to involve the parents of 16 and 17 year olds when it is
> appropriate to do so. This reflects the general principle that the way in
> which courts deal with young people aged 16 and 17 should take
> account of the stage of their development, and, in particular, their
> dependence on or independence from their parents.

7.2   Parental involvement under the 1991 Act encompassed attendance at court, liability to pay financial penalties on behalf of the young
offender and being bound over to exercise control over him/her.
More recently the focus has moved to poor parenting as a contributing factor in youth offending. This change of emphasis is reflected in
the Draft Guidance Document: *Parenting Orders* (paras 2.4, 2.6 and
2.7):

> Parents have an important role to play in preventing their children
> offending; they have a responsibility to the child, and to the
> community to take proper care and control of their children, and to do
> what they can to prevent offending. Some parents may need help,
> support, encouragement and direction in this and there are a number
> of aspects in the youth justice reform programme which seek to
> strengthen this.
>
> Research has shown that inadequate parental supervision is strongly
> associated with offending. For example a Home Office study[1] showed
> that 42% of juveniles who had low or medium levels of parental
> supervision had offended, whereas for those juveniles who had

---

1   Graham and Bowling (1995) *Young People and Crime,* Home Office Research
Study No 145.

experienced high levels of parental supervision the figure was only 20%. The same research showed that the quality of relationship between the parent and child is crucial. Research[2] also shows that the children of parents whose behaviour towards their children is harsh and erratic are twice as likely to offend.

In the United States, a study as long ago as 1973 showed that by training parents in negotiation skill, in sticking to clear rules and rewarding good behaviour, offending rates were halved[3] . . . The Government believes that for many parents whose children get into trouble, help from trained professionals and contact with other parents in the same situation may prove invaluable.

7.3   The possibility of providing such help to parents was introduced by the Crime and Disorder Act 1998. Parents may be asked to attend parenting classes as part of a rehabilitation programme following a final warning and as part of the new parenting order a court can require such attendance as well as impose requirements upon the parent with a view to preventing their children from offending.

7.4   The concept of parental involvement applies equally to the youth court, adult magistrates' court and the Crown Court. The application of the concept varies widely between different courts and different geographical regions and practitioners will be well advised to develop local knowledge about the prevailing attitudes of magistrates and judges in the courts where they appear to represent children and young persons.

Involvement in pre-court disposals

7.5   When a child or young person is given a final warning by the police, there will be a referral to the youth offending team to determine whether the young offender should participate in a rehabilitation programme.[4] This programme could involve asking the parent to attend parenting classes on a voluntary basis. It could also involve

2   Farrington 'Family backgrounds in aggressive youths', in Hersov et al. (ed.) *Aggressive and anti-social behaviour in childhood and adolescence.* Pergamon Press (1978).
3   Alexander and Parsons 'Short term behavioural intervention with delinquent families: impact on family process and recidivism', *Journal of Abnormal Psychology*, 81(3) (1973).
4   See para 6.33.

arranging for the social services department to provide help and support to the parent under the Children Act 1989 s17. The defence lawyer needs to be aware of any pre-court intervention as it may affect the court's decisions in relation to financial orders, bindovers and parenting orders.

Obligation to attend court

7.6   The Children and Young Persons Act 1933 s34A[5] imposes a duty upon the court to involve in the court proceedings the adult responsible for the care of a child or young person.

7.7   The purpose of this requirement is explained in Home Office Circular No 30/1992 as follows:

> There are a number of reasons why parents should be expected to attend court with their children. Their attendance:
> - provides support to their children in what may well be a confusing and intimidating experience;
> - ensures that parents understand the serious nature of the proceedings;
> - enables parents to participate in the proceedings as appropriate, and assist the court as necessary;
> - helps the court have confidence that any arrangements it makes will be properly understood and acted upon.

The obligation varies depending on the age of the defendant.

Defendants under 16

7.8   The court must require the attendance of the parent or guardian during all stages of the proceedings, unless and to the extent that it would be unreasonable, having regard to the circumstances of the case.[6]

Defendants aged 16 or 17

7.9   The court has a wider discretion in relation to 16- and 17-year-olds. With such defendants the court may require a parent or guardian to attend at court during all stages of the proceedings unless and to the

---

5   As inserted by Criminal Justice Act 1991 s56.
6   Children and Young Persons Act 1933 s34A(1)(b).

extent that it would be unreasonable in all the circumstances of the case.[7]

Discharging the responsibility to attend court

7.10 The duty to attend court may be discharged by the following:
- parents;
- guardian;
- a local authority.

Parents

7.11 'Parent' is not defined for the purposes of the Children and Young Persons Act 1933 s34A. By analogy with the Magistrates' Courts (Children and Young Persons) Rules 1992 SI No 2071 it is likely that the word should be construed as referring to a person with parental responsibility.

Guardians

7.12 'Guardian' is defined by the Children and Young Persons Act 1933 s107(1) as:

> any person, who in the opinion of the court having cognisance of any case in relation to the child or young person or in which the child or young person is concerned, has for the time being the care of the child or young person.

This definition would include step-parents, grandparents or other relatives who have day-to-day care of a child or young person.

Local authorities

7.13 By the Children and Young Persons Act 1933 s34A(2) a local authority may have an obligation to attend court with a defendant but only when:
- the authority has parental responsibility; and
- the defendant is in their care or accommodated by the authority under the Children Act 1989.

7.14 Parental responsibility has the same meaning as in the Children

---

7   Ibid, s34A(1)(a).

Act 1989.[8] A local authority will only have parental responsibility in the following circumstances:

– where a full care order under Children Act 1989 s31 is in force; or
– where an emergency protection order is in force.

7.15   When a local authority has an obligation to attend court, it should be discharged by the local authority social worker or other representative of the social services department with responsibility for the child or young person.[9] If the defendant is subject to a full care order but the local authority has placed him/her back at home, the obligation to attend court is shared by the parents and the authority.[10] In such circumstances it may be appropriate for both the parent(s) and a representative of the local authority to attend court.[11]

7.16   Where a child or young person has been remanded to local authority accommodation under Children and Young Persons Act 1969 s23, the authority does not acquire parental responsibility and therefore cannot be required to attend court. However, the authority will wish to consider whether it can fulfil its obligations to the court without arranging for the attendance of a representative.

Attending at all stages of the proceedings

7.17   The obligation is to attend at all stages of the proceedings and some courts may seek to enforce the responsibility to attend at every hearing. In practice, however, most courts will be concerned to see the responsibility to attend is discharged at any hearing where the liberty of the child or young person is at stake, either in the course of making a decision with regard to bail or sentence, or where substantive issues in the case are to be determined. This may include any first appearance at court when the question of whether bail should be granted will always arise and important preliminary issues will be dealt with such as confirmation of the defendant's name, address and date of birth. The court may be particularly concerned to ensure the attendance of a parent at a trial or other hearing where the child or young person may have to make decisions as to the conduct of the case or give evidence in the proceedings.

8   See para 4.17.
9   Home Office Circular No 30/1992 para 35.
10   Children and Young Persons Act 1933 s34A(2).
11   Home Office Circular No 30/1992 para 35.

Unreasonable to require attendance?

7.18 What is unreasonable is a question of fact for the court to decide in the circumstances of each individual hearing.

7.19 Where a parent fails to attend at a particular hearing, the court may accept that attendance would be unreasonable due for example to ill health or other unforeseen circumstances. Courts are generally more reluctant to accept that requiring attendance would be unreasonable when there is a general reason which will apply to all hearings. Relevant considerations could include:

- parental employment;
- other child care responsibilities;
- defendant estranged from his/her parent.

Enforcing the requirement to attend

7.20 The Children and Young Persons Act 1933 s34A states the court may require the parent or guardian to attend court. The term 'require' is not further defined in the Act.

7.21 The Magistrates' Courts (Children and Young Persons) Rules 1992 SI No 2071 r26 provides:

> where a child or young person is charged with an offence, or is for any other reason brought before a court, a summons or warrant may be issued by a court to enforce the attendance of a parent or guardian under section 34A of the Act of 1933, in the same manner as if an information were laid upon which a summons or warrant could be issued against a defendant under the Magistrates' Courts Act 1980 ...

For the purposes of this rule a parent is defined as:

- a local authority with parental responsibility; and
- in any other case, a parent with parental responsibility.[12]

'Guardian' has the same meaning as in Children and Young Persons Act 1933 s107(1) (see para 7.12).[13]

7.22 It is arguable that this rule is ultra vires insofar as it purports to give a youth court or adult magistrates' court the power to issue an arrest warrant against a parent or guardian. It is a fundamental rule of statutory interpretation that a power of arrest may only be created by express statutory authority. The power under the Magistrates'

12 Magistrates' Courts (Children and Young Persons) Rules 1992 SI No 2071 r2(2).
13 Ibid.

Courts Act 1980 s1 to issue an arrest warrant is given to a justice of the peace who receives an information that a person has committed or is suspected of having committed an offence. A parent or guardian who fails to attend court has not committed a criminal offence and it would therefore seem impossible to extend the scope of s1 merely by secondary legislation.

Liability for financial penalties

7.23   The power to order parents or guardians to pay financial orders on behalf of their children is set out in Children and Young Persons Act 1933 s55. The precise powers of the court depend once again on the age of the defendant.

Definition of parent and guardian

7.24   'Parent' has the same meaning as in the Family Law Reform Act 1987 s1, namely it applies to both biological parents, whether or not the father has parental responsibility.[14]

7.25   'Guardian' has the same meaning as in the Children and Young Persons Act 1933 s107(1) (see para 7.12). It does not include a local authority[15] or a limited company which is looking after the offender.[16]

Offenders aged under 16

7.26   The court *must* order the parent or guardian to pay the financial order unless:

– s/he cannot be found; or
– it would be unreasonable in all the circumstances of the case.[17]

7.27   The circumstances when ordering the parent or guardian to pay would be unreasonable is not defined in the Act; however, as a matter of practice guidance may be sought from Home Office Circular No 3/1983:

---

14   Children and Young Persons Act 1933 s55(6), as inserted by Crime and Disorder Act 1998 Sch 7 para 1(3).
15   *Leeds City Council v West Yorkshire Metropolitan Police* [1983] 1 AC 29, HL.
16   *Marlowe Child and Family Services Ltd v DPP* [1998] 2 Cr App R (S) 438; [1999] 1 FLR 997, QBD.
17   Children and Young Persons Act 1933 s55(1).

- whether the parents had neglected to exercise due care and control of the juvenile;
- whether any such neglect had caused or contributed directly or indirectly to the commission of the offence;
- whether it is desirable that the child or young person should bear the responsibility themselves;
- the relationship between the parent and juvenile and the likely effect on that relationship of ordering the parent or guardian to pay the sum adjudged; and
- the respective means of the parent or guardian and the juvenile.

7.28 The Divisional Court has also held that it would be unreasonable to order a parent to pay a financial penalty for a child who at the time of the offence was accommodated by the local authority under the Children Act 1989 s20. Although the parent still had parental responsibility, the local authority had de facto charge of the child's day-to-day management.[18] The same principle could be applied to school children who offend on school premises during school hours, when arguably the school has de facto care and control of the child or young person.

Offenders aged 16 or 17

7.29 The court *may* order the parent or guardian to pay the financial order unless:

- s/he cannot be found; or
- it would be unreasonable in all the circumstances of the case.[19]

As the court is not required to order the parent or guardian to pay the financial order, it may take into account not only the above factors, but also the maturity of the offender. Home Office Circular No 30/1992 para 9 suggests a number of relevant factors.[20]

Procedure

Determining responsibility

7.30 Where both parents live together the court may choose which of the parents should be ordered to pay the penalty. In practice it is likely to

---

18 *TA v Director of Public Prosecutions* [1997] 1 Cr App R (S) 1; [1996] Crim LR 606, QBD.
19 Children and Young Persons Act 1933 s55(1B).
20 Reproduced at para 19.6.

be a parent who is working. Where the parents are separated, the court is only likely to consider whether to order the parent who has a residence order in relation to the child or who has day-to-day care for him/her.

Giving the parent or guardian a right to be heard

7.31   The court cannot order the parent or guardian to pay without giving them an opportunity to be heard.[21] It is the practice in some courts to invite the defence lawyer to suggest why a financial order should not be made against the parents. The lawyer should consider carefully whether there is any potential conflict between his/her young client and the parent before accepting this invitation.

7.32   A parent or guardian would not be eligible for legal aid to be legally represented as criminal legal aid is limited to 'the accused or convicted person' in criminal proceedings.[22] The parent or guardian may be able to seek the advice of the duty solicitor provided that there is also a risk that the court is considering a parental bindover or parenting order.[23]

Making an order in the absence of the parent or guardian

7.33   A court may make an order against the parent or guardian in their absence where the court has required their attendance but they nonetheless failed to attend. The rules of natural justice would require that the parent or guardian is warned that attendance is being required at a hearing when the issue of their responsibility to pay any financial order will be determined.

Assessment of means

7.34   Where the court orders the parent or guardian to pay the financial order, the amount should be fixed in accordance with their means.[24] The maximum fine would be that applicable to the defendant.[25]

---

21 Children and Young Persons Act 1933 s55(2).
22 Legal Aid Act 1988 s21(1).
23 Legal Aid Board Duty Solicitor Arrangements 1997 para 50(2)(e).
24 Criminal Justice Act 1991 s57(3).
25 See para 18.19.

Right of appeal

7.35   The parent or guardian has a right of appeal against the making of an order. The right of appeal lies to the Crown Court in the case of a decision made by a youth or adult magistrates' court and to the Court of Appeal in the case of a decision made by a Crown Court judge.[26] Once again legal aid will not be available.

Liability of local authorities

7.36   A local authority may be ordered to pay a financial order instead of a child or young person but only if:

 – the authority has parental responsibility for the defendant; and
 – the defendant is in the authority's care or is accommodated by the authority under the Children Act 1989.[27]

Such occasions will be rare as parental responsibility is only acquired with a full care order.[28]

Reasonable for the local authority to pay?

7.37   The court has the power to order the local authority to pay unless it would be unreasonable to do so. The authority has the same right as a parent or guardian to assert unreasonableness. However, it must be prepared to provide evidence to support its assertion.

7.38   The principles upon which to decide whether it would be reasonable to order an authority to pay have been considered in two recent Divisional Court cases. In *D and R v DPP*[29] Leggatt LJ accepted that local authorities could not be liable in the same way as natural parents. Natural parents have had the responsibility for their child's upbringing since birth. In contrast:

> A local authority may often be entrusted with the care of, or be obliged to provide accommodation for, a young person who is already an offender, or who is of criminal or anti-social propensity. The steps that the local authority should or lawfully can take to restrain such a young person may well be limited.

26 Children and Young Persons Act 1933 s55(3) and (4).
27 Ibid, s55(5).
28 *North Yorkshire County Council v Selby Youth Court* [1994] 1 All ER 991, QBD.
29 (1995) 16 Cr App R (S) 1040; [1995] Crim LR 748.

Where therefore . . . the local authority is found to have done everything that it reasonably and properly could to protect the public from the young offender, it would be wholly unreasonable and unjust that it should bear a financial penalty.

In the subsequent case of *Bedfordshire County Council v DPP*[30] the court went even further and stated that a causal link between the authority's lack of care and the young person's offences would have to be established before a court should order the authority to pay the financial penalty.

Procedure

Right to be heard

7.39   The local authority has a right to be heard before any order is made against it. In the case of *Bedfordshire County Council v DPP*[31] the Divisional Court gave guidance on the procedure to follow when a court is minded to make a financial order against a local authority.

1) The court should notify the local authority in writing of its right to make representations and also supply the authority with any documents provided in support of a claim for compensation.
2) The local authority should notify the court whether there is any dispute regarding the amount of compensation or whether an order should be made.
3) If there is any dispute, a hearing should be arranged on reasonable notice to the local authority.
4) The local authority should supply the court and the prosecution with relevant documents which it intends to rely upon to assert unreasonableness.
5) The hearing should be as simple as possible.

Assessment of means

7.40   When assessing the means of a local authority, the disposable weekly income is deemed to be the maximum amount which could be determined in relation to a person of the same age as the offender.[32]

---

30 [1996] 1 Cr App R (S) 322; [1995] Crim LR 962.
31 Ibid.
32 Criminal Justice Act 1991 s57(4).

Right of appeal

7.41 The local authority has a right of appeal in the same way as a parent or guardian.

Binding over parents

7.42 The power to bind over parents was introduced by the Criminal Justice Act 1991. It appears to have been applied inconsistently in particular youth courts where some magistrates show a reluctance to impose such bindovers while others appear keen to impose them in most cases. It remains to be seen how courts will use bindovers once the new parenting order comes into force nationally (see below).

7.43 When a court is considering a bindover, the parent or guardian may seek the advice of the court duty solicitor.[33]

Definition of 'parent' and 'guardian'

7.44 The Criminal Justice Act 1991 contains no definition of either term.

Power

7.45 Following conviction for any offence the court has a power to bind over the parent or guardian of a child or young person:
– to take proper care of and exercise control over the offender; and
– where a community sentence has been passed, to ensure that the offender complies with the requirements of that sentence.

7.46 The court may require a recognisance of up to £1,000. In fixing the size of the recognisance the court must take into account among other things the means of the parent or guardian so far as they appear known.[34]

7.47 The period of the bindover is in the discretion of the court; however, no bindover may last for more than three years or beyond the offender's eighteenth birthday.[35]

7.48 A court may not bind over a parent or guardian without their consent. However, if consent is refused, and the court considers the

---

33 Legal Aid Board Duty Solicitor Arrangements 1997 para 50(2)(e).
34 Criminal Justice Act 1991 s58(5).
35 Ibid, s58(3).

refusal unreasonable, it may order the parent or guardian to pay a fine not exceeding £1,000.[36]

Exercise of the power

Offenders aged under 16

7.49 The court has a duty to bind over the parent or guardian if, having regard to the circumstances in the case, it considers it desirable in the interests of preventing the commission by the young offender of further offences.

7.50 If the court does not exercise its power in relation to the parents or guardian of an offender aged under 16 it must state in open court:

- that it is not satisfied that a bindover would help prevent the commission of further offences; and
- the reasons for that decision.[37]

7.51 It does not automatically follow that the conviction of a child or young person will result in the court exercising its power to bind over the parent or guardian. The court must act judicially and consider the particular circumstances of the case. Relevant criteria were suggested by Home Office Circular 30/1992:

> It is for the court to decide whether or not binding over the parents would help prevent the juvenile offending again, but the following factors may be relevant:
> - whether the juvenile is likely to be amenable to supervision and intervention by the parents;
> - whether the parents' authority over the juvenile would be strengthened;
> - whether the parents are physically in a position to exercise the necessary degree of care and control (e.g. the juvenile may be living away from the parents' home); and
> - the circumstances of the present offence (e.g. the juvenile, of previous good character, may have been drawn into an uncharacteristic slip in circumstances which are not likely to recur).

Offenders aged 16 or 17

7.52 The court has a discretion to bind over the parent or guardian if, having regard to the circumstances in the case, it considers it desir-

36 Ibid, s58(2)(b).
37 Ibid, s58(1)(b).

able in the interests of preventing the commission by the young offender of further offences. In the case of a 16- or 17-year-old, the court is not required to give reasons for its failure to bind over a parent or guardian.

Bindover to ensure compliance with a community sentence

7.53 This power was inserted in the Criminal Justice Act 1991 s58(2) by the Criminal Justice and Public Order Act 1994 Sch 9 para 50. It states:

> Where the court has passed on [the offender] a community sentence . . . it may include in the recognisance a provision that the [offender's] parent or guardian ensure that the [offender] complies with the requirements of that sentence.

The wording of the amendment makes it clear that:

- the power may only be exercised if the court has already decided to impose a parental bindover to prevent further offending; and
- there is no presumption that the requirement will be imposed on the parent or guardian of an offender under the age of 16.

Although it is not stated in the legislation, the bindover presumably expires with the end of the community order.

Variation or revocation of the order

7.54 Bindovers may be varied or revoked on the application of the parent or guardian, if the court considers that it would be in the interests of justice to do so, having regard to any change of circumstances since the order was made.[38] An obvious relevant change of circumstances would be that the child or young person no longer lives with the person bound over.

Right of appeal

7.55 The parent or guardian has a right of appeal against the making of a bindover. The appeal lies to the Crown Court from a decision of a youth court or adult magistrates' court and to the Court of Appeal from the decision of a Crown Court judge after a trial on indictment.[39]

---

38 Criminal Justice Act 1991 s58(8).
39 Ibid, s58(6) and (7).

Estreatment of the recognisance

7.56 Estreatment is the process whereby a recognisance is forfeited. In the case of a parental bindover, estreatment is initiated by way of complaint under the Magistrates' Courts Act 1980 s120.[40] The parent or guardian who entered into the recognisance will be summonsed to attend court. In practice it is likely to be the court itself which initiates the process.

Which court?

7.57 There has been some confusion as to the proper court to hear such a complaint under s120. It has been argued that it should be the adult magistrates' court because the youth court is a court of summary jurisdiction only able to deal with cases against children and young persons.[41] This is not the view taken by the Home Office, Lord Chancellor's Department and Crown Prosecution Service as expressed in a Home Office letter dated 9 May 1994 to the clerk to the justices in Leeds.[42] The letter said that the decision whether complaints would be heard in the youth court or adult magistrates' court should be made locally but a preference was indicated for such proceedings being in the youth court where magistrates ' ... are probably better able to judge whether the parent has tried to control the child or whether the child is out of parental control'. The authors prefer the latter view and would see no jurisdictional problem with the youth court dealing with the complaint.[43]

Legal aid

7.58 A parent or guardian facing estreatment proceedings may be represented by the duty solicitor.[44]

The hearing

7.59 Forfeiture is not automatic upon the young offender being found guilty of a further offence. The justices must enquire as to the extent

---

40 Ibid, s58(3).
41 See, for example, (1995) 159 JPN 611.
42 Reported in Gibson *et al The Youth Court One Year Onwards* (Waterside Press, 1994).
43 See discussion of the jurisdiction of the youth court at para 9.1.
44 Legal Aid Board Duty Solicitor Arrangements 1997 para 50(2)(e).

to which the parent or guardian is culpable.[45] The burden rests upon the parent or guardian that s/he exercised all reasonable control.

7.60   The court may order that the whole or part of the sum is to be forfeited. It may also order that the recognisance be remitted.[46] This would be appropriate when the court learns that the child or young person is no longer living with the parent who has been bound over.

Enforcement

7.61   Payment of any sum adjudged to be paid upon forfeiture will be enforced as if it were a fine.[47]

Appeal

7.62   The adjudication of forfeiture is not a conviction so there is no right of appeal to the Crown Court.[48]

Parenting order (pilot areas only)

7.63   Introduced by the Crime and Disorder Act 1998 this new order is being piloted in certain local authority areas between the autumn of 1998 and the spring of 2000.[49] A court shall not make a parenting order unless it has been notified by the Secretary of State that arrangements for implementing such orders are available in the area in which it appears to the court that the parent resides or will reside and the notice has not been withdrawn.[50]

7.64   A parenting order requires the parent or guardian:

- to attend counselling or guidance sessions (parenting classes) as specified by a responsible officer; and
- to comply with such requirements as are specified in the order.[51]

---

45 *R v Southampton Justices ex p Green* [1976] 1 QB 11; [1975] 2 All ER 1073.
46 Magistrates' Courts Act 1980 s120(3).
47 Ibid, s120(4).
48 *R v Durham Justices ex p Laurent* [1945] KB 33; [1944] 2 All ER 530.
49 For the pilot areas see Appendix 8.
50 Crime and Disorder Act 1998 s8(3).
51 Ibid, s8(4).

Definition of 'parent' or 'guardian'

7.65   'Parent' has the same definition as in the Family Law Reform Act 1987 s1 (see para 7.24)[52] 'Guardian' has the same definition as in the Children and Young Persons Act 1933 s107 (see para 7.12).[53] The Home Office assumes that the definition of guardian could include a local authority or a person caring for a child or young person on behalf of a local authority.[54] There is some doubt that this is the case in the light of the House of Lords' ruling in *Leeds City Council v West Yorkshire Metropolitan Police*[55] where it was held that the term 'guardian' as defined in the Children and Young Persons Act 1933 s107 could not be construed to include a local authority for the purposes of imposing liability for financial orders. Subsequent legislation expressly provided for local authorities to be liable for such orders. In the absence of such express provision in relation to parenting orders, it is submitted that a court would have no power to impose an order upon a local authority.

Responsible officer

7.66   A responsible officer may be one of the following:
- a probation officer;
- a social worker of a local authority social services department; or
- a member of a youth offending team.[56]

Power

Criminal cases

7.67   A court may impose a parenting order upon the parent or guardian of a child or young person when the child or young person is convicted of an offence and the court considers that such an order would be desirable in the interests of preventing the commission of any further offence by the child or young person.[57] If the court is of that opinion,

---

52 Home Office Draft Guidance document: *Parenting Orders*, para 3.6.
53 Crime and Disorder Act 1998 s117.
54 Home Office Draft Guidance document: *Parenting Orders*, paras 3.22–3.24.
55 [1982] 1 All ER 274; (1982) 146 JP 154; *sub nom Re Leeds City Council* (1982) 4 Cr App R (S) 26.
56 Ibid, s8(8).
57 Ibid, s8(1)(c).

it must make an order in relation to an offender under the age of 16.[58]

Civil cases

7.68 The order may also be imposed where:

- a child safety order is made in respect of a child;
- an anti-social behaviour order or sex offender order is made in respect of a child or young person; or
- the parent or guardian is convicted of failure to comply with a school attendance order or of failure to secure regular attendance at school of a registered pupil (offences contrary to the Education Act 1996 ss443 and 444 respectively).

7.69 A parenting order may be made where it would be desirable in the interests of preventing:

- a repetition of the kind of behaviour which led to a child safety order, an anti-social behaviour order or a sex offender order; or
- the commission of further offences under the Education Act 1996 ss443 and 444).

Desirable in the interests of preventing offending

7.70 It is not anticipated by the Home Office that the making of a parenting order will be desirable in the interests of preventing further offending in every case. The Draft Guidance document: *Parenting Orders* (para 3.4) states:

> The court may . . . wish to weigh up, for example, the extent to which the parent or guardian has previously been involved in any voluntary parenting classes or how much support and encouragement they have offered their child. The court may also wish to consider whether the parents are willing to receive other assistance and support from the local authority, on a voluntary basis, in which case the court may not consider it appropriate to make a parenting order.

7.71 The court may have a choice of adults against whom the order may be made. This could include both biological parents as well as the current carers of the child or young person. Where this is the case, the Draft Guidance document: *Parenting Orders* (para 3.8) states:

---

58 Ibid, s9(1)(a).

... the court will need to be satisfied that the parent(s) are in a position to help and support the child. This means that it would not be sensible nor practical for the court to make an order where this influence could not be exerted. For example, where one of the child's parents lives in a different town; where parents are separated or one parent does not have regular access to the child; or where the child lives with a relative, such as a grandparent.

Procedural requirements

Offenders aged under 16

7.72   Where the person convicted of the offence is under the age of 16 a court shall obtain and consider information about the person's family circumstances and the likely effect of a parenting order on those circumstances.[59]

7.73   If the court does not impose a parenting order it must state in open court why it is not doing so.[60]

All offenders

7.74   Before making the order, a court shall explain to the parent in ordinary language:
– the effect of the order and the requirements proposed to be included in it;
– the possibility of being fined if found in breach of any of the requirements of the order; and
– that the court may review the order on the application of the parent or responsible officer.[61]

Requirements of the order

7.75   The requirements which may be imposed upon a parent of a young offender are those which the court considers desirable in the interests of preventing further offending.[62] Guidance from the Home Office suggests that requirements could include the parent ensuring that the young offender:

59   Ibid, s9(2).
60   Ibid, s9(1)(b).
61   Ibid, s9(3).
62   Ibid, s8(7).

- attends school or extra-curricular activities;
- does not attend certain places (such as shopping centres) unsupervised;
- is at home during certain times, probably the evening, and that s/he is effectively supervised.[63]

7.76 The requirements specified in the order shall, as far as practicable, be such as to avoid:

- any conflict with the parent's religious beliefs; and
- any interference with the times, if any, at which the parent normally works or attends an educational establishment.[64]

Note that there is no requirement to avoid a conflict with the young offender's religious beliefs or his/her education or work commitments.

Discharge or variation

7.77 A court may discharge or vary the order on the application of either a parent or the responsible officer. When varying the order it may delete a requirement or insert a new condition (either in addition to or in substitution of an existing provision) that could have been included if the court had then had power to make the order.[65] Such an application is provided for by the Magistrates' Courts (Miscellaneous Amendments) Rules 1998 SI No 2167. Application is by way of complaint and involves the civil jurisdiction of the magistrates' court.[66]

7.78 Where a court dismisses an application for discharge, no further application to discharge the order may be made except with the consent of the court which made the order.[67]

---

63 Draft Guidance document: *Parenting Orders*, para 3.32.
64 Crime and Disorder Act 1998 s9(4).
65 Ibid, s9(5).
66 See Magistrates' Courts Act 1980 ss51–57 and Magistrates' Courts Rules 1981 SI No 552 (as amended) rr4 and 98.
67 Crime and Disorder Act 1998 s9(6).

Right of appeal

7.79 In the case of a parenting order imposed following the conviction of a child or young person, the parent has the same right of appeal against the making of the order as if it were a sentence imposed on him/her.[68] It would therefore be possible to appeal to the Crown Court or to appeal by way of case stated.

Enforcement

7.80 If a parent fails to comply with a requirement of a parenting order without a reasonable excuse for so doing, s/he shall be liable on summary conviction to a fine not exceeding level 3 on the standard scale.[69] The court could also make the parent the subject of a conditional discharge, probation order or a curfew order (if available).

7.81 Guidance issued by the Home Office anticipates that the responsible officer will report the alleged breach to the police, who will carry out a criminal investigation. The matter will then be referred to the Crown Prosecution Service to determine whether a prosecution should be brought.[70]

68 Ibid, s10(4).
69 Ibid, s9(7).
70 Draft Guidance document: *Parenting Orders*, paras 7.3–7.5.

Court procedure

For complete chapter contents, see overleaf

Commencing proceedings

8.1 There is no restriction upon who may commence proceedings against a child or young person, but in practice it would be very rare for a private prosecution to be brought against a person under the age of 18. The police will bring most prosecutions.

Notification to social services and probation

8.2 Before proceedings are commenced against a child or young person, notification should be given to the relevant social services department and probation service.

Social services

8.3 The Children and Young Persons Act 1969 s5 provides:

> (8) It shall be the duty of a person who decides to lay an information in respect of an offence in a case where he has reason to believe the alleged offender is a young person to give notice of the decision to the appropriate local authority unless he is himself that authority.
>
> (9) In this section –
>> 'the appropriate authority', in relation to a young person, means the local authority for the area in which it appears to the informant that the young person resides or, if the informant appears not to reside in the area of a local authority, the local authority in whose area it is alleged that the relevant offence or one of the relevant offences was committed.
>
> But nothing in this section shall be construed as preventing any council or other body from acting by an agent for the purposes of this section.

This provision has been considered by the Divisional Court in the case of *DPP v Cottier.*[1] Saville LJ held that notice could be given orally to the relevant social services department and that the section did not require notification to be effected by a particular stage in the proceedings. He further held that the purpose of the section was to allow the local authority to comply with its duty under Children and Young Persons Act 1969 s9 to provide to the court relevant background information regarding the young defendant.

---

1   [1996] 3 All ER 126; [1996] Crim LR 804, QBD.

Probation

8.4   The Children and Young Persons Act 1969 s34(2) provides:

> In the case of a person who has not attained the age of eighteen but who has attained such lower age as the Secretary of State may by order specify no proceedings for an offence shall be begun in any court unless the person proposing to begin the proceedings has, in addition to any notice to be given to a local authority in pursuance of section 5(8) of this Act, given notice of the proceedings to a probation officer for the area for which the court acts.

8.5   The lower age has been fixed as 10 years.[2]

8.6   Proceedings have been held to begin when the defendant is first brought before the court.[3] Notice, whether oral or in writing, should be served prior to that date so that the probation service is in a position to provide any possible help to the court by providing information regarding the young defendant.

The effect of failure to notify

8.7   Both of the above provisions have been held to be directory, and if the police fail to make the required notification the validity of the court proceedings are not affected.[4]

Requiring attendance at court

8.8   There are three ways of requiring attendance at court. These are by way of:

- charge;
- summons; or
- warrant.

Charge

8.9   A child or young person charged by the police must be handed a written notice of the offences with which s/he has been charged. If

---

2   Children and Young Persons Act 1969 (Transitional Modifications of Part I) Order 1970 SI No 1882.
3   *DPP v Cottier*, n1 above.
4   Ibid; confirmed in relation to s34(2) by the Court of Appeal in *R v Marsh* (1996) *Times*, 11 April.

the accused is a juvenile, the notice should be handed to the appropriate adult.[5]

8.10   There is no power for the police to require a parent or guardian to attend court with the child or young person.

Summons

8.11   Upon receiving an information a justice of the peace (or a justices' clerk[6]) may issue a summons requiring the attendance at court of any person suspected of having committed a criminal offence.[7]

8.12   A summons issued against a child or young person may also require the attendance of the parent or guardian.[8]

Warrant

8.13   Upon receiving a written information sworn on oath, a justice of the peace may issue a warrant for the arrest of a person suspected of committing a crime. The warrant will direct the police to bring the person arrested before the court.[9]

8.14   It is possible for the justices to endorse a warrant so that upon its execution the person arrested may be released on bail to attend court.[10]

Constitution of a youth court

8.15   The Children and Young Persons Act 1933 s45 provides:

> Courts of summary jurisdiction constituted in accordance with the provisions of the Second Schedule to this Act, and sitting for the purpose of hearing any charge against a child or young person or for the purpose of exercising any other jurisdiction conferred on youth courts by or under this or any other act, shall be known as youth courts and in whatever place sitting shall be deemed to be petty sessional courts.

---

5   PACE Code C para 16.3.
6   Justices' Clerks Rules 1970 SI No 231 r3.
7   Magistrates' Courts Act 1980 s1(1)(a).
8   Magistrates' Courts (Children and Young Persons) Rules 1992 SI No 2071 r26.
9   Magistrates' Courts Act s1(1)(b).
10 Ibid, s117.

Youth court panels

8.16　There are specific rules regarding the selection of youth court panels. These rules vary between England and Wales in general and Inner London (more specifically the Inner London Commission Area and the City of London).

England and Wales in general

8.17　The constitution of the court is governed by the Youth Courts (Constitution) Rules 1954.[11] Each petty sessional area must appoint justices specially qualified for dealing with juvenile cases to the youth court panel. Any stipendiary magistrate who exercises jurisdiction in a petty sessions area shall be an ex officio member of the panel.

8.18　Each youth court bench shall be constituted of not more than three justices and in normal circumstances shall include a man and a woman.[12] Exceptions to this general rule are provided for as follows:

- if at any sitting of the youth court no man or no woman is available owing to circumstances unforeseen when the justices were chosen, the other members of the panel may sit if they consider it inexpedient in the interests of justice to adjourn;[13] or
- a stipendiary magistrate may sit alone.[14]

8.19　The rules as to the constitution of a youth court are expressly subject to any general rule of law which grants jurisdiction to a single justice to act.[15] A single justice of the peace from the youth court panel may still, therefore, hear a bail application or act as an examining magistrate for the purposes of committal.

Inner London

8.20　The constitution of youth courts in the Inner London Commission Area is governed by the Children and Young Persons Act 1933 Sch 2, Part II. The general rule is that a bench should either consist of a metropolitan stipendiary magistrate sitting alone or consist of a chairman and two other members appointed by the Lord Chancellor

11　SI No 1711.
12　Ibid, r12(1).
13　Ibid, r12(3).
14　Ibid, r12(1)(a).
15　Ibid, r12(4).

to the youth panel.[16] The chairman (if applicable) may either be a metropolitan stipendiary magistrate or a lay justice nominated by the Lord Chancellor.[17] Where it appears to the chairman that a youth court cannot, without adjournment, be fully constituted, and that an adjournment would not be in the interests of justice, the chairman may sit with one other member (whether a man or a woman).

8.21   Unlike the constitution rules applicable outside the Inner London Commission Area, there is no express preservation of the jurisdiction of a single lay justice of the peace to hear certain cases. It is not clear whether a single justice could consider bail applications or commit a defendant for trial.

Procedure in the youth court

8.22   Youth courts should sit as often as may be necessary for the purposes of dealing with criminal cases against children or young persons.[18]

Separation of children and young persons from adult defendants

8.23   The Children and Young Persons Act 1933 s31 imposes an obligation upon the police, secure escort services and court administrators to ensure the separation of juvenile defendants from adult defendants. Arrangements should be made to ensure that no defendant under the age of 17 should be allowed to associate with an adult defendant (unless a relative or jointly charged) either while being conveyed to court or while waiting before or after attendance at court. In addition, a detained female juvenile should be under the care of a woman, while being conveyed to court or waiting at court.

8.24   The rule prohibiting a youth court from sitting in the same court-room within an hour either before or after the sitting of an 'adult' court has been abolished.[19]

---

16 Children and Young Persons Act 1933 Sch 2, Part II para 15(a).
17 Pursuant to the Inner London Youth Courts (Selection of Chairmen) Order 1990, SI No 1265.
18 Children and Young Persons Act 1933 s47(1).
19 Crime and Disorder Act 1998 s47(7) repealing Children and Young Persons Act 1933 s47(2).

Access to youth court hearings

8.25   The Children and Young Persons Act 1933 s47 restricts access to the sittings of the youth court. Only the following may have access:

- members and officers of the court;
- parties to the case before the court;
- solicitors and counsel representing the parties;
- witnesses to the case;
- other persons directly concerned in the case;
- bona fide representatives of newspapers or news agencies; and
- such other persons as the court may specially authorise to be present.

8.26   In a joint Home Office/Lord Chancellor's Department Circular entitled *Opening up Youth Court Proceedings* (issued 11 June 1998) youth courts are encouraged to make full use of their discretion to admit members of the public to the proceedings. The circular explains the government view that there should be a presumption that the victim, with a parent or other supporter if appropriate, should be admitted to the courtroom for the trial or preceding hearings unless there are good and sufficient reasons against this. Factors identified as going against this presumption include where:

- the defendant is particularly young or vulnerable;
- the defendant is charged with a number of offences and allowing a large number of victims to attend would be detrimental to youth court proceedings;
- at the sentencing hearing the court may wish to hear information regarding the young offender which is sensitive or of a personal nature.[20]

In the government's view, none of the above factors would automatically lead to the exclusion of victims from the courtroom, but they are considerations to be balanced by the court in each case against the benefits of openness. It is difficult to reconcile this guidance and the presumption of the benefits of openness with the guarantees of privacy contained in article 40(2)(b) of the United Nations Convention on the Rights of the Child.

8.27   It is submitted that where a court is considering allowing a victim to be present during the hearing, it should give the defence lawyer the opportunity to raise any objections before the decision is made.

20   *Opening up Youth Court Proceedings,* paras 9 and 10.

Informality

8.28   A defendant in a youth court will normally be referred to by his/her first name.

The oath

8.29   The form of the oath used in the youth court is modified.[21] The following wording should be used:

> I promise before Almighty God to tell the truth, the whole truth and nothing but the truth.

This wording should also be used by adult witnesses testifying in the youth court.

Terminology

8.30   The words 'conviction' and 'sentence' should not be used in relation to children and young persons dealt with in the youth or magistrates' court. Instead the terms 'finding of guilt' and 'order made upon a finding of guilt' should be used.[22]

Identification of the defendant

8.31   It is common practice at a first appearance for the clerk in court to verify the full name and address of the defendant. Where a person is brought before a court and it appears to the court that s/he is a child or young person, the court is required to make due inquiry as to his/ her age, and for that purpose shall take such evidence as may be forthcoming at the hearing of the case.[23]

Reporting restrictions in the youth court

8.32   The Children and Young Persons Act 1933 s49 imposes comprehensive reporting restrictions in relation to proceedings in the youth court. It also imposes such restrictions upon the following:

– proceedings on appeal from a youth court (including proceedings by way of case stated);

21 Children and Young Persons Act 1963 s28(1).
22 Children and Young Persons Act 1933 s59.
23 Ibid, s99(1).

- proceedings under s15 or s16 Children and Young Persons Act 1969 (proceedings for varying or revoking supervision orders); and
- proceedings on appeal from a magistrates' court arising out of proceedings under s15 or s16 of that Act (including proceedings by way of case stated).

8.33 The following prohibitions apply:

- no report shall be published which reveals the name, address or school of any child or young person concerned in the proceedings or includes any particulars likely to lead to the identification of any child or young person concerned in the proceedings; and
- no picture shall be published or included in a programme service as being or including a picture of any child or young person concerned in the proceedings.

Lifting the restrictions

8.34 The court which has proceedings before it may dispense to any specified extent with the requirements of this section if satisfied:

- it is appropriate to do so to avoid injustice to the child or young person;
- it is necessary to facilitate apprehension of a child or young person unlawfully at large; or
- it is in the interests of justice to do so after conviction.

To avoid injustice

8.35 The defence lawyer may wish to make an application regarding dispensation of reporting restrictions if it is considered that publicity for the case may prompt potential witnesses to come forward.

Child or young person unlawfully at large

8.36 The Crown Prosecution Service must apply to the relevant court on notice to the legal representative (if any) of the child or young person. Such an application may only be made if the defendant is charged with or has been convicted of:

- a violent offence;[24]

---

24 As defined by Criminal Justice Act 1991 s31(1).

- a sexual offence;[25] or
- an offence punishable in the case of a person aged 21 or over with imprisonment for 14 years or more.

8.37   Before making an order the court must be satisfied that:

- the child or young person is unlawfully at large; and
- it is necessary to dispense with those requirements for the purpose of apprehending him/her and bringing him/her before a court or returning him/her to the place in which s/he was in custody.[26]

8.38   A person shall be treated as unlawfully at large if, having been granted bail, s/he is liable to arrest (whether with or without a warrant).[27] The reference to the grant of bail would seem to exclude this section's application to cases where a juvenile absconds after being remanded to local authority accommodation.

Following conviction

8.39   For offences committed on or after 1 October 1997 the youth court has a power in relation to a child or young person convicted of an offence to dispense to any specified extent with the reporting restrictions where it is in the interests of justice to do so.[28] This power is considered in more detail in Chapter 15.

Breaching of a s49 order

8.40   If a report or picture is published or included in a programme service in contravention of s49 any editor, publisher, newspaper proprietor or broadcast company is liable on summary conviction to a fine not exceeding £5,000.[29]

Children and young persons in the adult courts

8.41   In general the child or young person is treated in the same way in the adult magistrates' court.

---

25 Ibid.
26 Children and Young Persons Act 1933 s49(5)(b).
27 Ibid, s49(11).
28 Ibid, s49(4A) as inserted by Crime (Sentences) Act 1997 s45.
29 Children and Young Persons Act 1933 s49(9).

Adult magistrates' court

8.42   Children or young persons appearing in the adult magistrates' court will not normally be required to stand in the dock. Usually the court clerk will ask the child or young person to sit in front of the dock with any adult accompanying him/her.

8.43   Practice varies as to whether the child or young person will be referred to by their first name.

Crown Court

8.44   Once again practice varies but it is the practice in some courts to allow the young defendant to sit outside the dock beside a parent or other adult and it may be decided to refer to the defendant by his/her first name during the proceedings. As there is no fixed practice the matter should be raised with the judge at the start of every case.

Reporting restrictions

8.45   Unlike in the youth court when a child or young person appears in the adult courts there is no automatic bar upon reporting. However, the court does have a power to prohibit the publication of details regarding the defendant or other children or young persons involved in the case. The Children and Young Persons Act 1933 s39(1) provides:

> In relation to any proceedings in any court . . . the court may direct that – (a) no newspaper report of the proceedings shall reveal the name address or school or include any particulars calculated to lead to the identification of any child or young person concerned in the proceedings, either as being the person by or against or in respect of whom the proceedings are taken, or as being a witness therein; (b) no picture shall be published in any newspaper as being or including a picture of any child or young person so concerned in the proceedings as aforesaid; except in so far (if at all) as may be permitted by the direction of the court.

The court's powers of prohibition have been extended to cover television broadcasts.[30]

8.46   In the magistrates' court the clerk will ask the justices to make an order under s39 and in the absence of any objection the order will be

---

30 Children and Young Persons Act 1963 s57(4).

made without further discussion. If such an order is made at the time of committal, the court clerk should forward with the depositions a notice that the order was made by the examining magistrates.[31] Any order made by the justices on committal will not extend beyond the first hearing at the Crown Court, consequently the judge should be asked to make a further order under s39 at the pleas and directions hearing. The question of whether the order should be lifted following conviction is considered in Chapter 15.

8.47   Publication of material in contravention of an order made under s39 is a summary offence punishable with a fine of up to £5,000.[32]

Taking a plea

8.48   When dealing with a child or young person a youth or magistrates' court is required to explain the nature of the proceedings and the substance of any charge in simple language suitable to the age and understanding of the young defendant.[33] The court is not required to give a detailed explanation of the charge but it should ensure that the essential elements of the offence are explained.[34]

8.49   Once the court is satisfied that the child or young person understands the charge, it should ask him/her whether s/he pleads guilty or not guilty to the charge.[35] If the defendant pleads not guilty, the court will normally adjourn so that the prosecution will have an opportunity to arrange for its witnesses to attend court. If the defendant pleads guilty, see Chapter 15.

Pleading by post

8.50   The Magistrates' Courts Act 1980 s12 allows certain cases to be disposed of without the defendant being required to attend. This procedure only applies to summary-only offences carrying a maximum of three months' imprisonment. In practice it is mainly used in road traffic cases. It only applies to defendants who have attained the age of 16.

---

31   Home Office Circulars Nos 18/1956 and 14/1965.
32   Children and Young Persons Act 1933 s39(2).
33   Magistrates' Courts (Children and Young Persons) Rules 1992 SI No 2071 r6.
34   *R v Blandford Justices ex p G (an Infant)* [1966] 1 All ER 1021, QBD.
35   Magistrates' Courts (Children and Young Persons) Rules 1992 SI No 2071 r7.

8.51 Once issued, the summons will be served by the prosecutor along with:

- an explanatory statement;
- a statement of the facts to be given to the magistrates; and
- any information regarding the accused which will be placed before the court.

The accused may then choose to attend the court in person or return the form accompanying the summons indicating a guilty plea along with mitigating factors and financial details.

8.52 It is not uncommon for young persons to be summonsed in error to attend the adult magistrates' court in relation to traffic matters. If a notification that an accused wishes to plead guilty under this provision is received by the clerk of the court, and the court has no reason to believe that the accused is a child or young person, then, if s/he is a child or young person s/he shall be deemed to have attained the age of 18 for the purposes of the proceedings.[36]

Changing plea

8.53 Any court has a common law power to allow a change of plea any time before sentence is passed.[37] This inherent jurisdiction still exists after a remit for sentence under the Children and Young Persons Act 1933 s56(1).[38] This power will be exercised where the plea was equivocal or it is otherwise in the interests of justice that the plea should be reopened.

Statutory time limits (pilot areas only)

8.54 Prosecution of Offences Act 1985 ss22, 22A and 22B (as amended by the Crime and Disorder Act 1998 ss43 to 45) allow for the possibility of statutory time limits applicable to children and young persons. Such statutory time limits have now been introduced by the

---

36 Children and Young Persons Act 1933 s46(1A).
37 *S (an Infant) v Recorder of Manchester* [1971] AC 481, HL.
38 *R v Stratford Youth Court ex p Conde* [1997] 1 WLR 113; (1997) 161 JP 308; [1997] 2 Cr App R 1, QBD.

Prosecution of Offences (Youth Court Time Limits) Regulations 1999 SI No 2743. These regulations came into force on 1 November 1999 but only in pilot areas.[39] There are three times limits.

Initial time limit

8.55   This runs from the date of the offender's arrest to the date fixed for his/her first court appearance. The maximum period for completion of this stage is 36 calendar days.[40] If the time limit would otherwise expire on a Saturday, Sunday, Christmas Day, Good Friday or any other bank holiday, it shall be treated as expiring on the first preceding day that is not one of these days.[41] For the purposes of the pilots, this time limit only applies if the offender was arrested in a pilot area.

8.56   The time limit is suspended for such time as the suspect is unlawfully at large:

- having escaped from arrest; or
- having been released on bail, fails to surrender him/herself at the appointed time.[42]

The time limit continues to run while a suspect is on police bail. Once the time limit has expired, s/he can only be charged if further evidence is obtained.[43]

8.57   It is possible to apply for an extension of the initial time limit. The application must be made to the youth court before the expiry of the time limit.[44] Written notice of the application must be served on the clerk of the court and the suspect (or his/her legal representative). There must be at least two days' notice.[45]

8.58   The application shall be made orally.[46] The court shall not grant an extension unless it is satisfied that:

- the need for the extension is due to some good and sufficient cause; and

---

39   See appendix 8 for pilot areas.
40   Prosecution of Offences (Youth Courts Time Limits) Regulations 1999 reg 5.
41   Ibid, reg 1(5).
42   Prosecution of Offences Act 1985 s22A(6).
43   Ibid, s22A(4).
44   Ibid, s22A(3).
45   Prosecution of Offences (Youth Courts Time Limits) Regulations 1999 reg 7(4).
46   Ibid, reg 7(3).

- the investigation has been conducted, and (where applicable) the prosecution has acted, with all due diligence and expedition.[47]

Both the prosecution and the accused have a right of appeal to the Crown Court against the decision of the youth court.[48] This right of appeal is only exercisable if the accused is charged.

8.59 Where the initial time limit expires after the accused has been charged but before s/he makes his/her first court appearance, the court shall stay the proceedings.[49]

Overall time limit

8.60 This runs from the date fixed for the offender's first appearance at court to the date fixed for the start of trial. The maximum period for completion of this stage is 99 calendar days.[50] If the time limit would otherwise expire on a Saturday, Sunday, Christmas Day, Good Friday or any other bank holiday, it shall be treated as expiring on the first preceding day that is not one of these days.[51]

8.61 The time limit is suspended for such time as the defendant is unlawfully at large, where s/he:

- escapes from the custody of a magistrates' court or the Crown Court; or
- having been released on bail, fails to surrender him/herself into the custody of the court at the appointed time.[52]

It is possible to apply for an extension of the overall time limit. Written notice of the application must be served on the clerk of the court and the defendant (or his/her legal representative). There must be at least two days' notice.[53] The application must be made orally.[54]

8.62 The court shall not grant an extension unless it is satisfied:

(a) that the need for the extension is due to:
   (i) the illness or absence of the accused, a necessary witness, a judge or a magistrate;

---

47 Prosecution of Offences Act 1985 s22A(3).
48 Ibid, s22(7) and (8).
49 Ibid, s22A(5).
50 Prosecution of Offences (Youth Courts Time Limits) Regulations 1999 reg 4.
51 Ibid, reg 1(5).
52 Prosecution of Offences Act 1985 s22(6) and (6A).
53 Prosecution of Offences (Youth Courts Time Limits) Regulations 1999 reg 7(4).
54 Ibid, reg 7(3).

(ii) a postponement which is occasioned by the ordering by the court of separate trials in the case of two or more offences; or

(iii) some other good and sufficient cause; and

(b) that the prosecution has acted with all due diligence and expedition.[55]

Both the prosecution and the accused have a right of appeal to the Crown Court against the decision of the youth court.[56] The hearing of any appeal by the prosecution must begin before the expiry of the limit in question.[57]

8.63   Where the overall time limit has expired before the date fixed for the start of the trial, the court shall stay the proceedings.[58]

Sentencing time limit

8.64   The sentencing time limit runs from conviction to sentence. The maximum period for completion of this stage is 29 calendar days. If the time limit would otherwise expire on a Saturday, Sunday, Christmas Day, Good Friday or any other bank holiday, it shall be treated as expiring on the first preceding day that is not one of these days.[59] The time limit applies where a defendant is to be sentenced in a pilot court and:

(a) was under the age of 18—

(i) at the time of his/her arrest for the offence;

(ii) (where s/he was not arrested for the offence) at the time of the laying of an information charging him/her with an offence; and

(b) is convicted of the offence in a pilot court on or after 1 November 1999.[60]

There is no sanction for exceeding the sentencing time limit.

55 Prosecution of Offences Act 1985 s22(3).
56 Ibid, s22(7) and (8).
57 Ibid, s22(9).
58 Ibid, s22(4).
59 Prosecution of Offences (Youth Courts Time Limits) Regulations 1999 reg 1(5).
60 Ibid, reg 6.

Re-institution of proceedings

8.65   Where proceedings have been stayed, fresh proceedings may be instituted within three months of the original ones being stayed.[61] Where the proceedings were stayed by a magistrates' court, they are re-instituted by the laying of a summons; where the proceedings were stayed by the Crown Court, they are re-instituted by preferring a bill of indictment.[62] If more than three months have passed, the prosecution must make an application to the court that stayed the original proceedings for them to be re-instituted.[63]

8.66   Fresh proceedings may be re-instituted notwithstanding the six-month time limit for the commencement of summary-only proceedings contained in Magistrates' Courts Act 1980 s127.[64] When proceedings are re-instituted, any previous disclosure by the prosecution and the service of any defence statement is deemed to have been done in the current proceedings. The fresh proceedings shall be subject to a new overall time limit.[65]

---

61 Prosecution of Offences Act 1985 s22B(2).
62 Ibid, s22B(3).
63 Ibid.
64 Ibid, s22B(4).
65 Ibid, s22B(5).

CHAPTER 9

Jurisdiction

For complete chapter contents, see overleaf

Youth court

General principle

9.1   The Children and Young Persons Act 1933 s46(1) establishes the following principle:

> Subject as hereinafter provided, no charge against a child or young person, and no application whereof the hearing is by rules made under this section assigned to youth courts, shall be heard by a court of summary jurisdiction which is not a youth court

A youth court is a court of summary jurisdiction assigned a special type of defendant defined by reference to age. It is the opinion of the authors that the above section should, therefore, be read as assigning certain matters to the youth court but not as exclusively defining the jurisdiction of the court.

What matters are assigned?

Charges and summonses

9.2   All informations involving defendants under the age of 18 must first be dealt with by a youth court, unless an adult is also one of the defendants (for which see below). In certain serious cases the case may ultimately be dealt with before a Crown Court.

Applications by rules made under s46

9.3   No rules have been made under this section assigning any applications to the youth court.

Complaints under MCA 1980 s115

9.4   This would be where the police have arrested a person under their common law powers to prevent a breach of the peace. Although not expressly assigned to the youth court, it is submitted that a child or young person should be brought before a youth court if one is sitting.

Magistrates' court

Child or young person in custody

9.5 In most parts of the country a youth court will only sit once a week or sometimes even less frequently. There will be occasions when the police have to place a child or young person before a court when a youth court is not sitting. This would occur when a child or young person is refused bail by the police after charge or when a warrant not backed for bail has been executed. In such circumstances the Children and Young Persons Act 1933 s46(2) provides that any justice or justices may entertain an application for bail or for a remand and may hear such evidence as is necessary for that purpose. The adult court must then remand the child or young person to the next sitting of the youth court for the same petty sessions area.

Charged with an adult

9.6 There are four exceptions to the general rule that a child or young person should appear before the youth court and these all relate to circumstances when an adult is involved in the case. A magistrates' court may deal with a child or young person if:

- the child or young person is jointly charged with an adult; or
- an adult is charged as an aider or abettor to the offence; or
- the child or young person is charged as the aider or abettor of an adult; or
- the child or young person is charged with an offence arising out of the same circumstances as those giving rise to proceedings against an adult.

Jointly charged with an adult

9.7 The Children and Young Persons Act 1933 s.46(1)(a) provides:

> [A] charge made jointly against a child or young person and a person who has attained the age of 18 shall be heard by a court of summary jurisdiction other than a youth court . . .

This provision is mandatory. It follows, therefore, that a youth court has no jurisdiction to deal with the child or young person in these circumstances.

9.8   It is not necessary for the charge to specify that the offence was committed 'jointly' or 'together with' the adult concerned.[1] In the case of taking without consent or aggravated vehicle-taking the driver and any passengers charged with allowing to be carried are jointly charged.[2]

Adult charged as aider and abettor

9.9   The Children and Young Persons Act 1933 s46(1)(b) provides:

> [W]here a child or young person is charged with an offence, the court may be heard by a court of summary jurisdiction other than a youth court if a person who has attained the age of eighteen years is charged at the same time with aiding, abetting, causing, procuring, allowing or permitting that offence . . .

This provision is permissive and therefore the youth court still retains jurisdiction if a child or young person appears before it.

Charged as an aider and abettor to an adult

9.10   The Children and Young Persons Act 1963 s18(1) provides:

> [A] magistrates' court which is not a youth court may hear an information against a child or young person if he is charged –
> (a) with aiding, abetting, causing, procuring, allowing or permitting an offence with which a person who has attained the age of eighteen is charged at the same time.

Once again, this provision is permissive and therefore the youth court retains jurisdiction and may deal with any child or young person who appears before it.

Charged with an offence arising out of the same circumstances

9.11   The Children and Young Persons Act 1963 s18(1) provides:

> [A] magistrates' court which is not a youth court may hear an information against a child or young person if he is charged –
> (b) with an offence arising out of circumstances which are the same as or connected with those giving rise to an offence with which a person who has attained the age of eighteen is charged at the same time.

1   *R v Rowlands* [1972] 1 All ER 306.
2   *R v Peterborough Justices ex p Allgood* (1994) 159 JP 627; (1994) *Times*, 25 November, QBD.

Once again this provision is permissive and therefore the youth court retains jurisdiction and may deal with any child or young person who appears before it.

Remittal to the youth court for trial

9.12 Where a child or young person is brought before an adult magistrates' court jointly charged with an adult, the court may remit him/her for trial in the youth court. This power arises in two circumstances:

– the court proceeds to summary trial and the adult defendant pleads guilty and the child or young person pleads not guilty; or
– the court proceeds to inquire into the information as examining magistrates and either commits the adult for trial or discharges him/her and in the case of the child or young person, proceeds to the summary trial of the information.[3]

In both cases the plea will be taken before the case is remitted to the youth court. The case may be remitted to a youth court acting for the same place as the remitting court or for the place where the accused habitually resides.

9.13 Where a child or young person is remitted for trial the remitting court may give such directions as appear to be necessary with respect to his/her custody or for his/her release on bail until s/he can be brought before the youth court.[4] There is no right of appeal against the order of remission.[5]

Crown Court

9.14 The general rule is that children and young persons should be dealt with in the more informal and less intimidating forum of a court of summary jurisdiction. However, there are exceptions to this rule. In summary, a child or young person may appear in the Crown Court for trial where s/he is:

– charged with an offence of homicide; or
– charged with a grave crime; or
– jointly charged with an adult.

---

3   Magistrates' Courts Act 1980 s29(2).
4   Ibid, s29(4)(b).
5   Ibid, s29(4)(a).

Each of these exceptions will be considered in more detail below.

Offences of homicide

Definition of homicide

9.15   There is no statutory definition of 'homicide'. There would be no question that the term included the offences of murder, manslaughter and probably infanticide. All these offences are punishable by life imprisonment and therefore on trial by indictment the Crown Court judge would have the powers of s53 detention available to him/her. It is arguable that a charge of attempted murder must be tried on indictment as well.[6]

9.16   The position is not so clear in relation to driving offences which result in death. These are causing death by dangerous driving, by careless driving while under the influence of drugs or alcohol or by aggravated vehicle-taking. It is the opinion of the editors of *Stone's Justices' Manual*[7] that the offence of causing death by dangerous driving is an offence of homicide. No further explanation is given nor is it explained why the other driving offences resulting in death are not also included. It is arguable that the driving offences should not be construed as offences of homicide and instead mode of trial should be considered only if the offence is punishable with s53 detention. This would only be in the case of an offender who has attained the age of 14 and has been convicted of an offence of causing death by dangerous driving or by careless driving while under the influence of drugs or alcohol.[8] It would not include causing death by aggravated vehicle-taking which is not a grave crime as the maximum penalty is only five years. To interpret the term 'homicide' in any other way would require a youth court to commit a child defendant to the Crown Court for trial when the judge would have no greater powers of punishment.

Committal of related offences

9.17   Where a child or young person is committed to stand trial for an offence of homicide, the court may also commit him for trial for any

---

6   See Criminal Attempts Act 1981 s2(2)(c).
7   Butterworths, 131st edition (1999).
8   Grave crimes by virtue of the Children and Young Persons Act 1933 s53(2)(b).

other indictable offence with which he is charged at the same time if the charges for both offences could be joined in the same indictment.[9]

Grave crimes

Definition of grave crime

9.18   A grave crime is defined by the Children and Young Persons Act 1933 s53(2) as being:

- an offence punishable in the case of an adult with imprisonment for 14 years or more;
- indecent assault upon a female contrary to the Sexual Offences Act 1956 s14;
- indecent assault upon a male contrary to the Sexual Offences Act 1956 s15; [10]
- (for offenders who have attained the age of 14) offences of causing death by dangerous driving or whilst under the influence of drink or drugs.

The definition would include robbery, residential burglary and handling stolen goods. Note it does not include non-residential burglary (maximum penalty 10 years).

9.19   A full list of offences which are grave crimes is produced in Appendix 4.

Factors to be taken into consideration

9.20   Certain principles may be extracted from the few occasions when the higher courts have considered the question of determining mode of trial in the youth court.

Facts of allegation

9.21   For the purposes of deciding jurisdiction the prosecution version of the allegation should be accepted. It is not appropriate for the court to

---

9   Magistrates' Courts Act 1980 s24(1A) as inserted by Crime and Disorder Act 1998 s47(6).

10   Only for offences committed on or after 1 October 1997: Crime(Sentences) Act 1997 s44.

consider evidence (even by being invited to read prosecution witness statements) to determine seriousness.[11]

Aggregating the seriousness of two or more grave crimes

9.22   There will be occasions when a youth court is considering mode of trial when more than one grave crime is before the court. The question then arises whether the court should consider the mode of trial for each offence separately or whether it is able to aggregate the seriousness of the various grave crimes. The Magistrates' Courts Act 1980 s24(1)(a) refers to the possibility of using s53 detention if the defendant 'is convicted of *the offence*'. It may be argued that this use of the singular prevents the court from aggregating offences for the purposes of mode of trial. Similar wording in a statutory section relating to committing adults for sentence was considered by the Divisional Court in *R v Rugby Justices ex p Prince*.[12] The court held that as the justices had to impose a separate sentence for each offence, they also had to consider each offence separately when deciding whether to commit for sentence. In this particular situation the Interpretation Act could not be used to construe 'offence' as a reference to 'offences'. The same question arose in *R v Hammersmith Juvenile Court ex p O (a Minor)*[13] in relation to s24(1)(a). The Divisional Court was referred to the *Rugby Justices* case in argument but in giving judgment May LJ chose not to rule upon the point.

Defendant's previous criminal convictions

9.23   No reference should be made by the prosecutor to the previous convictions of a defendant.[14]

Defendant's good character

9.24   Despite the above general principle, it is arguable that a defence lawyer may draw a court's attention to the defendant's good character. In the *South Hackney Juvenile Court* case (see n11), McNeill J said obiter:

---

11   *R v South Hackney Juvenile Court ex p RB and CB (Minors)* (1984) 77 Cr App R 294, QBD.
12   [1974] 1 WLR 736; (1974) 59 Cr App R 31, QBD.
13   (1987) 86 Cr App R 343; (1987) 151 JP 740, QBD.
14   *R v Hammersmith Juvenile court ex p O (a Minor)* see n13.

For my part, I would have thought it was open to a defendant, when appearing before a juvenile court and when attempting to persuade the [youth] court not to send him for trial, to draw the fact of his good character to their attention. I see no harm in it and I think it is a factor which could weigh with the justices when they are determining whether the powers that they have are sufficient in relation to the offence committed by the offender.

Guidelines

9.25 Unlike the mode of trial decision in the adult court there are no detailed guidelines which indicate when particular offences should not be dealt with summarily. The way a youth court should approach this decision has been considered by the Divisional Court in *R v Inner London Youth Court ex p Director of Public Prosecutions*.[15] This was an application for judicial review of the decision of justices sitting at Balham Youth Court to try summarily a 15-year-old charged with causing grievous bodily harm with intent. Sir Iain Glidewell stated that the question that the justices should ask themselves was as follows: 'Ought it to be possible to sentence the defendant in pursuance of the Children and Young Persons Act 1933 s53(2)?' He continued that, when dealing with serious charges, although not required by law, the justices would be well advised to seek their clerk's advice concerning the limits of their powers and the guidance available. Although in general a court would take into account the age of the witnesses and the desirability of disposing of the case expeditiously, such considerations could not outweigh the decision as to the proper penalty.

9.26 In the absence of offence-specific guidelines, youth courts have generally looked towards the general guidelines on the use of s53(2) detention provided by the Court of Appeal. These guidelines are contained in the decisions of *R v Fairhurst*[16] and *R v Mills*.[17]

Defendant aged 15–17 years

9.27 The court should ask itself: 'Is the offence so serious that in the case of this young offender a custodial sentence of more than two years would be merited?'

---

15 (1997) 161 JP 178; [1996] Crim LR 834, QBD.
16 (1986) 8 Cr App R (S) 346; [1986] 1 WLR 1374, CA.
17 [1998] 2 Cr App R 57; [1998] Crim LR 220, CA, reversing *R v Wainfur* [1997] 1 Cr App R (S) 43; [1996] Crim LR 674, CA.

9.28   The Court of Appeal has indicated that a youth court should never accept jurisdiction in relation to a young person charged with rape.[18]

Defendant aged 10–14 years

9.29   Until the implementation of secure training orders on 1 March 1998 the youth court had no custodial option available to it for this age range. A decision to accept jurisdiction was effectively a decision to rule out a custodial sentence. As custody was not available otherwise, the decisions in both *Fairhurst* and *Mills* accepted that a sentence of s53(2) detention for less than two years was permissible for offenders under the age of 15. Accordingly, when considering the question of jurisdiction, the youth court should simply ask itself the question: 'Is the offence so serious that a custodial sentence would be merited?'

9.30   Has the existence of a custodial option in the youth court changed the way that a youth court should approach the question of jurisdiction for defendants under the age of 15? It has been argued that no account should be taken of the availability of a secure training order because such an order is contingent on previous convictions, which are not a relevant consideration at the mode of trial stage.[19] Such an argument could equally be applied to detention and training orders which may only be imposed upon a defendant under the age of 15 if s/he is considered to be a persistent offender. A more pragmatic approach may be to allow the defence lawyer to draw the court's attention to the fact that the defendant could be sentenced to a secure training order (or detention and training order). Save in the most serious of offences, it could then be argued that committal for trial is not required as a custodial sentence of up to 24 months passed by the youth court would be adequate punishment for the offence.

9.31   It has also been argued before the Divisional Court that as a consequence of the introduction of secure training orders, s53 detention should no longer be used for less than two years in relation to offenders aged between 12 and 14.[20] No definitive ruling has been made.[21] If this argument is correct, youth courts should now retain jurisdiction of all offences charged against a defendant aged 10 to 14 unless the offence merited a sentence of two years or more.

18   Per Lane LCJ in *R v Billam* [1986] 1 WLR 349; (1986) 8 Cr App R (S) 48, CA.
19   F G Davies, *The Jurisdiction of Summary Courts to Try Children and Young Persons – A Further Update* (1998) 162 JPN 256 at 259.
20   See *R v Sheffield Youth Justices ex p M (a Minor)* CO/3343/97, 19.1.98, QBD, and *R v Liverpool Youth Court ex p C (a Minor)* CO/474/98, 7.5.98, QBD.
21   See para 21.74.

Procedure

9.32   In any case of a grave crime the issue of jurisdiction should be dealt with before any plea is taken from the defendant. It is for the prosecutor and/or court clerk to draw the court's attention to the fact that jurisdiction has to be decided. If a guilty plea is taken without dealing with the question of jurisdiction it is not open to the court to reopen the plea at a later stage.[22]

9.33   Although the detailed procedural requirements contained in the Magistrates' Courts Act 1980 ss18–23 do not apply, it is submitted that as far as possible they should be followed in the interests of fairness to the defendant. First, the prosecutor should present the facts dispassionately. S/he should then make representations as to the court's decision regarding jurisdiction but care should be taken not to invite the court to accept jurisdiction when it would be inappropriate to do so.[23] The defence lawyer should then be given the opportunity of making representations.

9.34   It should be noted that unlike the mode of trial criteria applicable to adults set out in Magistrates' Courts Act 1980 s19(3), the above criterion focuses on the individual offender. It is arguable that the court should consider whether to decline jurisdiction in relation to each offender separately. This may be of particular importance when there are several defendants charged with a variety of linked offences.

Committal of related offences

9.35   Where a child or young person is committed to stand trial for a grave crime, the court may also commit him/her for trial for any other indictable offence with which s/he is charged at the same time if the charges for both offences could be joined in the same indictment.[24]

9.36   If the grave crime is an either-way offence the court may commit any summary-only offences punishable by imprisonment or disqualification from driving if the offence arises out of similar circumstances to the either-way offence.[25]

---

22 *R v Herefordshire Youth Court ex p J (a Minor)* (1998) *Times*, 4 May, CO/334/97, 23.4.98, QBD.
23 *R v Learmouth* (1988) 10 Cr App R(S) 229; (1988) 152 JP 18, CA.
24 Magistrates' Courts Act 1980 s24(1A) as inserted by Crime and Disorder Act 1998 s47(6).
25 Criminal Justice Act 1991 s41(1).

Can the court change its mind?

9.37   Although rare in practice, a court may review its decision, either to reverse a decision to decline jurisdiction or to change from summary trial to commit the defendant.

9.38   A court may change its mind as to mode of trial if it appears to the court at any time before the conclusion of the evidence for the prosecution that the case is after all one which under s24(1) ought not to be tried summarily.[26] Evidence of the prosecution is evidence adduced to prove guilt and therefore it is not open to the court to review its decision regarding jurisdiction after a defendant has pleaded guilty to the offence.[27]

9.39   It has been suggested that a youth court may change its mind regarding the mode of trial not only by the above method but also if there has been a change of circumstances. This proposition is derived from the case of *R v Newham Juvenile Court ex p F (a Minor)*.[28] In that case jurisdiction had been accepted in relation to an armed robbery. On a subsequent hearing before a differently constituted bench the justices sought to reopen the question of jurisdiction and to commit for trial. Their decision was judicially reviewed. In giving judgment Stephen Brown LJ held that the justices had acted unlawfully. However, he proceeded to suggest obiter that the subsequent bench would have acted lawfully if they had changed the mode of trial after taking into account subsequent events including the fact that the defendant had committed another serious offence while on bail. This decision was considered by May LJ in *R v Hammersmith Juvenile Court ex p O (a Minor)*[29] in which he said, once again obiter, that subsequent offences should not be taken into consideration. It is submitted that the view of May LJ is preferable as it accords with the position applicable to adults.[30]

9.40   Where magistrates have commenced committal proceedings in respect of a child or young person they may revert to summary trial at any time before actually committing.[31] The practical significance of this provision is considered in relation to mode of committal (see para 9.54).

---

26   Magistrates' Courts Act 1980 s25(6).
27   *R v Dudley Justices ex p Gillard* [1986] AC 442.
28   (1987) 84 Cr App R 81; [1986] 1 WLR 939, QBD.
29   (1988) 86 Cr App R 343, QBD.
30   See *R v Colchester Justices ex p North Essex Building Company* [1977] 3 All ER 567; [1977] 1 WLR 1109.
31   Magistrates' Courts Act 1980 s25(7).

Jointly charged with an adult

Meaning of jointly charged

9.41 It is not necessary for the charge to specify that the offence was committed 'jointly' or 'together with' the adult concerned.[32] In the case of taking without consent or aggravated vehicle taking the driver and any passengers charged with allowing to be carried are jointly charged.[33]

9.42 Although s24(1)(b) only refers to committing a child or young person to stand trial with an adult when 'jointly charged' the Divisional Court in the case of *R v Coventry City Magistrates' Court ex p M (a Minor)*[34] assumed that there was a power to commit a child or young person to stand trial with an adult whom s/he is charged with aiding and abetting. There seems to have been no legal argument on the point during the hearing of the case.

Procedure

9.43 The procedure for determining the mode of trial for a child or young person jointly charged with an adult has unfortunately been made considerably more complicated as a result of the implementation of the Criminal Procedure and Investigations Act 1996 and the Crime and Disorder Act 1998. The proper procedure is determined by the procedure being employed in relation to the adult co-defendant.

Plea before venue

9.44 The court first needs to deal with plea before venue for the adult defendant.

Guilty plea indicated

9.45 Where the adult indicates a guilty plea, the court will normally take a plea from the child or young person. However, if the child or young person is charged with a grave crime, the court should decide

---

32 *R v Rowlands* [1972] 1 All ER 306.
33 *R v Peterborough Justices ex p Allgood* (1994) 159 JP 627; (1994) *Times*, 25 November, QBD.
34 (1992) 156 JP 809.

whether committal for trial is required under the Magistrates' Courts Act 1980 s24(1)(a) before the plea is taken.[35] If mode of trial is not considered before a plea is taken, it will be deemed that summary trial has been determined.[35A]

Not guilty or no plea indicated

9.46   If the adult defendant indicates a not guilty plea or refuses to indicate any plea, the court will then proceed to determine mode of trial for the adult pursuant to the principles set out the Magistrates' Courts Act 1980 ss18–23. As the child or young person has no right to elect jury trial s/he would have no right to make representations at this stage but the bench could exercise its discretion to allow any representations.

9.47   If the court decides to decline jurisdiction or the adult co-defendant elects jury trial, the child or young person may be committed to stand trial along with the adult co-defendant(s), if it is considered necessary in the interests of justice to do so.[36] If this happens s/he may also be committed to stand trial for any other indictable offence for which s/he is charged at the same time (whether jointly with the adult or not) if that other offence arises out of circumstances which are the same as or connected with those giving rise to the joint charge.[37] The court may also commit any summary-only offences punishable by imprisonment or disqualification from driving if the offence arises out of similar circumstances to the either-way offence.[38]

9.48   If the court decides not to commit the child or young person for trial, it may take a plea from him/her. If the child or young person pleads not guilty, s/he may be remitted for trial to the youth court.[39] If s/he pleads guilty, she should be remitted to the youth court for sentence, unless the case may be disposed of by way of a discharge, financial order or bindover.[40] In both cases the remittal may be to the youth court acting for the same place as the remitting court or for the place where the child or young person habitually resides.

---

35 *R v Tottenham Youth Court ex p Fawzy* [1998] 1 All ER 365, QBD.

35A *R v Herefordshire Youth Court ex p J (a minor)* (1998) *Times*, 4 May; CO/334/97, (1998) 23 April, QBD.

36 Magistrates' Courts Act 1980 s24(1)(b). For the meaning of 'interests of justice' see para 9.51.

37 Ibid, s24(2).

38 Criminal Justice Act 1988 s41(1).

39 Magistrates' Courts Act 1980 s29(2).

40 Children and Young Persons Act 1933 s56(1) and Children and Young Persons Act 1969 s7(8).

Sending for trial (indictable-only offences)

9.49 The Crime and Disorder Act 1998 s51 introduces a new procedure for dealing with adult defendants charged with an indictable-only offence. This new procedure in not generally in force but is being piloted in certain areas. Where in force, a magistrates' court is required to send an adult defendant charged with an indictable-only offence forthwith to the Crown Court for trial.[41] S/he may also be sent for trial on any either-way or summary-only offence with which s/he is charged which satisfies the 'requisite conditions', namely that the offence appears to the court to be related to the indictable-only offence or, in the case of a summary-only offence, that it is punishable with imprisonment or carries a power of disqualification from driving.[42]

9.50 Where an adult is sent for trial under the above procedure, a child or young person who appears before the court on the same or a subsequent occasion jointly charged with the adult with an indictable offence shall be sent for trial as well, if the court considers that it is in the interests of justice to do so.[43] The court may also send him/her for trial for any either-way or summary offence with which s/he is charged and which fulfils the 'requisite conditions' (for which see above).[44]

Interests of justice

9.51 When deciding whether it is in the interests of justice to commit or transfer a child or young person for trial along with an adult, the magistrates must act judicially[45] and the bench should invite separate representations from the prosecutor and the defence lawyer representing the child or young person.

9.52 When considering whether to commit a child or young person with an adult defendant guidance may be sought from the 1992 version[46] of the Code for Crown Prosecutors which stated that when a prosecutor was making representations to assist the court to determine the venue s/he would wish to take the following factors into account:

– the respective ages of the adult and the child or young person;
– the seriousness of the offence;

41   Crime and Disorder Act 1998 s51(1).
42   Ibid, s51(1) and (11).
43   Ibid, s51(5). For the meaning of 'interests of justice' see para 9.51.
44   Ibid, s51(6).
45   *R v Newham JJ, ex p Knight* [1976] Crim LR 323, QBD.
46   No reference is made to the prosecutor's role in determining mode of trial for a child or young person in the most recent version of the code (June 1994).

- the likely plea;
- whether there are existing charges against the child or young person before the youth court; and
- the need to deal with a child or young person as expeditiously as possible consistent with the interests of justice.

Committal for trial

9.53   With the implementation of the Criminal Procedure and Investigations Act 1996 it is now no longer possible to call witnesses to give live evidence at committal hearings. The consideration of evidence is now solely on written statements. The examining justices will be required to consider whether there is sufficient evidence for a trial if:

- the defendant is not legally represented; or
- if the defence lawyer requests that the court considers a submission that there is insufficient evidence to put the accused on trial by jury for the offence.

Form of committal

9.54   Defence lawyers will be familiar with considering whether to challenge the sufficiency of evidence in a committal hearing. An accused under the age of 18 has the same right to challenge the prosecution case at committal and all the same tactical considerations will apply to an accused who is a child or young person.

9.55   Where magistrates have commenced committal proceedings in respect of a child or young person they may revert to summary trial at any time before actually committing.[47]

9.56   McNeill J in *R v South Hackney Juvenile Court ex p R B and C B (Minors)*[48] suggested that at a committal hearing where the sufficiency of evidence is being challenged, it was open to the defence to make representations that the prosecution evidence did not indicate that the case needed to be committed to the Crown Court for trial and to invite the court to revert to summary trial.

---

47   Magistrates' Courts Act 1980 s25(7).
48   (1984) 77 Cr App R 294, QBD.

Transfer for trial

9.57 In certain circumstances where the alleged victim or a witness is a child, a committal hearing can be dispensed with. In such cases a transfer for trial takes place instead.

9.58 Transfer for trial may take place in relation to the following offences:

- an offence which involves an assault on, or injury or a threat of injury to a person;
- an offence under Children and Young Persons Act 1933 s1 (cruelty to persons under 16);
- an offence under the Sexual Offences Act 1956, the Indecency with Children Act 1960, the Sexual Offences Act 1967, the Criminal Law Act 1967 s54 or the Protection of Children Act 1978; and
- an offence which consists of attempting or conspiring to commit, or of aiding, abetting, counselling, procuring or inciting the commission of, an offence listed above.

Definition of child

9.59 Child is defined as follows:

- for a sexual offence it means a person under the age of 17; or
- in relation to other offences it means a person under the age of 14.[49]

9.60 If a video recording was made of the witness' evidence when s/he was under the relevant age, then the relevant age is increased by one year to 18 years and 15 years respectively.

Notice of transfer

9.61 To initiate the transfer for trial procedure, the Director of Public Prosecutions must serve a notice of transfer upon the relevant youth court or adult magistrates' court, certifying that s/he is of the opinion:

- that the evidence of the offence would be sufficient for the person charged to be committed for trial;
- that a child who is alleged –

49 Criminal Justice Act 1991 s53(6).

i) to be a person against whom the offence was committed; or
ii) to have witnessed the commission of the offence;
will be called as a witness at the trial; and

– that, for the purposes of avoiding any prejudice to the welfare of the child, the case should be taken over and proceeded with without delay by the Crown Court.[50]

The notice merely requires the DPP to state his/her opinion that the above criteria are satisfied. The decision to serve a notice of transfer shall not be subject to appeal or liable to be questioned in any court.[51]

9.62   A defendant who wishes to argue that there is insufficient evidence justifying a trial may apply to the Crown Court prior to arraignment to have the charge(s) dismissed.[52]

9.63   A notice for transfer may not be served once the justices have begun to inquire into the case as examining justices.[53]

Problems concerning jurisdiction

Accused attaining 18

9.64   Instances when the accused young person attains 18 after arrest can cause considerable procedural problems. The Children and Young Persons Act 1963 s29(1) provides:

> Where proceedings in respect of a young person are begun for an offence and he attains the age of eighteen before the conclusion of the proceedings, the court may deal with the case and make any order which it could have made if he had not attained that age.

Judicial opinion is divided as to whether this section applies to the whole court process or only the power to sentence. In *R v St Albans Juvenile Court ex p Godman*[54] Skinner J said obiter that s29(1) only applied to questions of disposal and not to questions of trial. Unfortunately he reached this view without the benefit of legal argument as both counsel in the case agreed with this view. In *R v*

---

50   Ibid, s53(1).
51   Ibid, s53(4).
52   Ibid, Sch 6 para 5.
53   Ibid, s53(2).
54   [1981] 2 All ER 311, QBD.

Amersham Juvenile Court ex p Wilson[55] Donaldson LJ took a contrary view:

> In the present case both counsel are equally agreed but in a contrary sense, namely that s29 does relate both to questions of trial and disposal. As they point out, the section in its original unamended form read 'the court may continue to deal', but Parliament when adding the words 'or for an offence' in 1969 deleted the words 'continue to'. This suggests that it now applies to the proceedings ab initio. Furthermore, the words 'deal with the case' stand as a phrase on their own and are used in contradistinction to the words 'make any order', the latter clearly covering all questions of disposal and leaving the earlier words as only really referable to questions of trial.

It is submitted that the view of Donaldson LJ, reached after the benefit of legal argument, is the preferable view.

9.65   The Children and Young Persons Act 1963 s29(1) does not solve all of the procedural problems that may arise. Some of the problems which may arise are considered below.

To which court should the police bail?

9.66   Donaldson LJ has given the following guidance:

> In our opinion, those who arrest and charge or lay an information against persons who are in the juvenile/adult borderline age group should take all reasonable steps to find out exactly when they will attain the age of [18]. If they are to be brought or summoned to appear before a court for the first time on a date when they will have attained the age of [18], the court selected or specified in the summons should be the adult court. If they have not attained the age of [18], it should be a [youth court].[56]

Attaining 18 prior to the first court appearance

9.67   There are occasions when a young person is charged with an offence and bailed to the youth court on a date when s/he will be under 18 years. The young person then fails to surrender to custody on the appointed day. Does the youth court still have jurisdiction to deal with the defendant who has subsequently attained 18, when s/he finally surrenders to court or when brought to court on a warrant?

9.68   The youth court could only retain jurisdiction if the provisions of the Children and Young Persons Act 1963 s29(1) could be relied on.

---

55   [1981] 2 All ER 315, QBD.
56   *R v Amersham Juvenile Court ex p Wilson* [1981] 2 All ER 315, at 320d.

The section may only be invoked if the proceedings have already begun. In *R v Billericay Justices ex p Johnson*[57] the Divisional Court held that proceedings had begun against a defendant when a summons was served upon him. In contrast, in *R v Amersham Juvenile Court ex p Wilson*[58] Donaldson LJ stated:

> [Section 29(1)] is wholly consistent with the statutory approach of classifying offenders as adult or [youth] by reference to their age when they first appear or are brought before a magistrates' court, provided that on the true construction of the section proceedings are 'begun' at that time and not at the earlier time when an information is laid or a charge preferred. We have no doubt that it should be so construed . . . It is on the defendant first appearing or being brought to court that his age is fixed for the purpose of all of these provisions.

This latter view has been confirmed recently in *R v Uxbridge Youth Court ex p H*.[59] In this case a 17-year-old had been charged with an offence and had then been bailed to the youth court. He failed to attend court on the day required and a warrant for his arrest was issued. The warrant was not executed until he had attained the age of 18. The youth court then purported to remit him to the adult magistrates' court. The defendant applied for judicial review of that decision. Rose LJ held that as the defendant had attained 18 before the day when the warrant was executed and the proceedings could be said to have begun, the youth court had no jurisdiction at all. It was not open to the youth court to remit the case to the adult court as no statutory power existed to do this.[60] Faced with such a situation, the police would have to recharge the accused so that proceedings could be re-commenced in the adult court.

New charges after the first appearance

9.69 It has been held in the case of *R v Chelsea Justices ex p DPP*[61] that any new charges preferred after the defendant has attained 18 must be laid in the adult court even if the new charges arise out of the same facts as the original charges. In this case a 16-year-old was charged with wounding and appeared before the (then) juvenile court. The

---

57 (1979) 143 JP 697.
58 [1981] 2 All ER 315.
59 (1998) *Times*, 7 April, CO/292/98, 19.3/98, QBD
60 It would appear that the new power to remit to the adult court under the Crime and Disorder Act 1998 s47(1) is not available either in such circumstances – see below.
61 [1963] 3 All ER 657; 128 JP 18, QBD.

case was adjourned during which time he attained the age of 17 which at that time would have made him an adult defendant. He was then charged with attempted murder. It was held that the juvenile court had no jurisdiction to hear the new charge and that it should have been laid before an adult magistrates' court.

Attaining 18 prior to the plea being taken

9.70   In the case of a defendant charged with an indictable offence who attains the age of 18 after the first court appearance the question arises whether s/he should be dealt with under the adult or youth court rules regarding mode of trial. The House of Lords held in the case of *R v Islington North Juvenile Court ex p Daley*[62] that the relevant age is the defendant's age on the day that the mode of trial is determined. If the defendant has attained 18 before that point in the case s/he has a right to elect jury trial. If the defendant has not attained 18 before the mode of trial is determined s/he shall be subject to the Magistrates' Courts Act 1980 s24. This principle applies equally to indictable-only offences.[63]

9.71   To prevent any doubt arising when dealing with a defendant in the youth court McNeill J in *R v Lewes Juvenile Court ex p Turner*[64] suggested the following practice should be followed:

> [W]here a person under the age of [18] pleads not guilty before a [youth] court, and the circumstances set out in s24 of the Magistrates' Courts Act 1980 do not apply, but when the [youth] court is not there and then able to take evidence in the trial which is to follow, the register of the court should be marked 'remanded for summary trial'. That to my mind, would be decisive and determinative of the date on which, for the purposes of the section, the defendant appeared or was brought before the court.

Remittal to the adult court

9.72   The Crime and Disorder Act 1998 s47(1) provides:

> Where a person who appears or is brought before a youth court charged with an offence subsequently attains the age of 18, the youth court may, at any time –
> (a) before the start of the trial; or
> (b) after conviction and before sentence,

---

62   [1983] 1 AC 347; (1982) 75 Cr App R 280; [1982] 3 WLR 344.
63   *R v Nottingham Justices ex p Taylor* (1991) 93 Cr App R 365, QBD.
64   (1984) 149 JP 186, QBD.

remit the person for trial, or as the case may be, for sentence to a magistrates' court (other than a youth court) acting for the same petty sessions area as the youth court.

For the above provision a trial starts when the court begins to hear prosecution evidence or, if the court accepts a guilty plea without so proceeding, when that plea is accepted.[65] It is not anticipated that the power to remit will be used in every case. The Home Office has stated that the power was introduced 'to ensure that young people are dealt with in the most appropriate way, according to their maturity, attitude and offending history, while avoiding unnecessary delay.'[66]

9.73   When a person is remitted under s47(1) the remitting youth court must adjourn proceedings in relation to the offence.[67] The Magistrates' Courts Act 1980 s128 and all other enactments (whenever passed) relating to remands or the granting of bail in criminal proceedings shall have effect in relation to the remitting youth court's power or duty to remand the defendant on the adjournment as if any reference to the court to or before which the person remanded is to be brought or appear after remand were a reference to the adult court to which s/he is being remitted.[68] There is no right of appeal against the decision to remit.[69]

9.74   Where remittal under s47(1) takes place, s47(4) provides:

> The other court may deal with the case in any way in which it would have power to deal with it if all proceedings relating to the offence which took place before the remitting court had taken place before the other court.

This subsection appears to have the potential to create some bizarre outcomes. For example, if a youth court accepted jurisdiction in relation to a robbery charge prior to the defendant's eighteenth birthday and s/he was then remitted for trial under s47(1), the adult magistrates' court would seem to have no option but to try the indictable-only charge.

9.75   It should be noted that s47(1) may only be used where the defendant appeared before the youth court prior to attaining the age of 18. It

---

65   Crime and Disorder Act 1998 s47(1), adopting the definition in the Prosecution of Offences Act 1985 s22(11B).
66   Home Office Circular 47/1998: *The Crime and Disorder Act 1998 – New Powers for Youth Courts* para 5.
67   Crime and Disorder Act 1998 s47(2)(b).
68   Ibid, s47(2)(c) and (3).
69   Ibid, s47(2)(a).

cannot, therefore, be used to solve the problem of a defendant bailed to the youth court who attains 18 before s/he appears or is brought before that court. In such circumstances the youth court would have no jurisdiction to deal with the defendant and there is no other statutory power to allow for a remittal to the adult magistrates' court.[70]

Accused wrongly before the court

9.76   Where a child or young person appears before an adult magistrates' court in circumstances where the court would not ordinarily have jurisdiction, the court may continue to determine the case. This situation might arise when an accused gave a false date of birth to the police. The Children and Young Persons Act 1933 s46(1)(c) provides:

> [W]here in the course of any proceedings before any court of summary jurisdiction other than a youth court, it appears that the person to whom the proceedings relate is a child or young person, nothing in this subsection shall be construed as preventing the court, if it thinks fit so to do, from proceeding with the hearing and determination of those proceedings.

Although this section gives the court discretion to proceed with the hearing, it is more common for the court to adjourn the hearing and remand to the next sitting of the youth court under the Children and Young Persons Act 1933 s46(2). The power to proceed would still seem to be subject to the provisions of the Children and Young Persons Act 1969 s7(8) which would require the defendant to be remitted to the youth court for sentence unless a discharge, fine or bindover was considered appropriate.

9.77   If an adult has lied about his/her age and appears before the youth court, the proceedings may still continue in that court. The Children and Young Persons Act 1933 s48(1) provides:

> A youth court sitting for the purpose of hearing a charge against a person who is believed to be a child or young person may, if it thinks fit to do so, proceed with the hearing and determination of the charge, notwithstanding that it is discovered that the person in question is not a child or young person.

If the court decides not to continue with the proceedings, there

---

70   *R v Uxbridge Youth Court ex p H* (1998) *Times*, 7 April, CO/292/98, 19.3.98.

would seem to be no statutory mechanism to transfer the case to an adult court.[71] The new power to remit a defendant to the adult court introduced by the Crime and Disorder Act 1998 s47(1) is of no avail as it only applies to situations where the defendant attains the age of 18 after the first appearance.[72] Accordingly, the prosecution would need to discontinue proceedings in the youth court and re-charge the adult.

71   Ibid.
72   See para 9.75.

Bail and remands

For complete chapter contents, see overleaf

Introduction

10.1   The rules regarding children and young persons in relation to bail and remands are frequently the source of misunderstanding. This chapter will cover the question of bail and how it affects children and young persons as well as examining what happens if the court refuses bail.

10.2   It should be emphasised at the outset that the Bail Act 1976 applies in its entirety to children and young people and as a result any court is under the same obligation to consider the question of bail as it would be with an adult defendant. It is only if the court refuses bail that the law is substantially different to that applying to an adult. Although the Criminal Justice Act 1991 extended the age range of the renamed youth courts, it created an anomaly in relation to bail by treating 17-year-olds differently to the younger age range of the youth court. In relation to bail and remands, 17-year-olds are treated as though they were adults. In contrast, younger defendants benefit from stringent rules designed to ensure that a remand to custody is always an absolute last resort. In the case of defendants under the age of 17 the Act therefore establishes a three-tier remand system:

–   bail with or without conditions;
–   remand to local authority accommodation with or without conditions; and
–   secure remand.

10.3   Whenever considering the question of bail and defendants under the age of 18 it is helpful to keep in mind the guidance issued by the Home Office at the time of the implementation of the Criminal Justice Act 1991:

> Removing children and young persons from home should be a course of last resort, and the Government believes that as many defendants as possible should be granted bail. In many areas bail information schemes are available. These provide detailed information which helps courts decide whether the general presumption in favour of bail should or should not be over-ruled. In some parts of the country community programmes, provided either by the voluntary sector or by local authorities, are available for work with defendants who might be at risk of being refused bail without some kind of support. Such programmes offer a range of measures of support for and work with juvenile defendants. The approach is similar to that used to good effect in specified activities programmes for convicted juvenile offenders. The Government believes that such programmes have an important part to

play in the arrangements for the remand of children and young persons.[1]

The right to bail

General principle

10.4   There is a general right to bail for any person in criminal proceedings.[2] This right applies to the following:

– an accused appearing before a magistrates' or youth court and the Crown Court;[3]
– a convicted person before any of these courts but only if the court is adjourning the case for the purpose of enabling reports to be prepared before sentence;[4] or
– an offender appearing before the court for alleged breach of a requirement of a probation, community service, combination or curfew order.[5]

A court must consider bail at every hearing and this obligation exists even if the accused does not apply for bail.

Serious cases

10.5   The generality of the right to bail has been revised in relation to very serious charges.

Homicide and rape cases

10.6   Special provisions apply to anyone charged with any of the following offences:

– murder;
– attempted murder;
– manslaughter;
– rape; or
– attempted rape.

1   Home Office Circular 30/1992 *Criminal Justice Act 1991: Young People and the Youth Court*, para 49.
2   Bail Act 1976 s4(1).
3   Ibid, s4(2).
4   Ibid, s4(4).
5   Ibid, s4(3).

Any court granting bail to a person charged with one of the above offences, where the prosecutor raised objections to bail, must give reasons for so doing and have those reasons recorded.[6] This rule does not effect the presumption in favour of bail for a child or young person charged with one of these offences

10.7   By the Criminal Justice and Public Order Act 1994 s25 there are restrictions on the granting of bail for a person charged with any of the above offences, if s/he has previously been convicted of one of those offences or convicted in Scotland of culpable homicide. If the previous offence was manslaughter or culpable homicide the person must have been sentenced to long-term detention under the Children and Young Persons Act 1933 s53(2) (detention in a young offenders' institution or a secure training order will not satisfy this criterion). If these pre-conditions are satisfied, the custody officer or court may only grant bail to the accused where there are exceptional circumstances which justify so doing. This provision does not rule out a non-custodial remand into local authority accommodation.

Treason

10.8   Bail may only be granted in a case of treason by a High Court judge or on the direction of the Home Secretary.[7]

Exception to the right to bail

10.9   Where there is a general right to bail the court may only refuse bail if it can identify one of the prescribed exceptions to that right which are contained in the Bail Act 1976 Sch 1. The exceptions vary depending on whether the offence is imprisonable or non-imprisonable, although there are some grounds which are common to all offences.

All cases

10.10   Bail may be refused if:

- the defendant has previously been released on bail and has subsequently been arrested for breach of the conditions of that bail;
- the defendant is already serving a criminal sentence;

6   Ibid, Sch 1 Part I, para 9A(1).
7   Magistrates' Courts Act 1980 s43.

- the court is satisfied that the defendant should be kept in custody for his/her own protection; or
- in the case of a juvenile, the court is satisfied that the defendant should be refused bail for his/her own welfare.

Cases where the defendant is charged with an imprisonable offence

10.11   Bail may be refused if the court is satisfied there are *substantial* grounds for believing that if granted bail the defendant would:

- fail to surrender to custody;
- commit an offence while on bail;
- interfere with witnesses or otherwise obstruct the course of justice, whether in relation to himself/herself or any other person.

10.12   When considering if there are substantial grounds for fearing one of the above, the court must take into account information available to it regarding the following:

- the nature and seriousness of the offence (and the probable means of dealing with the defendant for it);
- the character, antecedents (eg, criminal record), associations and community ties of the defendant;
- the defendant's previous record of complying with the obligation of bail;
- (except in the case of an adjournment for a pre-sentence report) the strength of the evidence against the defendant; and
- any other factor which the court considers relevant.[8]

10.13   Bail may also be refused if:

- the defendant is charged with an indictable-only or either-way offence and it appears to the court that s/he was on bail in criminal proceedings on the date of the offence;[9]
- the court is satisfied that it is not practicable to obtain sufficient information for the purposes of a bail decision for want of time since starting proceedings against him/her;[10] or
- the defendant has been convicted of an offence and the court is adjourning the matter for the preparation of a pre-sentence report,

8   Bail Act 1976 Sch 1 Part I para 9.
9   Ibid, Sch 1 Part I para 2A, as inserted by Criminal Justice and Public Order Act 1994 s26.
10   Bail Act 1976 Sch 1 Part I para 5.

but only if it appears to the court that it would be impracticable to complete the enquiries or make the report without keeping the defendant in custody.[11]

Non-imprisonable offences

10.14 Bail may be refused if the defendant has a previous history of failing to answer to bail and in view of that previous failure the court believes s/he would fail to surrender to custody.[12]

Where bail is refused

10.15 If a court refuses bail to a defendant it must give reasons for the refusal with a view to enabling the defendant to make another application for bail to another court.[13] The court is under an obligation to record the reasons for its decision and a magistrates' or youth court must supply a defendant with a copy of the reasons upon request.[14]

Conditional bail

Power to impose conditions

10.16 The Bail Act 1976 s3(6) provides that a person granted bail may be required by the court to comply with conditions both before bail is granted and afterwards. No condition may be imposed unless the court considers it *necessary* to impose conditions to ensure that s/he:

- answers bail;
- does not commit an offence while on bail;
- does not interfere with witnesses or otherwise obstruct the course of justice;
- makes himself/herself available for the purpose of preparing pre-sentence and other reports; or
- attends an interview with a solicitor before the time appointed for him/her to surrender to custody.

11 Ibid, Sch 1 Part I para 7.
12 Ibid, Sch 1 Part II para 2.
13 Ibid, s5(3).
14 Ibid, s5(4).

The court must give reasons for any conditions imposed.[15]

Practical considerations with young defendants

10.17   The defence lawyer should always ensure that when dealing with a child or young person, the court bears in mind the following:

- the obligation to consider the welfare of the child or young person under the Children and Young Persons Act 1933 s44;
- the impact on compulsory school attendance;
- that the terms are not onerous in view of the accused's age;
- that no condition requires financial expenditure which neither the accused nor his/her parents will be able to afford;
- that no condition requires the co-operation of another person (eg, parent or school teacher) unless they have expressly consented; and
- that the terms of any condition are precise and practicable.

Common conditions

10.18   Some of the more common conditions are as follows:

- residence;
- curfew;
- exclusion zone;
- non-association;
- not to contact witnesses;
- reporting;
- surety;
- security;
- co-operation with the preparation of reports; and
- to attend appointment with solicitor.

Residence

10.19   A court may impose a condition upon a defendant that s/he is to reside at a particular address while on bail. This condition is normally imposed if there are concerns about non-attendance at court. It is also the practice of some courts to impose the condition where it is hoped that imposing a condition to sleep every night at the parental home will ensure closer parental supervision.

---

15   Ibid, s5(3).

10.20   If the condition is to reside at a family address care should be taken that the condition does not interfere with the reasonable child care arrangements of the family. For example, where parents have separated but continue to share the responsibility of bringing up the defendant, a condition of residence could interfere with access arrangements. The defence lawyer should be alert to such problems and make sure the court is made aware of any problems such a condition would cause.

Reside as directed by social services

10.21   A significant number of children and young persons who appear before the courts are accommodated by the local authority. In such cases the defence lawyer should attempt to establish how permanent the current accommodation arrangements are. If a court wishes to impose a residence condition, it may be appropriate to suggest that the court bails the defendant 'to live as directed by [a named] social services department'. Such a flexible condition avoids any problems with the care plan and avoids the expense and inconvenience of returning to court for a bail variation application.

10.22   It has been held that when a child or young person is granted bail with a condition of residence to live as directed by the local social services department, s/he is accommodated by that local authority within the meaning of Children Act 1989 s20. It is submitted that if the young defendant is not already accommodated by a local authority the court has no power to order the authority to accommodate the defendant. However, there is nothing to stop the court from consulting with the authority and imposing such a condition if it is indicated that accommodation would be provided under s20.

Probation hostel

10.23   If a court bails a defendant with a condition that s/he resides at a bail hostel, the court may also impose a condition that the defendant complies with the conditions of the hostel.[16] Although in theory probation hostels accept defendants aged 16 and 17 on bail, in reality it is very difficult to obtain the necessary authorisation for placement.[17]

---

16   Bail Act 1976 s3(6ZA).
17   See para 19.119.

Curfew

10.24   This is a condition to remain indoors after a specified time in the evening until a specified time the following morning. It is imposed when the alleged offences were committed in the late evening or during the hours of darkness and the nature of the offences reveals a risk of similar occurrences if the defendant is at liberty at that time, for example if the defendant is charged with an office burglary committed at night when the premises were unoccupied or theft from a car in a quiet residential street at night.

10.25   Children's homes will already operate a curfew which is usually 10.30 pm or 11 pm. If an earlier curfew is likely to be imposed upon a defendant, the defence lawyer should establish whether the home runs evening activities outside the home. If this is the case and any curfew would prevent the defendant from taking part, it may be possible to persuade the court to vary the proposed curfew to allow the defendant to be outside the home after the curfew hour if accompanied by a member of staff.

10.26   An extreme example of this type of condition is where the defendant is not allowed to leave the premises at any time of the day unless accompanied by an adult. This is sometimes loosely referred to as a 24-hour curfew. Such a condition is extremely unlikely to be practicable if the condition of residence is at home with parents.

10.27   A curfew of this sort is only likely to be imposed in circumstances where a custodial sentence is a distinct possibility. Although such a curfew involves a considerable restriction of liberty, it will not be possible to count the time subject to the curfew towards any subsequent sentence. Accordingly the defence lawyer should consider whether the young defendant's interests would be best met by the court refusing bail and remanding to local authority accommodation. If the remand is to a children's home, the period spent there is likely to count towards any custodial sentence under Criminal Justice Act 1967 s67.[18]

Exclusion zone

10.28   This is a condition imposed either to deal with a fear of further offences or interference with witnesses. If the defendant's record and/ or current charges reveal a pattern of offending in a particular area, for

18   See para 22.25.

example shoplifting in the city centre, a court may consider forbidding the defendant from entering the area. If the concern is in relation to intimidating a particular witness the court may consider a condition not to go within a certain distance of the witness' home address or place of work.

10.29 If an exclusion zone is to be a possibility it is important that the defence lawyer takes instructions on the practical effect of such a condition. Will such a condition interfere, for example, with travelling to school or to constructive leisure activities?

Non-association

10.30 This is a condition not to associate with named people. It is usually imposed when the court is concerned that particular defendants have a history of offending together or it is feared that a concerted effort would be made by defendants to interfere with the administration of justice.

10.31 The defence lawyer should ensure that the court is aware of any practical problems that would arise from the imposition of such a condition, for example where the named people attend the same school, are neighbours or are part of the same extended family.

Not to contact witnesses

10.32 When the court considers that the defendant may try to intimidate a witness before any trial, it may impose a condition that the defendant is not to contact that witness. The condition is usually phrased in terms of no contact either directly or indirectly and will obviously cover telephoning the witness or having a family member or friend contact the witness.

10.33 Care should be taken to ensure that the condition is practicable, particularly if the defendant and witnesses attend the same school.

Reporting

10.34 When the court has good reason to fear that the accused may not surrender to his/her bail, the court may consider a condition of regular reporting to a specified police station. The frequency and times will be specified by the court.

10.35 Careful consideration should be given to the practicability of the condition and how onerous it will be for the accused in view of his/ her age. Particular problems may arise with the length of travelling time and the expense of travelling if public transport has to be used.

10.36   If the defendant is accommodated by a local authority in a children's home, it is submitted that a condition of signing at a police station is inappropriate. The police will be informed if the defendant absconds in any event and the condition will impose a considerable demand on the staff resources of the children's home who will have to accompany the defendant to the local police station.

Reporting as part of a bail support scheme

10.37   If a bail support centre exists in the locality, the defence lawyer may wish to seek to persuade the court to impose a condition of reporting to the scheme as an alternative to reporting to the police. In general it is likely that regular contact with a trained social worker will be more beneficial to the young defendant.

Surety

10.38   If the court is concerned about the risk of absconding one or more sureties may be taken before the defendant is granted bail.[19] A surety is a person who undertakes to guarantee the defendant's attendance at court. This guarantee is supported by the surety offering a sum of money, called the recognisance, which will be forfeited if the defendant fails to surrender to custody. Sureties may be taken in court before the magistrates, by a police inspector or by the governor of the remand centre or prison where the accused is held.

10.39   When considering whether a surety is suitable, the court may take the following into consideration:

– the surety's financial resources;
– his/her character and any previous convictions; and
– his/her proximity to the defendant (both in terms of relationship and geography).[20]

10.40   Before a court will accept a surety it will need to be satisfied that the proposed person is able to exercise sufficient influence over the defendant to ensure that s/he attends court. In the case of a child or young person the court will usually expect a parent or close relative to be the surety.

10.41   The defence lawyer should always ensure that the surety is a

19   Bail Act 1976 s3(4).
20   Ibid, s8(2).

suitable person and is prepared for the hearing. The following should be established:

- full name and address;
- relationship to defendant;
- what steps would be taken to ensure the defendant's attendance at court;
- amount of money available as recognisance;
- documentary proof of that money, eg, building society passbook;
- that the surety understands that all or part of the recognisance can be forfeited if the defendant absconds (and if the surety cannot pay the money as ordered by the court, s/he risks imprisonment); and
- whether the surety has any criminal convictions.

10.42   If the surety is taken in court, the surety will be asked to give sworn evidence regarding the above. Once satisfied with the surety's evidence a court will often indicate that the surety is accepted subject to police checks for criminal convictions. The court may indicate that a surety's obligation lasts only until the next hearing or until the disposal of the case.

10.43   If a surety cannot be taken immediately then the defendant cannot be released. In the case of a 17-year-old youth this would mean that s/he would be held in a remand centre or prison and in the case of a youth aged 16 years or under s/he would be remanded to local authority accommodation.[21] The defendant will be released on bail once the surety has been taken.

Security

If the court considers it unlikely that the defendant will surrender to custody, a security can be taken prior to his/her release.[22] A defendant would then have to lodge money, travellers' cheques or other valuables with the court to the value of the security required.

Co-operate with the preparation of a pre-sentence report

10.44   This is not a condition which would be imposed routinely following a conviction. However, if the child or young person has failed to attend appointments with the social worker or probation officer preparing the report, the court may want to adjourn again but this time imposing

---

21 Pursuant to Children and Young Persons Act 1969 s23 (see below).
22 Bail Act 1976 s3(5) as amended by Crime and Disorder Act 1998 s54(1).

such a condition. No doubt the court will wish to impress upon the defendant that missing any further appointments will result in the police being informed that s/he is in breach of bail, thus risking arrest.

Attend appointment with solicitor

10.45   The power to impose a condition to attend an appointment with a solicitor was created by the Crime and Disorder Act 1998 s54(2). The justification was to avoid unnecessary delays by ensuring that the unrepresented defendant obtained legal advice promptly, thus avoiding the need for further adjournments. The Home Office has confirmed that, in view of a solicitor's duty of confidentiality owed to the client, the court cannot expect the solicitor to report any breach of this condition to the police, instead the breach of the condition will be a factor to consider if a further application for an adjournment is made by the defence.[23]

Bail support

10.46   Bail support schemes provide support and supervision for defendants while on bail. Although still not very commonly available for adult defendants they are available for defendants aged under 18 in the majority of local authority areas.

Type of support

10.47   Most schemes which work with young offenders aim to help the defendants on the programme to comply with their conditions of bail and to provide constructive activities to occupy their time and lessen the risk of further offending. According to Gibson et al, *The Youth Court: One Year Onwards* (Waterside Press, 1994), the contents of bail support programmes vary across the country but may include:

- regular office reporting;
- monitored attendance at youth activities;
- monitoring of school attendance;
- programmes aimed at re-introducing the young defendant to school or to arrange specific educational provision;
- assistance with arranging training or finding employment;
- work with families to resolve conflicts and to ensure a continuing

---

23   Home Office Circular 34/1998 *New Bail Measures: Sections 54, 55 and 56 of the Crime and Disorder Act 1998*, paras 11 and 12.

home base for the young defendant and to involve the parents in taking more responsibility for their children's behaviour;

- supervision of any curfew imposed by the court;
- intensive supervision during the day; and
- placements with volunteers during the evening and weekends.

Importance of bail support

10.48 A defence lawyer who appears in the youth court should familiarise him/herself with the local bail support scheme. Whenever there is a risk that bail will be refused, it is advisable to make early contact with the scheme.

10.49 Particular problems arise when a young defendant appears at an adult Saturday remand court. In most parts of the country there is no emergency youth justice cover and so no possibility of presenting a bail support package to the court. Rather than proceed with a bail application which is doomed to failure, it might be worth arguing that the court does not have sufficient information upon which to make an application as the details of possible bail support are not known. The court could then be invited to postpone the bail decision under the Bail Act 1976 Sch 1 Part I para 5 and adjourn until the following Monday.

Parental surety

10.50 In the case of a defendant under the age of 17 the court may take a surety from a parent or guardian to ensure the defendant's compliance with any condition of bail imposed.[24] The parent or guardian must agree to stand surety and the recognisance must not be greater than £50. Such a surety may not be taken if the defendant will reach the age of 17 before the next hearing date.

10.51 A parental surety is normally sought by the court itself when it considers that there is a lack of parental control which is contributing to the defendant's offending. It is submitted that it is only an appropriate condition when there is clear evidence that the parent is in a position to exercise more supervision over his/her child.

10.52 The defence lawyer should consider carefully whether there is a conflict between the interests of his/her client, the defendant, and the parent if the court raises the possibility of such a surety. In particular

24 Bail Act 1976 s3(7).

the lawyer should consider how to respond to the court's invitation to comment on a proposed surety or to a request for details of a parent's means. Being seen to speak for the parent will inevitably result in the defence lawyer taking on the role of lawyer for the parent. As the parent stands to lose money as a direct result of the defendant's actions, it is doubtful that it is proper to act for both child and parent in such circumstances. Furthermore, there may very well be arguments against such a surety to put to the court. However, presenting such arguments is likely to be detrimental to the interests of the defendant.

Murder cases

10.53   In murder cases, if the court grants bail it shall impose a condition that the defendant undergoes a medical examination by two doctors unless it appears that suitable reports already exist. The court granting bail shall also impose a condition that the defendant attends at a particular place to enable the examinations to take place.[25]

Refusal of bail

10.54   The Children and Young Persons Act 1969 s23(1) provides:

> where–
>> (a) a court remands a child or young person charged with or convicted of one or more offences or commits him for trial or sentence; and
>> (b) he is not released on bail,
> the remand or committal shall be to local authority accommodation[26]

For the purposes of this section a young person is defined as 'a person who has attained the age of fourteen and is under the age of seventeen.[27] The situation in relation to accused persons under the age of 18 may be summarised as follows.

---

25   Ibid, s3(6A).
26   Subject to the provisions of Children and Young Persons Act 1969 s23(5).
27   Children and Young Persons Act 1969 s23(12).

17-year-olds

10.55 When a 17-year-old is refused bail, s/he is treated exactly like an adult and will be remanded into custody to be held in a prison, or remand centre (if one is available)

Juveniles

10.56 In the case of a defendant aged 16 or under, refusal of bail will normally result in a remand to local authority accommodation. The Children and Young Persons Act 1969 s23 has effect subject to:

 – Magistrates' Courts Act 1980 s37 (committal for sentence); and
 – Magistrates' Courts Act 1980 s128(7) (remand to police custody for further enquiries).[28]

In certain circumstances, when the stringent conditions of the Children and Young Persons Act 1969 s23(5) are satisfied, the court may make a secure remand.

Attaining 17 during the proceedings

10.57 If a defendant attains the age of 17 during a period of remand to local authority accommodation, it is the opinion of the authors that s/he would stay in that accommodation until the next hearing date. Thereafter, if the court refused bail again, s/he would be remanded to custody.

Remand to local authority accommodation

10.58 A remand to local authority accommodation will mean that a social services department will provide accommodation for the juvenile. Whilst remanded, the defendant will be treated for all procedural purposes as though s/he were remanded in custody.

Local authority accommodation

10.59 Local authority accommodation is defined by the Children Act 1989 s22.[29] It may include any of the following:

28 Ibid, s23(14).
29 See para 4.15.

- residential children's homes;
- remand foster placements;
- placement with members of the defendant's family.

In general, the local authority has considerable discretion as to the choice of accommodation, save that the court may stipulate that the defendant is not placed with a named individual (usually a parent).

To which authority?

10.60   The court must designate the local authority social services department which is to accommodate the defendant. In the case of a defendant already being looked after by a local authority, it shall be that authority. In all other cases it may be either:

- the authority in whose area it appears to the court that the defendant resides; or
- the authority in whose area the offence or one of the offences was committed.[30]

Obligations of the authority

10.61   In choosing how to accommodate the juvenile the local authority should bear in mind its obligations both to the court and to the juvenile.

Obligations to the court

10.62   The local authority must:

- ensure the juvenile's attendance at court;
- take all reasonable steps to protect the public from further offending by the juvenile.[31]

Obligations to the juvenile

10.63   A local authority has a duty to provide accommodation for a juvenile remanded to local authority accommodation.[32] While accommodated the juvenile is deemed to be 'a child who is looked after by a local

---

30   Children and Young Persons Act 1969 s23(2).
31   See para 4.43.
32   Children Act 1989 s21(2)(c)(i).

authority' within the meaning of the Children Act 1989 s22(1).[33] The local authority does not, however, acquire parental responsibility.[34]

Conditions on the remand

10.64　Having remanded the juvenile to local authority accommodation the court may require the juvenile to comply with such conditions as could be imposed under the Bail Act 1976 s3(6) if s/he were then being granted bail.[35] Before imposing any conditions upon the remand, the court must consult with the designated authority.

Consultation

10.65　Consultation for the purposes of s23 is defined as 'such consultation (if any) as is reasonably practicable in all the circumstances of the case'.[36]

Permissible conditions

10.66　Under the Bail Act 1976 s3(6) the court may only impose such conditions as it considers necessary:

- to ensure attendance at court;
- to prevent the commission of further offences;
- to avoid interference with witnesses or otherwise the obstruction of justice;
- to enable reports to be prepared for sentence; and
- to ensure that the defendant attends an appointment with his/her solicitor before the next court date.

Specifying the address

10.67　The remanding court may not impose a condition upon the juvenile to reside at a particular address.[37]

Sureties and securities

10.68　A court would be able to require the taking of a surety or the deposit of a security before the accused were released on bail. However, these

---

33 The local authority will need to implement a care plan and consult with the defendant and his/her parent(s) regarding the placement and plan: see para 4.23.
34 *North Yorkshire County Council v Selby Youth Court Justices* [1994] 2 FLR 169, QBD.
35 Children and Young Persons Act 1969 s23(7).
36 Ibid, s23(13)(b).
37 *Cleveland County Council v DPP* (1994) *Times*, 1 December, QBD.

powers are created by ss3(4) and 3(5) respectively. It is therefore submitted that a court would not be able to impose such conditions upon an accused as part of a remand into local authority accommodation.

Reasons for conditions imposed

10.69 When a court has imposed conditions upon a defendant as part of a remand into local authority accommodation it must explain to him/her *in open court* and in ordinary language why it is imposing those conditions. If the court is a youth or magistrates' court the stated reasons must be recorded in the court register and in the warrant of remand or commitment.[38]

Requirements on the authority

10.70 After consultation with the designated authority, the court may impose requirements upon the local authority to ensure that the defendant complies with his/her conditions of remand.[39] The court may stipulate that the authority shall not place the defendant with a named person (usually the parent or guardian whom the court considers is unable to exercise any control over the defendant).[40] No other negative requirements can be imposed upon the designated authority.

Secure remands

10.71 The Crime and Disorder Act 1998 ss97 and 98 introduce the possibility of a remand to local authority accommodation with a security requirement.[40A] Such a remand requires the designated local authority to place the defendant in secure accommodation.

10.72 A remand to local authority accommodation with a security requirement may not be imposed unless the defendant:

– has attained the age of 12;[41] and
– is legally represented.[41A]

---

38 Children and Young Persons Act 1969 s23(8).
39 Ibid, s23(9)(a).
40 Ibid, s23(9)(b).
40A Crime and Disorder Act 1998 (Commencement No 4) Order 1999 SI No 1279.
41 Children and Young Persons Act 1969 s23(5A) as inserted by Crime and Disorder Act 1998 s97(3).
41A Children and Young Persons Act 1969 s23(4A).

10.73 It may be imposed on both males and females but in the case of 15- and 16-year-old males, the remand will only be to a secure unit if the court:

- is notified that secure accommodation is available for the defendant; and
- is of the opinion that, by reason of his physical or emotional immaturity or a propensity of his to harm himself, it would be undesirable for the defendant to be remanded to a remand centre or prison.

If these further criteria are not satisfied, the remand will still be to a prison or remand centre.

Criteria for a secure remand

10.74 No secure remand can be made unless the following criteria are satisfied:

a) The defendant:
- is charged with or has been convicted of a violent or sexual offence, or an offence punishable in the case of an adult with imprisonment for a term of fourteen years of more,

or
- has a recent history of absconding while remanded to local authority accommodation, *and*
- is charged with or has been convicted of an imprisonable offence alleged or found to have been committed while he was so remanded; and

b) The court is of the opinion that only such a requirement would be adequate to protect the public from serious harm from him.

It is essential that both (a) and (b) are satisfied.

10.75 The criteria for a secure remand are complicated and need to be considered in detail. The criteria may be seen to fall into two parts. Paragraph (a) requires the court to identify facts from the defendant's past; paragraph (b) requires the court to look to the future and attempt to predict the level of risk the defendant poses to the public and whether that risk may be adequately contained in local authority accommodation.

'. . . has been convicted . . .'

10.76　The criterion may be satisfied not just by reference to the offences currently before the court but also by reference to the defendant's previous convictions.[42] This raises practical problems where the court is seeking to rely on a previous conviction but it does not have any details of the offence. As will be seen below, whether an offence satisfies the definition of a violent offence will depend on the circumstances of the offence. The Crown Prosecution Service may not be able to give the court any details of a previous conviction and the defence lawyer should argue in such circumstances that the conviction may not be relied upon to satisfy the criterion.

'Violent offence'

10.77　This is defined by the Criminal Justice Act 1991 s31 as:

> an offence which leads, or is intended or likely to lead, to a person's death or to physical injury to a person.

This definition does not include offences resulting in psychological injury only.[42A] Whether an offence is a violent one will depend on the individual circumstances of the offence.[43] In general the definition will be straightforward when dealing with offences against the person where actual physical injury is required as part of the offence. The situation may be less clear where the list of previous convictions reveals a conviction for common assault or assaulting a police officer in the execution of his/her duty. Such offence may be committed without any physical injury being likely or intended.

10.78　The same definition of a violent offence also applies where a court wishes to impose a longer than normal custodial sentence under the Criminal Justice Act 1991 s2(2)(b). In this context the phrase has been shown to be difficult to interpret. Some of the problem areas are considered below.

Driving offences

10.79　The offences of dangerous and careless driving will nearly always satisfy the definition of a violent offence. In many instances the offence of

---

42　*Re C (a Minor)* (1993) unreported, 22 October, per Kennedy LJ.
42A　*R v Robinson* (1992) 14 Cr App R (S) 448; [1993] 1 WLR 168, CA.
43　Ibid.

aggravated vehicle-taking will also be a 'violent offence', although there are likely to be occasions when the aggravated form of the offence is committed by reason of minor damage to another car when there was no likelihood of physical injury. In such instances it may be argued that the definition is not satisfied.

Threats to kill

10.80 An offence of threatening to kill which does not involve the infliction of actual physical injury is not a violent offence.[44]

'Sexual offence'

10.81 This is defined by the Criminal Justice Act 1991 s31[45] as follows:

- an offence under the Sexual Offences Act 1956, other than an offence under s30, 31 or 36 of that Act;
- an offence under the Mental Health Act 1959 s128;
- an offence under the Indecency with Children Act 1960;
- an offence under the Theft Act 1968 s9 of burglary with intent to commit rape;
- an offence under the Criminal Law Act 1977 s54;
- an offence under the Criminal Law Act 1977 s1 (conspiracy to commit any of the above);
- an offence under the Criminal Attempts Act 1981 s1 (attempting to commit any of the above); and
- an offence of inciting another to commit any of the above offences.

Prison term of 14 years or more

10.82 This would include robbery, if not already covered by the definition of a violent offence, as well as domestic burglary and handling stolen goods. It should be noted that the definition does not cover non-residential burglary (maximum sentence 10 years) and theft (maximum seven years).

10.83 This definition is the same as for grave crimes and the reader will find a full list of such offences in Appendix 4.

---

44 *R v Richart* (1995) 16 Cr App R (S) 977; [1995] Crim LR 574, CA.
45 As amended by Criminal Justice and Public Order Act 1994 s168(1) and Sch 9 para 45.

'. . . recent history of absconding . . .'

10.84   Each word in this phrase merits individual consideration:

Absconding

10.85   There is no statutory definition of absconding. It is likely to be interpreted loosely to mean any unauthorised absence from a children's
home or foster placement. In practice, absconding will often become
an issue when the prosecutor has been informed that the police computer indicates that a defendant has been reported 'missing from
care'. The defence lawyer should not accept this assertion on its own
as evidence that a child or young person has absconded in the past. All
children's homes impose a curfew and it is normal practice to report a
child as missing from care if s/he has not returned to the home by the
required time. If s/he returns to the home shortly afterwards the police
will be informed but the original computer entry will still exist. Being
late back to a placement in such circumstances cannot properly be
described as absconding.

History

10.86   Again there is no statutory definition but the term has been the subject
of judicial consideration in the context of two other statutory sections.
In *R v Crown Court at Southwark ex p Ager*[46] the Divisional Court had to
consider the meaning of the phrase 'a history of failure to respond to
non-custodial penalties' which was then contained in Criminal Justice
Act 1982 s1(4)(a), subsequently repealed. Judge J considered that the
word 'history' standing on its own suggested at least one previous
instance. The same view has been taken by the Family Division in the
unreported case of *R v Calder Justices ex p C (a Minor)*[47] which considered the criteria for authorising detention in secure accommodation under the Children Act 1989 s25.[48] The court considered that only
one instance of absconding would be sufficient to constitute a history
of such behaviour.

Recent

10.87   It is not enough that the court can identify instances when the defendant was absent from accommodation to which he was remanded.

46   (1990) 91 Cr App R 322.
47   (1993) unreported, 4 May.
48   See Chapter 11.

Those demonstrated instances must have been recent, a qualification which the court should be asked to construe in the context of the defendant's age and the rapid changes in his/her life. The defence advocate should seek to persuade the court to concentrate on any occasions in the last few months rather than dredging up occasions from several years earlier.

'. . . while remanded to local authority accommodation . . .'

10.88 A court cannot rely on any occasions when a child or young person has absconded from a foster placement or children's home, where the placement was purely for care reasons. However, a history of absconding from a care placement may be relevant if the criteria are satisfied in other ways and the court is considering whether any local authority accommodation is adequate to protect the public from serious harm.

Imprisonable offence

10.89 This is defined as an offence punishable in the case of an adult with imprisonment.[49] It is, therefore, irrelevant whether the court would be able to impose a custodial sentence upon the particular defendant in view of his/her age and sentencing restrictions in the youth court.

10.90 Note that the offence must have occurred during a period when the defendant had absconded from the local authority accommodation to which s/he was remanded.

'Serious harm'

10.91 This is defined by the Children and Young Persons Act 1969 s23(13)(c) as follows:

> Any reference, in relation to a person charged with or convicted of a violent or sexual offence, to protecting the public from serious harm from him shall be construed as a reference to protecting members of the public from death or serious personal injury, whether physical or psychological, occasioned by further such offences committed by him.

10.92 In relation to other offences there is no statutory definition but the defence lawyer may wish to refer the court to the Home Office's *Implementation Guidance: Court-ordered Secure Remands* (para 3.14):

49 Children and Young Persons Act 1969 s23(12).

'Serious harm' is not defined in relation to other offences. However, the definition for sexual and violent offences gives an indication of the gravity of the harm to which the public would need to be exposed from a young person in other circumstances before the test was likely to be satisfied.

10.93   The meaning of 'serious harm' in relation to offences not covered by the statutory definition has only been the subject of judicial consideration once in *R v Croydon Youth Court ex p G (a Minor)*.[50] A 15-year-old had appeared before the court charged with four domestic burglaries, handling stolen goods, criminal damage to a motor car and various motoring offences. These offences were allegedly committed over a three-month period. Since his first appearance at court he had breached the conditions of bail support and been arrested for failing to comply with the conditions of a remand to local authority accommodation. The justices remanded him into custody. The defendant applied for judicial review of that decision. In their affidavit the justices referred to the above statutory definition and said that they considered that any burglary caused psychological harm and that the number of offences allegedly committed by the defendant amounted to serious harm to the public in general. In quashing the remand into custody, Leggatt LJ stated:

> Though it would not be necessary to conclude that there was a risk of death or serious personal injury being caused, the Court would have to be satisfied that the young person whom they were minded to remand was liable to cause harm that could sensibly be described as serious on account of the nature of the offence or offences that might be committed and not merely of the risk of repetition.[51]

'. . . to protect the public . . .'

10.94   Section 23(5) gives no indication of how much of a general threat the defendant must present to the public. Guidance may perhaps be sought from the judicial authorities on the meaning of the term in similar statutory provisions in the Mental Health Act 1983 s43 and the Criminal Justice Act 1991 s2(2)(b). In both sections it has been decided that it is sufficient for the individual to pose a risk of serious harm to one member of the public.[52] As the wording and purpose of

---

50   (1995) *Times*, 3 May, QBD.
51   Court transcript p5.
52   *R v Birch*(1983) 11 Cr App R (S) 202, CA and *R v Hashi* (1995) 16 Cr App R (S) 121, CA (decisions on the Mental Health Act 1983 and Criminal Justice Act 1991 respectively).

the sections in these acts are similar to s23(5) it is likely that the same meaning would be given to the phrase in this context.

Identifying serious harm

10.95 The following propositions may be drawn from the judgment of Leggatt LJ in *R v Croydon Youth Court ex p G (a Minor)*(see above):

- the fact that a juvenile is charged with a violent or sexual offence or an offence punishable with 14 years or more does not by itself mean that he presents a risk of serious harm;
- a court may infer from the defendant's record that the public was liable to incur serious harm, having regard to the nature of the offences with which he has been charged, or of which he has been convicted, or the manner in which he had carried them out; and
- an apprehended series of offences, which individually could not constitute serious harm, could not be aggregated so as to render serious such harm as might be caused by them.

Satisfying the offence criterion

10.96 Handling stolen goods is an offence punishable with 14 years or more imprisonment but it will be exceedingly rare for the offence itself to indicate a risk of serious harm to the public. Leggatt LJ declared that domestic burglary would not necessarily satisfy the test and, to illustrate this, he gave the example of an offender who always burgles residential properties during the daytime, having checked that the occupants are out.

Relevance of the defendant's current offence(s) and previous record

10.97 An offender who has a criminal record which shows a pattern of street robberies with significant violence may have demonstrated by his record that he presents a risk of serious harm to the public. A single very serious offence allegedly committed by a young offender with no previous convictions is more problematic. In itself it may not be an indicator of potential risk.

Frequency of future offending

10.98 The court will often be faced with a young offender who is alleged to or has been found to offend frequently. It may have cogent grounds for fearing further multiple offences but that alone cannot satisfy the criterion of serious harm. The court must have reason to fear that the offender will commit a single offence which in itself will constitute serious harm to the public.

'Consultation'

10.99   This is defined by statute as:

> . . . such consultation (if any) as is reasonably practicable in all the circumstances of the case.[53]

This may seem a very limited requirement but the defence lawyer will wish to draw the court's attention to the view taken by Leggatt LJ:

> The point is not a formality. Its evident purpose is to inform the Court about the nature and suitability of the available local authority accommodation before it forms the opinion that only a remand centre would be adequate to protect the public from serious harm from a defendant.[54]

Alternative local authority accommodation

10.100   Even if the court is satisfied that the defendant presents a serious risk to the public, the court must still go on to examine what alternative non-secure accommodation options are available. Depending on the resources of the local authority, other accommodation may be available which will provide high levels of supervision for the defendant.

10.101   As soon as the defence lawyer realises that the court may be considering a secure remand, s/he should make contact with the designated local authority to establish what accommodation may be available. Since the reorganisation of social services departments to become service purchasers it is often a cumbersome process to identify a placement for any child. In many social services departments a placements officer will be involved in finding a placement and senior management will scrutinise the financial implications of any remand. The decision-making process may be even more complicated when the child concerned is accused of a violent or sexual offence where the authority must also assess the potential risk the defendant poses to other children in a residential setting.

---

53   Children and Young Persons Act 1969 s23(13)(b).
54   *R v Croydon Youth Court ex p G (a Minor)* (1995) *Times*, 3 May, court transcript p6.

Custodial remands for 15- and 16-year-old boys

10.102 Where the court is satisfied that the criteria of the Children and Young Persons Act 1969 s23(5) apply in relation to a 15- or 16-year-old boy, it will normally remand him to a prison or remand centre. The

---

Table 2: Maturity assessment objectives for 15-year-olds

1 Health
The young person is well, weight within normal limits for height. Ongoing health conditions and disabilities are being dealt with. The young person does not put their health at risk.

2 Education
The young person's educational attainments match their ability. They are acquiring leisure interests and participating in a range of activities. The young person has developed skills useful to employment.

3 Identity
The young person has a positive view of themselves and their abilities, has an understanding of their current situation. The young person has knowledge of their family of origin and can relate to their racial and ethnic background.

4 Family and social relationships
The young person has had continuity of care and has positive contact with birth family. The young person is able to make friendships with others of the same age.

5 Social presentation
The young person's appearance and behaviour is acceptable to young people and adults. The young person can communicate easily with others.

6 Emotional and behavioural development
The young person is free of serious emotional and behavioural problems or receiving effective treatment for all problems.

7 Self-care skills
The young person can function independently at a level appropriate to his/her age and ability.

Source: Department of Health, *Looking After Children*, 1995.

Table 3: Risk factors for suicide or self-harm in custody

- *Developmental immaturity*

- *Lack of stable background*
  Those who are in care or who have a history of broken placements have a significantly higher incidence of suicide and self-harm.

- *Victims of abuse*
  Victims of abuse, particularly sexual abuse, may have a sense of worthlessness and poor self-image.

- *History of truancy*
  As a result of bullying (as opposed to boredom or peer pressure).

- *The experience of loss*
  Whether by the death of a family member or broken relationship.

- *Social isolation*
  Not having contact with family, friends, social workers or other support networks.

- *Ethnic minority*
  May suffer racial abuse, which is a risk factor as it creates extra stress.

- *Gay young people*
  A vulnerable group, not directly as a result of their sexual orientation, but because of the lack of acceptance (and victimisation) they may experience.

- *History of previous self-harm*
  Teenagers who have already made a serious attempt on their lives are particularly likely to commit suicide. There are also risks when a member of the young person's family or friend has attempted or committed suicide.

- *Mental illness*
  Mentally ill young people are at particular risk; those suffering from depression or schizophrenia are very vulnerable. Sleeping difficulties, self-neglect, helplessness, confusion and cognitive rigidity are common signs of poor mental health.

- *Misuser of drugs, volatile substances or alcohol*
  The use of some illegal drugs increases impulsiveness.

- *No previous experience of custody*
- *Very short periods spent in the community between periods in custody*

Sources: A Liebling, *Risk and Prison Suicide* and J Lyon, *Teenage Suicide and Self-Harm* in H Kemshall and J Pritchard (eds), *Good Practice in Risk Assessment and Risk Management* (Jessica Kingsley Publishing, 1997).

court may, however, remand him to local authority accommodation with a security requirement if:

- it is of the opinion that, by reason of his physical or emotional immaturity or a propensity of his to harm himself, it would be undesirable for him to be remanded to a remand centre or prison;
- it is notified that a bed in a secure unit is available.[55]

Physical or emotional immaturity

10.103 Boys aged 15 and 16 will be at varying stages in their physical and emotional development. A proper assessment of a young person's maturity cannot be based on physical appearance alone. A more comprehensive assessment of an adolescent's development may be carried out by using the Department of Health's maturity assessment objectives (developed by the Dartington Social Research Unit) applicable to 15-year-olds (see Table 2 on p253). If the defendant has not met these objectives, he could be considered immature for his developmental age.

Risk of self-harm or suicide

10.103A Young prisoners do not cope well with the stresses of custody. Research has identified them as an 'at risk' group,[55A] particularly those on remand where the suicide rate is three times the rate in the general prison population.[55B] Some young people are more vulnerable

---

55 Children and Young Persons Act 1969 s23(5A) as inserted by Crime and Disorder Act 1998 s98.

55A A Liebling, *Risk and Prison Suicide* in H Kemshall and J Pritchard (eds), *Good Practice in Risk Assessment and Risk Management* (Jessica Kingsley Publishing, 1997).

55B H Grindrod and G Black, *Suicides at Leeds Prison: An inquiry into the deaths of five teenagers during 1988/89* (Howard League for Penal Reform, 1989). Between 1990 and 1998 14 boys aged 15 to 17 years have committed suicide in Prison Service establishments: see HM Inspectorate of Prisons, *Suicide is Everyone's Concern: A Thematic Review* (Home Office, 1999).

to self-harm and suicide than others. Some of the main risk factors relevant to young defendants are summarised in Table 3 on p254.

Assessment by the youth justice (or youth offending) team

10.104　Home Office guidance suggests that it is the responsibility of the designated local authority to draw the court's attention to the potential vulnerability of a young defendant.[55C] Draft guidance from the Youth Justice Board suggests that every child or young person at risk of a secure remand should be interviewed at court before the hearing. In the case of a 15- or 16-year-old boy this interview will involve an assessment of his vulnerability. The Board is developing the ASSET assessment tool to help court officers carry out this assessment in a comprehensive manner. The defence lawyer should establish that an assessment has been carried out and record the reasons given for the local authority's decision. Where the young client is not deemed to be vulnerable the defence lawyer should always ensure that this decision is justified. Where the conclusion is not accepted, s/he should be prepared to challenge the authority's assessment in court. This could involve cross-examining the representative of the youth justice (or youth offending) team.

Procedure in court

10.105　It should be noted that it is the court itself that must be satisfied that a young defendant is vulnerable. In practice, most youth courts are likely to accept that a defendant is vulnerable if this is the opinion of the local authority. In adult magistrates' courts and Crown Courts this may not be so straightforward. The defence lawyer, therefore, would be well advised to be prepared to make submissions to the court regarding the question of his/her client's vulnerability.

10.105A　Even where a court determines that a young defendant is vulnerable there may not be a place in a secure unit immediately available. In such circumstances, the remand will be to a remand centre or prison, but the defence lawyer should ask the court to remand for the shortest possible period to allow a place in a secure unit to be identified. The duty to have regard to a young person's welfare means that courts should be aware of the need to keep cases involving juveniles remanded in custody under constant review.[55D]

55C　*Implementation Guidance: Court-ordered Secure Remands*, para 3.18.
55D　Home Office Guidance, *Court-ordered Secure Remands*, para 3.23.

The contested bail application

10.106 The vast majority of occasions when children or young persons appear before a court there will be no problem regarding bail. However, in a significant minority of cases bail will be opposed by the prosecution either because of the seriousness of an individual offence or because of offending while on bail. In such circumstances a bail application can be extremely challenging as complex rules must be negotiated and an often complicated offending history must be dealt with.

Preparing the bail application

10.107 Before the hearing the defence lawyer should ensure that s/he speaks to:

- the prosecutor; and
- a representative of the youth justice (or youth offending) team.

Prosecutor

10.108 As youth courts are private hearings it is important to arrive before the court sits so that it is possible to speak to the prosecutor. As well as obtaining details of the current allegation, it is also important to establish what other information is held about the young defendant and what are the objections to bail. It is not uncommon to find prosecutors who are unfamiliar with the requirements of the Children and Young Persons Act 1969 s23(5) and it may be possible in preliminary negotiations to persuade him/her that there are no grounds to seek a secure remand.

Representative of the youth justice (or youth offending) team

10.109 All too frequently, defence lawyers fail to make use of this valuable resource. In many cases the youth justice officer will have had previous contact with the young defendant and will know him/her better than the lawyer. The officer will also have access to social services records which may provide useful background information. Most importantly, the officer may be able to provide resources in the form of accommodation or a bail support package. When the prosecution are vigorously opposing bail, a bail application supported by a youth justice officer with a well-presented bail support programme has a much greater chance of success.

Table 4: Preparing a bail application – checklist

General

1 Full name
2 Current address
3 Date of birth
4 Age
5 Remand rules applicable? juvenile/adult?

Domestic circumstances

6 Live at home?
   If yes:
   – name of parent(s)
   – occupation(s) and hours of work (if applicable)
   – able/willing to supervise bail conditions?
7 In care or looked after by local authority?
   If yes:
   – which local authority?
   – subject of full care order?
   – name of social worker/key worker?
   – reasons for being 'in care'.

Failure to surrender to custody

8 Does the client have previous conviction(s) for Bail Act offence(s)?
   If yes:
   – when?
   – penalty imposed?
   – what were the circumstances?
   – has s/he been granted bail since the last Bail Act offence?
9 Has the client previously surrendered to custody satisfactorily?
10 Possible conditions
   – a condition of residence? If client has no, or unsuitable address:
     – local authority willing to accommodate?
     – remand fostering scheme available?
     – (16- and 17-year-olds only) bail hostel available?
   – appropriate police station if reporting condition imposed?
   – reporting scheme as part of bail support?
   – where appropriate, the following information in respect of possible sureties: name; address; telephone number; occupation; relationship to client; any previous convictions; likely financial circumstances.
   – security?

Fear of further offences

11 Is client currently on bail?
    If yes:
    – date(s) imposed?
    – police or court bail?
    – alleged offence(s)?
    – how long on bail?
    – any conditions attached to bail?

12 Does client have previous convictions?
    If yes:
    – when and where sentence(s) imposed?
    – were any of them committed while on bail?
    – were any of them for similar offence(s) to offences(s) now charged?
    – have client's circumstances changed?

13 Have client's circumstances materially changed since these offence(s) allegedly committed?

14 How does client spend his/her week?
    – school
    – Youth Training Scheme
    – employment
    – structured leisure activities, eg, youth club, sports, etc
    – times of activities.

15 Possible conditions:
    – curfew? If so, would curfew be:
      – relevant (night time offending/to reinforce parental control)?
      – practicable?
    – not to go to scene of alleged crime? If so, would condition be:
      – relevant?
      – practicable?
    – availability of bail support?
    – parental surety?
    – are there other conditions that may be appropriate?

Interference with witnesses

16 Is the identity and address of any witness known to client?

17 Is there any history of threats allegedly made by client against any witness?

18 Possible conditions:
    – not to contact witness directly or indirectly? If so, would condition be feasible (eg, do the witness and defendant attend the same school)?
    – geographical exclusion? If so, would condition be practicable?

10.110   If the child or young person is appearing in the adult magistrates' court it is unlikely that a youth justice officer will be present at court. The court probation officer should be approached and asked to contact the relevant youth justice team. It may be necessary to persuade a member of the team to attend the court personally, particularly if a bail support package is to be proposed to magistrates unfamiliar with such programmes.

Instructions from the young defendant

10.111 As well as taking instructions specific to the allegation and the objections to bail, it is usually helpful to obtain more in-depth information regarding the young client's background. Relevant areas are contained in the checklist in Table 4 at pp258 and 259.

10.112   Such background information may indicate an underlying problem which if addressed is likely to lead to an end to the current offending. By seeking a bail support package which addresses those issues and problems, the objections to bail can be dealt with much more effectively.

10.113   Magistrates (particularly in adult courts) are sometimes reluctant to listen to descriptions of a young defendant's background and domestic circumstances. If faced with this response, the court should be reminded of its obligation under the Children and Young Persons Act 1933 s44 to have regard to the welfare of the child or young person.

The hearing

Structured decision-making

10.114 There is a real danger in bail hearings for juveniles that the very strict criteria of the 1969 Act are not applied because the prosecutor and the magistrates are allowed to turn the hearing into a discussion of why a secure remand should not be used. It is important for the defence lawyer to insist that the scheme of the legislation is followed. This requires the court to consider the following questions in order:

1) Are there substantial grounds for believing an objection to bail exists?
2) Can those objections be met adequately by conditional bail, perhaps with bail support?
3) If bail is refused, are the criteria of s23(5) applicable?

4) If yes, the court should consult with the local authority about possible accommodation and support available?

5) Is any type of local authority accommodation available which would be adequate to protect the public from serious harm from the defendant?

The court's decision-making process is shown as a flowchart in Table 5 at p263. As the provisions of the Children and Young Persons Act 1969 s23 only apply after a refusal of bail, the hearing should be split into two. First of all there should be a bail application and only if that is refused should there be further representations regarding a secure remand with the magistrates under a statutory duty to consult social services.

Presentation of the prosecution objections

10.115 The court has a duty to consider whether bail should be granted at each hearing whether or not the defence lawyer makes a bail application. The court will usually start by asking if the prosecutor has any objections to bail being granted. If any objections are raised, the prosecutor will usually start by summarising the allegation made against the defendant. A copy of the list of previous convictions (if any) will be handed to the court and the objections outlined with reference to the offence, previous record of the defendant and his/her current circumstances. Having heard the prosecutor's representations, the court will then hear the defence lawyer's representations regarding bail and any conditions.

10.116   In presenting the objections to bail the prosecutor may call a police officer to give evidence, although this will normally only be done in very serious cases. The strict rules of evidence do not apply and the court may consider hearsay evidence.[56] The defence may cross-examine any witness called as part of the prosecution presentation of objections to bail.

Procedural requirements

10.117 If, after consulting with the local authority, the court is of the opinion that the criteria of s23(5) are satisfied, the court must state in open court that it is of that opinion and explain to the defendant in open court and in ordinary language why it is of that opinion.[57] It is submitted

---

56 *R v Moles* [1981] Crim LR 170.
57 Children and Young Persons Act 1969 s23(6).

that the reasons given should be detailed and address the particular circumstances of the defendant and why the alternative accommodation would not be adequate.[58]

Options after a custodial remand

10.118 Once a defendant under the age of 18 has been remanded in custody, the reasons for that remand should be examined. It may, for example, be immediately obvious that a better bail support package would have been decisive. If this is the case, the defence lawyer needs to lobby the social services department for more resources to be allocated to the package. It should also be borne in mind that adult courts in general remand young defendants in custody much more frequently than youth courts and it may be important whether the defendant has now been remanded to the youth court.

10.119   Useful practical advice may be obtained from:

– the local youth justice (or youth offending) team;
– NACRO's Youth Crime Units; or
– the Children's Society Remand Review Initiative.

The options available depend on the age of the defendant.

17-year-olds

10.120 The options available are as follows:

– an immediate application for bail to a judge in chambers in the Crown Court or the High Court;
– a repeat bail application the following week; or
– a secure accommodation application.

Applications to judge in chambers

10.121 For a prompt re-hearing of the issues, such applications should be considered.[59]

Repeat bail applications

10.122 A defendant refused bail is always entitled to make one further bail application.[60] Thereafter, s/he may only apply for bail if it can be

58 To the authors' knowledge on two occasions High Court judges have given leave to move for judicial review on the basis that magistrates had given inadequate reasons. Neither application reached a full hearing.
59 See para 10.154.
60 Bail Act 1976 Sch 1 Part IIA para 2.

Table 5: A structural approach to bail for youth defendants

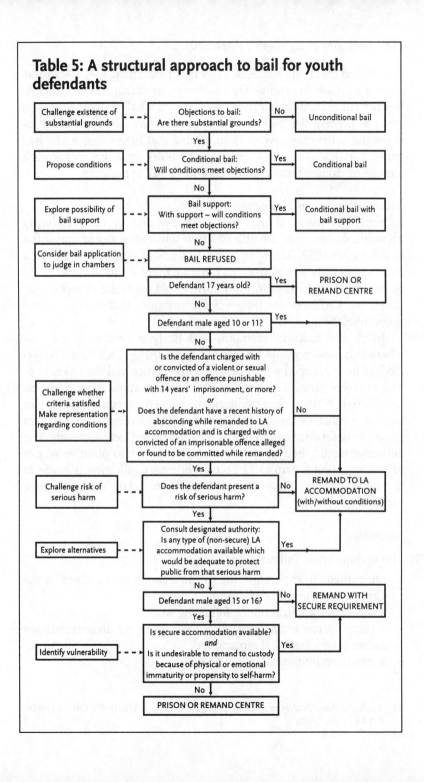

established that there has been a change of circumstances.[61] Attempts should be made to arrange for a bail support package to be available for any subsequent application, ideally with a bail support officer in court to present the package and to answer any questions and concerns the court may have. It is submitted that the existence of a bail support package or the presentation of a more intensive package is a change of circumstances justifying a fresh bail application.

Secure accommodation applications

10.123   Although 17-year-olds may not be remanded to local authority accommodation, they are still children within the definition of the Children Act 1989. Accordingly, if a 17-year-old was looked after by a local authority before a custodial remand, there would seem to be no reason in principle why a local authority could not make an application under the Children Act 1989 s25 for authority to detain in secure accommodation.

10.124   In view of financial restraints it is likely to be a very rare case where this option would be feasible. Nevertheless, where a 17-year-old has been charged with a very serious offence and the chances of bail are very slim, a secure accommodation application could be considered if there are substantial concerns regarding his/her welfare in custody. Such an application would require the court to grant the defendant bail to live as directed by the local authority. The authority would then need to exercise its power to place in secure accommodation for up to 72 hours while an application is made to the family proceedings court for authority to detain for up to three months.[62]

Juveniles

10.125   The options are as follows:

- an immediate application for bail to a judge in chambers in the Crown Court or the High Court;
- a repeat bail application the following week;
- an application for a remand to local authority accommodation rather than a custodial remand; or
- a secure accommodation application.

---

61   *R v Nottingham Justices ex p Davies* (1980) 71 Cr App R 178; [1981] QB 38; [1980] 2 All ER 775, QBD.
62   See Chapter 11.

Applications to judge in chambers

10.126 Once again such applications should ensure a prompt re-hearing of the bail application.[63]

Repeat bail application

10.127 As above for 17-year-olds.

Application for placement in local authority accommodation

10.128 It is arguable that, in contrast to applications for bail, there is no limit to the number of times an application can be made to the court for the issue of a custodial remand as opposed to a remand to local authority accommodation to be considered.[64]

10.129 The defence lawyer should ensure that the local authority takes an active part in the constant review of a juvenile's place of remand. The Department of Health has given the following advice:

> On each occasion that a juvenile is returned to the court for the remand to be reviewed, careful consideration should be given to advising the court whether alternative arrangements might be considered. For example, where a juvenile has been remanded to a penal establishment [under section 23(5)], the court may be willing to consider a remand to local authority accommodation if they are presented with a clear statement of how the juvenile would be accommodated within the care system in such a way that the public would be protected from the risk of further offending and that he would be produced in court when required.[65]

Bail enlargements

10.130 A youth or adult magistrates' court may remand the defendant in his/her absence in the following circumstances:

- when s/he has failed to attend through reason of illness or accident (applies to a defendant in custody or on bail);[66] or
- to enlarge the defendant's bail (that is appoint a later time for the defendant to surrender to custody).[67]

A court may also appoint a later time for a defendant to surrender to

---

63 See para 10.154.
64 See 'Does the *Nottingham Justices* rule apply to juveniles?' (1994) 158 JPN 233.
65 *The Children Act 1989 Guidance and Regulations* (HMSO, 1991) , Vol 1, Court Orders, para 6.39.
66 Magistrates' Courts Act 1980 s129(1).
67 Ibid, s129(3).

custody following a grant of bail by the police.[68] All the above powers may be exercised by justices' clerks under the Justices' Clerks Rules 1970 SI No 231.

Remanding in custody

General rule

10.131 When a youth or magistrates' court refuses bail the general rule is that the maximum period of remand is eight clear days.[69] This applies whether or not the defendant is subject to a secure remand.

Exceptions

10.132 There are two exceptions to this principle. Note that the former rule that these exceptions can only be applied if the defendant has attained the age of 17 has been removed by the Criminal Procedure and Investigations Act 1996 s52.[70]

28-day remand with consent

10.133 The court may refuse bail and remand a defendant to be produced within 28 days provided the defendant:

- is before the court;
- is legally represented in court; and
- consents not to be produced within eight days.[71]

28-day remand without consent

10.134 A court may remand in custody for up to 28 days without the defendant's consent provided:

- the defendant is before the court;
- s/he has previously been remanded for the same offence; and
- the court has set a date when it expects the next stage of the proceedings, other than a remand, to take place.[72]

---

68 Ibid, s43(1).
69 Ibid, s128(6).
70 This amendment only applies in cases where the offence was committed on or after 1 February 1997.
71 Magistrates' Courts Act 1980 s128(1) to (3).
72 Ibid, s128A(2).

10.135 Before making such a remand the court must:

- consider any representations the parties wish to make; and
- have regard to the total length of time which the defendant would spend in custody if it were to exercise the power.[73]

Remand to police custody

10.136 If a court refuses bail to a defendant it may remand him/her into the custody of the police if such a remand is 'necessary for the purpose of making inquiries into other offences'.[74] If so remanded s/he should be brought back to court as soon as the need ceases.

10.137 If the defendant is aged 17, the maximum period of such a remand is three days.[75] If the defendant is aged 16 or under, the maximum period is 24 hours.[76] It should be noted that this power of remand is not subject to the provisions of the Children and Young Persons Act 1969 s23 and therefore a refusal of bail would not mean a remand to local authority accommodation.[77]

10.138 The power is expressly stated to be subject to the right to bail contained in the Bail Act 1976. The court should first consider a full bail application and only if an exception to the right of bail is established should it then go on to consider whether there are grounds made out for a remand to police custody. If it is considered that there are such grounds, the court should still consider the length of the remand especially in view of the youth of the defendant(s). The defendant could already have spent considerably more than 24 hours in custody and a further remand to a police station to face further lengthy questioning could be oppressive.

Custody time limits

10.139 When a defendant is refused bail in the youth or magistrates' court the Prosecution of Offences (Custody Time Limits) Regulations 1987 SI No 299 reg 4 stipulates custody time limits. These limits, which apply equally to a juvenile remanded to local authority accommodation, are as follows.

---

73 Ibid.
74 Ibid, s128(7) and (8).
75 Ibid, s128(7).
76 Children and Young Persons Act 1969 s23(14)(b).
77 Ibid.

Either-way offences[78]

10.140 A maximum of 70 days between the defendant's first appearance and commencement of the summary trial or committal. If, before the expiry of 56 days, the court decides to proceed to summary trial, the maximum period between the defendant's first appearance and the commencement of the trial is 56 days.

Indictable-only offences

10.141 A maximum of 70 days between the defendant's first appearance and the date of committal.

Extension of the time limit

10.142 The prosecution may apply to the court for an extension to the time limit. This application must be made before the expiry of the time limit.

Procedure

10.143 The application may be made orally or in writing. Two days' notice must be given to the defence unless:

– the defence waives the requirement; or
– the court is satisfied that it is not practicable in all the circumstances to give such notice.

Grounds

10.144 The court must be satisfied that:

– there is good and sufficient cause for extending the time limit; and
– the prosecution has acted with all due expedition.

Expiry of the time limit

10.145 If no application is made for an extension or an extension is refused, the court must grant bail. The court may impose bail conditions but not a surety, security or other condition to be met before release.

---

78 This includes indictable-only offences which by virtue of the Magistrates' Courts Act 1980 s24 are triable summarily in the case of a child or young person: *R v Stratford Youth Court ex p S (a Minor)* [1998] 1 WLR 1758; 162 JP 552, QBD.

Appeals against bail by the prosecution

Right of appeal

10.146 Following a grant of bail[79] the prosecutor may appeal if the offence is:

- punishable by imprisonment of five years or more (in the case of an adult);
- taking without consent (Theft Act 1968 s12); or
- aggravated vehicle-taking (Theft Act 1968 s12A).[80]

The right of appeal only exists if the prosecutor made representations against the grant of bail before the magistrates' decision.[81]

Notice of appeal

10.147 Notice of the intention to appeal must be given orally to the magistrates at the conclusion of the proceedings and before the release from custody of the defendant.[82] Written confirmation of the notice of appeal must be served upon the court within two hours of the end of the hearing. If the written notice is not served within that period, the appeal is deemed to have been disposed of.[83]

10.148 Upon receiving oral notice of the intention to appeal the magistrates shall remand the defendant in custody. In the case of a defendant aged 16 or less this shall mean a remand to local authority accommodation.[84]

Legal aid

10.149 Legal aid for a prosecution appeal against bail is available under the Legal Aid in Criminal and Care Proceedings (General) Regulations 1989 SI No 344. It is covered by the criminal legal aid certificate issued by the magistrates' or youth court. Such an application is part of the core fee under the fixed fee regime.

---

79 This power is not available to challenge a court's failure to remand a juvenile in custody.
80 Bail (Amendment) Act 1993 s1(1).
81 Ibid, s1(3).
82 Ibid, s1(4).
83 Ibid, s1(5) and (7).
84 Ibid, s1(10)(b).

Procedure

10.150 The conduct of the hearing is governed by the Crown Court Rules 1982 SI No 1109 r11A. Notice of the hearing must be served upon:
  – the prosecutor;
  – the accused or his/her solicitor; and
  – the clerk of the youth or magistrates' court.

The appeal must be listed before a Crown Court judge within 48 hours of the oral notice of intention to appeal. In calculating this period Sundays, Christmas Day, Good Friday and bank holidays are ignored.[85]

10.151   The appeal is by way of re-hearing and the judge may remand the defendant in custody or grant bail with such conditions (if any) as s/he thinks fit.[86]

Defendant's presence

10.152 The defendant is not entitled to be present at the hearing of the appeal unless s/he is acting in person, or, in any other case of an exceptional nature, a Crown Court judge is of the opinion that the interests of justice require him/her to be present and the judge gives leave.[87]

Refusal of bail

10.153 If a Crown Court judge refuses bail on appeal and the case has not been committed for trial to the Crown Court, the prosecutor should invite the judge to remand the defendant for the same period as the magistrates would have been able to do if they had originally refused bail.[88] This will normally be for eight clear days.

Appeals for bail by the defence

Crown Court

10.154 Applications for bail are made to a Crown Court judge sitting in chambers. They are governed by the Crown Court (Amendment) Rules 1992 SI No 1847.

---

85   Ibid, s1(8).
86   Ibid, s1(9).
87   Crown Court Rules 1982 r11A(4).
88   *R v Governor of Pentonville Prison ex p Bone* (1994) *Times*, 15 November, QBD.

Legal aid

10.155 Legal aid for an application to a Crown Court judge in chambers is available under the Legal Aid in Criminal and Care Proceedings (General) Regulations 1989 SI No 344. It is covered by the criminal legal aid certificate issued by the magistrates' or youth court. Such an application is part of the core fee under the fixed fee regime.

Notice of application

10.156 Written notice of intention to apply for bail must be served on the Crown Prosecution Service and the relevant Crown Court at least 24 hours before the application. The notice must be in the form prescribed in Schedule 4 to the Rules. It will set out:

- the personal details of the applicant;
- the offences with which s/he is charged;
- details of any previous bail applications either to a court of summary jurisdiction or to a Crown Court;
- the objections to bail; and
- how it is proposed to meet those objections.

The notice should also be accompanied by:

- details of any surety;
- a list of any convictions recorded against the applicant; and
- a certificate of full bail argument issued by the youth or magistrates' court which refused bail.

Presence of applicant

10.157 The Crown Court Rules 1982 r19(5) states that the applicant shall not be entitled to be present on the hearing of his/her application unless the Crown Court gives leave.

Practical considerations

10.158 Before preparing any notice of application to the Crown Court it will be necessary for the defence lawyer to consider whether extra grounds will be needed for a successful application to a higher court. In particular, careful consideration should be given to any bail support package and whether its support can be improved.

10.159 It would be advisable to attempt to arrange for a youth justice social worker to be available at the court for the bail application. This will also allow the judge to ask questions regarding any bail support on offer.

10.160   A defence lawyer will always wish to proceed as quickly as possible when making a Crown Court bail application. Nevertheless, there may be delays caused by the Crown Prosecution Service or the Crown Court list office. These delays can be minimised by drawing the court's attention to the fact that the applicant is under 18 years of age. This may be done by sending the formal notice with a covering letter or even by telephoning the list office.

High Court

10.161   The application is made to a single judge in chambers. Such applications are governed by the Rules of the Supreme Court 1965 Ord 79. If refused, the application cannot be renewed before another judge or before the Divisional Court.

Legal aid

10.162   Applications to a judge of the High Court are not covered by criminal legal aid. Instead an application for civil legal aid must be made. It will be necessary to satisfy the Legal Aid Board that the application has a reasonable prospect of success. As the liberty of a person is involved it is possible to apply for emergency civil legal aid over the telephone. If granted, work can start immediately to prepare the application but the Legal Aid Board will seek an undertaking that the requisite application forms are returned within a specified number of working days.

Form of application

10.163   Application must be by way of a summons and it must be supported by an affidavit, usually sworn by the applicant's solicitor. This summons and affidavit must be served on the prosecution at least 24 hours before the return date, that is the date and time set for the hearing.

10.164   The summons should be in the form prescribed in the Rules of the Supreme Court, Ord 79 r9(2).[89] The affidavit should set out the history of the case so far, paying particular attention to the various bail applications made on behalf of the applicant. It should continue by outlining how the objections to bail could be met. Any documents which are enclosed with the application should be exhibited in the affidavit.

89 Form No 97 or 97A.

Presence of applicant

10.165 The Rules of the Supreme Court do not specify whether the applicant has any right to be present at the bail application. In practice s/he never is.

Review of bail granted

10.166 The Bail Act 1976 s5B allows the prosecutor to apply to a magistrates' or youth court for a review of court or police bail.

Power to apply

10.167 An application may only be made in relation to bail granted in respect of offences triable on indictment.[90] The application must be based on information not available to the court or custody sergeant who granted bail.[91]

Procedure

10.168 The application must be made on notice to the defendant but the court may proceed to consider the application even if the defendant does not attend.[92]

The court's powers

10.169 On hearing the application the court may:
- refuse to review the defendant's bail;
- vary the conditions of bail;
- impose conditions in respect of bail which has been granted unconditionally; or
- withhold bail.[93]

If the defendant is before the court s/he may be remanded in custody (subject to the provisions of the Children and Young Persons Act 1969 s23) or if absent a warrant for his/her arrest may be issued.[94]

---

90 Bail Act 1976 s5B(2).
91 Ibid, s5B(3).
92 Ibid, s5B(4).
93 Ibid, s5B(1).
94 Ibid, s5B(6).

When a defendant is arrested on the warrant s/he must be brought before a justice of the peace acting for the area where s/he was arrested within 24 hours. The justice shall then remand the defendant in custody (again subject to the provisions of the Children and Young Persons Act 1969 s23).[95]

Failing to answer bail

10.170 Any person bailed by either a custody officer or court is under a duty to surrender to custody.[96] The Bail Act 1976 makes it a criminal offence to fail to answer bail and empowers the court to issue a warrant for the defendant's arrest.

When has a defendant surrendered to his/her bail?

10.171 Surrendering to bail is defined as 'surrendering [himself/herself] into the custody of the court or of the constable (according to the requirements of the grant of bail) at the time and place for the time being appointed for [him/her] to do so'.[97] This definition is satisfied if the defendant arrives at the court building at or before the time specified but only if s/he also reports to the court employee who records the attendance of defendants. This will normally be the court usher or list caller.[98] Once the defendant has reported in this way s/he has answered bail and if s/he subsequently leaves the court building before the case is called this is not a breach of bail, although it may be a contempt of court. In such circumstances a warrant may still be issued under the Bail Act 1976 s7(2).

10.172 It should be noted that bail is granted to a particular time and if the defendant arrives at court after that time the condition to surrender to bail has been breached.

Bail Act offences

10.173 The Bail Act 1976 s6 creates two criminal offences relating to the failure to surrender to bail. The defendant is guilty of an offence if s/he:

---

95 Ibid, s5B(7) and (8).
96 Ibid, s3(1).
97 Ibid, s2(2).
98 *DPP v Richards* [1988] QB 701; [1988] 3 All ER 406.

- fails to surrender to custody without reasonable cause: s6(1); or
- having failed to surrender to custody with reasonable cause, fails to surrender to the appointed place as soon after the appointed time as is reasonably practicable: s6(2).

The second offence would be committed, for example, if a defendant was too ill to come to court on the day appointed but failed to surrender to the court as soon as s/he had recovered.

10.174　If the defendant is convicted of a Bail Act offence in a magistrates' court, the maximum penalty in the case of an adult is three months' imprisonment.[99] In the case of a child or young person detention in a young offender institution would be available.[100] If the defendant is convicted before the Crown Court, the offence is treated as a contempt of court and the maximum penalty for an adult is 12 months' imprisonment.[101] In the case of a child or young person there is some doubt whether a contempt of court may be punished by a custodial sentence.[102]

10.175　The burden of proving reasonable cause rests upon the defendant.[103] Although it is good practice to give a defendant a copy of the bail date, failure to give written notice of the bail decision cannot constitute reasonable cause.[104] It has also been held that it is not reasonable cause if the defendant mistakenly believes that the hearing date is later and so fails to attend court.[105]

A court's powers on the non-attendance of the defendant

10.176　Faced with the non-appearance of the defendant, the court will first seek confirmation that s/he was properly bailed to that time and place. If satisfied that this was the case, the court may:

- adjourn and enlarge the defendant's bail to a new court date;[106] or
- issue a warrant for the defendant's arrest.[107]

99　Bail Act 1976 s6(7).
100　Note that when detention and training orders are implemented, the minimum sentence will be four months and therefore it would appear that no custodial sentence could be imposed.
101　Bail Act 1976 s6(7).
102　See para 18.115.
103　Bail Act 1976 s6(3).
104　Ibid, s6(4).
105　*Laidlaw v Atkinson* (1986) *Times*, 2 August.
106　Magistrates' Courts Act 1980 s129.
107　Bail Act 1976 s7(1) (if the defendant surrendered to custody but then left the building, a warrant can still be issued under s7(2)).

10.177   Many courts will only consider enlarging a defendant's bail if there is information before the court that there is reasonable cause for the non-attendance, for example that s/he is too ill to attend. In the case of a child or young person, it is submitted that a court should be willing to be more flexible and consider the wider circumstances. As a parent or guardian is also expected to attend, the court should be asked to consider what responsibility can be reasonably placed upon the defendant. This will depend upon the age of the child or young person. If the defendant is known to be accommodated by a social services department, enquiries should be made through the youth justice officer or probation officer to see whether the reason for non-attendance may be established.

10.178   If the court decides to issue a warrant, it has a choice whether it should be backed for bail. Many courts demonstrate a marked reluctance to consider a warrant backed for bail. Nevertheless, the court's duty to consider the welfare of a child or young person requires a more flexible approach. The defence lawyer may wish to bring to the court's attention:

- the age of the defendant;
- whether in view of the youth of the defendant s/he would be expected to travel with a parent;
- the likely penalty (if the offence is minor);
- whether the child or young person has attended the court before and, therefore, whether it is likely s/he knows where it is; and
- if the defendant has previous convictions, whether the list reveals previous Bail Act offences.

The defence lawyer should also ensure that the court is aware that a warrant not backed for bail which is executed early in the weekend will result in the child or young person spending two nights in a police cell as the warrant gives the custody officer no discretion to transfer to local authority accommodation under the Police and Criminal Evidence Act 1984 s38(6).[108]

Execution of a Bail Act warrant

10.179   Once a warrant has been issued the defendant may come before the court voluntarily, by surrendering to the warrant, or as a result of being arrested by the police. Once before the court a decision must be taken whether a Bail Act charge will be preferred.

108   See para 5.194.

10.180   The Practice Direction (Bail: Failure to Surrender)[109] sets out the procedure to be followed when considering a Bail Act charge. First, the
direction distinguishes between failing to surrender to bail granted by
the police and bail granted by the court. In the case of police bail, the
Bail Act offence should be preferred by way of charge or information
and is subject to the normal six-month time limit.[110] In the case of court
bail, the failure to attend is tantamount to defiance of the court and no
charge or information needs to be preferred nor is the matter subject
to the six-month time limit.

10.181   The direction also sets out the procedure to follow in court. In the
case of police bail the charge is preferred at the discretion of the
prosecutor, whereas, in the case of court bail, the court invites representations from the prosecutor and then has a discretion to initiate
proceedings if it considers it proper to do so. If proceedings are then
initiated the prosecutor will conduct them and call evidence should
the matter be contested. Any trial regarding a Bail Act offence should
normally take place immediately after the disposal of the substantive
offence.

10.182   It is the practice of many courts to invite an explanation for the
non-attendance before the decision whether to initiate proceedings is
taken. This is good practice, particularly when dealing with a child or
young person. The Bail Act offences impose a high standard upon
defendants and it could very well be unrealistic to impose that standard on such a young defendant. Inviting an explanation before initiat-
ing proceedings allows the court to make allowance for explanations
which are reasonable in view of the defendant's age but which would
not strictly be accepted as 'reasonable cause' within the definition of
the Bail Act 1976 s6.

10.183   If proceedings are initiated, the matter should be put to the
defendant and s/he must give a clear indication of whether the offence
is admitted. S/he should then be given an opportunity to put forward
any mitigating circumstances.

Failure to attend after a local authority remand

10.184   When a juvenile is refused bail and remanded to local authority
accommodation, s/he is technically in custody. No specific legal

109   [1987] 1 WLR 79.
110   Magistrates' Courts Act 1980 s127.

obligation to attend court is therefore imposed upon the juvenile but an implied requirement is imposed upon the local authority to ensure that s/he is produced at the time and place. The juvenile does not commit a Bail Act offence if s/he fails to attend court and a s7 warrant may not be issued.

Absconding during the period of remand

10.185 During the period of remand to local authority accommodation a defendant who has absconded may be arrested without warrant.[111] Once arrested the absconder should be conducted to the local authority accommodation or to such other place as the designated local authority shall direct. Taking the absconder to the accommodation shall be at the authority's expense.

10.186   It is not clear what the police should do if the child or young person is not only an absconder but has also been arrested under the Children and Young Persons Act 1969 s23A in breach of a condition of that remand. Do the provisions of s32(1A) or s23A of the 1969 Act take precedence? The legislation is silent on the point, although in practice it is likely that the custody officer would choose to send the juvenile to court under s23A.

10.187   It is a criminal offence knowingly to compel, persuade, incite or assist another person to become or continue to be absent from local authority accommodation to which s/he has been remanded. The offence is summary only and is punishable by six months imprisonment or a fine at level five.[112]

Procedure on non-appearance of defendant

10.188 The court will normally wish to establish why the local authority has not brought the defendant to court. If it is clear that s/he will not be brought to court that day the youth or adult magistrates' court should mark the register 'defendant not produced'.[113] The court will then go on to consider whether it should issue a warrant under the Magistrates' Courts Act 1980 s13. Such a warrant may only be issued if the

---

111 Children and Young Persons Act 1969 s32(1A)(b)(ii).
112 Ibid, s32(3).
113 Not 'unlawfully at large' as the period of remand has ended and in any event a magistrates' court has no power to issue declaratory statements of status (see 'Practical Points' (1995) 159 JPN 660).

information is on oath. In the Crown Court there is no comparable statutory power to issue a warrant for the defendant's arrest.

Breach of conditions: enforcement

10.189 The conditions of bail or a remand to local authority accommodation can be enforced by the police but it should be noted that unlike failing to answer bail this is not a criminal offence.

10.190   The Bail Act 1976 s7(3) allows a constable to arrest without warrant a person released in criminal proceedings with a duty to surrender to the custody of a court if:

- s/he has reasonable grounds for believing that the accused is not likely to surrender to custody;
- s/he has reasonable grounds for believing that the accused is likely to break any conditions of bail;
- s/he has reasonable grounds for suspecting that the accused has broken any of the conditions of bail; or
- in a case where the accused was released on bail with one or more sureties, if a surety notifies the police in writing that the accused is unlikely to surrender to custody and the surety wishes to be relieved of the obligations of a surety.

When the accused has been remanded to local authority accommodation with conditions, the Children and Young Persons Act 1969 s23A allows a constable to arrest without warrant the accused but only if the constable has reasonable grounds for suspecting that s/he has broken any of the conditions of the remand.

Procedure on arrest

10.191 On arrest under either provision the custody officer is under an obligation to detain the child or young person at the police station until a court hearing can be arranged. As bail has not been refused by the custody officer following charge, the Police and Criminal Act 1984 s38(6) does not apply and there should not be a transfer to local authority accommodation.

10.192   The police must then bring the accused before a justice of the peace for the petty sessions area where the accused was arrested as soon as practicable and in any event within 24 hours of the arrest (for the purposes of calculating this time limit Christmas Day, Good Friday and any Sunday are ignored). If the arrest takes place within 24 hours of the time when the accused is due to surrender to custody, then the police should ensure that s/he is taken before the court which originally remanded him/her. If the accused is not produced before the court within the specified 24-hour period, then the court has no jurisdiction to deal with the alleged breach.[114]

Court procedure for breach of bail conditions

10.193   When the accused appears, the Bail Act s7(5) requires the court to consider whether the accused is likely to surrender to custody, or whether s/he has broken or is likely to break any of the conditions of bail. If the court is of that opinion, it may:

- refuse bail (in which case a 17-year-old will be remanded in custody and a defendant 16 or under will be remanded to local authority accommodation);
- grant bail subject to different conditions; or
- grant bail subject to the same conditions.[115]

If the court is not of the opinion that one of the factors in s7(5) is likely, then it must grant the defendant bail on the same conditions as before.

10.194   The way the hearing should be conducted has been examined by the Divisional Court in *R v Liverpool City Justices ex p DPP*.[116] It set out the following principles:

- there is no requirement for evidence to be given on oath and subjected to cross-examination;
- the Act contemplates the constable who has arrested the accused bringing him/her before the court and stating the grounds for believing that the accused has broken the conditions of bail; this may very well involve the giving of hearsay evidence;
- in fairness the court will allow the accused the opportunity to respond to what the constable says;
- the hearing may be before one justice of the peace; and
- there is no power to adjourn the proceedings, and therefore the court must reach a decision on the information available to it.

---

114   *R v Governor of Glen Parva Young Offenders Institution ex p G (a Minor)* [1998] 2 Cr App R 349; [1998] QB 877; [1998] 3 WLR 12; sub nom *In re G (a Minor)* 162 JP 225, QBD.
115   Bail Act 1976 s7(5).
116   (1992) 95 Cr App R 222.

Court procedure for breach of remand conditions

10.195 The Children and Young Persons Act 1969 s23A requires a court to determine whether any condition of the remand has been broken. If the court is of the opinion that a condition has been broken, the court must remand the accused. If the court is not of that opinion, then it must remand the accused into local authority accommodation, again on the same conditions unless an application for variation is made by the accused or the designated authority. No guidance has been given for the procedure to be followed during such a hearing but it is submitted that the guidelines in the *Liverpool City Justices* case are equally applicable.

10.196　In most circumstances the fact that the conditions of a local authority remand have been breached does not give the court any greater powers to remand in custody. For a custodial remand the criteria of s23(5) must still be satisfied and breach of remand conditions is only relevant so far as it may affect the court's assessment as to the adequacy of local authority accommodation to protect the public from serious harm.

Applications for variation of conditions

Police bail

10.197 Application for the variation of bail conditions imposed by the police may be made to:

- the custody officer who imposed the conditions or another custody officer serving at the same police station;[117] or
- the magistrates' court or youth court.[118]

In either case, the applicant risks the imposition of more onerous bail conditions being imposed, and in the case of an application to a court, the court does have the power to withdraw bail altogether.

Application to a custody officer

10.198 This might be considered where there has been a clear change of circumstances since the original grant of conditional bail, for example a condition of residence at the parental home was imposed and

---

117　Bail Act 1976 s3A(4).
118　Magistrates' Courts Act 1980 s43B.

the accused is now estranged from his/her parents and due to be accommodated by the local authority or a curfew was imposed and the accused has now obtained a job which requires him/her to be away from home after the time the curfew comes into force.

10.199   If the accused simply objects to the necessity of particular conditions, it is not expected that a custody officer will overrule a colleague and it is preferable therefore to a make an application direct to court.

Application to a court

10.200 Written notice must be served upon the custody officer at the police station where the accused was bailed and upon the court.[119] From a practical point of view a copy of the notice should also be sent to the Crown Prosecution Service. The notice must:

– contain a statement of the grounds upon which the application is made;
– specify the offence with which the defendant was charged; and
– specify the reasons given by the custody officer for imposing the bail conditions.[120]

No minimum period of notice is prescribed but it is unlikely to be practicable to make the application unless at least 24 hours notice is given. The time fixed for the hearing shall be not later than 72 hours after receipt of the application (no account being taken of Christmas Day, Good Friday, any bank holiday or any Saturday or Sunday).[121]

10.201   There may be problems in obtaining legal aid prior to an attendance at court as the court will not be in a position to process the application until a charge sheet has been received from the police.

Court bail

10.202 An application may be made to a court which granted conditional bail for the conditions of bail to be varied. The application may be made by the accused or somebody on his behalf as well as the prosecutor.

10.203   The application must be on notice to the court and the prosecution. No minimum period of notice is specified but in practice the court and prosecutor will need to be given reasonable time to ensure that their files are in court. It is the normal practice of most courts to

119   Magistrates' Courts Rules 1981 SI No 552 r84A(1).
120   Ibid.
121   Ibid, r84A(4).

consider applications before the main business of the day. The accused or his/her lawyer makes the application explaining why there has been a change of circumstances requiring the change of conditions. The prosecutor will be asked whether there is any objection to the variation and the court will then reach its decision.

10.204 The accused should be aware that upon an application for variation of bail conditions the court has the power to remove bail altogether. As the application may be made on behalf of the accused, it is not necessary for him/her to be present in court during the application. It is, however, wise to advise him/her to attend. The court may be reluctant to vary conditions if the defendant is not in court to have the new conditions explained to him/her. Attending court voluntarily (along with any parent or guardian) for the application also demonstrates that the child or young person takes the question of his/her bail conditions seriously.

High Court: jurisdiction

10.205 If a magistrates' court or youth court impose conditional bail, the accused may apply to the High Court for the removal or variation of those conditions.[122] The procedure for this is the same as a High Court application for bail.

Remand conditions

10.206 After an accused has been remanded in local authority accommodation with conditions, the accused or the designated authority may apply for the conditions to be varied or revoked.[123] In addition the designated authority may apply for any requirements imposed upon itself to be varied or revoked.[124]

10.207 The application must be made to a relevant court which is defined as 'the court by which [the accused] was so remanded, or any magistrates' court having jurisdiction for the place where [s/he] is for the time being.'[125]

10.208 A designated local authority may apply to the relevant court for a declaration that the criteria for a secure remand apply.[126] This power

---

122 Note that no such application may be made to the Crown Court.
123 Children and Young Persons Act 1969 s23(11).
124 Ibid.
125 Ibid, s23(12).
126 Ibid, s23(9A).

exists under the current provisions for a custodial remand and will also apply to 15- and 16-year-old males under the provisions to be introduced under the Crime and Disorder Act 1998 ss97 and 98. Such an application might be made when the juvenile refused bail behaves in such a way that the local authority considers it can no longer perform its duties to protect the public from injury.

Secure accommodation

For complete chapter contents, see overleaf

Introduction

11.1 This chapter considers the use of secure accommodation in all other contexts other than a court-directed remand to local authority accommodation with a security requirement.[1] The use of secure accommodation by local authorities is controlled by the Children Act 1989 s25 and the Children (Secure Accommodation) Regulations 1991 SI No 1505. Within the context of criminal proceedings secure accommodation may be used for a looked after child when s/he has been:

- detained by the police and transferred to local authority accommodation;
- remanded to local authority accommodation;
- bailed to reside as directed by a local authority and subsequently placed in local authority accommodation;
- made subject to a supervision order with a residence requirement.

It should be noted that local authorities are subject to a general duty to take reasonable steps to avoid the need for children in their area to be placed in secure accommodation.[2]

Definition

11.2 The Children Act 1989 defines 'secure accommodation' as 'accommodation provided for the purpose of restricting liberty'.[3] Such accommodation must be registered with the Department of Health and at present is run by local authorities, although there is now provision for secure accommodation to be run by other bodies.[4]

Placement in secure accommodation

11.3 A child may only be placed in secure accommodation in strictly defined circumstances.

---

1   For which see para 10.71.
2   Children Act 1989 Sch 2 Part I para 7(c).
3   Ibid, s25(1).
4   Criminal Justice and Public Order Act 1994 s19.

General criteria

11.4   The Children Act 1989 s25(1) provides:

> A child who is being looked after by a local authority may not be placed, and, if placed, may not be kept in accommodation provided for the purpose of restricting liberty ('secure accommodation') unless it appears:
> (a) that–
> > (i)   he has a history of absconding and is likely to abscond from any other description of accommodation; and
> > (ii)   if he absconds he is likely to suffer significant harm; or
> (b) that if he is kept in any other description of accommodation he is likely to injure himself or other persons.

Child

11.5   This means any person under the age of 18.[5]

Looked after

11.6   This obviously includes children subject to full care orders under the Children Act s31 and children looked after by a local authority under s22(1).[6] A defendant remanded on bail with a condition to reside as directed by a local authority is 'looked after' by that authority and, therefore, may be placed in secure accommodation.[7]

11.7   It should be noted that young people aged 16 or 17 who are accommodated in children's homes under the Children Act 1989 s20(5) are not subject to the power to place in secure accommodation.[8]

History of absconding

11.8   One previous instance of absconding is sufficient.[9]

---

5   Children Act 1989 s105.
6   Note that a 'looked after' child is defined as a child in the care of a local authority or a child provided with accommodation by the authority for a continuous period of 24 hours. It is arguable that this prevents the placement in secure of a child not previously looked after by the authority.
7   *Re C (a Minor) (Secure Accommodation: Bail)* [1994] 2 FCR 1153, FD.
8   Children (Secure Accommodation) Regulations 1991 SI No 1505 (amended by 1992 SI No 2117) reg 5(2)(a).
9   *R v Calder Justices ex p C (a Minor)* unreported, 4 May 1993.

Any other description of accommodation

11.9　As with the criteria for a remand with a security requirement this is an important consideration.[10] The court must satisfy itself that no other accommodation available is suitable. The local authority should therefore be in a position to identify what other accommodation has been considered and to explain why the other options are not considered adequate.

11.10　The Department of Health has issued guidance to local authorities considering the exercise of their powers under s25:

> Restricting the liberty of children is a serious step which must be taken only when there is no appropriate alternative. It must be a 'last resort' in the sense that all else must first have been comprehensively considered and rejected – never because no other placement was available at the relevant time, because of inadequacies in staffing, because the child is simply being a nuisance or runs away from his accommodation and is not likely to cause significant harm in doing so, and never a form of punishment. It is important, in considering the possibility of a secure placement, that there is a clear view of the aims and objectives of such a placement and those providing the accommodation can fully meet those aims and objectives. Secure placements, once made, should be only for so long as is necessary and unavoidable. Care should be taken to ensure that children are not retained in security simply to complete a pre-determined assessment of 'treatment' programme.[11]

Significant harm

11.11　The Children Act 1989 s105 states that the definitions and guidance in s31 of the Act shall apply.[12]

Modified criteria for detained and remanded children

11.12　The Children (Secure Accommodation) Regulations 1991 SI No 1505 reg 6 modify the criteria for the use of secure accommodation in the case of:

1) a detained juvenile transferred to local authority accommodation under the Police and Criminal Evidence Act 1984 s38(6); and

---

10　See para 10.100.
11　Department of Health, *The Children Act 1989: Guidance and Regulations* (HMSO, 1991) Vol 4, Residential Care, para 8.5.
12　See para 4.26.

2) a defendant refused bail and remanded to local authority accommodation under the Children and Young Persons Act 1969 s23 who is either:

– charged with or convicted of a violent or sexual offence or an offence punishable in the case of an adult with imprisonment for a term of 14 years or more; or

– who has a recent history of absconding while remanded to local authority accommodation, and is charged with or has been convicted of an imprisonable offence alleged or found to have been committed while he was so remanded.

The criteria in (2) above are the same as those required before a court can remand a juvenile with a security requirement under Children and Young Persons Act 1969 s23(5).[13] In such cases the criteria for the use of secure accommodation are reduced to read as follows:

A child who is being looked after by a local authority may not be placed, and if placed, may not be kept, in accommodation provided for the purposes of restricting liberty . . . unless it appears that any accommodation other than that provided for the purpose of restricting liberty is inappropriate because–

(a) the child is likely to abscond from such other accommodation, or

(b) the child is likely to injure himself or other people if he is kept in any such other accommodation.

Children under the age of 13

11.13 The Children (Secure Accommodation) Regulations 1991 SI No 1505 reg 4 provides:

A child under the age of 13 years shall not be placed in secure accommodation unless it has been approved by the Secretary of State for such use and approval that is subject to such terms and conditions as he sees fit.

In practice, where a local authority is considering the use of secure accommodation for a child of this age, the advice of the Social Services Inspectorate at the Department of Health should be sought in the first instance. Out of office hours there is provision for approval to be sought through the Department of Health duty service.

13 See para 10.74.

Placement without court authority

11.14   When the criteria are satisfied, a local authority may place a child in secure accommodation for a maximum of 72 hours (in any 28-day period) without seeking the authority of a court.[14] If the authority wishes to keep the child in secure accommodation for a longer period it must seek the authority of a court.

Role of the court

11.15   The court's duty is to determine whether any relevant criteria for keeping a child in secure accommodation are satisfied.[15] If a court determines that any such criteria are satisfied, the court is required to make an order authorising the child to be kept in secure accommodation and specifying the maximum period for which s/he may be kept.[16]

11.16   The role of the court has been considered by the Court of Appeal in *Re M (Secure Accommodation Application)*.[17] The court held that it was the duty of the court to put itself in the position of a reasonable local authority and consider, first, whether the criteria were satisfied and, secondly, whether it would be in accordance with the local authority's duty under Children Act 1989 s22(3) to safeguard and promote the welfare of the child by placing him/her in secure accommodation. Although the welfare of the child was a relevant consideration, it could not be the paramount one as the local authority was permitted to exercise its powers in relation to the child to protect members of the public from serious injury.[18]

Which court?
Remand under CYPA 1969 s23

11.17   The Criminal Justice Act 1991 s60(3) provides:

> In the case of a child or young person who has been remanded or committed to local authority accommodation by a youth court or a

14   Children (Secure Accommodation) Regulations 1991 SI No 1505 reg 10(1).
15   Children Act 1989 s25(3).
16   Ibid, s25(4).
17   [1995] 2 All ER 407; [1995] 1 FLR 418; [1995] 2 FCR 373.
18   See Children Act 1989 s22(6).

magistrates' court other than a youth court, any application under section 25 of the Children Act 1989 (use of accommodation for restricting liberty) shall . . . be made to that court.

The application for authority to place in secure accommodation must, therefore, be made to a youth court or magistrates' court and not a family proceedings court.

11.18   In *Liverpool City Council v B*[19] the question arose whether the application had to be made to the particular court which remanded the defendant. Ewbank J sitting in the Family Division held that the term 'that court' in s60(3) was a generic term and allowed an application to any court of that type. The section merely required that the application be made to a youth court as opposed to a family proceedings court. It has been suggested that a court to which a case has been remitted under the Children and Young Persons Act 1933 s56(1) may not consider an application under s25 until it has remanded the defendant.[20] A similar practical problem may arise when an adult magistrates' court has remanded a child or young person to a youth court under the Children and Young Persons Act 1933 s46(2).

11.19   Where a juvenile is committed to stand trial there is no provision for the Crown Court to authorise the use of secure accommodation under the Children Act 1989 s25. It is the view of the Home Office that as a result of s60(3) such authority should be sought from the youth court or adult magistrates' court which committed the juvenile.[21]

Civil

11.20   In other circumstances an application for authority to place in secure accommodation must be made to a family proceedings court.[22] Rather confusingly this also applies to a defendant remanded on bail with a condition of residence as directed by social services.[23]

---

19 [1995] 1 WLR 505; [1995] 2 FLR 84.
20 (1992) 156 JPN 208.
21 *Implementation Guidance: Court-ordered Secure Remands*, para 3.10.
22 Children (Allocation of Proceedings) Order 1991 SI No 1677 art 3(1)(a) and Children Act 1989 s92.
23 *Re W (Secure Accommodation Order: Jurisdiction)* [1995] 2 FCR 708, FD.

Legal aid

11.21 No court may authorise the use of secure accommodation for a child who is not legally represented unless, having been informed of the right to apply for legal aid and having had an opportunity to do so, s/he has refused to do so.[24] Legal aid must be granted where a child is brought before a court on an application for authority to detain in secure accommodation.[25]

11.22 The Department of Health also gives the following guidance:

> Children should be encouraged to appoint a legal representative in such proceedings and given every assistance to make such arrangements . . . The child in such circumstances should have details of local solicitors on the Law Society's [Children Panel] made available to him and should be assisted in making contact with the solicitor of his choice.

11.23 Non-means, non-merit tested legal aid is available for the child in relation to a secure accommodation application. The defence solicitor should complete form CLAIM4. As long as the completed form is received by the Legal Aid Board within three working days, the legal aid certificate will cover all work done from the date when the form was signed by the solicitor.

11.24 It is the opinion of the Legal Aid Board that a form CLAIM4 need not be completed if the child is already represented in criminal proceedings to which the s25 application relates as any secure accommodation would come within the scope of the criminal legal aid order as defined by the Legal Aid Act 1988 s19(2).[26]

Powers of the court

Interim orders

11.25 On any adjournment of the hearing of an application for authority to place in secure accommodation the court may make an interim order permitting the child to be kept during the period of the adjournment in secure accommodation.[27]

---

24 Children Act 1989 s25(6).
25 Legal Aid Act 1988 s15(3B) as inserted by Children Act 1989 s99.
26 *Legal Aid Handbook 1998/99* (Sweet & Maxwell, 1998), Notes for Guidance, para 8.03.
27 Children Act 1989 s25(5).

Length of authorisation

11.26   This depends on whether the application is made in a remand case or a civil case.

Remand to local authority accommodation under CYPA 1969 s23

11.27   The authorisation may only be for the period of the remand and in any event no longer than 28 days.[28] Authority must therefore be sought at every remand hearing.[29]

Civil

11.28   Authority may be given in the first instance for up to three months.[30] On subsequent applications the court may authorise a child to be kept in secure accommodation for a further period not exceeding six months at any one time.[31]

11.29   For the purposes of calculating the period of authorisation any interim order must be included.[32]

Procedure

Youth or adult magistrates' court

11.30   The procedure is governed by the Magistrates' Courts (Children and Young Persons) Rules 1992 Part III.[33]

Notice of application

11.31   The local authority making the application must send the relevant court a notice specifying:

– the grounds for the application; and
– the name and addresses of the people upon whom notice must be served.

No minimum period of notice of the application is specified.

---

28   Children (Secure Accommodation) Regulations 1991 SI No 1505 reg 13.
29   This will cause considerable practical problems during the course of a Crown Court trial.
30   Children (Secure Accommodation) Regulations 1991 SI No 1505 reg 11.
31   Ibid, reg 12.
32   *C (a Minor) v Humberside County Council and another* (1994) *Times* 24 May.
33   SI No 2071.

11.32 Notice of the application along with the time and date of the hearing must also be given to the following:

- the child who is the subject of the application;
- the parent or guardian[34] of the child, if the whereabouts of such parent or guardian is known to the local authority or can be readily ascertained; and
- where the father and mother of the child were not married to each other at the time of the birth, any person who is known to the local authority to have made an application to acquire parental responsibility which has not yet been determined.[35]

Failure to give the requisite notices may render any authority to detain in secure accommodation invalid.[36]

Guardian ad litem

11.33 There is no provision permitting a court to appoint a guardian *ad litem*.

The hearing

11.34 As far as practicable the court must arrange for copies of any reports in support of the local authority's application to be made available to:

- the defence lawyer;
- the parent or guardian; and
- the child or young person, unless the court considers that it is impracticable to do so having regard to his/her age and understanding or undesirable to do so having regard to potential serious harm which might thereby be suffered by him/her.[37]

11.35 The court must inform the child or young person of the general nature both of the proceedings and the grounds upon which they are brought. Such an explanation must be in terms suitable for his/her age and understanding.[38] If a child or young person is not legally represented, the court must allow a parent or guardian to conduct the case on the defendant's behalf, unless the child or young person

---

34 For the definition of parent and guardian in these rules see para 7.24.
35 Rule 14(2) and (3).
36 Cf, *D v X City Council* [1985] FLR 275.
37 Rule 21(1).
38 Rule 17.

requests otherwise.[39] If it thinks it appropriate the court may allow another relative or other responsible person to conduct the case on behalf of the child or young person.[40]

11.36 The procedure for the hearing is set out in the Magistrates' Courts Rules 1981 SI No 552 r14. It should start with the local authority representative addressing the court and thereafter calling any evidence in support of the application. Written statements or reports will have to be adduced in evidence to support the application. At the conclusion of the evidence for the local authority, the lawyer for the child or young person may address the court and thereafter call any evidence. The local authority may call rebuttal evidence. At the conclusion of the evidence, the defence lawyer may address the court if s/he has not already done so. Either party may with the leave of the court address the court a second time. If leave is obtained, the address by the defence should precede that of the local authority.

11.37 The child or young person may be excluded from the hearing unless s/he is conducting his/her own case, if the court considers that evidence will be presented which it is not in the interests of the child or young person to hear. Any evidence relating to the character or conduct of the child or young person must be given in his/her presence.

11.38 If a court determines that the criteria for detention in secure accommodation are satisfied, it must then go on to consider the length of the period of authorisation. In reaching this decision it must take into consideration such information as it considers necessary for the purpose, including such information regarding the background of the child or young person provided by the local authority pursuant to its obligations under the Children and Young Persons Act 1969 s9.[41]

Family proceedings court

11.39 An application to the family proceedings court for authorisation to detain in secure accommodation is governed by the Family Proceedings Courts (Children Act 1989) Rules 1991 SI No 1395 (as amended by SI 1991 No 1991 and SI 1992 No 2068). An application under s25 is defined as specified proceedings.[42]

39 Rule 18(1).
40 Rule 18(2).
41 Rule 21(2): for the duty under s9 see para 16.4.
42 Rule 2(2)(a).

Notice of application

11.40 The local authority must file a notice of application on the prescribed form with the clerk of the justices with sufficient copies for each respondent.[43]

11.41 Notice of the application along with the time and place of the hearing must be served upon the following:

- the child or young person; and
- any parent with parental responsibility.

A minimum period of one day's notice must be given.[44]

Guardian ad litem

11.42 As the application for authorisation falls within the definition of specified proceedings, a guardian ad litem should be appointed by the clerk to the court as soon as practicable after the commencement of the proceedings, unless it is considered unnecessary so to do in order to safeguard the interests of the child.[45] Once a guardian has been appointed, the defence solicitor is required to act on the instructions received from the guardian. If the child wishes to give contrary instructions to those of the guardian, the solicitor may act upon the child's instructions, if, having taken into account the views of the guardian, the solicitor considers that the child is able, having regard to his/her understanding, to give instructions on his/her own behalf.[46]

The hearing

11.43 The child need not be present during the application. It has been suggested that the court should only allow his/her attendance if it is satisfied that it would be in the interests of the child.[47]

11.44 Subject to any directions from the justices' clerk the various parties to the proceedings should address the court in the following order:

---

43 Family Proceedings Rules 1991 SI No 1247 (as amended) r4.4.
44 Family Proceedings Courts (Children Act 1989) Rules 1991 r4(1)(b) and Sch 2 column (ii).
45 Rule 10(1).
46 Rule 12(1)(a).
47 *Re W (a Minor) (Secure accommodation order: attendance at court)* [1994] 2 FLR 1092, FD.

- the representative of the local authority making the application;
- any person with parental responsibility;
- the guardian ad litem;
- the child, if there is no guardian ad litem.[48]

Before the court announces its decision the justices' clerk must record in writing the names of the justices constituting the bench and the reasons for the court's decision and any finding of fact.[49]

Right of appeal

11.45   The defendant has a right of appeal against the authorisation of detention in secure accommodation. The local authority may also appeal the denial of authorisation. Irrespective of the court which heard the original application, the right of appeal lies to the Family Division of the High Court.[50]

Review of secure placement

11.46   A local authority looking after a child in secure accommodation is required to review the placement in such accommodation within one month of the start of the placement and then at intervals not exceeding three months.[51] This review is separate from the statutory review process required in relation to a looked after child.

11.47   The authority is required to appoint three persons to review the placement. At least one of those persons must be neither a member nor an officer of the authority by or on behalf of which the child is being looked after. Having regard to the welfare of the child in question, the persons appointed to review the placement shall satisfy themselves as to whether or not:

- the criteria for keeping the child in secure accommodation continue to apply;
- the placement continues to be necessary; and
- any other description of accommodation would be appropriate.[52]

---

48   Rule 21(3).
49   Rule 21(5).
50   Children Act 1989 s94(1).
51   Children (Secure Accommodation) Regulations 1991 SI No 1505 reg 15.
52   Ibid, reg 16(1).

11.48   If practicable the local authority must ascertain the wishes and feelings of:

- the child;
- any parent;
- anyone with parental responsibility;
- persons having had care of the child;
- the independent visitor (if appointed); and
- the authority managing the secure accommodation.[53]

The authority shall, if practicable, provide information to those it has consulted about what action in intends to take in relation to the child in the light of the review.[54]

---

53   Ibid, reg 16(2).
54   Ibid, reg 16(3).

The trial process

For complete chapter contents, see overleaf

Introduction

12.1　The trial of a child or young person will most commonly take place in the youth court. A smaller number will take place in the Crown Court or in the adult magistrates' court with one or more adults.

12.2　The trial of a child or young person presents particular problems for the defence lawyer. Taking instructions on the facts of the case may be more difficult than in the case of an adult client; the parent may be involved in the trial process and wish to intervene in the solicitor/client relationship; the age of the defendant may have implications for the evidential and procedural requirements in the trial; and his/her limited maturity will influence the tactical approach to the trial and the question of whether the juvenile should be advised to give evidence.

Pre-trial preparation

Taking instructions

12.3　The main difficulties in taking instructions from a child or young person arise from lack of opportunity and impaired communication. Young clients frequently fail to maintain adequate contact with the defence lawyer before trial, failing to make and/or keep appointments. This may be due to a chaotic lifestyle, lack of maturity, failure to take the proceedings seriously, fear of the consequences or a parental failure to ensure arrangements are made. As a consequence lawyers should achieve as much as possible in any contact with the client during the proceedings. There may be only one or two hearings before the trial date but these should be used as fully as possible to take instructions and consider trial preparation. Many youth courts and most Crown Courts have private interview rooms where conditions of confidentiality can be achieved and, as waiting periods at court may be prolonged, instructions may be taken quite fully at the early hearings. At adult magistrates' courts interview rooms are far less common and it may be impossible to achieve appropriate conditions.

12.4　The defence lawyer will always need to bear in mind the age and level of understanding of the child or young person when taking instructions. The practical considerations of taking instructions from a young client are considered in more detail in Chapter 2.

Advance disclosure

12.5   Advance disclosure of the prosecution case is only strictly required in respect of either-way offences.[1] Although this may be rigidly observed in the case of adult defendants, many Crown Prosecution Service branches will make voluntary disclosure in most cases involving a child or young person. This will rarely be automatic and defence lawyers should, therefore, write to the relevant office to request disclosure in all cases. This will greatly facilitate the taking of instructions in even the simplest case.

12.6   Where the prosecution refuse to make advance disclosure, consideration should be given to making detailed representation in favour of voluntary disclosure, based on the facts of the particular case and the principle that the welfare of the child or young person is best served by consideration of the prosecution case before the trial date. In the case of indictable-only offences to be tried in a youth court, it should also be pointed out that full disclosure would take place in the case of an adult tried on indictment and therefore it would be unfair to the child or young person to be placed is a less advantageous position.

Evidential considerations

Exclusion of evidence

12.7   The common law and the Police and Criminal Evidence Act 1984 ss76 and 78 apply to children and young persons just as much as they apply to adult defendants. In addition to the various reasons for excluding evidence applicable to defendants of all ages,[2] the defence lawyer needs to consider whether any comments made by a juvenile in the absence of an appropriate adult are admissible. PACE Code C para 11.14 requires that any interview of a juvenile must be conducted in the presence of an appropriate adult unless it is an emergency covered by Code C para 11.1 or Annex C. It follows that any interview conducted in the absence of an appropriate adult risks being excluded at trial.

---

1   Magistrates' Courts (Advance Information) Rules 1985 SI No 601 as amended by SI 1992 No 2072.
2   See Levenson, Fairweather and Cape, *Police Powers* (LAG, 3rd edn, 1996), Chapter 11.

Urgent interviews

12.8   If the police claim to have interviewed under one of the exceptions the defence lawyer should examine whether those grounds existed and also in the case of an interview in the police station that the requisite authority was obtained.

Questioning at the time of arrest

12.9   The courts have been willing to exclude admissions made by a juvenile at the time of arrest on the basis that the conversation amounted to an interview[3] but in another case the court ruled that the conversation which followed the arrest was not an interview but 'questions at or near the scene of a suspected crime to elicit an explanation which if true would exculpate the suspect'.[4]

12.10   The question has been most recently considered by the Court of Appeal in the case of *R v Weekes*[5] in which Farquharson LJ stated:

> It is very difficult . . . to draw a line between what is an interview for the purposes of the Code and what is not. When a police officer is in the street seeking information and trying to establish whether there are grounds for arresting a suspect, it is absurd to suppose that before questioning a juvenile he has to wait until a parent has been summoned to the scene. Such enquiries are not within the meaning of the word 'interview' as contemplated by the Code.
>
> But if the police officer persists in his questioning, beyond the point it is necessary for his purposes at the time, it may be that the protection of the Code is invoked, even though the conversation is taking place in the street or in a police car on the way to the police station. Like most of these problems it depends on the judge's assessment of the position in the light of all the circumstances. Is the nature, length, sequence and place where the enquiries takes place such that the person questioned is entitled to the protection of the provisions of the Code concerning interviews?
>
> The essence of the matter is whether fairness demands that in the circumstances of a particular case the provisions of the Code should be implemented; in other words, one does not construe the word 'interview' as one would in a statute. One looks at what is fair in the light of the provisions of the Code.

Farquharson LJ obviously takes a very pragmatic view of the ques-

---

3   For example, *R v Delroy Fogah* [1989] Crim LR 141, Snaresbrook Crown Court.
4   *R v Maguire (Jason)* (1990) 90 Cr App R 115, CA.
5   (1993) 97 Cr App R 227.

tion of when an appropriate adult's presence is required. This judgment was delivered before the 1995 edition of the Police and Evidence Act Codes inserted Code C para 11.1A which clarified the definition of an interview. Although it is probably still correct to say a police officer may question a juvenile in the street in suspicious circumstances as soon as the officer suspects the juvenile of a specific offence s/he should caution the juvenile and any further conversation constitutes an interview as defined by Code C para 11.1A.

Modifying the procedure at trial

12.11 The European Convention on Human Rights art 6 guarantees an accused person a fair hearing. In *V v UK*[5A] the European Court of Human Rights stated that it was not sufficient for the purposes of art 6 that a child defendant was represented by skilled and experienced lawyers. Taking account of the young defendant's age, level of maturity and intellectual and emotional capacities, the trial court should take steps to promote the defendant's ability to understand and participate in the proceedings.

12.12 The steps that need to be taken will depend on:

– the particular defendant; and
– the venue and complexity of the trial.

Age, level of maturity and capacities of the defendant

12.13 Prior to the trial hearing the defence lawyer should always consider the level of maturity and intellectual capacities of the client. If possible, enquiries should be made to establish the client's educational attainment. Where there is any doubt concerning the client's ability to participate in the trial process, the defence lawyer will need to obtain a psychological assessment of the young client.

Venue and complexity of the trial

12.14 The demands made on a young defendant by the trial process will vary enormously. Greater demands will be placed on a young defendant where:

5A Judgment delivered 16 December 1999 (Application no 24888/94) (see (1999) *Times*, 17 December). See also para 3.26ff.

- the trial is in the Crown Court rather than the youth court;
- the trial involves many witnesses;
- the trial is likely to be lengthy for other reasons;
- the defendant is likely to testify; or
- the defendant has few sources of social support.[5B]

Possible modifications

12.15 There are many possible modifications to trial procedure which will help a young defendant to understand and participate in the proceedings more effectively. A checklist of possible modifications is contained in Table 6 on p308. Whether any of these modifications is appropriate will depend, of course, on the particular young defendant and the circumstances of the trial.

Doli incapax

12.16 As discussed in Chapter 4 the presumption of *doli incapax* has been abolished for offences committed on or after 30 September 1998. The trial advocate still needs to be alert to the possibility that the presumption will still apply to offences committed before that date where the defendant was under the age of 14. The existence of the presumption of *doli incapax* will influence the cross-examination of prosecution witnesses and the formulation of submissions at the close of the prosecution case.

12.17 In cases where doli incapax still applies, the prosecution must satisfy the court that the presumption has been rebutted beyond reasonable doubt. This burden must be discharged by the close of the prosecution case as is clear from the opinion of Lord Lowry in *C (a Minor) v DPP*[6]:

> It is quite clear that as the law stands, the Crown must, *as part of the prosecution case*, show that the child is *doli capax* before the child can have a case to meet. [original emphasis]

At the close of the prosecution case, when the defence propose to submit that the prosecution have not rebutted the presumption and additionally that there is no prima facie case in relation to one or

5B For a detailed analysis of the situational demands of the trial process for a young defendant, see T Grisso, *Forensic Analysis of Juveniles* (Professional Resource Press, 1998).
6 [1995] 2 Cr App R 1, HL.

Table 6: Modifications to the trial procedure – checklist

To reduce the formality of the proceedings
- Refer to defendant by his/her first name.
- Removal of wigs and gowns by judge and barristers (in Crown Court).
- Allow defendant to leave dock.

To enable the defendant to follow the testimony of prosecution witnesses
- Ask all witnesses and advocates to avoid as much as possible complex language during the course of evidence.
- Help the young defendant to concentrate during the proceedings by adjourning for short breaks regularly.

To facilitate communication between defendant and his/her lawyer
- Allow defendant to sit next to trial advocate.
- Encourage young defendant to seek explanations when development in proceedings is not understood.
- Adjourn on regular basis to allow the trial advocate to check his/her client's understanding.

To minimise the potential distress and inhibition caused by a public trial
- Imposition of reporting restrictions (Children and Young Persons Act 1933 s39).
- Exercise of common law power to sit *in camera*.

To facilitate the effective testimony of the young defendant
- Use of simple language in examination-in-chief and cross-examination.
- Questions to contain only one idea.
- Use of screen while defendant testifying.
- Clearing court (if public hearing) while defendant testifies in a case involving an offence against, or any conduct contrary to, decency or morality (Children and Young Persons Act 1933 s37).

To ensure adequate social support during the trial
- Presence of a parent or guardian in close proximity to defendant.
- Access to parent, guardian or other carer during adjournments in the court day.

more of the charges, the court might be invited to deal first with the *doli incapax* issue. If the court finds that the presumption has not been rebutted, the case against the accused child must be discharged and there would be no need to hear the submission on the charges. The defence may take the view that this approach has the advantage of clarity and simplicity in the presentation of the relevant issues.

12.18   Alternatively the court has an unfettered discretion to proceed to hear submissions on *doli incapax* and on the charges at the same time. It is essential that defence advocates are alert to this and that any submission on *doli incapax* is clearly distinguished from a submission in relation to the charges. The court should then be invited to consider whether the presumption has been rebutted first.

Failure to mention facts relied on at the trial

12.19   The Criminal Justice and Public Order Act 1994 s34 allows a court to draw such inferences as appear proper where at any time before an accused was charged with an offence s/he failed to mention a relevant fact relied on in his/her defence in those proceedings.

12.20   The fact must be one which, in the circumstances existing at the time, the accused could reasonably be expected to mention. When a very young accused failed to mention such facts, there are a number of factors which might be relevant in persuading the court that no inference should be drawn.

Did the accused understand the caution?

12.21   The new caution is complicated. A survey carried out with A-level students found that a significant proportion did not understand its meaning. The full implications of any caution given in the absence of a legal adviser may not have been understood by a child or young person and this must be carefully checked with the young client when taking instructions in preparation for trial.

What facts did the child or young person have while being questioned?

12.22   Section 34 only permits the drawing of inferences where the fact was actually known to the suspect at the time of any questioning under caution. The actual knowledge of the particular child or young person must be carefully checked. The relevance of facts which might have been obvious to an adult may be less so to a child or young person.

Was it reasonable for the child or young person to have withheld facts?

12.23 Even where the child or young person is aware of the relevant facts, there may be good reason why s/he did not mention them. The test of whether it was reasonable to mention facts is subjective and therefore the failure should be assessed in the light of the age of the accused. Circumstances which might carry no weight at the trial of an adult may be highly material in the trial of a child or young person. A young suspect might fail to mention relevant facts because of a fear of parental disapproval or of getting friends into trouble. There may be reasons specific to childhood such as truanting from school or fear of bullies. The reason for failing to mention facts may be the young suspect's acceptance of advice from a lawyer, parent or other appropriate adult. In view of the age difference the adult will inevitably exercise authority or great influence over the child or young person. It may, therefore, be argued that accepting advice from an adult in such circumstances would be reasonable.

What was the condition of the accused?

12.24 Where a child or young person is suffering from a condition which justifies failure to mention relevant facts, this must be fully presented to the court. Such conditions may include a learning disability, drug abuse, medical or mental illness. All such conditions might provide adequate reasonable grounds to justify failure to mention facts later relied on at trial.

12.25 It may be necessary to adduce expert medical or psychiatric/ psychological evidence or to call a teacher or social worker. If the child or young person has been assessed as having special educational needs, the defence lawyer may wish to obtain a copy of the statement as a first step in exploring this issue. The statement will include assessments by teachers, doctors, child therapists and educational psychologists. If no copy of the statement is available at home, a copy may be requested from the relevant education authority.[7]

What happened at the charging procedure?

12.26 Different rules apply to the failure to mention facts at the charging procedure. The court may draw such inferences as appear proper

7 See para 14.12.

where, on being charged with the offence or officially informed that s/he might be prosecuted for it, an accused failed to mention any fact relied on in his/her defence in those proceedings.[8]

12.27   Where an accused child or young person is charged without the benefit of legal advice, it may be argued that it would be unreasonable to expect the significance of this stage to be apparent to him/her. It should, however, be noted that this provision does not depend on the accused understanding the legal implications of silence; the section is based on the assumption that an innocent person (of whatever age) would normally be expected to volunteer facts which tend to show innocence. This assumption should be at its weakest in the case of a child or young person who may have many reasons, including fear of parental reaction, for remaining silent.

12.28   Where failure to mention facts at the charging stage is the result of legal advice, the defence advocate should argue that a child or young person could not be reasonably expected to reject such advice. Similar considerations apply if the suspect was told to remain silent by a parent or other appropriate adult.

Failure to account for marks, etc, or presence at the scene

12.29   No inference may be drawn unless from a failure to account for articles, marks etc and presence at the scene of a crime unless a special warning has been given.[9] The rules regarding the contents of a special warning are highly complex and are frequently ignored by interviewing officers. The defence lawyer should always listen to a taped interview to check that the form of any special warning complies with the requirements of the Codes of Practice. The lawyer should also consider the form of words used by the officer and whether it is likely that the child or young person would have understood the actual warning given.

12.30   Failures to account for information under ss36 and 37 may form part of the prosecution case and inferences may be drawn, whatever the nature of the case. The prosecutor may, therefore, open the facts by mentioning these failures.

12.31   Sections 36 and 37 do not include any reasonableness criterion which may justify the failure by the accused to account for presence, objects, etc. However, this does not prevent the defence advocate from

8   Criminal Justice and Public Order Act 1994 s34(1)(b).
9   PACE Code C para 10.5B.

putting forward circumstances which the court might accept as nullifying any need to draw an inference.

The trial

Role of the parent or guardian

12.32 Where the defendant is under 16 year of age, a parent must attend unless the court dispenses with this requirement.[10] This may cause particular problems when the parent is also a witness in the proceedings. This must be considered in advance and arrangements need to be made for the other parent or another adult relative or friend to attend in addition to the witness/parent.

12.33 When a parent is present during the trial s/he will normally sit beside the young defendant. The parent should be advised that any comments the child or young person makes to the parent should be communicated to the advocate so that an assessment may be made of its relevance and further instructions taken. With a defence lawyer present the parent will not be expected to play any part in the trial itself (other than as a witness) and this should be adequately explained before the trial commences. In contrast, where the child or young person is not legally represented, the court must allow the parent or guardian to conduct the case on behalf of the defendant.[11]

Taking instructions during the trial

12.34 It may be necessary to take instructions as the trial proceeds, either because the prosecution failed to disclose in advance or because new matters arise. Depending on the age of the defendant it may be necessary to request that the trial is stood down so that instructions may be taken in private and away from the pressure of the courtroom; or even to apply for an adjournment to another date. The court may be more indulgent of such delay in the case of a child or young person as long as it is in the interests of justice but this is not an invariable approach. Some courts may need to be presented with strong reasons for such an application and the defence lawyer should

---

10 Children and Young Persons Act 1933 s34A.
11 Magistrates' Courts (Children and Young Persons) Rules 1992 SI No 2071 r5(1).

always remind the court of its duty to consider the welfare of the child or young person.[12]

Failure to give evidence

12.35 The Criminal Justice and Public Order Act 1994 s35 allows a court to draw such inferences as appear proper from the failure of the accused to give evidence or refusal without good cause to answer questions while in the witness box. This section does not apply in three circumstances set out in the Act.

The accused is under the age of 14

12.36 This exception only applies in the case of defendants tried for offences committed before 30 September 1998.[13] Section 35 does not specify when the age of the accused should be determined but it has generally been taken to be the age of the accused at the time of the trial. Taking this further, it should probably be construed to mean the age of the accused when the opportunity to give evidence at the trial arises.

Physical or mental condition

12.37 Where it appears to the court that the physical or mental condition of the accused makes it undesirable that s/he should give evidence, no inference may be drawn against the accused.

12.38 This provision applies to all accused persons of whatever age. 'Physical or mental condition' is not further defined in the section. This means that mental condition need not be limited to mental illness but could arguably include learning disability or very limited communication skills. The court will require evidence to be adduced before accepting that this ground is made out. The Court of Appeal in *R v Cowan*[14] held:

> It could not be proper for a defence advocate to give to the jury reasons for his client's silence at trial in the absence of evidence to support such reasons.

12.39 In *R v Friend*[15] it was argued that the low IQ of a 15-year-old defendant charged with murder meant that no adverse inference

---

12 Children and Young Persons Act 1933 s44.
13 Crime and Disorder Act 1998 s35 and Sch 9 para 2.
14 [1995] 2 Cr App R 513; [1995] 3 WLR 881; [1995] 4 All ER 939.
15 [1997] 2 Cr App R 231; [1997] 2 All ER 1011.

should be drawn from his failure to testify. Expert psychological evidence was called to show that the defendant had an IQ of between 56 to 63 (comparable to a mental age of about nine years). He was also virtually illiterate with a reading age of a six-year-old. Based on this expert evidence it was contended that it would be wrong to leave the possibility of drawing an adverse inference to the jury. The judge disagreed. He pointed out that there was no evidence that the defendant was unusually suggestible and that it was not unknown for nine-year-old witnesses to testify in the Crown Court. Applying a test of *Wednesbury* unreasonableness, the Court of Appeal refused to interfere with the judge's decision. Otton LJ stated that it would only be in very rare cases that a judge would have to consider whether it is undesirable for an accused to give evidence on account of his/her mental condition. He continued that in the majority of such cases there would be evidence that the accused was unfit to plead.[16]

Statutory warning

12.40 No inference may be drawn unless the court is satisfied at the conclusion of the prosecution case that the accused is aware that s/he can give evidence and that an adverse inference may be drawn if s/he does not.[17] The younger the accused, the more important it is this is observed and that the position is explained to the accused in non-technical language.

The child or young person as witness

Competence

12.41 A child witness shall give unsworn evidence.[18] A witness, who is a young person, must give sworn evidence in the same way as an adult witness.

12.42 The former statutory requirement upon a court to enquire whether a witness of tender years had sufficient intelligence and understanding to be a witness of truth has been repealed.[19] A court shall receive a child's evidence unless it appears to the court that the

---

16 [1997] 2 Cr App R 231, at 239–240. For fitness to plead see para 3.28.
17 Criminal Justice and Public Order Act 1994 s35(2). See also *R v Price* [1996] Crim LR 736, CA.
18 Criminal Justice Act 1988 s33A(1).
19 Criminal Justice Act 1991 s52 repealing Children and Young Persons Act 1933 s38(1).

child is incapable of giving intelligible testimony.[19A] If there is any doubt about a young witness' understanding, the court should ask him/her questions to establish the issue, before the start of the testimony proper. In the Crown Court this should be done by the judge in the presence of the jury and the accused.[20]

Compellability

12.43 A competent witness may be compelled to attend court to testify. In the youth court this will be done by the issue of a summons or arrest warrant under the Magistrates' Courts Act 1980 s97. A magistrates' court has no discretion to refuse to issue a witness summons against a child or young person once it has determined that the witness could give useful evidence. The duty to consider the welfare of a child or young person cannot be relevant at this stage. The welfare principle is, however, relevant at the moment when it is desired to call the child or young person.[21]

12.44 If a witness under the age of 18 attending or brought before the court refuses to give evidence, the court's powers are extremely limited. In the case of an adult the witness may be fined or committed to custody.[22] Children and young persons are excluded from this power by virtue of the Criminal Justice Act 1982 s1(1). They are similarly excluded from the power to commit to custody for contempt of court.[23]

Video recordings of children's evidence

12.45 By the Criminal Justice Act 1988 s32A a pre-recorded video interview between a child witness (other than the accused) and an adult may be admitted in relation to certain offences as evidence of anything of which the child could have given evidence in chief. Such video evidence may only be given in trials in the Crown Court or the youth court.[24]

19A Criminal Justice Act 1988 s33A(2A).
20 *R v Dunne* (1929) 99 LJKB 117.
21 *R v Highbury Corner Magistrates' Court ex p Deering* (1997) 161 JP 138; [1997] Crim LR 59, QBD.
22 Magistrates' Courts Act 1980 s97(4).
23 See para 18.115.
24 The use of video-recordings is governed by the Crown Court Rules 1982 SI No 1109 r23C and in the case of youth courts by the Magistrates' Courts (Children and Young Persons) Rules 1992 SI No 2071 r24. See also *Practice Note* [1992] 3 All ER 909.

Child witness

12.46   A child is defined as follows:
  - for a sexual offence it means a person under the age of 17; and
  - in relation to other offences it means a person under the age of 14.

12.47   If the video recording was made of the witness' evidence when s/he was under the relevant age, then the relevant age is increased by one year to 15 years and 18 years respectively.[25]

Applicable offences

12.48   Video testimony may be received in relation to the following offences:
  - an offence which involves an assault on, or injury or a threat of injury to a person;
  - an offence under Children and Young Persons Act 1933 s1 (cruelty to persons under 16);
  - an offence under the Sexual Offences Act 1956, the Indecency with Children Act 1960, the Sexual Offences Act 1967, the Criminal Law Act 1967 s54 or the Protection of Children Act 1978; and
  - an offence which consists of attempting or conspiring to commit, or of aiding, abetting, counselling, procuring or inciting the commission of, an offence listed above.

Leave of the court

12.49   Video testimony may only be admitted with the leave of the court. Such leave may not be granted if it appears to the court that:
  - the child witness will not be available for cross-examination;
  - any rules regarding the disclosure of the video evidence have not been complied with; or
  - having regard for all the circumstances of the case, it is not in the interests of justice to admit the recording.[26]

Evidence through television link

12.50   By virtue of the Criminal Justice Act 1988 s32A a witness (other than the accused) who is under the age of 14 or is to be cross-examined following the admission of a video recording of testimony by him/

25   Criminal Justice Act 1988 s32A(7).
26   Ibid, s32A(3).

her may give evidence by way of a live television link. This provision applies to trials in both the Crown Court and the youth court, but only for the applicable offences listed above (see para 12.48).[27]

Proceeding in the absence of the defendant

12.51 A youth court or adult magistrates' court may proceed with a trial in the absence of the defendant.[28] Before the justices decided to proceed in absence they should consider all the circumstances of the case. In *R v Dewsbury Magistrates' Court ex p K (a Minor)*[29] the Divisional Court considered a youth court's decision to proceed in absence. The defendant was 16 years old. He had been charged with domestic burglary and remanded to local authority accommodation. He had no history of failing to attend court. His trial was listed and it was accepted that he knew of the hearing date. In fact he did not attend and the prosecutor applied for the trial to go ahead in the defendant's absence. The application was granted and the defence lawyer had then withdrawn. The hearing continued. While the justices were deliberating the accused arrived at court. This fact was not relayed to the justices until after they had found the case proved at 1.05pm. That same afternoon the defence applied for the conviction to be set aside under the Magistrates' Courts Act 1980 s142. The application was refused and judicial review of this refusal was sought on behalf of the accused.

12.52 In their affidavit the justices explained that they had acceded to the request to proceed in absence because they were satisfied that the accused was aware of the trial date, he had failed to notify the court or his solicitor of the reasons for his non-attendance and a large number of witnesses had attended for a full day's hearing. McCowan LJ held that the convenience of the court could not outweigh the facts that the defendant was 16, facing a very serious charge where he risked if convicted a custodial sentence, had not been put on bail and had no record of non-attendance. He further commented that a danger of proceeding in the defendant's absence was that inadmissible evidence would be heard for want of anyone to challenge it.

27 The use of live television links is governed by the Crown Court Rules 1982 SI No 1109 r23A and in the youth court by the Magistrates' Courts (Children and Young Persons) Rules 1992 SI No 2071 r23.
28 Magistrates' Courts Act 1980 s11(1).
29 (1994) *Times*, 16 March.

CHAPTER 13

Sentencing: general principles

Seriousness of the offence

13.1   The Criminal Justice Act 1991 created a framework for sentencing which takes as its most important criterion the seriousness of the offence. Once the court has assessed the seriousness of the offence it must then consider any information about the personal circumstances of the offender which may act as mitigation. The Act further imposes minimum levels of seriousness before a sentence may impose a custodial sentence or a community sentence. These minimum levels of seriousness are referred to as the custody and the community sentence thresholds.

13.2   It is fundamental to the scheme of the Act that consideration of an offender's personal mitigation can mean that a sentence below a particular threshold is more appropriate. This is clearly illustrated by the case of *R v Cox*.[1] In this case an 18-year-old was convicted of reckless driving. The Court of Appeal held that the offence itself was so serious that custody was justified but taking into account the appellant's age and other personal mitigation, a custodial sentence should not have been imposed. Taylor LCJ said:

> We have reached the conclusion that only a custodial sentence could be justified for this offence . . . That, however, is not the end of the matter. Section 1(2) enjoins the court not to pass a custodial sentence unless it is of the opinion that the criteria of seriousness are met. The court is not *required* to pass such a sentence even when they are. Although an offender may qualify for a custodial sentence by virtue of section 1(2), the court is still required to consider whether such a sentence is appropriate having regard to the mitigating factors available and relevant to the offender (as opposed to such factors as are relevant to the offence).

This principle would apply equally to an offence sufficiently serious to warrant a community penalty, but where personal mitigation is available so that a fine or discharge is more appropriate.

Determining offence seriousness

13.3   The court will start by determining an 'entry point' for the offence, that is the broad band of sentences appropriate for an average offence of that type. Once the sentencing range is established, the

---

1   (1993) 14 Cr App R (S) 479.

court will go on to identify any aggravating or mitigating features related to the offence itself.

13.4   National guidelines have been produced for the sentencing of adult offenders.[2] No guidelines exist specifically for use in the youth court. The defence lawyer must, therefore, become familiar with the practice in his/her local courts. The severity of sentencing can vary enormously.[3]

Statutory aggravating factors

13.5   In addition to the above general features derived from case law, the Criminal Justice Act 1991 s29 provides:

> (1) In considering the seriousness of any offence, the court may take into account any previous convictions of the offender or any failure of his to respond to previous sentences.
> (2) In considering the seriousness of any offence committed while the offender was on bail, the court shall treat the fact that it was committed in those circumstances as an aggravating factor.

The court may take into account any previous offences, including those for which the offender was conditionally discharged or given probation.[4]

Previous convictions

13.6   The court is given a discretion to take into account any previous convictions of the offender. Prior to the implementation of the 1991 Act the Court of Appeal had held that a court should not impose a sentence disproportionate to the seriousness of the current offence(s) because of the offender's record. This would be to sentence the offender more than once for his/her previous offences.[5] Instead the Court of Appeal adopted the concept of progressive loss of mitigation which suggested that each new offence reduced the effect of any mitigation available to the offender. In the absence of any judicial decisions regarding the interpretation of s29(1), it is not clear whether this principle still exists. It is submitted that it is in keeping with the general philosophy of the 1991 Act.

2   Magistrates' Association, *Sentencing Guidelines* (1993).
3   A NACRO survey in the early 1990s revealed that across the country the proportion of youth court defendants who received a youth court sentence varied between 2 per cent and 19 per cent.
4   Criminal Justice Act 1991 s29(4) to (6).
5   *R v Queen* (1983) 3 Cr App R (S) 245.

Table 7: Offence seriousness: aggravating and mitigating features

Nature of offence

- category of offence
- amount of violence used, manner of infliction, whether sadistic, degree of injury and effect on victim
- whether weapon carried or used
- value of property stolen or damaged, whether any property recovered
- the need for deterrence

Characteristics of victim

- whether vulnerable (because younger child, elderly or disabled) and deliberately selected
- whether public servant (especially police officers)
- whether abuse of trust

Intention and motive

- whether premeditated or spontaneous
- whether aware of likely injury, likely damage or effect on victim
- whether provoked
- whether racial motivation
- degree of duress, pressure or stress on offender

Role in offence

- ringleader or minor role
- whether organised gang/group offence
- whether offender involved younger children in offence

Location and time

- in a public place or crowded location, frightened onlookers
- whether burglary during hours of darkness or while victim at home
- prevalence of offence in area

Gain to offender

- whether offender benefited considerably or little

Alcohol/drugs

- role of alcohol or drugs in the offence

Attitude to offence

- whether guilt, remorse, concern for victim, desire for/making of reparation or compensation

Failure to respond to previous sentences

13.7 Again the court has a discretion to take into account the response to previous sentences. Once again the lack of response to previous sentences should not result in a sentence disproportionate to the seriousness of the current offence(s).

13.8 The defence lawyer may be able to explain to the court why there has been a poor response to previous penalties. There may have been problems at home, or the child or young person was not attending school at the time. Any change in circumstances which would suggest that the offender will respond better to the proposed penalty should be brought to the court's attention.

Offending while on bail

13.9 Unlike the above two factors, offending whilst on bail must be treated by the court as an aggravating factor.

Personal mitigation

13.10 The Criminal Justice Act 1991 s28 states:

(1) Nothing in this Part shall prevent a court from mitigating an offender's sentence by taking into account any such matters as, in the opinion of the court, are relevant in mitigation of sentence.

(2) Without prejudice to the generality of subsection (1) above, nothing in this Part shall prevent a court –

(a) from mitigating any penalty included in an offender's sentence by taking into account any other penalty included in the sentence; or

(b) in a case of an offender who is convicted of one or more other offences, from mitigating his sentence by applying any rule of law as to the totality of sentences.

13.11 This clearly allows a court to take into account any personal mitigation advanced on behalf of a child or young person. Relevant factors could include:

- the welfare of the child or young person;
- plea of guilty;
- full co-operation with police;
- youth;
- previous good character;
- signs of reform or settling down;

- completed previous supervision;
- additional hardship caused by conviction;
- keeping of all bail conditions;
- remand in custody has had impact;
- custody would damage family relationships, accommodation, education, training or job;
- ill-health;
- having voluntary help for alcohol, drugs or gambling problems; or
- unrelated worthy conduct.

Welfare of the child or young person

13.12   The welfare principle enshrined in the Children and Young Persons Act 1933 s44(1) conflicts with the due process framework of the Criminal Justice Act 1991. The starting point must always be the seriousness of the offence and a more restrictive sentence should never be imposed merely because the court has welfare concerns regarding the child or young person. Rather than resorting to the coercive means of a criminal sentence, such concerns should be addressed by the social services department by treating the child as a child in need or, in more extreme cases, by care proceedings before the family proceedings court.

13.13   The principle may also be relevant to the question of the appropriateness of a community sentence. For example, a community sentence which involves group-work with other offenders could be detrimental to a young, criminally inexperienced offender.

13.14   The welfare principle is both a factor relevant to personal mitigation and a reason for giving greater weight to other mitigation arising out of the young offender's background and personal circumstances. The court should take it into account when considering the custody threshold as well as the length of any custodial sentence. The principle cannot override the need for a deterrent sentence if the seriousness of the offence and other circumstances require it.[6]

Plea of guilty

13.15   There has long been a practice by the courts that credit is given

6   *R v Ford* (1976) 82 Cr App R 303, CA.

when an offender pleads guilty.[7] This has now been given statutory force by the Criminal Justice and Public Order Act 1994 s48:

> (1) In determining what sentence to pass on an offender who has pleaded guilty to an offence in proceedings before that or another court a court shall take into account–
>   (a) the stage in the proceedings for the offence at which the offender indicated his intention to plead guilty, and
>   (b) the circumstances in which this indication was given.
> (2) If, as a result of taking into account any matter referred to in subsection (1) above, the court imposes a punishment on the offender which is less severe than the punishment it would otherwise have imposed, it shall state in open court that it has done so.

It is clear that, although the court is required to take account of the plea of guilty, it is not required to impose a less severe punishment.

Stage in the proceedings

13.16 A court will give the maximum discount when the defendant indicates a guilty plea at the earliest opportunity. This is generally construed to apply to the start of the proceedings. The later that the indication is left, the less discount will be given.

Circumstances in which the indication given

13.17 Taking earlier case law as a guide[8] it would be expected that a discount could be withheld or curtailed in the following circumstances:

- the defendant enters a tactical plea on the day of the trial;
- the defendant did not have a realistic defence and therefore had no choice but to plead guilty; or
- the defendant disputed a material fact requiring a *Newton* hearing.

Form of discount for a guilty plea

13.18 Court of Appeal decisions suggest that reductions in a custodial sentence should be in the order of a quarter to a third to reflect the fact that a defendant pleads guilty. The Magistrates' Association's *Sentencing Guidelines* (1993) also suggest a reduction of a third for a timely plea of guilty. This reduction will obviously be smaller if the court identifies any of the factors mentioned above.

---

7   For example, *R v Buffrey* (1992) 14 Cr App R (S) 511, CA.
8   For example, *R v Hollington* (1985) 7 Cr App R (S) 364 and *R v Costen* (1989) 11 Cr App R (S) 182.

13.19   It could be argued that an admission of guilt from a defendant lacking maturity should attract the maximum discount:

> [I]t is right that all people, and perhaps particularly young offenders at the stage in the development of this young man [age 16], should be given maximum credit for their admission, their frankness and their plea.[9]

13.20   The use in s48 of 'less severe' punishment does also contemplate the possibility of sentencers reducing the proposed sentence below the custody threshold and instead imposing a community sentence.

Co-operation with the police

13.21   This is usually considered as part of the mitigation when the defendant has either admitted the offence in circumstances where it would have been difficult and time consuming for the police to gather evidence or where the defendant has admitted other offences for which the police did not suspect him/her. In extreme examples where the defendant surrendered and confessed to an offence for which s/he was not suspected, the discount upon any sentence could exceed 50 per cent.[10]

Youth

13.22   The age of the offender will usually be a significant consideration in mitigation. Its relevance has been summarised as follows:

> Age does play a part in the sentencing process in appropriate circumstances. That is generally so when the court deals with criminal behaviour by young people. A difference of two and a half years or five years at that stage of development in the life of a person can be quite considerable in respect of responsibility for wrongdoing and its consequences and appreciation of its seriousness.[11]

13.23   The following factors may lead a court to reduce the proposed sentence because of the offender's youth:

- Young people are generally more easily influenced by their peers than adults, therefore it is more likely that they will be led into criminal activity.

---

9   *R v Metcalfe* (1986) 8 Cr App R (S) 110, per MacPherson J.
10   *R v Claydon* (1993) 15 Cr App R (S) 526, CA.
11   *R v Pritchard* (1989) 11 Cr App R (S) 421, CA per Watkins LJ.

- They have less experience of life, therefore they may not appreciate the consequences of their actions in the way that a mature adult would do.
- Offending for many young people is a passing phase. To allow the young person an opportunity to grow out of his/her offending without acquiring a serious criminal record, sentencing disposals should be kept to a minimum and involve the minimum intervention in the offender's life, commensurate with the duty to protect the public.
- As young offenders do not have significant emotional resources, a custodial sentence will have a greater impact than upon a mature adult. The impact of even the shortest custodial sentence will be significant.

Additional hardship caused by conviction

13.24 When dealing with adult offenders sentencers have been willing to mitigate any sentence if the offence has resulted in a loss of employment. This would be equally applicable to young offenders and should include a loss of a training place too. It could have a wider application. As a result of an offence committed at school the young offender may have been permanently excluded from school. Increasingly it is proving difficult to place excluded pupils back into mainstream schools and as a consequence a young person may be left with limited tuition leading to few or no qualifications.

Has kept all bail conditions

13.25 Although the fact that an offender has been subject to restrictive bail conditions is not a factor to be taken into account when determining the length of a custodial sentence, it may still be highly relevant. Successful compliance with onerous bail conditions may demonstrate an ability to comply with a high tariff community penalty. Furthermore, it may establish that the young offender is not a risk to the public if sufficient supervision in the community is provided.

Remand in custody has had impact

13.26 It may be possible to demonstrate to the court that a young offender has changed substantially as a result of a remand in custody or into secure accommodation. It would also be important to make the court aware of any particular problems, such as bullying, suffered by the young person while on remand.

Damaging effect of custody

13.27 Imposing a custodial sentence upon a young offender may have a devastating effect upon the relationship with the offender's family and any dependants. It may also result in the loss of the offender's accommodation, education, training or employment.

Relationship with family

13.28 The younger the offender the more important family contact will be. Removal from a close-knit family to a custodial institution can only have a damaging effect upon the development of a child or young person.

Dependants

13.29 Exceptional adverse effects upon dependants should be brought to the court's attention. This could be the effect upon an offender's own children or a disabled or sick parent for whom the offender is caring.

Accommodation

13.30 Young offenders living independently stand to lose their accommodation if imprisoned. Some local authorities will allocate housing to care-leavers as young as 16 or 17 years old. Imposing even the shortest custodial sentence puts that accommodation at risk. Rent arrears may accrue and in many inner city areas there will be the constant threat of squatters moving in.

Education, training or employment

13.31 Courts are under a statutory duty to consider the welfare of the child or young person and in particular to ensure suitable education and training. Any custodial sentence will inevitably disrupt an education course and result in the loss of a job or training course. As young people are at the start of their employment careers, such disruption will have even greater consequences. It may be useful to obtain reports from teacher, trainers or employers to confirm good progress and identify future prospects which will be jeopardised by a custodial sentence.

Ill-health

13.32 The fact that the offender suffers from a serious illness may be relevant mitigation. However, there has been a reluctance to accept that ill-health is sufficient reason for not imposing a custodial sentence. Nevertheless, it is accepted that an illness which will make serving a custodial sentence a severe hardship may be a reason to reduce a sentence below the custody threshold,[12] as would the fact that the offender suffered from an illness requiring specialist treatment unavailable in custody without which s/he could die.[13]

Having voluntary help for alcohol, drugs or gambling problems

13.33 The fact that offences were committed to feed an addiction is not mitigation.[14] Nevertheless, evidence that a young offender has taken the initiative to deal with the problem shows considerable maturity and a desire to reform.

Unrelated worthy conduct

13.34 Decisions of the Court of Appeal have given a sentencing discount for meritorious conduct while awaiting trial (for example, saving children from a fire[15]). This principle has been extended to cover the conduct of a young offender's parents. In *R v Catterall*[16] the father of a 19-year-old informed the police that his son was dealing in ecstasy. The Court of Appeal reduced the sentence passed by the trial judge making specific reference to the father's actions in serving the public interest.

Length of sentence

Concurrent or consecutive?

13.35 When passing sentence upon an offender convicted of more than one offence, the court must impose a separate sentence for each offence. Sentences may be ordered to run concurrently or consecutively to each other. In addition they may be ordered to run concurrently or consecutively to existing sentences. On passing sentence the court must indicate whether a sentence is to run concurrently or consecutively. If it is not specified at the time, the sentence is presumed to run concurrently.

---

12 *R v Leatherbarrow* (1992) 13 Cr App R (S) 632, CA.
13 *R v Green* (1992) 13 Cr App R (S) 613, CA.
14 *R v Lawrence* (1988) 10 Cr App R (S) 463, CA.
15 *R v Reid* (1982) 4 Cr App R (S) 280, CA.
16 (1993) 14 Cr App R (S) 724; (1993) *Times*, 29 March, CA.

13.36   In general, offences arising out of the same criminal trans-
action will be dealt with by concurrent sentences. A consecutive
sentence may be appropriate in the following circumstances:

- where the second offence was committed whilst on bail for the
  first;
- for an offence of violence against a police officer or member of the
  public in an attempt to resist arrest for another offence;
- where the offender carries a firearm to carry out another offence.

Totality of sentence

13.37   When cases of multiplicity of offences come before the court, the
court must not content itself by doing the arithmetic and passing the
sentence which the arithmetic produces. It must look at the totality of
the criminal behaviour and ask itself what is the appropriate sentence
for all the offences.[17]

This principle applies as much to financial orders and community sentences as it does to custodial sentences. It is of particular
relevance to young offenders who have not previously served a custodial sentence.[18]

---

17 *Per* Lawton LJ, quoted in Thomas, *Principles of Sentencing* (Heineman, 1979).
18 *R v Koyce* (1979) 1 Cr App R (S) 21, CA.

CHAPTER 14
Sentencing strategies

For complete chapter contents, see overleaf

Introduction

14.1 Preparing for the sentencing hearing of a child or young person can in many cases be considerably more complicated than in the case of an adult defendant. The youth of the client may mean that it is more difficult to obtain relevant information from him/her. The welfare principle will mean that a number of agencies may provide information to the court and be in a position to offer support to the young person to prevent further offending. As a consequence the defence lawyer must be prepared both to work closely with the youth justice (or youth offending) team and to lobby for resources to ensure that the best package is offered to the court.

14.2 This chapter offers some practical advice about preparing the mitigation for a young offender and also examines the particular problems faced when dealing with young offenders charged with sexual offences or who have drug or mental health problems.

14.3 It is important to bear in mind that the Crown Prosecution Service's duty to review a prosecution continues up until the accused is convicted. Bearing in mind the duty to have regard to the welfare of the child or young person under the Children and Young Persons Act 1933 s44 it may, therefore, be appropriate in certain cases to make representations to the prosecutor before a young defendant enters a guilty plea. If substantial new information is to be provided, the defence lawyer will have to ask the court to adjourn while written submissions are made and considered.

Preparing mitigation

Obtaining background information

14.4 The defence lawyer should aim to collect information regarding the following:

- family circumstances;
- care history (if any);
- care plan (if relevant);
- education;
- training;
- employment/career plans;
- leisure activities;

- financial resources; and
- offending history.

A detailed checklist is contained in Table 8 at p335.

Sources of information

14.5   The first source of information will obviously be the young client. However, obtaining background information about a young client can be considerably more difficult than in the case of an adult client. Many young defendants have troubled home lives or care histories. As a result they may be unable or reluctant to discuss what may be painful memories. The defence lawyer may, therefore, need to ask the young client for permission to talk to:

- parent(s) or other carers;
- youth justice (or youth offending) team;
- social worker;
- teachers.

14.6   Any information obtained from other sources will obviously have to be checked with the young client. It is not good practice to rely upon the author of the pre-sentence report to provide all the relevant background information for the court. The report writer may not produce a very comprehensive report and in any event the current National Standards emphasise assessing the offence and protection of the public at the expense of personal background.

Supervising officer

14.7   Where a child or young person has had recent contact with the youth justice (or youth offending) team it may be useful to contact the team member who had contact with him/her. The information provided may avoid the need for a pre-sentence report. A good response in the past could also be good mitigation.

Social worker

14.8   A child or young person may have contact with a social worker because of support offered to the family or because the child or young person has been looked after by the local authority. In some cases the social services files will cover most of the young client's life.

14.9   Where it is known that the young client has contact with a social

Table 8: Preparing personal mitigation – checklist

- *Family*
  Composition.
  Principal carer(s) – current and previous.
  Parental occupation(s).
  Achievements/criminal history of siblings.
  Problems in home life (eg, domestic violence, parental drug dependency or mental disorder).
  History of social services intervention (eg, 'placement at risk' register).

- *Care history (if relevant)*
  History of periods when 'looked after' child.
  Reason for being looked after.
  Type and number of placements.
  Care plan.
  Relationship with current social worker.

- *Health and developmental problems*
  Physical conditions or disabilities.
  Any history of psychiatric problems.

- *Schooling*
  History.
  Truancy.
  Exclusions.
  Achievements (academic, sporting or extra-curricular) and examination prospects/results.
  Statement of special educational need (if any).

- *Training/employment*
  Periods in training – YTS or Modern Apprenticeship.
  Vocational qualifications (eg, NVQ or City and Guilds).
  History of paid employment (if any).
  Career plans.

- *Leisure*
  Use of leisure time.
  Involvement in organised youth activities (eg, amateur sport leagues or youth clubs).

- *Financial resources*

- *Offending history*
  Types of offences.
  Dates of offences.
  Disposals.
  History of contact with youth justice/offending team (if any).

worker, the defence lawyer would be well advised to contact him/her. It would be useful to establish:

- the history of contact between the young client and the local authority;
- the number and types of placement (if any); and
- the current care plan.

14.10 In cases where the client has had a very troubled history in care, the defence lawyer may wish to gain access to the social services files. Access to a social service file is governed by the Access to Personal Files Act 1987 and the Access to Personal Files (Social Services) Regulations 1989 SI No 206. Any person may seek disclosure by the local authority of personal information relating to the applicant held by it. Where the request for information is made by a minor, the authority must be satisfied that s/he has sufficient understanding to make the application. The local authority may withhold information in specified circumstances. The defence lawyer could request access to the files on behalf of the young client.

Teacher

14.11 After parents or other carers, teachers are the adults who spend most time with the majority of children and young persons. They may, therefore, be a useful source of information about a young client. Teachers will often be willing to provide a more personal assessment of a pupil than that contained in a pre-sentence report. Research has demonstrated that youth court magistrates do place great store on the views of teachers.[1]

14.12 Contacting a teacher may also reveal that the young client has a statement of special educational needs. Such statements will normally have attached various expert reports by, among others, an educational psychologist. If the young client does already have a copy of the statement, his/her parent or guardian may request a copy from the local education department.[1A]

Character witnesses

14.13 It may also be fruitful to identify potential character witnesses from whom statements may be taken or letters of support obtained. Such

---

1 C Ball and J Connolly, 'Requiring School Attendance: A Little Used Sentencing Power' [1999] Crim LR 183.
1A Education (School Records) Regulations 1989 SI No 1261.

statements may still be of considerable use even if the writer gives some negative information about the offender. As much as anything, their importance is in identifying good qualities and a chance of rehabilitation. Possible referees could include:

- a family friend;
- a foster parent or care worker;
- a school teacher;
- a youth training scheme supervisor;
- an employer (including Saturday/holiday/after school jobs);
- a youth worker;
- a religious leader;
- a community leader; or
- a sports coach (eg, amateur youth league, etc).

Frequent offenders

14.14 When a lawyer represents a child or young person who has been arrested and charged with many offences, the greatest challenge can simply be to keep track of all the offences. Cases may be in different courts, some awaiting sentence, some awaiting trial. In addition, there may be many outstanding cases at police stations.

14.15 Traditionally lawyers organise their caseload by reference to individual court cases rather than individual clients, and it may therefore be difficult to maintain a clear picture of the young client's cases. Yet the defence lawyer is likely to be the only person who is in a position to be aware of the full picture. Preparing a schedule of outstanding offences may help to provide a clear picture of the cases. With fast-tracking of defendants deemed to be persistent young offenders, it may also help the defence lawyer to prepare a strategy to deal with all the cases expeditiously and most advantageously for the young client.

14.16 The defence lawyer will wish to make full use of the power to remit for sentence so that offences can be collected together for sentence. S/he may also wish to make representations to the prosecution that it is not in the public interest to continue with the prosecution of some offences, in the light of the likely penalty. Similar arguments could be used to persuade a prosecutor to agree to offences being taken into consideration at another court.

14.17 If a child or young person is given a custodial sentence and other offences are still outstanding, the defence lawyer should again consider writing to the prosecution suggesting discontinuance.

Alternatively, some police forces may wish to speak to the young offender with a view to 'clearing up' outstanding offences. It has also been held that if the prosecution decides to proceed with offences known to be outstanding, the police should not wait until after the offender serves his/her sentence before charging him/her with the other offences. Instead prompt steps should be taken to initiate proceedings.[2]

Serious offenders

14.18   Save in the case of murder, the defence lawyer should never assume that a lengthy custodial sentence is inevitable when a defendant is convicted of a very serious offence. By adopting a proactive role and preparing a well thought out alternative to custody, it may well be possible to persuade a Crown Court judge not to impose a lengthy custodial sentence.

On committal

14.19   The defence lawyer should ensure that the relevant social services department has activated the Home Office's early warning system so that in the event of the child or young person receiving a sentence of detention under s53(2) and (3), a place in a local authority secure unit is more likely to be available.[3]

Exploring the alternatives

14.20   The defence lawyer will need to be familiar with the various local projects and establishments available in the area. Whether a particular option is realistic in a particular case will depend to a large extent on local resources, the willingness of the social services department or probation service to pay and the reputation that a project or establishment has in the eyes of local Crown Court judges.

14.21   Possible alternatives to a custodial sentence include:
 – high tariff community penalties;
 – community orders with residence requirements;
 – secure accommodation orders; and
 – community orders with a requirement as to psychiatric treatment.

2 *R v Fairfield* (1987) 9 Cr App R (S) 49, CA.
3 See para 22.20ff.

High tariff community penalties

14.22 These would include:
- a supervision order with specified activities;
- a probation order with a requirement to attend day centre; and
- a combination order.

Community orders with residence requirements

14.23 These could include:
- a supervision order with a requirement to reside in local authority accommodation; and
- a probation order with a condition of residence.

14.24 The Court of Appeal has upheld the use of a three-year probation order with a condition of residence in a semi-secure children's home for a 17-year-old convicted of s18 GBH where the victim was hit several times on the head with a piece of wood resulting in a fractured skull.[4] In considering the case Taylor LCJ described the establishment's regime as follows:

> Frontier House is described as a semi-secure children's unit, which has an intense learning programme, aimed at challenging, developing and controlling behaviour. The ration there is of two staff to each young person. The object is to ensure a high degree of monitoring and restriction of liberty. The offender was never allowed out, for example, from the unit unaccompanied, and only then on one occasion per week. The unit was a considerable distance away from his family, so that he was in a position of very restricted liberty at Frontier House.

In upholding the sentence he took into account the tough regime and the fact that the defendant had successfully spent 16 months in the unit by the time of the appeal.

Secure accommodation

14.25 If a local authority is willing to allocate the resources to pay for secure accommodation, a court could be asked to consider a supervision order with a condition of residence in local authority accommodation, in the expectation that the local authority would then apply to the family proceedings court for authority to detain the offender. Such an arrangement would ensure that the offender is kept in a

4 *Attorney-General's Reference No 15 of 1994* (1995) 16 Cr App R (S) 619.

child care establishment while ensuring that the public are protected. As the authority to detain in secure accommodation is permissive only, the local authority would have discretion to remove the offender from secure accommodation when it is considered that the public are no longer at risk.

Young offenders dependent on alcohol, drugs or substances

Identifying resources

14.26   Although there are many drug rehabilitation organisations, most provide a service directed at adults. Such projects may not meet the special needs of adolescents. It may therefore be difficult to identify suitable community-based or residential projects for young offenders. Depending on location, resources may be available from social services, local health authorities or the voluntary sector. Details of specialist projects may be found in the *ISTD Handbook of Community Programmes for Young and Juvenile Offenders.*[5]

Sentencing disposals

14.27   The court could consider any of the following options:
- supervision order with specified activities (involving drug counselling);
- probation order with requirement as to treatment for drug or alcohol dependency (16 years and over);
- drug treatment and testing order (16 years and over).

In extreme cases it may be possible to persuade a court to impose a supervision order with a requirement to reside in local authority accommodation where the local authority would then seek a secure accommodation order from the family proceedings court.

Mentally disordered offenders

14.28   The prevalence of diagnosable mental disorder among adolescents is estimated to be as high as 25 per cent with 7 per cent to 10 per cent

5   Waterside Press (2nd edn, 1998).

having moderate to severe problems.[7] Research evidence suggests that there may be a significant number of young offenders with psychiatric problems who would benefit from treatment. In one survey carried out at Manchester Youth Court, 7 per cent of the 192 young defendants were found to have a psychiatric problem requiring treatment.[8] The defence lawyer should always be alert to the possibility that a young client would benefit from treatment. If there is a history of contact with psychiatric services or evidence of mental disorder, consideration should be given to obtaining a report from an adolescent psychiatrist.

Diversion

14.29 Home Office Circulars 66/90 and 12/95 emphasise the importance of diverting mentally disordered offenders from the criminal justice system. The forms of diversion suggested are:

- cautioning;
- voluntary admission psychiatric hospital;
- compulsory admission to psychiatric hospital under the Mental Health Act 1983 ss2 or 3; or
- use of criminal psychiatric disposals (hospital and guardianship orders).

In the case of children and young persons there may also be the option of a secure accommodation order.[9]

Sentencing disposals

14.30 Where a child or young person has been charged with a criminal offence, the possible disposals include:

- absolute discharge;
- supervision order with a requirement to receive psychiatric treatment;

---

7 PJ Graham, 'Behavioural and Intellectual Development in Childhood Epidemiology' (1986) *British Medical Bulletin*, 42, 2, 155–62.

8 M Dolan et al, 'Health status of juvenile offenders. A survey of young offenders appearing before the juvenile courts' (1999) 22 *Journal of Adolescence* 137–144.

9 For a consideration of the relative advantages of seeking a secure accommodation order or detention under the Mental Health Act 1983, see S Bailey and A Harbour, 'The Law and a Child's Consent to Treatment (England and Wales)' (1998) *Child Psychology & Psychiatry Review*, Volume 4, No 1, 1999.

- probation order with a requirement as to treatment for mental condition (16 years and over);
- hospital order;
- guardianship order (16 years and over); and
- restriction order.

If there is concern about an offender presenting a risk to the public, there is always the possibility of the local authority seeking authority to place him/her in secure accommodation. Such an option could be pursued in conjunction with a sentencing proposal of a community penalty.

Sexual offenders

14.31   The phenomenon of adolescent sexual offending has been neglected until very recently, yet adolescents make up a significant proportion of the total number of sexual offenders dealt with by the criminal justice system. In 1992, 16 per cent of sex offenders who were cautioned or found guilty were under the age of 18.[10] Moreover, research suggests that a much higher proportion of sexual offences committed against children are committed by perpetrators under the age of 18.[11-12]

Child protection

14.32   Previous Department of Health guidance contained in *Working Together under the Children Act 1989* (HMSO, 1991) suggested that referrals to child protection agencies should be made when a child or young person is accused of sexual offences. Upon receipt of the referral there should be a child protection conference in respect of the alleged abuser. The more recent draft guidance *Working Together to Safeguard Children* issued by the Department of Health no longer suggests that a child protection conference should be convened automatically. Instead it recommends that there should be a co-ordinated approach on the part of youth justice, child welfare, education and health agencies which involves an assessment of the needs of the child or young person accused of abusive behaviour. This assessment could lead to the convening of a child protection conference.

10   *Criminal Statistics: England and Wales* (Cm 2410, HMSO, 1993).
11-12   Research in Liverpool based on interviews with children revealed that 36 per cent of the perpetrators were under the age of 18: Horne, L et al 'Sexual abuse of children by children' (1991) *Journal of Child Law* 3, pp147–51.

14.33   The assessment of the needs of a child or young person could be highly beneficial as it results in appropriate help for the young client. However, it also raises problems when criminal proceedings are pending. The defence lawyer is often put in the invidious position of being forced to decide whether the young client's best interests will be met by co-operation with any child protection assessment to gain access to therapeutic services or a refusal to co-operate which may avoid incriminating information being disclosed to the police or courts.

Diversion

14.34   There is considerable variation in local practice in relation to diverting sexual offenders from the youth justice system. In some police areas the view is taken that early intervention in the form of compulsory supervision as part of a criminal sentence is in the best interests of the child or young person. The defence lawyer should note that a caution for a sexual offence involving a minor will still result in a requirement to register as a sex offender.[13]

14.35   It should be noted that recent government guidance advises police forces not to prosecute young people under the age of 18 for prostitution unless there is evidence that they are 'willingly involved'.[14]

Identifying resources

14.36   It may be difficult to identify suitable community-based or residential projects for young offenders. Depending on location, resources may be available from social services, local health authorities or the voluntary sector. Details of specialist projects may be found in the *ISTD Handbook of Community Programmes for Young and Juvenile Offenders*.[15]

Sentencing options

14.37   The sentencing options are as follows.

---

13 See para 24.21.
14 Home Office/Department of Health, *Draft Guidance on Children Involved in Prostitution*.
15 Waterside Press (2nd edn, 1998).

Probation

14.38   Offenders who have attained the age of 16 may be sentenced to a probation order with a requirement that they attend a probation day centre or activities for longer than the normal maximum of 60 days. Such programmes will be designed for adult sex offenders and may not be suitable for young offenders.

Supervision

14.39   A supervision order with an additional requirement of specified activities may be imposed. Here the maximum programme would be 90 days.

Custody

14.40   Young sex offenders have been made subject to longer than normal sentences under the Criminal Justice Act 1991 s2(2)(b).[17] For an offence committed on or after 30 September 1998, the court may also impose an extended sentence which includes a further period (the extension period) for which the offender will be subject to licence.[18]

Sex offender order

14.41   A chief officer of police may apply for a sex offender order against any person whom it appears to him/her fulfils the following conditions:
   – s/he is a sex offender; and
   – s/he has acted, since the relevant date, in such a way as to give reasonable cause to believe that an order is necessary to protect the public from serious harm from him/her.[19]

'Sex offender' is defined as a person who has been convicted of or cautioned for a sexual offence as defined by the Sex Offenders Act 1997 Sch 1 (see para 24.20). The definition also includes a person found not guilty of such an offence by reason of insanity or found to be under a disability and to have done the act charged and to a person convicted abroad of a sexual offence as defined by the 1997 Act.[20]

---

17   *R v K* (1995) 16 Cr App R (S) 966, CA.
18   Crime and Disorder Act 1998 s58. See also Criminal Justice Act 1991 s44 as inserted by Crime and Disorder Act 1998 s59.
19   Crime and Disorder Act 1998 s2(1).
20   Ibid, s3(1).

14.42 'Relevant date' is defined as the date or, as the case may be, the latest date on which the offender has been convicted of a sexual offence or 1 September 1997 if later.[21]

14.43 Application is made to an adult magistrates' court (not a youth court). Assistance by way of representation (ABWOR) is available for the defendant. An appeal against a sex offender order may be made to the Crown Court.[22]

21 Ibid, s3(2).
22 Ibid, s4(1).

CHAPTER 15

Sentencing: powers and procedure

For complete chapter contents, see overleaf

Youth court

Available sentences

15.1   The youth court has an extensive range of sentencing options available to it. It can impose the following sentences:
   - absolute and conditional discharges;
   - fine;
   - reparation order (pilot areas only);
   - attendance centre order;
   - curfew order (pilot areas only);
   - supervision order;
   - action plan order (pilot areas only);
   - probation order;
   - community service order;
   - combination order;
   - drugs treatment and testing order (pilot areas only);
   - detention in a young offender institution;
   - secure training order; or
   - detention and training order (to be implemented).

15.2   There is no restriction upon a youth court's powers in relation to community orders. In the case of detention in a young offenders institution, the youth court is restricted in the case of one or more summary-only offences to a total of six months' detention, or the maximum penalty for the offences, if less.[1] In the case of either-way or indictable-only offences the maximum period of detention for one offence is six months and for more than one offence it is 12 months' detention.[2] There would seem to be no similar restriction on the youth court's powers to impose a secure training order or a detention and training order.

Committal for sentence

15.3   A youth court may commit a young person aged 15 to 17 to the Crown Court for sentence. The Magistrates' Courts Act 1980 s37(1) provides:

---

1   Magistrates' Courts Act 1980 s31(1).
2   Ibid, s133.

Where a person who is not less than 15 but under 18 years old is convicted by a magistrates' court of an offence punishable on conviction on indictment with a term of imprisonment exceeding six months, then, if the court is of the opinion that he should be sentenced to a greater term of detention in a young offender institution than it has power to impose, the court may commit him in custody or on bail to the Crown Court for sentence.

Changing age during the proceedings

15.4 The relevant age is that on the date of conviction and therefore a 14-year-old defendant who attains the age of 15 after his/her conviction would not be liable to be committed to the Crown Court for sentence.

15.5 Should the offender turn 18 after the determination of mode of trial but before the finding of guilt it would seem that the youth court may use the Magistrates' Courts Act 1980 s38 to commit the offender for sentence. This section is limited to offenders who have attained the age of 18 by the date of conviction and who are convicted of offences triable either way. It would seem that an offender convicted of an indictable-only offence after s/he has attained the age of 18 cannot be committed for sentence under any circumstances.

Remanding the offender

15.6 The offender may be committed for sentence on bail or in custody. In the case of a 15- or 16-year-old offender (male or female) refused bail the remand is still to custody as the Children and Young Persons Act 1969 s23 (provisions for a remand to local authority accommodation) does not apply.[3]

Committing the offender for sentence in relation to other offences

15.7 At the same time the youth court may commit the offender to be dealt with for other offences which are before the youth court and the court has power to deal with.[4] For such offences the Crown Court is limited to the powers which would have been available to the youth court if it had not committed.

---

3   Children and Young Persons Act 1969 s23(14).
4   Criminal Justice Act 1967 s56(1).

Grave crimes

15.8　A committal for sentence under this provision does not allow the Crown Court to sentence the defendant to extended detention under the Children and Young Person Act 1933 s53(2) and (3).[5]

Introduction of detention and training orders

15.9　When the detention and training order is introduced, s37 will be repealed.[6] As the youth court will be able to impose a detention and training order for up to 24 months there will obviously be no need to commit an offender for sentence.[7]

Remittal for sentence

15.10　Having convicted a child or young person, a youth court may remit the case for sentence to the youth court local to the offender's home. The Children and Young Persons Act 1933 s56(1) provides:

> Any court by or before which a child or young person is found guilty of an offence other than homicide may, and, if it is not a youth court, shall unless satisfied that it would be undesirable to do so, remit the case to a youth court acting for the place where the offender was committed for trial, or, if he was not committed for trial, to a youth court acting either for the same place as the remitting court or for the place where the offender habitually resides and, where any such case is so remitted, the offender shall be brought before a youth court accordingly, and that court may deal with him in any way in which it might have dealt with him if he had been tried and found guilty by that court.

Discretion to remit

15.11　A youth court may have a good reason for not exercising its power under this section, for example, if the defendant can be sentenced immediately or it is considered desirable to sentence co-defendants from different areas together to avoid disparity of sentence. However, in the absence of such reasons it is desirable for the case to be remitted. The young defendant (and parent or guardian) will then not have to travel so far to court and s/he will appear before a youth

---

5　*R v McKenna* (1985) 7 Cr App R (S) 348, CA.
6　Crime and Disorder Act 1998 s120(2) and Sch 10. Implementation is expected in June 2000.
7　See para 21.54.

court where a representative of the local social services department (or youth offending team) is available to identify any outstanding welfare concerns.

Where the offender habitually resides

15.12 Courts will usually interpret this to be the petty sessions area where the young offender is currently living at the time of the conviction. However, it is fairly common that offenders accommodated by a local authority are actually residing outside the area of that authority. In such circumstances it is suggested that the court consider remitting to the petty sessions area served by the local authority accommodating the young offender. The use of 'habitually' does seem to allow a more practical interpretation of this power.[8]

Attaining the age of 18 prior to conviction

15.13 Although the power to remit under s56(1) is only available to a court dealing with a child or young person, the Children and Young Persons Act 1963 s29(1) would seem to allow the court to remit for sentence an offender who has attained the age of 18 prior to conviction. This section allows a court to deal with the case and make any order which it could have made if the offender had not attained the age of 18.

Right of appeal

15.14 There is no right of appeal against the decision to remit but the offender retains the right to appeal against the conviction. In addition s/he may appeal against any decision of the court to which the case is remitted as if s/he had been found guilty by that court.[9] In practice this will mean that any appeal against conviction will have to wait until the offender is sentenced by the second court. A notice of appeal would then be lodged with the clerk to the court receiving the remittal.

Remittal for sentence to the adult magistrates' court

15.15 If a young person attains the age of 18 during the proceedings s/he may be remitted to the adult court to be sentenced.[10]

---

8 Cf, the definition of 'ordinarily resident' in the Children Act 1989 s105(6) (see Chapter 4).
9 Children and Young Persons Act 1933 s56(2).
10 Crime and Disorder Act 1998 s47(1). This power is considered at para 9.72.

Magistrates' court

Available sentences

15.16 In practice a magistrates' court is limited by the Children and Young Persons Act 1969 s7(8) to the following disposals:
- absolute discharge;
- conditional discharge;
- fine;
- parental bindover; or
- any other order the court has the power to make when absolutely or conditionally discharging an offender.

Remittal for sentence

15.17 Where a magistrates' court finds a child or young person guilty of an offence, it must remit the case to a youth court under the Children and Young Persons Act 1933 s56(1) unless it is of the opinion that the case is one which can properly be dealt with by one of the above orders.[11] If remittal for sentence is to take place there seems to be no reason why the magistrates' court cannot order a pre-sentence report to be prepared for the next hearing in the youth court. This has the advantage of reducing the number of future hearings and consequently avoiding unnecessary delays.

To which youth court?

15.18 The Children and Young Persons Act 1933 s56(1) allows a magistrates' court to remit a child or young person to either the youth court acting for the same petty sessions area or the court acting for the area where the offender habitually resides.[12]

Right of appeal

15.19 There is no right of appeal against the decision to remit but the offender retains the right to appeal against the conviction. In addition s/he may appeal against any decision of the court to which the case is remitted as if s/he had been found guilty by that court.[13] In practice this will mean that any appeal against conviction will have to

---

11 Children and Young Persons Act 1969 s7(8) as amended by Crime and Disorder Act 1998 Sch 8 para 16.
12 For a consideration of 'habitually resides' see para 15.12.
13 Children and Young Persons Act 1933 s56(2).

wait until the offender is sentenced by the second court. A notice of appeal would then be lodged with the clerk to the court receiving the remittal.

Crown Court

Available sentences

15.20 The Crown Court has all the powers available to the youth court (as listed above) and in addition it has available the sentences of extended detention under Children and Young Persons Act 1933 s53(2)[14] and indeterminate detention during Her Majesty's Pleasure. In the case of detention in a young offender institution the Crown Court's powers are limited to sentencing a 15- to 17-year-old to a maximum of 24 months' detention irrespective of the number of offences.[15]

Remittal for sentence

15.21 Having convicted a child or young person, a Crown Court should remit him/her for sentence to a youth court under Children and Young Persons Act 1933 s56(1), unless the judge is satisfied that it would be undesirable to do so. Guidance on the exercise of this discretion was provided in *R v Lewis*[16] where Lane LCJ stated:

> Possible reasons that it would be undesirable to do so are as follows – these of course are by no means comprehensive: that the judge who presided over the trial will be better informed as to the facts and circumstances; that there is, in the sad and frequent experience of this Court, a risk of unacceptable disparity if co-defendants are to be sentenced in different courts on different occasions; thirdly, that as a result of the remission there will be delay, duplication of proceedings and fruitless expense; and finally the provisions for appeal which are, as to conviction in the Crown Court an appeal to the Court of Appeal (Criminal Division) and as to orders made in the [youth court] an appeal to the Crown Court.

---

14 On trial by indictment only: see below.
15 Criminal Justice Act 1982 s1B(2), as amended by Criminal Justice and Public Order Act 1994 s17.
16 (1984) 79 Cr App R 94; (1984) 6 Cr App R (S) 44, CA.

However, it may become desirable to remit the case where a report has to be obtained and the Judge will be unable to sit when the report becomes available . . .

15.22 Some commentators have taken the decision in *Lewis* as authority to say that a Crown Court should never remit a child or young person to a youth court for sentence. However, the last sentence of the quotation above demonstrates that Lord Lane did contemplate circumstances when it would be appropriate to remit the young offender for sentence. As the formality of the procedure and language usually makes the Crown Court unsuited to young offenders, it is submitted that the court should always consider carefully whether grounds such as those identified by Lord Lane exist in the case to make it unreasonable to remit.

15.23 It would obviously make little sense to remit for sentence a child or young person who was committed to the Crown Court after a youth court declined jurisdiction under Magistrates' Courts Act 1980 s24(1)(a) in relation to a grave crime. However, if the child or young person appears in the Crown Court after a magistrates' court committed him/her to stand trial jointly with an adult, there may very well be persuasive reasons why a remittal should be considered. When all defendants plead guilty relevant considerations may include:

– the judge will not have any special knowledge of the case;
– an adjournment for the preparation of pre-sentence reports may be necessary in any event;
– disparity of sentence is almost inevitable when sentencing a child or young person at the same time as an adult;
– the youth court will have special knowledge of the availability and nature of special programmes and activities designed for young offenders;
– the extra expense of a remittal may be balanced against the saving of a cheaper hearing in the youth court without the need for representation by both a barrister and solicitor; and
– with a plea of guilty, there is no duplication of appeal rights.

15.24 A further factor in favour of remittal is that the defendant may have other offences (possibly more serious ones) for sentence before a youth court. Remittal would allow all these offences to be dealt with together whereas there is no power to commit these matters to the Crown Court for sentence unless the youth court considers it appropriate under Magistrates' Courts Act 1980 s37. Administrative convenience would not be a valid reason for the exercise of this power.

Sentencing procedure

Disparity of sentence

15.25 When a court has before it more than one defendant it will normally be desirable to ensure that all co-defendants are sentenced together to avoid the risk of disparity of sentence and the consequent possibility of appeal.[17] For example, when one defendant pleads guilty while others plead not guilty, sentencing should normally be adjourned until after the conclusion of the trial. It is submitted, however, that this principle is less persuasive in the youth court where sentencing is much more defendant orientated and welfare concerns may favour prompt disposal of the case for the defendant pleading guilty or remittal to a local youth court.

Adjourning cases for sentence

15.26 In order to avoid unnecessary delay in dealing with young offenders the Crime and Disorder Act 1998 reversed case law dealing with some aspects of sentencing procedure. The Magistrates' Courts Act 1980 s10(3A)[18] now provides:

> A youth court shall not be required to adjourn any proceedings for an offence by reason only of the fact–
> (a) that the court commits the accused for trial for another offence; or
> (b) that the accused is charged with another offence.

Accused committed for trial for another offence

15.27 Where a defendant comes before the youth court for a number of unrelated offences, it is possible for the court to commit the offender for trial in relation to a grave crime thereby leaving other matters in the youth court. The youth court will then need to decide whether to proceed to sentence on the remaining matters. The court needs to balance the desirability of disposing with cases promptly against the risk of practical problems arising for the sentencing judge at the Crown Court. Problems are most likely to arise at the Crown Court where the youth court imposes a custodial

---

17 *R v Weekes* (1980) 2 Cr App R (S) 377, CA.
18 As inserted by Crime and Disorder Act 1998 s47(5).

sentence for offences which post-date the grave crime committed for trial.[19]

Sentencing offences together

15.28   Some young offenders may have a large number of outstanding cases before the courts at any one time. In *R v Bennett*[20] the Court of Appeal gave some guidance applicable to such situations. If a defence lawyer is aware that a client has other outstanding cases awaiting sentence s/he should do everything possible to ensure that all outstanding offences are dealt with in the same court, by the same sentencer and on the same occasion. Such an approach both saves public money and avoids the unsatisfactory result that a community penalty is quickly followed by a custodial sentence for other outstanding offences. This guidance cannot, of course, override the defence lawyer's duty of confidentiality owed to the client and there will be occasions when it is not in the interests of the defendant to have all outstanding cases brought together for sentence.

15.29   In the youth court, the guidance in *Bennett* must now be read in the light of s10(3A). It should be noted that a youth court is not prohibited from adjourning to link up cases. The effect of s10(3A) is simply to emphasise that there is no presumption that an adjournment should take place to join up proceedings. It is submitted, however, that there will be many occasions when an adjournment would be the most sensible option to allow matters to be linked together. In many instances such a course of action will not involve significant delay.

Exercising the discretion to adjourn

15.30   The discretion to adjourn should be exercised judicially. It would not be so exercised if it was done for no other purpose than to ensure that the defendant attains a particular age before the next hearing date, thus giving the court increased sentencing powers.[21]

---

19   These practical problems may be seen in *R v Abdul Khan* (1994) 158 JP 760, CA, but note that the guidance to youth courts given by Smith J has now been reversed by Magistrates' Courts Act 1980 s10(3A).
20   *R v Bennett* (1980) 2 Cr App R (S) 96, CA.
21   *Arthur v Stringer* (1986) 8 Cr App R (S) 329, QBD.

Statutory time limits (pilot areas only)

15.30A Where the Prosecution of Offences Act 1985 s22A is in force,[21A] there is a statutory time limit which runs from conviction to sentence. The maximum period for completion of this stage in the proceedings is 29 calendar days.[21B] If the time limit would otherwise expire on a Saturday, Sunday, Christmas Day, Good Friday or any other bank holiday, it shall be treated as expiring on the first preceding day that is not one of these days.[21C]

15.30B   The time limit applies where a defendant is to be sentenced in a pilot court and:

   (a) was under the age of 18–
       (i) at the time of his/her arrest for the offence; or
       (ii) (where s/he was not arrested for the offence) at the time of the laying of an information charging him/her with an offence; and
   (b) is convicted of the offence in a pilot court on or after 1 November 1999.[21D]

There is no sanction for exceeding the sentencing time limit, but Home Office guidance suggests that, where the date fixed for sentencing falls after the expiry of the time limit, it would be good practice for a court to state that the time limit no longer applies and to give reasons why a longer period is required in the particular case. The guidance suggests that possible reasons for a longer period being required would be the need to obtain the victim's views where a reparation or action plan order is being considered or where complex psychiatric assessments are required.[21E]

Establishing the factual basis

After a trial

15.31 When a child or young person has been found guilty after a trial the case will often be adjourned for a remittal to another court or the

---

21A For pilot areas see appendix 8.
21B Prosecution of Offences (Youth Courts Time Limits) Regulations 1999 SI No 2743 reg 6 (see appendix 2).
21C Ibid, reg 1(5).
21D Ibid, reg 6.
21E *Home Office Statutory Time Limits: Guidance for Pilots*, para 59.

preparation of a pre-sentence report. S/he will then come before a different bench to the one which heard the evidence at trial. The court will sentence on the basis of the facts as set out by the prosecution, unless the trial bench indicated that certain elements of the allegation were not proved.

On a guilty plea

15.32   Upon a guilty plea it is the duty of the prosecution to give the court a summary of the offence which reveals not only any aggravating features but also any mitigating ones. The prosecutor should warn the defence lawyer if details of any aggravating features are to be given to the bench when it is anticipated that those features will be disputed. If a plea is to be tendered on facts different from those of the prosecution it is the duty of the defence lawyer to notify the prosecutor prior to the hearing. In practice, the defence version will often be accepted as the basis for sentence.

Resolving factual disputes

15.33   When the prosecution will not accept the factual basis of the plea, the court may resolve the issue based on the information before it. Lane LCJ considered the options in the case of *R v Newton*.[22] Faced with a factual dispute the court had the following options:

1) to have a trial on the issue (for example, when the dispute is whether an assault was with the necessary intent for a charge under Offences Against the Person Act 1861 s18);
2) to hear submissions from both the prosecution and the defence; and
3) for the sentencer to hear evidence and determine the factual dispute (a *Newton* hearing).

Hearing submissions

15.34   If there is a substantial conflict between the two versions of events, the court should accept the defendant's version of events as much as possible, otherwise a *Newton* hearing should be held.

22   (1982) 77 Cr App R 13.

Newton hearing

15.35   Such a hearing will only be held if the difference on facts makes a material difference to the sentence.[23] Ultimately the decision whether to hold a *Newton* hearing rests with the court, not the prosecution or the defence.[24] A defendant risks losing any credit for a guilty plea if his/her version of events is not accepted by the sentencer.[25]

15.36   At a *Newton* hearing the prosecution must prove any disputed facts beyond reasonable doubt. The usual rules of evidence apply, but as the hearing is not to determine guilt adverse inferences under the Criminal Justice and Public Order Act 1994 may not be drawn from the exercise of the right to silence.

Offences to be taken into consideration

15.37   It is not uncommon with persistent young offenders that the police charge him/her with a small number of offences and suggest that other offences should be taken into consideration (often referred to as TICs). A court may take into consideration other offences admitted by the defendant when it is sentencing. Normally these offences to be taken into consideration will be of a similar nature to those for which the defendant is being sentenced. Such offences are associated offences for the purposes of determining the seriousness of the offences to which the defendant has pleaded guilty.[26]

15.38   A schedule of the offences to be taken into consideration will be prepared and shown to the defendant before the sentencing hearing. It is important that the defence lawyer checks that the child or young person agrees that s/he is responsible for each offence on the list. If the list is accepted it should be signed by the defendant. In court the signed list should be handed to the court clerk who will confirm orally that the defendant admits all the offences contained in the list and that s/he wishes them to be taken into consideration by the magistrates when sentencing. When the bench announces sentence, it should make specific reference to the offences being

---

23   *R v Sweeting* (1987) 9 Cr App R (S) 372, CA.
24   *R v Costley* (1989) 11 Cr App R (S) 357, CA.
25   *R v Costen* (1989) 11 Cr App R (S) 182, CA.
26   Criminal Justice Act 1991 s31(2).

taken into consideration and the court register should be noted accordingly.

Police antecedents

15.39   This is a generic term for information regarding the defendant which is collected by the police. On charge the police will usually take very brief personal details regarding the accused and it is still the practice that this information be read out to a Crown Court judge following conviction. In the youth court this practice is much less common. Nevertheless, the antecedents are still important for the list of previous convictions and cautions supplied.

Previous convictions

15.40   It is the duty of the prosecution to provide the court with a list of previous convictions. In some youth courts the social services department will also provide a list of convictions recorded against a child or young person.

15.41   Before a sentencing bench is given details of any recorded convictions the list should be shown to the defence lawyer and the defendant. It should be determined that the defendant accepts the convictions listed. The defence lawyer should also check that every matter listed is in fact a conviction. It is not unknown for the police to provide courts with a computer print-out of all their contacts with a particular child or young person. Such a list will include arrests for which no further action was taken or charges which resulted in acquittals.

15.42   If the list is accepted the prosecutor will often hand in the list although it is considered better practice to read out only the relevant convictions, ignoring those which are spent under the Rehabilitation of Offenders Act 1974.[27] If the printed list contains irrelevant matters, the defence lawyer should object to a list being handed to the bench.

15.43   If the defendant disputes that s/he is the person named on the list of previous the prosecution will have to prove the defendant is indeed the person against whom the convictions are recorded. This is normally done by a fingerprint analysis.[28] If individual offences are dis-

27   See Chapter 24.
28   Criminal Justice Act 1948 s39.

puted then the court should ignore them for the purposes of sentencing, unless the prosecution indicates it wishes to prove the conviction by obtaining a memorandum of conviction from the relevant court. In such circumstances the sentencing hearing would have to be adjourned.

Previous cautions

15.44 Previous cautions may be cited but only if relevant to the offence(s) before the court.[29] Care should be taken to distinguish between convictions and cautions, which should be listed on separate sheets of paper.[30]

15.45 The defence lawyer should check that any cautions listed are in fact formal cautions. It is the practice in some police areas to produce lists of cautions which include various forms of informal warnings. These should not be cited in court, most importantly because there may not have been a formal admission of guilt. Consideration should also be given to whether the cautions listed are relevant to the offence(s) before the court for sentence. In the opinion of the authors a narrow test of relevance should be adopted and only cautions for the same or very similar offences should be cited.

Reprimands or warnings

15.46 Where a child or young person has previously been arrested in a pilot area for provisions of the Crime and Disorder Act 1998 s/he may have received a reprimand or warning under s65 of the Act.[31] The prosecutor may cite in court a reprimand, warning or failure by the defendant to participate in a rehabilitation programme in the same circumstances as a conviction may be cited.[32]

15.47 The defence lawyer should confirm with the defendant that the cited reprimand or warning is accepted. S/he should also attempt to establish whether a rehabilitation programme was offered following a warning. The fact that such a programme was not offered should be brought to the sentencing court's attention as it demonstrates that no intervention by the youth offending team took place prior to an appearance at court.

15.48 If it is claimed that the defendant did not participate in a

---

29 *National Standards for Cautioning (Revised)* Note 6A.
30 Ibid.
31 See Chapter 6.
32 Crime and Disorder Act 1998 s66(5).

rehabilitation programme, the defence lawyer should attempt to confirm whether this is accepted by the child or young person and his/her parent. Any explanation for the non-participation needs to be identified. Where there is a good excuse (for example, the family moved to a new address outside the area of the youth offending team or an adult carer was too ill to escort a child to the programme) this needs to be brought to the court's attention.

15.49   It should also be noted that where there has been non-participation in a rehabilitation programme, there is no defence of reasonable excuse. Moreover, the decision whether to record non-participation rests solely with the youth offending team organising the programme.

The sentencing hearing

15.50   In general the procedure for sentencing a child or young person is the same as for an adult, however, the Magistrates' Courts (Children and Young Persons) Rules 1992 (SI No 2071) impose specific requirements upon justices sitting both in the youth court and in the adult magistrates' court.

Presence in court

15.51   Usually an offender will be present in court throughout his/her sentencing hearing. The same would apply to any parent or guardian present. However, it is possible for the justices to require the young offender or the parent/guardian to withdraw from court if it is considered necessary in the interests of the child or young person.[33] Such a break with the principles of natural justice would only happen in the most unusual of circumstances.

15.52   On rare occasions the defence lawyer may wish to invite a youth court to use this power to hear submissions or some mitigation in the absence of the defendant. It may be considered important to provide the court with information about a parent's terminal illness or a traumatic incident experienced by the young defendant. It may be extremely distressing for a young defendant to hear such information related dispassionately in the courtroom. If it is not possible to provide the information in written form, the lawyer should seek the

---

33 Magistrates' Courts (Children and Young Persons) Rules 1992 SI No 2071 r10(2)(e).

client's consent to providing the information in the defendant's absence. In the authors' opinion the client should still be made aware of the general nature of the information that will be given in his/her absence.

Consideration of reports

15.53   Any reports may be received and considered without being read aloud.[34] In normal circumstances a copy of the report will have been made available to the young offender, his/her parent or guardian as well as the defence lawyer.[35]

Making a statement

15.54   The court must give the child or young person and his/her parent or guardian, if present, an opportunity to make a statement.[36] This right is rarely exercised when the young offender is legally represented.

Passing sentence

15.55   Having considered its sentence, the court must inform the defence lawyer and child or young person of the manner in which it proposes to dispose of the case. Representations by the defence lawyer, child or young person or parent/guardian must be allowed.[37] The final sentence must then be announced and its general effect and nature explained to the child or young person.[38]

Deferring sentence

15.56   A court may defer sentence if it considers it would be in the interests of justice to do so, having regard to the nature of the offence and the character and circumstances of the defendant.[39]

---

34   Ibid, r10(2)(d).
35   Access to the reports is considered in more detail in Chapter 16.
36   Magistrates' Courts (Children and Young Persons) Rules 1992 SI No 2071 r10(2)(a).
37   Ibid, r11(1).
38   Ibid, r11(2).
39   Powers of Criminal Courts Act 1973 s1.

Is deferment appropriate?

15.57 The purpose of a deferment is to enable the court to have regard to the offender's conduct after conviction (including, where appropriate, the making of reparation for the offence) or to any change in his/her circumstances.[40]

15.58 In the case of children and young persons deferring sentence should be used sparingly. As Lane LCJ said in *R v George*[41] the court should have a clear idea of the purpose of the deferment and it should not just be used to avoid a difficult decision. On many occasions a short supervision order would serve the same purpose by providing regular supervision of the offender's conduct as well as providing practical support. However, a deferment may be appropriate where the court's expectations are not sufficiently precise to include in the requirements of a supervision order. Such expectations commonly include:

- staying out of trouble;
- co-operating with parents or the social services department;
- attending school;
- finding training or employment; and
- making reparation for the offence.

15.59 Deferring sentence can have practical disadvantages for a young offender. The court may be expecting a substantial change in the offender's lifestyle, yet without a supervision order being in place there may be very little support from the local authority. A deferment of up to six months will seem like a very long time to a young offender and postpones the time when s/he will end his/her contact with the criminal courts as well as delaying the time when the conviction will be spent under the Rehabilitation of Offenders Act 1974.

Procedure on deferment

15.60 The court must fix a date for the deferment which should not be more than six months later. It should also indicate to the defendant what expectations it has. A careful note of these expectations should be made in the court register and it is good practice to give the defendant a written copy of them.[42]

---

40 Ibid.
41 (1984) 6 Cr App R (S) 211, CA.
42 *R v George*, see n41.

Consent

15.61 The defendant must consent to the deferment. If such consent is not obtained, it may mean that the eventual sentencing court has no power to impose any penalty at all.[43]

Pre-sentence reports

15.62 On deferring sentence it is common for the court to order that a pre-sentence report is prepared for the date of the sentencing hearing. This report will not only consider the defendant's attitude to the offence and background information but it will also describe how well the defendant has fulfilled the court's expectations.

No remand on bail

15.63 When a court defers sentence it cannot remand the defendant on bail.

Powers of the sentencing court

15.64 On passing sentence the court may deal with the offender in any way in which the court which deferred sentence could have dealt with him/her.[44] The court dealing with the deferred sentence may still decide to commit the offender for sentence under Magistrates' Courts Act 1980 s37.[45]

15.65 The relevant age for the purposes of sentence is the age of the offender at the date of conviction, not the date of final sentence.[46]

Commission of further offences

15.66 If the defendant is convicted of further criminal offences during the period of deferment, the court dealing with the new offences may sentence the defendant for the deferred offences too, except that a youth court may not sentence for offences deferred by a Crown Court and a Crown Court may not pass a sentence for offences deferred by a youth court which is longer than that available originally to the youth court.[47]

---

43 *R v McQuaide* (1974) 60 Cr App R 239, CA.
44 Powers of Criminal Courts Act 1973 s1(8)(a).
45 Ibid, s1(8)(b).
46 Cf, *R v Danga* (1992) 13 Cr App R (S) 408, CA.
47 Powers of Criminal Courts Act 1973 s1(4A).

Procedure at the final hearing

15.67   It is good practice that the same justices or judge sit at the deferred hearing. At the deferred sentencing hearing the court should start by ascertaining the purpose of the deferment and any requirements imposed on the defendant by the deferring court. Any pre-sentence report should be considered.

15.68   The court should then determine whether the defendant has substantially complied with or attempted to comply with those expectations. If there has been substantial compliance, then the defendant has a legitimate expectation that s/he will not receive a custodial sentence. If there has not been substantial compliance, the court should carefully outline in which areas the defendant has failed.[48]

15.69   If the young offender does not attend court for the final hearing a summons or warrant may be issued for his/her arrest.[49]

Naming and shaming

15.70   The protection from publicity normally given to children and young persons appearing in criminal proceedings may be lifted upon conviction. Increasingly the lifting of the reporting restrictions is being seen as part of the sentencing process, either as a means of encouraging young offenders to face up to the consequences of their offending or as part of a deterrent sentence.

15.71   The United Nations Convention on the Rights of the Child art 40(2)(b)(vii) establishes for defendants under the age of 18 the right to privacy at all stages of criminal proceedings. More specifically, the Beijing Rules r8 recommends that, in principle, information leading to the identification of an offender under the age of 18 should not be published. In the recent decision of *V v UK* the European Court of Human Rights noted these provisions and considered that they represented 'an international tendency in favour of the protection of the privacy of juvenile defendants'.[49A] When the Human Rights Act 1998 is implemented, it is submitted that these international standards should be a major factor to take into account when a court is considering whether to lift reporting restrictions.

48   *R v George* (1984) 6 Cr App R (S) 211, CA.
49   Powers of Criminal Courts Act 1973 s1(5).
49A   ECHR (application no 24888/94) official transcript, para 77 (see (1999) *Times*, 17 December). The judgment is available on the court's website – see appendix 7.

Youth court

15.72 For offences committed on or after 1 October 1997 the youth court has a power to dispense to any specified extent with the reporting restrictions where it is in the interests of justice to do so.[50] This power extends to proceedings relating to any of the following:

- the prosecution or conviction of any of the offence;
- the manner in which the offender, or his/her parent or guardian, should be dealt with in respect of the offence;
- the enforcement, amendment, variation or revocation or discharge of any order made in respect of the offence;
- where an attendance centre order is made in respect of the offence, the enforcement of any rules made under the Criminal Justice Act 1991 s16(3); or
- where a secure training order is made, the enforcement of any requirement of the supervision part of that order.

Before exercising this power the court must give all parties an opportunity to make representations and must take such representations into account when making its decision.[51]

Exercise of the power

15.73 Guidance has been issued on the use of this power in a joint Home Office/Lord Chancellor's Department circular.[52] The circular reminds youth court magistrates of the duty to prevent offending and the duty to have regard to the welfare of the child or young person. It continues:

Lifting reporting restrictions could be particularly appropriate in cases where:
- the nature of the young person's offending is persistent or serious or has impacted on a number of people or his or her community in general;
- alerting others to the young person's behaviour would prevent further offending by him or her.

There will of course be circumstances in which the lifting of reporting restrictions will not be in the best interests of justice. Factors which courts will wish to consider are whether:

---

50 Children and Young Persons Act 1933 s49(4A).
51 Ibid, s49(4B).
52 *Opening Up Youth Court Proceedings* (issued 11 June 1998).

- naming the young offender would reveal the identity of a vulnerable victim and lead to unwelcome publicity for that victim;
- publicity may put the offender or his/her family at risk of harassment or harm;
- the offender is particularly young or vulnerable;
- the offender is contrite and has shown himself or herself ready to accept responsibility for his or her actions by, for example, an early guilty plea.[53]

Remedies if reporting restrictions lifted

15.74   The decision to lift reporting restrictions following conviction would seem to be an order made on conviction within the meaning of the Magistrates' Courts Act 1980 s108. It should therefore be possible to appeal the decision to the Crown Court.

15.75   When the youth court has made an order to lift reporting restrictions, the defence lawyer must act quickly if the decision is to be challenged otherwise any damage will be done when the local press report the young offender's name. If there is a risk that the details will be published the same day, a notice of appeal should be lodged immediately. The lawyer should then ask the youth court to suspend its decision pending the appeal. The appeal proceedings before the Crown Court will be automatically covered by reporting restrictions.[54]

Crown Court

15.76   A Crown Court judge may consider whether to revoke the order imposing reporting restrictions after a child or young person has been convicted of a particularly serious offence. There may even be a request from a representative of the press for the order to be lifted.

15.77   The Divisional Court considered when it might be proper to lift the reporting restrictions in the case of *R v Leicester Crown Court ex p S (a Minor)*[55] which involved a 12-year-old boy convicted of arson causing damage estimated at £2.5 million. Watkins LJ stated:

> In our judgment, the correct approach to the exercise of the power given by section 39 is that proceedings should not be restricted unless there are reasons to do so to outweigh the legitimate interest of the

53 Ibid, paras 16 and 17.
54 By virtue of Children and Young Persons Act 1933 s49(2)(b).
55 (1992) 94 Cr App R 153; [1993] 1 WLR 111.

public in receiving fair and accurate reports of criminal proceedings and knowing the identity of those in the community who have been guilty of criminal conduct and who may, therefore, present a danger or threat to the community in which they live. The mere fact that the person before the court is a child or young person will normally be a good reason for restricting reports of the proceedings in the ways permitted by section 39 and it will, in our opinion, only be in rare and exceptional cases that directions under section 39 will not be given or having been given will be discharged.

This formulation of principle was subsequently considered by the Court of Appeal (constituted as a Divisional Court) in *R v Lee*.[56] The defendant in this case was a 14-year-old boy convicted of robbery and possession of a firearm. These offences were committed while he was on bail for rape. Referring to the opinion of Watkins LJ that the restrictions should only be lifted in 'rare and exceptional cases', Lloyd LJ stated:

For our part, we would not wish to see the court's discretion fettered so strictly. There is nothing in section 39 about rare or exceptional cases.

This latter view has been preferred by the Divisional Court in *R v Central Criminal Court ex p S and P (Minors)*[57]

15.78 When considering whether to lift reporting restrictions the judge must consider all relevant factors. The judge must have regard to the welfare of the child or young person. Considerable weight should be given to the age of the offender and to the potential damage to a young person of public identification as a criminal before s/he has the benefit or burden of adulthood.[58] The court should also consider the damage caused to any rehabilitation programme proposed in a custodial setting or in the community by adverse publicity.[59] It may also be relevant in the case of sex offenders to consider any increased risk of physical attack while in custody occasioned by publicity which names the offender.[60] In the case of very serious offences it is permissible to consider naming the offender so that it serves as a deterrent

---

56 (1993) 96 Cr App R 188; [1993] 1 WLR 103.
57 (1998) *Times*, 26 October, CO/2702/98, (1998) 16 October, Kennedy LJ, Sullivan, J, QBD.
58 *R v Inner London Crown Court ex p Barnes (Anthony)* (1995) *Times*, 7 August, QBD.
59 *R v Leicester Crown Court ex p S (a Minor)*, n55 above.
60 *R v Central Criminal Court ex p S and P (Minors)*, n57 above.

to others, but it would be improper to allow his/her naming solely to ensure that the severity of any sentence was reported widely.[61] The judge should consider any grounds of appeal against sentence before deciding whether to lift the reporting restrictions as a successful appeal is likely to result in a re-trial.[61A]

Remedies if a s39 order is lifted

15.79   A member of the press who wishes to challenge the existence of reporting restrictions may appeal to the Court of Appeal by virtue of the Criminal Justice Act 1988 s159. The defendant, however, cannot use this provision and moreover it would seem that s/he cannot seek to have the restrictions re-imposed by the Court of Appeal as part of an appeal against sentence as the power under s39 only applies to proceedings before the court making the order.[62]

15.80   The only possible remedy may be to seek judicial review of the decision to remove the reporting restrictions. However, it has been questioned on a number of occasions whether judicial review is an available remedy. It has been argued that the making of a s39 order is a matter which relates to trial on indictment and therefore the High Court's jurisdiction is excluded by the Supreme Court Act 1981 s29(3). In *R v Leicester Crown Court ex p S (a Minor)*[63] this argument was rejected and in successive decisions the jurisdiction of the High Court does not seem to have been challenged.[64] More recently the debate has been reopened. Judicial review was held to be available in *R v Cardiff Crown Court ex p M (a Minor)*.[65] A s39 order was considered to be a separate child protection power and therefore not a matter relating to trial on indictment. This argument was rejected by a differently constituted court in the subsequent case of *R v Winchester Crown Court ex p B (a Minor)*[66] which held that a s39 order was in fact integral to the administration of justice so that the Supreme Court Act 1981 s29(3) applied. Subsequently in *Re H, Re D*[66A] the divisional court has once again held that judicial review is available at

61   *R v Inner London Crown Court ex p Barnes (Anthony)*, n58 above.
61A *Re H, Re D* (1999) *Times*, 13 August, QBD.
62   *R v Lee*, n56 above
63   See n55 above.
64   See *R v Lee* (n56 above); *R v Inner London Crown Court ex p Barnes* (n58) and *R v Central Criminal Court ex p S and P (Minors)* (n57).
65   162 JP 527, QBD.
66   [1999] 1 WLR 788, QBD.
66A (1999) *Times*, 13 August, QBD.

least after conviction and sentence. It is the opinion of the authors that this view is to be preferred. In the light of the decision in *R v Lee*[67] that there is no effective right of appeal to the Court of Appeal, the contrary view that the making of a s39 order relates to a matter of trial on indictment deprives the young offender of any means of challenging the decision to lift the reporting restrictions.

15.81   In *R v Leicester Crown Court ex p S (A Minor)*[68] Watkins LJ suggested that the Divisional Court would interfere with the decision of the Crown Court judge if s/he had failed to take into account relevant matters; failed to give reasons for the decision to lift the s39 order or if the decision was *Wednesbury* unreasonable.[69] If there is any risk that the young offender's name will be published that same day or the following morning, the judge should be asked to suspend the lifting of the s39 order until leave to move for judicial review can be applied for.

67 See para 15.79.
68 See n55.
69 (1992) Cr App R 153, at p157.

CHAPTER 16

Reports

For complete chapter contents, see overleaf

Introduction

16.1 Reports play a very important role in the sentencing of children and young persons. In many cases background information is needed before the court is in a position to comply with its statutory duty to consider the welfare of the defendant under the Children and Young Persons Act 1933 s44.

16.2 A youth court is required to consider available background information regarding an offender before disposing of a case. If sufficient information is not available the court will usually adjourn to obtain a pre-sentence report, and more unusually an education or medical report. In certain circumstances the court is required to obtain a pre-sentence report before passing a custodial sentence or some community penalties.

16.3 The information contained in a report obviously depends on the co-operation of the offender. Nevertheless, the quality of reports concerning children and young persons varies alarmingly. The defence lawyer can play a role in identifying sources of information regarding the offender. S/he should also attempt to contact the report writer before the report is finalised to discuss the contents and the recommendation.

Obligation to consider background information

16.4 The Children and Young Persons Act 1969 s9 places a duty upon local authority social services departments and local education authorities to make investigations and provide information relating to the home surroundings, school record, health and character of the child or young person appearing before a criminal court. Normally no such information would be made available unless there has been a finding of guilt.

16.5 A youth court is under an obligation to consider the background of the young offender. The Magistrates' Courts (Children and Young Persons) Rules 1992 r10(2) states:

a) ...

b) the court shall take into consideration all the available information as to the general conduct, school record and medical history of the relevant minor and, in particular, shall take into account such information as aforesaid which is provided in pursuance of section 9 of the Act of 1969,

c) if such information as aforesaid is not fully available, the court shall consider the desirability of adjourning the proceedings for such inquiry as may be necessary.

This obligation must be seen in the context of the general duty to consider the welfare of the child or young person imposed on all courts.[1] A youth court will normally seek the background information required by adjourning the case and requesting written reports regarding the defendant.

Adjourning for reports

Power to adjourn

16.6 A youth court or magistrates' court may adjourn after conviction to obtain further information regarding the offender. The maximum period of that remand is three weeks if the defendant is in custody (or remanded in local authority accommodation) and four weeks if remanded on bail.[2]

16.7 This power must be considered in the light of Children and Young Persons Act 1933 s48(3) which provides:

> When a youth court has remanded a child or young person for information to be obtained with respect to him, any youth court acting for the same petty sessional division or place–
> (a) may in his absence extend the period for which he is remanded, so, however, that he appears before a court or a justice of the peace at least once in every twenty-one days;
> (b) when the required information has been obtained, may deal with him finally.

This provision seems to conflict with the power granted under Magistrates' Courts Act 1980 s10(3). However, the editors of *Justice of the Peace* argue persuasively that s48(3) must take precedence as Magistrates' Courts Act 1980 s152 states that any procedural rule contained in the 1980 Act is subject to any rule specifically relating to a youth court.[3]

Is an adjournment necessary?

16.8 Because of the welfare ethos in the youth court pre-sentence reports are ordered in some circumstances where no such report would be

1 Children and Young Person Act 1933 s44(1).
2 Magistrates' Courts Act 1980 s10(3).
3 (1995) 159 JPN 292.

considered in an adult magistrates' court. A defence lawyer should always consider, therefore, whether it may be possible to persuade the court to dispose of the case without adjourning for reports. It may be possible, for example, to arrange for the supervisor of an existing community sentence to provide a letter for the court hearing describing the response to supervision or the other requirement of the sentence. Alternatively, if a supervisor is at court, s/he could be asked to provide a short oral report about the offender's progress.

Indications of seriousness

16.9   It is the practice in most courts for an indication of seriousness to be given before adjourning for reports. This practice is of great benefit to the writer of a pre-sentence report as it allows a more focused report to be prepared. Such an indication should always be noted by the defence lawyer for the benefit of the advocate at the sentencing hearing.

Implied promises

16.10   It has been held to be good practice when adjourning for reports before sentence if the court warns the defendant that the request for reports in itself does not indicate that custody has been ruled out.[4] Nevertheless, if the court fails to give this warning, it will not by itself raise in the defendant's mind a legitimate expectation that s/he will not be given a custodial sentence.[5] This is even more the case if the adjournment for a report was required by the provisions of the Criminal Justice Act 1991.[6] However, if the court postpones sentence so that an alternative to custody can be examined and that alternative is found to be satisfactory, then the court ought to adopt the alternative.[7] The test is whether the court's actions have led the defendant to expect that a particular community penalty will be imposed if the assessment is favourable.[8]

Failure to co-operate with the preparation of reports

16.11   In normal circumstances reports will be prepared without any significant practical problems. However, in a small number of cases the

4   *R v Norton and Claxton* (1989) 11 Cr App R (S) 143, CA.
5   *R v Moss* (1983) 5 Cr App R (S) 209, CA.
6   *R v Woodin* [1994] Crim LR 72, CA.
7   *R v Gillam* (1980) 2 Cr App R (S) 267, CA.
8   *R v Stokes* (1983) 5 Cr App R (S) 449, CA.

young offenders may fail to co-operate with the report writer. Report writers are expected to offer an offender at least two appointments during the period of any remand after conviction.[9] If these appointments are not kept, the report writer will submit a letter to the court detailing the missed appointments. This is generally referred to as a non-report.

16.12 Faced with such non-cooperation, the court has two powers:

- to impose a condition of bail that the young offender should co-operate with the preparation of the report; or
- to refuse bail.

Condition of bail

16.13 The court may impose a condition that the young offender must co-operate with the preparation of the report. If the report writer is able to suggest a particular appointment, it is open to the court to phrase the condition to require attendance at that appointment. Such a condition should not be imposed as a matter of routine.

16.14 Once such a condition has been imposed, failure to attend appointments as required is a breach of bail which makes the offender liable for arrest by the police to be returned to court. Furthermore, the social worker or probation officer preparing the report will be expected by the court to report any missed appointments to the police as a breach of bail.

16.15 When an up-to-date report is considered important, the defence lawyer may wish to draw the court's attention to this power and emphasise that the risk of arrest by the police should act as a powerful incentive to the young offender to attend the necessary appointments.

Refusal of bail

16.16 If a court refuses bail to a 17-year-old, s/he will be remanded into custody. If it refuses bail to a juvenile, s/he will be remanded to local authority accommodation under the Children and Young Persons Act 1969 s23. If the sole reason for refusing bail is the failure to co-operate with the preparation of reports, it is unlikely that the criteria of s23(5) will be satisfied justifying a custodial remand.

16.17 As part of a remand to local authority remand, the court may

9 *National Standards for the Supervision of Offenders in the Community* (1995), paras 36 to 39.

impose a condition upon the offender requiring co-operation with the preparation of the report.[10] This would have the same practical effect as a bail condition.

16.18   If exercise of neither of the above powers produces the desired result, the court may seek to sentence without an up-to-date report. This may not be possible and the requirements of the Criminal Justice Act 1991 ss3 and 7 must be considered (see below).

Pre-sentence reports

Definition

16.19   A pre-sentence report is defined as a report in writing submitted by a social worker or probation officer which is intended to assist the court in determining the most suitable method of dealing with an offender.[11] There is a statutory duty to provide such reports imposed on both social workers[12] and probation officers.[13]

Format

16.20   The Home Office, Welsh Office and the Department of Health have jointly issued the *National Standards for the Supervision of Offenders in the Community* (1995). These prescribe the layout of the report as follows:

- *Introduction* – recording the sources of information in the report;
- *Offence analysis* – including an assessment of the offender's culpability, attitude to the offence, impact on the victim and awareness of the offence's consequences;
- *Relevant information about the offender* – selective coverage focusing on information relevant to the offending behaviour (or any pattern of it), the likelihood of further offending and the offender's capacity or motivation to change;
- *Risk to the public of re-offending* – distinguishing the nature and seriousness of possible further offences and the likelihood of their occurring and having regard to possible patterns of offending behaviour, the offender's capacity or motivation to change and the

---

10   Children and Young Persons Act 1969 s23(7).
11   Criminal Justice Act 1991 s3(5).
12   Children and Young Persons Act 1969 s9.
13   Powers of Criminal Courts Act 1973 Sch 3 para 8.

availability of programmes or activities which could reduce the risk or impact of further offending; and
- *Conclusion.*

Preparing a report on a child or young person

16.21 The *National Standards* (1995) also provides specific guidance regarding the preparation of pre-sentence reports (PSRs) for young offenders.

> In considering possible disposals the report writer should have particular regard to the individual's maturity where it has an influence on offending or the risk of re-offending. In the case of 16 and 17 year olds the report writer should consider which of the sentences available to the Youth Court is most suitable for the individual offender.

> Where the offender is of school age, in every case the report writer should obtain information from the school, pupil referral unit or local education authority, concerning a pupil's attendance, behaviour and performance, for use in the *relevant information about the offender* section of the report. In cases where the court orders additional information from the school this should be attached to the PSR.

> A PSR written on a child or young person should take account of any *care plan* prepared for that individual under the Children Act 1989 and must address the child or young person's relationship with his or her parent(s) or person(s) with parental responsibility and the degree to which they are responsible for the child or young person and should be involved in the supervision. When a PSR is being prepared on a child or young person it will usually be desirable for the parent to be interviewed as well as the offender.

> PSRs have an important role to play in providing information and advice to the courts which can help them to decide upon the desirability or otherwise of proposing a bindover.[14]

When is a pre-sentence report required?

16.22 The requirements to obtain a pre-sentence report depend on the type of sentence being considered.

Custody

16.23 The Criminal Justice Act 1991 s3(1) requires a court to obtain and consider a pre-sentence report before determining that an offence is

14 Part 2: Pre-sentence Reports, paras 36 to 39.

so serious that only a custodial sentence can be justified or determining the length of that sentence. This requirement has been modified by the Criminal Justice and Public Order Act 1994 Sch 9 para 40 so that, when sentencing a child or young person, the court must obtain a pre-sentence report unless:

- in the case of an indictable-only offence, if the court considers it unnecessary in the circumstances of the case; or
- in all other cases, if a previous pre-sentence report is available to be considered (if more than one report is available the court should consider the most recent).

16.24   A pre-sentence report is not required before imposing a custodial sentence under the Criminal Justice Act 1991 s1(3) upon an offender who has refused to consent to a community penalty.[15] Failure to obtain a pre-sentence report as required by the above rules does not invalidate the sentence passed, but on appeal the appellate court shall obtain such a report unless it is considered that the sentencing court was justified in deciding that a report was unnecessary or that it now appears that no report is required.[16]

Community sentences

16.25   No pre-sentence report is required before a court may sentence a defendant to any of the following sentences:

- attendance centre order;
- supervision order (without any further requirements); or
- probation order (without any additional requirements).

16.26   The Judicial Studies Board has advised magistrates that as a matter of good practice a pre-sentence report should be obtained before imposing any supervision order, even though not required by law.

16.27   The Criminal Justice Act 1991 s7 imposes obligations upon a court in relation to the ordering of pre-sentence reports. A court must obtain a pre-sentence report to assess a defendant's suitability for any of the following:

- supervision order with requirements;
- probation order with additional requirements;

---

15   *R v Meredith* [1994] Crim LR 142, CA.
16   Criminal Justice Act 1991 s3(4) and (4A).

- community service order; or
- combination order.[17]

16.28 The Criminal Justice and Public Order Act 1994 has modified this requirement and a court need not now order a report:

- in the case of an indictable-only offence, if the court considers it unnecessary in all the circumstances; or
- in all other cases, if a previous pre-sentence report is available to be considered (if more than one report is available the most recent should be considered).[18]

16.29 Failure to obtain a pre-sentence report as required by the above rules does not invalidate the sentence passed but on appeal the appellate court shall obtain such a report unless it is considered that the sentencing court was justified in deciding that a report was unnecessary or that it now appears that no report is required.[19]

Other penalties

16.30 No pre-sentence report is required before a court may sentence a defendant to the following sentences:

- absolute discharge;
- conditional discharge; or
- fine.

Sentencing without an up-to-date pre-sentence report

16.31 The Magistrates' Association issued guidance on the power to dispense with a pre-sentence report at the time that the amendment was introduced in 1995.[20] It reminds justices that the 1991 Act, as amended, still contains a statutory presumption in favour of obtaining and considering a report and that it would be good practice to explain in open court why a report was not being ordered. Specifically in relation to young offenders the Association concludes:

> Research and experience show that the situation and circumstances of young people can change dramatically over quite short periods of

17 Ibid, s7(3).
18 Ibid, s7(3B).
19 Ibid, s3(4) and (4A) and s7(4) and (5).
20 *Discretion to Dispense with a Pre-sentence Report and the New National Standard* (The Magistrates' Association, January 1995, 95/1).

time. This is true both of juveniles and of young adults. The Magistrates' Association has taken the view that there will be few cases in which it would be wise to dispense with PSRs whether for juveniles or young adults or to rely on previous reports.

16.32   In the quest for speedier proceedings, an inter-departmental government circular has been issued which does address the issue of using old reports in the youth court.[21] It reminds magistrates of the possibility of using an old report in certain circumstances. The guidance then goes further and suggests that magistrates should avoid acceding to routine requests for adjournments to provide up-to-date reports where an old report exists. When considering such a request the magistrates should take into account whether the request is likely to cause delays in sentencing and whether a verbal update might be more appropriate.[22]

Indictable-only offences

16.33 The Criminal Justice Act 1991 s3 imposes a stringent test upon the sentencer. Before imposing a custodial sentence without a pre-sentence report, the justices or judge must be satisfied that the contents of any report would not alter their views on either the proposed sentence or its length. The defence lawyer may further argue that sentencing without a report ignores the statutory obligation to consider the welfare of the child or young person.

16.34   Guidance from the Court of Appeal suggests that it will be a rare case where a child or young person should properly be sentenced without a report, even for very serious offences. In the case of *R v Rogan*[23] a 16-year-old of good character pleaded guilty to arson being reckless as to whether life would be endangered. He threw a petrol bomb into a house where a family was sleeping. The trial judge sentenced him to eight years s53(2) detention. On appeal Curtis J stated that although it was permissible to sentence without a report, this would rarely be the correct course with an offender who was so young or where the offence was so serious that the court was properly considering a long sentence.

---

21 *Tackling Delays in the Youth Justice System* (issued 15 October 1997 jointly by the Lord Chancellor's Department, Home Office, Department of Health, Welsh Office, Attorney-General and the Department for Education and Employment).
22 Ibid, para 39.
23 (1994) *Independent*, 11 April, CA.

Using an old report

16.35   The use of an old report may be unsatisfactory for a number of reasons. An old report will not deal with the defendant's attitude to the current offence(s) which could reveal unusual immaturity on the part of the defendant. As many defendants who come before the youth court regularly have troubled and unstable backgrounds, the information contained in a previous report may rapidly become out of date. With significant changes in an adolescent's life, or even simply increasing maturity, community penalties previously discounted may now be suitable for the defendant.

Specific sentence reports

16.35A   Before a court may impose a reparation order or an action plan order, it must obtain and consider a written report prepared by a member of a youth offending team. This written report is often referred to as a specific sentence report to distinguish it from a full pre-sentence report.

16.35B   When prepared in anticipation of a reparation order being made, the report must indicate:

- the type of work that is suitable for the young offender; and
- the attitude of the victim or victims to the requirements proposed to be included in the order.[23A]

16.35C   When prepared in anticipation of an action plan order being made, the report must indicate:

- the requirements proposed by the youth offending team member to be included in the order;
- the benefits to the young offender that the proposed requirements are designed to achieve; and
- the attitude of a parent or guardian of the young offender to the proposed requirements.[23B]

Where the offender is under the age of 16, the report should also include information about his/her family circumstances and the likely effect of the order on those circumstances.[23C]

23A   Crime and Disorder Act 1998 s68(1).
23B   Ibid, s70(1)(a).
23C   Ibid, s70(1)(b).

Education reports

16.36　A court may order a written report from the offender's school or from the local education authority. Local practice in relation to such reports varies enormously. In some local authority areas an education report is not requested but the writer of the pre-sentence report will routinely contact an offender's school and incorporate relevant information into the report. However, even where such local arrangements exist a court may still seek a report regarding an offender's schooling if there is concern regarding the adequacy of educational provision. This applies in particular when an offender is currently excluded from school.

Department of Education guidance

16.37　In the past there has been considerable concern regarding the content of educational reports as surveys have discovered an alarming proportion of reports containing irrelevant and often highly prejudicial information.[23D]

16.38　As a result of this concern the Department of Education (as it then was) issued guidance to schools regarding the preparation of such reports.[24] Teachers preparing the report are advised that the report should:

- be comprehensive, unbiased and factual;
- have a primarily educational focus;
- be specific to the school experience; and
- substantiate any judgements or opinions.

16.39　The guidance suggests that a court report should cover:

- the pupil's academic achievement (including specific reference to any statement of special educational need);
- attendance;
- behaviour;
- health; and
- home surroundings.

The contents of the report should always be discussed with the pupil and, if practicable, with his/her parent or guardian.

23D　NACRO, *School Reports to the Juvenile Court: Could Do Better* (1988).
24　*School Reports to the Courts* (Department of Education, 1992).

Medical reports

Adjourning for a report

16.40 By the Magistrates' Courts Act 1980 s30 a youth or adult magistrates' court may adjourn to allow a psychiatric report to be prepared. The period of adjournment may be for a maximum of four weeks if the defendant is on bail; three weeks if in custody or remanded to local authority accommodation.

16.41 This power should be considered in conjunction with Children and Young Persons Act 1933 s48(3), which probably means that the defendant must attend court personally at least every three weeks.

16.42 The power may only be exercised if:

- the offence is imprisonable;
- the court is satisfied that the accused did the act or made the omission charged; and
- the court is of the opinion that an inquiry ought to be made into his/her physical or mental condition.

16.43 If the court remands the defendant on bail it may impose conditions requiring him/her:

- to undergo a medical examination by a duly qualified practitioner; and
- for that purpose, to attend such an institution or place as the court directs, and where the inquiry is into his/her mental condition, to comply with any other directions which may be given to him/her for that purpose by any person (or class of persons) specified by the court.

Remand to hospital

16.44 A youth court may remand a defendant to hospital for the preparation of a psychiatric report on his/her mental condition.

16.45 The power may only be exercised if:

- the accused has been found guilty of an imprisonable offence or the court is satisfied that s/he did the act or made the omission charged or the accused has consented;[25]
- the court is satisfied, on the written or oral evidence of a registered medical practitioner, that there is reason to suspect that the

25 Mental Health Act 1983 s35(2).

accused is suffering from mental illness, psychopathic disorder, severe mental impairment or mental impairment; and

– the court is of the opinion that it would be impracticable for a report on his/her mental condition to be made if s/he were remanded on bail.[26]

A remand to hospital may not be for more than 28 days at a time and for no more than 12 weeks in total. The court may terminate the remand at any time if it appears to the court that it is appropriate to do so.[27]

When is a medical report required?

16.46　The sentencing court must consider a medical report before imposing any of the following orders:

– custodial sentence (upon defendant who appears mentally disordered);
– longer than normal sentence under Criminal Justice Act 1991 s2;
– hospital order (or interim hospital order);
– guardianship order; or
– supervision or probation order with requirement of treatment for mental condition.

Custodial sentence upon mentally disordered offender

16.47　Before passing a custodial sentence upon a defendant who appears to be mentally disordered, the court must obtain and consider a medical report unless, in the circumstances of the case, the court is of the opinion that it is unnecessary.[28]

Medical report

16.48　This is a report concerning the offender's mental condition. It need not be in writing[29] and therefore could be delivered orally by a court duty psychiatrist.

16.49　　Before passing a custodial sentence a custodial sentence on a defendant who appears to be mentally disordered the court must consider:

26　Ibid, s35(3).
27　Ibid, s35(7).
28　Criminal Justice Act 1991 s4(1) and (2).
29　Ibid, s4(5).

- any information before it which relates to his/her mental condition (whether given in a medical report, pre-sentence report or otherwise); and
- the likely effect of such a sentence on that condition and on any treatment which may be available for it.[30]

Longer than normal custodial sentence

16.50 Although the Court of Appeal has upheld a longer than normal sentence passed without consideration of a psychiatric report, the general principle is that such a report should be obtained. The obligation to consider the welfare of the child or young person should ensure that any court considering the exercise of this power would obtain a report.

Access to reports

16.51 Access to copies of pre-sentence reports are governed by the Crime (Sentences) Act 1997 s50 and the Magistrates' Courts (Children and Young Persons) Rules 1992 SI No 2071.

16.52 The Act provides that a copy of a pre-sentence report shall be given to:

- the offender or his/her defence lawyer; and
- to the prosecutor.[31]

16.53 If the offender is under 17 and is not represented by a defence lawyer, a copy of the report need not be given to him but shall be given to his/her parent or guardian, if present in court.[32]

16.54 Access to separate education or medical reports would seem not to be covered by s50.

Rights of offender

16.55 The Magistrates' Courts (Children and Young Persons) Rules 1992 SI No 2071 r10(3)(c) requires a court to arrange for copies of any written report before the court to be made available to the young offender. There is no guidance as to when these copies should be made available.

30 Ibid, s4(3).
31 Crime (Sentences) Act 1997 s50(2).
32 Ibid, s50(3).

16.56   The *National Standards* (1995) require the social services department or probation service to give a copy of the pre-sentence report to the young offender.[33] They further seem to assume that in many cases the contents of the report will have been discussed with the young offender prior to the report's completion.[34]

16.57   A court may direct that a copy of any report should not be disclosed to the child or young person, if it considers that disclosure is:

– impracticable having regard to his/her age and understanding; or
– undesirable having regard to potential serious harm which might thereby be suffered by him/her.[35]

16.58   Such a direction would also bind the defence lawyer representing the child or young person.

16.59   If the child or young person has been denied access to a copy of the report, the court must still tell him/her the substance of any part of the information given to the court bearing on his character or conduct which the court considers to be material to the manner in which the case should be dealt with unless it appears to be impracticable to do so having regard to his/her age and understanding.[36]

Rights of parent or guardian

16.60   The Magistrates' Courts (Children and Young Persons) Rules 1992 r10(3)(b) require the court to ensure that a copy of the pre-sentence report is made available to any parent or guardian *who is present at the hearing*. It would seem, therefore, that the right to sight of the report only exists on the day of the sentencing hearing. Nevertheless, most social services departments consider it to be good practice to allow a parent or guardian the opportunity to see a draft of a report prior to its completion.

16.61   The court may never refuse access to a copy of the pre-sentence report to a parent or guardian present at the sentencing hearing.

Access by the prosecutor

16.62   The prosecutor will only receive a copy of the pre-sentence report on the day of the sentencing hearing. No information obtained by

33 *National Standards for the Supervision of Offenders in the Community* (1995), Part 2 para 41.
34 Ibid, para 11.
35 Magistrates' Courts (Children and Young Persons) Rules 1992 r10(3)(c).
36 Ibid, r10(4)(a).

reading a pre-sentence report may be used or disclosed otherwise than for the purpose of making representations to the court concerning matters contained in the report.[37] The prosecutor is only likely to make such representations if the young defendant's account of the offence is disputed. As a matter of practice some youth justice teams require the prosecutor to return the copy of the pre-sentence report at the end of the hearing.

Access by defence lawyer

16.63 The Magistrates' Courts (Children and Young Persons) Rules 1992 require the court to ensure that copies of any written reports are made available to the young offender's legal representative.[38]

16.64 The defence lawyer would clearly prefer to have a copy of the pre-sentence report prior to the day of the sentencing hearing to allow for better preparation. This is particularly true when the hearing is complicated by multiple offences or there is a serious risk of custody. Having read the report the defence lawyer may wish to clarify points raised in the report or to seek further information regarding a suggested disposal. S/he may even identify a need for the report writer to attend court to be cross-examined.

16.65 Unfortunately, the 1992 rules do not specify when a copy of the reports should be provided to the defence lawyer. In some parts of the country local arrangements have been made for the disclosure of the report before the day of the sentencing hearing but in many parts of the country disclosure is routinely refused. A defence lawyer may wish to ask for a copy of the pre-sentence report when discussing the report with the writer. Alternatively, there would seem to be nothing to stop the defence lawyer asking the justices who request the report to direct that a copy should be supplied to the defence lawyer prior to the day of the sentencing hearing.

Use beyond the sentencing hearing

16.66 Subject to below, a pre-sentence report should be treated as a confidential document, subject to no wider disclosure without the offender's consent.[39]

---

37 Crime (Sentences) Act 1997 s50(5).
38 Magistrates' Courts (Children and Young Persons) Rules 1992 r10(3)(b).
39 *National Standards for the Supervision of Offenders in the Community* (1995) Part 2 para 43.

Disclosure to the Prison Service

16.67   The *National Standards* suggest that a copy of a pre-sentence report should be forwarded to the Prison Service if an offender receives a custodial sentence.[40]

Use of reports for other purposes

16.68   The Court of Appeal has suggested that interviews conducted in the course of preparing a pre-sentence report are 'in a confidential relationship and made in the interests of the child'. Accordingly it would be contrary to the public interest for information contained in a pre-sentence report to be used for any purpose other than the sentencing of the child or young person.[41]

Challenging the contents of a report

16.69   The defence lawyer should always go through the contents of a report with his/her client. S/he will also wish to discuss its contents with any parent or guardian present. If the client disagrees with the factual content of the report, the errors may be dealt with when addressing the bench in mitigation. If it is necessary to challenge the opinions expressed in the report, the author of the report may have to be called to be cross-examined. Ultimately it is up to the sentencing bench or judge to determine whether the report is adequate for the purposes of the Criminal Justice Act 1991.[42]

16.70   If a report is considered to have been inadequate the child or young person (or a parent or guardian on his/her behalf) may make a complaint to the relevant social services department or probation service. A complaints system must be established for this purpose.[43]

40   Ibid, Part 2 para 42.
41   *Lenihan v West Yorkshire Metropolitan Police* (1981) 3 Cr App R (S) 42.
42   *R v Okinikan* (1993) 96 Cr App R 431, CA.
43   *National Standards for the Supervision of Offenders in the Community* (1995) Introduction.

CHAPTER 17

Youth offender panels

For complete chapter contents, see overleaf

Introduction

17.1 Introduced by the Youth Justice and Criminal Evidence Act 1999, the referral order will be the mandatory sentence for most first-time defendants who plead guilty. It will even apply to non-imprisonable offences, such as, fare evasion and offences under the Road Traffic Act 1988. The Act creates a unique disposal. When the defendant pleads guilty s/he will be referred to a youth offending panel established by the youth offending team. The court will specify the length of the referral but it will be for the panel to draw up a contract with the offender specifying the reparation and activities that the young offender will carry out. Compliance will be monitored by the youth offending team. If the contract is successfully completed, the offender's conviction is immediately spent under the Rehabilitation of Offenders Act 1974. If the offender fails to comply with a contract drawn up, s/he will be returned to the youth court to be re-sentenced.

17.2 The government has decided that defence lawyers have no place in the meetings of youth offending panels, arguing that their presence would put an obstacle in the way of the panel dealing directly with the young offender.[1] It is arguable, however, that the panel hearing is still part of the sentencing process because the panel has wide powers which can restrict a young offender's liberty and these powers are comparable to many community sentences available to the youth court. The fact that the legislation refers to agreeing a contract cannot obscure the fact that, in reality, the panel is likely to be imposing conditions upon the young offender. The denial of a right to legal representation may, therefore, be in breach of article 6(3)(c) of the European Convention on Human Rights.

17.3 As in reality most defendants will not be able to pay for legal representation, the defence practitioner must strive to ensure that the defendant's legal interests are protected as much as possible. This could include preparing the client and his/her parents for the panel meeting by explaining the procedure and the panel's powers. It may also be appropriate to send written representations to the panel on the young offender's behalf.

17.4 Youth offending panels will not be implemented nationally in the first instance. Instead, they will be piloted, probably from June 2000. A court may only refer a young offender to a youth offending

---

1 Home Office *No More Excuses – a new approach to tackling youth crime in England and Wales*, Cmnd 3809, para 9.37.

panel if it has been notified by the Secretary of State that arrangements for the implementation of referral orders are available in the area in which it appears to the court that the offender resides or will reside.[2]

Referral order

17.5   Referral orders can only be made by a youth court or an adult magistrates' court. If a Crown Court judge wishes to make a referral order, the offender will have to be remitted for sentence to a youth court under Children and Young Persons Act 1933 s56.

17.6   A referral order cannot be made if:

– the penalty for the offence is fixed by law; or
– the offender has previously been convicted of a criminal offence in any court in the United Kingdom or been bound over in criminal proceedings in England and Wales or in Northern Ireland to keep the peace or to be of good behaviour.[3]

For the purposes of this legislation, a conditional discharge is counted as a conviction.[4]

Compulsory referral conditions

17.7   Referral to a youth offender panel must take place where the offender pleads guilty to the offence and to any associated offence(s).[5]

Discretionary referral conditions

17.8   A court may also refer an offender to a panel where s/he has pleaded guilty to at least one of the offences for which s/he is being dealt with.[6]

Alternative disposals

17.9   If the conditions for the making of a referral order are satisfied, the court may still impose one of the following disposals:

2   Youth Justice and Criminal Evidence Act 1999 s1(4). For the pilot areas see appendix 8.
3   Ibid s2(1)(b)–(c) and (2)(b)–(c).
4   Ibid s2(5).
5   Ibid ss1(2) and 2(1).
6   Ibid ss1(3) and 2(2).

- an absolute discharge;
- a hospital order;
- a custodial sentence.[7]

Prohibited disposals

17.10 When the court makes a referral order, it may not also impose any of the following:

- a community sentence;
- a fine;
- a reparation order;
- a conditional discharge;
- a bindover to keep the peace or be of good behaviour;
- a parental bindover; or
- a parenting order.[8]

Where the compulsory referral conditions apply, the court may not defer sentence.[9]

Power to adjourn or remit

17.11 Where the compulsory referral conditions are satisfied, the court may not be sure whether one of the other permitted disposals would be more appropriate. In such circumstances, before making a final decision about the appropriate disposal, the court may do any of the following:

- adjourn for pre-sentence reports;
- remit to the youth court for sentence;
- remand to hospital for reports;
- make an interim hospital order.[10]

Procedural requirements

17.12 When making a referral order the court must:

- specify the youth offending team responsible for implementing the order;
- require the offender to attend each of the meetings of the panel;
- require the attendance of an appropriate person; and

7 Ibid, s1(1).
8 Ibid, s4(4) and (5).
9 Ibid, s4(7).
10 Ibid.

- specify the length of time within which the contract between offender and panel shall have effect; and
- explain to the offender in ordinary language the effect of the order and the consequences of failure to agree a contract or breach of any contract made.

Determining the length of the contract

17.13   When considering the length of the referral order, the court must take into account the seriousness of the offence and any personal mitigation put forward on behalf of the defendant.[11] As the disposal may only be made when a guilty plea has been entered, it would seem that the duty to give a discount for a guilty plea is largely redundant.

17.14   In most cases where the referral conditions are satisfied, the defence lawyer will have to be prepared to mitigate immediately after plea, as it is very unlikely that the court will consider adjourning for reports unless the offence may merit a custodial sentence.

Determining the basis of plea

17.15   The young offender is unlikely to be legally represented in the meetings of the youth offending panel, therefore, it is important that the basis of plea is clear at the time that it is entered. To avoid problems later on, it is suggested that the court could be asked to make a written record of the agreed facts of the offence which could then be forwarded to the youth offending team convening the panel.

Attendance of an appropriate person

17.16   On making a referral order in relation to an offender under the age of 16, the court must require the attendance of at least one appropriate person.[12] The court need not require attendance if it is satisfied that it would be unreasonable to do so.[13] Where the offender is aged 16 or 17, the court may require the attendance of an appropriate person.

17.17   'Appropriate person' is defined as follows:

- any parent or guardian of the young offender;
- in the case of a looked-after child, a representative of the relevant local authority.

---

11   Criminal Justice Act 1991 ss1 and 28.
12   Youth Justice and Criminal Evidence Act 1999 s5(1) and (2).
13   Ibid, s5(3).

17.18 'Guardian' has the same meaning as that contained in the Children and Young Persons Act 1933 (for which see para 7.12).[14]

17.19 Where more than one appropriate person exists, the court may require more than one to attend. If the appropriate person required to attend the panel meetings is not present when the court makes the referral order, s/he shall be sent a copy of the order straight away.[15]

Youth offender panel

17.20 Where a referral order has been made, it is the duty of the specified youth offending team to establish a panel for the offender and to arrange meetings of that panel.[16]

17.21 At each of its meetings a panel shall consist of at least:

- one member appointed by the youth offending team from among its members; and
- two members so appointed who are not members of the team.[17]

The Secretary of State may issue regulations setting out the qualification criteria for the panel members drawn from the local community.[18]

Before the first panel meeting

17.21A A representative of the youth offending team should contact the young offender withn five working days of the referral order being made. An assessment of the offender's circumstances should be carried out (or updated). This will involve completion of the ASSET profile. The youth offending team representative should also collate information regarding the offender's family circumstances as well his/her education and health needs. It is intended that all this background information will be available to the panel members.[18A] The defence lawyer may wish to submit further written information to the youth offending team on behalf of the young offender.

---

14 Ibid, s5(8).
15 Ibid, s5(7).
16 Ibid, s6(1).
17 Ibid, s6(3).
18 Ibid, s6(4).
18A Home Office, *The Referral Order: Draft Guidance to Youth Offending Teams*, paras 3.4 and 3.5.

17.21B   In addition to the assessment of the young offender, a youth offending team representative should contact the victim of the offence to explain the panel procedure and to establish whether s/he wishes to participate in the panel meeting or in any reparation.[18B]

Attendance at panel meetings

17.22   The specified youth offender team must notify the offender and any appropriate person of the time and place at which they are required to attend the meeting. The panel may also allow the following to attend:

– a person over 18 chosen by the offender;
– a person who is capable of having a good influence on the offender; and
– a victim of the offence.

Adult chosen by the offender

17.23   The offender has the right to nominate, with the agreement of the panel, a person over the age of 18 to accompany him/her to the panel meetings.[19] The same person need not attend each meeting of the panel. This adult could be a sibling, family friend or possibly even a children's rights advocate.

17.24   As the defence lawyer is unlikely to attend the panel meetings, it is important to advise the young offender of the right to nominate an adult to attend with him/her. The lawyer may need to help the client to identify a suitable adult. If a person is identified immediately it would be advisable to inform the representative of the youth offending team so that any notification can be sent to the adult.

Person capable of having a good influence upon the offender

17.25   The panel may also invite any other adult who appears to be capable of having a good influence on the offender.[20] Such an invitation would not appear to require the consent of either the young offender or his/her parent or guardian.

Victim of offence

17.26   The panel may invite any person who appears to the panel to be a victim of, or otherwise affected by, the offence, or any of the offences,

18B Ibid, para 3.10ff.
19   Youth Justice and Criminal Evidence Act 1999 s7(3).
20   Ibid, s7(4)(b).

in respect of which the offender was referred to the panel.[21] Where a victim wishes to attend the meeting, the panel may allow him/her to be accompanied by one person. The choice of person to accompany the victim is subject to the agreement of the panel.[22]

Presence of a lawyer

17.27   The Youth Justice and Criminal Evidence Act 1999 does not expressly prohibit legal representation of the young offender at the panel hearings, however, legal aid will not be available and, consequently, the vast majority of young offenders will have no choice but to attend the panels without legal representation.

17.28   Defence lawyers who are instructed privately or agree to act *pro bono* should be aware that youth offender panels are strongly advised to exclude legal representation:

> Young people will not be legally represented at a youth offender panel meeting as this could seriously hinder the process of the panel. The purpose of the panel process is to encourage the direct involvement of the young person in order to give them a real opportunity to take responsibility for both the offending behaviour, and their future behaviour.
>
> The panel should be alert to attempts to introduce a legal representative in the guise of the offender's support. However, the panel should not seek to prevent the attendance of lawyers who have a genuine role as a parent, carer, adult supporter or victim. In such cases the panel will need to ensure that the young person speaks for himself during the course of the panel meetings.[22A]

Failure of offender to attend meetings

17.29   If the offender fails to attend any part of a meeting the panel may:

- adjourn the meeting to such place and time as it may specify; or
- end the meeting and refer the offender back to the appropriate court.[23]

The young offender does not commit a criminal offence by not attending. There is also no power to require attendance, for example, by the issuing of an arrest warrant.

---

21   Ibid, s7(4)(a).
22   Ibid, s7(5).
22A Home Office, *The Referral Order: Draft Guidance to Youth Offending Teams*, paras 3.31 and 3.32. Compare *R v Cornwall CC ex p LH* [2000] 1 FLR 237, where it was held that a rigid policy of excluding lawyers representing parents from child protection conferences was unlawful.
23   Youth Justice and Criminal Evidence Act 1999 s7(3).

Failure of appropriate person to attend meetings

17.30   Where the appropriate person does not attend the panel meetings, there is no power to compel attendance by the issue of a warrant. However, a person who fails to attend without good reason when required to do so by a court, may be summonsed by that court for contempt under Magistrates' Courts Act 1980 s63.

Youth offender contract

17.31   At the first meeting of the panel, the members of the panel shall seek to reach agreement with the offender on a programme of behaviour. The aim of this programme is the prevention of re-offending by the offender.[24]

Terms of the programme

17.32   The programme may include provision for any of the following:
- financial or other reparation to any person who appears to the panel to be a victim of, or otherwise affected by, the offence or any of the offences, for which the offender was referred to the panel;
- the offender to attend mediation sessions with any such victim or other person;
- the offender to carry out unpaid work or service in or for the community;
- the offender to be at home at times specified in the programme;
- attendance by the offender at a school or other educational establishment or at a place of work;
- the offender to participate in specified activities;
- the offender to present him/herself to specified persons at times and places specified in or determined under the programme;
- the offender to stay away from specified places or persons (or both);
- enabling the offender's compliance with the programme to be supervised and recorded.[25]

The programme may not however provide:
- for the monitoring of the offender's whereabouts (electronically or otherwise); or

24   Ibid, s8(1).
25   Ibid, s8(2).

– for the offender to have imposed on him/her any physical restriction on his/her movements.[26]

No condition requiring anything to be done to or with any victim or other person affected by the offence(s) may be included in the programme without the consent of the victim or other person.[27]

Record of the programme

17.33 Where a programme has been agreed between the offender and the panel, the panel shall cause a written record of the programme to be prepared immediately. This record should be in language capable of being readily understood by, or explained to, the offender. The offender will then be expected to sign the agreed contract. It is not clear whether it would be open to the young offender to seek an adjournment of the panel meeting at that point to obtain legal advice on the contents of the draft programme.

Youth offender contract

17.34 Once the record has been signed by both the offender and a member of the panel on behalf of the panel, the terms of the programme take effect as the terms of a 'youth offender contract'.[28] A copy of the record must be given or sent to the offender.[29] There is surprisingly no similar requirement to give a copy to the parent or guardian.

17.35 The contract will take effect from the day when it is signed for the length of the referral order made by the court.[30] It is the duty of the specified youth offending team to make arrangements for supervising the offender's compliance with the terms of the contract and to ensure that records are kept of that compliance.[31]

Failure to agree contract

17.36 It is clearly intended that a youth offender contract will be agreed at the first meeting of the panel. However, where it is considered appropriate to do so, the panel may end the first meeting without

26 Ibid, s8(3).
27 Ibid, s8(4).
28 Ibid, s8(6).
29 Ibid.
30 Ibid, s9(3)–(5).
31 Ibid, s14(2).

reaching agreement and resume consideration of the offender's case at a further meeting of the panel.[32]

17.37   Where is appears to the panel at the first of any such further meeting that there is no prospect of agreement being reached with the offender within a reasonable period after the making of the referral order, the panel may chose to refer the offender back to the appropriate court to be re-sentenced.[33] Before exercising this power it is suggested that the panel could end the meeting and advise the young offender to seek legal advice before the panel meets again to consider his/her case.

17.38   If at a meeting of the panel agreement is reached with the offender but s/he does not sign the record and his/her failure to do so appears to the panel to be unreasonable, the panel shall end the meeting and refer the offender back to the appropriate court.[34]

Progress meetings

17.39   At any time after a youth offender contract has taken effect and before the expiry of the period for which the contract has effect, the panel may request the specified youth offending team to arrange a further meeting of the panel. Such meetings are referred to as progress meetings.[35]

Request initiated by the panel

17.40   A progress meeting may be requested if it appears to the panel to be expedient to review:

- the offender's progress in implementing the programme of behaviour contained in the contract; or
- any other matter arising in connection with the contract.[36]

A progress meeting must be requested if it appears to the panel that the offender is in breach of any terms of the contract.[37]

Request initiated by the young offender

17.41   The panel must request a progress meeting if the offender has notified the panel that:

32   Ibid, s10(1).
33   Ibid, s10(2).
34   Ibid, s10(3).
35   Ibid, s11(1).
36   Ibid, s11(2).
37   Ibid, s11(3)(b).

- s/he wishes to seek the panel's agreement to a variation in the terms of the contract, or
- s/he wishes the panel to refer him/her back to the appropriate court with a view to the referral order being revoked on account of a significant change in his/her circumstances making compliance with any youth offender contract impractical.[38]

17.42   The example of a significant change of circumstances given in the legislation is the offender being taken to live abroad. While youth offending panels are being piloted, a move to an area where they are not in operation would also seem to be a significant change of circumstances making compliance impractical.

Final meeting

17.43   When the compliance period of a youth offender contract is due to expire, the youth offending team must arrange a final meeting of the panel. This meeting must take place before the expiry of the contract.[39] It can take place in the absence of the offender.[40]

17.44   At the final meeting the panel shall:

- review the extent of the offender's compliance with the terms of the contract; and
- decide, in the light of that review, whether the offender's compliance with those terms justifies the conclusion that, by the time the contract expires, s/he will have satisfactorily completed the contract.[41]

The final meeting may not be adjourned to a time after the end of the period of the youth offender contract.[42]

17.45   If the panel determines that the offender's compliance has been satisfactory, it shall give him/her written confirmation of its decision.[43] This will also mean that the referral order will be discharged as from the end of the period of the contract.[44] If the panel concludes that the offender's compliance has not been satisfactory, it shall refer him/her back to the appropriate court.[45]

38   Ibid, s11(3)(a).
39   Ibid, s12(1).
40   Ibid, s12(5).
41   Ibid, s12(2).
42   Ibid, s12(6).
43   Ibid, s12(2).
44   Ibid, s12(3).
45   Ibid, s12(4).

Appealing decisions of the panel

17.46 There is no right of appeal against any of the decisions of the panel; however, it is likely that the panel would be subject to judicial review. This might be appropriate where the panel has exceeded its statutory powers or acted contrary to the rules of natural justice.

Referral back to appropriate court

17.47 A youth offending panel may refer an offender back to court if:
- the offender fails to attend any panel meeting;
- it appears that there is no prospect of agreement being reached with the offender within a reasonable time after the making of the referral order;
- the offender unreasonably refuses to sign a contract which has been agreed at a meeting;
- the offender unreasonably refuses to sign an amended contract;
- the panel considers that the offender is in breach of the contract;
- the offender requests such a referral with a view to the referral order being revoked on account of a significant change in circumstances making compliance with any contract impractical.

Which court?

17.48 Any referral to the 'appropriate court' is to the youth court acting for the petty sessions area in which it appears to the youth offender panel that the offender resides or will reside. Where the offender will have attained the age of 18 by the time of the first court appearance, the referral should be to the adult magistrates' court for the same area.[46]

Requiring the offender's attendance

17.49 Where the appropriate court receives a report from the panel alleging non-compliance with the terms of the contract, a justice may:
- issue a summons requiring the offender to appear at the place and time specified in it; or
- if the report is substantiated on oath, issue a warrant for the offender's arrest.[47]

46 Ibid, Sch 1 para 1(2).
47 Ibid, Sch 1 para 3(1) and (2).

Detention and remand of an arrested offender

17.50   Where an offender is arrested on a warrant and cannot be brought immediately before the appropriate court, the person in whose custody s/he is held may make arrangements for his/her detention in a place of safety[48] for a period of not more than 72 hours from the time of the arrest. The offender shall be brought before a youth court (adult magistrates' court if s/he has attained the age of 18) within that period.

The hearing

17.51   The court must decide whether:

- the panel was entitled to make any finding of fact; and
- any exercise of discretion was reasonably exercised.[49]

In performing this role it is not clear whether the court is acting as a tribunal of fact requiring the alleged breach to be proved or as a supervisory body only rejecting wholly unreasonable decisions. As the young offender would have no access to legal representation at the panel meeting, it is submitted that the former role should be adopted by the court.

Powers of the court

17.52   If the court upholds the panel's decision to refer the offender back to court it may revoke the referral order.[50] If further referral orders were made at a subsequent sentencing hearing, these orders would also be automatically revoked.[51]

17.53   When a court revokes a referral order, it may deal with the offender in any manner in which s/he could have been dealt with for that offence by the court which made the referral order.[52] This means that the relevant age is the age on the date of conviction for the offence. When sentencing the court must have regard to:

48   'Place of safety' means a community home provided by a local authority or a controlled community home, any police station, or any hospital, surgery, or any other suitable place, the occupier of which is willing temporarily to receive a child or young person: Children and Young Persons Act 1933 s107(1).
49   Youth Justice and Criminal Evidence Act 1999 Sch 1 para 5(1).
50   Ibid, Sch 1 para 5(2).
51   Ibid, Sch 1 para 5(3).
52   Ibid, Sch 1 para 5(5)(a).

- the circumstances of the offender's referral back to the court; and
- the extent to which the offender complied with any contract that had been agreed.[53]

The court may not revoke a referral order and sentence the offender unless s/he is present before it.[54]

Appeal

17.54   Where the offender is re-sentenced for the original offence, s/he may appeal any sentence to the Crown Court.[55]

The effect of further convictions

17.55   When a defendant subject to a referral order appears before a court for other offences, the court has two options:

- to extend the compliance period of the existing referral order; or
- to revoke the order.

Extending the compliance period of the referral order

17.56   The power of the court to do this depends on whether the offence was committed before or after the making of the referral order. The period of compliance may not be extended beyond 12 months.[56] The court may not, therefore, exercise this power where the original referral order was for the maximum 12 months.

Offences committed before the making of the referral order

17.57   Where the defendant is under the age of 18, the court may sentence him/her by making an order extending the compliance period of the existing referral order. This power may only be exercised if this is the only other time that the defendant has been sentenced in a court in any part of the United Kingdom.[57]

---

53   Ibid, Sch 1 para 5(5)(b).
54   Ibid, Sch 1 para 5(6).
55   Ibid, Sch 1 para 6.
56   Ibid, Sch 1 para 13(1).
57   Ibid, Sch 1 para 11.

Offences committed after the making of the referral order

17.58   Where the defendant is under the age of 18, the court may sentence him/her by making an order extending the compliance period of the existing referral order, but only if it is satisfied, on the basis of a report made by the panel, that there are exceptional circumstances which indicate that, even though the offender has re-offended, extending his/her compliance period is likely to prevent further re-offending.[58] If the court is satisfied that this exception exists, it must state in open court that it is so satisfied and why it is.[59]

Revocation of the referral order

17.59   When a defendant is sentenced for another offence other than by way of an absolute discharge or an extension of the referral order, any existing referral order is automatically revoked.[60]

17.60   If it appears to be in the interests of justice, the court may deal with the offender for the offence in respect of which the referral order was made in any manner in which s/he could have been dealt with for that offence by the court which made the order.[61] The relevant age is, therefore, the offender's age at the time when s/he entered a guilty plea to the original offence. When re-sentencing the court shall have regard to the extent of the offender's compliance with the youth offending contract.[62] If on re-sentence the defendant is committed for sentence to the Crown Court, the sentencing judge is limited to the sentencing powers of the court which made the original referral order.[63]

58   Ibid, Sch 1 para 12(1) and (2)(a).
59   Ibid, Sch 1 para 12(2)(b).
60   Ibid, Sch 1 para 14(1).
61   Ibid, Sch 1 para 14(3).
62   Ibid, Sch 1 para 14(4) and (5)(b).
63   Ibid, Sch 1 para 14(5)(a).

CHAPTER 18

Discharges, financial orders and other powers

For complete chapter contents, see overleaf

Absolute and conditional discharges

18.1   The Powers of Criminal Courts Act 1973 s1A(1) states:

> Where a court by or before which a person is convicted of an offence (not being an offence the sentence for which is fixed by law) is of the opinion, having regard to the circumstances including the nature of the offence and the character of the offender, that it is inexpedient to inflict punishment, the court may make an order either–
> (a) discharging him absolutely;
> (b) if the court thinks fit, discharging him subject to the condition that he commits no offence during such period, not exceeding three years from the date of the order, as may be specified in the order.

Absolute discharge

18.2   This disposal is very rare. It is imposed where the offender is considered to be blameless or guilty only because of a technicality. With the policy of diversion from the criminal justice system it is unlikely that a court will have before it a young offender whose offence could be considered to warrant an absolute discharge.

18.3   It is the practice of some courts to use an absolute discharge as the nominal sentence for an offence dealt with at the same time that a custodial sentence is imposed upon the offender. Other courts achieve the same result by announcing that no separate penalty has been imposed.

Conditional discharge

18.4   When a court imposes a conditional discharge upon an offender it should announce the length of the discharge and explain to the offender in ordinary language that if s/he commits another offence during the period of conditional discharge s/he will be liable to be sentenced for the original offence.[1-2]

18.5   In the past, conditional discharges have been frequently used when dealing with young offenders as they were seen to maintain the principle of diversion. With the recent emphasis on early intervention to prevent offending their use is likely to decline (see also para 18.6).

1–2 Powers of Criminal Courts Act 1973 s1A(3).

Restrictions on the use of a conditional discharge

18.6 Where a child or young person has received a warning within two years of the date of the commission of the current offence, the court shall not conditionally discharge him/her unless it is satisfied that there are exceptional circumstances relating to the offence or the offender which justify its doing so.[3] Where a court does discharge the young offender in such circumstances, it must state in open court the reasons for considering that there are exceptional circumstances.[4]

Effect of a discharge

18.7 A discharge is not deemed to be a conviction except for the purposes of the proceedings in which the order was made and any subsequent proceedings for breach of the discharge.[5] This applies even if the child or young person is re-sentenced for the offence.[6]

Security for good behaviour

18.8 When making an order for a conditional discharge the court may allow any person who consents to do so to give security for the good behaviour of the offender, if it thinks it is expedient for the purpose of the reformation of the offender.[7]

18.9 This power is extremely rarely used and would seem to be largely redundant in the case of children and young persons as the court already has a general power to bind over a parent or guardian.[8]

Breach of a conditional discharge

18.10 An offender will be in breach of a conditional discharge if s/he is convicted of a further offence which occurred during the period of conditional discharge. When this has happened the offender is liable to be sentenced for the original offence and the sentencing court will have available to it all sentencing powers that would be available if the

---

3 Crime and Disorder Act 1998 s56(4)(a).
4 Ibid, s56(4)(b).
5 Powers of Criminal Courts Act 1973 s1C(1).
6 Ibid, s1C(2).
7 Ibid, s12(1)
8 Children and Young Persons Act 1933 s55.

offender had just been convicted of the offence.[9-10] This could mean that a young offender has now attained the age of 15 and has therefore become eligible for detention in a young offender institution. In such circumstance the defence lawyer would wish to draw the court's attention to the offender's age at the date of the original conviction.

18.11   When an offender is sentenced for an offence following a breach of a conditional discharge, the discharge shall cease to have effect.[11]

18.12   The procedure for dealing with the breach depends upon whether the discharge was imposed by a magistrates' court or Crown Court.

Discharge imposed by youth court or magistrates' court

18.13   The breach of the discharge will usually be discovered by the court which is dealing with the new offence, conviction for which puts the offender in breach. In practice it is therefore more convenient for this court to deal with the breach. This is possible provided the court obtains the consent of the original court to deal with the breach.[12] A Crown Court does not need to obtain the consent of a magistrates' court or youth court before dealing with a breach.[13]

18.14   If such consent is obtained, the offender will be asked to confirm that s/he admits both the fact that the conditional discharge was imposed and that the new conviction means that the discharge has been breached. If the breach is admitted the court may proceed to sentence. If the breach is not admitted the original conviction would have to be proved by the production of a memorandum of conviction.

18.15   It is also possible for the original court to deal with the breach. This is the case even if the original court was a youth court and the offender has now attained the age of 18.[14]

18.16   Upon receipt of an information a justice of the peace for the original court may issue a summons requiring the offender to appear before the court at a time specified if it appears that the offender has been convicted of an offence committed during the period of discharge and s/he has been dealt with for this new offence. A warrant for the offender's arrest may be issued if the information is in writing and sworn.[15]

9–10   Powers of Criminal Courts Act 1973 s1B(6) and (8).
11   Ibid, s1B(7).
12   Ibid, s1B(8).
13   Ibid, s1B(7).
14   Children and Young Persons Act 1933 s48(2).
15   Powers of Criminal Courts Act 1973 s1B(1) and (3).

18.17   If a youth court conditionally discharges a young person for an indictable-only offence and the offender has attained the age of 18 before s/he is dealt with for any breach, the court's powers on re-sentence are limited to those available for an offence triable either-way which has been tried summarily.[16] This means that the maximum custodial sentence would be six months' detention.

Discharge imposed by the Crown Court

18.18   When an offender is convicted of an offence before a magistrates' or youth court which places him/her in breach of a conditional discharge imposed by a Crown Court, the justices may commit the offender on bail or in custody, to appear at the Crown Court.[17] If an offender is committed the court shall send a memorandum of the conviction entered in the court register to the Crown Court. This memorandum should be signed by the clerk of the court. The new offence may also be committed to the Crown Court under Criminal Justice Act 1967 s56.[18]

Fine

Power to fine

18.19   In the youth court or magistrates' court an offender convicted of an offence may be fined. If the offence is summary only, the court's powers will be limited depending on the level of the offence and the standard scale.

Level on the scale	Amount of fine £
1	200
2	500
3	1,000
4	2,500
5	5,000

16 Ibid, s1B(9).
17 Ibid, s1B(5).
18 *R v Penfold* [1995] Crim LR 666, CA.

For offences triable on indictment there is a statutory maximum of
£5,000.

18.20   The Magistrates' Courts Act 1980 s36 imposes lower maxima
when fining children and young persons. An offender under the age
of 14 is subject to a maximum of £250 and an offender aged 14 to 17
is subject to a maximum of £1,000. In the Crown Court the judge is
not subject to a statutory maximum. The Crown Court judge is
required to fix a period of imprisonment to be served in default of
payment of the fine.[19] In relation to a child or young person this
requirement would seem to be redundant as a child or young person
may not be imprisoned for default nor may detention in a young
offender institution be ordered.[20]

A fine or one day

18.21   It is common for justices to impose a fine but declare that an alternative period of imprisonment may be served. This disposal is most
commonly used where the offender has already spent a period of
time in custody.

18.22   This disposal is not available in relation to a child or young person
as there is no power to commit a child or young person to prison for
default[21] and the power to commit to detention for default only exists
if the offender is not less than 18 years of age.[22] The disposal would of
course be available to a court dealing with a young offender who has
attained the age of 18 during the proceedings.

Ordering the parent or guardian to pay

18.23   The Children and Young Persons Act 1933 s55 requires a court to
order a parent or guardian to pay any fine imposed against an
offender aged under 16 and gives the court a discretion to order such
payment in the case of an offender aged 16 or 17. If a local authority
has parental responsibility it, rather than the young offender, may be
ordered to pay the fine. This power and the criteria for considering its
use are considered in detail in Chapter 7.

---

19   Powers of Criminal Courts Act 1973 s31(2).
20   Criminal Justice Act 1982 s9; see also *R v Basid* [1996] Crim LR 67, CA.
21   Ibid, s1(1).
22   Ibid, s9.

Determining the level of the fine

18.24 The Criminal Justice Act 1991 s18 provides:

(1) Before fixing the amount of the any fine, a court shall inquire into the financial circumstances of the offender.

(2) The amount of any fine fixed by a court shall be such as, in the opinion of the court, reflects the seriousness of the offence.

(3) In fixing the amount of any fine, a court shall take into account the circumstances of the case including, among other things, the financial circumstances of the offender so far as they are known, or appear, to the court.

The court must, therefore, take into consideration:

– the seriousness of the offence; and
– the means of the person ordered to pay the fine.

Seriousness of the offence

18.25 Section 18(2) refers to the level of the fine reflecting the seriousness of the offence. The court is therefore required to consider any aggravating or mitigating features of the offence as well as any personal mitigation before fixing the level of the fine. Account should also be taken of any guilty plea. It should be noted that the section makes no reference to associated offences and it would seem that the level of a fine should be fixed solely by reference to the individual offence, subject to the principle of the totality of the sentence.

Means

18.26 When ordering the young offender to pay the fine, the court will assess his/her means; when ordering the parent or guardian to pay, the court will assess their means.

18.27 The court is required to inquire into the means of the person who is to be ordered to pay the fine before any order may be made. This can often be a very cursory examination of a person's income and outgoings and a defence lawyer would be advised to prepare a detailed schedule of the income and outgoings of a young offender living independently before the court hearing.

18.28 If the person ordered to pay does not have the means to pay the fine ordered immediately, the court may order that the full amount be paid within a specified period or it may order the payment of the fine in instalments. In normal circumstances it should be possible to pay the fine in 12 months, but there is nothing wrong in principle with a period of payment longer than a year, provided that it was not an undue burden and too severe a punishment, having regard to the nature of the offence and the offender.[23]

18.29   When ordering payment by instalments the court may fix a return date when the offender must attend court for payments of the fine to be reviewed. The court may also place the offender under the supervision of a person appointed by the court to ensure payment is made. Both of these powers are considered below.

18.30   Where the offender lacks the money to pay both a fine and a compensation order, a court should give priority to a compensation order.[24]

Rehabilitation of Offenders Act

18.31   It should be noted that an offence for which a child or young person is found guilty and fined is only spent after the expiry of two-and-a-half years from the date of the conviction. This contrasts with a conditional discharge where the offence is spent at the end of the period of discharge. Defence lawyers should ensure that courts bear this difference in mind when selecting the appropriate penalty. It could have a significant effect on a young person's ability to obtain employment.

Compensation order

Power to order compensation

18.32   Following a conviction a court is empowered to order the offender to pay compensation to the victim of the offence. Such an order is referred to as a compensation order and it may be made along with another sentence or on its own. If a court does not make a compensation order, it is required to state in open court why it has not done so.[25] It is not necessary for a request for compensation to be made to the court before the power may be exercised.

18.33   If there is more than one claimant for compensation, individual

---

23   *R v Olliver and Olliver* (1989) 11 Cr App R (S) 10; [1989] Crim LR 387, CA.
24   Powers of Criminal Courts Act 1973 s35(4A).
25   Powers of Criminal Courts Act 1973 s35(1).

orders should be made[26] and the available money apportioned between the various complainants on a pro rata basis.[27] It is, however, possible in rare cases to select certain complainants to receive the money available for compensation.[28]

Ordering the parent or guardian to pay

18.34 The Children and Young Persons Act 1933 s55 requires a court to order a parent or guardian to pay any compensation imposed against an offender aged under 16 and gives the court a discretion to order such payment in the case of an offender aged 16 or 17. If a local authority has parental responsibility it may be ordered to pay the compensation instead of the young offender. This power and the criteria for considering its use are considered in detail in Chapter 7.

What loss may be compensated?

18.35 The offender may be required to pay for:

> ... any personal injury, loss or damage resulting from that offence or any other offence which is taken into consideration by the court in determining sentence or to make payments for funeral expenses or bereavement in respect of a death resulting from any such offence, other than a death due to an accident arising out of the presence of a motor vehicle on a road.[29]

Personal injury

18.36 Guidance for common injuries may be found in the appendix to the Home Office Circular 53/1993 *Compensation in the Criminal Courts*. An award may be made if the injury may fairly be said to have resulted from the offence. For example it was held lawful to order an offender convicted of affray to pay compensation to a person injured during the disturbance even though it could not be shown that the offender directly caused the injury.[30]

18.37 A victim may also be compensated for any distress and anxiety caused by the offence.[31] The circular offers the following guidance:

26 *R v Grundy* [1974] 1 WLR 139.
27 *R v Miller* [1976] Crim LR 694
28 *R v Amey* (1982) 4 Cr App R (S) 694.
29 Powers of Criminal Courts Act 1973 s35.
30 *R v Taylor* (1993) 14 Cr App R (S) 276.
31 *Bond v Chief Constable of Kent* [1983] 1 All ER 456.

The assessment of compensation in such cases is not always easy, but some factors which can be taken into account are any medical or other help required, the length of any absence from work and a comparison with the suggested levels of compensation for physical injury.

Items of sentimental value

18.38 Home Office Circular 53/1993 gives the following guidance:

[I]n the case of stolen or damaged items of sentimental value or where the value can no longer be ascertained, it may be possible to draw common sense comparisons with other property losses and the likely effect on the victim. The fact that an exact value cannot be established should not necessarily deter courts from attempting to assess compensation and from making an order; victims will otherwise take away the impression that their losses have been ignored.

Motor vehicles

18.39 Compensation arising out of the presence of a motor vehicle on a road may only be ordered if:

- it is in respect of damage to property resulting from an offence under the Theft Act 1968; or
- it is in respect of injury, loss or damage as respects which the offender is uninsured in relation to the use of the vehicle, and compensation is not payable under any arrangements to which the Secretary of State is a party (ie, agreements with the Motor Insurers' Bureau).

Compensation may be ordered for the loss of an owner's no claims bonus.[32]

Determining the amount of the order

Determining the loss

18.40 By Powers of Criminal Courts Act 1973 s35(1A):

Compensation . . . shall be of such amount as the court considers appropriate, having regard to any evidence and to any representations that are made by or on behalf of the accused or the prosecutor.

32 Powers of Criminal Courts Act 1973 s35(3).

If the loss claimed by the complainant is not accepted by the offender, the court should not make a compensation order without receiving any evidence.[33] The claim will usually be supported by documentary evidence, for example a repair bill for materials and labour. The court should enquire whether the offender (or his/her parent or guardian) accepts the stated amount of loss. If s/he does not, the court should attempt to resolve the dispute on the evidence available, however, a complicated investigation where the court is asked to resolve questions of fact and law should not be undertaken.[34] In such circumstances the complainant should be left to pursue his/her civil remedies.

Means

18.41 A court must have regard to the offender's means so far as they appear or are known to the court before determining the amount of any compensation order.[35] When the parent or guardian is ordered to pay it is their means which should be assessed.

18.42 If the means of the person ordered to pay are insufficient to pay the compensation ordered immediately the court may allow time to pay or may order payment by instalments. According to Home Office Circular 53/1993, wherever possible the period of payment should not be more than 12 months. However, there is nothing wrong in principle with a period of payment longer than a year, provided that it was not an undue burden and too severe a punishment, having regard to the nature of the offence and the offender.[36]

18.43 Where the offender lacks the money to pay both a fine and a compensation order, a court should give priority to a compensation order.[37] All defendants found guilty of an offence are jointly and severally responsible for any loss; therefore, if more than one defendant is being sentenced for an offence, it is quite proper for the court to order one to pay all the compensation if s/he is the only one who has any means.[38]

---

33 *R v Horsham Justices ex p Richards* (1985) 7 Cr App R (S) 158, QBD.
34 *Hyde v Emery* (1984) 6 Cr App R (S) 158, QBD.
35 Powers of Criminal Courts Act 1973 s35(4).
36 *R v Olliver and Olliver* (1989) 11 Cr App R (S) 10; [1989] Crim LR 387, CA.
37 Powers of Criminal Courts Act 1973 s35(4A).
38 *R v Beddow* (1987) 9 Cr App R (S) 235, CA.

Costs

Prosecution costs

18.44   A court may order an accused convicted of an offence to pay such prosecution costs as the court considers 'just and reasonable'.[39] In the case of an offender under the age of 17, the amount of any costs ordered to be paid shall not exceed the amount of any fine imposed.[40]

18.45   By the Children and Young Persons Act 1933 s55 a court which decides to make an order as to costs must make that order against the parent or guardian of an offender aged under 16 years unless they cannot be found or it would be unreasonable to do so. For offenders aged 16 or 17 the court has a discretion to order the parent or guardian to pay the costs. If the offender is in the care of a local authority or accommodated by the authority and the authority has parental responsibility, the court may order it to pay the costs of the prosecution. This power is considered in more detail in Chapter 8.

Defence costs

18.46   A court may order the costs incurred in defending the proceedings to be paid out of central funds in the following situations:

   – where any information charging a person with an offence is not proceeded with;
   – where a defendant is discharged at committal proceedings;
   – where any information is dismissed at summary trial.[41]

In normal circumstances a defendant may expect to receive his/her costs to be paid out of central funds in any of the circumstances listed above.[42]

18.47   Defence costs may also be claimed if the prosecution serves a written notice of discontinuance under the Prosecution of Offences Act 1985 s23. It is not necessary for the accused to return to court to claim his/her costs; instead a written request may be made to the clerk of the court.[43]

---

39   Prosecution of Offences Act 1985 s18.
40   Ibid, s18(5).
41   Ibid, s16.
42   *R v Birmingham Juvenile Courts ex p H* (1992) *Times*, 4 February.
43   *DPP v Denning* [1991] Crim LR 699; [1991] 3 All ER 439.

Enforcement of financial orders

Enforcement against the offender

18.48 If the young offender was ordered to pay the fine, compensation order or costs personally, any enforcement proceedings will be against the child or young person.

18.49 Enforcement proceedings against a child or young person should be undertaken by the youth court unless the offender has attained the age of 18, in which case the appropriate court is the adult magistrates' court.[44]

Enforcement against the parent or guardian

18.50 If the parent or guardian has been ordered to pay the financial order under the Children and Young Persons Act 1933 s55 or under the Magistrates' Courts Act 1980 s82 after enforcement proceedings against the child or young person, the magistrates' court has the power to enforce the order. Enforcement proceedings in these circumstances may only be against the parent or guardian not against the child or young person. The court will have all the powers considered below except deduction from income support and the imposition of an attendance centre order (assuming the parent or guardian is over the age of 25).

Means enquiry

18.51 If the young offender is in default the court may issue a summons requiring the child or young person to attend at a specified time and date or the court may issue a warrant for his/her arrest.[45] In normal circumstances the court will first issue a summons against the child or young person and only if s/he fails to attend will a warrant be issued. If on sentence a return date was set and the child or young

---

44 Moore and Wilkinson in *Youth Court: A Guide to the Law and Practice* (2nd edn, 1995, FT Law and Tax) argue that the youth court may not have jurisdiction as default is not a charge and therefore not assigned to the court under the Children and Young Persons Act 1933 s46(1). The authors' view is that s46(1) does not exclusively define the jurisdiction of the youth court. For more see para 9.1.

45 Magistrates' Courts Act 1980 s83(1).

person does not attend as required, the court is much more likely to issue a warrant straightaway.

18.52   When the defaulter is before the court, s/he will be asked to go into the witness box and take the oath. The court will then ask why the money has not been paid. It will also carry out a means enquiry. If the young person is living independently or for any other reason has significant financial commitments, it is advisable for any defence lawyer or social worker attending with him/her to prepare a list of income and outgoings before going into court.

Powers of the court

18.53   The court has the following powers in relation to a child or young person in default:

- remission of whole or part of a fine;
- giving more time to pay;
- making a money payment supervision order;
- imposing an attachment of earnings order;
- issuing a distress warrant;
- imposing an attendance centre order;
- imposing a community service order;
- imposing a curfew order;
- ordering the offender's parent/guardian to enter into a recognisance to ensure payment; and
- ordering the parent/guardian to pay.

For offenders who have attained the age of 18, all the above powers are available as well as:

- ordering deductions from the offender's Income Support; and
- committing the offender to detention in a young offender institution for default.

Remission

18.54   This power only applies to fines; not compensation orders and costs. By the Magistrates' Courts Act 1980 s85 a court may remit the whole or any part of the fine, but only if it thinks it just to do so having regard to a change of circumstances which has occurred since the date of conviction, for example the loss of employment or a youth training placement.

Time to pay

18.55 Either on the offender's application or the court's own motion a court may allow further time to pay. The proceedings can be adjourned to a fixed return date to monitor the payments.[46]

Money payment supervision order

18.56 By the Magistrates' Courts Act 1980 s88(1) a magistrates' court or youth court may place a person ordered to pay a financial order under the supervision of such person as the court may from time to time appoint. This money payment supervision order does not need the consent of the offender and lasts as long as s/he remains liable to pay the sum or any part of it, unless the order is discharged by the court or a transfer of fine order is made.[47] The duty of the supervisor is to advise and befriend the offender with a view to inducing him/her to pay, and if required, to report to the court as to the offender's conduct and means.[48]

Attachment of earnings

18.57 If a young person is known to be working the court may consider an attachment of earnings order. This is an order to the defaulter's employer to deduct a specified amount each week at source and to pay this direct to the court. The employer is entitled to make an administrative charge of 50p for each deduction. Before making such an order the court must conduct a means enquiry. The court will fix a normal deduction rate and a protected earnings rate. If in any one week the defaulter's earnings drop below the protected rate then no deduction will be made.

18.58 If a court is considering an attachment of earnings order the defence lawyer should prepare a financial statement detailing the young person's income and outgoings. It should also be checked whether the young person's employment will be at risk if the employer discovers that s/he has a criminal record. In view of the low wages often paid to young people it may become apparent after the means enquiry that any normal deduction rate which could be reasonably imposed would be uneconomic especially when the employer's administrative charge is taken into account.

46 Ibid, s86(1).
47 Ibid, s83(2) and (3).
48 Magistrates' Courts Rules 1981 SI No 552 r56.

Distress warrant

18.59   Upon default of payment of a financial order a court may issue a warrant of distress for the purpose of levying the sum outstanding. This warrant will then be passed to bailiffs who will visit the defaulter's address empowered to seize such of the defaulter's property as is required to satisfy payment of the outstanding money. The bailiffs are entitled to add their costs to the money owed.

18.60   Justices are entitled to require evidence that a defaulter has goods before issuing a distress warrant.[49] In the case of a child or young person, it is submitted that justices should always insist on such evidence before issuing the warrant. If there is evidence before the justices that the defaulter has sufficient assets to satisfy the sum owed, then a warrant should be issued before considering an attendance centre order or a warrant of commitment (if the defaulter has attained the age of 18).[50]

Attendance centre order

18.61   Where a court would have a power to commit an adult defaulter to prison, the court may impose an attendance centre order upon a defaulter under the age of 25. The detailed rules relating to an attendance centre order are considered in Chapter 19.

18.62   The use of the phrase 'where a court would have power ... to commit' incorporates all the pre-conditions which must be satisfied before a committal may take place. These are considered in detail below but, in summary, before a court may impose an attendance centre for default, it must:

– conduct an enquiry into the offender's means;
– be satisfied that the default is due to the offender's wilful refusal or culpable neglect; and
– have considered or tried all other methods of enforcing payment of the sum and it appears to the court that they are inappropriate or unsuccessful.

18.63   After a making of an attendance centre order for default, payment of the outstanding money means that the order ceases to have effect. If part of the money is paid, the total number of hours that the offender is required to attend shall be reduced proportionately, 'that is to say by such number of complete hours as bears to the total

49   *R v German* (1891) 56 JP 358.
50   *R v Birmingham Justices ex p Bennett* [1983] 1 WLR 114; 147 JP 279.

number the proportion most nearly approximating to, without exceeding, the proportion which the part bears to the said sum'.[51] The Magistrates' Courts (Children and Young Persons) Rules 1992 SI No 2071 r27 allows the clerk of the court to accept full payment of the sum outstanding, but the officer in charge of the attendance centre may take receipt of any sum of money less than the total provided that the sum offered will result in the reduction of the order by at least one hour.

Community service order

18.64 Where a court would have a power to commit an adult defaulter to prison, the court may impose a community service order upon a defaulter who has attained the age of 16.[52] The detailed rules relating to a community service order are considered in Chapter 19. It should be noted that the minimum order that can be imposed for default is 20 hours.[53]

18.65 The use of the phrase 'where a magistrates' court has power . . . to issue a warrant of commitment' incorporates all the pre-conditions which must be satisfied before a committal may take place. These are considered in detail below but, in summary, before a court may impose a community service order for default, it must:

- conduct an enquiry into the offender's means;
- be satisfied that the default is due to the offender's wilful refusal or culpable neglect; and
- have considered or tried all other methods of enforcing payment of the sum and it appears to the court that they are inappropriate or unsuccessful.

The period of community service imposed shall not exceed the number of hours specified below:[54]

Amount	Number of hours
An amount not exceeding £200	40 hours
An amount exceeding £200 but not exceeding £500	60 hours
An amount exceeding £500	100 hours

---

51 Criminal Justice Act 1982 s17(13).
52 Crime (Sentences) Act 1997 s35(1) and (2).
53 Ibid, s35(5)(a).
54 Ibid, s35(6).

If the defaulter pays all the sum outstanding, the community service order shall cease to have effect. If a part of the sum is paid, the total number of hours to which the order relates shall be reduced proportionately.[55]

Curfew order

18.66 Where a court would have a power to commit an adult defaulter to prison, the court may impose a curfew order.[56] The detailed rules relating to a curfew order are considered in Chapter 19. It should be noted that such an order may only be imposed upon a defaulter who has attained the age of 16.[57]

18.67 The use of the phrase 'where a court would have power ... to commit' incorporates all the pre-conditions which must be satisfied before a committal may take place. These are considered in detail below but, in summary, before a court may impose an attendance centre for default, it must:

– conduct an enquiry into the offender's means;
– be satisfied that the default is due to the offender's wilful refusal or culpable neglect; and
– have considered or tried all other methods of enforcing payment of the sum and it appears to the court that they are inappropriate or unsuccessful.

The length of the curfew order is limited by reference to the amount of the outstanding financial order as follows:[58]

Amount	Number of days
An amount not exceeding £200	20 days
An amount exceeding £200 but not exceeding £500	30 days
An amount exceeding £500 but not exceeding £1,000	60 days
An amount exceeding £1,000 but not exceeding £2,500	90 days
An amount exceeding £2,500	120 days

If the defaulter pays all the sum outstanding the curfew order shall cease to have effect. If a part of the sum is paid, the total

55 Ibid, s35(13).
56 Ibid, s35(1) and (2).
57 Ibid, s35(10).
58 Ibid, s35(9).

number of days to which the order relates shall be reduced proportionately.[59]

Recognisance by parent/guardian

18.68 A court may order the parent or guardian of an offender aged under 18 to enter into a recognisance to ensure that the defaulter pays so much of the sum as remains unpaid.[60] The parent or guardian must consent.[61]

18.69 Before making such an order the court must:

- conduct an enquiry into the offender's means;
- be satisfied that the default is due to the offender's wilful refusal or culpable neglect; and
- have considered or tried all other methods of enforcing payment of the sum and it appears to the court that they are inappropriate or unsuccessful.

18.70 For the purposes of this section 'guardian' is defined as 'a person appointed, according to law, to be his guardian, or by order of a court of competent jurisdiction.[62] It does not include a local authority which is looking after a child or young person.[63]

Ordering parent/guardian to pay

18.71 A court may order the parent or guardian[64] of an offender aged under 18 to pay the sum remaining instead of the defaulter.[65] Before making such an order the court must:

- conduct an enquiry into the offender's means;
- be satisfied that the default is due to the offender's wilful refusal or culpable neglect; and
- have considered or tried all other methods of enforcing payment of the sum and it appears to the court that they are inappropriate or unsuccessful.

59 Ibid, s35(13).
60 Magistrates' Courts Act 1980 s81(1)(a).
61 Ibid, s81(2)(a).
62 Ibid, s81(8).
63 *R v Barnet Juvenile Court ex p Barnet London Borough Council* (1982) 4 Cr App R (S) 221; [1982] Crim LR 592, QBD.
64 For the definition of guardian, see above.
65 Magistrates' Courts Act 1980 s81(1)(b).

18.72   The court may not make such an order unless it is satisfied in all the circumstances that it is reasonable to do so.[66] As the original sentencing court decided it was not appropriate to order the parent or guardian to pay the financial order, it is likely to be rare for a subsequent court to then consider it to be reasonable to order such payment.

Deductions from income support

18.73   The Criminal Justice Act 1991 s24 allows the court to apply to the Department of Social Security asking for the Benefit Agency to deduct money from the offender's income support or income-based jobseeker's allowance. This power only exists when the offender is entitled to income support. Moreover, by the Fines (Deductions from Income Support) Regulations 1992[67] reg 7 no deduction may be made unless at the date of application by the court the offender is aged not less than 18.

18.74   It would seem that the power does not apply to parents or guardians who have been ordered to pay the financial order.

Committal for default

18.75   The Criminal Justice Act 1982 s9 allows a court to commit an offender aged 18 to 20 to detention in a young offender institution for default in payment of a financial order. The power may be exercised where an adult defaulter could be committed to prison.

18.76   The power to commit for default is contained in Magistrates' Courts Act 1980 s76. This power is restricted by s82 of the Act in relation to defaulters of all ages. In addition s88(4) imposes further restrictions in relation to money payment supervision orders.

18.77   Before a defaulter may be committed, the court must have conducted a means enquiry in the defaulter's presence on at least one occasion since conviction.[68] Before a commitment for default may be considered the court must have placed the young offender under supervision unless 'the court is satisfied that it is undesirable or impracticable to place him under supervision'. A warrant of commitment may not then be issued unless:

---

66   Ibid, s81(2)(b).
67   SI No 2182.
68   Magistrates' Courts Act 1980 s82(3).

- in the case of an offence punishable with imprisonment, the offender appears to the court to have sufficient means to pay the sum forthwith; or
- the court –
  i) is satisfied that the default is due to the offender's wilful refusal or culpable neglect; and
  ii) has considered or tried all other methods of enforcing payment of the sum and it appears to the court that they are inappropriate or unsuccessful.[69]

18.78   If a money payment supervision order has been made the court may not commit a defaulter under the age of 21 unless the court has considered an oral or written report from the supervisor regarding the offender's conduct and means.[70]

18.79   A committal to detention for default may not be made against a person under the age of 21 unless the court is of the opinion that no other method of dealing with him/her is appropriate. In forming such an opinion the court must take into account all such information about the circumstances of the default (including any aggravating or mitigating factors) as is available to it. In addition the court may take into account any information about the defaulter.[71] If the court does commit the defaulter to detention it is required to state in open court the reason for its opinion that no other method of dealing with him/her is appropriate. The stated reasons must be recorded in the warrant of commitment and the court register.[72]

'Wilful refusal or culpable neglect'

18.80   The phrase has been considered in the case of *R v Poole Justices ex p Benham*[73] when it was held to constitute:

> . . . something more than negligence, it must be sufficiently blameworthy to justify immediate imprisonment in the absence of mitigating factors.

The court should satisfy itself that money was available but was not paid to the court and that this was due to a failure which demonstrates an avoidable choice to use the money for other purposes. In

69   Ibid, s82(4).
70   Ibid, s88(6).
71   Criminal Justice Act 1982 s1(5).
72   Ibid, s1(5A).
73   (1991) *Times*, 10 October, QBD.

the context of young offenders, the defence lawyer should establish whether paid employment or training has been available and if not whether the defaulter has been eligible for welfare benefits. If the defaulter lives alone a financial statement should be prepared to show income and outgoings. Young people frequently have problems learning how to budget effectively and this is made worse by the lower rates of welfare benefits payable to claimants under the age of 26. The court should be made aware of any evidence of budgeting problems, for example arrears of rent, community charge or utilities which would point to a lack of means. It is submitted that 'culpable neglect' should not be found in relation to a young person in such circumstances.

Reparation order (pilot schemes only)

18.81 No court shall make a reparation order unless it has been notified by the Secretary of State that arrangements for implementing such orders are available in the petty sessions area proposed to be named in the order.[74]

18.82 A reparation order requires the offender to make reparation specified in the order to either a person or persons specified in the order (the victim(s) of the offence) or the community at large.[75] It is supervised by a responsible officer, defined as a probation officer, social worker of a local authority social services department or a member of a youth offending team.[76]

Pre-conditions

18.83 A reparation order may be passed upon a child or young person convicted of any offence for which the sentence is not fixed by law.[77] A reparation order is not a community sentence therefore the court does not need to consider whether the offence is serious enough to merit such an order.

---

74 Crime and Disorder Act 1998 s67(3). The pilot areas where reparation orders are in force are listed in appendix 8. They are expected to be in force in the rest of England and Wales in June 2000.
75 Ibid, s67(2).
76 Ibid, s67(10).
77 Ibid, s67(1).

Presumption in favour of reparation

18.84   There is a statutory presumption that a reparation order will be made on passing sentence unless one of the following sentences are passed:

- a custodial sentence;
- a community service order or a combination order;
- a supervision order with additional requirements imposed under ss12 to 12C of the Children and Young Persons Act 1969;
- an action plan order.[78]

Age

18.85   A reparation order may be imposed upon any offender aged 10 to 17.[79]

Length of order

18.86   The order shall not require the offender to work for more than 24 hours in aggregate.[80] It must be completed within three months of the date of sentence.[81]

Procedural requirements

18.87   Before making a reparation order the court shall obtain and consider a written report by a probation officer, social worker or a member of a youth offending team. The report should indicate the type of work suitable for the offender and the attitude of the victim or victims to the proposed requirements.[82]

18.88   Before making the order the court shall explain to the offender in ordinary language:

- the effect of the order and of the requirements proposed to be included in it;
- the consequences of a breach of the order; and
- that the court has power to review the order on the application either of the offender or of the responsible officer.[83]

78 Ibid, s67(4).
79 Ibid, s67(1).
80 Ibid, s67(5)(a).
81 Ibid, s67(8)(b).
82 Ibid, s68(1).
83 Ibid, s68(2).

The court shall give reasons if it does not make a reparation order in a case where it has power to do so.[84]

18.89　The order must name the petty sessions area in which it appears that the offender resides or will reside and specify the responsible officer who will supervise the offender.[85]

Requirements of the order

18.90　The requirements specified in the order shall be such as in the opinion of the court are commensurate with the seriousness of the offence, or the combination of the offence and one or more offences associated with it.[86]

18.91　Draft guidance issued by the Home Office[87] suggests that reparation may vary from a letter of apology to several hours a week of practical activity which benefits an individual victim or the community at large. Where possible, the nature of the reparation should be linked as closely as possible to the type of offence itself. The guidance gives the following examples:

- A 15-year-old offender breaks into a newsagent's shop, vandalises the shop and daubs graffiti on the walls. Having been found guilty by the court of these offences he is sentenced to a reparation order which, with the agreement of the newsagent, requires the offender to clean the graffiti from the walls, and to spend one hour under supervision every Saturday morning for two months helping the newsagent to sort out his stock.

- A 12-year-old offender is terrorising an elderly lady by constantly vandalising her garden and shouting abusive language at her. He is sentenced to a reparation order which requires him, with the victim's agreement, to meet with the victim in order to hear her describe the effect that his behaviour has had on her and to allow him to explain why he has behaved in this way, and to apologise. This meeting might be arranged and supervised by the local victim/offender mediation service.

- A 16-year-old offender has caused minor damage to a local children's playground. The court sentences her to a reparation order. As there is no obvious, specific victim in this case, the reparation

---

84　Ibid, s67(11).
85　Ibid, s67(9).
86　Ibid, s67(8).
87　*Reparation Orders: Guidance.*

is designed to benefit the community at large, many of whom use the playground; the offender is required to spend one hour every weekend under supervision helping to repair the damage she has caused.

18.92 As far as is practicable the requirements of the order shall be such as to avoid:

- any conflict with the offender's religious beliefs;
- any interference with the times, if any, at which the offender usually works or attends school or any other educational establishment; or
- any conflict with the requirements of any community order to which s/he may be subject.[88]

Binding over

18.93 Binding over is a procedure whereby the court seeks to avoid antici- pated breaches of the peace by asking a person to enter into an agreement to be of good conduct for a specified period of time not exceeding three years. As part of this agreement the person being bound over will enter into a recognisance for a specified sum of money. If the court subsequently finds that the person has broken the agreement s/he is liable to forfeit some or all of the recognisance in a procedure called 'estreatment'.

18.94 In relation to children and young persons the courts have powers to bind over both the young defendant and the parent or guardian. The circumstances when these powers arise are different and they will, therefore, be considered separately.

The young defendant

18.95 Any court with a criminal jurisdiction may bind over a person before it. Two distinct powers exist:

- on complaint under the Magistrates' Courts Act 1980 s115; and
- under common law powers.

Magistrates' Courts Act 1980 s115

18.96 A person usually appears before the court under this section after the police have exercised their common law powers of arrest when a

88 Crime and Disorder Act 1998 s67(7).

breach of the peace has taken place. If the police consider there is a continuing risk of a breach of the police the person will be held in custody until s/he may be brought before a court.

Which court?

18.97   The hearing of complaints under this section is not a matter which has been specifically assigned to the youth court under Children and Young Persons Act 1933 s46 and therefore it could be argued that a child or young person should be taken before the adult magistrates' court. As discussed elsewhere the authors consider that s46 does not exclusively define the competence of the youth court and it would clearly be preferable for a youth court to deal with any alleged breach.

Procedure

18.98   In court the defendant will be asked whether s/he admits the breach of the peace. If it is admitted the court will proceed to consider whether to bind over the defendant. If the breach is not admitted it must be proved beyond reasonable doubt that there had been a use of violence or the threat of violence.[89]

Appeal

18.99   There is a right of appeal against a bindover to the Crown Court.[90] The appeal is by way of a complete rehearing.

Common law powers

18.100   These powers of the court are a form of preventative justice when the court has material before it leading it to the conclusion that there is a risk of a breach of the peace in the future. The power may be exercised after the prosecution discontinues proceedings, when a defendant is convicted or even when there is an acquittal.

18.101   If the court is considering binding over a defendant it is good practice to warn him/her and give an opportunity for representations to be made either by the defendant or his/her lawyer. Unless the court intends to fix the recognisance at a trivial sum the court should allow the defendant to give information about his/her means.

---

89   *Percy v DPP* (1994) *Times,* 13 December, QBD.
90   Magistrates' Courts (Appeals from Binding Over Orders) Act 1956.

Can a child or young person be compelled to consent to be bound over?

18.102 In the case of adults the court may imprison anyone who refuses to be bound over. In the case of children and young persons this power does not exist. In *Veater v Glennon*[91] it was held that no other sanction existed and accordingly a bindover could not be imposed. Notwithstanding this decision, a bindover may be imposed if the child or young person agrees to be bound over.[92]

18.103 *Veater v Glennon* predates the Criminal Justice Act 1982 and it may be questioned whether it still accurately describes the law. Section 1(1) of the Act forbids the use of imprisonment for anyone under the age of 21. Section 17 of the same Act allows a court to impose an attendance centre order upon a person under the age of 21:

> (1) ... [W]here a court –
> (a) would have power, but for section 1 above, ... to commit such a person to prison ... for failing to do or abstain from doing anything required to be done or left undone ...

It could be argued that this section gives a court the power to impose an attendance centre order upon a child or young person who refuses to be bound over.

Application to children and young persons

18.104 When a child or young person is charged with a minor assault or public order offence in circumstances where a caution is unrealistic, the defence lawyer may wish to canvas the possibility of the prosecution being discontinued if the young defendant consents to being bound over. It is not necessary for the defendant to admit a past use of violence to justify a court binding him/her over.[93]

The parent or guardian

18.105 A court may bind over the parent or guardian of a child or young person in the following circumstances:

- after a finding of guilt, to ensure good behaviour;
- on the imposition of a community sentence, to ensure attendance.

---

91 [1981] 1 WLR 567; [1981] 2 All ER 306; 145 JP 158, QBD.
92 *Conlan v Oxford* (1983) 5 Cr App R (S) 237; (1984) 148 JP 97.
93 *Hourihane v Metropolitan Police Commissioner* (1995) *Independent*, 18 January.

The power to bind over in these circumstances is considered in detail in Chapter 7.

Estreatment

18.106 Estreatment is the legal process by which some or all of the recognisance may be forfeited to the court. Proceedings start by way of complaint and the person who entered into the recognisance will be summonsed to attend court.

Child or young person

18.107 Estreatment proceedings against a child or young person is not a matter which is expressly assigned to the youth court under the Children and Young Persons Act 1933 s46(1). Nevertheless, it is the opinion of the authors that the appropriate court to hear the proceedings would be the youth court.[94]

Parent or guardian

18.108 Estreatment proceedings against a parent or guardian are considered in Chapter 7.

Contempt of court

What constitutes contempt?

18.109 The Contempt of Court Act 1981 s12 provides that it is a contempt of court where a person:

- wilfully insults the justice or justices, any witnesses or officer of the court or any solicitor or counsel having business in the court, during his or their sitting or attendance at court or in going to or returning from the court; or
- wilfully interrupts the proceedings of the court or otherwise misbehaves in court.

'Otherwise misbehaves' could include assaulting anyone concerned in the proceedings and disrespectful behaviour which impairs the authority of the court.

18.110   It is also a contempt of court for a witness to refuse to give evi-

94 See para 9.1.

dence without just cause. It would be a defence to show that the witness was refusing to testify because of duress[95] or because of a well-founded fear of attack.[96]

Procedure

18.111 Faced with gross contempt of the court which is disrupting proceedings, a court may take immediate action by detaining the contemnor to stop the disruption. This power would also seem to apply to children and young persons. However, it must be stressed that it would only extend to detention in the court cells until at the latest the end of the court sitting.

18.112 Before any final decision as to how the contempt will be dealt with, the contemnor has the right to legal representation. For this purpose non-means tested legal aid may be granted.[97] The court should not act in the heat of the moment, but instead should leave itself some time for reflection. Before reaching a final decision as to whether to impose any sanction, the court should allow the contemnor the opportunity to apologise for his/her behaviour.[98]

18.113 If the court is dealing with a witness who refuses to give evidence, it should allow a period for reflection perhaps even overnight and the witness should be allowed the opportunity to have legal advice.

What sanctions are available against a child or young person?

18.114 It is not completely clear what sanctions are available but in any event it would seem the court's powers are extremely limited.

Detention in a young offender institution

18.115 No one under the age of 18 may be imprisoned for contempt of court.[99] The Criminal Justice Act 1982 s1A allows a court to sentence a person aged 15 to 17 convicted of an imprisonable offence to detention in a young offender institution. A person found to be in contempt of court is not a person convicted of an offence[100] and therefore

---

95 *R v K* (1984) 148 JP 410.
96 *R v Lewis (James John)* (1993) 96 Cr App R 412.
97 Legal Aid Act 1988 s29.
98 *R v Moran* (1985) 81 Cr App R 51.
99 Criminal Justice Act 1982 s1(1).
100 *R v Byas* [1995] Crim LR 439, CA.

there is no power to detain a young person for contempt. If a person has attained the age of 18 s/he may be committed to detention for contempt pursuant to the Criminal Justice Act 1982 s9(1).

Community penalty

18.116   As a finding of contempt is not 'a conviction for an offence' it is not possible to impose a probation order upon the contemnor as being convicted of an offence is a pre-condition for the sentence.[101] The same principle would seem to rule out the imposition of a community service order, combination order or curfew order. By virtue of the Criminal Justice Act 1982 s17 it would be possible to impose an attendance centre order, but this is prohibited by the Contempt of Court Act 1981 s14(2A) 'if it appears to the court, after considering any available evidence, that [the contemnor] is under 17 years of age'.

Financial order

18.117   It would seem that a fine is the only penalty available for a person under the age of 17. It would also seem to be possible to bind over the person if a further breach of the peace is feared.

Forfeiture order

General power

18.118   Courts have a general power to order the forfeiture of property used in the connection of crime. The Powers of Criminal Courts Act 1973 s43(1) provides:

> Subject to the following provisions of this section, where a person is convicted of an offence, and–
> (a) the court by or before which he is convicted is satisfied that any property which has been lawfully seized from him or which was in his possession or under his control at the time when he was apprehended for the offence or when a summons in respect of it was issued–
>   (i)   has been used for the purpose of committing, or facilitating the commission of any offence; or
>   (ii)   was intended by him to be used for that purpose; or
> (b) the offence, or an offence which the court has taken into

---

101   *R v Palmer* (1992) 13 Cr App R (S) 595; [1992] 1WLR 568.

consideration in determining his sentence, consists of unlawful possession of property which–

(i)   has been lawfully seized from him; or

(ii)   was in his possession or under his control at the time when he was apprehended for the offence of which he has been convicted or when a summons in respect of that offence was issued,

the court may make an order under this section in respect of that property, and may do so whether or not it also deals with the offender in respect of the offence in any other way and without regard to any restrictions on forfeiture in an enactment contained in an Act passed before the Criminal Justice Act 1988.

A court may order the forfeiture of, for example, a screwdriver used to break into cars or cans of spray paint used to put graffiti on trains.

Specific powers

18.119   There also exist a number of specific powers of forfeiture available to the courts. The ones most applicable to young offenders are as follows:

- forfeiture of drugs;
- forfeiture of offensive weapons; and
- forfeiture of firearms and prohibited weapons.

Drugs

18.120   By the Misuse of Drugs Act 1971 s27 a court may, following a conviction under that Act or for a drug trafficking offence, order the forfeiture of anything shown to the satisfaction of the court to relate to the offence.

Offensive weapons

18.121   By the Prevention of Crime Act 1953 s1(2) a court may order the forfeiture and disposal of any weapon which is the subject of a conviction under s1(1) of that Act.

Firearms and prohibited weapons

18.122   By the Firearms Act 1968 s52 a court may order the forfeiture and disposal of any firearms found in the possession of a person:

- convicted of an offence under the Act (except an offence relating to the possession of an air weapon);

- sentenced to detention in a young offender institution;
- ordered to enter into a recognisance to keep the peace or be of good behaviour, a condition of which is that s/he shall not possess, use or carry a firearm; or
- subject to a probation order containing a requirement that s/he shall not possess, use or carry a firearm.

Schedule 6 to the Act extends the power to order forfeiture to offences involving the unlawful possession of airguns. The court may also order the cancellation of any firearms or shotgun certificate.

Restitution order

18.123 A court may order property found in the possession of an offender to be seized to make good the loss suffered as a result of the offence for which sentence is being passed. The Theft Act 1968 s28(1) provides:

> Where goods have been stolen, and either a person is convicted of any offence with reference to the theft (whether or not stealing is the gist of his offence) or a person is convicted of any other offence but such an offence as aforesaid is taken into consideration in determining his sentence, the court by or before which the offender is convicted may on the conviction (whether or not the passing of sentence is in other respects deferred) exercise any of the following powers–
>
> (a) the court may order anyone having possession or control of the goods to restore them to any person entitled to recover them from him; or
>
> (b) on the application of a person entitled to recover from the person convicted any other goods directly or indirectly representing the first-mentioned goods (as being the proceeds of any disposal or realisation of the whole or part of them or of goods so representing them), the court may order those other goods to be delivered or transferred to the applicant; or
>
> (c) the court may order that a sum not exceeding the value of the first-mentioned goods shall be paid, out of any money of the person convicted which was taken out of his possession on his apprehension, to any person who, if those goods were in the possession of the person convicted, would be entitled to recover them from him.

By s28(4) the court should not make an order unless satisfied that the relevant facts sufficiently appear from evidence given at the trial or the available documents. An application for a restitution order should not be entertained after sentence has been passed.[102] It is not necessary to show that the money is the proceeds of the offence for which sentence is being passed.[103]

18.124   In the case of children and young persons the most likely use for a restitution order would seem to be in relation to any money found on the offender at the time of arrest or during a s18 search of the offender's home address.

Hospital order

18.125 This order may be made either by a youth court or the Crown Court. The order transfers the offender to a psychiatric hospital where s/he is treated as being detained under the Mental Health Act in the same way as civil patients.

18.126   The court may make a hospital order if:

- the court is satisfied, on the written or oral evidence of two registered medical practitioners, that the offender is suffering from mental illness, psychopathic disorder, severe mental impairment or mental impairment;
- the mental disorder from which the offender is suffering is of a nature or degree which makes it appropriate for him/her to be detained in a hospital for medical treatment and, in the case of psychopathic disorder or mental impairment, that such treatment is likely to alleviate or prevent a deterioration of his/her condition; and
- the court is of the opinion, having regard to all the circumstances including the nature of the offence and the character and antecedents of the offender, and to the other available methods of dealing with him/her, that the most suitable method of disposing of the case is by means of a hospital order.[104]

When a court is considering making a hospital order, the defendant should, except in the rarest circumstances, be legally represented.[105]

---

102   *R v Church* (1970) 55 Cr App R 65, CA.
103   *R v Lewis* [1975] Crim LR 353.
104   Mental Health Act 1983 s37(2).
105   *R v Blackwood* (1974) 59 Cr App R 170, CA.

Guardianship order

18.127   A guardianship order may be made by either a youth court or a Crown Court. The offender must have attained the age of 16.[106] The court may only make the order if it is satisfied that the relevant social services department or other person is willing to receive the offender into guardianship.[107]

18.128   The pre-conditions for the making of a guardianship order are as for a hospital order, except that there is no requirement that the mental disorder must be treatable. A guardianship order gives the local authority social services department or other person nominated in the order the power to determine the young person's place of residence, education or training. The young person may also be required to attend for treatment.

Restriction order

18.129   A restriction order is a hospital order where the court orders that the offender's release shall be subject to special restrictions. A restriction order may only be made by a Crown Court judge. The order may only be made when making a hospital order if it appears to the court, having regard to the nature of the offence, the antecedents of the offender and the risk of his/her committing further offences if set at large, that it is necessary for the protection of the public from serious harm from him/her.[108] Before the order can be made at least one of the medical practitioners must give evidence orally before the court.[109]

18.130   A youth court or adult magistrates' court which has convicted a defendant, may commit him/her to the Crown Court with a view to a restriction order being made, but only if:

- s/he has attained the age of 14 by the date of conviction;
- the offence is imprisonable in the case of an adult;
- the conditions for a hospital order are satisfied (see above); and
- it appears to the court, having regard to the nature of the offence, the antecedents of the offender and the risk of his/her committing

---

106   Mental Health Act 1983 s37(2)(a)(ii).
107   Ibid, s37(6).
108   Ibid, s41(1).
109   Ibid, s41(2).

further offences if set at large, that if a hospital order is made a restriction order should also be made.[110]

18.131 If committal is made under this power, the offender shall be committed in custody to the Crown Court.[111] If the offender has not attained the age of 17, it is submitted that committal to custody should be construed subject to the provisions of the Children and Young Persons Act 1969 s23.

Recommendation for deportation

18.132 A youth court or Crown Court may recommend that an offender should be deported, but only if:

– the offender is not a British citizen; [112]
– s/he has attained the age of 17 by the date of conviction; [113]
– the offence is imprisonable in the case of an adult.

Procedure

18.133 A person liable to deportation must be given at least seven days' written notice. This is usually given by the police at the time of charge. If this has not been done, the case must be adjourned for seven days.

18.134 The offender should be given warning that the court is considering exercising the power to recommend deportation. The defence lawyer will need to address the issue specifically. The court must give reasons for its decision to recommend deportation.[114] Once a court has recommended deportation, the offender is automatically detained under the Immigration Act 1971 unless the court grants bail.

---

110 Ibid, s43(1).
111 Ibid.
112 Defined in the British Nationality Act 1981, Part I: EU nationals may only be deported in limited circumstances specified in EU Directive 64/221 arts 3 and 9 (see also *R v Bouchereau* [1978] QB 732).
113 A person is deemed to have attained the age of 17 if, on consideration of any available evidence, s/he appears to the court to have done so: Immigration Act 1971 s6(3)(a).
114 *R v Rodney* (1996) 2 Cr App R (S) 230, CA and *R v Bozat* [1997] 1 Cr App R (S) 270, CA.

Grounds for recommendation

18.135 The court must be of the opinion that the offender's continuing presence in the United Kingdom would be detrimental to the community, and relevant considerations include the seriousness of the offence, the offender's record and the likely detrimental effect upon third parties.[115]

18.136 A recommendation may be inappropriate if the young offender has spent all his formative years in the United Kingdom.[116] In the case of a young person regard must be had to the right to family life contained in article 8 of the European Convention on Human Rights. It is arguable that a young person should not be deported to a country where s/he has never lived and where his/her family live in the United Kingdom.[117]

Appeal

18.137 A recommendation for deportation may be appealed in the same way as any other part of the sentence. Representations may also be made to the Immigration and Nationality Department to persuade the Home Secretary not to act upon the recommendation.

Binding over to come up for judgment

18.138 This common law power is only available to the Crown Court. On conviction the offender may be bound over on specified conditions. A recognisance will also be taken. If the offender breaks any of the conditions during a specified period, s/he may be brought back before the court for sentence.

18.139 The power has been used to require an offender to leave the country. In *R v Williams*[118] an 18-year-old had been convicted of theft and he had a number of previous convictions. He was British-born of Jamaican parents. The Crown Court judge bound him over to come up for judgment on condition that he accompanied his mother to Jamaica and did not return to the United Kingdom for

---

115 *R v Nazari* [1980] 1 WLR 1366, CA
116 *R v Dudeye* unreported, 24 March 1999, 97/08498/X2.
117 See, eg, *Lamguindaz v UK* (1994) 17 EHRR 213.
118 [1982] 1 WLR 1398, CA.

five years. Lane LCJ held that such a condition could not be imposed upon the defendant as he was a British citizen and it should generally be used sparingly, for example to require an offender to return to a country of which he was a citizen and where s/he usually resided.

Disqualification and endorsement of driving licences

18.140 When a person is found guilty of a road traffic offence and certain other offences related to motor vehicles the court has extra powers on sentencing which relate to the offender's driving licence. These powers are:

- – to impose penalty points;
- – to endorse the offender's licence; or
- – to disqualify the offender from driving.

The Crime (Sentences) Act 1997 s39 has also introduced a power to disqualify an offender for any offence (see below).

Penalty points

18.141 For most road traffic offences the court is required to impose penalty points in addition to any other sentence. The number of penalty points to be imposed vary depending on the offence.

18.142 If an offender does not have a driving licence or is too young to apply for one, the court should still impose penalty points for the offence. The Driving Vehicle Licence Agency will then be informed and any licence issued subsequently will be endorsed with any outstanding points.

Endorsement

18.143 An endorsement is a record on the offender's licence that s/he has been found guilty of an offence. The endorsement will also record how many penalty points have been imposed for the offence. For many road traffic offences the court is required to order the endorsement. No endorsement is made if the offender is disqualified at the same time; instead the fact that s/he is now disqualified is recorded.

Disqualification

18.144 An offender may be disqualified by a court as part of the sentence or s/he may be disqualified as a result of an accumulation of penalty points by what is usually termed the 'totting up' system. For any endorsable offence the court will have a discretionary power to order disqualification. In addition some offences require the court to disqualify.

Discretionary disqualification

18.145 All offences which carry penalty points give the court a discretion to disqualify. The power should only be exercised in cases involving bad driving, persistent motoring offences or the use of the vehicle for the purposes of crime.[119] With young defendants the court should also consider the serious consequences that disqualification may have on his/her future employment prospects.

Mandatory disqualification

18.146 Certain offences carry a mandatory disqualification. In such cases the minimum disqualification is for 12 months.[120] If an offender has been convicted of two offences carrying a mandatory disqualification and involving alcohol (offences of driving with excess alcohol, drunk in charge or failing to give a specimen) in a 10-year period, the minimum period of disqualification following the second conviction is three years.[121]

Interim disqualification

18.147 It is possible to make an interim disqualification where the court::

- commits the offender for sentence to the Crown Court;
- defers sentence; or
- adjourns for the preparation of a pre-sentence report.[122]

Although not specifically mentioned, it is arguable that the power applies when a court remits for sentence under the Children and Young Persons Act 1933 s56(1).

---

119 *R v Callister* [1993] RTR 70 per Morland J.
120 Road Traffic Offenders Act 1988 s34(1).
121 Ibid, s34(3).
122 Ibid, s26(1) and (2).

Totting up

18.148 If an offender receives 12 or more penalty points in respect of offences committed within three years of the latest offence(s), the court must disqualify him/her for a minimum period of six months.[123] If the offender has a previous disqualification imposed within three years of the commission of the current offence(s), the minimum period of disqualification is 12 months. If there are two such disqualifications, the minimum is two years' disqualification.

Length of period of disqualification

18.149 Subject to the minimum periods of disqualification applicable in certain circumstances, the following principles apply:

- where there is a real chance that the ability to drive will improve a young offender's employment prospects, the court should keep any disqualification to a minimum; [124]
- a lengthy period of disqualification should be avoided, particularly when imposed at the same time as a custodial sentence as it may have an adverse effect upon the defendant's chances of rehabilitation; [125]
- with defendants who seem incapable of leaving motor cars alone, a lengthy period of disqualification will only invite the offender to commit further offences in relation to motor cars which would be counter-productive and so contrary to the public interest;[126] and
- where a defendant's record demonstrates that his/her driving constitutes a risk to the public, a lengthy period of disqualification is proper to enable the young offender to mature.[127]

Disqualification as a sentence for any offence

18.150 The court by or before which a person is convicted of an offence may, in addition to or instead of dealing with him/her in any other way, order him/her to be disqualified, for such period as it thinks fit, for

---

123 Ibid, s35.
124 *R v Apsden* [1975] RTR 456.
125 *R v Russell* [1993] RTR 249, CA.
126 *R v Thomas* [1983] 1 WLR 1490 (two years under totting up procedure reduced to 12 months).
127 *R v Gibbons* (1987) 9 Cr App R (S) 21, CA. See also *R v Sharkey and Daniels* (1995) 16 Cr App R (S) 257, CA, where five years' disqualification upheld after convictions for aggravated vehicle taking.

holding or obtaining a driving licence.[128] A court which makes such an order shall require the offender to produce any driving licence held by him/her.[129]

18.151   Although not specifically dealt with in the statute, this power is presumably only exercisable where the offender is of sufficient age to be able to hold a driving licence.

128 Crime (Sentences) Act 1997 s39(1).
129 Ibid, s39(4).

Table 9: Disqualification and endorsement

Offence	Disqualification	Penalty points
Road Traffic Act 1988		
Dangerous driving: s2	Mandatory [130]	3–11
Careless driving: s3	Discretionary	3–9
Driving while unfit: s4(1)	Mandatory	3–11
Drunk in charge: s4(2)	Discretionary	10
Driving with excess alcohol: s5(1)	Mandatory	3–11
Failing to give specimen for breath test: s6	Discretionary	4
Failing to give specimen for laboratory test: s7	Mandatory	3–11
No headgear: s16	–	–
Failing to comply with traffic directions: s35	Discretionary [131]	3
Using vehicles in dangerous condition: s40A	Discretionary	3
No test certificate: s47	–	–
Driving otherwise than in accordance with licence: s87(1)	Discretionary	3–6
Causing or permitting above: s87(2)	–	–
Driving whilst disqualified: s103(1)(b)	Discretionary	6
Driving without insurance: s143	Discretionary	6–8
Failing to stop after accident s170(4)		
Theft Act 1968		
Aggravated vehicle taking: s12A	Mandatory	3–11
Theft/attempted theft of motor vehicle	Discretionary	–
Taking without consent: s12	Discretionary	–
Going equipped to steal (in relation to the theft of motor vehicles): s25	Discretionary	–

130 Offender must be required to take special driving test before s/he may receive full licence.
131 If directions given by a police officer or traffic warden.

CHAPTER 19

Community sentences

For complete chapter contents, see overleaf

General

Definition

19.1 A community sentence is defined as a sentence which consists of or includes one or more community orders. A community order is defined[1] as any of the following:

- attendance centre order;
- supervision order;
- action plan order (pilot areas only);
- curfew order;
- probation order;
- community service order;
- combination order; or
- drug treatment and testing order (pilot areas only).

Statutory restrictions

19.2 The Criminal Justice Act 1991 imposes the following restrictions upon a court in relation to community orders:

6.–(1) A court shall not pass on an offender a community sentence [. . .] unless it is of the opinion that the offence, or the combination of the offence and one or more offences associated with it, was serious enough to warrant such a sentence.

(2) Subject to subsection (3) below, where a court passes a community sentence –

(a) the particular order or orders comprising or forming part of the sentence shall be such as in the opinion of the court is, or taken together are, the most suitable for the offender; and

(b) the restrictions on liberty imposed by the order or orders shall be such as in the opinion of the court are commensurate with the seriousness of the offence, or the combination of the offence and one or more offences associated with it.

(3) In consequence of the provision made by section 11 below with respect to combination orders, a community sentence shall not consist of or include both a probation order and a community service order.

7.–(1) In forming any such opinion as is mentioned in subsection (1) or (2) (b) of section 6 above, a court shall take into account all such information about the circumstances of the offence or (as the case

---

1   By Criminal Justice Act 1991 s31(1).

may be) of the offence or offences associated with it, (including any aggravating or mitigating factors) as is available to it.

(2) In forming any such opinion as is mentioned in subsection (2)(a) of that section, a court may take into account any information about the offender which is before it.

Serious enough to warrant such a sentence

19.3   To determine whether a community sentence is warranted the court is required to consider firstly the seriousness of the offence and any offences associated with it. In making this assessment the court must consider the aggravating and mitigating features known to the court. Relevant features are considered in Chapter 13. Having made this initial assessment, the court is then required to consider any personal mitigation and reduce its assessment accordingly. If the court is still considering a community sentence, it must proceed to consider the most suitable sentence for the offender.

Suitability

19.4   In assessing an offender's suitability for a particular community sentence the court is required to take into account any information about the offender which is before it. It may wish to consider the following:

- the risk of re-offending and the likely seriousness of further offences;
- the need and scope for intervention, including help with particular problems as part of a programme to reduce offending (eg, alcohol, drugs, aggression, sexual offending, social skills, employment/training, accommodation, education, personal/ family relationships and finances/budgeting);
- the need for work to confront offending behaviour;
- the need for psychiatric treatment;
- the maturity (or stage of development) of the offender;
- the composition of groups in any group activity to which referral is being considered;
- previous experience of this particular sentence; and
- whether the sentence stands a realistic prospect of completion by the offender.

The gender of the young offender may also be relevant as many community order schemes will be ill-equipped to cater for female offenders.

19.5 When considering the prospects for success of an order, it is important to bear in mind that many young offenders who appear before the courts lead chaotic lives and the restrictions of even a short community order will make considerable demands on them.[2] In a discussion paper *Community Sentences and the Restriction of Liberty* (March 1993) produced jointly by the Magistrates' Association, Association of Chief Officers of Probation and the Justices' Clerks' Society, sentencers were reminded of the usefulness of even very short sentences:

> Orders involving a low level of restriction or intervention can be profoundly effective in changing attitudes and reducing the likelihood of further offending. The satisfactory completion of a short community order can represent a considerable achievement for an offender whose earlier experiences have all been of failure; and many offenders can use short periods of supervision to resolve practical or relationship problems which have contributed to their offending. In each case, long term benefits accrue.

19.6 The question of suitability is of particular relevance when considering the community sentence options for 16- and 17-year-olds. The Home Office Circular 30/1992 *Criminal Justice Act 1991: Young People and the Youth Court* para 9 gives useful guidance:

> Under the Act, when a court decides to pass a community sentence on an offender of any age it must ensure that the sentence matches the seriousness of the offence, and that the particular sentence imposed is the one which is most suitable for the offender. In deciding which is the most suitable community sentence for a 16 or 17 year old, courts will need to take account both of the offender's circumstances and of the stage of his/her emotional, intellectual, social and physical development in the transition from childhood to adulthood. This decision will be a particularly difficult one to make. Factors likely to be relevant include:
> - the offender's continuing dependence on or independence from his or her parents;
> - whether he/she is leading a stable independent life, and has family responsibilities of his/her own;
> - whether he/she is still in full-time education or in or seeking employment;
> - the general pattern of his/her social behaviour and his/her leisure interests and activities;

---

2 A point accepted by the Government in its White Paper *Crime, Justice and Protecting the Public* (1990).

  – the nature of his/her relationship with friends and associates;
  – whether he/she accepts personal responsibility for his/her actions;
  – his/her attitude towards the offence and any victim; and
  – whether he/she is intellectually impaired.
Information about and assessment of these factors in pre-sentence reports will be particularly helpful to the courts in reaching their decision.

Restriction of liberty commensurate with seriousness

19.7   This criterion applies to both the length of any order and the nature of any additional requirements imposed. The sentencer will have to balance these two (sometimes conflicting) requirements. It is submitted, however, that offence seriousness must provide the 'sentencing ceiling'. This would mean that a court should first make an assessment of offence seriousness and then choose between the community penalties which reflect that seriousness. It would never be appropriate to choose a welfare-orientated penalty such as a supervision order merely to deal with perceived welfare concerns if the seriousness of the offence does not merit it.

Practical considerations for young offenders

19.8   As well as taking full account of the above statutory criteria the defence lawyer will also wish to consider with his/her client:

  – continuity of contact with statutory agencies;
  – the client's perception of the various community orders available locally; and
  – the period required to expire before the conviction is spent.

Continuity

19.9   For many young offenders, especially those who have been in care, there has been a long history of frequently changing adult carers and professionals. Such constant change reduces the child or young person's sense of security and is often bitterly resented. If a relationship has developed between a professional linked to one community order and an offender, there is perhaps a better chance of continuing success. If a different order is being proposed, the defence lawyer should ensure that full consideration has been given to the value of continuity of contact.

Perception

19.10 Certain community programmes for offenders may have a good reputation locally, particularly among the young offender's peer group. An offender may know somebody who already attends a programme proposed. Such personal considerations may make a substantial difference to a teenager's attendance.

Attendance centre order

19.11 The Criminal Justice Act 1982 s17 provides that an attendance centre order may be imposed:

- on conviction for any imprisonable offence;
- in default of payment of any fine or order for compensation or costs;
- for failure to comply with any requirements of a probation order.

It may also be imposed as a sanction for failure to comply with the requirements of a supervision order.[3]

19.12 An attendance centre order is intended to:

- punish the offender by imposing a restriction on liberty (in the form of a loss of leisure time);
- provide the offender with occupation and instruction designed to assist him/her to acquire or develop personal responsibility, self-discipline, skills and interests; and
- enable the offender to develop social skills when living in the community and to make better use of leisure time, through group projects organised in a disciplined environment.[4]

Attendance centres are usually run by police officers and frequently make use of school premises. They usually operate on alternate Saturdays. Traditionally there has been a considerable emphasis on physical activities, although other practical activities such as first aid, DIY and group discussions are organised too.

Pre-conditions

19.13 An attendance centre order may be imposed upon a child or young person by a youth court or by a Crown Court. It may only be imposed if:

3 Children and Young Persons Act 1969 s15(3)(a)(i).
4 *National Standard for Attendance Centres* (1995) para 4.

- the offence is imprisonable;
- the offence, or the combination of the offence and associated offences, is serious enough;
- the order is the most suitable for the offender;
- the court has been notified by the Secretary of State that an attendance centre is available for the reception of persons of the offender's description;[5]
- the court is satisfied that the centre is reasonably accessible to the offender, having regard to his age, the means of access available to him/her and any other circumstances.[6]

A pre-sentence report is not required before an attendance centre order is imposed.

Available for the reception of persons of the offender's description

19.14   This means that the court must be satisfied that a centre exists which caters both for the age of the offender and his/her gender.

19.15   Attendance centres may be classed as either junior or senior centres. Junior centres cater for all offenders aged 10 to 15. In addition, subject to local arrangements, they may also cater for offenders aged 16 and 17. Senior centres cater for offenders aged 18 to 20, and may also accept offenders aged 16 and 17. Junior centres usually run for two hours each session whereas senior centres may run for three-hour sessions. Most centres cater for males only but in larger conurbations some mixed centres exist. The Home Office maintains a directory of attendance centres[7] and each court should be aware of the facilities available in its vicinity.

19.16   If there is a choice of a junior and senior centre available for an offender aged 16 or 17, Home Office Circular 72/1992 suggests that the offender should always be sent to the senior centre if the order is for more than 24 hours and in the case of a shorter order the court should select the centre according to suitability. When considering suitability the circular suggests the court take into account the maturity of the offender.

Reasonably accessible

19.17   The court is clearly expected to make enquiries of the offender and

5   Criminal Justice Act 1982 s17(1).
6   Ibid, s17(7).
7   *Directory of Attendance Centres in England and Wales* (Home Office, 1995).

his/her parent or guardian to ascertain how the offender would travel to the centre if the order were imposed.

19.18   The Home Office has provided guidance to courts regarding reasonable distances for travelling to attendance centres. Offenders should not usually be expected to travel for more than 90 minutes each way, although courts may consider that less-demanding travelling requirements are appropriate to younger attendees.[8]

19.19   In normal circumstances the cost of travelling to the centre must be borne by the offender or his/her parents, but in cases of hardship officers in charge of the centre may pay all or part of the expenses incurred.[9]

Age

19.20   An attendance centre order may be imposed upon any offender aged between the ages of 10 and 20 (or 25 if the order is being imposed for fine default).[10]

19.21   When the offender changes age during the proceedings it is not clear what should be taken to be the relevant age. This is relevant to the maximum number of hours that may be imposed. The general principle in sentencing is that the relevant age is that on the date of conviction.[11] To ensure a consistency of approach it is the opinion of the authors that the same rule should be applied here. This would mean that an offender aged 15 at the time of conviction but who attains the age of 16 before sentence would be subject to a maximum of 24 hours.

Length of the order

19.22   By the Criminal Justice Act 1991 s6(2)(b) the length of the order shall be such as is, in the opinion of the court, commensurate with the seriousness of the offence, or the combination of the offence and other offences associated with it.

Minimum

19.23   The minimum number of hours shall be 12 unless the offender is aged under 14 and, having regard to the offender's age or any other

---

8   *National Standard for Attendance Centres* (1995) para 11.
9   Ibid, para 12.
10   Where the age of the offender is in doubt see para 3.9ff.
11   See para 3.48.

circumstances, the court is of the opinion that 12 would be excessive.[12]

Maximum

19.24   The aggregate number of hours shall not exceed 12 except where the court is of opinion, having regard to all the circumstances, that 12 hours would be inadequate. In such circumstances the court may order attendance to a maximum of 24 hours for an offender under 16 years of age and up to 36 hours for an offender aged 16 or over.[13]

Multiple orders

19.25   It is possible for a court to impose an attendance centre order upon an offender who is still completing an existing attendance centre order. If a court does this, it may determine the number of hours for the new order without regard to the number specified in the previous order or to the fact that the previous order is still in effect.[14]

Procedural requirements

19.26   On sentencing an offender the court must specify the centre and the day and time of the first attendance which should be recorded in the order.[15] Subsequent times will be fixed by the officer in charge of the centre. The offender is not required to consent to the order.

Requirements of the order

19.27   The offender is required to attend the centre as directed initially by the court and thereafter by the officer in charge of the centre.[16] S/he may not be required to attend the centre on more than one occasion on each day. The times of attendances should be such as to avoid interference, as far as is practicable, with the offender's schooling and any employment.[17]

---

12   Criminal Justice Act 1982 s17(4).
13   Ibid, s17(5).
14   Ibid, s17(6).
15   Ibid, s17(9).
16   Ibid, s17(9) and (10).
17   Ibid, s17(8).

Variation

19.28 Either the offender or the officer in charge of the centre may apply to a court for the petty sessions area where the centre is situated for a variation of the order.[18] The court may vary the starting date of the order or the time when the offender is required to attend. It may also change the centre specified in the order.[19] A copy of any variation order should be supplied to the offender and the officer in charge of the centre.[20] The Home Office Circular 30/1992 contemplates an application for variation being made if the offender changes address or the centre in the original order closes.

Discharge

19.29 Both the offender and the officer in charge of the centre may apply to a court for the order to be discharged.[21] Such an application may be made to a magistrates' court or youth court for the petty sessions area where the centre is situated or to the court which made the order.[22] Where it is a Crown Court order and there is included in the order a direction that the power to discharge the order is reserved to that court, any application must be made to that Crown Court.[23]

19.30 On discharge the court has the power to deal with the offender in any manner in which s/he could have been dealt with for the offence if the order had not been made.[24] There is surprisingly no statutory requirement to take account of the extent to which the order has been completed prior to discharge but it is submitted that the court should take this into account as it would if the discharge had followed breach proceedings.[25]

19.31 The Home Office Circular 72/1992 contemplates an application for discharge of the order when the young offender's circumstances change and s/he is no longer able to attend the centre, for example when a Saturday job has been found.

---

18 Ibid, s18(1).
19 Ibid, s18(6).
20 Ibid, s18(8).
21 Ibid, s18(1).
22 Ibid, s18(3).
23 Ibid, s18(4).
24 Ibid, s18(4A).
25 Cf, s19(5A) – see para 20.13.

Supervision order

19.32   The supervision order is the most significant youth court sentence. With its wide range of additional requirements it can be the suitable disposal for a relatively minor offence as well as the disposal for some of the most serious offences. The supervision order is seen as the specialist order to provide supervision to young offenders where the offending behaviour needs to be addressed in the context of adolescence. This view is reinforced by the current *National Standards for the Supervision of Offenders in the Community* (1995) which give the following guidance as to the aims and objectives of a supervision order:

> The aims that should be pursued by probation services and social services departments in supervision are:
> - to encourage and assist the child or young person in his or her development towards a responsible and law-abiding life, thereby promoting the welfare of the offender and seeking
> - to secure the rehabilitation of the offender
> - to protect the public from harm from the offender
> - to prevent the offender from committing further offences.
>
> To achieve these aims and to ensure effective supervision, supervising officers and those working under their direction should address the following objectives:
>
> - enabling and encouraging the young offender to understand and accept responsibility for his or her behaviour and its consequences;
> - ensuring the involvement, wherever possible, of the parents, guardian, family or other carers in the supervision of the young offender;
> - helping the young offender to resolve personal difficulties linked with offending (eg. problems within the family or at school) and to acquire positive new skills;
> - making the young offender aware of the impact of the crime committed on its victim, the community and the offender himself or herself;
> - motivating and assisting the young offender towards a greater sense of personal responsibility, discipline and self-respect, and to aid re-integration as a law-abiding member of the community;
> - ensuring that the young offender understands the difference between right and wrong; and
> - ensuring that the supervision programme is demanding and effective.

Pre-conditions

19.33   A supervision order may only be imposed if the court considers that:
- the offence, or the combination of the offence and associated offences is serious enough; and
- the order is the most suitable for the offender.

Consent

19.34   The requirement to obtain the consent of the offender or his/her parent or guardian has been abolished by the Crime (Sentences) Act 1997 s38(1) in relation to all additional requirements except a requirement as to mental treatment.

Age

19.35   A supervision order may be imposed upon any offender under 18 years of age.[26] The relevant age will be that at the date of conviction. By virtue of the Children and Young Persons Act 1963 s29(1), however, a young offender who attains 18 during the proceedings may still be dealt with as though s/he had not attained that age and therefore a supervision order may be available.

Length of the order

19.36   There is no minimum period for an order. However, in practical terms it is unlikely that a court would impose a supervision order for less than six months. The maximum period is three years from the date the order was made by the court.[27] By the Criminal Justice Act 1991 s6(2)(b) the length of the order shall be such as is, in the opinion of the court, commensurate with the seriousness of the offence, or the combination of the offence and other offences associated with it. It therefore follows that a court should not impose a supervision order because of welfare concerns unless the seriousness of the offence warrants it, and equally, the period of supervision should not be extended beyond that which is commensurate with the seriousness of the offence by reference to the offender's welfare.

---

26 Children and Young Persons Act 1969 s7(7): where the offender's age is in doubt, see para 3.9ff.
27 Ibid, s17.

Procedural requirements

19.37   The court shall in the order name the area of the local authority and the petty sessions area in which it appears the supervised person resides or will reside.[28] A court may make an order placing the offender under the supervision of a local authority designated in the order, a probation officer or a member of a youth offending team.[29] A court shall not designate a local authority as the supervisor unless the authority agrees or it appears to the court that the supervised person resides or will reside in the area of the authority.[30] Where the supervisor is to be a probation officer, s/he shall be an officer appointed for or assigned to the petty sessions area named in the order.[31] Where a supervision order places a person under the supervision of a member of a youth offending team, the supervisor shall be a member of the team established by the local authority within whose area it appears to the court that the supervised person resides or will reside.[32]

19.38   Before a court can impose an additional requirement under s12A(3) (specified activities, reparation order, residence as directed, night restriction or refraining requirement) upon an offender aged under 16, the court must obtain and consider information about the offender's family circumstances and the likely effect of the requirements on those circumstances.[33]

19.39   A copy of the order shall be sent forthwith:

   - to the supervised person, and if the supervised person is a child, to his/her parent or guardian;
   - to the supervisor;
   - where the supervised person is required to reside with an individual or to undergo treatment by or under the direction of an individual or at any place, to the individual or the person in charge of that place; and
   - if the petty sessions area named in the order is not that for which the court acts, to the clerk to the justices for the petty sessions area so named (and the clerk shall also be sent such documents and

28   Ibid, s18(2)(a).
29   Ibid, s11.
30   Ibid, s13(1).
31   Ibid, s13(3).
32   Ibid, s13(4).
33   Ibid, s12A(6)(c).

information relating to the case as the court considers likely to be of assistance to them).[34]

Requirements of the order

19.40 The imposition of a supervision order does not in itself impose any requirements upon the offender, however, by the Children and Young Persons Act 1969 s18(2) the court may impose requirements which it considers appropriate for facilitating the performance by the supervisor of his/her duty to advise, assist and befriend the supervised person. The Magistrates' Courts (Children and Young Persons) Rules 1992 SI No 2071, r29(2) prescribes the following requirements which may be included in an order:

(a) That he/she shall inform the supervisor at once of any change in his/her address or employment;

(b) That he/she shall keep in touch with the supervisor in accordance with such instructions as may from time to time be given by the supervisor, and in particular, that he/she shall, if the supervisor so requires, receive visits from the supervisor at his/her home.

Failure to include such requirements in the supervision order is likely to cause difficulties if the supervised person fails to co-operate with the order.

19.41 The court may impose additional requirements as part of the supervision order. By the Criminal Justice Act 1991 s6(2)(b) the restrictions on liberty imposed by the order with any additional requirements must be such as are, in the opinion of the court, commensurate with the seriousness of the offence, or the combination of the offence and other offences associated with it. These additional requirements may be:

- to attend a specified place at specified times (Intermediate Treatment): s12(2)(b);
- to take part in specified activities (Intermediate Treatment): s12A(3)(a);
- to make reparation to specified persons or the community at large: s12A(3)(aa);
- to remain at a specified place or places between 6pm and 6am (a night restriction): s12A(3)(b);
- to refrain from taking part in specified activities: s12A(3)(c);

34 Ibid, s18(3).

- to live at a particular place (residence as specified): s12(2)(a) and s12A(3)(a);
- to live in local authority accommodation: s12AA;
- to receive psychiatric treatment: s12B; and
- to attend school or comply with other arrangements for his/her education: s12C.

Supervision orders with an additional requirement of specified activities as a direct alternative to custody have been abolished.[35]

Intermediate treatment

19.42   This is a generic term for a range of programmes run by social services departments, and increasingly voluntary organisations, which are designed for offenders under the age of 18. The Department of Health encouraged such programmes to develop local initiatives in conjunction with the relevant youth court magistrates and as a result the types of programmes available vary enormously across the country. Most programmes will have one-to-one sessions to address offending behaviour, some will also run group sessions to discuss offending and its effects upon victims. Programmes will often have a practical element where offenders can learn vocational skills such as carpentry. Less frequently there may be specialist projects such as motor vehicle schemes or victim compensation schemes.[36] It would be advisable for the defence lawyer to make contact with the local youth justice team (or youth offending team) or even directly with the local scheme itself to find out what activities are available.

19.43   The court may impose two types of Intermediate Treatment, the difference being whether the court or the supervisor specify the exact nature of the programme. It is important to distinguish between the two types of order but unfortunately there is no universally accepted terminology. It has been decided to use the terms non-specified activities and specified activities in this work largely because it keeps as close as possible to the terminology used in the 1969 Act. However, in some parts of the country the terms discretionary and non-stipulated activities are also employed.

---

35   Crime and Disorder Act 1998 s72.
36   For further information see *The ISTD Handbook of Community Programmes for Young and Juvenile Offenders* (Waterside Press, 2nd edn, 1998).

Non-specified activities: s12(2)(b)

19.44   A requirement for non-specified activities leaves the supervisor with the discretion as to the type of activities to include in the programme and the times and frequency of contact. Although the court would be required to consider a pre-sentence report before imposing non-specified activities, it is not required to have consulted the supervisor about the feasibility of such a requirement. It is, however, submitted that it would be best practice to consult in any event.

19.45   The requirement may be for any period up to a maximum of 90 days. If a requirement to reside as specified under the same subsection is imposed the aggregate of the requirements must not exceed 90 days.[37]

Specified activities: s12A(3)(a)

19.46   Before imposing a specified activities requirement the court must:

(i)   consult the supervisor as to:
       – the offender's circumstances;
       – the feasibility of securing compliance with the requirements;
(ii)   be satisfied in the light of the supervisor's report that the requirements are necessary for securing the good conduct of the supervised person or for preventing a repetition by him/her of the same offence or the commission of other offences.[38]

19.47   A specified activities requirement requires the offender to attend on specified times and days for particular activities. Prior to sentencing the court will have considered a specified activities programme which will set out the type of activity proposed for each session during the programme. By imposing such a requirement the court removes the discretion from the supervising officer and should the programme need to be varied for any reason the supervising officer will have to apply to the court for a variation of the order.

19.48   The requirement may be for any period up to a maximum of 90 days. If a night restriction or reparation requirement is also imposed the aggregate of the requirements must not exceed 90 days.[39]

19.49   The court may not impose a specified activities requirement upon an offender under the age of 16 unless it has obtained and considered

37   Children and Young Persons Act 1969 s12(3).
38   Ibid, s12A(6)(a) and (b).
39   Ibid, s12A(5).

information about the offender's family circumstances and the likely effect of the requirements on those circumstances.[40]

Reparation: s12A(3)(aa)

19.50   The offender is required to make reparation specified in the order to a person or persons or to the community at large. This provision is not yet in force.[41]

19.51   Before imposing a reparation requirement the court must:

(i)   consult the supervisor as to:
  – the offender's circumstances;
  – the feasibility of securing compliance with the requirements;

(ii) be satisfied in the light of the supervisor's report that the requirements are necessary for securing the good conduct of the supervised person or for preventing a repetition by him/her of the same offence or the commission of other offences.[42]

The requirement may be for any period up to a maximum of 90 days. If a specified activities or night restriction requirement is also imposed the aggregate of the requirements must not exceed 90 days.[43]

19.52   The court may not impose a reparation requirement upon an offender under the age of 16, unless it has obtained and considered information about the offender's family circumstances and the likely effect of the requirements on those circumstances.[44]

Night restriction: s12A(3)(b)

19.53   Before imposing a night restriction the court must:

(i)   consult the supervisor as to:
  – the offender's circumstances;
  – the feasibility of securing compliance with the requirements;

40   Ibid, s12A(6)(c).
41   According to the Home Office's *Introductory Guide to the Crime and Disorder Act 1998* this provision will be implemented at the end of the piloting of reparation orders (for which see para 18.81). This is expected to be in June 2000.
42   Children and Young Persons Act 1969 s12A(6)(a) and (b).
43   Ibid, s12A(5)(a).
44   Ibid, s12A(6)(c).

(ii) be satisfied in the light of the supervisor's report that the requirements are necessary for securing the good conduct of the supervised person or for preventing a repetition by him/her of the same offence or the commission of other offences.[45]

19.54 There are complicated rules relating to the requirement which may be summarised as follows:

- the restriction may not be for more than 30 days in total (an overnight restriction counting as one day's restriction);[46]
- a restriction may not be for any time falling after three months following the making of the supervision order;[47]
- the supervised person may not be required to remain at a place for longer than 10 hours on any one night;[48] and
- one of the places specified as part of the restriction must be the place where the offender lives.[49]

19.55 The supervised person may go out during the currency of a night restriction if accompanied by a parent or guardian, supervisor or some other person specified in the order.[50] The court may not impose a requirement as part of a night restriction that the offender is to live with a specified individual nor is the restriction to be imposed if it would require the co-operation of a person other than the supervisor unless that person consents to its inclusion.[51]

19.56 The court may not impose a night restriction requirement upon an offender under the age of 16 unless it has obtained and considered information about the offender's family circumstances and the likely effect of the requirements on those circumstances.[52]

19.57 This requirement is rarely imposed as it is generally perceived that it would not be feasible to enforce it.

Refraining from specified activities: s12A(3)(c)

19.58 Again, this is an additional requirement which is very rarely imposed. It may conceivably be considered where there has been shown to be a

---

45 Ibid, s12A(6)(a) and (b).
46 Ibid, s12A(11).
47 Ibid, s12A(10).
48 Ibid, s12A(9).
49 Ibid, s12A(8).
50 Ibid, s12A(12).
51 Ibid, s12A(7).
52 Ibid, s12A(6)(c).

pattern of offending linked to a particular leisure activity, for example football matches.

19.59   Before imposing a requirement that the supervised person refrain from specified activities the court must:

(i)   consult the supervisor as to:
   –   the offender's circumstances;
   –   the feasibility of securing compliance with the requirements;
(ii) be satisfied in the light of the supervisor's report that the requirements are necessary for securing the good conduct of the supervised person or for preventing a repetition by him/her of the same offence or the commission of other offences.[53]

The court may not impose an additional requirement to refrain from specified activities upon an offender under the age of 16, unless it has obtained and considered information about the offender's family circumstances and the likely effect of the requirements on those circumstances.[54]

Residence as specified: s12(2)(a) and s12A(3)(a)

19.60   A court may impose two types of requirement upon a supervised person. These are as follows:

   –   to comply with the supervising officer's directions to live at a specified place: s12(2)(a);
   –   to live at a place specified by the court: s12A(3)(a).

19.61   Before imposing a requirement under s12A(3)(a), the court must:

(i)   consult the supervisor as to:
   –   the offender's circumstances;
   –   the feasibility of securing compliance with the requirement;
(ii) be satisfied in the light of the supervisor's report that the requirement is necessary for securing the good conduct of the supervised person or for preventing a repetition by him/her of the same offence or the commission of other offences.[55]

---

53   Ibid, s12A(6)(a) and (b).
54   Ibid, s12A(6)(c).
55   Ibid, s12A(6)(a) and (b).

In the case of an offender under the age of 16, the court may not impose a condition to reside as specified under s12A(3)(a) unless it has obtained and considered information about the offender's family circumstances and the likely effect of the requirements on those circumstances.[56]

19.62   The practical difference between the requirements is that with the first the supervising officer is left with discretion as to how the requirement will be implemented, whereas with the second the court imposes a requirement which may only be amended by an application to the court for a variation of the order. In either case the supervised person may not be required to comply with such a direction for more than 90 days. Should a non-specified or specified activities requirement be imposed at the same time the aggregate of the two requirements must not exceed 90 days.[57]

Residence in local authority accommodation: s12AA

19.63   A court may impose a requirement upon a supervised person to live for a specified period (not exceeding six months) in local authority accommodation.[58] The court must designate the authority which is to receive the supervised person. The designated authority should be the authority in whose area the supervised person resides.[59] The requirement may stipulate that the supervised person is not to live with a named person.[60]

19.64   The pre-conditions for imposing a requirement of residence in local authority accommodation were amended in the Crime and Disorder Act 1998. As of 1 April 1999 such a requirement may only be made if the following pre-conditions are satisfied:

– the court has first consulted with the designated authority;[61]
– a supervision order has previously been made in respect of the child or young person;
– the supervision order in existence includes an additional requirement contained in s12, 12A or 12C of the Children and

---

56 Ibid, s12A(6)(c).
57 Ibid, s12(3).
58 Ibid, s12AA(1) and (5).
59 Ibid, s12AA(2).
60 Ibid, s12AA(4).
61 Ibid, s12AA(3).

Young Persons Act 1969 (any requirement other than a requirement for psychiatric treatment);

- the supervised person has either failed to comply with the additional requirement or been found guilty of an offence committed
  while that order was in force;
- the court is satisfied that –
  i) the failure to comply with the requirements, or the behaviour
     which constituted the offence, was due to a significant extent to
     the circumstances in which the supervised person was living;
     and
  ii) the imposition of the residence requirement will assist in his/
      her rehabilitation;[62] and
- the supervised person is legally represented at the hearing when
  the court is considering whether or not to impose the residence
  requirement.[63]

19.65   The last condition can be ignored if the child or young person has
been informed of his/her right to apply for legal aid and s/he has
failed to do so or, having applied, the application has been refused
because his financial resources were such that it did not appear that
he needed assistance.

19.66   A residence requirement may be imposed along with any of the
other requirements mentioned in ss12, 12A or 12C of the Act.[64]

Local authority accommodation

19.67   This is defined as 'accommodation provided by or on behalf of a local
authority (within the meaning of the Children Act 1989)'.[65] This could
include a placement with family, relatives or any suitable person (for
example a foster parent) as well as accommodation in a children's
home.[66]

19.68   The court has no power to specify a particular placement for the
offender. The order, therefore, leaves the social services department
with considerable discretion subject to the court naming a particular
person with whom the offender is not to reside.

---

62 Ibid, s12AA(6).
63 Ibid, s12AA(9).
64 Ibid, s12AA(11).
65 Ibid, s70(1).
66 Children Act 1989 s23(2).

Application

19.69 This requirement clearly involves a substantial restriction of liberty and this fact is reflected in the legislation by the fact that the offender must be legally represented before it may be imposed. The court should only impose such a requirement where there has been a full assessment of the young offender's home circumstances. The Department of Health has given the following guidance on the use of this requirement:

> The purpose of the residence requirement is not punitive; it is designed to help a young person to work through his problems. A young person's circumstances may contribute to his offending: for example, he may be living rough and stealing to survive; he may have experienced a lack of parental control; or his life at home may be unsatisfactory in other respects. The residence requirement is designed to remove such a young person from the surroundings that are contributing to his offending behaviour, and to place him in local authority accommodation while the local authority enables him to work through the problems associated with his home surroundings. The aim must be to assist the young person to deal with his problems, and to stop him re-offending, even when he does return to his home surroundings. It therefore follows that the role of the social workers responsible for him must be to care for and assist him, and not simply to act as warders.[67]

In the past, requirements to reside in local authority accommodation have been little used. The defence lawyer may wish to explore their use in cases where a defendant is facing a custodial sentence. Their use as an alternative to a custodial sentence could be further enhanced if the local authority were to consider placement in secure accommodation. To do this the local authority would have to seek authority from a family proceedings court under the Children Act 1989 s25.[68]

Requirement to receive psychiatric treatment

19.70 Before imposing this additional requirement to a supervision order, the court must be satisfied, on the evidence of a medical practitioner approved under the Mental Health Act 1983 s12, that the mental condition of the supervised person is such as requires and may be

---

67 *The Children Act 1989 Guidance and Regulations* (HMSO, 1991), Vol 1, Court Orders, para 6.26.
68 See Chapter 11.

susceptible to treatment but is not such as to warrant his/her detention under a hospital order.[69]

19.71   The court may require the supervised person to submit to treatment of one of the following descriptions:

- treatment by or under the direction of a fully registered medical practitioner specified in the order;
- treatment as a non-resident patient at a place specified in the order; or
- treatment as a resident patient in a hospital or mental nursing home (but not a special hospital).[70]

The court must specify the period for which the supervised person must comply with the requirement. The requirement may presumably last as long as the supervision order itself, except that it may not continue in force after the supervised person has attained the age of 18.[71]

19.72   The court must be satisfied that arrangements have been or can be made for the treatment proposed. In the case of treatment as an in-patient, the court must also be satisfied that a bed will be available. In the case of a supervised person who has attained the age of 14, s/he must consent to the inclusion of the requirement.[72]

Requirement as to education

19.73   A court may require a supervised person of compulsory school age to comply, for as long as s/he is of that age and the requirement remains in force, with the arrangements made for his/her education by his/her parents. These arrangements must be approved by the local education authority.

19.74   Before including such a requirement in a supervision order the court must:

- first consult with the supervisor as to the offender's circumstances;[73]
- consult with the local education authority with regard to the proposal to include the requirement and satisfy itself that, in the opinion of the authority, arrangements exist for the child or young

---

69   Children and Young Persons Act 1969 s12B(1).
70   Ibid.
71   Ibid, s12B(2).
72   Ibid, s12B(2)(b).
73   Children and Young Persons Act 1969 s12C(4).

person to receive efficient full-time education suitable to his/her age, ability and aptitude and to any special needs s/he may have;[74] and

- having regard to the circumstances of the case, consider the requirement necessary for securing the good conduct of the supervised person or for preventing a repetition by him/her of the same offence or the commission of other offences.[75]

This additional requirement appears to be very rarely used by magistrates.[76]

Variation

19.75 An application may be made to the relevant court by the supervisor or the offender.[77] If the court considers it appropriate, it may:

- cancel any additional requirement; or
- insert in the order (either in addition to or in substitution for any of its provisions) any provision which could have been included in the order if the court had then had power to make it and were exercising the power.[78]

19.76 The court's power to vary the original supervision order is limited in two respects.[79] After three months from the original date of sentence the court may not insert a condition requiring the offender to receive psychiatric treatment (although such a condition already in force may be varied). Secondly, it may not impose a curfew condition in respect of any day which falls outside the period of three months after the date of original sentence.

Which court?

19.77 The application should be made to the relevant court. This is defined by the Children and Young Persons Act 1969 s15(11) as follows:

- in the case of an offender who has not attained 18, a youth court;
- in the case of an offender who has attained 18, a magistrates' court.

---

74 Ibid, s12C(2).
75 Ibid, s12C(4).
76 In 1995 only 22 such orders were made: see Ball, C and Connolly, J *Requiring School Attendance: A Little Used Sentencing Power* [1999] Crim LR 183.
77 The parent or guardian may make the application on behalf of the offender: Children and Young Persons Act 1969 s70(2).
78 Ibid, s15(1).
79 Ibid, s15(2).

The section does not specify the relevant petty sessions area, but it is submitted that the most appropriate area would be that where the supervised person is now residing or if not known the area for the local authority named in the order.

Discharge

19.78   The supervisor may apply to the relevant court for the length of the order to be shortened or for the order to be discharged. Once again the court may grant the application if it appears appropriate. Such an application may be granted in the absence of the supervised person.[80]

19.79   The *National Standards for the Supervision of Offenders in the Community* (1995) give the following guidance:

> Early termination of a supervision order should be considered where the offender has made good progress in achieving the objectives set out for the order and where there is not considered to be a significant risk of re-offending and/or of serious harm to the public. Early termination should not be considered before at least half the order has been successfully completed without breach or re-offending.

Action plan order (pilot areas only)

19.80   Action plan orders were introduced by the Crime and Disorder Act 1998. They are currently being piloted in certain areas.[81] They are intended to be 'a short but intensive and individually tailored response to offending behaviour, so that the causes of that offending as well as the offending itself can be addressed'.[82]

19.81   The Home Office has issued guidance to the courts and youth offending teams operating in the pilot areas:

> The action plan order is . . . intended to be issued for relatively serious offending but it is also intended to offer an early opportunity for targeted intervention to help prevent further offending. For young people whose offending is serious enough to justify a community sentence, the action plan order should be considered as a first option.[83]

No court shall make an action plan order unless it has been notified by the Secretary of State that arrangements for implementing such

---

80   Ibid, 16(5).
81   See appendix 8.
82   Home Office, *Draft Guidance on Action Plan Orders*, para 2.1.
83   Ibid, para 2.3.

orders are available in the petty sessions area proposed to be named in the order and the notice has not been withdrawn.[84]

Pre-conditions

19.82 An action plan order may be imposed by a youth court or a Crown Court. It may be imposed for any offence, the penalty for which is not fixed by law, but only if:

- the offence, or the combination of the offence and associated offences, is serious enough;
- the order is the most suitable for the offender; and
- the court is of the opinion that it is desirable to pass such an order in the interests of securing the offender's rehabilitation or of preventing the commission by him/her of further offences.[85]

Age

19.83 An action plan order may be passed upon any offender aged 10 to 17.[86] The age of a person shall be deemed that which it appears to the court to be after considering any available evidence.[87]

Length of order

19.84 The order shall last for a period of three months beginning with the date of the order.[88]

Procedural requirements

19.85 Before making an action plan order, a court shall obtain and consider a written report by a probation officer, social worker of a local authority social services department or a member of a youth offending team, indicating:

- the requirements proposed to be included in the order;
- the benefits to the offender that the proposed requirements are designed to achieve; and

---

84 Crime and Disorder Act 1998 s69(3).
85 Ibid, s69(2).
86 Ibid, s69(1).
87 Ibid, s69(2)(a).
88 Ibid, s69(2)(a)

- the attitude of a parent or guardian of the offender to the proposed requirements.[89]

In the case of offenders under the age of 16, the report should also contain information regarding the offender's family circumstances and the likely effect of the order on those circumstances.[90]

19.86   Before making an action plan order, a court shall explain to the offender in ordinary language:

- the effect of the order and of the requirements proposed to be included in it;
- the consequences which may follow if the order is breached; and
- that the court has power to review the order on the application of either the offender or the responsible officer.[91]

19.87   An action plan order may not be imposed upon a young offender already the subject of another action plan order.[92] It also cannot be combined with any of the following orders:

- a custodial sentence;
- a probation order;
- a community service order;
- a combination order;
- a supervision order; or
- an attendance order.[93]

Requirements of order

19.88   A young offender subject to an action plan order may be required to do any of the following:

- participate in activities specified in the requirements or directions at a time or times so specified;
- present him/herself to a person or persons specified in the requirements or directions at a place or places and at a time or times so specified;
- attend an attendance centre specified in the requirements or directions for a specified number of hours (only in case of imprisonable offence);

89   Ibid, s70(1)(a).
90   Ibid, s70(1)(b).
91   Ibid, s70(2).
92   Ibid, s70(4)(a).
93   Ibid, s70(4)(b).

- stay away from a place or places specified in the requirements or directions;
- comply with any arrangements for his/her education specified in the requirements or directions;
- make reparation specified in the requirements or directions; or
- attend any review hearing as fixed by the court.[94]

19.89 As far as is practicable the requirements of the order shall be such as to avoid:

- any conflict with the offender's religious beliefs;
- any interference with the times, if any, at which the offender usually works or attends school or any other educational establishment; or
- any conflict with the requirements of any community order to which s/he may be subject.[95]

Review hearing

19.90 Immediately after making an action plan order, a court may fix a further hearing for a date not more than 21 days after the making of the order. The court may also direct the responsible officer to make at that hearing a report (oral or written) as to the effectiveness of the order and the extent to which it has been implemented.

19.91 The Home Office has given the following advice to courts in pilot areas regarding the use of review hearings:

> This further hearing is discretionary; it is not expected that courts will feel it necessary in every case. Its purpose is to allow the court to review the initial stages of the action plan order, and to make any alterations – variations or cancellations of certain requirements, and/or their replacement with alternative ones – in the action plan which are necessary or appropriate. It will also allow the court an opportunity to encourage the young person to complete the order successfully and to provide positive feedback on progress with the order so far. In deciding whether to hold such a further hearing, the court may wish to consider:
>
> (i)   any recommendation from the report writer;
> (ii) the attitude of the young person and his or her parents/guardians to the action plan order and its requirements. It

---

94 Crime and Disorder Act 1998 s69(5).
95 Ibid, s69(6).

may be that the court feel that some might need particular
encouragement or oversight; and

(iii)   ... the possibility of victim/offender mediation.[96]

At the review hearing the court shall consider the responsible
officer's report and may, on the application of the responsible officer
or the offender vary the order by cancelling any provision contained
in it or by inserting in it (either in addition to or in substitution for
any of its provisions) any provision that the court could originally
have included in it.

Variation and discharge

19.92   An application for variation or discharge of the order may be made by
either the offender or the responsible officer.[97] Application should be
made to the youth court acting for the petty sessions area named in
the order.[98]

19.93   The order may be varied by inserting in it (in addition to or substitution for) any provision which could have been included in the
order if the court had then had the power to make it and were exercising the power.[99] Home Office draft guidance suggests that this power
might be exercised where an offender moves to a different area or a
particular requirement of the order is proving unsuccessful and the
responsible officer believes it could be usefully replaced with an
alternative requirement.[100]

19.94   Where an application for discharge of an action plan order has
been dismissed, no further discharge application may be made without the consent of the youth court acting for the petty sessions area
named in the order.[101]

19.95   An offender may appeal to the Crown Court against any decision
to vary the requirements of the order or to dismiss an application to
discharge the order. The right of appeal does not extend to appealing
a decision:

– discharging the order;
– cancelling a requirement of the order;

96 Home Office, *Draft Guidance on Action Plan Orders*, para 8.2.
97 Crime and Disorder Act 1998 Sch 5 para 2(1).
98 Ibid, Sch 5 para 1.
99 Ibid, Sch 5 para 2(1).
100 Home Office, *Draft Guidance on Action Plan Orders*, para 9.2.
101 Crime and Disorder Act 1998 Sch 5 para 2(2).

- altering the relevant petty sessions named in the order; or
- changing the responsible officer.[102]

Curfew order

19.96 The Criminal Justice Act 1991 s12(1) states:

> Where a person of or over the age of sixteen years is convicted of an offence (not being an offence for which the sentence is fixed by law) the court by or before which he is convicted may make a curfew order, that is to say, an order requiring him to remain, for periods specified in the order, at a place so specified.

Curfew orders have been piloted in certain areas for some years. As of 1 December 1999 they are available to all courts in England and Wales.[103]

19.97 As well as the power to order an offender to stay indoors at a particular time the court has the power to monitor compliance by the means of electronic tagging of the offender.[104] The Home Secretary may contract with private firms to operate any tagging system under licence. These firms will also initiate any breach proceedings if the offender fails to observe the conditions of the order.

Pre-conditions

19.98 A curfew order may only be imposed if the court considers:

- the offence, or the combination of the offence and associated offences to be serious enough; and
- the order to be the most suitable for the offender;

The order may be imposed for any offence whether or not it is imprisonable.

Age

19.99 Under the Criminal Justice Act 1991, a curfew order may only be imposed upon an offender who has attained the age of 16. The Crime (Sentences) Act 1997 s43 has made provision for the minimum age

---

102 Ibid, Sch 5 paras 5(7) and 4(9).
103 Criminal Justice Act 1991 (Commencement No 4) Order 1994 SI No 3191 and Curfew Order (Responsible Officer) Order 1999 SI No 3155.
104 Criminal Justice Act 1991 s13, see para 19.103.

to be reduced to 10 years. This lower age limit is being piloted in a small number of areas.[105] The relevant age is the age at the date of conviction for the offence.[106]

Length of the order

19.100 The order may not last beyond six months from the day on which it was made.[107]

Procedural requirements

19.101 The court is not required to obtain a pre-sentence report before imposing a curfew order. However, before making the order, the court is required to obtain and consider information about the place proposed to be specified in the order (including information as to the attitude of the persons likely to be affected by the enforced presence there of the offender).[108] It is submitted that this is particularly important in the case of young offenders where the court is likely to be requiring them to remain in the parental home.

19.102 Before making the order, the court shall explain to the offender in ordinary language:

- the effect of the order (including the effect of any electronic tagging);
- the fact that on breach the court may impose a fine, community service order or re-sentence; and
- that the court has the power to review the order at the application of either the supervisor or the offender.[109]

An offender need not consent before a curfew order is imposed.

Electronic tagging

19.103 In addition to the curfew order, the court may include a requirement for securing the electronic monitoring of the offender's whereabouts during the curfew periods specified in the order. The court may not include an electronic monitoring requirement unless:

---

105 See appendix 8.
106 If the offender's age is in doubt, see para 3.9ff.
107 Criminal Justice Act 1991 s12(2)(a).
108 Ibid, s12(6).
109 Ibid, s12(5).

- it has been notified by the Secretary of State that electronic monitoring arrangements are available in the area in which the place proposed to be specified in the order is situated; and
- it is satisfied that the necessary provision can be made under those arrangements.[110]

Requirements of the order

19.104 The order will specify the period of each day when the offender must not leave a place (usually, but not necessarily, the offender's home address). More than one place may be specified and the court may specify different times for different days of the week. The order may not specify a period of less than two hours or more than 12 hours in any one day.[111] The requirements of a curfew order shall, as far as is practicable, be such as to avoid:

- any conflict with the offender's religious beliefs; or
- any conflict with the requirements of any other community order to which s/he may be subject; and
- any interference with the times, if any, at which s/he usually works or attends school or any other educational establishment.[112]

Variation

19.105 Application may be made by either the offender or his/her supervisor to a youth court (or to a magistrates' court if the offender has attained 18) for the variation of a curfew order.[113] The court may:

- substitute another place for the one named in the order;
- cancel any requirement; and
- insert in the order (either in addition or in substitution for any existing requirements) any requirements which the court could include if it were then making the order.[114]

A court may not vary the requirements of a curfew order by extending the curfew periods beyond the end of six months after the date of the original order.[115]

---

110   Ibid, s13(2).
111   Ibid, s12(2)(b).
112   Ibid, s12(3).
113   Ibid, Sch 2 paras 12 and 13.
114   Ibid.
115   Ibid, Sch 2 para 13(2)(b).

494   *Defending young people / chapter 19*

Revocation

19.106 Application may be made either by the offender or the responsible officer to a youth court (or to a magistrates' court if the offender has attained 18) for the curfew order to be revoked. If, after having regard to the circumstances which have arisen since the imposition of the order, the court is satisfied that it would be in the interests of justice that the order be revoked or that the offender be dealt with in another manner, it may:

– revoke the order; or
– revoke the order and deal with the offender, for the offence in respect of which the order was made, in any manner in which it could deal with him/her if s/he had just been convicted by the court of the offence.[116]

If the order was made by the Crown Court, the court may not revoke the order itself but it may commit the offender to the Crown Court for that purpose.[117] In either case if a court does re-sentence the offender, the extent to which s/he complied with the curfew order must be taken into account.[118]

19.107   No application for revocation may be made by the offender while an appeal against sentence is pending.[119]

Probation order

19.108 The Powers of Criminal Courts Act 1973 s2(1) provides:

> Where a court by or before which a person of or over the age of sixteen is convicted of an offence (not being an offence for which the sentence is fixed by law) is of the opinion the supervision of the offender by a probation officer is desirable in the interests of –
> (a) securing the rehabilitation of the offender; or
> (b) protecting the public from harm from him/her; or preventing the commission by him/her of further offences,
> the court may make a probation order, that is to say, an order requiring him to be under the supervision of a probation order for a period specified in the order of not less than six months nor more than three years.

116   Ibid, Sch 2 para 7(1) and (2).
117   Ibid, Sch 2 para 7(2) (b).
118   Ibid, Sch 2 paras 7(4) and 8(4)
119   Ibid, Sch 2 para 7(8).

Pre-conditions

19.109 A probation order may be imposed for any offence whether imprisonable or non-imprisonable. However, it may not be imposed unless the court considers:

- the offence, or the combination of the offence and associated offences to be serious enough;[120] and
- the order to be the most suitable for the offender.[121]

Age

19.110 A probation order may only be imposed upon an offender who has attained the age of 16. The relevant age is that at the date of conviction for the offence.[122]

Length of the order

19.111 A probation order may be imposed for any period between six months and three years. By the Criminal Justice Act 1991 s6(2)(b) the court is required to determine the length of the order by reference to the seriousness of the offence.

Procedural requirements

19.112 No pre-sentence report is required before the imposition of a probation order without any additional requirements. A report is, required, however, if such additional requirements are to be imposed.[123]

19.113 Before making an order the court shall explain to the offender in ordinary language:

- the requirements imposed by the order;
- that if s/he breaches any of the requirements, the court may impose a fine, a community service order of up to 60 hours or revoke the order and re-sentence; and
- that the order may be varied at the application of either the supervising officer or the probationer.[124]

---

120 Criminal Justice Act 1991 s6(1).
121 Ibid, s6(2)(a).
122 Powers of Criminal Courts Act 1973 s2(1): if the offender's age is in doubt see para 3.9ff.
123 See para 16.27.
124 Powers of Criminal Courts Act 1973 s2(3).

19.114   A probation order shall specify the petty sessions area in which the offender resides or will reside. The probation service for that petty sessions area will then be responsible for the supervision of the order. The court shall forthwith give the court probation officer a copy of the order and s/he shall give a copy to:

- the offender;
- the probation officer responsible for the offender's supervision; and
- the person in charge of an institution in which the offender is required by the order to reside.[125]

Requirements of the order

19.115 A probation order imposes general requirements. These require the offender to keep in touch with the probation officer responsible for his/her supervision in accordance with such instructions as s/he may from time to time be given by the officer and to inform the officer of any change of address.[126]

19.116   By virtue of the Powers of Criminal Courts Act 1973 Sch 1A a court may impose additional requirements upon an offender sentenced to a probation order. These requirements may include the following:

- residence requirements;
- requirements to participate in activities;
- requirements to attend a probation centre;
- requirements for sex offenders;
- requirements as to treatment for mental condition; and
- requirements as to drugs or alcohol dependency.

19.117   By the Criminal Justice Act 1991 s6(2)(b) the restriction of liberty imposed by these additional requirements shall be such as in the opinion of the court are commensurate with the seriousness of the offence, or the combination of the offence and other offences associated with it.

Residence requirements

19.118 A court may attach to the probation order a requirement to live at a place specified by the court.[127] The type of accommodation where the

---

125   Ibid, s2(3).
126   Ibid, s2(6).
127   Ibid, Sch 1A para 1(1).

offender may be required to reside is not specified by the legislation. As well as being a probation hostel or other institution dealing with offenders, it could presumably also cover a requirement for a young offender to reside with a named member of the family. If the required residence is a probation hostel or other institution, the order must specify the period for which the offender is required to reside there. Before making a probation order with a residence requirement the court shall consider the home surroundings of the offender.

19.119   The Home Office has issued guidance on the use of a residence requirement for offenders aged 16 or 17.[128] Authority for the placement of such a young offender in a probation hostel should be given by an assistant chief probation officer. Before considering whether such a requirement is appropriate the following factors should be considered:

- whether the young person is still in full-time education;
- in the case of female offenders, whether the living accommodation for each sex is distinct and separate;
- whether other residents may present a risk to the young offender (in particular the risk from sex offenders must be considered); and
- hostels aim to move residents on to permanent accommodation as soon as possible – this may not be suitable for young offenders who may not be ready for such independence.

Requirements to participate in activities

19.120   An offender may be required to:

1) present himself/herself to a person or persons specified in the order at a place or places so specified;
2) participate in activities specified in the order on a day or days so specified or during the probation period or a portion of it as specified.[129]

19.121   In (1) above the offender is required to attend as directed by the supervising probation officer for not more than 60 days in the aggregate.[130] While attending as required, s/he must comply with the instructions of the person in charge.[131]

19.122   The court may only impose such a requirement if:

128 Home Office Circular 44/1993 *Admission of 16- and 17-year-olds to Approved Probation/Bail Hostels.*
129 Powers of Criminal Courts Act 1973 Sch 1A para 2(1).
130 Ibid, Sch 1A para 2(4)(a).
131 Ibid, Sch 1A para 2(4)(b).

- it has consulted a probation officer; and
- it is satisfied that it is feasible to secure compliance with the requirement.[132]

Requirements to attend a probation centre

19.123 A court may require an offender during the probation period to attend at a probation centre on not more than 60 days.[133] A probation centre is defined as 'premises at which non-residential facilities are provided for use in connection with the rehabilitation of offenders . . .'[134] Attendance at such a centre may include attendances elsewhere than at the centre for the purpose of participating in activities in accordance with instructions given by, or under the authority of, the person in charge of the centre.[135]

19.124   A court shall not include such a requirement in a probation order unless:

- it has consulted a probation officer; and
- it is satisfied that arrangements can be made for the offender's attendance at a centre and the person in charge of the centre consents to the inclusion of the requirement.[136]

19.125   An offender subject to such a requirement shall be required:

- to attend the centre in accordance with instructions given by the probation officer responsible for his/her supervision; and
- while attending there to comply with instructions given by, or under the authority of, the person in charge of the centre.

19.126   The instructions given to an offender should, so far as practicable, be such as to avoid any interference with the times, if any, at which the offender usually works or attends school or other educational establishment.[137]

Requirements for sex offenders

19.127 A court has the power in the case of an offender convicted of a sexual offence to impose a requirement to participate in activities or attend a

132   Ibid, Sch 1A para 2(2).
133   Ibid, Sch 1A para 3(1) and (3).
134   Ibid, Sch 1A para 3(7)(a).
135   Ibid, Sch 1A para 3(5).
136   Ibid, Sch 1A para 3(2).
137   Ibid, Sch 1A para 3(4).

probation centre for any period beyond the normal maximum period of 60 days.[138] For this purpose sexual offence has the same meaning as the Criminal Justice Act 1991 s31(1).[139]

Requirements as to treatment for drug or alcohol dependency

19.128 A court may include a requirement that an offender shall submit, during the whole period of the probation order or during such part of the period as may be specified in the order, to treatment with a view to the reduction or elimination of the offender's dependency on drugs or alcohol.[140] The court may only impose such a requirement if it is satisfied:

- that the offender is dependent on drugs or alcohol;
- that the dependency caused or contributed to the offence in respect of which the order is proposed to be made; and
- that the dependency is such as requires and may be susceptible to treatment.[141]

Dependent on drugs or alcohol

19.129 Dependent includes 'having a propensity towards the misuse of drugs or alcohol'.[142]

Treatment

19.130 The probation order must specify the type of treatment to be followed. It may comprise any of the following:

- treatment as a resident in an institution specified in the order;
- treatment as a non-resident in an institution specified in the order; and
- treatment by or under the direction of such person having the necessary qualifications or experience.[143]

19.131 The court shall not impose such a requirement unless it is satisfied that arrangements have been made for the treatment intended to

---

138 Ibid, Sch 1A para 4(1).
139 Ibid, Sch 1A para 4(2): see para 10.81.
140 Ibid, Sch 1A para 6(2).
141 Ibid, Sch 1A para 6(1).
142 Ibid, Sch 1A para 6(9).
143 Ibid, Sch 1A para 6(3).

be specified in the order (including arrangements for the reception of the offender as a resident).[144]

19.132   Once treatment has started, the person responsible for that treatment may, with the consent of the offender, arrange for his/her admittance to an institution not named in the order if it is considered that treatment can be better or more conveniently given.[145]

Requirement as to treatment for mental condition

19.133   Where it appears that a young offender is mentally ill, the court may impose a requirement to submit to treatment for that mental illness.[146]

Medical evidence

19.134   The court must be satisfied, on the evidence of a medical practitioner approved under the Mental Health Act 1983 s12, that the mental condition of the offender is such as requires and may be susceptible to treatment but is not such as to warrant the making of a hospital order or guardianship order.[147]

Type of treatment

19.135   The treatment required in the order must be of the description of one of the following:

– treatment as a resident patient in a mental hospital;
– treatment as a non-resident patient at such institution or place as may be specified in the order; or
– treatment by or under the direction of such duly qualified medical practitioner as may be so specified.[148]

The actual nature of the treatment may not be specified by the court beyond the categories listed above.

Length of the requirement

19.136   The court may require the offender to submit to the treatment during the whole of the probation period or such part of that period as is specified in the order.[149]

144   Ibid, Sch 1A para 6(4).
145   Ibid, Sch 1A para 6(6).
146   Ibid, Sch 1A para 5(2).
147   Ibid, Sch 1A para 5(1).
148   Ibid, Sch 1A para 5(3).
149   Ibid, Sch 1A para 5(2).

Procedural requirements

19.137 A requirement as to treatment for mental condition may not be imposed unless the court is satisfied that arrangements have been made for the treatment intended to be specified in the order.[150]

Amendment

19.138 Application may be made by either the offender or his/her supervisor to a youth court (or to a magistrates' court if the offender has attained 18) for the amendment of the requirements of a probation order.[151] The court may:

- substitute another petty sessions area for the one named in the order;
- cancel any requirement; or
- insert in the order (either in addition or in substitution for any existing requirements) any requirements which the court could include if it were then making the order.[152]

19.139 A court may not amend the order:

- by reducing the probation period, or by extending that period beyond the end of three years from the date of the original order; or
- by inserting in it a requirement that the offender shall submit to treatment for his/her mental condition, or his/her dependency on drugs or alcohol, unless the amending order is made within three months after the date of the original order.[153]

Revocation

19.140 Application may be made either by the offender or the supervisor to a youth court (or to a magistrates' court if the offender has attained 18) for the probation order to be revoked. If, after having regard to the circumstances which have arisen since the imposition of the order, the court is satisfied that it would be in the interests of justice that the order be revoked or that the offender be dealt with in another manner, it may:

150 Ibid, Sch 1A para 5(4).
151 Criminal Justice Act 1991 Sch 2 paras 12 and 13.
152 Ibid, Sch 2 paras 12(2) and 13(1).
153 Ibid, Sch 2 para 13(2)(a).

- revoke the order; or
- revoke the order and deal with the offender, for the offence in respect of which the order was made, in any manner in which it could deal with him/her if s/he had just been convicted by the court of the offence.[154]

If the order was made by the Crown Court, the court may not revoke the order itself but it may commit the offender to the Crown Court for that purpose.[155] In either case if a court does re-sentence the offender, the extent to which s/he complied with the probation order must be taken into account.[156]

19.141　　In relation to early termination the 1995 *National Standards for the Supervision of the Offender in the Community* give the following guidance:

> Early termination of a probation order should be considered:
>
> (a) where the offender has made good progress in achieving the objectives set out for the order and where there is not considered to be a significant risk of re-offending and/or of serious harm to the public. Early termination on these grounds should not be considered until at least half the order has been completed without breach or re-offending; or
>
> (b) where the supervising officer considers that the offender should be re-sentenced because the order is no longer appropriate.

Community service order

19.142　*The National Standards for the Supervision of Offenders in the Community* (1995) states that the purpose of a community service order is to prevent further offending by re-integrating the offender into the community through:

- punishment – by means of positive and demanding unpaid work and keeping to disciplined requirements; and
- reparation to the community – by undertaking socially useful work.

19.143　　The work is done under the supervision of the probation service and can involve painting and decorating, gardening and other manual tasks. There is a special emphasis on making good the damage

154　Ibid, Sch 2 para 7(1) and (2)(a).
155　Ibid, Sch 2 para 7(2)(b).
156　Ibid, Sch 2 paras 7(4) and 8(4).

caused by crime (for example, removing graffiti from public places or housing estates).

Pre-conditions

19.144 An order may not be imposed unless:
- the offence is imprisonable;[157]
- the court considers the offence, or the combination of the offence and associated offences to be serious enough;[158] and
- the court considers the order to be the most suitable for the offender.[159]

Age

19.145 A community service order may not be imposed upon an offender who has not attained the age of 16 years.[160] The relevant age is the age at the date of conviction.

Length of the order

19.146 By the Criminal Justice Act 1991 s6(2)(b) the length of the order shall be such as is, in the opinion of the court, commensurate with the seriousness of the offence, or the combination of the offence and other offences associated with it.

Minimum

19.147 The aggregate shall not be less than 40 hours.[161]

Maximum

19.148 The aggregate shall not be more than 240 hours.[162]

Multiple orders

19.149 The court may impose more than one community service order at the same time. If it does so, it may specify that the orders are to run

---

157 Powers of Criminal Courts Act 1973 s14(1).
158 Criminal Justice Act 1991 s6(1).
159 Ibid, s6(2).
160 Powers of Criminal Courts Act 1973 s14(1).
161 Ibid, s14(1A)(a).
162 Ibid, s14(1A)(b).

concurrently or consecutively. A court may also impose a community service order upon an offender already subject to such an order. The court may then specify that the new order is to run concurrently with the existing order or to run consecutively. If the order is made consecutively it is undesirable for the offender to be subject to orders totalling more than 240 hours.[163] This principle refers to the hours of the various orders rather than the actual number of hours which remain to be completed.[164]

Procedural requirements

19.150 Before making a community service order the court must explain to the offender in ordinary language:

- the purpose and effects of the order (and in particular the requirements of the order outlined below);
- the consequences if the offender is found to be in breach of the order – the court may impose a fine, a further 60 hours community service or revoke the order and re-sentence the offender; and
- that the order may be varied or discharged at the application of both the offender and the supervising officer.[165]

A court may not make a community service order unless the offender consents to the order and the court, having heard (if it thinks it necessary) from a probation officer or social worker, is satisfied that the offender is a suitable person to perform the order.[166] As young offenders aged 16 and 17 will be at various stages of maturity it is submitted that a court should always consult a probation officer or social worker before imposing an order. The best way to achieve this consultation would be to order a pre-sentence report with a specific request for the offender to be assessed for community service.

19.151 On making the order the court shall forthwith give copies of the order to a probation officer assigned to the court who shall then give the offender and the supervising officer a copy.[167]

---

163 *R v Evans* [1977] 1 All ER 228; [1977] 1 WLR 27; 141 JP 141.
164 *R v Anderson* [1990] Crim LR 130, CA.
165 Powers of Criminal Courts Act 1973 s14(5).
166 Ibid, s14(2).
167 Ibid, s14(6).

Requirements of the order

19.152 An offender subject to a community service order shall:
- keep in touch with the supervising officer in accordance with such instructions as s/he may from time to time be given by that officer and notify the officer of any change of address; and
- perform for the number of hours specified in the order such work at such times as s/he may be instructed by the supervising officer.[168]

19.153 Most community service schemes operate during the week as well as on some evenings and Saturdays. The order should involve a minimum work rate of five hours a week (calculated as an average over the order) and no more than 21 hours should be worked in any one week. The times when the offender is required to work should, as far as practicable, avoid any conflict with the offender's religious beliefs or with the times s/he usually attends school or work.[169]

19.154 The order should be completed within one year of the date of sentence.[170] If the order is to run beyond this the supervisor should apply to the court for an extension. This may be granted if it appears to the court that it would be in the interests of justice to do so having regard to circumstances which have arisen since the order was made.[171]

Amendment

19.155 Application may be made by either the offender or his/her supervisor to a youth court (or to a magistrates' court if the offender has attained 18) for the substitution of a different petty sessions area to the one specified in the order. The court may only substitute the new petty sessions area if it is satisfied that provision exists for the offender to perform such work in that area.[172]

Revocation

19.156 Application may be made either by the offender or the supervisor to a youth court (or to a magistrates' court if the offender has attained 18)

168   Ibid, s15(1).
169   Ibid, s15(3).
170   Ibid, s15(2).
171   Criminal Justice Act 1991 Sch 2 para 15.
172   Ibid, Sch 2 para 12(4).

for the community service order to be revoked. If, after having regard to the circumstances which have arisen since the imposition of the order, the court is satisfied that it would be in the interests of justice that the order be revoked or that the offender be dealt with in another manner, it may:

- revoke the order; or
- revoke the order and deal with the offender, for the offence in respect of which the order was made, in any manner in which it could deal with him/her if s/he had just been convicted by the court of the offence.[173]

If the order was made by the Crown Court, the court may not revoke the order itself but it may commit the offender to the Crown Court for that purpose.[174] In either case, if a court does re-sentence the offender, the extent to which s/he complied with the community service order must be taken into account.[175]

Combination order

19.157　Introduced by the Criminal Justice Act 1991, the combination order is intended to be a high tariff community penalty. It requires the offender to be under the supervision of a probation officer as well as to carry out community service. Although the current National Standards give little guidance as to the circumstances when a combination order would be appropriate, it may still be useful to refer to the 1992 National Standards introduced to coincide with the implementation of the 1991 Act. These state that a combination order would be most appropriate for an offender who has:

- committed an offence which is among the most serious for which a community sentence may be imposed;
- clearly identified areas of need that have contributed to the offending and which can be dealt with by probation supervision; and
- a realistic prospect of completing such an order, including both the probation and community service elements.

173　Ibid, Sch 2 para 7(1) and (2)(a).
174　Ibid, Sch 2 para 7(2)(b).
175　Ibid, Sch 2 paras 7(4) and 8(4).

Pre-conditions

19.158 A combination order may only be imposed if:

- the offence is imprisonable;[176]
- the court considers the offence, or the combination of the offence and associated offences to be serious enough;[177]
- the court is of the opinion that the making of the order is desirable in the interests of –
  (a) securing the rehabilitation of the offender; or
  (b) protecting the public from further harm from him/her or preventing the commission by him/her of further offences;[178]
- the court considers the order to be the most suitable for the offender.[179]

Age

19.159 The offender must have attained the age of 16.[180] The relevant age is that at the date of conviction.

Length of the order

19.160 By the Criminal Justice Act 1991 s6(2)(b) the length of the order shall be such as is, in the opinion of the court, commensurate with the seriousness of the offence, or the combination of the offence and other offences associated with it.

19.161   The probation element of the order may be for a minimum of 12 months and a maximum of three years.[181] The community service element may be for a minimum in the aggregate of 40 hours and a maximum in the aggregate of 100 hours.[182]

Requirements of the order

19.162 The offender will be required to comply with the requirements imposed by both the probation element and the community service element. These will be as follows:

176 Ibid, s11(1).
177 Ibid, s6(1).
178 Ibid, s11(1) and (2).
179 Ibid, s6(2)(a).
180 Ibid, s11(1); if the offender's age is in doubt see para 3.9ff.
181 Ibid, s11(1)(a).
182 Ibid, s11(1)(b).

- to keep in touch with the probation officer responsible for his/her supervision in accordance with such instructions as s/he may from time to time be given by the officer and to inform the officer of any change of address.
- keep in touch with the community service supervising officer in accordance with such instructions as s/he may from time to time be given by that officer and notify the officer of any change of address; and
- perform for the number of hours specified in the order such work at such times as s/he may be instructed by the supervising officer.

The probation part of the order may include any of the additional requirements as permitted by the Powers of Criminal Courts Act 1973 Sch 1A.[183]

19.163   To ensure close liaison between the officers supervising the two elements of the order, the *National Standards for the Supervision of Offenders in the Community* suggest that the probation service should appoint a supervising officer with overall responsibility for the order.

Amendment

19.164 Application may be made by either the offender or his/her supervisor to a youth court (or to a magistrates' court if the offender has attained 18) for the amendment of the requirements of a combination order. The court may:

- substitute another petty sessions area for the one named in the order;
- cancel any requirement;
- insert in the order (either in addition or in substitution for any existing requirements) any requirements which the court could include if it were then making the order.[184]

19.165   A court may not amend the probation part of the order:

- by reducing the probation period, or by extending that period beyond the end of three years from the date of the original order; or

---

183 See para 19.116.
184 Criminal Justice Act 1991 Sch 2 paras 12(1) and 13(1).

–   by inserting in it a requirement that the offender shall submit to treatment for his/her mental condition, or his/her dependency on drugs or alcohol, unless the amending order is made within three months after the date of the original order.[185]

A court may only substitute a new petty sessions area in the community service part of the order if it is satisfied that provision exists for the offender to perform such work in that area.[186]

Revocation

19.166   Application may be made either by the offender or the supervisor to a youth court (or to a magistrates' court if the offender has attained 18) for the combination order to be revoked. If, after having regard to the circumstances which have arisen since the imposition of the order, the court is satisfied that it would be in the interests of justice that the order be revoked or that the offender be dealt with in another manner, it may:

–   revoke the order; or
–   revoke the order and deal with the offender, for the offence in respect of which the order was made, in any manner in which it could deal with him/her if s/he had just been convicted by the court of the offence.[187]

If the order was made by the Crown Court, the court may not revoke the order itself but it may commit the offender to the Crown Court for that purpose.[188] In either case if a court does re-sentence the offender, the extent to which s/he complied with the requirements of the combination order must be taken into account.[189]

19.167   If the supervisor is applying for the revocation of the order because of good progress, *National Standards* state that such an application may only be made when the community service element of the order has been completed and then only in accordance with the criteria for early termination which are applicable to probation orders.

---

185   Ibid, Sch 2 para 13(2).
186   Ibid, Sch 2 para 12(4).
187   Ibid, Sch 2 para 7(2).
188   Ibid, Sch 2 para 7(2)(b).
189   Ibid, Sch 2 paras 7(4) and 8(4).

Drug treatment and testing order (pilot areas only)

19.168 The order was introduced in the Crime and Disorder Act 1998 and is being piloted until the spring of 2000.[190] No court shall make a drug treatment and testing order unless it has been notified by the Secretary of State that arrangements for implementing such orders are available in the petty sessions area proposed to be named in the order and the notice has not been withdrawn.[191]

Pre-conditions

19.169 A drug treatment and testing order may be imposed by a youth court or a Crown Court. It may be imposed for any offence, the penalty for which is not fixed by law, but only if:

- the offence, or the combination of the offence and associated offences, is serious enough;
- the order is the most suitable for the offender;
- the court is satisfied that the offender is dependent on or has a propensity to misuse drugs; and
- his/her dependency or propensity is such as requires and may be susceptible to treatment.

Age

19.170 A drug treatment and testing order may only be imposed upon an offender who has attained the age of 16.[192] The relevant age is that on the date of conviction. The age of a person shall be deemed that which it appears to the court to be after considering any available evidence.[193]

Length of the order

19.171 The length of the order shall be such as is, in the opinion of the court, commensurate with the seriousness of the offence, or of the combination of the offence and other offences associated with it.[194]

---

190 For the pilot areas see appendix 8.
191 Crime and Disorder Act 1998 s61(3).
192 Ibid, s61(1).
193 Ibid, s117(3).
194 Criminal Justice Act 1991 s6(2)(b).

19.172   The order shall be for a minimum of six months and a maximum of three years.[195]

Procedural requirements

19.173 Before making a drug treatment and testing order, the court must explain to the offender in ordinary language:

- the effect of the order and of the requirements proposed to be included in it;
- the consequences which may follow if the offender fails to comply with any of the requirements;
- that the court has power to review the order on the application either of the offender or of the responsible officer; and
- that the order will be periodically reviewed at intervals as provided for in the order.[196]

The offender must agree to comply with the requirements of the order.[197]

19.174   A court shall not make a drug treatment and testing order unless it is satisfied that arrangements have been or can be made for the treatment intended to be specified in the order (including arrangements for the reception of the offender where s/he is to be required to submit to treatment as a resident).[198]

19.175   The order must specify the petty sessions area in which it appears to the court that the offender resides or will reside.[199] Copies of the order must be given to a probation officer assigned by the court and s/he shall give a copy to the offender, to the treatment provider and to the responsible officer.[200]

Requirements of the order

19.176 The offender is required to submit during the whole period of the order to treatment by or under the direction of a specified person. The treatment should have the aim of reducing or eliminating the

195 Crime and Disorder Act 1998 s61(2)(a) – the Secretary of State may by order amend the minimum or maximum period: s61(7).
196 Ibid, s64(1).
197 Ibid.
198 Ibid, s62(3).
199 Ibid, s62(6).
200 Ibid, s64(3).

offender's dependency on or propensity to misuse drugs.[201] It may be residential treatment at an institution specified in the order or treatment as an out-patient at such institution or place, and at such intervals, as specified in the order.[202]

19.177   The offender is also required during the period of the order to provide samples of urine for the purposes of ascertaining whether s/he has any drug in his/her body.[203] These samples must be given at such times or in such circumstances as determined by the treatment provider. The court will specify the minimum number of samples to be provided in any one month.[204]

Periodic reviews

19.178 The court must order review hearings which must take place at least once a month. The offender must attend the hearings and the responsible officer must provide a written report to the court describing the offender's progress on the order.[205]

19.179   At a review hearing the court may amend any requirement or provision of the order.[206] The offender must consent to any amendment of the order.[207] If such consent is not forthcoming the court may revoke the order and deal with the offender for the offence in respect of which the order was made in any manner in which it could deal with him/her if the offender had just been convicted by the court of the offence.[208] If re-sentencing the offender, the court must take into account the extent to which the offender has complied with the requirements of the order.[209] A custodial sentence may be imposed notwithstanding the restrictions imposed by the Criminal Justice Act 1991 s1(2).[210] In the case of an indictable-only offence the maximum penalty on re-sentence is six months' detention.[211]

201 Ibid, s62(1).
202 Ibid, s62(2).
203 Ibid, s62(4).
204 Ibid, s62(5).
205 Ibid, s63(1).
206 Ibid, s63(2).
207 Ibid, s63(3).
208 Ibid, s63(4).
209 Ibid, s63(5)(a).
210 Ibid, s63(5)(b).
211 Ibid, s63(6).

Revocation of community sentences following further offending

19.180 By the Criminal Justice Act 1991 Sch 2 para 8 a Crown Court may revoke an existing relevant order and re-sentence the offender, if it appears to the court to be in the interests of justice to do so, having regard to circumstances which have arisen since the order was made.

19.181   A relevant order is defined as the following:

- probation order;
- community service order;
- combination order;
- curfew order; and
- drug treatment and testing order.[212]

This power may only be exercised if, while a relevant order is in force:

- the offender is convicted by the Crown Court of a new offence; or
- a youth or magistrates' court commits the offender to the Crown Court for sentence for a new offence.[213]

It should be noted that a youth court or magistrates' court may not revoke an existing relevant order and re-sentence because of further offending, nor may such a court commit the offender to the Crown Court under Sch 2 for the Crown Court to revoke the relevant order.[214]

Interests of justice

19.182 It will not always be in the interests of justice either to revoke the existing relevant order or to re-sentence the offender. In *R v Cawley*[215] the Court of Appeal considered the appeal of a young offender (aged over 18) who was sentenced to two years' detention in a young offender institution for offences committed before an existing probation order was imposed. The Crown Court judge had also revoked this probation order and imposed a consecutive sentence of detention. The Court of Appeal declared that it would seldom if ever be in the interests of justice to re-sentence an offender for offences for

212 Criminal Justice Act 1991 Sch 2 para 1(1).
213 Ibid, Sch 2 para 8(1).
214 *R v Adams* [1994] Crim LR 73, CA.
215 [1993] Crim LR 797, CA.

which s/he was placed on probation after the commission of the crime for which s/he was subsequently sentenced, even if it were appropriate to revoke the probation order. The court went further and held in this particular case it would be appropriate that the probation order should still be in place when the offender emerged from custody and it quashed the revocation of the probation order.

While a relevant order is in force

19.183   The crucial date is the date when the offender falls due to be sentenced before the Crown Court. The power may not be exercised if the subsequent offences were committed during the currency of the relevant order but that order has expired or been completed by the time that sentencing in the Crown Court takes place.[216]

216   *R v Bennett* [1993] Crim LR 802, CA.

Table 10.3 Supervision order – additional requirements

Order/sentence	Length	Pre-conditions
Supervision order CYPA 1969 s12(1)	Up to 3 years	Offence(s) seriousness – Suitability
Additional requirements		
Inform supervisor of change of residence or employment Keep in touch with supervisor as per instruction – receive visits s18(2)(b)		If the court considers it appropriate
SO + Non-specific activities (IT) s12(2) SO + Reside as directed by supervisor s12(2)	Up to 90 days	Offence(s) seriousness – Suitability
SO + Specified activities s12A(3)(a) SO + Reside as directed by court s12A(3)(a) SO + Refraining conditions s12A(3)(c)	Up to 90 days	Offence(s) seriousness – Suitability – If under 16 consider family circumstances Necessary to ensure good conduct and prevention of offending Consultation with supervisor regarding circumstances and feasibility of compliance Agreement of any other person whose co-operation is required
SO + Night restrictions s12A(3)(b)	Up to 30 days in first months Maximum 10 hours per night between 6 pm and 9 am at place(s) specified	Offence(s) seriousness – Suitability – If under 16 consider family circumstances Necessary to ensure good conduct and prevention of offending Consultation with supervisor regarding circumstances and feasibility of compliance Agreement of any other person whose co-operation is required

Continued overleaf

Table 10 (continued)

Order/sentence	Length	Pre-conditions
SO + Residence requirement s12AA	Six months	Offence 'is in the opinion of the court serious' Designate local authority where young person resides – consult local authority Previous SO + s12A(3) requirement or a residence requirement Offence committed while order in force – Offence punishable with imprisonment Behaviour due to a significant extent to home circumstance (but not where imprisonable offence)
SO + Psychiatric treatment s12BB	For periods specified in the order, or up to 18	Offence(s) seriousness – Suitability – Consent of offender if over 14 Evidence of registered medical practitioner – Availability of treatment
SO + School attendance s12C	Period of order up to school leaving age	Offence(s) seriousness – Suitability – Must be of school age – Availability of suitable education facilities Necessary to ensure good conduct and prevention of offending – Consultation with supervisor regarding circumstances necessary to secure good conduct or preventing offending
SO + Reparation s12A(aa) NOT IN FORCE	90 days	Offence(s) seriousness – Suitability – If under 16 consider family circumstances Necessary to ensure good conduct and prevention of offending Consultation with supervisor regarding circumstances and feasibility of compliance Agreement of any other person whose co-operation is required Where reparation is to the victim, his/her consent

CHAPTER 20

Breach proceedings

For complete chapter contents, see overleaf

Introduction

20.1   Failure to comply with the requirements of any community order may lead to breach proceedings. Courts are given the power to impose a sanction for the breach and the offender may be re-sentenced for the original offence. The revised *National Standards for the Supervision of Offenders in the Community* (1995) expect enforcement action to be instituted after no more than two formal warnings (copies of which should be sent to the offender's parent or guardian). Such a rigid enforcement of community penalties is likely to result in a high proportion of children and young persons being the subject of breach proceedings. It is therefore an area of law with which the defence lawyer needs to be familiar.

20.2   The enforcement powers of the courts in relation to children and young persons are unfortunately complicated. Although the Criminal Justice Act 1991 introduced a uniform breach procedure for probation, community service, combination and curfew orders, it preserved separate procedures for supervision and attendance centre orders. The Crime and Disorder Act 1998 further complicated the situation by introducing yet another procedure for the new youth court sentences: the reparation order and the action plan order.

Attendance centre order

20.3   Breach proceedings are regulated by Criminal Justice Act 1982 s19. They may be instituted for:

- failure to attend the centre as required by the order; or
- breach of the Attendance Centre Rules 1995 SI No 3281 which cannot be adequately dealt with under those rules.[1]

Requiring attendance

20.4   The officer in charge of the centre must apply by way of information. If it appears that the offender has failed to attend in accordance with the order or while attending he has committed a breach of the Attendance Centre Rules 1995, which cannot be adequately dealt with under those rules, a justice of the peace may:

---

1   Criminal Justice Act 1982 s19(3).

- issue a summons requiring the offender and the parent or guardian to attend court; or
- if the information is in writing and on oath, issue a warrant for the offender's arrest.[2]

In normal circumstances the court would first issue a summons and only if the offender failed to attend as required would the officer in charge swear the information and request a warrant for the offender's arrest.

Which court?

20.5   The application for the summons should be made to a court acting for a relevant petty sessions area. This is defined as:

- the area where the attendance centre is situated; or
- the area covering the youth court which originally imposed the order.[3]

If the offender has attained 18 by the time that breach proceedings are to be instituted then the adult magistrates' court should deal with the application.

Before the hearing

20.6   The defence lawyer should obtain a copy of the original order and the summons to establish the nature of the alleged breach. S/he should also attempt to contact the officer in charge of the centre and establish the history of attendance (if any) and whether the centre is prepared to have the young offender back to complete the order. It may be possible to negotiate for the young offender to attend while breach proceedings are pending.

20.7   The young offender should also be asked if there is any reason for any failure to attend to establish whether there was 'reasonable excuse'. Documentary evidence may have to be obtained before the hearing.

The hearing

20.8   The court must establish whether the offender has:

- failed to attend without reasonable excuse; or

2   Ibid, s19(1).
3   Ibid, s19(2).

– while attending committed a breach of the Attendance Centre Rules 1995 which cannot be adequately dealt with under those rules.[4]

The offender will first be asked by the clerk of the court whether s/he admits the breach. If it is admitted, the officer in charge will give to the court the dates of non-attendance or details of any other breach of the centre's rules. If the breach is not admitted the court will have to hear evidence and reach a finding of fact on the usual criminal burden of proof, namely beyond reasonable doubt. The burden of establishing a reasonable excuse for non-attendance rests upon the offender but the evidential test will be to prove the excuse on the balance of probabilities.

20.9   At any time the court may adjourn the proceedings. This may even be done before the breach has been put to the offender.

Powers of the court

20.10   If the court is satisfied that the offender is in breach, it may allow the order to continue and for the breach it may:

– take no action at all; or
– fine the offender up to £1,000 (£250 in the case of an offender under the age of 14).[5]

Alternatively the court may decide that the offender should be re-sentenced for the offence. If the original order was made by a youth court, the court may revoke it and re-sentence the offender for the original offence.[6] If the original order was made by a Crown Court, the court may commit the offender to that court either on bail or in custody.[7]

Allowing the order to continue

20.11   If the offender indicates that s/he will comply with the order, it will often be possible to persuade a youth court to adjourn the proceedings for a month to monitor attendance. If attendance is then regular and satisfactory, the defence lawyer should seek to persuade the bench that it would not be in the interests of the child or young person to impose any extra penalty for the breach.

4   Ibid, s19(3).
5   Ibid.
6   Ibid, s19(3)(a).
7   Ibid, s19(3)(b).

Revocation and re-sentencing

20.12 When the court revokes an attendance centre order, the Criminal Justice Act 1982 s19(3)(a) states that it:

> ... may ... deal with [the offender], for the offence in respect of which the order was made, in any manner in which [s/he] could have been dealt with for that offence by the court which made the order if the order had not been made.

The offender must, therefore, be re-sentenced on the basis of his/her age at the time of the original sentencing hearing and it is important that the defence lawyer establishes when the original finding of guilt was made and based on that determine which sentences would have been available to the court at that time.

20.13 When re-sentencing the offender, the court is required to take into account the extent to which s/he has complied with the requirements of the order.[8] The court should, therefore, reduce any new sentence in proportion to the extent that the attendance order has been completed. In the case of an offender who has wilfully and persistently failed to comply with the requirements of the order the court may impose a custodial sentence notwithstanding the restrictions on the use of custodial sentences contained in the Criminal Justice Act 1991 s1(2).[9] Where the court re-sentences the offender, it shall revoke the attendance order if it is still in force.[10]

Breach of an order imposed by the Crown Court

20.14 Breach proceedings are started in the usual way by the issue of a summons or warrant by a youth or adult magistrates' court. If the breach is proved to the satisfaction of the court, in addition to the power to impose a fine it may commit the offender to the Crown Court either on bail or in custody. If an offender is committed in these circumstances the court should send the Crown Court a certificate signed by a justice of the peace setting out the details of the offender's failure to attend or breach of the rules.[11] This signed certificate is admissible as evidence during the Crown Court proceedings, however, the breach must still be proved before the Crown Court.

---

8 Ibid, s19(5A)(a).
9 Ibid, s19(5A)(b); for more see para 21.4.
10 Ibid, s19(5B).
11 Criminal Justice Act 1982 s19(4).

20.15   On re-sentence the Crown Court may deal with the offender, for the offence in respect of which the order was made, in any manner in which it could have dealt with him/her for that offence if it had not made the order.[12] This means that the relevant age for the purposes of re-sentence is the offender's age on the date of the original conviction.

Breach of an order imposed following breach of a supervision order

20.16   If the offender is subject to an attendance centre order because s/he breached the conditions of a supervision order, the court's powers on re-sentencing are more limited. The Children and Young Persons Act 1969 s16A(2) amends the court's powers as follows:

> [The] court . . . deal with [the offender], in any manner in which he could have been dealt with by the court which made the order if the order had not been made.

The amendment restricts the court to the sentencing options available when the previous court was dealing with the breach of the supervision order. In the case of a supervision order made before 30 September 1998 this would mean the options were limited to a fine or another attendance centre order.

Right of appeal on re-sentence

20.17   A right of appeal against the re-sentence exists to the Crown Court in the case of a decision of a youth court or magistrates' court and to the Court of Appeal in the case of a decision of a Crown Court.[13]

Supervision order

20.18   Breach proceedings are regulated by Children and Young Persons Act 1969 s15. They may be instituted when the young offender has failed to comply with a requirement of the order.

20.19   The *National Standards* (1995) provide the following guidance regarding the enforcement of supervision orders:

> The overall purpose of enforcement is to seek to secure and maintain the child or young person's co-operation and compliance with the order in order to ensure successful completion of the order achieving

12 Ibid, s19(5).
13 Ibid, s19(6).

the aims and objectives set out in paragraphs 6 and 7. The process of enforcement should, where appropriate, involve the parent(s) or other carer(s), and encourage the child or young person to accept discipline, but should retain the degree of flexibility demanded by the individual's age, stage of development and degree of responsibility for his or her actions. Any action taken to enforce the order should take full account of the welfare of the child or young person. [original emphasis][14]

The *National Standards* (1995) also require breach proceedings to be instituted after two written warnings about non-compliance.

Initiating proceedings

20.20 The supervisor should make an application to court. No form is required for the application, but it is preferable that the application is in writing and it should clearly identify the alleged breach.[15]

Which court?

20.21 The application should be made to the relevant court for the petty sessions area for the time being named in the supervision order.[16] Relevant court is defined as follows:

- in the case of an offender who has not attained 18, a youth court;
- in the case of an offender who has attained 18, a magistrates' court.[17]

A youth court may still deal with breach proceedings in relation to a young offender who attains the age of 18 while the supervisor's application is pending.[18] In such circumstances the court shall deal with the application as if the offender had not attained the age of 18.

Requiring attendance at court

20.22 On receiving an application the court may issue:

- a summons requiring the supervised person (and parent or guardian, if still under 18) to attend court at a specified time and place;

---

14 *National Standards for the Supervision of Offenders in the Community* (1995) Part 4 para 27.
15 Ibid, Part 4 para 31.
16 Children and Young Persons Act 1969 s16(11).
17 Ibid, s15(11).
18 Ibid, s16(11): the term 'pending' is not defined, but it is arguable that an application is pending as soon as it is received by the relevant court.

- a warrant under the Children and Young Persons Act 1969 s16(2); or
- a warrant under the Magistrates' Court Act 1980 s1.

Warrant under CYPA 1969 s16(2)

20.23   On application of the supervisor a justice of the peace may issue a warrant for the arrest of the supervised person under s16(2) Children and Young Persons Act 1969. When the supervised person is arrested under such a warrant the police:

- may arrange for his/her detention in a place of safety[18A] for a period of not more than 72 hours from the time of arrest; and
- shall within that period bring the supervised person before a justice of the peace, unless s/he can be brought before the relevant court within that time.[19]

20.24   When the supervised person is brought before a justice of the peace under the above provision, the justice may:

- direct that the supervised person be released forthwith; or
- remand him/her to local authority accommodation.[20]

If there is a remand to local authority accommodation, the justice must designate the authority named in the supervision order.[21] Unlike the normal provisions for a remand to local authority accommodation, under the Children and Young Persons Act 1969 s23 this provision also applies to 17-year-olds. If the supervised person has attained the age of 18 s/he may not be remanded to local authority accommodation but s/he may be remanded to custody.[22]

Before the hearing

20.25   The defence lawyer should first establish whether the supervision order is still in force as the court has no power to deal with a breach

---

18   Ibid, s16(11): the term 'pending' is not defined, but it is arguable that an application is pending as soon as it is received by the relevant court.
18A 'Place of safety' means a community home provided by a local authority or a controlled community home, any police station, or any hospital, surgery, or any other suitable place, the occupier of which is willing temporarily to receive a child or young person (Children and Young Persons Act 1933 s107(1)).
19   Children and Young Persons Act 1969 s16(3).
20   Ibid, s16(3A).
21   Ibid, s16(3B).
22   Ibid, s16(3C).

after the order has expired. S/he should also obtain a copy of the original supervision order to:

- determine the exact requirements imposed upon the supervised person (no requirements are imposed automatically by the legislation);
- establish when the order was made (a court may only re-sentence an offender for an order made before 30 September 1998 in very limited circumstances); and
- (in the case of an order made before 30 September 1998) to check whether the order was certified as imposed as a direct alternative to custody under the Children and Young Persons Act 1969 s12D.

Before the hearing it is often helpful to approach the officer presenting the breach proceedings. In the light of the *National Standards* guidance quoted above at para 20.19, it may be possible to persuade the presenting officer to agree to an adjournment of the proceedings to give the supervised person a chance to comply with the order.

The hearing

20.26 If the proceedings do continue, the presenting officer should explain to the court the nature of the breach. The supervised person will then be asked if s/he admits the breach. If the breach is denied the presenting officer must prove the breach to the satisfaction of the court. This should be done observing the usual criminal rules of evidence and to the usual criminal standard of proof, that is beyond reasonable doubt.

Powers of the court

20.27 If the breach is admitted or proved, the court's powers vary depending upon the date on which the order was imposed.

Orders imposed prior to 30 September 1998

20.28 The court may vary the requirements or it may discharge the order. Whether or not the court exercises these powers, in relation to the breach, it may:

- take no action;
- impose a fine not exceeding £1,000 (maximum of £250 if aged under 14 years); or
- impose an attendance centre order.

If the court discharges the supervision order, it may only re-sentence the offender (save for orders made as a direct alternative to custody, for which see below), if s/he has attained the age of 18. In such circumstances, the Children and Young Persons Act 1969 s15(3)(b) provides that the court:

> . . . may . . . make an order imposing on him any punishment, other than detention in a young offender institution, which it could have imposed on him if it–
> (i) had then had power to try him for the offence in consequence of which the supervision order was made; and
> (ii) had convicted him in the exercise of that power.

The court must, therefore, sentence on the basis of the offender's age at the time of the discharge of the order.

Direct alternative to custody (s12D)

20.29   If the court which made the supervision order made a statement that the order with an additional requirement of specified activities was being made as a direct alternative to custody, the court dealing with the breach proceedings has greater powers. To be a valid s12D order the court must have stated in open court:

- that it was making the order instead of a custodial sentence;
- that it was satisfied that –
  (i)   the offence of which s/he has been convicted, or the combination of that offence and one or more offences associated with it, was so serious that only a supervision order containing such a requirement or a custodial sentence can be justified for that offence; or
  (ii) the offence was a violent or sexual offence and only a supervision order containing such a requirement or such a sentence would be adequate to protect the public from serious harm from him; and
- why it was so satisfied.

The greater powers of the court on re-sentence only exist if a breach of the specified activities requirement is proved to the satisfaction of the court. It is not enough that the supervised person has failed to attend appointments with his/her supervisor. An offender cannot breach a supervision order under s12D by committing further offences during the currency of the order.

20.30   If there is any dispute as to whether the original order was declared to be imposed as a direct alternative to custody, the Children and Young Persons Act 1969 s15(6) stated that the certificate made under s12D shall be evidence of the making of the statement. It is, therefore, important for the defence lawyer to check that the certificate is valid and that its wording complies with the requirements of s12D. As the court's powers to pass a custodial sentence depend upon a valid certificate, it is submitted that any deficiency or ambiguity in the certificate should be decided in the offender's favour.

20.31 Where the court decides to discharge the order, the Children and Young Persons Act 1969 s15 provides:

> (4) . . . [T]he court may, if it also discharges the supervision order, make an order imposing on him any sentence which it could have imposed on him if it –
> (a) had then had power to try him for the offence in consequence of which the supervision order was made; and
> (b) had convicted him in the exercise of that power.
> (5) In a case falling within subsection . . . (4) above where the offence in question is of a kind which the court has no power to try, or has no power to try without appropriate consents, the sentence imposed by virtue of that provision –
> . . .
> (c) shall not in any event exceed a custodial sentence for a term of six months and a fine of £5,000.

The court may, therefore, impose any sentence including a custodial sentence. The relevant age is that at the time of re-sentence. The maximum of six months' detention in a young offender institution would seem to preclude a committal for sentence under the Magistrates' Courts Act 1980 s37. Where the offender has attained the age of 18, the adult magistrates' court may still re-sentence even if the offence is indictable only.[23] It too may not impose a custodial sentence which exceeds six months. Where the original s12D order was imposed by a Crown Court, there is no provision to commit the offender for re-sentence.

20.32 It should be emphasised that the fact that a previous court certified an order as being a direct alternative to custody does not mean that upon discharge, a custodial sentence is inevitable. It is submitted that the court is still under a duty to consider the facts of the offence to reach its own view of the seriousness of the offence and then it should consider the personal mitigation known to it. It is open to the defence lawyer to argue that positive changes in the young offender's

---

23 Ibid, s15(5).

life, particularly a substantial reduction in offending, are sufficient reason for a court to consider other forms of punishment.

20.33   In re-sentencing the court must also take into account:

- any plea of guilty to the original offence;[24] and
- the extent to which the offender has complied with the requirements of the supervision order as required by s15(8).

The court need not take into account any time spent on remand before the imposition of the original supervision order before imposing a custodial sentence as this should be deducted automatically from the sentence by the custodial institution.[25]

Orders made on or after 30 September 1998

20.34   The court may vary the requirements or it may discharge the order. Whether or not the court exercises these powers, in relation to the breach, it may:

- take no action;
- impose a fine not exceeding £1,000 (maximum of £250 if aged under 14 years);
- impose an attendance centre order; or
- impose a curfew order (age of offender permitting).[26]

If the court decides to discharge a youth court supervision order, it may deal with the offender for the original offence in any manner in which s/he could have been dealt with by the court which made the order if the order had not been made.[27]

20.35   The offender must, therefore, be re-sentenced on the basis of his/her age at the time of the original sentencing hearing and it is important that the defence lawyer establishes when the original finding of guilt was made and based on that determine which sentences would have been available to the court at that time.

20.36   If the supervision order was made by a Crown Court, the youth court or magistrates' court may commit the offender in custody or release him/her on bail until s/he can be brought or appear before the Crown Court.[28] Where a youth or adult magistrates' court commits the offender to the Crown Court, it shall send a certificate signed

---

24 As required by the Criminal Justice and Public Order Act 1994 s48.
25 Criminal Justice Act 1967 s67: see para 22.32.
26 Children and Young Persons Act 1969 s15(3).
27 Ibid, s15(3)(b).
28 Ibid, s15(3)(c).

by a justice of the peace giving particulars of the supervised person's failure to comply with the requirements of the order. Such a certificate shall be admissible as evidence of the failure before the Crown Court. If it is proved to the satisfaction of the Crown Court that the supervised person has failed to comply with the requirements of the order, the Crown Court may deal with him/her for the offence in respect of which the order was made, in any manner in which it could have dealt with him/her for that offence if it had not made the order.[29] Again the relevant age is the age at the date of the original conviction.

Right of appeal

20.37 The supervised person may appeal from the youth court or the adult magistrates' court to the Crown Court against any sanction imposed for breach of the requirements of a supervision order or against any sentence imposed following discharge of the order.[30] In the case of a Crown Court order, any sentence passed following discharge of the supervision order may be appealed to the Court of Appeal.[31]

Reparation and action plan orders

20.38 Breach proceedings for reparation and action plan orders are covered by the Crime and Disorder Act 1998 Sch 5.

Which court?

20.39 To commence breach proceedings an application should be made by the responsible officer to the appropriate court.[32] 'Appropriate court' is defined by Sch 5 para 1 as 'the youth court acting for the petty sessions area for the time being named in the order'. There appears to be a lacuna in the legislation in relation to offenders who have attained the age of 18. Where a young offender attains the age of 18 while an application is pending, Sch 5 para 5(6) states that the youth court retains the jurisdiction to deal with the breach proceedings. However, where the offender has attained the age of 18 prior to any breach proceedings commencing, it would appear that no court has

---

29 Ibid, s15(5).
30 Ibid, s16(8).
31 Criminal Appeal Act 1968 s9(1).
32 Crime and Disorder Act 1998 Sch 5 para 3(1).

jurisdiction to hear the application. The youth court no longer has jurisdiction as it cannot deal with applications relating to persons who have attained the age of 18; the adult magistrates' court has no jurisdiction as it does not satisfy the definition of an 'appropriate court' contained in Sch 5 para 1.

Requiring attendance at court

20.40 On the application of the responsible officer an appropriate court may issue:

- a summons requiring the young offender (and parent or guardian, if still under the age of 18) to attend at a specified time and place;
- a warrant under Sch 5 para 4(2); or
- a warrant under the Magistrates' Courts Act 1980 s1.

A warrant under Sch 5 para 4(2) may only be issued if the complaint is substantiated on oath and the court is satisfied that either a summons cannot be served or that the summons was served on the young offender within a reasonable time before the hearing.[33]

20.41 Where a young offender is arrested in pursuance of a warrant issued under Sch 5 para 4(2) and cannot be brought immediately before the appropriate court, the person in whose custody s/he is:

- may make arrangements for his/her detention in a place of safety[33A] for a period of not more than 72 hours from the time of arrest; and
- shall within that period bring him/her before a youth court.

Where a young offender is brought before a youth court other than the appropriate court, that court may release him/her forthwith or remand him/her to local authority accommodation.[34] Where the offender is aged 18 or over at the time when s/he is brought before the court, s/he shall not be remanded to local authority accommodation but may instead be remanded into custody.[35]

---

33 Ibid, Sch 5 para 4(3).
33A 'Place of safety' means a community home provided by a local authority or a controlled community home, any police station, or any hospital, surgery, or any other suitable place, the occupier of which is willing temporarily to receive a child or young person (Children and Young Persons Act 1933 s107(1)).
34 Ibid, Sch 5 para 4(5).
35 Ibid, Sch 5 para 4(6).

Powers of the court

20.42   If while a reparation order or action plan order is in force it is proved to the satisfaction of the court that the offender is in breach of the order, the court may allow the order to continue and for the breach it may:

- take no action at all;
- fine the young offender up to £1,000 (£250 in the case of an offender under the age of 14);
- impose an attendance centre order; or
- impose a curfew order (age of offender permitting).[36]

Alternatively the court may decide that the offender should be re-sentenced for the offence. If the order was made by a youth court, the court may discharge the order and re-sentence the offender for the original offence.[37] If the order was made by a Crown Court, the court may commit the offender to that court on bail or in custody.[38]

Allowing the order to continue

20.43   If the offender indicates that s/he will comply with the order, it will often be possible to persuade a youth court to adjourn the proceedings for a month to monitor attendance. If attendance is then regular and satisfactory, the defence lawyer should seek to persuade the bench that it would not be in the interests of the child or young person to impose any extra penalty for the breach.

Discharge and re-sentencing

20.44   When the court discharges a reparation order or action plan order it may deal with the offender in any manner in which s/he could have been dealt with by the court which made the order if the order had not been made.[39]

20.45   The offender must, therefore, be re-sentenced on the basis of his/her age at the time of the original sentencing hearing and it is important that the defence lawyer establishes when the original finding of guilt was made and based on that determine which sentences would have been available to the court at that time.

36 Ibid, Sch 5 para 3(2).
37 Ibid, Sch 5 para 3(2)(b).
38 Ibid, Sch5 para 3(2)(c).
39 Ibid, Sch 5 para 3(2)(b).

20.46 When sentencing the offender the court is required to take into account the extent to which s/he has complied with the requirements of the order.[40] The court should, therefore, reduce any new sentence in proportion to the extent that the reparation order or action plan order has been completed.

Breach of an order imposed by the Crown Court

20.47 Breach proceedings are started in the usual way by the issue of a summons or warrant by the youth court. If the breach is proved to the satisfaction of the court, in addition to the power to impose a sanction for the breach, it may commit the offender to the Crown Court either on bail or in custody.[41] If an offender is committed in these circumstances the youth court should send the Crown Court a certificate signed by a justice of the peace giving particulars of the offender's failure to comply with the requirement in question and such other particulars of the case as may be desirable.[42] A certificate purporting to be so signed shall be admissible as evidence of the failure of the breach before the Crown Court.[43]

20.48 Breach proceedings are heard by a Crown Court judge sitting alone. If it is proved to the satisfaction of the court that the offender has failed to comply with the requirements of the order, it may deal with him/her in any manner in which it could have dealt with him/her for the original offence if it had not made the order.[44] Where the Crown Court re-sentences an offender, it shall revoke the original order, if it is still in force.[45]

Right of appeal

20.49 The young offender may appeal to the Crown Court against:

- any sanction imposed for failure to comply with the requirements of the order;
- the new sentence imposed by the youth court following discharge of the order.[46]

---

40 Ibid, Sch 5 para 3(7).
41 Ibid, Sch 5 para 3(2)(c).
42 Ibid, Sch 5 para 2(3).
43 Ibid, Sch 5 para 2(3).
44 Ibid, Sch 5 para 2(4).
45 Ibid, Sch 5 para 2(5).
46 Ibid, Sch 5 para 5(7).

In the case of a Crown Court order, any sentence passed following discharge of the reparation order or action plan order may be appealed to the Court of Appeal.[47]

Other community sentences

20.50 The Criminal Justice Act 1991 Sch 2 creates a unified scheme for dealing with the enforcement of the following community sentences:

- curfew order;
- probation order;
- community service order;
- combination order; and
- drug treatment and testing order.

Separate rules exist for attendance centre orders, supervision orders, reparation orders and action plan orders. These are dealt with above.

National Standards

20.51 The various *National Standards* for the relevant orders all require the supervisor to keep a record of all contact with the offender and to note any unauthorised absences. Any explanation given by an offender for an absence should also be along with any reason why it was not accepted as reasonable. This will then be formally recorded as an instance of non-compliance. A formal warning should then be given to the offender. This should be in writing and in the case of a young person a copy should be sent to the offender's parent or guardian. At most, two warnings within a 12-month period may be given by the supervisor before breach proceedings are instituted. In the case of a serious breach (involving an attempt to avoid the completion of the order or serious misconduct) breach proceedings may be instituted without prior warning.

Instituting proceedings

20.52 All breach proceedings start in the youth court or magistrates' court even if the order was made by a Crown Court.

20.53   If the offender has attained the age of 18, proceedings will start in

47 Criminal Appeal Act 1968 s9(1).

the magistrates' court, otherwise they should start in the youth court. In the case of a probation, community service order, combination order or drug treatment and testing order, the proceedings should be instituted in the court for the petty sessions area specified in the order; in the case of a curfew order it should be the court for the petty sessions area where the offender is required to be during the specified times.[48]

Requiring attendance

20.54 If it appears to a justice of the peace on information that an offender has failed to comply with any of the requirements of the order, the justice may:

- issue a summons requiring the offender to appear at the place and time specified in it; or
- if the information is in writing and on oath, issue a warrant for his/her arrest.[49]

It would usually be the case that a summons would be issued in the first instance and only if the offender failed to attend court would a warrant be issued.

Before the hearing

20.55 The defence lawyer should establish the exact nature of the alleged breach and obtain a copy of the original order. The easiest way to do this is by contacting the supervisor of the order. If possible a full history of the offender's contact with the supervisor under the order should be obtained. It should also be established whether the supervisor is willing to have the young offender back to continue the order. *National Standards* certainly contemplate the offender continuing with an order after breach proceedings have been initiated and the court will be obliged to take such compliance into account if considering re-sentencing the offender. If the supervisor is not prepared to have the young offender back, the reasons for this should be noted.

20.56 Having spoken to the supervisor, instructions should be taken from the young person to establish which if any of the alleged breaches are accepted. It should also be considered whether there is a

48 Criminal Justice Act 1991 Sch 2 para 1(1).
49 Ibid, Sch 2 para 2(1).

reasonable excuse for any of the breaches. Documentary evidence of this must be obtained before the court hearing. It should also be discussed with the young person whether it would be advisable to continue with the order while awaiting the court hearing. The young person should be advised that the court is obliged to take such attendances into account even if it decides to re-sentence and it will be much harder for the court to decide that the offender has wilfully and persistently failed to comply with the requirements of the order.

The hearing

20.57 The court must be satisfied that the offender has failed without reasonable excuse to comply with any of the requirements of the relevant order. The court will ask the young offender whether s/he admits or denies the breaches alleged in the information. If the breaches are admitted, the court will then proceed to hear details of the breach from the supervisor and then invite any representations from the offender, his/her parent or guardian or any lawyer present. If the breaches are denied, the matter will usually be adjourned for the issue to be resolved at a trial. The breach will then have to be proved on the criminal burden of proof and subject to the usual criminal rules of evidence.

Powers of youth or adult magistrates' court

20.58 If the youth or magistrates' court is satisfied that the offender has failed to comply with any requirement without reasonable excuse, it may allow the order to continue and for the breach:

- take no action;
- impose a fine not exceeding £1,000;
- impose a community service order of 40–60 hours (if the existing order is a community service order, the total of both orders must not exceed 240 hours);
- if the existing order is a probation order, impose an attendance centre order in addition.[50]

If the order was made by a youth court, the court may revoke the order and re-sentence for the original offence. If the order was made

50 Ibid, Sch 2 para 3(1).

by a Crown Court, the court may commit the offender either on bail or in custody[51] to be dealt with by the Crown Court.[52]

Powers of the Crown Court

20.59   If the Crown Court judge is satisfied that the offender has failed without reasonable excuse to comply with any of the requirements of an order, s/he may allow the order to continue and deal with the breach in any of the ways discussed above, or revoke the order and re-sentence the offender for the original offence.[53]

What constitutes a breach of the requirements?

20.60   An offender required by a probation order to submit to treatment for a mental condition or a dependency on drugs or alcohol shall not be treated as having failed to comply with that requirement on the ground only that s/he has refused to undergo any surgical, electrical or other treatment if, in the opinion of the court, his/her refusal was reasonable having regard to all the circumstances.[54]

20.61   An offence committed after a community order has been imposed can never be treated as a breach of the order.[55]

Re-sentencing

20.62   The court may deal with the offender in any manner in which it could deal with him if s/he had just been convicted by or before the court of the offence. It must, however, take into account:

- any plea of guilty to the original offence;[56]
- any time spent on remand prior to the imposition of the order being revoked;[57] and
- the extent to which the offender has complied with the requirements of the order.[58]

---

51   If the offender is aged under 17, this would be a remand to local authority accommodation as required by Children and Young Persons Act 1969 s23.
52   Criminal Justice Act 1991 Sch 2 para 4.
53   Ibid, Sch 2 para 4(1).
54   Ibid, Sch 2 para 5(2).
55   Ibid, Sch 2 para 5(1).
56   As required by Criminal Justice and Public Order Act 1994 s48.
57   *R v McDonald* (1988) 10 Cr App R (S) 458, CA.
58   Criminal Justice Act 1991 Sch 2 paras 3(2)(a) and 4(2)(a) for the youth/ magistrates' court and the Crown Court respectively.

Is a pre-sentence report required?

20.63　When re-sentencing the offender, the Criminal Justice Act 1991 ss3 and 7 would apply and the court may be required to consider a pre-sentence report. If the original sentencing hearing was some time ago, the defence lawyer will wish to argue that a new report should be ordered to give up-to-date information concerning the young offender.

20.64　　If the court is invoking the Criminal Justice Act 1991 s1(3) to impose a custodial sentence, then a pre-sentence report is not required by s3 of the Act.[59]

Extent to which the offender has complied

20.65　In taking into account the extent of the offender's compliance the court must consider not only the number of hours for which the offender has attended community service or a probation activity, but also how far s/he has accepted the supervision of a probation or combination order.[60] No guidance has yet been given as to how the compliance will actually affect the length of any custodial sentence subsequently imposed.

Powers of the court

20.66　The youth court (or adult magistrates' court, if the offender has attained the age of 18) may deal with the offender for the offence in any manner which it could deal with him/her if s/he had just been convicted by or before the court of the offence.[61] The relevant age is, therefore, that on re-sentencing and not the age when the offender was originally convicted of the offence.

Sentencing to custody

20.67　The fact that the original sentencing court did not impose a custodial sentence does not mean that the offence itself is not so serious that only a custodial sentence could be justified.[62] It may be, therefore, that after reviewing the seriousness of the offence and the weight to be

---

59　*R v Meredith* (1994) 15 Cr App R (S) 528, CA.
60　*R v Neville* [1993] Crim LR 463, CA.
61　Criminal Justice Act 1991 Sch 2 para 3(1)(d).
62　*R v Cox* (1993) 14 Cr App R (S) 479, CA; *R v Oliver and Little* [1993] Crim LR 147, CA.

attached to the personal mitigation, the court now determines that a custodial sentence is indeed the only sentence justified.

20.68   Even if the court determines that the offence is not so serious, it may still sentence the offender to a custodial sentence under Criminal Justice Act 1991 s1(3) if it considers s/he has wilfully and persistently failed to comply with the requirements of the order.

Wilfully and persistently failed to comply

20.69   In the absence of any case law on the interpretation of the phrase 'wilfully and persistently' it may be helpful to consider the dictionary definitions. The *Concise Oxford English Dictionary* gives the following definitions:

> wilful, *adjective*, (Of action or state) for which compulsion or ignorance or accident cannot be pleaded as excuse, intentional, deliberate, due to perversity or self-will.
> persistent, *adjective*, enduring, constantly repeated.

It should be noted that the court must find that both are satisfied before assuming the offender has refused to consent to a community penalty requiring his/her consent.

20.70   Any explanation as to why the young offender has not complied with the order should be put to the court, even if it could not constitute a reasonable excuse. Such explanations may show that the offender's non-compliance was not wilful. It is also submitted that erratic compliance may not be persistent.

Table 11: Breach proceedings – powers of court

Community service	Pre-conditions	Powers of court	Notes
Attendance centre order	1 Offender has failed *without reasonable excuse* to attend in accordance with the order.	Take no action. Fine (max: £1,000, £250 if a child).	On re-sentence the court must take into account the extent to which the offender has complied with the order.
	Or		
	2 While attending, the offender has committed a breach of the Attendance Centre Rules 1995.	Revoke order and re-sentence. (If Crown Court order) commit the offender to the Crown Court to be dealt with.	Relevant age is that at date of original conviction.
Supervision order (imposed on or after 30 September 1998)	1 Order must still be in force. 2 Offender has failed to comply with requirements of the order.	1 Allow the order to continue and for the breach: – take no action; – impose a fine; – impose an ACO; – impose a curfew order (16 years and over)	No requirement automatically imposed by statute. Check what requirements imposed.
		2 Discharge the order and impose a sanction as above. 3 Discharge the order and re-sentence.	Relevant age is that at date of original conviction.
		4 (If Crown Court order) commit the offender to the Crown Court to be dealt with.	

Continued overleaf

Table 11 (continued)

Community service	Pre-conditions	Powers of court	Notes

Reparation order
Action plan order
	1 Order must still be in force.
	2 Offender has failed to comply with requirements of order.
		1 Allow the order to continue and for the breach:
		  – take no action;
		  – impose a fine;
		  – impose an ACO; or
		  – impose a curfew order (16 years and over).
		2 Discharge the order and re-sentence.
		3 (If Crown Court order) commit the offender to the Crown Court to be dealt with.
			On re-sentence:
			– the relevant age is that at the date of original conviction;
			– the court must take into account the extent to which the offender has complied with the order.

Probation order
Community service order
Combination order
Curfew order
Drug treatment and testing order
	Offender has failed *without reasonable excuse* to comply with the requirements of the order.	1 Allow the order to continue and for the breach:
		  – take no action;
		  – impose a fine;
		  – impose CSO (40 to 60 hours);
		  – impose curfew order;
		  – (in case of probation) impose an ACO.
		2 Revoke order and sanction as above.
		3 Revoke order and re-sentence.
		4 (If Crown Court order) commit offender to Crown Court to be dealt with.
			On re-sentence:
			– the court has the powers available on the date of revocation;
			– the court must take into account the extent to which the offender has complied with the order;
			– time spent on remand before the imposition of the community sentence must be deducted from final custodial sentence.

Custodial sentences

For complete chapter contents, see overleaf

General

Definition

21.1   In relation to offenders under the age of 21 a custodial sentence is defined by the Criminal Justice Act 1991 s31(1) as any of the following:

- detention in a young offender institution;
- secure training order;
- detention and training order (not in force);
- detention under the Children and Young Persons Act 1933 s53(2) and (3);
- custody for life; or
- detention during Her Majesty's pleasure.

Offender to be legally represented

21.2   A court may not impose a sentence of detention in a young offender institution, detention under the Children and Young Persons Act 1933 s53(2), a secure training order or a detention and training order unless the offender is legally represented.[1]

21.3   An offender is treated as legally represented if, but only if, s/he has the assistance of counsel or a solicitor to represent him/her in the proceedings in that court at some time after s/he was found guilty and before s/he is sentenced. This statutory requirement may be ignored if the offender either:

- has applied for legal aid and the application was refused on the ground that it did not appear his/her means were such that s/he required assistance; or
- having been informed of his right to apply for legal aid and had the opportunity to do so, he refused or failed to apply.

It is submitted that a young offender aged under 16, for whom the parent or guardian is required to provide details of income, could not be said to have failed to apply for legal aid if the parent/guardian has failed to provide the required details or make the necessary contributions to the order.

---

1   Criminal Justice Act 1982 s3(1).

Statutory restrictions

21.4   The Criminal Justice Act 1991 s1 imposes upon all courts certain restrictions before a custodial sentence may be imposed upon an offender of any age:

(1) This section applies where a person is convicted of an offence punishable with a custodial sentence other than one fixed by law or falling to be imposed under section 2(2), 3(2) or 4(2) of the Crime (Sentences) Act 1997.

(2) Subject to subsection (3) below, the court shall not pass a custodial sentence on the offender unless it is of the opinion–

(a) that the offence, or the combination of the offence and one or more offences associated with it, was so serious that only such a sentence can be justified for the offence; or

(b) where the offence is a violent or sexual offence, that only such a sentence would be adequate to protect the public from serious harm from him.

(3) Nothing in subsection (2) above shall prevent the court from passing a custodial sentence on the offender if he fails to express his willingness to comply with a requirement which is proposed by the court to be included in a probation order or supervision order and which requires an expression of such willingness.

21.5   A custodial sentence may, therefore, only be imposed if:

- the offence is so serious;
- the offence is violent or sexual and it is necessary for the protection of the public; or
- the offender has failed to express willingness to comply with a requirement of a community sentence.

Each of these grounds will be considered in more detail below.

Offence seriousness

21.6   This is the most common reason for imposing a custodial sentence. A court must firstly consider the seriousness of the offence and any offences associated with it. In making this assessment the court must consider the aggravating and mitigating features known to the court. Relevant features are considered in Chapter 13. Having made an initial assessment, the court is then required to consider any personal mitigation and reduce its assessment accordingly. A custodial sentence may only be imposed if the court is still of the opinion that the offence is so serious that only such a sentence can be justified.

21.7 Since the implementation of the Criminal Justice Act 1991 the Court of Appeal has considered what test to apply to determine 'so serious that only such a sentence can be justified'. In *R v Cox*[2] Lord Taylor CJ adopted the description previously given by Lawton LJ in considering a similar provision for young offenders, now repealed:

> The kind of offence which when committed by a young person would make all right thinking members of the public, knowing all the facts, feel that justice had not been done by the passing of any sentence other than a custodial one.[3]

Protection of the public (violent and sexual offences)

21.8 The definition of violent and sexual offences as well as that for serious harm is contained in the Criminal Justice Act 1991 s31(1).[4]

Procedural requirements

21.9 Any sentencer considering imposing a longer than normal sentence should warn the lawyer representing the offender and allow representations before passing sentence.[5] A psychiatric report should usually be obtained and considered before imposing a longer than normal sentence.[6] Any court contemplating proceeding without one should be reminded of the statutory duty to consider the welfare of the child or young person.

Application to children or young persons

21.10 As the youth court's sentencing powers are limited to six months for any one offence and 12 months for any two or more indictable offences it is extremely unlikely that such a court would impose a longer than normal sentence. It may, however, be a consideration for committing the young offender for sentence to the Crown Court under the Magistrates' Courts Act 1980 s37 so that detention powers of up to 24 months are available. Nevertheless, the limits on sentencing would mean that any longer than normal sentence would still

2 [1993] 1 WLR 188.
3 *R v Bradbourn* (1985) 7 Cr App R (S) 180, CA (consideration of s1(4A)(c) Criminal Justice Act 1982, now repealed).
4 See paras 10.77 et seq and 10.81 for a fuller discussion of the terms.
5 *R v Baverstock* [1993] 1 WLR 202, (1993) 14 Cr App R (S) 471, CA.
6 *R v Fawcett* (1995) 16 Cr App R (S) 55, CA; but cf, *R v Hashi* (1995) 16 Cr App R (S) 121, CA.

be only a matter of a few months longer and in such circumstances it could be questioned whether committal for sentence is warranted in view of the minimal extra protection of the public achieved.

21.11 The ability of the Crown Court to impose s53(2) detention when a child or young person is tried on indictment will possibly allow for greater use of longer than normal sentences. The case of *R v K*[7] demonstrates the circumstances in which the power has been found to have been appropriately used. The appellant, aged 16, pleaded guilty to raping his six-year-old sister. He had previously been placed in care because he had been sexually abusing his sister and 12-year-old brother. While in care he had received counselling and was allowed home when he seemed to be responding. After his return to the family home he committed the rape on his sister. At sentence in the Crown Court the judge considered a psychiatric report which stated that the appellant was a danger and would remain so for at least a decade. The Crown Court judge sentenced him to three years s53 detention for the rape and a further five years for the protection of the public. The fact that the rape had taken place so soon after the period in care was considered to support the need for a longer than normal sentence. On appeal, the appropriateness of using s2(2)(b) was upheld but the total sentence was reduced to six years.

Refusal to express willingness to comply with additional requirements

21.12 The Criminal Justice Act 1991 s1(3) is the only exception to the principle that a custodial sentence can only be justified in terms of the offence. It allows the court to sentence an offender to a custodial sentence irrespective of the seriousness of the offence.

21.13 The offender is required to express willingness to comply with the following requirements:

- supervision order with requirement as to mental treatment;
- probation order with requirement to submit to treatment for mental condition; and
- probation order with requirement as to treatment for drug or alcohol dependency.

It is the opinion of the authors that s1(3) requires the express refusal of the offender in court at the sentencing hearing. The sub-section

---

7   (1995) 16 Cr App R (S) 966, CA.

could not be satisfied merely by a pattern of failed appointments for assessment by the relevant agency or medical practitioner.

Determining the length of the sentence

21.14 Having determined that only a custodial sentence is justified, the court must then consider the length of that sentence. The Criminal Justice Act 1991 s2 provides:

(1) This section applies where a court passes a custodial sentence other than one fixed by law or falling to be imposed under section 2(2) of the Crime (Sentences) Act 1997.

(2) Subject to sections 3(2) and 4(2) of that Act the custodial sentence shall be–

(a) for such term (not exceeding the maximum) as in the opinion of the court is commensurate with the seriousness of the offence, or the combination of the offence and one or more offences associated with it; or

(b) where the offence is a violent or sexual offence, for such longer term (not exceeding the maximum) as in the opinion of the court is necessary to protect the public from serious harm from the offender.

Commensurate with the seriousness of the offence

21.15 The court is still required to take into account any personal mitigation when determining the length of sentence. In particular with young offenders the courts have always been anxious to ensure that any custodial sentence is for the shortest possible period.

Relevance of statutory minima

21.16 Detention in a young offender institution and a secure training order are both subject to statutory minimum terms (two months and six months respectively). When detention and training orders are implemented they will be subject to a minimum term of four months. In relation to detention in a young offender institution the minimum term has been held to apply to each offence rather than the aggregate term.[8] The language used in the statutes dealing with secure training orders and detention and training orders are very similar and it is submitted that the minimum terms applicable to

8 *R v Kent Youth Court ex p K (a Minor)* [1999] 1 WLR 27; [1999] Crim LR 168, QBD.

these sentences also apply to each offence rather than the aggregate term.

21.17 The defence lawyer needs to be alert to the possibility that these restrictions may rule out the use of a custodial sentence. A court may have decided that only a custodial sentence is justified for the offence, even taking into account personal mitigation. However, it may then be conceded that the seriousness of the offence does not warrant a sentence of the minimum or above. In such circumstances the court is not in a position to pass a custodial sentence and will be forced to impose a community penalty.

Giving of reasons

21.18 When any court passes a custodial sentence it must state in open court that it is of the opinion, either:

- that the offence or the combination of that offence and one or more offences associated with it, is so serious that only such a sentence can be justified; or
- in the case of a violent or sexual offence, that only such a sentence would be adequate to protect the public form serious harm from the offender.[9]

21.19 The reason for the custodial sentence need not be stated if the offender has refused to consent to a community sentence. A youth court must record the stated reasons for passing a custodial sentence in the court register.[10]

21.20 If a longer than normal sentence is passed the court is required to state in open court and in ordinary language why it is of the opinion that such a sentence is required.[11]

Mandatory minimum sentences

21.21 The Crime (Sentences) Act 1997 introduced the concept of mandatory minimum sentences for some offenders. A mandatory minimum sentence may only be imposed upon an offender who has attained the age of 18, however, convictions for offences committed when younger than 18 may be relevant. Mandatory minimum sentences are considered in more detail at para 24.9.

9 Criminal Justice Act 1991 s1(4).
10 Ibid, s1(5)
11 Ibid, s2(3)

Detention in a young offender institution

21.22   This sentence will be abolished for offenders under the age of 18 with the introduction of detention and training orders on 1 April 2000.[11A]

Pre-conditions

21.23   Before a sentence of detention in a young offender institution may be passed:

- the young offender must be legally represented;
- the court must be of the opinion that the offence is so serious that only a custodial sentence is justified; or
- in the case of a violent or sexual offence, it is necessary for the protection of the public from serious harm from the offender; and
- the period of detention should be at least two months.

Age

21.24   By the Criminal Justice Act 1982 s1 a sentence of imprisonment may not be passed upon an offender aged under 21 years. Instead, by virtue of s1A of the Act an offender under 21 but not less than 15 years of age may be sentenced to detention in a young offender institution.[12] The relevant age of the offender is the age on the date of conviction, that is the date the offender enters a plea of guilty or is found guilty at trial.[13]

21.25   This rule requires particular vigilance from the defence lawyer in the case of a client who has recently attained the age of 15. It may be that there are a number of offences to be sentenced and the dates of conviction vary. It may be that the dates of conviction for the more serious offences pre-date the offender's fifteenth birthday. Although all the offences may be considered when assessing seriousness (they are all associated offences), it will be difficult to justify a sentence of detention unless the offences post-dating the birthday would warrant custody in themselves.

11A   Crime and Disorder Act 1998 (Commencement No 6) Order 1999 SI No 3426. Existing sentences of detention in a young offender institution will not be affected.

12   Where the offender's age is in doubt see para 3.9ff.

13   *R v Danga* [1992] QB 476; [1992] 2 WLR 277; (1992) 13 Cr App R (S) 408, CA.

Minimum and maximum terms

Offender aged under 18

21.26   A court may not sentence an offender aged under 18 to detention in a young offender institution for a term less than two months. A sentence for less would be unlawful. This minimum term applies to the sentence for each offence.[14] There is one statutory exception to this minimum. That is in the case of an offender who fails to comply with the requirements of his/her young offender's licence. The penalty for such non-compliance is up to 30 days detention in a young offender institution.[15]

21.27   The maximum term of detention (available only to the Crown Court) is 24 months.[16] Furthermore, the total term of detention in a young offender institution passed upon an offender must not exceed 24 months irrespective of the number of offences.[17] If the total term exceeds 24 months, the period in excess shall be treated as remitted. This would have the effect of reducing the total to 24 months.

Total term

21.28   The Criminal Justice Act 1982 s1B(6) defines the total term as:

   (a) in the case of an offender sentenced (whether or not on the same occasion) to two or more terms of detention in a young offender institution which are consecutive or wholly or partly concurrent, the aggregate of those terms;
   (b) in the case of any other offender, the term of the sentence of detention in a young offender institution in question.

The total term has been held to include the aggregate of a sentence of detention for a substantive offence and a Bail Act offence[18] and a substantive offence and a consecutive period of detention ordered under the Criminal Justice Act 1991 s40 when the main offence was committed during the 'at risk' period after release from custody.[19]

---

14 *R v Kent Youth Court ex p K (a Minor)* [1999] 1 WLR 27; [1999] Crim LR 168, QBD.
15 Criminal Justice Act 1991 s65(6).
16 Criminal Justice Act 1982 s1B(2)(b).
17 Ibid, s1B(4).
18 *R v Starkey* [1994] Crim LR 380, CA.
19 *R v Foran* [1995] Crim LR 751, CA.

Discount for a guilty plea

21.29   When detention in a young offender institution was limited to an aggregate of 12 months, the Court of Appeal developed an exception to the principle that credit should be given for a plea of guilty. It was held that where a Crown Court judge was dealing with a grave crime for which s53(2) detention may have been appropriate but s/he chose not to impose such a sentence, the judge could then impose the maximum term of detention in a young offender institution even if the offender had pleaded guilty as s/he was already receiving a considerable benefit from not being sentenced to s53(2) detention.[20]

Offender has attained 18 before sentence

21.30   The relevant date is once again the date of conviction.[21] Therefore, if the offender attains 18 after conviction the minimum term is still two months and the total term must not exceed 24 months. However, if the offender attains 18 before conviction at trial, the minimum term of detention is only three weeks and the maximum term is that available for the offence.

Procedural requirements

21.31   The Criminal Justice Act 1991 s3 requires the court to obtain and consider a pre-sentence report before passing a sentence of detention in a young offender institution, unless, in the case of an indictable only offence, it is considered unnecessary in all the circumstances, and in the case of all other offences the court has considered a previous report. The need for a report is considered at para 16.22ff.

21.32   On passing sentence the magistrates or judge must state in open court that they are of the opinion:

- that the offence or the combination of that offence and one or more offences associated with it, is so serious that only such a sentence can be justified; or
- in the case of a violent or sexual offence, that only such a sentence

---

20   *R v Reynolds* (1985) 7 Cr App R (S) 335 distinguishing *R v Stewart* (1983) 5 Cr App R (S) 320 and *R v Pilford* (1985) 7 Cr App R (S) 23.
21   *R v Starkey* [1994] Crim LR 380, CA.

would be adequate to protect the public form serious harm from the offender.

21.33 In any event the court must explain to the offender in open court and in ordinary language why a sentence of detention is being passed upon him/her. If the court is a youth court it shall record the reasons for imposing a custodial sentence in the warrant of commitment and in the court register.[22]

Secure training order

21.34 This sentence is only available for offences committed on or after 1 March 1998.[23] It will be abolished with the implementation of detention and training orders on 1 April 2000.[23A]

21.35 A secure training order is divided into two equal parts. The first half is served in a secure training centre; the second half is served under supervision. A secure training centre is a place in which:

> . . . offenders not less than 12 but under 17 years of age in respect of whom secure training orders have been made under section 1 Criminal Justice and Public Order Act 1994 may be detained and given training and education and prepared for their release.[24]

Pre-conditions

21.36 A court may not impose a secure training order unless:

- the accused is legally represented;[25]
- the offence before the court is imprisonable;[26]
- the court is of the opinion that the offence, or the combination of the offence, and one or more offences associated with it, was so serious that only a custodial sentence can be justified;[27]
- the court is of the opinion that the offence was sufficiently serious

22 Criminal Justice Act 1991 s1(5).
23 Criminal Justice and Public Order Act 1994 (Commencement No 12 and Transitional Provisions) Order 1998 SI No 277 para 4.
23A Crime and Disorder Act 1998 (Commencement No 6) Order 1999 SI No 3426. Existing secure training orders will not be affected.
24 Prison Act 1952 s43(1)(d), as inserted by Criminal Justice and Public Order Act 1994 s5(2).
25 Criminal Justice Act 1982 s3(1); see para 21.2.
26 Criminal Justice and Public Order Act 1994 s1(2)(a).
27 Criminal Justice Act 1991 s1(2)(a).

to warrant the minimum period of the order, namely six months;[28] and

– the court is of the opinion that the criteria of the Criminal Justice and Public Order Act 1994 s1(5) are satisfied.

21.37   The Criminal Justice and Public Order Act s1(5) provides:

The court shall not make a secure training order unless it is satisfied–

(a)   that the offender was not less than 12 years of age when the offence for which he is to be dealt with by the court was committed;

(b)   that the offender has been convicted of three or more imprisonable offences; and

(c)   that the offender, either on this or a previous occasion–

    (i)   has been found by a court to be in breach of a supervision order under the Children and Young Persons Act 1969, or

    (ii)   has been convicted of an imprisonable offence committed whilst he was subject to such a supervision order.

The Act gives no further guidance upon these criteria which are likely to cause considerable practical problems.

Age at date of offence

21.38   This is an unusual criterion as the relevant age is usually that on the date of conviction.

Convicted of three or more imprisonable offences

21.39   It is not clear whether these three offences all have to be previous convictions or whether the current offence may be included. It is also not clear whether offences taken into consideration may be counted. A formal caution could never be used to satisfy the criterion.

21.40   It would seem that a conditional discharge cannot satisfy the criterion either. This is because the Powers of Criminal Courts Act 1973 s1C states that a discharge is not a conviction save for proceedings under that Act (in relation to re-sentencing for breach of a period of conditional discharge). Whether or not this a drafting oversight is not clear, but the position may be contrasted with the express exception to s1C in relation to considering previous convictions to determine the seriousness of an offence[29] and in relation to the statutory prohibition

---

28   Criminal Justice and Public Order Act 1994 s1(3).

29   Criminal Justice Act 1991 s29, as inserted by Criminal Justice and Public Order Act 1994 Sch 9 para 44.

on bail for persons accused of certain offences.[30] This omission is all the more striking when it is considered that the other two exceptions were both introduced by the same 1994 Act.

Supervision order

21.41 It should be noted that it is not necessary for the offender to be subject to a supervision order when the court is considering a secure training order. The criterion merely requires that at some time in the past the offender was either found to be in breach of the requirements of a supervision order or that s/he committed an imprisonable offence while subject to the order.

21.42 The first of the two limbs may only be satisfied if breach proceedings were initiated and the offender either admitted the breach or was found to be in breach. If the proceedings were adjourned without the breach being put to the offender it is submitted that this cannot satisfy the criterion.

Age

21.43 A court may make a secure training order upon an offender aged not less than 12 but under 15 years of age.[31] The court must also be satisfied that the offender was not less than 12 years old when the offence for which s/he is being dealt with by the court was committed. If the offender attains 15 after conviction, it is submitted that the court would still be able to sentence him/her to a secure training order.[32]

Length of the order

21.44 On making a secure training order the court shall specify the length of the order. The minimum order is six months and the maximum is two years. The minimum term applies to each offence.[33] As only half the order is served at the secure training centre, this means that the offender may lose his/her liberty for a period of between three and

30 Criminal Justice and Public Order Act 1994 s25.
31 The age of the offender shall be deemed to be that which it appears to the court to be after considering any available evidence: Criminal Justice and Public Order Act 1994 s1(9). Where the offender's age is in doubt see para 3.9ff.
32 Cf, *R v Danga* (1992) 13 Cr App R (S) 408; *R v Robinson* (1993) 14 Cr App R (S) 448 and *R v Starkey* [1994] Crim LR 380.
33 Cf, *R v Kent Youth Court ex p K (a Minor)* [1999] 1 WLR 27; [1999] Crim LR 168, QBD and see para 21.16.

12 months. The order is not subject to the provisions of the Criminal Justice Act 1991 s33, and therefore there is no provision for early release from the custodial part of the order.

Procedural requirements

21.45 The court must obtain and consider a pre-sentence report before imposing a secure training order unless, in the case of an indictable-only offence, it is not considered necessary or, in any other case, an existing report is considered.[34]

21.45A A court may not impose a secure training order upon a young offender without first establishing whether accommodation in a secure training centre or secure unit is immediately available for him/her.[34A] The relevant enquiries should be made to the Juvenile Offenders Unit of the Home Office.[34B]

21.46 When a court passes a secure training order, it must state in open court and in ordinary language that it is of the opinion:

- that the offence or the combination of that offence and one or more offences associated with it, was so serious that only a custodial sentence could be justified;[35] and
- that the criteria of s1(5) were satisfied.[36]

A youth court should record the stated reasons for passing the secure training order in the court register.[37]

Detention and training order (not in force)

21.47 Detention and training orders will be implemented on 1 April 2000.[37A] Half the order is served in custody; the other half is served under supervision in the community.

---

34 Criminal Justice Act 1991 s3(1).
34A Secure Training Order (Transitory Provisions) Order 1998 SI No 1928 art 2.
34B Home Office letter dated 5 August 1998 – for contact details see appendix 7.
35 Criminal Justice Act 1991 s1(4).
36 Criminal Justice and Public Order Act 1994 s1(7).
37 Criminal Justice Act 1991 s1(5).
37A Crime and Disorder Act 1998 (Commencement No 6) Order 1999 SI No 3426.

Age

21.48 On implementation the order will be available to young offenders aged between 12 and 17 inclusive.[38]

21.49 There is provision for the age limit to be reduced to include 10- and 11-year-olds. This may be done by the Home Secretary by statutory instrument.[39]

Pre-conditions

21.50 A court may not impose a detention and training order unless:

- the accused is legally represented;[40]
- the offence before the court is imprisonable;[41]
- the court is of the opinion that the offence, or the combination of the offence and one or more offences associated with it, was so serious that only a custodial sentence can be justified;[42] and
- the court is of the opinion that the offence was sufficiently serious to warrant the minimum period of the order, namely four months.[43]

Defendants aged 12 to 14

21.51 In the case of a defendant below the age of 15 the court must also be of the opinion that s/he is a persistent offender.[44] The term 'persistent offender' is not defined. It is possible that the courts will apply the ordinary dictionary definition ('enduring, constantly repeated'[45]) or they may adopt the Home Office definition used for identifying young offenders who should be fast tracked (sentenced on three previous occasions for an imprisonable offence[46]).

Defendants aged 10 or 11

21.52 If the use of detention and training orders are extended to 10- and 11-year-olds, they may only be imposed if the court is of the opinion that:

---

38 Crime and Disorder Act 1998 s73(2).
39 Ibid, s60(2)(b).
40 Criminal Justice Act 1982 s3(1).
41 Crime and Disorder Act 1998 s73(1)(a).
42 Criminal Justice Act 1991 s1.
43 Crime and Disorder Act 1998 s73(5).
44 Ibid, s73(2)(a).
45 *Concise Oxford Dictionary* (Oxford University Press, 10th edn, 1999).
46 See para 1.46.

- the child is a persistent offender;[47] and
- only a custodial sentence would be adequate to protect the public from further offending by him/her.[48]

Length of order

Minimum term

21.53   The minimum term is four months.[49]

Maximum term

21.54   The maximum term is 24 months. It should be noted that the youth court is not limited by the usual restrictions on imposing custodial sentences.[50] It may, therefore, impose a detention and training order of up to 24 months for a single offence, provided that the term of the order does not exceed the maximum term of imprisonment that the Crown Court could (in the case of an offender aged 21 or over) impose for the offence.[51]

Determining the length of the order

21.55   The term of a detention and training order shall be four, six, eight, 10, 12, 18 or 24 months.[52] A court may not impose a term exceeding 24 months.[53]

Aggregate term

21.56   A court has the same power to pass consecutive detention and training orders as if they were sentences of imprisonment. This applies where the offender:

- is being sentenced for more than one offence at the same time; or
- is already subject to a detention and training order.

A court may not make in respect of an offender a detention and training order the effect of which would be that s/he would be subject

---

47 See para 21.51.
48 Crime and Disorder Act 1998 s73(2)(b).
49 Ibid, s73(5). It is submitted that this minimum term applies to each offence rather than the aggregate term: see para 21.16.
50 Magistrates' Courts Act 1980 s133.
51 Crime and Disorder Act 1998 s73(6).
52 Ibid, s73(4).
53 Ibid, s74(3).

to orders for an aggregate term which exceeds 24 months. Where the aggregate term of the orders to which an offender would otherwise be subject exceeds 24 months, the excess shall be treated as remitted.[54]

Time spent on remand

21.57 Detention and training orders are not covered by the normal rules for deducting time spent on remand from a sentence passed by the court. Instead, when determining the term of the order, the court must take into account any period for which the offender has been remanded in custody in connection with the offence, or any other offence the charge for which was founded on the same facts or evidence.[55] A reference to being remanded in custody shall include any period where the young offender was:

- held in police detention;
- remanded to or committed to custody by an order of a court;
- remanded or committed to local authority accommodation under the Children and Young Persons Act 1969 s23 and placed and kept in secure accommodation; or
- remanded, admitted or removed to hospital under s35, 36, 38 or 48 of the Mental Health Act 1983.[56]

Procedural requirements

21.58 The court must obtain and consider a pre-sentence report before imposing a detention and training order unless, in the case of an indictable-only offence, it is not considered necessary or, in any other case, an existing report is considered.[57]

21.59 When a court passes a detention and training order, it must state in open court and in ordinary language that it is of the opinion:

- that the offence or the combination of that offence and one or more offences associated with it, was so serious that only a custodial sentence could be justified;[58] and
- that the criteria of the Crime and Disorder Act 1998 s73(2) (see paras 21.50 and 21.51) are satisfied.[59]

---

54 Ibid, s74(4).
55 Ibid, s74(5).
56 Ibid, s74(6).
57 Criminal Justice Act 1991 s3(1).
58 Ibid, s1(4).
59 Crime and Disorder Act 1998 s74(1).

A youth court should record the stated reasons for passing the detention and training order in the court register.[60]

Place of detention

21.60 The period of detention under the order can be served in a young offender institution, secure training centre or a secure unit. The choice of institution is at the discretion of the Home Office.[61]

Detention under the Children and Young Persons Act 1933 s53(2) and (3)

Availability of the sentence

Applicable offences

21.61 Detention under s53(2) and (3) applies to the following:
- any offence punishable in the case of an adult with imprisonment for 14 years or more (except where the sentence is fixed by law);[62]
- indecent assault upon a woman, contrary to Sexual Offences Act 1956 s14;
- indecent assault upon a male contrary to Sexual Offences Act 1956 s15;[62A]
- causing death by dangerous driving, contrary to Road Traffic Act 1988 s1; or
- causing death by careless driving while under the influence of drink or drugs, contrary to Road Traffic Act 1988 s3A.

Age

21.62 In general this sentence is available for all young offenders aged 10 to 17. It should be noted, however, that in relation to the offences under the Road Traffic Act 1988 ss1 and 3A it is only available to offenders aged 14 to 17.

21.63 The relevant age for the purposes of s53(2) is the age on the date of conviction.[63] This means that the sentence must still be imposed

---

60 Criminal Justice Act 1991 s1(5).
61 See para 22.24.
62 A comprehensive list of offences may be found in appendix 4.
62A Only for offences committed on or after 1 October 1997.
63 *R v Robinson* (1993) 14 Cr App R (S) 448, CA.

upon an offender who attains the age of 18 between the date of conviction and the date of sentence. By the Children and Young Persons Act 1963 s29(1) the court is also given the discretion to use the sentence in the case of a young person who attains the age of 18 after proceedings have commenced but prior to conviction.

21.64 As the relevant age is the age at the date of conviction, the sentence is not available in relation to offences under the Road Traffic Act 1988 ss1 and 3A for an offender who is convicted at the age of 13 but attains 14 by the time of sentence.

Convicted on indictment

21.65 Detention under s53(2) and (3) is only available when the young offender has been committed to stand trial on indictment at the Crown Court. This will be when:

- the offence was one of homicide;
- the offence was a grave crime and a youth court considered that the powers of s53 should be available; or
- the young offender was jointly charged with an adult and the magistrates' court considered it to be in the interests of justice that the young offender stand trial together with the adult.

21.66 Detention under s53(2) and (3) will never be available to a Crown Court judge when the young person is before the court following a committal for sentence under the Magistrates' Court Act 1980 s37.[64]

No other method suitable

21.67 The Crown Court judge is required to consider whether any other disposal would be suitable to deal with the offender. The defence lawyer should consider the possibility of preparing an alternative sentencing package (for which see Chapter 14).

Place of detention

21.68 Once sentenced to detention under s53(2) and (3), the young offender may be detained in any establishment as determined by the Home

---

63 *R v Robinson* (1993) 14 Cr App R (S) 448, CA.
64 *R v McKenna* (1985) 7 Cr App R (S) 348, CA; *R v Corcoran* (1986) 8 Cr App R (S) 118, CA; *R v Learmonth* (1988) 10 Cr App R (S) 229, CA.

Office. This will usually be either a local authority secure unit, a young offender institution or a youth treatment centre run by the Department of Health. The type of establishment will be determined in the early part of the sentence as part of the allocation procedure.[65]

Guidelines

21.69   The principles for the use of detention under s53(2) and (3) are mainly contained in the judgments of Lane LCJ in *R v Fairhurst*[66] and Bingham LCJ in *R v Mills*.[67] The relevant principles are set out below.

General principles

21.70   On the one hand there exists the desirability of keeping youths under the age of [18] out of long terms of custody. This is implicit in the provisions of the Criminal Justice Act 1982 already referred to. On the other hand it is necessary that serious offences committed by youths of this age should be met with sentences sufficiently substantial to provide both the appropriate punishment and also the necessary deterrent effect, and in certain cases to provide a measure of protection to the public.

A balance has to be struck between these objectives. In our view it is not necessary, in order to invoke the provisions of section 53(2) of the Children and Young Persons Act 1933, that the crime committed should be one of exceptional gravity, such as attempted murder, manslaughter, wounding with intent, armed robbery or the like.[68]

Offenders aged 15 to 17

21.71   The provisions of section 53(2) and (3) may be properly invoked where the crime committed is one within the scope of the section, and is one that not only calls for a sentence of detention but detention for a longer period than 24 months.

The court should not exceed the 24 month limit for detention in a young offender institution without much careful thought; but if it

---

65   See para 22.20.
66   (1986) 8 Cr App R (S) 346; [1986] 1 WLR 1374; [1987] 1 All ER 46; [1987] Crim LR 60.
67   [1998] 2 Cr App R 57; [1998] 1 WLR 363; [1998] Crim LR 220.
68   *R v Fairhurst* (1986) 8 Cr App R (S) 346, per Lane LCJ at p349.

concludes that a longer sentence, even if not a much longer sentence, is called for, then the court should impose whatever it considers the appropriate period of detention under section 53(2) and (3).[69]

21.72   An exception to this two-year threshold may exist in cases where the offender is exceptionally vulnerable. However, a court should not impose detention under s53(2) and (3) for a period less than two years unless:

– there was clear and compelling evidence to show that detention in a young offender institution is for demonstrable reasons clearly unsuitable; and

– it was in receipt of a clear current indication that there is a place for the defendant in a secure unit and the unit was willing to accept him/her.[70]

21.73   Save in quite exceptional circumstances, this power should not be exercised in the case of a defendant aged over 15 at the date of conviction.[71]

Offenders aged under 15

21.74   [W]here an offender is aged under 15 and thus ineligible for [detention in a young offender institution], a detention sentence of less than two years may well be appropriate.[72]

It has been suggested that this principle needs to be modified following the implementation of secure training orders. In *R v Sheffield Youth Justices ex p M (a Minor)*[73] it was argued that the fact that Parliament had passed the Criminal Justice and Public Order Act 1994 s1 (see para 21.34) indicated that it was intended that only those young offenders who satisfied the pre-conditions for a secure training order should be subject to a custodial sentence of less than two years. In response Kennedy LJ pointed out that secure training orders were not yet in force but he did comment *obiter*:

. . . I am prepared to assume, without in any way deciding, that the scheme of section 1 [of the Criminal Justice and Public Order Act

---

69 [1998] 2 Cr App R 57, per Bingham LCJ at p65.
70 *R v B (a Minor) (Sentence: Jurisdiction)* [1999] 1 WLR 61; sub nom *R v Brown* [1999] 1 Cr App R (S) 132, CA.
71 Ibid.
72 *R v Fairhurst* (1986) 8 Cr App R (S) 346, per Lane LCJ at p349.
73 CO/3343/97, 19.1.98, QBD. The case is reported at (1998) *Times*, 29 January

1994] is intended, once it comes into force, to set out the criteria for a custodial sentence in respect of a person of not less than 12 but under 15 years, and that it would not, in practice at least, be open to a court simply to resort to section 53 if the preconditions in subsection (5) were not satisfied.

In contrast, when the same argument was raised in *R v Liverpool Youth Court ex p C (a Minor)*[74] Smedley J declared *obiter* that where the criteria for a secure training order are not made out, the sentencing court would still have to consider the appropriateness of passing a sentence of detention under s53(2) and (3).

Sentencing for more than one grave crime together

21.75   [W]here more than one offence is involved for which section 53(2) is available, but the offences vary in seriousness, provided that at least one offence is sufficiently serious to merit section 53(2) detention, detention sentences of under two years' duration, whether concurrent or consecutive, may properly be imposed in respect of the other offences (see *Gaskin* (1985) 7 Cr App R (S) 28).[75]

Sentencing grave crimes together with non-grave crime

21.76   Where there are two offences committed by a 15 or 16 [or 17] year old and one of them (A) carries a maximum sentence of 14 years and the other (B) carries a lower maximum, then generally speaking it is not proper to pass a sentence of section 53(2) detention in respect of offence A which would not otherwise merit it in order to compensate for the fact that 12 months' [detention in a young offender institution] is grossly inadequate for offence B. Where, however, it can be truly said that the defendant's behaviour giving rise to offence B is part and parcel of the events giving rise to offence A such a sentence may properly be passed.[76]

Consecutive sentence of detention in a young offender institution

21.77   If one or more offences fall within section 53(2) and (3) and merit an order for detention under that section, and other offences do not fall within section 53(2) and (3) but merit an order of detention in a young offender institution, the sentencing court may properly and without causing administrative difficulty sentence the offender to a term of detention in a young offender institution consecutively to an order of

74 Unreported, CO/474/98, 7.5.98
75 *R v Fairhurst* (1986) 8 Cr App R (S) 346, per Lane LCJ at p349.
76 Ibid.

detention under section 53(2) and (3), unless the order under that section is of indefinite duration. Consecutive sentences should not, however, be imposed in this way on offenders aged 15: such offenders may be detained in secure accommodation and difficulties could result if a consecutive sentence in a young offender institution were passed.[77]

A Crown Court judge may impose a term of detention under s53(2) and (3) on an offender already serving a sentence of detention in a young offender institution, even though the combined total term would exceed two years.[78]

Concurrent sentence of detention in a young offender institution

21.78   Since the possibility exists that terms of detention under s53(2) and (3) and under section 1B [detention in a young offender institution] might be served in different places, we consider it generally undesirable to impose terms concurrently under both sections. Where some of the offences fall within s53(2) and (3) and other offences are 'associated' but do not fall within the section, it will usually be preferable to impose a term under section 53(2) and (3) which takes account of the associated offences or offences which do not fall within that section. In such a case the practice recommended by the court in the *Fairhurst* case of imposing no separate penalty for the lesser offence should be adopted. If the court is minded to impose concurrent terms under the two sections, it should before doing so make quite sure that no administrative difficulty will result, particularly in the case of a 15-year-old offender.[79]

When detention and training orders replace detention in a young offender institution, it will possible for the offender to serve both sentences in the same types of institution. There will, therefore, no longer be any practical reason why the two sentences could not be passed concurrently.

Determining the length of detention

21.79   In determining the length of a sentence of detention under s53(2) and (3), the court is still required to take into account the criteria of the Criminal Justice Act 1991 s2(2), namely that the length of sentence must be:

77   *R v Mills* [1998] 2 Cr App R 57, per Bingham LCJ at p67.
78   *R v O'Meara* [1999] 1 Cr App R (S) 35, CA.
79   *R v Mills* [1998] 2 Cr App R 57, per Bingham LCJ at p68.

- for such term as in the opinion of the court is commensurate with the seriousness of the offence, or the offence and one or more offences associated with it; or
- where the offence is a violent or sexual offence, for such longer term as in the opinion of the court is necessary to protect the public from serious harm from the offender.

Light at the end of the tunnel

21.80 Although the court will often be dealing with extremely serious offences, consideration should still be given to the youth of the offender. In *R v Storey*[80] Mustill J stated the principle which has been followed on many occasions.

> There is another principle to which effect must, in our opinion, be given. These are young men not of outstanding intellectual attainments, and perhaps not very gifted in imagination. It is important, when using the powers under the Act, that the court should not impose a sentence, which, the far end of it, would to young men like this seem completely out of sight. True it always lies in the administrative powers of the appropriate authorities to release the offender substantially before the end of the period fixed by the court. Nevertheless it is not always easy for a 16 year old to appreciate this. The court must take care to select a duration for the order upon which the offender can fix his eye, so that he could buckle down to taking advantage of the structured environment in a place like Aycliffe School, with a view to emerging from it in the foreseeable future improved by his study there.

Deterrence

21.81 Using detention under s53(2) and (3) to impose a deterrent sentence has been held to be compatible with the court's statutory duty to consider the welfare of the child or young person.[81] It has been established that the possibility of a deterrent sentence survived the Criminal Justice Act 1991[82] and the Court of Appeal have further confirmed that a deterrent sentence may be proper in the context of detention under s53(2) and (3).[83] Nevertheless, the court should take account of the offender's youth:

---

80 (1984) 6 Cr App R (S) 104, CA.
81 *R v Ford* (1976) 82 Cr App R 303, CA, per Scarman LJ.
82 *R v Cunningham* (1993) 14 Cr App R (S) 404, CA.
83 *R v Marriott and Shepherd* (1995) 16 Cr App R (S) 428; *R v Arrowsmith* [1996] 16 Cr App R (S) 6.

It is not inappropriate to impose a deterrent sentence; there may be a very real need to deter others and indeed young others from offending in a like manner. But when one is passing . . . a deterrent sentence, it is necessary to keep a balance between that aspect of the matter, the youth of the offender and the effect of a long sentence upon the perception of the offender, it being trite to observe that young offenders see time stretching ahead of them in a different way to that in which adults see it.[84]

Detention for life

21.82   It is possible to order that a young offender be detained for life under s53(2) and (3), provided the maximum for the offence permits.[85] After the Criminal Justice Act 1991 it would seem that a life sentence is only possible if the offence is violent or sexual and the court considers that a longer than normal sentence is required for the protection of the public.[86]

Criteria

21.83   A life sentence may be imposed in preference to a lengthy determinate sentence when the offender is a person of mental instability who is likely to reoffend and present a grave danger to the public and in view of the instability of the offender's mental condition s/he will remain a potential danger for a long or uncertain period.

21.84   When considering the case of a 17-year-old, the Court of Appeal expressed the view that:

[A] sentence of life imprisonment should be imposed only in exceptional cases where the offender is subject to a marked degree of mental instability, and that it is not in fact a merciful way of dealing with an offender, particularly a young offender, to sentence him to life imprisonment or custody for life without giving him a determinate sentence so that he will at least have a release date towards which he can work.[87]

Nevertheless, where the available evidence before the court cannot give any assurances to the court as to when the child or young person

---

84   *R v Marriott and Shepherd*, above, n83, per Ebsworth LJ.
85   *R v Abbot* (1963) 47 Cr App R 110, CA.
86   Criminal Justice Act 1991 s2.
87   *R v Turton* (1986) 8 Cr App R (S) 174, per Drake J.

will cease to present a serious danger to the public, detention for life has been upheld on appeal.[88]

21.85   A psychiatric and/or psychological report should be obtained and considered before imposing detention for life.[89]

The specified period

21.86   When a discretionary life sentence is passed, the judge must usually specify the minimum period the offender is required to serve before the Parole Board may consider release on licence.[90] This is referred to as the specified part (or more loosely the tariff). The Court of Appeal has confirmed that this requirement does apply to life sentences under s53(2) and (3).[91]

21.87   Before determining the specified period, the trial judge should invite representations from defence counsel as to the appropriate length. The judge should give reasons for the period specified.[92] The young offender may appeal the length of the relevant period to the Court of Appeal.

Fixing the specified period for a child or young person

21.88   Lord Browne-Wilkinson in the case of *R v Secretary of State for the Home Department ex p Venables*[93] gave general guidance on the factors to take into consideration when fixing the specified period:

> In setting the judicialised tariff period . . . the judge is directed to specify such a period as is 'appropriate' taking into account the seriousness of the offence. The section does not say that that is the only matter to be taken into account. No doubt the judge, in fixing the period, will also take into account all other normal sentencing considerations. In relation to a child sentenced to detention for life the judge is bound by s44(1) of the [Children and Young Persons Act 1933] . . . to have regard to the welfare of the child. Therefore, in imposing such a tariff he must take into account the need for flexibility in the treatment of the child and, in so doing, will set the minimum tariff so as to ensure that at the earliest possible moment

---

88   *R v Bryson* (1973) 58 Cr App R 464; *R v Bell* (1989) 11 Cr App R (S) 472, [1990] Crim LR 206.
89   *R v Pither* (1979) 1 Cr App R (S) 209, CA.
90   Crime (Sentences) Act 1997 s28 (replacing Criminal Justice Act 1991 s34).
91   *R v Lomas* [1995] Crim LR 576.
92   *Practice Direction (Crime: Life Sentences)* [1993] 1 WLR 223.
93   [1997] 3 WLR 23, at p52D-E.

the matter comes under consideration of the Parole Board who will be able to balance the relevant factors including the development and progress of the child.

The sentencing judge should first determine the length of a notional determinate sentence. Having regard to the welfare of the child or young person this notional sentence should be reduced by one-half (rather than one-third) to arrive at a suitable specified period.[94] When determining the specified period the judge must have regard to any period spent in custody before sentence as this will not be automatically deducted from the specified period.[95]

Procedural requirements

21.89   The Criminal Justice Act 1991 s3 requires the court to obtain and consider a pre-sentence report before passing a sentence of detention in a young offender institution, unless, in the case of an indictable-only offence, it is considered unnecessary in all the circumstances, and in the case of all other offences the court has considered a previous report. The need for a report is considered in Chapter 16.

21.90   Before passing a sentence of detention under s53(2) and (3) the court must state that it is of the opinion, either:

– that the offence or the combination of that offence and one or more offences associated with it, is so serious that only such a sentence can be justified; or

– in the case of a violent or sexual offence, that only such a sentence would be adequate to protect the public from serious harm from the offender.[96]

21.91   If a longer than normal sentence has been passed under the Criminal Justice Act 1991 s2(2) (violent or sexual offences only), the judge must:

– state in open court that s/he is of the opinion that a longer than normal sentence is needed for the protection of the public and why s/he is of that opinion; and

– explain to the offender in open court and in ordinary language why the sentence is for such a term.[97]

94   *R v M, R v L* [1998] 2 All ER 939, CA.
95   Ibid.
96   Criminal Justice Act 1991 s1(4).
97   Ibid, s2(3).

It should also be noted that it is essential that the Crown Court judge makes it clear that s/he is using the extended powers of s53(2) and (3). There have been a surprising number of cases where the judge passed lengthy sentences of custody without specifying that s/he was using s53(2) and (3). In such cases the Court of Appeal has ruled that the Criminal Justice Act 1982 s1B(5) automatically remits the part of the sentence in excess of the statutory maximum for detention in a young offender institution (currently 24 months).[98] It has been held, however, that the mistake may be rectified if the case is brought back before the sentencing judge within the 28 days required by the Supreme Court Act 1981 s47(2).[99]

Detention during Her Majesty's pleasure

21.92   The Children and Young Persons Act 1933 s53(1) provides that detention during Her Majesty's pleasure is the mandatory sentence for murder where the offender was under the age of 18 at the time of the offence. When sentence is passed the offender may be detained at the discretion of the Secretary of State.[100] The sentence is indeterminate.

21.93   The nature of the sentence of detention during Her Majesty's pleasure has been reviewed by the House of Lords in *R v Secretary of State for the Home Department ex p Venables*.[101] It was concluded that the sentence was not purely reformative in character and that, therefore, the Home Secretary was entitled to set an initial tariff which reflected the need for retribution and deterrence. When setting this initial tariff the Home Secretary is required to have regard to the welfare of the child or young person. It was considered that the welfare of the young offender did require that his/her continued detention should be kept under review and that the period to be served to meet the needs of retribution and deterrence should be capable of being reduced in the light of the offender's progress and personal development. In the light of the judgment the then Home Secretary, Michael

---

98   *R v Edgell* (1993) 15 Cr App R (S) 509 and *R v Venison* (1993) 15 Cr App R (S) 624.

99   *R v Anderson* (1991) 13 Cr App R (S) 325. This problem will survive the implementation of detention and training orders as an identical provision is contained in Crime and Disorder Act 1998 s74(4) .

100   The young offender may be detained in the same types of institutions as those used for offenders detained under s53(2) and (3): see para 21.68.

101   [1997] 3 WLR 23.

Howard announced an amended procedure for the setting and review of the tariff.[102] This procedure is summarised below.

Determining the tariff

21.94 After conviction the judge will simply announce that the offender is to be detained during Her Majesty's pleasure. Subsequently the judge submits a written report to the Home Office summarising the issues in the case and giving a recommendation for the minimum period that should be served to mark the seriousness of the offence (the tariff period). A copy of this report is also sent to the Lord Chief Justice for his opinion regarding the appropriate period. Before the Home Secretary determines the length of the tariff, the substance of the sentencing judge's report will be disclosed to the young offender, who then has six months in which to submit written representations regarding the proposed tariff period.[103]

Reviewing the tariff period

21.95 The Home Office will receive annual progress reports on each offender detained during Her Majesty's pleasure. When the offender has served half his/her tariff period, representations from the offender will be invited. A Home Office minister will then consider a report regarding the offender's progress along with any representations. In complex cases an independent psychiatric report on the offender will also be commissioned. When considering whether to reduce the offender's tariff the Home Secretary will look for evidence of:

– significant alteration in the offender's maturity and outlook since the commission of the offence;
– risks to the offender's continued development that cannot be sufficiently mitigated or removed in the custodial environment;
– any matter that calls into question the basis of the original decision to set a tariff at a particular level (for example, about the circumstance of the offence itself or the offender's state of mind at the time).

---

102 22 July 1994.
103 Representations should be sent to the Tariff Unit at Prison Service Headquarters – for address see appendix 7.

21.96   An offender's tariff will only be reduced if the Home Secretary considers that the offender's welfare would be seriously prejudiced by his/her continued detention and that the public interest in the offender's welfare outweighs the public interest in a further period of imprisonment lasting at least until the expiry of the provisionally set tariff.

Release on licence

21.97   Towards the end of the tariff period, the offender's case is referred to the Parole Board by the Home Office. The Parole Board may direct that the offender be released on licence, but only if:

– the offender's tariff has expired; and
– the Board is satisfied that it is no longer necessary for the protection of the public that the prisoner should be confined.[104]

If the Parole Board directs that an offender should be released, it shall be the duty of the Secretary of State to release him/her on licence.[105]

European Convention on Human Rights

21.98   The procedure for setting the tariff has recently been held by the European Court of Human Rights to be in breach of arts 5 and 6 of the Convention.[106] The court ruled that the fixing of the tariff amounts to a sentencing exercise. The fact that the tariff was set by the Home Secretary was, therefore, a breach of art 6.1 as he was not an impartial tribunal independent of the executive. The court also ruled that the two applicants had been deprived, since their convictions, of the opportunity to have the lawfulness of their detention reviewed by a judicial body as required by art 5.4.

21.99   At the time of writing no Government announcement has been made in response to this decision. It is likely that legislation will be required to remove the Home Secretary's role in the setting of the tariff as well as establishing a judicial panel to review the continued detention of young offenders convicted of murder.

104   Crime (Sentences) Act 1997 s28(6).
105   Ibid, s28(5).
106   *V and T v UK* – decision of the court delivered on 16 December 1999 (application nos 24888/94 and 24724/94) (see (1999) *Times*, 17 December).

Serving a custodial sentence

For complete chapter contents, see overleaf

Types of secure institution

22.1   There are four types of institution where a young offender may serve his/her sentence.

Young offender institution

22.2   The regime in a young offender institution is governed by the Young Offender Institution Rules 1988 SI No 1422 (as amended) made under the Prisons Act 1952 s47.

22.3   Following recent severe criticism of the quality of the regime for juvenile prisoners in young offender institutions,[1] the Prison Service has started a major reorganisation of its institutions. It is planned that juvenile prisoners will be detained separately from older young offenders. In addition, 'enhanced regimes' are being established for juvenile prisoners deemed to be vulnerable. The first such regime was established at HMYOI Huntercombe in June 1999; two further units are planned.[2]

22.4   Young offender institutions are subject to inspection by HM Inspectorate of Prisons.

Secure training centre

22.5   At the time of writing two secure training centres have been opened – Medway in Chatham, Kent and Rainsbrook in Onley, Northamptonshire. Both of these centres are operated by *Rebound*, a subsidiary of the security firm *Group 4 Securitas*. A third site has been identified at Medomsley at Consett, County Durham. Two further centres are planned for the North West and South West. Each centre is designed to hold 40 trainees.

22.6   The regime at a secure training centre is governed by the Secure Training Centre Rules 1998 SI No 472 made under the Prisons Act 1952 s47. The Home Office has also confirmed that secure training centres will be run in conformity with the underlying principles of the Children Act 1989.

22.7   Secure training units are subject to inspection by the Social Services Inspectorate and OFSTED.

---

1   See HM Prison Inspectorate reports – *Young Prisoners: A Thematic Review* (Home Office, 1998) and Report on HMYOI and RC Feltham (Home Office, 1999).
2   Letter from the Prison Service Section 53 Casework Unit to the first author.

Secure unit

22.8   Secure units are all currently run by local authorities.[4] They tend to be small institutions – the largest holding less than 40 young people. In total there are 460 beds in England and Wales. About a third of these beds are used for young people detained under the Children Act 1989 s25 on welfare grounds.

22.9   Secure units are run by local authorities in accordance with the principles of the Children Act 1989. They are subject to inspection by the Social Services Inspectorate.

Glenthorne Youth Treatment Centre

22.10 Glenthorne YTC is situated in the West Midlands. It is a secure child care establishment run by the Youth Treatment Service, an executive unit of the Department of Health. The centre holds up to 40 young people.

Allocation to secure institutions

Current arrangements

22.11 The procedure by which a young offender is allocated to a secure institution currently depends on the type of custodial sentence passed by the court.

Offender sentenced to detention in a young offender institution

22.12 The offender will normally serve the sentence in a young offender institution no matter how vulnerable s/he is.[5] The Secretary of State may from time to time direct that an offender shall be detained in a prison or remand centre instead of a young offender institution.[6] If the offender is still under the age of 18, this may only be for a temporary purpose.[7]

---

4   Criminal Justice and Public Order Act 1994 s19 introduced the possibility of voluntary or private organisations running secure units.
5   Criminal Justice Act 1982 s1C(1).
6   Ibid, s1C(2).
7   Ibid, see also *R v Accrington Youth Court ex p Flood* [1998] 1 WLR 156, QBD.

22.13   The Home Office Circular 94/1992 sets out the arrangements for male offenders under the age of 18 who have been sentenced to detention in a young offender institution. Such prisoners are to be referred to as juvenile young offenders and they should be committed straight from court to a Prison Service establishment with a designated juvenile unit.

22.14   The circular states that it is the responsibility of the court to telephone the appropriate institution as soon as possible after sentence to ascertain whether a place is available. If no place is available the Prison Service Tactical Management and Planning Unit should be contacted for alternative arrangements to be made. If reception on the same day is impracticable the offender may be held at the nearest institution which would normally receive prisoners under the age of 18 on remand. Transfer to a designated juvenile unit must take place the following day.

22.15   The circular assumes that a juvenile young offender would remain in the institution of reception until the completion of his/her sentence unless:

– an alternative juvenile unit is located closer to the offender's home area, in which case s/he will be transferred there as soon as a place becomes available;
– his/her maturity or demeanour suggests that an individual would benefit by being transferred to a young offender institution for young adults.

At the time of writing there is considerable demand for beds in institutions suitable for juvenile offenders. This circular, therefore, does not seem to be observed fully.

Offender sentenced to a secure training order

22.16   The allocation of young offenders sentenced to a secure training order is currently managed by the Juvenile Offenders Unit at the Home Office.[8]

22.17   The offender should be transferred to a centre straight from court. However, if no place is immediately available, the court may commit the offender to such place and on such conditions as the Secretary of State may direct for such period (not exceeding 28 days) as the court may specify or until his/her transfer to a secure training

---

8   For contact details see appendix 7.

centre.[9] In practice the committal will be a local authority secure unit.

22.18 If no place in a secure training centre becomes or will become available before the expiry of the committal period, the court may, on application, extend the period of committal for up to 28 days.[10] It is not clear who should make the application nor what happens if no place is available at the end of the 28-day period.

22.19 The period of detention in the secure training centre under the order shall be reduced by the period an offender spends committed to a secure unit.[11]

Offender sentenced to detention under s53(2) and (3)

22.20 Young offenders detained under 53(2) and (3) may be detained in any institution as directed by the Home Office. At present this will be in one of the following:

– a young offender institution;
– a secure unit; or
– Glenthorne Youth Treatment Centre.

The allocation of young offenders detained under s53(2) and (3) is currently managed by the Section 53 Casework Unit based at Prison Service Headquarters.[12] Prison Service Circular Instruction 31/1987 suggests that in general those under sixteen-and-a-half will be allocated to secure units while those who are older would remain in young offender institutions. If an older offender is exceptionally immature, vulnerable or had no previous convictions, allocation to a secure unit may be possible.

22.21 In practice the above guidelines have not been followed for some time. This was challenged by way of judicial review by two juvenile prisoners in *R v Secretary of State for the Home Department ex p J (a Minor)*.[13] In an affidavit filed for the proceedings the Prison Service stated that only the most vulnerable and needy offenders over the age of 15 are placed in secure units. In deciding whether to place an offender in a secure unit, the Prison Service would take into account, the following factors:

– the nature of the offence;

9 Criminal Justice and Public Order Act 1994 s2(2)(a).
10 Ibid, s2(2)(b).
11 Ibid, s2(2)(c).
12 For contact details see appendix 7.
13 (1998) *Times*, 2 December, CA.

- the length of the sentence;
- the maturity of the detainee and his/her ability to cope in a structured environment;
- the previous behaviour of the young person in detention;
- any history of self-harm or other vulnerability;
- educational needs;
- health needs (both physical or psychological); and
- proximity to family and other support.[14]

If it is considered likely that a child or young person will receive a sentence of detention under 53(2) and (3), early warning can be given to the Section 53 Casework Unit. The youth justice (or youth offending) team should forward any relevant reports and background information. It is important it emphasise any reasons why the child or young person should be considered vulnerable.

22.22   The importance of using the early warning system has been emphasised by the Howard League's Troubleshooter Project.[15] Activating the system has no detrimental effect upon the young person as the court is not informed of the notification and its use can make a significant difference to the treatment of young offenders who actually receive a s53 sentence.

22.23   Following sentence at the Crown Court an offender aged under 15 should be allocated straight to a secure unit or to Glenthorne YTC. For older offenders, who do not start their sentences in secure accommodation, there should be an allocation meeting held within a month of the start of the sentence. The meeting may be attended by a youth justice officer, allocated social worker, institution probation officer or the prison officer acting as the offender's personal officer. The pre-sentence report will be considered along with any reports prepared specially for the meeting. These could include medical and psychiatric reports. The offender and his/her parent or guardian can also attend.

Arrangements from 1 April 2000

22.24   On 1 April 2000 the Youth Justice Board for England and Wales will take over responsibility for the management of the juvenile secure

14   Affidavit of Mr Le Marechal quoted by Collins J in the Queen's Bench Division judgment in *R v Secretary of State for the Home Department ex p J (a Minor)* (unreported, CO/1163/98, 3.7.98).
15   *The Howard League Troubleshooter Project: Report of the First Year* (Howard League, 1995).

estate. This change in management will coincide with the abolition of both detention in a young offender institution as a sentence for those under 18 and secure training orders. Instead the new detention and training order will be introduced. The period of detention under this order shall be served in such secure accommodation as may be determined by the Secretary of State or by such other person as may be authorised (the Youth Justice Board for England and Wales).[16] Secure accommodation means:

- a secure training centre;
- a young offender institution;
- a local authority secure unit; or
- any other accommodation provided for the purpose of restricting liberty as the Secretary of State may direct.[17]

At the time of writing the final arrangements for the allocation of juvenile prisoners has not been determined. The Youth Justice Board has published two consultation papers setting out their views on how the secure estate should be managed. The second of these papers suggests that the Youth Justice Board would enter into contracts and service-level agreements with secure institutions to provide places for juvenile prisoners. The Board would then monitor standards and contract compliance by those institutions. The placement of young offenders should be the responsibility of the Board but would, where practicable, be delegated to youth offending teams. The Board would issue guidance on matching individual offenders to particular institutions and would maintain a database of institutions and a clearing house system to facilitate placement. The Board would retain a consultancy role in relation to the more complex cases.[18]

Effect of time spent on remand

22.25   Where a young offender is sentenced to detention in a young offender institution, to a secure training order or to detention under s53(2) and (3), the Criminal Justice Act 1967 s67(1) provides that the

---

16 Crime and Disorder Act 1998 s75(1).
17 Ibid, s75(7).
18 *Improving the Juvenile Secure Estate through Commissioning and Purchasing*: A Report by the Youth Justice Board for England and Wales to the Home Secretary (published July 1999).

actual time to be served in custody will be treated as reduced by the relevant period. This is defined as the following:

- any period during which the offender was in police custody in connection with the offence for which the sentence was passed;
- any period for which s/he was remanded in custody for the offence; or
- any period when the offender was remanded or committed to local authority accommodation and placed in accommodation provided for the purpose of restricting liberty.[19]

Time in police custody

22.26   This includes time spent in the police station as a suspect prior to charge, time spent after charge if bail was refused and any time spent in a police station following a court remand to police custody.

22.27   In the case of young offenders who have been sentenced to a custodial sentence for a series of offences committed over a period of time, there may be a significant number of days to be deducted from the sentence. The defence lawyer may be the only person who would be able to calculate the time spent in police custody and s/he should be prepared to confirm the figure in writing to the Prison Service.

Time spent remanded in custody

22.28   This will not count if the offender is serving a custodial sentence at the same time.

Remanded in LA accommodation provided for the purpose of restricting liberty

22.29   This has been held to include not just secure accommodation (ie, 'accommodation which is provided in the community home for the purpose of restricting liberty and is approved for that purpose by the Secretary of State') but also other forms of local authority accommodation where the regime is 'highly structured and closely supervised'.[20]

22.30   The Home Office has issued a Circular to Governors[21] giving

---

19 Criminal Justice Act 1967 s67(1).
20 *R v Collins* (1995) 16 Cr App R (S) 156; [1994] Crim LR 872, CA.
21 IG 51/1995.

advice on the criteria to be used for assessing whether particular accommodation satisfies the test. The circular states:

3) Remand time must now also be counted in cases where a juvenile has been held in local authority accommodation which is not certified as secure, but which has restricted that person's liberty.
4) The following criteria constitute good evidence that a juvenile's liberty was restricted to such a degree that time spent in such accommodation should count towards a sentence:
    (i) The accommodation was a Children's Home, subject to the Children's Homes Regulations 1991
    (ii) He/she was not permitted to live at home with parents
    (iii) He/she was not permitted to leave
    (iv) Education was provided on the premises

The court has defined a regime in such accommodation as highly structured and closely supervised. Further evidence may include curfew arrangements.

A Department of Health letter to Directors of Social Services (16 May 1995) described the above criteria proposed by the Home Office and advised that '[i]n practice this will mean all placements in community homes'.[21A] Each local authority is under a duty to calculate the period of remand in such accommodation and to pass that information on to the institution where the offender is being detained.

Calculating the relevant time on re-sentence

22.31   The Criminal Justice Act 1967 s67(1) provides that if an offender is being re-sentenced following revocation of a probation or community service order or breach of a conditional discharge, any period on remand before the passing of the order should not be deducted from the custodial sentence passed. Instead, the court imposing the custodial order on re-sentence should take into account any time spent on remand prior to the original order and reduce the order accordingly.[22]

22.32   It should be noted that supervision, attendance centre, reparation and action plan orders are not covered by this exception and any remand time before the imposition of the original sentence should, therefore, still be deducted from the final custodial sentence.

21A This interpretation has been confirmed in *R v Home Office ex p A (a Minor)* (1999) *Times*, 22 September, QBD.
22   *R v McDonald* (1988) 10 Cr App R (S) 458, CA.

Detention and training orders

22.33 The Criminal Justice Act 1967 s67(1) does not apply to detention and training orders. Instead the sentencing court may take into account time spent on remand when determining the length of the order.[23]

Offender serving detention in a YOI or under CYPA s53(2) and (3)

Temporary release

22.34 Whilst serving a sentence of detention in a young offender institution there is provision for a young offender to be released temporarily. This may be done in the following ways:

- compassionate licence;
- resettlement licence; and
- facility licence.

Compassionate licence

22.35 This allows a serving prisoner to be released for a specific compassionate reason such as a family funeral or a visit to a sick or dying relative.

Resettlement licence

22.36 This has replaced home leave. For young offenders it is available to all prisoners (not just those serving sentences over 12 months as with adult prisoners). For prisoners serving sentences under 12 months they may be considered either three months from the date of sentence or four weeks before the automatic date of release, whichever is the sooner. For prisoners serving between 12 months and four years, they will have to serve one-third of the sentence before being considered. For those serving over four years, they will have to serve half of the sentence.

23 See para 21.57.

Facility licence

22.37 This allows a prisoner to be released to attend outside classes or training courses. It may also be used to allow prisoners to attend work experience or to participate in community service projects run by groups such as Community Service Volunteers.

22.38 The prisoner must have served at least a quarter of the sentence before being able to apply for a facility licence.

Release from custody

22.39 The provisions differ depending on the length of the sentence. The actual release date may be delayed if the offender has lost remission for bad behaviour.

Sentence of 12 months or less

22.40 The offender will be released unconditionally after serving half of the sentence imposed by the court.[24] The rest of the sentence is spent in the community subject to recall for further offending.

Sentence over 12 months and under four years

22.41 The offender will be released automatically after half the sentence has been served but s/he will be subject to supervision on licence until s/he has served three-quarters of the sentence.[25]

Sentence of four years or more

22.42 The offender must be released on licence after serving two-thirds of the sentence.[26] The period of licence will last until three-quarters of the sentence has been served.[27] In addition the offender may be released earlier at any time after serving half the sentence upon the recommendation of the Parole Board.[28]

24 Criminal Justice Act 1991 s33(1)(a) as modified by s43(4).
25 Ibid, ss33(1)(b) and 37(1).
26 Ibid, s33(2).
27 Ibid, s37(1).
28 Ibid, s35(1).

Post-release supervision

22.43   Offenders released before the end of the sentence may be subject to two types of supervision in the community.

Licence conditions

22.44   An offender released before s/he has served three-quarters of the custodial sentence may be required to observe conditions as part of his/her licence. This power does not exist if the offender was sentenced to 12 months or less[29] (or, if the offender had attained the age of 18 by the date of conviction, less than 12 months[30]).

22.45   Failing to comply with any condition of the licence is a non-imprisonable summary offence. Proceedings may be instituted by way of summons or warrant.[31]

22.46   If it is proved that the offender has failed to comply with the conditions of the licence, the court may impose any penalty available for a non-imprisonable offence, ie:

- discharge;
- fine (not exceeding £1,000);
- supervision order; and
- probation order.[32]

Whether or not a penalty is imposed for the breach, the court may suspend the licence for a period of up to six months and order that the offender be recalled to custody for the period of the suspension.[33] On the suspension of the licence, the offender may be detained in pursuance of his/her sentence and, if the matter was proved in absence, the offender will be deemed to be unlawfully at large.[34]

Supervision of young offenders under CJA 1991 s65

22.47   As well as the above provisions for supervision on licence, the Criminal Justice Act 1991 s65 imposes a minimum period of supervision upon all offenders aged under 22 who are released from a sentence of detention in a young offender institution or s53 detention. This

---

29   Ibid, s43(4).
30   Ibid, s37(2).
31   Subject to the provisions of Magistrates' Courts Act 1980 s1. See paras 8.11 to 8.14.
32   Criminal Justice Act 1991 s38(1).
33   Ibid, s38(2).
34   Ibid, s38(3).

period of supervision, often termed young offender licence, exists even if the custodial sentence was for less than 12 months.

22.48   The period of the supervision runs from three months from the date of release, unless the young offender is subject to supervision under licence, in which case the s65 supervision does not start until the expiry of the supervision under licence and in any event it expires at the end of three months from the offender's release from custody.

22.49   On release, conditions may be imposed on the young offender as part of the supervision. These conditions must be specified in a written notice given to the young offender on release.[35] Non-compliance with the requirements of the supervision is a summary offence.[36] Proceedings may be instituted by way of summons or warrant under Magistrates' Courts Act 1980 s1. If it is proved that the offender has failed to comply with a requirement of supervision without reasonable excuse, the court is limited to the following disposals:

– a fine (not exceeding £1,000); or
– detention in a young offender institution for up to 30 days.[37]

Offender subject to a secure training order

Release from custody

22.50   The offender will normally serve half the order in the centre and the second half on supervision in the community.[38] There is no power to extend the period of detention if the offender misbehaves.

22.51   The Home Secretary may order the early release of a child or young person, subject to a secure training order if satisfied that exceptional circumstances exist which justify the offender's release on compassionate grounds. Having been released under this provision, the offender remains under supervision for the remainder of the order.[39]

---

35 Ibid, s65(5).
36 Ibid, s65(6).
37 The usual minimum of two months' detention does not apply: Criminal Justice Act 1982 s1A(4).
38 Criminal Justice and Public Order Act 1994 s1(4).
39 Ibid, s2(6).

Supervision of offender following release from the centre

22.52   For the second part of the order the offender is required to be under supervision. This may be carried out by a social worker, probation officer or 'such other person as the Secretary of State may designate'.[40] This latter category would cover employees of voluntary and profit-making organisations franchised to carry out the work. If the supervisor is a social worker s/he shall be appointed from the local authority where the offender resides for the time being.[41] Similarly, if the supervisor is a probation officer, s/he shall be appointed from the probation service which covers the petty sessions area where the offender resides for the time being.[42] Before being released from the secure training centre, the offender shall be given a written notice specifying the category of person for the time being responsible for his/her supervision and any requirements with which s/he must for the time being comply.[43]

Breach of requirements of supervision

22.53   If an offender fails to comply with the requirements of supervision, the supervisor may initiate breach proceedings.

Requiring attendance

22.54   Where it appears on information to a justice of the peace that an offender subject to a secure training order has failed to comply with the requirements of the supervision, the justice may:

- issue a summons requiring the offender (and his/her parent or guardian) to attend before the youth court on a day and time specified in the summons; or
- if the information is in writing and on oath, issue a warrant for the offender's arrest.[44]

It would be expected that the youth court would initially issue a summons and only if the offender failed to attend would the supervisor swear the information and request a warrant. The court may issue the warrant with or without bail.

40   Ibid, s3(2).
41   Ibid, s3(4).
42   Ibid, s3(5).
43   Ibid, s3(7).
44   Ibid, s4(1).

Which court?

22.55 The supervisor may seek a summons from a youth court for a relevant petty sessions area. The court is in a relevant petty sessions area:

- if the secure training centre is situated in it;
- the offender resides for the time being in it; or
- if the order was made by a youth court acting for it.[45]

Procedure

22.56 When the offender is before the court, the supervisor will outline how the requirements of the supervision have been breached. The offender will then be asked whether s/he admits the breach. If the breach is not admitted the supervisor will have to prove the breach to the satisfaction of the court. It should be noted that the legislation provides for no defence of reasonable excuse. If the breach is admitted or proved the court may:

- do nothing about the breach;
- fine the offender up to £1,000 (£250 if the offender is still under the age of 14); or
- order the offender to be detained in a secure training centre for up to three months or for the remainder of the order, whichever is the shorter.[46]

In the first two possibilities the supervision presumably continues, although the Act does not deal specifically with the point.

Offender subject to a detention and training order

Release from custody

22.57 The offender will normally serve the first half of the sentence in custody and the second half under supervision in the community.[47]

---

45 Ibid, s4(2).
46 Ibid, s4(3).
47 Crime and Disorder Act 1998 s75(2).

Early release on compassionate grounds

22.58   The Secretary of State may at any time release the offender if he is satisfied that exceptional circumstances exist which justify the offender's release on compassionate grounds.[48]

Early release for good progress

22.59   The Secretary of State may release the offender:

–   in the case of an order for a term of eight months or more but less than 18 months, one month before the halfway point of the term of the order; and

–   in the case of an order for a term of 18 months or more, one month or two months before that point.[49]

Delayed release for bad behaviour

22.60   The Secretary of State may apply to a youth court for the period of detention to be extended. If the youth court grants such authority the offender must be released:

–   in the case of an order for a term of eight months or more but less than 18 months, one month after the halfway point of the term of the order; and

–   in the case of an order for a term of 18 months or more, one month or two months after that point.[50]

The youth court which should hear this application is not specified.

Supervision following release

22.61   The period of supervision begins with the offender's release and ends when the term of the order ends. During the period of supervision the young offender will be under the supervision of a probation officer, a social worker of a local authority social services department or a member of a youth offending team.[51] Any probation officer appointed shall be from the petty sessions area within which the offender resides for the time being.[52] Any social worker or member of

48   Ibid, s75(3).
49   Ibid, s75(4).
50   Ibid, s75(4).
51   Ibid, s76(3).
52   Ibid, s76(4).

a youth offending team appointed shall be from the local authority area within whose area the offender resides for the time being.[53]

22.62 Before being released on supervision the young offender must be given a notice specifying:

- the category of person responsible for his/her supervision; and
- any requirements with which s/he must comply while on supervision.[54]

Breach of requirements of supervision

22.63 Where a detention and training order is in force in respect of an offender and it appears on information to a justice of the peace that the offender has failed to comply with requirements of supervision, the justice may:

- issue a summons requiring the offender to appear before a youth court; or
- if the information is in writing and on oath, issue a warrant for the offender's arrest.[55]

Which court?

22.64 The supervisor may seek a summons from a youth court for a relevant petty sessions area. The court is in a relevant petty sessions area if:

- the order was made by the youth court acting for it; or
- the offender resides in it for the time being.[56]

Procedure

22.65 When the offender is before the court, the supervisor will outline how the requirements of the supervision have been breached. The offender will then be asked whether s/he admits the breach. If the breach is not admitted the supervisor will have to prove the breach to the satisfaction of the court. It should be noted that the legislation provides for no defence of reasonable excuse. If the breach is admitted or proved the court may:

---

53 Ibid, s76(5).
54 Ibid, s76(6).
55 Ibid, s77(1).
56 Ibid, s77(2).

- do nothing about the breach;
- fine the offender up to £1,000 (£250 if the offender is still under the age of 14); or
- order the offender to be detained in such secure accommodation as determined by the Secretary of State for up to three months or for the remainder of the order, whichever is the shorter.[57]

In the first two possibilities the supervision presumably continues, although the Act does not deal specifically with the point.

Recall to custody for further offending

22.66   If the young offender commits further offences during the currency of his/her custodial sentence s/he may be recalled to custody for the remainder of the sentence. The statutory provisions for this vary depending on the sentence originally passed. They are as follows:

- YOI detention or detention under s53(2) and (3): Criminal Justice Act 1991 s40; and
- detention and training order: Crime and Disorder Act 1998 s78.

Note that there is no such recall provision for offenders sentenced to a secure training order.

22.67   The details of both of these statutory provisions are very similar. The court may order the recall of an offender if s/he commits an imprisonable offence during the currency of the existing custodial sentence. The power may be exercised on conviction for the new offence even if the custodial sentence has by then expired. Recall may be ordered even if the court imposes no penalty for the new offence. The period of recall may not exceed the period between the date of the new offence and the end of the custodial sentence. For example, an offender commits a burglary on 1 January, during the currency of a custodial sentence due to expire on 1 March. He is convicted of the offence on 15 March. On top of any sentence for the burglary, the court may order the offender's recall to custody for a period of up to two months.

---

57   Ibid, s77(3).

CHAPTER 23

Appeals

For complete chapter contents, see overleaf

Introduction

23.1   A child or young person has the same rights of appeal as an adult. Save in the case of appeal by way of case stated, the young offender may exercise his/her right of appeal in his/her own name. No parental consent is required.

23.2   A child or young person found guilty in the youth court or magistrates' court may appeal his/her conviction and/or sentence to the Crown Court. On a point of law either a conviction or sentence may be challenged in the Divisional Court by way of case stated or judicial review. A person tried in the Crown Court may appeal conviction or sentence to the Court of Appeal (Criminal Division).

23.3   Following conviction and sentence the defence lawyer is under a duty to advise his/her client of any grounds of appeal. This advice is covered by the existing criminal legal aid certificate.

Appeal to the Crown Court

23.4   Following sentence in the youth court or adult magistrates' court a child or young person may appeal his/her conviction and/or sentence to the Crown Court.[1]

Legal aid

23.5   Legal aid for an appeal may be granted by the magistrates' court from which the appeal originates or by the Crown Court which will hear the appeal.[2] An application for legal aid should be lodged with the youth court at the same time as the notice of appeal. Legal aid is almost invariably granted to a child or young person for an appeal to the Crown Court.

Notice of appeal

23.6   A written notice of appeal should be served upon the clerk to the justices and the prosecutor.[3] The notice should state in the case of an

---

1   Magistrates' Courts Act 1980 s108.
2   Legal Aid in Criminal and Care Proceedings (General) Regulations 1989 SI No 344 reg 18(1).
3   Crown Court Rules 1982 SI No 1109 (as amended) r7(2).

appeal arising out of conviction of a youth court whether the appeal is against conviction or sentence or both.[4]

Time limit

23.7   Notice of intention to appeal must be lodged within 21 days of the date of the court's order, that is the sentence of the court.[5] This time limit applies even if the appeal is against conviction only, except in the case of a deferred sentence where the time limit for an appeal against conviction runs from the date when the sentence is deferred and not from the day when final sentence is passed.[6]

Calculating the time limit

23.8   The 21-day time limit is calculated by excluding the day of the court's order but including the 21st day thereafter. This means that if a court sentences a young offender on the 1st of the month, the notice of appeal must be received by the court clerk before midnight on the 22nd.[7]

Appealing out of time

23.9   If the notice of appeal is not lodged within this period, an application must be made to the Crown Court for leave to appeal out of time. This application must be in writing and it must explain the reasons why the appeal was not lodged in time. If leave is then granted the Crown Court will notify the clerk to the justices. It is for the defence lawyer to notify the Crown Prosecution Service that an extension to the time limit has been granted.

Bail pending appeal

23.10   Where magistrates have imposed a custodial sentence upon a child or young person, they may grant him/her bail pending the determination of the appeal provided a written notice of appeal has been received.[8] If the magistrates refuse bail, a further application may be

4   Ibid, r4(a).
5   Ibid, r7.
6   Ibid, r7(3).
7   Ibid.
8   Magistrates' Courts Act 1980 s113.

made to the Crown Court.[9] Bail will only be granted in exceptional circumstances.[10]

Withdrawing an appeal

23.11 An appeal may be withdrawn at any time by serving written notice upon the justices' clerk and the chief clerk at the Crown Court.[11]

The appeal hearing

23.12 Appeals are heard by a Crown Court judge sitting with two lay magistrates. Appeals against conviction are complete re-hearings of the evidence and the burden of proof is on the prosecution.

Powers of the court

23.13 On hearing an appeal against sentence, the Crown Court may confirm, reverse or vary any part of the decision appealed against.[12] The sentence may be increased; it may not, however, exceed the maximum sentence which the magistrates' court could have imposed.[13]

23.14 If only part of a sentence is appealed, the whole sentence is still at large and the Crown Court may increase the penalty in relation to any part of the sentence.[14]

Appealing by way of case stated

23.15 A child or young person may apply to the Divisional Court of the High Court to argue that a conviction or sentence of a youth court or adult magistrates' court was wrong in law or in excess of jurisdiction.[15] Once an application for case stated has been made the applicant loses the right to appeal to the Crown Court.[16]

---

9 Supreme Court Act 1981 s81(1)(b).
10 *R v Watton* (1978) 68 Cr App R 293, CA.
11 Crown Court Rules 1982 SI No 1109 r11.
12 Supreme Court Act 1981 s48(2).
13 Ibid, s48(4).
14 *Dutta v Westcott* [1987] QB 291.
15 Magistrates' Courts Act 1980 s111(1).
16 Ibid, s111(4).

Legal aid

23.16   Civil legal aid must be applied for. In view of the short time limit for making the application, an application for emergency legal aid should be made by fax using form APP 11. An application for full civil legal aid will then have to be made using form APP 1. To provide details of the client's financial circumstances a form MEANS 4 (MEANS 1 if the client has attained the age of 16) should be completed.

Litigation friend

23.17   Litigants under the age of 18 in civil proceedings are treated as litigants under a disability. A litigation friend (previously known as 'next friend') is therefore required for a child or young person to appeal by way of case stated.[17]

23.18   The litigation friend will usually be a parent or guardian. If the applicant is looked after by a local authority, it may be appropriate to ask a social worker who knows the young person to act as the litigation friend. If neither a parent or social worker is willing to act, any other responsible adult may be approached. If no other adult known to the young client is suitable, it may be possible to persuade the Official Solicitor of the Supreme Court to act as the litigation friend.

The application

23.19   The application must be in writing and must be sent to the clerk to the justices. It must identify the question or questions of law or jurisdiction on which the opinion of the High Court is sought. If it is thought that the court could not have reached its decision on the evidence, the application should identify the particular finding(s) of fact which it is claimed cannot be supported by the evidence.[18]

23.20   The application must be signed by or on behalf of the applicant. There is no required form for the application and it can be simply contained in the form of a letter to the court.

---

17   CPR Part 21.2.
18   Ibid, r76(2).

Time limits

23.21 The application should be received by the court within 21 days of the date of the decision which is being challenged.

Bail pending appeal

23.22 Where magistrates have imposed a custodial sentence upon a child or young person, they may grant him/her bail pending the determination of the appeal provided a written request to state a case has been received.[19] If the magistrates refuse bail, a fresh application may be made to a High Court judge in chambers.

Procedure for stating a case

23.23 The procedure is governed by the Magistrates' Courts Rules 1981 SI No 552 rr77 and 78. In summary, the procedure is as follows:

- upon receipt of the application the court should produce a draft case which should be served upon the applicant's lawyer and the Crown Prosecution Service as respondent within 21 days;
- the parties have 21 days in which to submit representations and amendments;
- within a further 21 days the court serves the final version of the case upon the applicant's solicitor;
- the applicant's solicitor should then lodge it at the Crown Office of the Divisional Court within 10 days;
- within four days thereafter the applicant's solicitor must notify the respondent that the appeal has been lodged and forward a copy of the case.

There is provision for the granting of extensions to these time limits.[20]

The content of a case

23.24 The case must include the facts as found by the justices and the question or questions of law or jurisdiction on which the opinion of the High Court is sought. A statement of evidence should not usually

19 Magistrates' Courts Act 1980 s113.
20 Magistrates' Courts Rules 1980 SI No 552 r79.

be included.[21] If, however, it is contended that a particular finding of fact cannot be supported by the evidence before the court, the disputed finding of fact should be specified and a statement of evidence included.[22]

Powers of the Divisional Court

23.25   Upon the hearing and determination of the case, the Divisional Court may:

- reverse, affirm or amend the determination of the youth or adult magistrates' court; or
- remit the matter to the justice(s) with the opinion of the court.[23]

Appeal to the Court of Appeal

Legal aid

23.26   The legal aid certificate which covers representation in the Crown Court automatically covers an advice on appeal against conviction and/or sentence. This advice should usually be in writing and should be drafted by counsel instructed in the case. If counsel advises that there are grounds for an appeal, the legal aid certificate also covers the drafting of the grounds of appeal.

23.27   Legal aid to be represented at the appeal is granted by the Registrar of Criminal Appeals. It is usually only granted once leave has been given. In the case of an appeal against sentence, legal aid will only be granted for representation by counsel.

Notice of appeal

23.28   Notice of appeal should be sent to the Chief Clerk at the Crown Court. The following documents should be included:

- notice of appeal; and
- grounds of appeal signed by counsel.

The notice of appeal is usually completed by the solicitor. It may be

---

21   Ibid, r81(1).
22   Ibid, r81(2) and (3).
23   Supreme Court Act 1981 s28A(3).

signed personally be the appellant or his/her solicitor.[24] The grounds of appeal will usually be drafted by counsel and may be supported by a written advice on appeal.

Time limits

23.29 Notice of appeal should be received by the court within 28 days of the decision which is being appealed. In the case of an appeal against conviction this time limit starts to run from the day when the jury returns its verdict even if sentence is then adjourned for the preparation of pre-sentence reports.

23.30 If the notice is not lodged within that time, an application for leave to appeal out of time must be made. An explanation for the delay must be included in the grounds of appeal.

Leave to appeal

23.31 In normal circumstances the application will be considered by a single judge reading the written application. The decision of the judge will be sent directly to counsel who drafted the grounds of appeal and to the appellant.

23.32 If the application is refused, the appellant has the right to renew the application before a full court. Oral arguments may be made at this hearing but legal aid will not be available and therefore a young appellant is only likely to be legally represented if the barrister involved is willing to appear without payment.

23.33 Both a single judge or the full court on refusing leave to appeal may make directions that the time spent in custody pending the determination of an appeal should not count towards the custodial sentence.[25] This power may not be exercised where leave to appeal or a certificate for appeal has been granted.[26] A direction concerning loss of time would not usually be made where leave is refused after an application where the grounds are settled by counsel and supported by a written advice.[27] There is a greater danger of a direction being

---

24 If signed by the solicitor, s/he must certify that the appellant has been advised that the Court of Appeal may order that the time spent awaiting the appeal hearing should not count towards the sentence.

25 *Criminal Appeal Act 1968* s29(1).

26 Ibid, s29(2).

27 *Practice Direction (Crime: Sentence: Loss of Time)* [1980] 1 WLR 270.

made where an appellant renews his/her application for leave to the full court.[28]

Powers of the court

23.34   In an appeal against conviction the Court of Appeal may quash the conviction,[29] and, if it appears to be in the interests of justice, order a retrial.[30]

23.35   In an appeal against sentence the Court may, if it thinks that the appellant should be sentenced differently for the offence(s), quash any sentence or order and in its place pass such sentence as is appropriate, provided that a Crown Court had power to impose the sentence. The Court may not deal with the appellant more severely than the original sentence.[31]

Appeals against sentence by the prosecution

23.36   The Attorney-General may ask the Court of Appeal to review a sentence passed because it is considered to be unduly lenient.[32] This power only exists if the sentencing of the offender took place in the Crown Court. The offence must be in one of the following categories:

- an indictable-only offence; or
- an either-way offence mentioned in a statutory instrument issued by the Secretary of State (currently indecent assault, threats to kill and cruelty to a person under 16).

The power to appeal an unduly lenient sentence applies to children and young persons even though by virtue of the Magistrates' Courts Act 1980 s24 indictable-only offences may be tried summarily.[33]

Procedure

23.37   The Attorney-General must give notice of an application for leave to refer a case to the Court of Appeal within 28 days of sentence being passed. The offender has no right to be present at any leave hearing.

---

28   *R v Wanklyn* (1984) *Times*, 11 November, CA.
29   Criminal Appeal Act 1968 s2(2).
30   Ibid, s7(1).
31   Ibid, s11(3).
32   Criminal Justice Act 1988 s35.
33   *Attorney-General's Reference No 3 of 1993* (1993) 14 Cr App R (S) 739; [1993] Crim LR 472, CA.

If leave is granted, legal aid will be granted to the offender to oppose the reference.

Grounds for increasing a sentence

23.38 In considering references of sentences as unduly lenient the Court of Appeal has adopted the test of whether the sentence is outside the range of sentences which a judge, applying his/her mind to all relevant factors, could reasonably consider appropriate.[34] Even if the court reaches the conclusion that the sentence was unduly lenient, it is not obliged to increase the sentence. Developments since the date of sentence may mean that an increased sentence would be unfair to the offender.

Other remedies

Rectification of mistakes

23.39 A youth or adult magistrates' court may vary or rescind a sentence or other order imposed or made by it, if it appears to be in the interests of justice to do so.[35] This power may be exercised by any subsequent bench at any time.[36] As the power is in relation to an offender, it would appear that the power may only be exercised after conviction.

23.40 A power to rectify mistakes also exists in the Crown Court where it is commonly referred to as the slip rule.[37] Unlike the power in a magistrates' court, it may only be exercised by the same judge within 28 days of the original decision.

Judicial review

23.41 Magistrates' courts and youth courts are creations of statute and are therefore subject to the supervisory jurisdiction of the Divisional Court. The court may exercise this jurisdiction when the youth or magistrates' court:

---

34 *Attorney-General's Reference No 4 of 1989* (1989) 11 Cr App R (S) 517.
35 Magistrates' Courts Act 1980 s142 as amended by Criminal Appeal Act 1995 s25.
36 The previous limitation that the power must be exercised within 28 days by substantially the same bench has been deleted by the Criminal Appeal Act 1995 s25.
37 Supreme Court Act 1981 s47(2).

- has acted outside its statutory powers (ultra vires);
- has breached the rules of natural justice;
- has wrongly exercised its discretion by taking into account irrelevant factors or ignoring relevant factors; or
- has acted irrationally or wholly unreasonably.

Judicial review is a discretionary remedy governed by the Supreme Court Rules 1965, Ord 53. The procedure for such an application is beyond the scope of this book.[38]

Habeas corpus

23.42   The writ of habeas corpus is a means of challenging the lawfulness of the detention of a person. Application must be made to the Divisional Court of the High Court and it will issue if the person detained is detained without any authority or the purported authority is beyond the powers of the person authorising the detention.[39]

23.43   The procedure for applying for a writ is governed by the Supreme Court Rules 1965 Order 54. This is beyond the scope of this book.[40]

---

38 See Manning, *Judicial Review Proceedings* (LAG, 1995).
39 *R v Home Secretary ex p Cheblak* [1991] 1 WLR 890, CA
40 See *Supreme Court Practice 1999* (Sweet & Maxwell).

CHAPTER 24

Having a criminal record

For complete chapter contents, see overleaf

Introduction

24.1 Having a criminal record potentially affects employment prospects and access to some other services such as insurance and credit from financial institutions. As many young clients are approaching the age when they will be seeking employment, a criminal record will be a matter of concern for them and their parents. The defence lawyer should be prepared to advise on the consequences of any criminal conviction.

24.2 Unlike some jurisdictions, there is no rule that removes a young person's criminal record when s/he attains the age of 18. Instead the general policy has been to allow most offenders to be formally rehabilitated by the passage of time. This policy has been given effect by the Rehabilitation of Offenders Act 1974. Parallel to this general policy are a number of provisions aimed to protect the public from certain offenders. Local authorities and probation services have long kept registers of offenders who have committed violent or sexual offences against children (schedule 1 offences). More recently offenders convicted of a wide range of sex offences have been required to register with the police under the Sex Offenders Act 1997. Both of these schemes apply to offenders aged under 18. The restrictions they impose on the offender can have long-term consequences for the child or young person. The effects of having a criminal record will be felt even more acutely with the establishment of the Criminal Records Agency. For the first time any employer will be able to obtain independent confirmation of a job applicant's criminal record.

Rehabilitation of Offenders Act 1974

24.3 The intention of the Act is to provide a mechanism whereby a person convicted of a criminal offence may be rehabilitated for most official purposes. This is effected by deeming offences to have been 'spent' after a fixed period of time.

Spent convictions

24.4 The Act provides that a criminal conviction becomes spent after a certain period of time. The rehabilitation period depends upon the sentence imposed by the court and is set out in s5 of the Act. The period starts to run in most cases from the date of conviction. As a further concession to youth, the rehabilitation period is halved where the sentence was imposed on a person who was under 18 years of age at the date of conviction.[1]

24.5   Once a conviction is spent, the Act deems that the person concerned shall be treated as though s/he were never convicted of the offence. In practical terms a spent conviction need not be declared when applying for a job or for services (eg, mortgages, credit, insurance etc).[2]

24.6   Convictions are never spent for the purposes of criminal proceedings.[3] *Practice Direction (Crime: Spent convictions)*[4] states, however, that any conviction which is spent should be marked as such and should only be referred to in open court with the consent of the judge. The same practice was extended to the magistrates' court by Home Office Circular 98/1975.

Excluded sentences

24.7   Certain sentences may never be rehabilitated. These include:

– detention during Her Majesty's pleasure; and
– detention under s53(2) and (3) exceeding 30 months.[5]

Excluded occupations

24.8   The provisions of the Act do not apply in relation to the following professions and occupations:

– all health professionals;
– veterinary surgeons;
– pharmacists;
– solicitors and barristers;
– accountants;
– probation officers;
– prison staff;
– police officers;
– traffic wardens;
– teachers;

1   Rehabilitation of Offenders Act 1974 s5(2)(a).
2   Ibid, s4.
3   Ibid, s7(2)(a).
4   [1975] 1 WLR 1065.
5   Rehabilitation of Offenders Act 1974 s5(1).

Table 12: Rehabilitation of Offenders Act 1974

Rehabilitation Periods

Sentence	Period
Absolute discharge	six months
Conditional discharge	one year or until the order expires, whichever is the longer
Fine or compensation order	two-and-a-half years
Reparation order	two-and-a-half years
Attendance centre order	one year after the order ceases
Curfew order	two-and-a-half years
Action plan order	two-and-a-half years
Supervision order	one year or until the order ceases, whichever is the longer
Probation order	two-and-a-half years
Community service order	two-and-a-half years
Combination order	two-and-a-half years
Secure training order	one year after the date on which the order ceases to have effect
YOI detention:	
– less than six months	three-and-a-half-years
– six to 30 months	five years
Detention and training order: if aged 15 or over:	
– less than six months	three-and-a-half years
– six to 24 months	five years
if aged less than 15	one year after the date on which the order ceases to have effect
Detention under CYPA 1933 s53(2):	
– less than six months	three years
– six to 30 months	five years

Unless otherwise specified, the rehabilitation period runs from the date of conviction.

- employees of social services departments (or voluntary organisations) who in the course of ordinary duties would have access to
various vulnerable groups (eg, elderly, mentally ill, disabled etc);
- any employment concerned with the provision of services to persons under the age of 18.[6]

Mandatory sentences

24.9   The Crime (Sentence) Act 1997 introduced a number of minimum
mandatory sentences for offenders. Although the provisions in the
Act only apply to offenders who have attained the age of 18, they can
be triggered by convictions for offences committed when the
offender was under the age of 18. The defence lawyer may, therefore,
need to advise a young client of the future implication of a conviction.

Mandatory sentence for domestic burglary

24.10   Where an offender is convicted of a domestic burglary committed
after the commencement of this provision and at the time when the
offence was committed s/he was 18 or over and had been convicted
on two separate occasions in England and Wales of offences of
domestic burglary (both having been committed after the implementation of this provision), the court must impose a custodial sentence
for a minimum term of three years unless the court is of the opinion
that such a sentence would be unjust having regard to specific
circumstances which relate to any of the offences or to the offender.[7]

24.11   This provision came into force on 1 December 1999.[7A]

Mandatory sentence for class A drug trafficking

24.12   Where an offender is convicted of a class A drug trafficking offence
committed after 1 October 1997 and at the time when the offence was
committed s/he was 18 or over and had been convicted on two separate occasions in any part of the United Kingdom of class A drug
trafficking offences, the court must impose a custodial sentence for a
minimum term of seven years unless the court is of the opinion that

---

6   Rehabilitation of Offenders Act 1974 (Exceptions) Order 1975 SI No 1023 Sch 1.
7   Crime (Sentence) Act 1997 s4(1) and (2).
7A Crime (Sentences) Act 1997 (Commencement No 3) Order 1999 SI No 3096.

such a sentence would be unjust having regard to specific circumstances which relate to any of the offences or to the offender.[8]

Mandatory life sentence for a second conviction for a serious crime

24.13 Unless there are considered to be exceptional circumstances relating either to the offences or the offender, a court must impose a life sentence where a person is convicted of a serious offence committed after 1 October 1997 and at the time when that offence was committed s/he was 18 or over and had been convicted in any part of the United Kingdom of another serious offence.[9]

24.14 An offence committed in England and Wales is defined as a serious offence for the purposes of this provision if it is one of the following:

- an attempt to murder, a conspiracy to murder or an incitement to murder;
- soliciting murder;
- manslaughter;
- wounding, or causing grievous bodily harm with intent;
- rape or an attempt to commit rape;
- unlawful sexual intercourse with a girl under 13;
- an offence under s16 (possession of a firearm with intent to injure), s17 (use of a firearm to resist arrest) or s18 (carrying a firearm with criminal intent) of the Firearms Act 1968; and
- robbery, where at some time during the commission of the offence, the offender had in his/her possession a firearm or imitation firearm.[10]

Schedule 1 offenders

24.15 Special provisions relate to persons convicted of offences against children and young persons which are specified in the Children and Young Persons Act 1933 Sch 1. These offences include:

- murder or manslaughter of a child or young person;
- infanticide;

8 Ibid, s3(1) and (2).
9 Ibid, s2(1) and (2).
10 Ibid, s2(5).

- any offence involving bodily injury to a child or young person;
- common assault or battery;
- any offence against a child or young person under the Sexual Offences Act 1956 ss2 to 7, 10 to 16, 19, 20, 22 to 26, 28;
- gross indecency with a child under 14.

The list of offences indicate that the aim of the provisions is to ensure that local authorities can carry out their child protection duties more effectively. Children and young persons who offend against their age peers will fall within the definition of schedule 1 offender, without in most cases posing a continuing risk to minors.

Registers of schedule 1 offenders

24.16   Most local authority social services departments maintain registers of schedule 1 offenders known to be living in their areas. The fact that a schedule 1 offender is known to live in the same household as children may prompt a child protection investigation. The fact that a person is on the schedule 1 offenders' list may also rule out certain types of employment involving contact with children as well as the possibility of fostering or adopting children.[11] Classification would stay with the offender for life.

Release from custody

24.17   Guidance to the Prison Service[12] requires prison officers to identify any prisoner of whatever age who has schedule 1 convictions. This includes not just the current offence(s), but also previous convictions. The local social services department and probation service should be notified. Classification as a schedule 1 offender will restrict the opportunities for temporary release and parole. It could also result in licence conditions prohibiting the offender from living in a household containing children.

24.18   This whole procedure can be dispensed with but only if the Director of Social Services for the area where the offender lives certifies in writing to the Prison Service that no child protection issues are involved. The guidance suggests an example would be cases of minor

11 Children (Protection from Offenders) (Miscellaneous Amendments) Regulations 1997 SI No 2308 and see Local Authority Circular LAC (97)17 for further guidance.
12 *Release of Prisoners Convicted of Offences Against Children or Young Persons under the Age of 18* (IG 54/1994).

physical violence between young persons of similar age or development. Because of the serious consequences of being classified as a schedule 1 offender, the defence lawyer should make representations to the relevant social services department asking that confirmation is sent to the young offender institution where the young offender is being held.

Sex Offenders Act 1997

24.19 The Act came into force on 1 September 1997.[13] Although popularly thought of as a 'paedophile register' it potentially catches a wide range of children and young persons within its remit.

Applicable offences

24.20 The Act applies to the following offences:
- offences under the following provisions of the Sexual Offences Act 1956:
  -s1 (rape);
  -s5 (unlawful sexual intercourse with a girl under the age of 13);
  -s6 (unlawful sexual intercourse with a girl between 13 and 16) (does not apply to offences committed by a person under 20);
  -s10 (incest by a man) (does not apply where the other party is aged 18 or over);
  -s14 (indecent assault on a woman) (does not apply where the other party is aged 18 or over, unless the offender is or has been sentenced to detention for a term of 30 months or more, or is admitted to a hospital subject of a restriction order);
  -s15 (indecent assault on a man) (does not apply where the other party is aged 18 or over, unless the offender is, or has been sentenced to detention for a term of 30 months or more, or is admitted to a hospital subject of a restriction order);
  -s16 (assault with intent to commit buggery) (does not apply where the other party is aged 18 or over);
  -s28 (causing or encouraging prostitution of, intercourse with, or indecent assault on a girl under 16);
- indecent conduct towards a young child (Indecency with Children Act 1960 s1);

13 Sex Offenders Act 1997 (Commencement) Order 1997 SI No 1920.

- inciting girl under 16 to have incestuous sexual intercourse (Criminal Law Act 1977 s54);
- making/distributing/publishing indecent photographs of children (Protection of Children Act 1978 s1);
- importation of indecent photographs of children (Customs and Excise Management Act 1979 s170);
- possession of indecent photographs of children (Criminal Justice Act 1988 s160).[14]

Notification requirement

24.21   The notification requirement applies to a person, if after the commencement of the Act s/he is:

- convicted of a sexual offence listed above;
- cautioned in respect of such an offence; or
- found not guilty of such an offence by reason of insanity, or to be under a disability and to have done the act charged against him in respect of such an offence.[15]

It also applies to an offender who at the date of commencement is serving a custodial or community sentence for a sexual offence listed above or is subject to supervision after being released from a custodial sentence for such an offence.[16]

Length of requirement of notification

24.22   The period for which an offender is subject to a requirement of notification depends on the sentence received for the offence. It is referred to as the applicable period.

24.23   The applicable period for offenders aged under 18 on the date of conviction are as follows:[17]

---

14   Sex Offenders Act 1997 Sch 1 para 1.
15   Ibid, s1(1).
16   Ibid, s1(3).
17   Ibid, s1(4) as modified by s4(2).

Disposal	Applicable period
Sentence of s53 detention for a term of 30 months or more	Indefinite
Restriction order	Indefinite
Custodial sentence for a term of more than six months but less than 30 months	Five years
Custodial sentence for a term of six months or less	Three-and-a-half years
Non-custodial sentence and caution	Two-and-a-half years

Certificates

24.24 The court before which the offender is convicted will certify that the offence is one for which the registration requirement applies.[18] In the case of a caution the police officer administering the caution will issue a certificate confirming that the offence is one to which the registration requirement applies.[19]

Notification to police

24.25 An offender of any age to whom the notification requirement applies must give his/her local police station the following information:

– his/her name;
– any other names used;
– date of birth; and
– home address.[20]

This must be done within 14 days of the date of conviction or receiving a caution.[21] The offender must also notify the local police station within 14 days, if s/he changes his/her name or home address or if s/he stays at another address for a qualifying period (defined as a period of 14 days or two or more periods in any period of 12 months, which (taken together) amount to 14 days).[22]

18 Ibid, s5(2).
19 Ibid, s5(3).
20 Ibid, s2(1).
21 Ibid.
22 Ibid, s2(2).

24.26   A offender who fails to notify the police without reasonable excuse or who knowingly gives the police false information is guilty of a summary only offence.[23] In the case of a person who is under the age of 18 the offence is non-imprisonable.[24]

Obligations on the parent or guardian

24.27   In the case of an offender aged under 18 the sentencing court may direct that, until s/he attains that age, the person with parental responsibility shall be deemed to be authorised to comply with the notification requirements and will be liable in the offender's stead for any non-compliance.[25] This would seem to include being liable to a term of imprisonment for a term not exceeding six months.[26]

Certificates under the Police Act 1997

24.28   The Police Act 1997 introduces a new system of certificates which will detail information held on police computer records. The intention is that applicants for jobs will be required to provide certificates to their prospective employers. A fee will be paid for the issuing of the certificate. The new system is due to be introduced in 2001 and will be managed by a new Criminal Records Agency.

24.29   The Act creates three types of certificate.

Criminal conviction certificate

24.30   This will be by far the most common type of certificate. It details convictions recorded against the applicant or confirms that no conviction is recorded.[27] The certificate does not list any conviction which is spent under the provisions of the Rehabilitation of Offenders Act 1974 s5.[28] This type of certificate could be required by any employer.

---

23   Ibid, s3(1).
24   Ibid, s4(4).
25   Ibid, s4(3).
26   Ibid, s3(1).
27   Police Act 1997 s112(1).
28   Ibid, s112(3).

Criminal record certificate

24.31 This certificate details both convictions and cautions and will include offences which are spent.[29] Criminal record certificates will normally be required from applicants seeking employment in an occupation specified in the Rehabilitation of Offenders Act 1974 (Exceptions) Order 1975 SI No 1023 Sch 1.[30]

Enhanced criminal record certificate

24.32 This type of certificate will only be issued if the job involves work (paid or unpaid) which involves regularly caring for, training, supervising or being in sole charge of persons under 18. It will not only include convictions and cautions recorded against the offender but also police intelligence which could include unsubstantiated allegations.

---

29 Ibid, s113.
30 See para 24.8.

Measures to prevent youth crime and disorder

For complete chapter contents, see overleaf

Introduction

25.1　The Crime and Disorder Act 1998 has introduced a range of measures intended to reduce the incidence of crime and disorder. The following have implications for young people under the age of 18:

- anti-social behaviour orders;
- powers to remove truants to designated premises;
- child curfew schemes; and
- child safety orders.

Although not strictly criminal powers, these provisions have been included in this second edition as their operation will involve both the police and youth offending teams. They will therefore indirectly draw children and young persons into the ambit of the youth justice system. The anti-social behaviour order and child safety order significantly extend the remit of criminal law and youth justice. While made in civil proceedings, breach of an anti-social behaviour order is a criminal offence, and breach of a child safety order can lead to the placing of children under 10 in public care for 'offending behaviour'. Government guidance suggests that local authorities consider the use of these measures in their youth justice plans, and advocates the involvement of youth offending teams when young people are made the subject of orders.

25.2　The defence lawyer will need to be aware both of the law relating to these measures and the consequences for a young client who may have been the subject of these in the past or may be currently affected by them.

The anti-social behaviour order

25.3　The Crime and Disorder Act 1998 s1 introduces the anti-social behaviour order. It is akin to an injunction and is designed to prevent serious anti-social behaviour of a criminal or near-criminal kind. The anti-social behaviour order came into force in England and Wales on 1 April 1999.[1]

1　Crime and Disorder Act 1998 (Commencement No 3 and Appointed Day) Order 1998 SI No 3264.

Applicable age

25.4 An anti-social behaviour order may be made against any persons aged 10 or over.[2] In relation to children and young persons, Home Office guidance suggests:

> [I]t is unlikely that there will be many instances where anti-social behaviour orders will be appropriate against the younger age groups of juveniles eg, 10–11 year olds except where the child's behaviour is part of anti-social behaviour by a family or group which includes older people. In the case of the older age group of 12–17 year olds, however, it is envisaged that applications may be made more routinely particularly if other measures have failed to prevent the offending and anti-social behaviour.[3]

Power

25.5 An application for an anti-social behaviour order may be made by a relevant authority (defined as either the council for the local government area or any chief officer of police any part of whose police area lies within that area) if it appears to the applicant that:

– the person has acted, since the commencement date, in an anti-social manner, that is to say, in a manner that caused or was likely to cause harassment, alarm or distress to one or more persons not of the same household as him/herself; and

– such an order is necessary to protect persons in the local government area in which the harassment, alarm or distress was caused or was likely to be caused from further anti-social acts by him/her.[4]

Before applying for an order the applicant must consult with the other relevant authority.[5] Although not required by statute, Home Office guidance suggests that in the case of a child or young person the applicant should also consult with the relevant social services department and youth offending team.[6] The guidance also notes that there exists a range of other measures available to deal with anti-social behaviour. In particular there is the requirement under the

---

2   Crime and Disorder Act 1998 s1(1).
3   *Anti-social Behaviour Orders – Guidance*, para 5.9.
4   Crime and Disorder Act 1998 s1(1).
5   Ibid, s1(2).
6   *Anti-social Behaviour Orders – Guidance*, paras 3.15 and 5.9.

Children Act 1989 s17 for local authorities to assess and meet the needs of children in need.[7]

Applying for an order

25.6 Application for an anti-social behaviour order is made to the adult magistrates' court whose commission area includes the place where it is alleged that the harassment, alarm or distress was caused or was likely to be caused.[8] Application cannot be made to a youth court. A separate application must be made against each single named individual. The application must be in writing and in the prescribed form.[9]

25.7 A summons must be served on the person against whom the application is made. The summons should be served in person or sent by first class post to his/her last known address. A person with parental responsibility should also receive a copy of the summons.[10] A parent or guardian may be required to attend the hearing.[11]

Legal representation

25.8 Defendants may receive advice and assistance from the court duty solicitor under the Legal Aid Board Duty Solicitor Arrangements 1997.

25.9 A defendant may also receive assistance by way of representation (ABWOR).[12] ABWOR may be refused where it appears:

– unreasonable that approval should be granted in the circumstances of the case; or

– it is not in the interests of justice that approval should be granted.[13]

The Legal Aid Board has issued guidance which emphasises that representation by the duty solicitor should be the norm. The grant of ABWOR may be appropriate where the application for an anti-social behaviour order raises complicated issues of fact, law or procedure

---

7 Ibid, para 3.15.
8 Ibid, s1(3).
9 Magistrates' Courts (Sex Offender and Anti-Social Behaviour Orders) Rules 1998 SI No 2682 Sch 4.
10 *Anti-social Behaviour Orders – Guidance*, para 5.6.
11 Children and Young Persons Act 1933 s34A: see para 7.6.
12 Legal Advice and Assistance (Scope) Regulations 1989 SI No 550 reg 7.
13 Legal Advice and Assistance Regulations 1989 SI No 340 reg 22(6A).

(eg, where the defendant is mentally disordered or where a contested hearing will involve professional witnesses or the statutory defence of reasonableness). It is submitted that the youth of the defendant is also a relevant consideration especially in light of the statutory duty to have regard to the welfare of the child or young person.[15]

The hearing

25.10　Procedure at the hearing is governed by the Magistrates' Courts Act 1980 ss53–55. If the defendant is present, the court will ascertain whether the application is contested. If it is, the applicant will have to call evidence to prove the grounds for the application.

25.11　As the proceedings are by way of complaint, it is generally assumed that the civil burden of proof will apply, namely that the complainant must prove the grounds on a balance of probabilities. It should be noted however that the civil standard of proof may vary depending on the conduct alleged. Where criminal behaviour is alleged, a higher burden of proof has been required in certain circumstances.[16]

25.12　Government guidance suggests that the court should only grant adjournments in exceptional circumstances. Where evidence is contested the defence lawyer may have to ask for an adjournment to prepare properly for the hearing. In support of the application for an adjournment it may be useful to draw the court's attention to the Home Office's acceptance that the imposition of an anti-social behaviour order is a serious matter.[17]

25.13　If the defendant does not attend court, a warrant for his/her arrest may be issued provided the complaint has been substantiated on oath.[18] Instead the court may proceed in the defendant's absence. In either case the court must be satisfied that the summons was served upon the defendant within a reasonable time of the hearing.

15　Children and Young Persons Act 1933 s44.
16　See, for example, *Halford v Brooks* (1991) *Times,* 3 October.
17　*Anti-social Behaviour Orders – Guidance,* para 2.6.
18　Magistrates' Courts Act 1980 s55.

Defence of reasonableness

25.14   When considering whether the grounds for an anti-social behaviour order are made out, the court shall disregard any act of the defendant which s/he shows was reasonable in the circumstances.[19]

Length of the order

25.15   An anti-social behaviour order has a minimum length of two years. There is no maximum period, although the Home Office recommends that orders should be for a fixed duration.[20]

Requirements of the order

25.16   The prohibitions that may be imposed are those necessary for the purpose of protecting from further anti-social acts by the defendant persons in the local government area as well as persons in any adjoining local government area specified in the application for the order.[21]

25.17   The Home Office has offered the following guidance:

> It is important to note that any prohibitions contained in the order must be only those necessary for the purpose of protecting persons in the local government area from further anti-social acts of the same kind by the defendant. This is likely to be restricted to a prohibition on the kind of behaviour that led to the order being sought, but care will be needed in drafting the order to ensure it cannot easily be circumvented by, for example, carrying out behaviour similar to the prohibited behaviour, but which is not specifically prohibited by the order. Prohibitions should be specific in time and place so that it is readily apparent both to the defendant and to those enforcing the order what does or does not constitute a breach. Orders should contain a prohibition on inciting/encouraging the commission of specified anti-social acts within the meaning of the Act, including where appropriate by minors in the household, and by others over whom the person subject to the anti-social behaviour order has control. Any requirements in the order must be *negative*. There is no power to compel an individual to do anything, only *not* to take particular actions.[22]

19 Crime and Disorder Act 1998 s1(5).
20 *Anti-social Behaviour Orders – Guidance*, para 6.11.
21 Crime and Disorder Act 1998 s1(6).
22 *Anti-social Behaviour Orders – Guidance*, para 6.10.

Parenting orders

25.18 When making an anti-social behaviour order on someone under 18 the court may make a parenting order.[23]

Right of appeal

25.19 A defendant has a right of appeal against the making of an anti-social behaviour order. An appeal is made to the Crown Court.[24]

Discharge or variation

25.20 The defendant or the applicant may apply by complaint to the court which made the anti-social behaviour order for it to be varied or discharged by a further order.[25] Except with the consent of both parties, no order shall be discharged before the end of the period of two years beginning with the date of service of the order.[26] Variation does not require the agreement of both parties. The procedure for discharge and variation of orders is covered by the Magistrates' Court (Sex Offender and Anti-social Behaviour Orders) Rules 1998 SI No 2682.

Breach of the requirements of the order

25.21 It is a criminal offence for a person to do anything which s/he is prohibited from doing by an anti-social behaviour order without a reasonable excuse. The offence is triable either way and is punishable in the case of a child or young person by a fine or two years' detention.[27] The court may not conditionally discharge the defendant.[28]

25.22 A prosecution for an alleged breach of the requirements of an order is a matter for the police. The case will be referred to the Crown Prosecution Service and in the case of a child or young person, the case will be heard in the youth court.

---

23 Ibid.
24 Crime and Disorder Act 1998 s4.
25 Crime and Disorder Act 1998 s1(8).
26 Ibid, s1(9).
27 Ibid, s1(10).
28 Ibid, s1(11).

Powers to remove truants to designated premises

25.23   The need to deal with the phenomenon of truancy has been explained by the Government as follows:

> Truancy carries costs both for the children involved and for society more widely. Truants are more likely than others to leave school with few or no qualifications, are more likely to be out of work and are more likely to become homeless. Truancy is also closely associated with crime. The Audit Commission found that a quarter of school age offenders have truanted significantly. A Metropolitan Police study found that 5% of offences were committed by children in school hours.[29]

Truancy patrols with education welfare officers and police officers working jointly have been a feature in some areas for a number of years. However, truancy is not an offence and in reality police have had limited powers. The Crime and Disorder Act 1998 s16 gives police officers the power to return truants to their schools or to other premises designated by the local authority. The section was implemented on 1 December 1998.[30]

Authorising the use of the power

25.24   The power to remove truants is not a power that may be exercised at any time. It may only be exercised when:

- the local authority have designated premises to which children and young persons may be taken; or
- a police officer of at least the rank of superintendent has authorised the use of the power.[31]

In practice the power is only likely to be used for short periods of time when a campaign against truancy is to be mounted.

---

29   Home Office *Guidance Document: Power for the Police to Remove Truants*, para 2.1.
30   Crime and Disorder Act 1998 (Commencement No 2 and Transitional Provisions) Order 1998 SI No 2327 art 4(1).
31   Crime and Disorder Act 1998 s16(1) and (2).

Exercising the power

25.25 A constable may remove a child or young person to designated premises or to the school from which the child or young person is absent if the constable has reasonable cause to believe that a child or young person found by him/her in a public place in a specified area during a specified period:

- is of compulsory school age; and
- is absent from a school without lawful authority.[32]

Although not specified in the Act, Home Office guidance states that the power should be exercised by police officers in uniform, who where practicable should be accompanied by an education representative such as an education welfare officer.[33]

Compulsory school age

25.26 A person ceases to be of compulsory school age at the end of the school year in which s/he attains the age of 16.[34]

Absent from school without lawful authority

25.27 A pupil's absence from a school shall be taken to be without lawful authority unless it falls within one of the reasons set out in the Education Act 1996 s444, namely:

- leave;
- sickness;
- unavoidable cause; or
- day set apart for religious observance.[35]

Pupils on leave could include pupils on work experience placements arranged through the school and traveller children with leave of absence granted for purposes of travelling. Pupils excluded from school would be absent from school with authority and, therefore, not subject to the power to remove.

Designated premises

25.28 Designated premises could include the following:

---

32 Ibid, s16(3).
33 Home Office *Guidance Document: Power for the Police to Remove Truants*, para 4.7.
34 Education Act 1996 s8.
35 Crime and Disorder Act 1998 s16(4).

- the school from which the child or young person is absent;
- the education welfare service office; or
- offices within a shopping precinct maintained by the local education authority for the duration of the truancy operation.[36]

The designated premises will not include police stations.[37]

Public place

25.29   'Public' place has the same meaning as in Part II of the Public Order Act 1986.[38] This includes:

- any highway; and
- any place to which at the material time the public or section of the public has access, on payment or otherwise, as of right or by virtue of express or implied permission.

This definition would include shopping centres, parks, amusements arcades and cinemas.

Reasonable force

25.30   The Crime and Disorder Act 1998 s16 does not make truancy a criminal offence, nor does it create a power of arrest and detention. The Government has, however, given some guidance on the use of force when exercising this power.

> [T]here may be occasional cases in which suspected truants refuse to comply. In such cases, if the constable has reasonable grounds for believing that the child or young person is absent from school without authority, the power under section 16 will enable the officer to use such force as is necessary in the circumstances. What reasonable force might be will depend on the circumstances. It must be proportionate to the nature of the power and the behaviour of the child or young person concerned. If the child or young person resists with violence, that in itself might be an offence of assault and other powers would come into play.[39]

---

36 The Crime and Disorder Act – Guidance Document: *Power for the Police to Remove Truants*, para 4.9.
37 Home Office *Guidance Document: Power for the Police to Remove Truants*, para 4.9.
38 Crime and Disorder Act 1998 s16(5).
39 The Crime and Disorder Act – Guidance Document: *Power for the Police to Remove Truants*, para 4.16.

Child curfew schemes

25.31   The Home Office has explained the rationale for child curfew schemes as follows:

> The Government believes that early intervention before habits become ingrained and before a child has started to identify himself or herself as an offender will often be more effective than waiting until that child is old enough to end up in the criminal justice system.
>
> The Government believes that for a number of reasons children under the age of 10 should not be out late at night unsupervised. It may place them at risk and can create problems for the local community because such children, particularly when gathered in large groups, may become involved in anti-social or potentially criminal behaviour. Such behaviour should not be tolerated because people should have the right to live in a society which is safe and trouble free.[40]

The Crime and Disorder Act 1998 s14 allows local authorities to develop local child curfew schemes. It came into force on 30 September 1998.[41]

25.32   In consultation with the police and local community, a local authority can produce a local child curfew scheme. Before a scheme may be implemented, it must be submitted to the Home Secretary for his approval. If the scheme is approved the local authority may impose a curfew notice.

Curfew notice

25.33   A curfew notice bans children of a specified age being in a public place during specified hours unless they are under the effective control of a parent or a responsible person aged 18 or over.[42]

25.34   Any curfew notice shall be given by posting the notice in some conspicuous place or places within the specified area. The local authority may also use other means it considers desirable for giving publicity to the notice (eg, leafleting local homes or advertising in the local news media).

---

40   Guidance Document: *Local Child Curfews*, para 2.1 and 2.3.
41   Crime and Disorder Act 1998 (Commencement No 2 and Transitional Provisions) Order 1998 SI No 2327 art 2(1).
42   Crime and Disorder Act 1998 s14(2).

Length of notice

25.35   A curfew notice may apply for a maximum of 90 days.[43]

Applicable age

25.36   Child curfews are only applicable to children up to the age of 10.

Specified hours

25.37   A child curfew notice may apply to any time period between the hours of 9.00 pm and 6.00 am.[44] The notice may specify different hours in relation to children of different ages.[45]

Public place

25.38   'Public place' has the same meaning as in Part II of the Public Order Act 1986.[46] This includes:

–   any highway; and
–   any place to which at the material time the public or section of the public has access, on payment or otherwise, as of right or by virtue of express or implied permission.

Enforcement of the curfew

25.39   The Home Office suggests that the primary responsibility for enforcing a local child curfew will rest with the police, but that special operations in conjunction with the local authority and social services department might be mounted.

Removal of the child to his/her place of residence

25.40   Where a constable has reasonable cause to believe that a child is in contravention of a ban imposed by a curfew notice, s/he may remove the child to the child's place of residence unless s/he has reasonable cause to believe that the child would, if removed to that place, be likely to suffer significant harm.[47] Where the constable considers that

---

43   Crime and Disorder Act 1998 s14(1).
44   Ibid, s14(2).
45   Ibid, s14(6).
46   Ibid, s14(8).
47   Ibid, s15(1) and (3). For the definition of 'significant harm' see para 4.26.

significant harm is likely, s/he may take the child into police protection.[48]

Duty of local authority to investigate

25.41   Where a constable has reasonable cause to believe that a child is in contravention of a ban imposed by a curfew notice, s/he shall as soon as practicable, inform the local authority for the area that the child has contravened the ban.[49] Upon receiving such notification the social services department is under a duty to make such enquiries as they consider necessary to enable them to decide whether they should take action to promote the child's welfare.[50] Such enquiries must be commenced within 48 hours of the authority receiving the notification from the police.[51] As a result of these enquiries the social services department could offer support, or could apply to the family proceedings court for a child safety order (see below), or, if the threshold criteria are satisfied, a supervision or care order.

The child safety order (pilot areas only)

25.42   A child safety order places a child under the age of 10 under the supervision of a responsible officer and requires the child to comply with specified requirements. It is designed to protect children under 10 who are at risk of becoming involved in crime or who have already started to behave in an anti-social or criminal manner.[52]

25.43   A court shall not make a child safety order unless it has been notified by the Secretary of State that arrangements for implementing such orders are available in the area in which it appears to the court that the child resides or will reside and the notice has not been withdrawn.[53] This order is currently being piloted in certain local authority areas.[54] It is likely to be introduced throughout England and Wales in April 2000.

---

48   Children Act 1989 s46: see para 4.20.
49   Crime and Disorder 1998 s15(1) and (2).
50   Children Act 1989 s47(1)(a)(iii) as inserted by Crime and Disorder Act 1998 s15(4).
51   Ibid.
52   Home Office Draft Guidance Document: *Child Safety Orders* para 2.2.
53   Crime and Disorder Act 1998 s11(2).
54   For the pilot areas see appendix 8.

Applying for the order

25.44   To obtain a child safety order the local authority with social services responsibility must apply to a magistrates' court sitting as a family proceedings court.[55] The procedure will be covered by the Family Proceedings Courts (Children Act 1989) Rules 1991 SI No 1395. The applications for child safety orders are not specified proceedings for the purposes of the Children Act 1989 s41. Consequently, the child is not a party to the proceedings and no guardian ad litem will be appointed. Notice of the application should be served on any person who is believed to have parental responsibility.

Grounds for an order

25.45   To make a child safety order the court must be satisfied that one or more of the following conditions are fulfilled:

- the child has committed an act which, if s/he had been aged 10 or over, would have constituted an offence;
- a child safety order is necessary for the purpose of preventing the commission by the child of an offence;
- the child has contravened a ban imposed by a curfew notice; and
- the child has acted in a manner that caused or was likely to cause harassment, alarm or distress to one or more persons not of the same household as himself.[56]

The hearing

25.46   Where the grounds for the application are contested by any of the respondents present, the local authority must establish those grounds to the civil burden of proof, namely on a balance of probabilities.[57]

25.47   Before making a child safety order, a court shall obtain and consider information about the child's family circumstances and the likely effect of the order on those circumstances.[58]

---

55   Crime and Disorder Act 1998 s11(6).
56   Ibid, s11(3).
57   Ibid, s11(6)
58   Ibid, s12(1).

Length of the order

25.48   The maximum period permitted for a child safety order is normally three months.[59] Where the court is satisfied that the circumstances of the case are exceptional, the order may be for a maximum of 12 months.[60]

25.49   The Home Office provides the following advice:

> The local authority will need to provide compelling evidence to justify the making of a longer order given that three months' effective supervision in the life of a child under 10 is a substantial period which, if properly structured, should prove to be effective. By their nature, exceptional circumstances cannot be precisely defined although these might arise in a situation where the child's actions would, if they had been committed by a child aged 10 or over, be criminally very serious.[61]

Responsible officer

25.50   A responsible officer may be one of the following:

– a social worker of a local authority social services department; or
– a member of a youth offending team.[62]

Requirements of the order

25.51   The requirements that may be specified are those which the court considers desirable in the interests of:

– securing that the child receives appropriate care, protection and support and is subject to proper control; or
– preventing any repetition of the kind of behaviour which led to the child safety order being made.[63]

25.52   The Home Office suggests that the order could include requirements that the child:

– attend school or extra-curricular activities;
– avoid contact with disruptive and possibly older children;

---

59   Ibid, s11(4).
60   Ibid.
61   Draft Guidance Document: *Child Safety Orders*, para 5.2.
62   Crime and Disorder Act 1998 s11(8).
63   Ibid, s11(5).

- do not attend certain places (such as shopping centres) unsupervised;
- be at home during certain times, probably the evenings; or
- attend particular courses to address specific problems.[64]

25.53   The requirements specified in the order shall, as far as practicable, be such as to avoid:

- any conflict with the parent's religious beliefs; and
- any interference with the times at which the child normally attends school.[65]

Note there is no requirement to avoid a conflict with the child's religious beliefs, where these are different to those of the parent with whom the child lives.

Procedural requirements

25.54   Before making the order, a court shall explain to the parent or guardian of the child in ordinary language:

- the effect of the order and the requirements proposed to be included in it;
- the consequences that may follow if the child fails to comply with the requirements of the order; and
- the court may review the order on the application of the parent, guardian or responsible officer.[66]

The Home Office suggests that, where appropriate, the order should also be explained to the child.[67] Unless family proceedings courts change their practice regarding the attendance at court of children under the age of 10, it is unlikely that this possibility will arise.

Parenting order

25.55   When making a child safety order, the court may also make a parenting order against the child's parent or guardian.[68]

---

64 Home Office Guidance Document: *Child Safety Orders*, para 3.15.
65 Crime and Disorder Act 1998 s12(3).
66 Ibid, s12(2).
67 Home Office Draft Guidance Document: *Child Safety Orders*, para 3.11.
68 Crime and Disorder Act 1998 s8(1)(a) and (2): see para 7.63.

Discharge or variation

25.56 The court which made the order may discharge or vary the order on the application of either the parent or guardian of the child or the responsible officer.[69] When varying the order the court may delete a requirement or insert a new condition (either in addition to or in substitution of an existing provision) that could have been included if the court had then had power to make the order.[70] The procedure for an application to vary or discharge the order is covered by the Magistrates' Courts (Miscellaneous Amendments) Rules 1998 SI No 2167.

25.57 Home Office guidance suggests that orders may be varied where:

– the child moves;
– the requirements are not effective in meeting the objectives of the order; or
– the child has made good progress.[71]

Where a court dismisses an application for discharge, no further application to discharge the order may be made except with the consent of the court which made the order.[72]

Breach of the requirements of the order

25.58 Where a child safety order is in force and it is proved to the satisfaction of the court which made the order, or another magistrates' court acting for the same petty sessions area, on the application of the responsible officer, that the child has failed to comply with any requirement included in the order, the court may:

– vary the order (by cancelling any provision or by inserting any provision that could have been included in the order if the court had then had power to make it and were exercising the power); or
– discharge the order and make a care order.[73]

The power to make a care order applies whether or not the court is satisfied that the usual threshold criteria contained in the Children Act 1989 s31(2) are satisfied.[74]

---

69 Ibid, s12(4).
70 Ibid.
71 Draft Guidance: *Child Safety Orders*, para 7.2.
72 Crime and Disorder Act 1998 s12(5).
73 Ibid, s12(6).
74 Ibid, s12(7).

Right of appeal

25.59   An appeal against the making of a child safety order is made to the High Court.[75]

---

75   Ibid, s13(1).

APPENDICES

continued overleaf

Extracts from legislation

Children and Young Persons Act 1933

Separation of children and young persons from adults in police stations, courts, etc

31 (1) Arrangements shall be made for preventing a child or young person while detained in a police station, or while being conveyed to or from any criminal court, or while waiting before or after attendance in any criminal court, from associating with an adult (not being a relative) who is charged with any offence other than an offence with which the child or young person is jointly charged, and for ensuring that a girl (being a child or young person) shall while so detained, being conveyed, or waiting, be under the care of a woman.

(2) In this section and section 34 of this Act, 'young person' means a person who has attained the age of fourteen and is under the age of seventeen years.

Attendance at court of parent of child or young person charged with an offence, etc

34 (1) [*Repealed.*]

(2) Where a child or young person is in police detention, such steps as are practicable shall be taken to ascertain the identity of a person responsible for his welfare.

(3) If it is practicable to ascertain the identity of a person responsible for the welfare of the child or young person, that person shall be informed, unless it is not practicable to do so –
(a) that the child or young person has been arrested;
(b) why he has been arrested; and
(c) where he is being detained.

(4) Where information falls to be given under subsection (3) above, it shall be given as soon as it is practicable to do so.

(5) For the purposes of this section the persons who may be responsible for the welfare of a child or young person are –
(a) his parent or guardian; or
(b) any other person who has for the time being assumed responsibility for his welfare.

(6) If it is practicable to give a person responsible for the welfare of the child or young person the information required by subsection (3) above, that person shall be given it as soon as it is practicable to do so.

(7) If it appears that at the time of his arrest a supervision order, as defined in 643

section 11 of the Children and Young Persons Act 1969 or Part IV of the Children Act 1989, is in force in respect of him, the person responsible for his supervision shall also be informed as described in subsection (3) above as soon as it is reasonably practicable to do so.

(7A) If it appears that at the time of his arrest the child or young person is being provided with accommodation by or on behalf of a local authority under section 20 of the Children Act 1989, the local authority shall also be informed as described in subsection (3) above as soon as it is reasonably practicable to do so.

(8) The reference to a parent or guardian in subsection (5) above is in the case of a child or young person in the care of a local authority, a reference to that authority.

(9) The rights conferred on a child or young person by subsections (2) to (8) above are in addition to his rights under section 56 of the Police and Criminal Evidence Act 1984.

(10) The reference in subsection (2) above to a child or young person who is in police detention includes a reference to a child or young person who has been detained under the terrorism provisions; and in subsection (3) above – arrest – includes such detention.

(11) In subsection (10) above 'the terrorism provisions' has the meaning assigned to it by section 65 of the Police and Criminal Evidence Act 1984.

Attendance at court of parent or guardian

34A (1) Where a child or young person is charged with an offence or is for any other reason brought before a court, the court –

  (a) may in any case; and

  (b) shall in the case of a child or a young person who is under the age of sixteen years,

require a person who is a parent or guardian of his to attend at the court during all the stages of the proceedings, unless and to the extent that the court is satisfied that it would be unreasonable to require such attendance, having regard to the circumstances of the case.

(2) In relation to a child or young person for whom a local authority have parental responsibility and who –

  (a) is in their care; or

  (b) is provided with accommodation by them in the exercise of any functions (in particular those under the Children Act 1989) which stand referred to their social services committee under the Local Authority Social Services Act 1970,

the reference in subsection (1) above to a person who is a parent or guardian of his shall be construed as a reference to that authority or, where he is allowed to live with such a person, as including such a reference.

In this subsection 'local authority' and 'parental responsibility' have the same meanings as in the Children Act 1989.

Power to prohibit publication of certain matter in newspapers

39 (1) In relation to any proceedings in any court the court may direct that –

(a) no newspaper report of the proceedings shall reveal the name, address, or school, or include any particulars calculated to lead to the identification, of any child or young person concerned in the proceedings, either as being the person by or against or in respect of whom the proceedings are taken, or as being a witness therein;

(b) no picture shall be published in any newspaper as being or including a picture of any child or young person so concerned in the proceedings as aforesaid;

except in so far (if at all) as may be permitted by the direction of the court.

(2) Any person who publishes any matter in contravention of any such direction shall on summary conviction be liable in respect of each offence to a fine not exceeding level 5 on the standard scale.

(3) In this section 'proceedings' means proceedings other than criminal proceedings.

Assignment of certain matters to youth courts

46 (1) Subject as hereinafter provided, no charge against a child or young person, and no application whereof the hearing is by rules made under this section assigned to youth courts, shall be heard by a court of summary jurisdiction which is not a youth court:

Provided that –

(a) a charge made jointly against a child or young person and a person who has attained the age of eighteen years shall be heard by a court of summary jurisdiction other than a youth court; and

(b) where a child or young person is charged with an offence, the charge may be heard by a court of summary jurisdiction which is not a youth court if a person who has attained the age of eighteen years is charged at the same time with aiding, abetting, causing, procuring, allowing or permitting that offence; and

(c) where, in the course of any proceedings before any court of summary jurisdiction other than a youth court, it appears that the person to whom the proceedings relate is a child or young person, nothing in this subsection shall be construed as preventing the court, if it thinks fit so to do, from proceeding with the hearing and determination of those proceedings.

(1A) If a notification that the accused desires to plead guilty without appearing before the court is received by the justices' chief executive for a court in pursuance of section 12 of the Magistrates' Courts Act 1980 and the court has no reason to believe that the accused is a child or young person, then, if he is a child or young person he shall be deemed to have attained the age of eighteen for the purposes of subsection (1) of this section in its application to the proceedings in question.

(2) No direction, whether contained in this or any other Act, that a charge shall be brought before a youth court shall be construed as restricting the powers of any justice or justices to entertain an application for bail or

for a remand, and to hear such evidence as may be necessary for that purpose.

(3) [*Repealed.*]

Miscellaneous provisions as to powers of youth courts

48 (1) A youth court sitting for the purpose of hearing a charge against a person who is believed to be a child or young person may, if it thinks fit to do so, proceed with the hearing and determination of the charge notwithstanding that it is discovered that the person in question is not a child or young person.

(2) The attainment of the age of eighteen years by a person in whose case an order for conditional discharge has been made, shall not deprive a youth court of jurisdiction to enforce his attendance and deal with him in respect of the commission of a further offence.

(3) When a youth court has remanded a child or young person for information to be obtained with respect to him, any youth court acting for the same petty sessions area or place –

(a) may in his absence extend the period for which he is remanded, so, however, that he appears before a court or a justice of the peace at least once in every twenty-one days;

(b) when the required information has been obtained, may deal with him finally.

(4) A youth court may sit on any day for the purpose of hearing and determining a charge against a child or young person in respect of an indictable offence.

(5) [*Repealed.*]

(6) [*Repealed.*]

Restrictions on reports of proceedings in which children or young persons are concerned

49 (1) No matter relating to any child or young person concerned in proceedings to which this section applies shall while he is under the age of 18 be included in any publication if it is likely to lead members of the public to identify him as someone concerned in the proceedings.

(2) The proceedings to which this section applies are –

(a) proceedings in a youth court;

(b) proceedings on appeal from a youth court (including proceedings by way of case stated);

(c) proceedings under section 15 or 16 of the Children and Young Persons Act 1969 (proceedings for varying or revoking supervision orders); and

(d) proceedings on appeal from a magistrates' court arising out of proceedings under section 15 or 16 of that Act (including proceedings by way of case stated).

(3) In this section 'publication' includes any speech writing, relevant programme or other communication on whatever form, which is addressed to the public at large or any section of the public (and for this purpose every relevant pro-

gramme shall be taken to be so addressed), but does not include an indictment or other document prepared for use in particular legal proceedings.

(3A) The matters relating to a person in relation to which the restrictions imposed
by subsection (1) above apply (if their inclusion in any publication is likely to
have the result mentioned in that subsection) include in particular –

(a) his name,

(b) his address,

(c) the identity of any school or other educational establishment attended by
him,

(d) the identity of any place of work, and

(e) any still or moving picture of him.

(4) For the purposes of this section a child or young person is concerned in any
proceedings if he is –

(a) a person against or in respect of whom the proceedings are taken, or,

(b) a person called, or proposed to be called, to give evidence in the
proceedings.

(4A) If a court is satisfied that it is in the public interest to do so, it may, in
relation to a child or young person who has been convicted of an offence, by
order dispense to any specified event with the restrictions imposed by subsection (1) above in relation to any proceedings before it to which this
section applies by virtue of subsection (2)(a) or (b) above, being proceedings
relating to –

(a) the prosecution or conviction of the offender for the offence;

(b) the manner in which he, or his parent or guardian, should be dealt with
in respect of the offence;

(c) the enforcement, amendment, variation, revocation or discharge of any
order made in respect of the offence;

(d) where an attendance centre order is made in respect of the offence, the
enforcement of any rules made under section 16(3) of the Criminal
Justice Act 1982; or

(e) where a detention and training order is made, the enforcement of any
requirements imposed under section 76(6)(b) of the Crime and Disorder
Act 1998.

(4B) A court shall not exercise its power under subsection (4A) above without –

(a) affording the parties to the proceedings an opportunity to make representations; and

(b) taking into account any representations which are duly made.

(5) Subject to subsection (7) below, a court may, in relation to proceedings
before it to which this section applies, by order dispense to any specified
extent with the requirements of this section in relation to a child or young
person who is concerned in the proceedings if it is satisfied –

(a) that it is appropriate to do so for the purpose of avoiding injustice to the
child or young person; or

(b) that, as respects a child or young person to whom this paragraph applies
who is unlawfully at large, it is necessary to dispense with those
requirements for the purpose of apprehending him and bringing him
before a court or returning him to the place in which he was in custody

(6) Paragraph (b) of subsection (5) above applies to any child or young person who is charged with or has been convicted of –
   (a) a violent offence,
   (b) a sexual offence, or
   (c) an offence punishable in the case of a person aged 21 or over with imprisonment for fourteen years or more.

(7) The court shall not exercise its power under subsection (5)(b) above –
   (a) except in pursuance of an application by or on behalf of the Director of Public Prosecutions; and
   (b) unless notice of the application has been given by the Director of Public Prosecutions to any legal representative of the child or young person.

(8) The court's power under subsections (4A) or (5) above may be exercised by a single justice.

(9) If a publication includes any matter in contravention of subsection (1) above, the following persons shall be guilty of an offence and liable on summary conviction to a fine not exceeding level 5 on the standard scale –
   (a) where the publication is a newspaper or periodical, any proprietor, any editor and any publisher of the newspaper or periodical;
   (b) where the publication is a relevant programme –
      (i) any body corporate or Scottish partnership engaged in providing the programme service in which the programme is included; and
      (ii) any person having functions in relation to the programme corresponding to those of an editor of a newspaper;
   (c) in the case of any other publication, any person publishing it.

(9A) Where a person is charged with an offence under subsection (9) above it shall be a defence to prove that at the time of the alleged offence he was not aware, and neither suspected nor had reason to suspect, that the publication included the matter in question.

(9B) If an offence under subsection (9) above committed by a body corporate is proved–
   (a) to have been committed with the consent or connivance of, or
   (b) to be attributable to any neglect on the part of, an officer, the officer as well as the body corporate is guilty of the offence and liable to be proceeded against and punished accordingly.

(9C) In subsection (9B) above 'officer' means a director, manager, secretary or other similar officer of the body, or a person purporting to act in any such capacity.

(9D) If the affairs of a body corporate are managed by its members, 'director' in subsection (9C) above means a member of that body.

(9D) Where an offence under subsection (9) above is committed by a Scottish partnership and is proved to have been committed with the consent or connivance of a partner, he as well as the partnership shall be guilty of the offence and shall be liable to be proceeded against and punished accordingly.

(10) In any proceedings under section 15 or 16 of the Children and Young Persons Act 1969 (proceedings for varying or revoking supervision orders) before a magistrates' court other than a youth court or on appeal from such a court it shall be the duty of the magistrates' court or the appellate court to

announce in the course of the proceedings that this section applies to the proceedings; and if the court fails to do so this section shall not apply to the proceedings.

(11) In this section –

'legal representative' means an authorised advocate or authorised litigator, as defined by section 119(1) of the Courts and Legal Services Act 1990;

'picture' includes a likeness however produced;

'relevant programme' means a programme included in a programme service, within the meaning of the Broadcasting Act 1990;

'sexual offence' has the same meaning as in section 31(1) of the Criminal Justice Act 1991;

'specified' means specified in an order under this section;

'violent offence' has the same meaning as in section 31(1) of the Criminal Justice Act 1991;

and a person who, having been granted bail, is liable to arrest (whether with or without a warrant) shall be treated as unlawfully at large.

[(12–14) *Not reproduced.*]

Power to order parent or guardian to pay fine, etc

55 (1) Where –

(a) a child or young person is convicted or found guilty of any offence for the commission of which a fine or costs may be imposed or a compensation order may be made under section 35 of the Powers of Criminal Courts Act 1973; and

(b) the court is of opinion that the case would best be met by the imposition of a fine or costs or the making of such an order, whether with or without any other punishment,

it shall be the duty of the court to order that the fine, compensation or costs awarded be paid by the parent or guardian of the child or young person instead of by the child or young person himself, unless the court is satisfied –

(i) that the parent or guardian cannot be found; or

(ii) that it would be unreasonable to make an order for payment, having regard to the circumstances of the case.

(1A) Where but for this subsection –

(a) a court would order a child or young person to pay a fine under section 15(3)(a) of the Children and Young Persons Act 1969 (failure to comply with requirement included in supervision order); or

(b) a court would impose a fine on a child or young person under section 19(3) of the Criminal Justice Act 1982 (breach of attendance centre order, or attendance centre rules); or

(bb) a court would impose a fine on a child or young person under paragraph 3(1)(a) or 4(1)(a) of Schedule 2 to the Criminal Justice Act 1991 (breach of requirement of a relevant order (within the meaning given by that Schedule) or of a combination order);

(c) a court would impose a fine on a child or young person under section 4(3) of the Criminal Justice and Public Order Act 1994 (breach of requirements of supervision under secure training order), or

(d) a court would impose a fine on a child or young person under section 77(3) of the Crime and Disorder Act 1998 (breach of requirements of supervision under detention and training order) or paragraph 3 of Schedule 5 to that Act (breach of requirements of reparation order or action plan order),

it shall be the duty of the court to order that the fine be paid by the parent or guardian of the child or young person instead of by the child or young person himself, unless the court is satisfied –

(i) that the parent or guardian cannot be found; or

(ii) that it would be unreasonable to make an order for payment, having regard to the circumstances of the case.

(1B) In the case of a young person who has attained the age of sixteen years, subsections (1) and (1A) above shall have effect as if, instead of imposing a duty, they conferred a power to make such an order as is mentioned in those subsections.

(2) An order under this section may be made against a parent or guardian who, having been required to attend, has failed to do so, but, save as aforesaid, no such order shall be made without giving the parent or guardian an opportunity of being heard.

(3) A parent or guardian may appeal to the Crown Court against an order under this section made by a magistrates' court.

(4) A parent or guardian may appeal to the Court of Appeal against an order made under this section by the Crown Court, as if he had been convicted on indictment and the order were a sentence passed on his conviction.

(5) In relation to a child or young person for whom a local authority have parental responsibility and who –

(a) is in their care; or

(b) is provided with accommodation by them in the exercise of any functions (in particular those under the Children Act 1989) which stand referred to their social services committee under the Local Authority Social Services Act 1970,

references in this section to his parent or guardian shall be construed as references to that authority.

In this subsection 'local authority' and 'parental responsibility' have the same meanings as in the Children Act 1989.

(6) In relation to any other child or young person, references in this section to his parent shall be construed in accordance with section 1 of the Family Law Reform Act 1987.

Power of other courts to remit juvenile offenders to youth courts

56 (1) Any court by or before which a child or young person is found guilty of an offence other than homicide, may and, if it is not a youth court, shall unless satisfied that it would be undesirable to do so, remit the case to a youth court acting for the place where the offender was committed for trial, or, if he was not committed for trial, to a youth court acting either for the same place as the remitting court or for the place where the offender habitually resides; and, where any such case is so remitted, the offender shall be brought before a youth court accordingly, and that court may deal with him in any way in which it might have dealt with him if he had been tried and found guilty by that court.

(1A) References in subsection (1) above to an offender's being committed for trial include references to his being sent for trial under section 51 of the Crime and Disorder Act 1998.

(2) Where any case is so remitted –

    (a) the offender shall have the same right of appeal against any order of the court to which the case is remitted as if he had been found guilty by the court, but shall have no right of appeal against the order of remission; and

    (b) [*Repealed.*]

(3) A court by which an order remitting a case to a youth court is made under this section may give such directions as appear to be necessary with respect to the custody of the offender or for his release on bail until he can be brought before the youth court, and shall cause to be transmitted to the justices' chief executive for the youth court a certificate setting out the nature of the offence and stating that the offender has been found guilty thereof, and that the case has been remitted for the purpose of being dealt with under this section.

Children and Young Persons Act 1963

Jurisdiction of magistrates' courts in certain cases involving children and young persons

18   Notwithstanding section 46(1) of the principal Act (which restricts the jurisdiction of magistrates' courts which are not youth courts in cases where a child or young person is charged with an offence) a magistrates' court which is not a youth court may hear an information against a child or young person if he is charged –

    (a) with aiding, abetting, causing, procuring, allowing or permitting an offence with which a person who has attained the age of eighteen is charged at the same time; or

    (b) with an offence arising out of circumstances which are the same as or connected with those giving rise to an offence with which a person who has attained the age of eighteen is charged at the same time.

Children and Young Persons Act 1969

Restrictions on criminal proceedings for offences by young persons

5 (1)–(7) [*Repealed.*]

    (8) It shall be the duty of a person who decides to lay an information in respect of an offence in a case where he has reason to believe that the alleged offender is a young person to give notice of the decision to the appropriate local authority unless he is himself that authority.

    (9) In this section –

'the appropriate local authority', in relation to a young person, means the local authority for the area in which it appears to the informant in question that the young person resides or, if the young person appears to the informant not to reside in the area of a local authority, the local authority in whose area it is alleged that the relevant offence or one of the relevant offences was committed;

[*Other definitions repealed.*]

Alterations in treatment of young offenders, etc

7 (1)–(4) [*Repealed.*]

(5) An order sending a person to an approved school shall not be made after such day as the Secretary of State may by order specify for the purposes of this subsection.

(6) Sections 54 and 57 of the Act of 1933 (which among other things enable a child or young person found guilty of an offence to be sent to a remand home or committed to the care of a fit person) shall cease to have effect.

(7) Subject to the enactments requiring cases to be remitted to youth courts and to section 53(1) of the Act of 1933 (which provides for detention for certain grave crimes), where a child or a young person is found guilty of any offence by or before any court, that court or the court to which his case is remitted shall have power –

(a) [*Repealed*];

(b) to make a supervision order in respect of him; or

(c) [*Repealed*];

and, if it makes such an order as is mentioned in this subsection while another such order made by any court is in force in respect of the child or young person, shall also have power to discharge the earlier order.

(7A)–(7C) [*Repealed.*]

(8) Without prejudice to the power to remit any case to a youth court which is conferred on a magistrates' court other than a youth court by section 56(1) of the Act of 1933, in a case where such a magistrates' court finds a child or young person guilty of an offence it shall be the duty of the court to exercise that power unless the case falls within subsection (8A) or (8B) of this section.

(8A) The case falls within this subsection if the court would, were it not to so remit the case, be required by section 1(2) of the Youth Justice and Criminal Evidence Act 1999 to refer him to a youth offender panel (in which event the court may, but need not, so remit the case).

(8B) The case falls within this subsection if the court would not be so required to refer him to such a panel in the event of its not so remitting the case.

(9) The reference in subsection (8) above to a person's parent shall be construed in accordance with section 1 of the Family Law Reform Act 1987 (and not in accordance with section 70(1A) of this Act).

Supervision orders

11   Any provision of this Act authorising a court to make a supervision order in respect of any person shall be construed as authorising the court to make an order placing him under the supervision of –

(a) a local authority designated by the order;

(b) a probation officer; or

(c) a member of a youth offending team,

and in this Act 'supervision order' shall be construed accordingly and 'supervised person' and 'supervisor', in relation to a supervision order, mean respectively the person placed or to be placed under supervision by the order and the person under whose supervision he is placed or to be placed by the order.

Power to include requirements in supervision orders

12 (1) A supervision order may require the supervised person to reside with an individual named in the order who agrees to the requirement, but a requirement imposed by a supervision order in pursuance of this subsection shall be subject to any such requirement of the order as is authorised by the following provisions of this section or by section 12A, 12B or 12C below.

(2) Subject to section 19(12) of this Act, a supervision order may require the supervised person to comply with any directions given from time to time by the supervisor and requiring him to do all or any of the following things –

(a) to live at a place or places specified in the directions for a period or periods so specified;

(b) to present himself to a person or persons specified in the directions at a place or places and on a day or days so specified;

(c) to participate in activities specified in the directions on a day or days so specified;

but it shall be for the supervisor to decide whether and to what extent he exercises any power to give directions conferred on him by virtue of this subsection and to decide the form of any directions; and a requirement imposed by a supervision order in pursuance of this subsection shall be subject to any such requirement of the order as is authorised by subsection 12B(1) of this Act.

(3) The total number of days in respect of which a supervised person may be required to comply with directions given by virtue of paragraph (a), (b) or (c) of subsection (2) above in pursuance of a supervision order shall not exceed 90 or such less number, if any, as the order may specify for the purposes of this subsection; and for the purpose of calculating the total number of days in respect of which such directions may be given the supervisor shall be entitled to disregard any day in respect of which directions were previously given in pursuance of the order and on which the directions were not complied with.

(4) Directions given by the supervisor by virtue of subsection (2)(b) or (c) above shall, as far as practicable, be such as to avoid –

(a) any conflict with the offender's religious beliefs or with the requirements of any other community order (within the meaning of Part I of the Criminal Justice Act 1991) to which he may be subject; and

(b) any interference with the times, if any, at which he normally works or attends school or any other educational establishment.

Young offenders

12A(1) This subsection applies to any supervision order made under section 7(7) of this Act unless it requires the supervised person to comply with directions given by the supervisor under section 12(2) of this Act.

(2) [*Repealed.*]

(3) Subject to the following provisions of this section and to section 19(13) of this Act, a supervision order to which subsection (1) of this section applies may require a supervised person –

(a) to do anything that by virtue of section 12(2) of this Act a supervisor has power, or would but for section 19(12) of this Act have power, to direct a supervised person to do;

(aa) to make reparation specified in the order to a person or persons so specified or to the community at large;

(b) to remain for specified periods between 6 pm and 6 am –
   (i) at a place specified in the order; or
   (ii) at one of several places so specified;

(c) to refrain from participating in activities specified in the order –
   (i) on a specified day or days during the period for which the supervision order is in force; or
   (ii) during the whole of that period or a specified portion of it.

(4) Any power to include a requirement in a supervision order which is exercisable in relation to a person by virtue of this section or the following provisions of this Act may be exercised in relation to him whether or not any other such power is exercised.

(5) The total number of days in respect of which a supervised person may be subject to requirements imposed by virtue of subsection (3)(a), (aa) or (b) above shall not exceed 90.

(6) The court may not include requirements under subsection (3) above in a supervision order unless –

(a) it has first consulted the supervisor as to –
   (i) the offender's circumstances; and
   (ii) the feasibility of securing compliance with the requirements, and is satisfied, having regard to the supervisor's report, that it is feasible to secure compliance with them;

(b) having regard to the circumstances of the case, it considers the requirements necessary for securing the good conduct of the supervised person or for preventing a repetition by him of the same offence or the commission of other offences; and

(c) if the supervised person is under the age of sixteen, it has obtained and considered information about his family circumstances and the likely effect of the requirements on those circumstances.

(7) The court shall not include in such an order by virtue of subsection (3) above –

(a) any requirement that would involve the co-operation of a person other than the supervisor and the supervised person unless that other person consents to its inclusion; or

(aa) any requirement to make reparation to any person unless that person –

    (i) is identified by the court as a victim of the offence or a person otherwise affected by it; and

    (ii) consents to the inclusion of the requirement; or

(b) any requirement requiring the supervised person to reside with a specified individual; or

(c) any such requirement as is mentioned in section 12B(1) of this Act.

(8) The place, or one of the places, specified in a requirement under subsection (3)(b) above ('a night restriction') shall be the place where the supervised person lives.

(9) A night restriction shall not require the supervised person to remain at a place for longer than 10 hours on any one night.

(10) A night restriction shall not be imposed in respect of any day which falls outside the period of three months beginning with the date when the supervision order is made.

(11) A night restriction shall not be imposed in respect of more than 30 days in all.

(12) A supervised person who is required by a night restriction to remain at a place may leave it if he is accompanied –

(a) by his parent or guardian;

(b) by his supervisor; or

(c) by some other person specified in the supervision order.

(13) A night restriction imposed in respect of a period of time beginning in the evening and ending in the morning shall be treated as imposed only in respect of the day upon which the period begins.

(14) In this section 'make reparation' means make reparation for the offence otherwise than by the payment of compensation.

Requirement for young offender to live in local authority accommodation

12AA (1) Where the conditions mentioned in subsection (6) of this section are satisfied, a supervision order may impose a requirement ('a residence requirement') that a child or young person shall live for a specified period in local authority accommodation.

(2) A residence requirement shall designate the local authority who are to receive the child or young person and that authority shall be the authority in whose area the child or young person resides.

(3) The court shall not impose a residence requirement without first consulting the designated authority.

(4) A residence requirement may stipulate that the child or young person shall not live with a named person.

(5) The maximum period which may be specified in a residence requirement is six months.

(6) The conditions are that –
- (a) a supervision order has previously been made in respect of the child or young person;
- (b) that order imposed –
  - (i) a requirement under section 12, 12A or 12C of this Act; or
  - (ii) a residence requirement;
- (c) he fails to comply with that requirement, or is found guilty of an offence committed while that order was in force; and
- (d) the court is satisfied that –
  - (i) the failure to comply with the requirement, or the behaviour which constituted the offence, was due to a significant extent to the circumstances in which he was living; and
  - (ii) the imposition of a residence requirement will assist in his rehabilitation;

except that sub-paragraph (i) of paragraph (d) of this subsection does not apply where the condition in paragraph (b)(ii) is satisfied.

(7)–(8) [*Repealed.*]

(9) A court shall not include a residence requirement in respect of a child or young person who is not legally represented at the relevant time in that court unless –
- (a) he was granted a right to representation funded by the Legal Services Commission as part of the Criminal Defence Service for the purposes of those proceedings but the right was withdrawn because of his conduct; or
- (b) he has been informed of his right to apply for such representation for the purpose of the proceedings and has had the opportunity to do so, but nevertheless refused or failed to apply.

(10) In subsection (9) of this section –
- (a) 'the relevant time' means the time when the court is considering whether or not to impose the requirement; and
- (b) 'the proceedings' means –
  - (i) the whole proceedings; or
  - (ii) the part of the proceedings relating to the imposition of the requirement.

(11) A supervision order imposing a residence requirement may also impose any of the requirements mentioned in sections 12, 12A, 12B or 12C of this Act.

(12) [*Repealed.*]

Requirements as to mental treatment

12B (1) Where a court which proposes to make a supervision order is satisfied, on the evidence of a registered medical practitioner approved for the purposes of section 12 of the Mental Health Act 1983, that the mental condition of a supervised person is such as requires and may be susceptible to treatment but is not such as to warrant the making of a hospital order or guardianship order within the meaning of that Act, the court may include in the supervision order a requirement that the supervised person shall, for a period specified in the order, submit to treatment of one of the following descriptions so specified, that is to say –

(a) treatment by or under the direction of a registered medical practitioner specified in the order;

(aa) treatment by or under the direction of a chartered psychologist specified in the order;

(b) treatment as a non-resident patient at an institution or place specified in the order; or

(c) treatment as a resident patient in a hospital or mental nursing home within the meaning of the Mental Health Act 1983, but not a special hospital within the meaning of that Act.

(1A) In subsection (1) of this section 'registered medical practitioner' means a fully registered person within the meaning of the Medical Act 1983 and 'chartered psychologist' means a person for the time being listed in the British Psychological Society's Register of Chartered Psychologists.

(2) A requirement shall not be included in a supervision order in pursuance of subsection (1) above –

(a) in any case, unless the court is satisfied that arrangements have been or can be made for the treatment in question and, in the case of treatment as a resident patient, for the reception of the patient;

(b) in the case of an order made or to be made in respect of a person who has attained the age of 14, unless he consents to its inclusion;

and a requirement so included shall not in any case continue in force after the supervised person becomes 18.

(3) Subsections (2) and (3) of section 54 of the Mental Health Act 1983 shall have effect with respect to proof for the purposes of subsection (1) above of a supervised person's mental condition as they have effect with respect to proof of an offender's mental condition for the purposes of section 37(2)(a) of that Act.

Requirements as to education

12C(1) Subject to subsection (3) below, a supervision order to which section 12A(1) of this Act applies may require a supervised person, if he is of compulsory school age, to comply, for as long as he is of that age and the order remains in force, with such arrangements for his education as may from time to time be made by his parent, being arrangements for the time being approved by the local education authority.

(2) The court shall not include such a requirement in a supervision order unless it has consulted the local education authority with regard to its proposal to include the requirement and is satisfied that in the view of the local education authority arrangements exist for the child or young person to whom the supervision order will relate to receive efficient full-time education suitable to his age, ability and aptitude and to any special educational need he may have.

(3) Expressions used in subsection (1) above and in the Education Act 1996 have the same meaning there as in that Act.

(4) The court may not include a requirement under subsection (1) above unless

it has first consulted the supervisor as to the offender's circumstances and, having regard to the circumstances of the case, it considers the requirement necessary for securing the good conduct of the supervised person or for preventing a repetition by him of the same offence or the commission of other offences.

12D   [*Repealed.*]

Selection of supervisor

13 (1) A court shall not designate a local authority as the supervisor by a provision of a supervision order unless the authority agree or it appears to the court that the supervised person resides or will reside in the area of the authority.

(2) [*Repealed.*]

(3) Where a provision of a supervision order places a person under the supervision of a probation officer, the supervisor shall be a probation officer appointed for or assigned to the petty sessions area named in the order in pursuance of section 18(2)(a) of this Act and selected under arrangements made under section 4(1)(d) of the Probation Service Act 1993 (arrangements made by Probation Committee).

(4) Where a provision of a supervision order places a person under the supervision of a member of a youth offending team, the supervisor shall be a member of a team established by the local authority within whose area it appears to the court that the supervised person resides or will reside.

Duty of supervisor

14   While a supervision order is in force it shall be the duty of the supervisor to advise, assist and befriend the supervised person.

Variation and discharge of supervision orders

15 (1) If while a supervision order is in force in respect of a supervised person it appears to a relevant court, on the application of the supervisor or the supervised person, that it is appropriate to make an order under this subsection, the court may make an order discharging the supervision order or varying it –

(a) by cancelling any requirement included in it in pursuance of section 12, 12A, 12AA, 12B, 12C or 18(2)(b) of this Act; or

(b) by inserting in it (either in addition to or in substitution for any of its provisions) any provision which could have been included in the order if the court had then had power to make it and were exercising the power.

(2) The powers of variation conferred by subsection (1) above do not include power –

(a) to insert in the supervision order, after the expiration of three months beginning with the date when the order was originally made, a requirement in pursuance of section 12B(1) of this Act, unless it is in substitution for such a requirement already included in the order; or

(b) to insert in the supervision order a requirement in pursuance of section 12A(3)(b) of this Act in respect of any day which falls outside the period of three months beginning with the date when the order was originally made.

(3) If while a supervision order made under section 7(7) of this Act is in force in respect of a person it is proved to the satisfaction of a relevant court, on the application of the supervisor, that the supervised person has failed to comply with any requirement included in the supervision order in pursuance of section 12, 12A, 12AA, 12C or 18(2)(b) of this Act, the court –

  (a) whether or not it also makes an order under subsection (1) above, may order him to pay a fine of an amount not exceeding £1,000, or make in respect of him –

    (i) subject to section 16A(1) of this Act, an order under section 17 of the Criminal Justice Act 1982 (attendance centre orders) or;

    (ii) subject to section 16B of this Act, an order under section 12 of the Criminal Justice Act 1991 (curfew orders);

  (b) if the supervision order was made by a magistrates' court, may discharge the order and deal with him, for the offence in respect of which the order was made, in any manner in which he could have been dealt with for that offence by the court which made the order if the order had not been made; or

  (c) if the order was made by the Crown Court, may commit him in custody or release him on bail until he can be brought or appear before the Crown Court.

(4) Where a court deals with a supervised person under subsection (3)(c) above, it shall send to the Crown Court a certificate signed by a justice of the peace giving –

  (a) particulars of the supervised person's failure to comply with the requirement in question; and

  (b) such other particulars of the case as may be desirable;

and a certificate purporting to be so signed shall be admissible as evidence of the failure before the Crown Court.

(5) Where –

  (a) by virtue of subsection (3)(c) above the supervised person is brought or appears before the Crown Court; and

  (b) it is proved to the satisfaction of the court that he has failed to comply with the requirement in question,

that court may deal with him, for the offence in respect of which the order was made, in any manner in which it could have dealt with him for that offence if it had not made the order.

(6) Where the Crown Court deals with a supervised person under subsection (5) above, it shall discharge the supervision order if it is still in force.

(7) A fine imposed under subsection (3) or (5) above shall be deemed for the purposes of any enactment, to be a sum adjudged to be paid by a conviction.

(8) In dealing with a supervised person under subsection (3) or (5) above, the court shall take into account the extent to which that person has complied with the requirements of the supervision order.

(8A) Where a supervision order has been made on appeal, for the purposes of subsection (3) above it shall be deemed –

  (a) if it was made on an appeal brought from a magistrates' court, to have been made by that magistrates' court;

(b) if it was made on an appeal brought from the Crown Court or from the criminal division of the Court of Appeal, to have been made by the Crown Court;

and, in relation to a supervision order made on appeal, subsection (3)(b) above shall have effect as if the words 'if the order had not been made' were omitted and subsection (5) above shall have effect as if the words 'if it had not made the order' were omitted.

(9) If a medical practitioner by whom or under whose direction a supervised person is being treated for his mental condition in pursuance of a requirement included in a supervision order by virtue of section 12B(1) of this Act is unwilling to continue to treat or direct the treatment of the supervised person or is of opinion –

(a) that the treatment should be continued beyond the period specified in that behalf in the order; or

(b) that the supervised person needs different treatment; or

(c) that he is not susceptible to treatment; or

(d) that he does not require further treatment,

the practitioner shall make a report in writing to that effect to the supervisor.

(10) On receiving a report under subsection (9) above, the supervisor shall refer it to a relevant court and on such a reference, the court may make an order cancelling or varying the requirement.

(11) In this section 'relevant court' means –

(a) in the case of a supervised person who has not attained the age of eighteen, a youth court;

(b) in the case of a supervised person who has attained that age, a magistrates' court other than a youth court.

(12) The provisions of this section shall have effect subject to the provisions of section 16 of this Act.

Provisions supplementary to s15

16 (1) Where the supervisor makes an application or reference under the preceding section to a court he may bring the supervised person before the court, and subject to subsection (5) of this section a court shall not make an order under that section unless the supervised person is present before the court.

(2) Without prejudice to any power to issue a summons or warrant apart from this subsection a justice may issue a summons or warrant for the purposes of securing the attendance of a supervised person before the court to which any application or reference in respect of him is made under the preceding section; but subsections (3) and (4) of section 55 of the Magistrates' Courts Act 1980 (which among other things restrict the circumstances in which a warrant may be issued) shall apply with the necessary modifications to a warrant under this subsection as they apply to a warrant under that section and as if in subsection (3) after the word 'summons' there were inserted the words 'cannot be served or'.

(3) Where the supervised person is arrested in pursuance of a warrant issued by virtue of the preceding subsection and cannot be brought immediately

before the court referred to in that subsection, the person in whose custody he is –

(a) may make arrangements for his detention in a place of safety for a period of not more than seventy-two hours from the time of the arrest (and it shall be lawful for him to be detained in pursuance of the arrangements); and

(b) shall within that period, unless within it the supervised person is brought before the court aforesaid, bring him before a justice;

(3A) Where a supervised person is brought before a justice under subsection (3) of this section, the justice may –

(a) direct that he be released forthwith; or

(b) subject to subsection (4A) of this section, remand him to local authority accommodation.

[(3B) and (3C) *Repealed.*]

(4) Subject to subsection (4A) of this section, where an application is made to a youth court under section 15(1) of this Act, the court may remand (or further remand) the supervised person to local authority accommodation if –

(a) a warrant has been issued under subsection (2) of this section for the purpose of securing the attendance of the supervised person before the court; or

(b) the court considers that remanding (or further remanding) him will enable information to be obtained which is likely to assist the court in deciding whether and, if so, how to exercise its powers under section 15(1).

(4A) Where a supervised person has attained the age of eighteen at the time when he is brought before a justice under subsection (3) of this section, or has attained that age at a time when (apart from this subsection) a youth court could exercise its powers under subsection (4) of this section in respect of him, he shall not be remanded to local authority accommodation but may instead be remanded–

(a) to a remand centre, if the justice or youth court has been notified that such a centre is available for the reception of persons under this subsection; or

(b) to a prison, if the justice or youth court has not been so notified.

(4B) A court or justice remanding a person to local authority accommodation under this section shall designate, as the authority who are to receive him, the authority named in the supervision order.

(5) A court may make an order under the preceding section in the absence of the supervised person if the effect of the order is one or more of the following, that is to say –

(a) discharging the supervision order;

(b) cancelling a provision included in the supervision order in pursuance of section 12, 12A, 12AA, 12B or 12C or section 18(2)(b) of this Act;

(c) reducing the duration of the supervision order or any provision included in it in pursuance of the said section 12, 12A, 12AA, 12B or 12C;

(d) altering in the supervision order the name of any area;

(e) changing the supervisor.

(6) A youth court shall not –

   (a) exercise its powers under subsection (1) of the preceding section to make an order discharging a supervision order or inserting in it a requirement authorised by section 12, 12A, 12AA, 12B or 12C of this Act or varying or cancelling such a requirement except in a case where the court is satisfied that the supervised person either is unlikely to receive the care or control he needs unless the court makes the order or is likely to receive it notwithstanding the order;

   (b) exercise its powers to make an order under subsection (10) of the preceding section except in such a case as is mentioned in paragraph (a) of this subsection;

   (c) exercise its powers under the said subsection (1) to make an order inserting a requirement authorised by section 12B(1) of this Act in a supervision order which does not already contain such a requirement unless the court is satisfied as mentioned in the said section 12B(1) on such evidence as is there mentioned.

(7) Where the supervised person has attained the age of fourteen, then except with his consent a court shall not make an order under the preceding section containing provisions which insert in the supervision order a requirement authorised by section 12B(1) of this Act or which alter such a requirement already included in the supervision order otherwise than by removing it or reducing its duration.

(8) The supervised person may appeal to the Crown Court against –

   (a) any order made under the preceding section by a relevant court (within the meaning of that section), except an order made or which could have been made in the absence of the supervised person and an order containing only provisions to which he consented in pursuance of the preceding subsection;

   (b) the dismissal of an application under that section to discharge a supervision order.

(9) Where an application under the preceding section for the discharge of a supervision order is dismissed, no further application for its discharge shall be made under that section by any person during the period of three months beginning with the date of the dismissal except with the consent of a court having jurisdiction to entertain such an application.

(10) [*Repealed.*]

(11) In this and the preceding section references to a youth court or any other magistrates' court, in relation to a supervision order, are references to such a court acting for the petty sessions area for the time being named in the order in pursuance of section 18(2)(a) of this Act; and if while an application to a youth court in pursuance of the preceding section is pending the supervised person to whom it relates attains the age of eighteen, the court shall deal with the application as if he had not attained the age in question.

Application of sections 17 to 19 of Criminal Justice Act 1982

16A (1) The provisions of section 17 of the Criminal Justice Act 1982 (attendance centre orders) shall apply for the purposes of section 15(3)(a) of this Act but as if –

(a) in subsection (1), for the words from 'has power' to 'probation order' there were substituted the words 'considers it appropriate to make an attendance centre order in respect of any person in pursuance of section 15(3)(a) of the Children and Young Persons Act 1969';

(b) for references to an offender there were substituted references to a supervised person; and

(c) subsection (13) were omitted.

(2) Sections 18 and 19 of the Criminal Justice Act 1982 (discharge and variation of attendance centre order and breach of attendance centre orders or attendance centre rules) shall also apply for the purposes of section 15(3)(a) of this Act but as if –

(a) for the references to an offender there were substituted references to the person in respect of whom the attendance centre order has been made; and

(b) there were omitted –

(i) from subsection (4A) of section 18 and subsections (3) and (5) of section 19, the words, 'for the offence in respect of which the order was made,' and 'for that offence'; and

(ii) from subsection (4B) of section 18 and subsection (6) of section 19, the words 'for an offence'.

Application of section 12 of Criminal Justice Act 1991, etc

16B (1) The provisions of section 12 of the Criminal Justice Act 1991 (curfew orders shall apply for the purposes of section 15(3)(a) of this Act but as if –

(a) in subsection (1), for the words from the beginning to 'before which he is convicted' there were substituted the words 'Where a court considers it appropriate to make curfew order in respect of any person in pursuance of section 15(3)(a) of the Children and Young Persons Act 1969, the court'; and

(b) in subsection (8), for the words 'on conviction' there were substituted the words 'on the date on which his failure to comply with a requirement included in the supervision order was proved to the court'.

(2) Schedule 2 to the Criminal Justice Act 1991 (enforcement, etc of community orders), so far as relating to curfew orders, shall also apply for the purposes of that section but as if –

(a) the power conferred on the magistrates' court by each of paragraphs 3(1)(d) and 7(2)(b) to deal with the offender for the offence in respect of which the order was made were a power to deal with the offender, for his failure to comply with a requirement included in the supervision order in any manner in which the relevant court could deal with him for that failure to comply if it had just been proved to the satisfaction of the court;

(b) the power conferred on the Crown Court by paragraph 4(1)(d) to deal with the offender for the offence in respect of which the order was made were a power to deal with the offender, for his failure to comply with such a requirement, in any manner in which that court could deal with him for that failure to comply if it had just been proved to its satisfaction;

(c) the reference in paragraph 7(1)(b) to the offence in respect of which the order was made were a reference to the failure to comply in respect of which the curfew order was made; and

(d) the power conferred on the Crown Court by paragraph 8(2)(b) to deal with the offender for the offence in respect of which the order was made were a power to deal with the offender, for his failure to comply with a requirement included in the supervision order in any manner in which the relevant court (if that order was made by a magistrates' court) or the Crown Court (if that order was made by the Crown Court) could deal with him for that failure to comply if it had just been proved to the satisfaction of that court.

(3) For the purposes of the provisions mentioned in subsection (2)(a) and (d) above, applied by that subsection, if the supervision order is no longer in force the relevant court's powers shall be determined on the assumption that it is still in force.

(4) In this section 'relevant court' has the same meaning as in section 15 above.

Termination of supervision

17   A supervision order shall, unless it has previously been discharged, cease to have effect in any case, on the expiration of the period of three years, or such shorter period as may be specified in the order, beginning with the date on which the order was originally made.

Supplementary provisions relating to supervision orders

18 (1) A court shall not make a supervision order unless it is satisfied that the supervised person resides or will reside in the area of a local authority; and a court shall be entitled to be satisfied that the supervised person will so reside if he is to be required to so reside by a provision to be included in the order in pursuance of section 12(1) of this Act.

(2) A supervision order –

(a) shall name the area of the local authority and the petty sessions area in which it appears to the court making the order, or to the court varying any provision included in the order in pursuance of this paragraph, that the supervised person resides or will reside; and

(b) may contain such prescribed provisions as the court aforesaid considers appropriate for facilitating the performance by the supervisor of his functions under section 14 of this Act, including any prescribed provisions for requiring visits to be made by the supervised person to the supervisor,

and in paragraph (b) of this subsection 'prescribed' means prescribed by rules under section 144 of the Magistrates' Courts Act 1980.

(3) A court which makes a supervision order or an order varying or discharging a supervision order shall forthwith send a copy of its order –

(a) to the supervised person and, if the supervised person is a child, to his parent or guardian; and

(b) to the supervisor and any person who has ceased to be the supervisor by virtue of the order; and

(c) to any local authority who is not entitled by virtue of the preceding paragraph to such a copy and whose area is named in the supervision order in pursuance of the preceding subsection or has ceased to be so named by virtue of the court's order; and

(d) where the supervised person is required by the order, or was required by the supervision order before it was varied or discharged, to reside with an individual or to undergo treatment by or under the direction of an individual or at any place, to the individual or the person in charge of that place; and

(e) where a petty sessions area named in the order or discharged order in pursuance of subsection (2) of this section is not that for which the court acts, to the justices' chief executive for the petty sessions area so named;

and, in a case falling within paragraph (e) of this subsection, shall also send to the justices' chief executive in question such documents and information relating to the case as the court considers likely to be of assistance to them.

(4) Where a supervision order –

(a) requires compliance with directions given by virtue of section 12(2) of this Act; or

(b) includes by virtue of section 12A(3) of this Act a requirement which involves the use of facilities for the time being specified in a scheme in force under section 19 of this Act for an area in which the supervised person resides or will reside,

any expenditure incurred by the supervisor for the purposes of the directions or requirements shall be defrayed by the local authority whose area is named in the order in pursuance of subsection (2) of this section.

Remands and committals to local authority accommodation

[*Consolidated version of section 23 as amended by Crime and Disorder Act 1998 s97–applicable to boys aged 12 to 14 and girls aged 12 to 16.*]

23 (1) Where –

(a) a court remands a child or young person charged with or convicted of one or more offences, transfers proceedings against him for trial or commits him for sentence; and

(b) he is not released on bail,

then, unless he is declared by the court, after consultation with a probation officer or a social worker of a local authority social services department, to be a person to whom subsection (5) below applies he shall be remanded or committed to local authority accommodation; and in the following provisions of this section, any reference (however expressed) to a remand shall be construed as including a reference to a committal.

(2) A court remanding a person to local authority accommodation shall designate the local authority who are to receive him; and that authority shall be –

(a) in the case of a person who is being looked after by a local authority, that authority; and

(b) in any other case, the local authority in whose area it appears to the court that he resides or the offence or one of the offences was committed.

(3) Where a person is remanded to local authority accommodation, it shall be lawful for any person acting on behalf of the designated authority to detain him.

(4) Subject to subsections (5) and (5A) below, a court remanding a person to local authority accommodation may, after consultation with the designated authority, require that authority to comply with a security requirement, that is to say, a requirement that the person in question be placed and kept in secure accommodation.

(5) A court shall not impose a security requirement except in respect of a child who has attained the age of twelve, or a young person, who (in either case) is of a prescribed description, but only if –

(a) he is charged with or has been convicted of a violent or sexual offence, or an offence punishable in the case of an adult with imprisonment for a term of fourteen years or more; or

(b) he has a recent history of absconding while remanded to local authority accommodation, and is charged with or has been convicted of an imprisonable offence alleged or found to have been committed while he was so remanded,

and (in either case) the court is of opinion that only remanding him to a remand centre or prison would be adequate to protect the public from serious harm from him.

(5A) A court shall not impose a security requirement in respect of a child or young person who is not legally represented in the court unless –

(a) he was granted a right to representation funds by the Legal Services Commission as part of the Criminal Defence Service but the right was withdrawn because of his conduct; or

(b) having been informed of his right to apply for such representation and had the opportunity to do so, he refused or failed to apply.

(6) Where a court declares a person to be one to whom subsection (5) above applies, it shall be its duty –

(a) to state in open court that it is of such opinion as is mentioned in that subsection; and

(b) to explain to him in open court and in ordinary language why it is of that opinion;

and a magistrates' court shall cause a reason stated by it under paragraph (b) above to be specified in the warrant of commitment and to be entered in the register.

(7) A court remanding a person to local authority accommodation may, after consultation with the designated authority, require that person to comply with any such conditions as could be imposed under section 3(6) of the Bail Act 1976 if he were then being granted bail.

(8) Where a court imposes on a person any such conditions as are mentioned in subsection (7) above, it shall be its duty to explain to him in open court and

in ordinary language why it is imposing those conditions; and a magistrates' court shall cause a reason stated by it under this subsection to be specified in the warrant of commitment and to be entered in the register.

(9) A court remanding a person to local authority accommodation may, after consultation with the designated authority, impose on that authority requirements –

(a) for securing compliance with any conditions imposed on that person under subsection (7) above; or

(b) stipulating that he shall not be placed with a named person.

(9A) Where a person is remanded to local authority accommodation, a relevant court may, on the application of the designated authority, declare him to be a person to whom subsection (5) above applies; and on its doing so, he shall cease to be remanded to local authority accommodation and subsection (4) above shall apply.

(10) Where a person is remanded to local authority accommodation, a relevant court –

(a) may, on the application of the designated authority, impose on that person any such conditions as could be imposed under subsection (7) above if the court were then remanding him to such accommodation; and

(b) where it does so, may impose on that authority any requirements for securing compliance with the conditions so imposed.

(11) Where a person is remanded to local authority accommodation, a relevant court may, on the application of the designated authority or that person, vary or revoke any conditions or requirements imposed under subsection (7), (9) or (10) above.

(12) In this section –

'court' and 'magistrates' court' include a justice;

'imprisonable offence' means an offence punishable in the case of an adult with imprisonment;

'prescribed description' means a description prescribed by reference to age or sex or both by an order of the Secretary of State;

'relevant court', in relation to a person remanded to local authority accommodation, means the court by which he was so remanded, or any magistrates' court having jurisdiction in the place where he is for the time being;

'secure accommodation' means accommodation which is provided in a community home, a voluntary home or a registered children's home for the purpose of restricting liberty, and is approved for that purpose by the Secretary of State;

'sexual offence' and 'violent offence' have the same meanings as in Part I of the Criminal Justice Act 1991;

'young person' means a person who has attained the age of fourteen years and is under the age of seventeen years.

but, for the purposes of the definition of 'secure accommodation', 'local authority accommodation' includes any accommodation falling within section 61(2) of the Criminal Justice Act 1991.

(13) In this section –

(a) any reference to a person who is being looked after by a local authority shall be construed in accordance with section 22 of the Children Act 1989;

(b) any reference to consultation shall be construed as a reference to such consultation (if any) as is reasonably practicable in all the circumstances of the case; and

(c) any reference, in relation to a person charged with or convicted of a violent or sexual offence, to protecting the public from serious harm from him shall be construed as a reference to protecting members of the public from death or serious personal injury, whether physical or psychological, occasioned by further such offences committed by him.

(14) This section has effect subject to –

(a) [*Repealed.*]

(b) section 128(7) of that Act (remands to the custody of a constable for periods of not more than three days),

but section 128(7) shall have effect in relation to a child or young person as if for the reference to three clear days there were substituted a reference to twenty-four hours.

Remands and committals: alternative provision for 15- or 16-year-old boys

[*Consolidated version of section 23 as amended by Crime and Disorder Act 1998 s98–applicable to boys aged 15 and 16 only.*]

23 (1) Where –

(a) a court remands a child or young person charged with or convicted of one or more offences, transfers proceedings against him for trial or commits him for sentence; and

(b) he is not released on bail,

then unless he is declared by the court, after consultation with a probation officer or a social worker of a local authority social services department, to be a person to whom subsection (5) below applies, then unless he is remanded to a remand centre or a prison in pursuance of subsection (4)(b) or (c) below, he shall be remanded or committed to local authority accommodation; and in the following provisions of this section, any reference (however expressed) to a remand shall be construed as including a reference to a committal.

(2) A court remanding a person to local authority accommodation shall designate the local authority who are to receive him; and that authority shall be –

(a) in the case of a person who is being looked after by a local authority, that authority;

(b) in any other case, the local authority in whose area it appears to the court that he resides or the offence or one of the offences was committed.

(3) Where a person is remanded to local authority accommodation, it shall be lawful for any person acting on behalf of the designated authority to detain him.

(4) Where a court, after consultation with a probation officer, a social worker

of a local authority social services department or a member of a youth offending team, declares a person to be one to whom subsection (5) below applies –

  (a) it shall remand him to local authority accommodation and require him to be placed and kept in secure accommodation, if–

   (i) it also, after such consultation, declares him to be a person to whom subsection (5A) below applies; and

   (ii) it has been notified that secure accommodation is available for him;

  (b) it shall remand him to a remand centre, if paragraph (a) above does not apply and it has been notified that such a centre is available for the reception from the court of persons to whom subsection (5) below applies; and

  (c) it shall remand him to a prison, if neither paragraph (a) nor paragraph (b) above applies.

(4A) A court shall not declare a person who is not legally represented in the court to be a person to whom subsection (5) below applies unless –

  (a) he was granted a right to representation funded by the Legal Services Commission as part of the Criminal Defence Service but the right was withdrawn because of his conduct; or

  (b) having been informed of his right to apply for such representation and had the opportunity to do so, he refused or failed to apply.

 (5) This subsection applies to a person who –

  (a) is charged with or has been convicted of a violent or sexual offence, or an offence punishable in the case of an adult with imprisonment for a term of fourteen years or more; or

  (b) has a recent history of absconding while remanded to local authority accommodation, and is charged with or has been convicted of an imprisonable offence alleged or found to have been committed while he was so remanded,

 if (in either case) the court is of opinion that only remanding him to a remand centre or prison, or to local authority accommodation with a requirement that he be placed and kept in secure accommodation, would be adequate to protect the public from serious harm from him.

(5A) This subsection applies to a person if the court is of opinion that, by reason of his physical or emotional immaturity or a propensity of his to harm himself, it would be undesirable for him to be remanded to a remand centre or a prison.

 (6) Where a court declares a person to be one to whom subsection (5) above applies, it shall be its duty–

  (a) to state in open court that it is of such opinion as is mentioned in that subsection; and

  (b) to explain to him in open court and in ordinary language why it is of that opinion;

 and a magistrates' court shall cause a reason stated by it under paragraph (b) above to be specified in the warrant of commitment and to be entered in the register.

 (7) A court remanding a person to local authority accommodation may, after

consultation with the designated authority, require that person to comply with any such conditions as could be imposed under section 3(6) of the Bail Act 1976 if he were then being granted bail.

(8) Where a court imposes on a person any such conditions as are mentioned in subsection (7) above, it shall be its duty to explain to him in open court and in ordinary language why it is imposing those conditions; and a magistrates' court shall cause a reason stated by it under this subsection to be specified in the warrant of commitment and to be entered in the register.

(9) A court remanding a person to local authority accommodation may, after consultation with the designated authority, impose of that authority requirements–

(a) for securing compliance with any conditions imposed on that person under subsection (7) above; or

(b) stipulating that he shall not be placed with a named person.

(9A) Where a person is remanded to local authority without the imposition of a security requirement, a relevant court may, on the application of the designated authority, declare him to be a person to whom subsection (5) above applies; and on its doing so, subsection (4) above shall apply.

(10) Where a person is remanded to local authority accommodation, a relevant court –

(a) may, on the application of the designated authority, impose on that person any such conditions as could be imposed under subsection (7) above if the court were then remanding him to such accommodation; and

(b) where it does so, may impose on that authority any requirements for securing compliance with the conditions so imposed.

(11) Where a person is remanded to local authority accommodation, a relevant court may, on the application of the designated authority or that person, vary or revoke any conditions or requirements imposed under subsection (7), (9) or (10) above.

(12) In this section –

'court' and 'magistrates' court' include a justice;

'imprisonable offence' means an offence punishable in the case of an adult with imprisonment;

'prescribed description' means a description prescribed by reference to age or sex or both by an order of the Secretary of State;

'relevant court', in relation to a person remanded to local authority accommodation, means the court by which he was so remanded, or any magistrates' court having jurisdiction in the place where he is for the time being;

'secure accommodation' means accommodation which is provided in a community home, a voluntary home or a registered children's home for the purpose of restricting liberty, and is approved for that purpose by the Secretary of State;

'sexual offence' and 'violent offence' have the same meanings as in Part I of the Criminal Justice Act 1991;

'young person' means a person who has attained the age of fourteen years and is under the age of seventeen years;

but, for the purposes of the definition of 'secure accommodation', 'local authority accommodation' includes any accommodation falling within section 61(2) of the Criminal Justice Act 1991.

Liability to arrest for breaking conditions of remand

23A (1) A person who has been remanded or committed to local authority accommodation and in respect of whom conditions under subsection (7) or (10) of section 23 of this Act have been imposed may be arrested without warrant by a constable if the constable has reasonable grounds for suspecting that that person has broken any of those conditions.

(2) A person arrested under subsection (1) above –
  (a) shall, except where he was arrested within 24 hours of the time appointed for him to appear before the court in pursuance of the remand or committal, be brought as soon as practicable and in any event within 24 hours after his arrest before a justice of the peace for the petty sessions area in which he was arrested; and
  (b) in the said excepted case shall be brought before the court before which he was to have appeared.

In reckoning for the purposes of this subsection any period of 24 hours, no account shall be taken of Christmas Day, Good Friday or any Sunday.

(3) A justice of the peace before whom a person is brought under subsection (2) above –
  (a) if of the opinion that that person has broken any condition imposed on him under subsection (7) or (10) of section 23 of this Act shall remand him; and that section shall apply as if he was then charged with or convicted of the offence for which he had been remanded or committed;
  (c) if not of that opinion shall remand him to the place to which he had been remanded or committed at the time of his arrest subject to the same conditions as those which had been imposed on him at that time.

Bail Act 1976

Incidents of bail in criminal proceedings

3 (1) A person granted bail in criminal proceedings shall be under a duty to surrender to custody, and that duty is enforceable in accordance with section 6 of this Act.

(2) No recognisance for his surrender to custody shall be taken from him.

(3) Except as provided by this section –
  (a) no security for his surrender to custody shall be taken from him,
  (b) he shall not be required to provide a surety or sureties for his surrender to custody, and
  (c) no other requirement shall be imposed on him as a condition of bail.

(4) He may be required, before release on bail, to provide a surety or sureties to secure his surrender to custody.

(5) He may be required before release on bail, to give security for his surrender to custody. The security may be given by him or on his behalf.

(6) He may be required to comply, before release on bail or later, with such requirements as appear to the court to be necessary to secure that –
   (a) he surrenders to custody,
   (b) he does not commit an offence while on bail,
   (c) he does not interfere with witnesses or otherwise obstruct the course of justice whether in relation to himself or any other person,
   (d) he makes himself available for the purpose of enabling inquiries or a report to be made to assist the court in dealing with him for the offence.
   (e) before the time appointed for him to surrender to custody, he attends an interview with an authorised advocate or authorised litigator, as defined by section 119(1) of the Courts and Legal Services Act 1990;

   and, in any Act, 'the normal powers to impose conditions of bail' means the powers to impose conditions under paragraph (a), (b) or (c) above.

(6ZA) Where he is required under subsection (6) above to reside in a bail hostel or probation hostel, he may also be required to comply with the rules of the hostel.

(6A) In the case of a person accused of murder the court granting bail shall, unless it considers that satisfactory reports on his mental condition have already been obtained, impose as conditions of bail –
   (a) a requirement that the accused shall undergo examination by two medical practitioners for the purpose of enabling such reports to be prepared; and
   (b) a requirement that he shall for that purpose attend such an institution or place as the court directs and comply with any other directions which may be given to him for that purpose by either of those practitioners.

(6B) Of the medical practitioners referred to in subsection (6A) above at least one shall be a practitioner approved for the purposes of section 12 of the Mental Health Act 1983.

(7) If a parent or guardian of a child or young person consents to be surety for the child or young person for the purposes of this subsection, the parent or guardian may be required to secure that the child or young person complies with any requirement imposed on him by virtue of subsection (6) or (6A) above but –
   (a) no requirement shall be imposed on the parent or the guardian of a young person by virtue of this subsection where it appears that the young person will attain the age of 17 before the time to be appointed for him to surrender to custody; and
   (b) the parent or guardian shall not be required to secure compliance with any requirement to which his consent does not extend and shall not, in respect of those requirements to which his consent does extend, be bound in a sum greater than £50.

(8) Where a court has granted bail in criminal proceedings that court or, where that court has committed a person on bail to the Crown Court for trial or to be sentenced or otherwise dealt with, that court or the Crown Court may on application –
   (a) by or on behalf of the person to whom bail was granted, or
   (b) by the prosecutor or a constable,

vary the conditions of bail or impose conditions in respect of bail which has been granted unconditionally.

(8A) Where a notice of transfer is given under section 4 of the Criminal Justice Act 1987, subsection (8) above shall have effect in relation to a person in relation to whose case the notice is given as if he had been committed on bail to the Crown Court for trial.

(8B) Subsection (8) above applies where a court has sent a person on bail to the Crown Court for trial under section 51 of the Crime and Disorder Act 1998 as it applies where a court has committed a person on bail to the Crown Court for trial.

(9) This section is subject to subsection (2) of section 30 of the Magistrates' Courts Act 1980 (conditions of bail on remand for medical examination).

(10) Where a custody time limit has expired this section shall have effect as if –

(a) subsections (4) and (5) (sureties and security for his surrender to custody) were omitted;

(b) in subsection 6 (conditions of bail) for the words 'before release on bail or later' there were substituted the words 'after release on bail'.

Conditions of bail in case of police bail

3A (1) Section 3 of this Act applies, in relation to bail granted by a custody officer under Part IV of the Police and Criminal Evidence Act 1984 in cases where the normal powers to impose conditions of bail are available to him, subject to the following modifications.

(2) Subsection (6) does not authorise the imposition of a requirement to reside in a bail hostel or any requirement under paragraph (d) or (e).

(3) Subsections (6ZA), (6A) and (6B) shall be omitted.

(4) For subsection (8), substitute the following –

'(8) Where a custody officer has granted bail in criminal proceedings he or another custody officer serving at the same police station may, at the request of the person to whom it was granted, vary the conditions of bail; and in doing so he may impose conditions or more onerous conditions.'

(5) Where a constable grants bail to a person no conditions shall be imposed under subsections (4), (5), (6) or (7) of section 3 of this Act unless it appears to the constable that it is necessary to do so for the purpose of preventing that person from –

(a) failing to surrender to custody, or

(b) committing an offence while on bail, or

(c) interfering with witnesses or otherwise obstructing the course of justice, whether in relation to himself or any other person.

(6) Subsection (5) above also applies on any request to a custody officer under subsection (8) of section 3 of this Act to vary the conditions of bail.

General right to bail of accused persons and others

4 (1) A person to whom this section applies shall be granted bail except as provided in Schedule 1 to this Act.

(2) This section applies to a person who is accused of an offence when –

(a) he appears or is brought before a magistrates' court or the Crown Court in the course of or in connection with proceedings for the offence, or

(b) he applies to a court for bail in connection with the proceedings.

This subsection does not apply as respects proceedings on or after a person's conviction of the offence or proceedings against a fugitive offender for the offence.

(3) This section also applies to a person who, having been convicted of an offence, appears or is brought before a magistrates' court to be dealt with under Part II of Schedule 2 to the Criminal Justice Act 1991 (breach of requirement of probation, community service, combination or curfew order).

(4) This section also applies to a person who has been convicted of an offence and whose case is adjourned by the court for the purpose of enabling inquiries or a report to be made to assist the court in dealing with him for the offence.

(5) Schedule 1 to this Act also has effect as respects conditions of bail for a person to whom this section applies.

(6) In Schedule 1 to this Act 'the defendant' means a person to whom this section applies and any reference to a defendant whose case is adjourned for inquiries or a report is a reference to a person to whom this section applies by virtue of subsection (4) above.

(7) This section is subject to section 41 of the Magistrates' Courts Act 1980 (restriction of bail by magistrates' court in cases of treason).

(8) Where a custody time limit has expired this section shall have effect as if, in subsection (1), the words 'except as provided in Schedule 1 to this Act' were omitted.

Supplementary provisions about decisions on bail

5 (1) Subject to subsection (2) below, where –

(a) a court or constable grants bail in criminal proceedings, or

(b) a court withholds bail in criminal proceedings from a person to whom section 4 of this Act applies, or

(c) a court, officer of a court or constable appoints a time or place or a court or officer of a court appoints a different time or place for a person granted bail in criminal proceedings to surrender to custody, or

(d) a court or constable varies any conditions of bail or imposes conditions in respect of bail in criminal proceedings, that court, officer or constable shall make a record of the decision in the prescribed manner and containing the prescribed particulars and, if requested to do so by the person in relation to whom the decision was taken, shall cause him to be given a copy of the record of the decision as soon as practicable after the record is made.

(2) Where bail in criminal proceedings is granted by endorsing a warrant of arrest for bail the constable who releases on bail the person arrested shall make the record required by subsection (1) above instead of the judge or justice who issued the warrant.

(3) Where a magistrates court or the Crown Court –

(a) withholds bail in criminal proceedings, or

(b) imposes conditions in granting bail in criminal proceedings, or

(c) varies any conditions of bail or imposes conditions in respect of bail in criminal proceedings,

and does so in relation to a person to whom section 4 of this Act applies, then the court shall, with a view to enabling him to consider making an application in the matter to another court, give reasons for withholding bail or for imposing or varying the conditions.

(4) A court which is by virtue of subsection (3) above required to give reasons for its decision shall include a note of those reasons in the record of its decision and shall (except in a case where, by virtue of subsection (5) below, this need not be done) give a copy of that note to the person in relation to whom the decision was taken.

(5) The Crown Court need not give a copy of the note of the reasons for its decision to the person in relation to whom the decision was taken where that person is represented by counsel or a solicitor unless his counsel requests the court to do so.

(6) Where a magistrates' court withholds bail in criminal proceedings from a person who is not represented by counsel or a solicitor, the court shall –

(a) if it is committing him for trial to the Crown Court, inform him that he may apply to the High Court or to the Crown Court to be granted bail;

(b) in any other case, inform him that he may apply to the High Court for that purpose.

(7) Where a person has given security in pursuance of section 3(5) above and a court is satisfied that he failed to surrender to custody then, unless it appears that he had reasonable cause for his failure, the court may order the forfeiture of the security.

(8) If a court orders the forfeiture of a security under subsection (7) above, the court may declare that the forfeiture extends to such amount less than the full value of the security as it thinks fit to order.

(9) A security which has been ordered to be forfeited by a court under subsection (7) above shall, to the extent of the forfeiture –

(a) if it consists of money, be accounted for and paid in the same manner as a fine imposed by that court would be;

(b) if it does not consist of money, be enforced by such magistrates' court as may be specified in the order.

(10) In this section 'prescribed' means, in relation to the decision of a court or an officer of a court, prescribed by Supreme Court rules, Courts-Martial Appeal rules, Crown Court rules or magistrates' courts rules, as the case requires or, in relation to a decision of a constable, prescribed by direction of the Secretary of State.

(11) This section is subject, in its application to bail granted by a constable, to section 5A of this Act.

Supplementary provisions in cases of police bail

5A (1) Section 5 of this Act applies, in relation to bail granted by a custody officer under Part IV of the Police and Criminal Evidence Act 1984 in cases where the normal power to impose conditions of bail are available to him, subject to the following modifications.

(2) For subsection (3) substitute the following –

'(3) Where a custody officer, in relation to any person, –

(a) imposes conditions in granting bail in criminal proceedings, or

(b) varies any conditions of bail or imposes conditions in respect of bail in criminal proceedings,

the custody officer shall, with a view to enabling that person to consider requesting him or another custody officer, or making an application to a magistrates' court, to vary the conditions, give reasons for imposing or varying the conditions.'

For subsection (4) substitute the following –

'(4) A custody officer who is by virtue of subsection (3) above required to give reasons for his decision shall include a note of those reasons in the custody record and shall give a copy of that note to the person in relation to whom the decision was taken.'

(3) Subsections (5) and (6) shall be omitted.

Reconsideration of decisions granting bail

5B (1) Where a magistrates' court has granted bail in criminal proceedings in connection with an offence, or proceedings for an offence, to which this section applies or a constable has granted bail in criminal proceedings in connection with proceedings for such an offence, that court or the appropriate court in relation to the constable may, on application by the prosecutor for the decision to be reconsidered –

(a) vary the conditions of bail,

(b) impose conditions in respect of bail which has been granted unconditionally, or

(c) withhold bail.

(2) The offences to which this section applies are offences triable on indictment and offences triable either way.

(3) No application for the reconsideration of a decision under this section shall be made unless it is based on information which was not available to the court or constable when the decision was taken.

(4) Whether or not the person to whom the application relates appears before it, the magistrates' court shall take the decision in accordance with section 4(1) (and Schedule 1) of this Act.

(5) Where the decision of the court on a reconsideration under this section is to withhold bail from the person to whom it was originally granted the court shall –

(a) if that person is before the court, remand him in custody, and

(b) if that person is not before the court, order him to surrender himself forthwith into the custody of the court.

(6) Where a person surrenders himself into the custody of the court in

compliance with an order under subsection (5) above, the court shall remand him in custody.

(7) A person who has been ordered to surrender to custody under subsection (5) above may be arrested without warrant by a constable if he fails without reasonable cause to surrender to custody in accordance with the order.

(8) A person arrested in pursuance of subsection (7) above shall be brought as soon as practicable, and in any event within 24 hours after his arrest, before a justice of the peace for the petty sessions area in which he was arrested and the justice shall remand him in custody.

In reckoning for the purposes of this subsection any period of 24 hours, no account shall be taken of Christmas Day, Good Friday or any Sunday.

(9) Magistrates' court rules shall include provision–

   (a) requiring notice of an application under this section and of the grounds for it to be given to the person affected, including notice of the powers available to the court under it;

   (b) for securing that any representations made by the person affected (whether in writing or orally) are considered by the court before making its decision; and

   (c) designating the court which is the appropriate court in relation to the decision of any constable to grant bail.

Offence of absconding by person released on bail

6   (1) If a person who has been released on bail in criminal proceedings fails without reasonable cause to surrender to custody he shall be guilty of an offence.

(2) If a person who –

   (a) has been released on bail in criminal proceedings, and

   (b) having reasonable cause therefor, has failed to surrender to custody,

   fails to surrender to custody at the appointed place as soon after the appointed time as is reasonably practicable he shall be guilty of an offence.

(3) It shall be for the accused to prove that he had reasonable cause for his failure to surrender to custody.

(4) A failure to give to a person granted bail in criminal proceedings a copy of the record of the decision shall not constitute a reasonable cause for that person's failure to surrender to custody.

(5) An offence under subsection (1) or (2) above shall be punishable either on summary conviction or as if it were a criminal contempt of court.

(6) Where a magistrates' court convicts a person of an offence under subsection (1) or (2) above the court may, if it thinks –

   (a) that the circumstances of the offence are such that greater punishment should be inflicted for that offence than the court has power to inflict, or

   (b) in a case where it commits that person for trial to the Crown Court for another offence, that it would be appropriate for him to be dealt with for the offence under subsection (1) or (2) above by the court before which he is tried for the other offence, commit him in custody or on bail to the Crown Court for sentence.

(7) A person who is convicted summarily of an offence under subsection (1) or

(2) above and is not committed to the Crown Court for sentence shall be liable to imprisonment for a term not exceeding three months or to a fine not exceeding level 5 on the standard scale or to both and a person who is so committed for sentence or is dealt with as for such a contempt shall be liable to imprisonment for a term not exceeding 12 months or to a fine or to both.

(8) In any proceedings for an offence under subsection (1) or (2) above a document purporting to be a copy of the part of the prescribed record which related to the time and place appointed for the person specified in the record to surrender to custody and to be duly certified to be a true copy of that part of the record shall be evidence of the time and place appointed for that person to surrender to custody.

(9) For the purposes of subsection (8) above –

(a) 'the prescribed record' means the record of the decision of the court, officer or constable made in pursuance of section 5(1) of this Act;

(b) the copy of the prescribed record is duly certified if it is certified by the appropriate officer of the court or, as the case may be, by the constable who took the decision or a constable designated for the purpose by the officer in charge of the police station from which the person to whom the record relates was released;

(c) 'the appropriate officer' of the court is –

(i) in the case of a magistrates' court, the justices' chief executive;

(ii) in the case of the Crown Court, such officer as may be designated for the purpose in accordance with arrangements made by the Lord Chancellor;

(iii) in the case of the High Court, such officer as may be designated for the purpose in accordance with arrangements made by the Lord Chancellor;

(iv) in the case of the Court of Appeal, the registrar of criminal appeals or such other officer as may be authorised by him to act for the purpose;

(v) in the case of the Courts-Martial Appeal Court, the registrar or such other officer as may be authorised by him to act for the purpose.

Liability to arrest for absconding or breaking conditions of bail

7 (1) If a person who has been released on bail in criminal proceedings and is under a duty to surrender into the custody of a court fails to surrender to custody at the time appointed for him to do so the court may issue a warrant for his arrest.

(2) If a person who has been released on bail in criminal proceedings absents himself from the court at any time after he has surrendered into the custody of the court and before the court is ready to begin or to resume the hearing of the proceedings, the court may issue a warrant for his arrest; but no warrant shall be issued under this subsection where that person is absent in accordance with leave given to him by or on behalf of the court.

(3) A person who has been released on bail in criminal proceedings and is

under a duty to surrender into the custody of a court may be arrested without warrant by a constable –

(a) if the constable has reasonable grounds for believing that that person is not likely to surrender to custody;

(b) if the constable has reasonable grounds for believing that that person is likely to break any of the conditions of his bail or has reasonable grounds for suspecting that that person has broken any of those conditions; or

(c) in a case where that person was released on bail with one or more surety or sureties, if a surety notifies a constable in writing that that person is unlikely to surrender to custody and that for that reason the surety wishes to be relieved of his obligations as a surety.

(4) A person arrested in pursuance of subsection (3) above –

(a) shall, except where he was arrested within 24 hours of the time appointed for him to surrender to custody, be brought as soon as practicable and in any event within 24 hours after his arrest before a justice of the peace for the petty sessions area in which he was arrested; and

(b) in the said excepted case shall be brought before the court at which he was to have surrendered to custody.

In reckoning for the purposes of this subsection any period of 24 hours, no account shall be taken of Christmas Day, Good Friday or any Sunday.

(5) A justice of the peace before whom a person is brought under subsection (4) above may, subject to subsection (6) below, if of the opinion that that person –

(a) is not likely to surrender to custody, or

(b) has broken or is likely to break any condition of his bail,

remand him in custody or commit him to custody, as the case may require, or alternatively, grant him bail subject to the same or to different conditions, but if not of that opinion shall grant him bail subject to the same conditions (if any) as were originally imposed.

(6) Where the person so brought before the justice is a child or young person and the justice does not grant him bail, subsection (5) above shall have effect subject to the provisions of section 23 of the Children and Young Persons Act 1969 (remands to the care of local authorities).

(7) Where a custody time limit has expired this section shall have effect as if, in subsection (3), paragraphs (a) and (b) were omitted.

SCHEDULE 1: PERSONS ENTITLED TO BAIL: SUPPLEMENTARY PROVISIONS

PART I – DEFENDANTS ACCUSED OR CONVICTED OF IMPRISONABLE OFFENCES

Defendants to whom Part I applies

1 Where the offence or one of the offences of which the defendant is accused or convicted in the proceedings is punishable with imprisonment the following provisions of this Part of this Schedule apply.

Exceptions to right to bail

2   The defendant need not be granted bail if the court is satisfied that there are substantial grounds for believing that the defendant, if released on bail (whether subject to conditions or not) would –
   (a) fail to surrender to custody, or
   (b) commit an offence while on bail, or
   (c) interfere with witnesses or otherwise obstruct the course of justice, whether in relation to himself or any other person.

3   The defendant need not be granted bail if the court is satisfied that the defendant should be kept in custody for his own protection or, if he is a child or young person, for his own welfare.

4   The defendant need not be granted bail if he is in custody in pursuance of the sentence of a court or of any authority acting under any of the Services Acts.

5   The defendant need not be granted bail where the court is satisfied that it has not been practicable to obtain sufficient information for the purpose of taking the decisions required by this Part of this Schedule for want of time since the institution of the proceedings against him.

6   The defendant need not be granted bail if, having been released on bail in or in connection with the proceedings for the offence, he has been arrested in pursuance of section 7 of this Act.

Exception applicable only to defendant whose case is adjourned for inquiries or a report.

7   Where his case is adjourned for inquiries or a report, the defendant need not be granted bail if it appears to the court that it would be impracticable to complete the inquiries or make the report without keeping the defendant in custody.

Restriction of conditions of bail

8   (1) Subject to sub-paragraph (3) below, where the defendant is granted bail, no conditions shall be imposed under subsections (4) to (7) (except subsection (6)(d)) or (e) of section 3 of this Act unless it appears to the court that it is necessary to do so for the purpose of preventing the occurrence of any of the events mentioned in paragraph 2 of this Part of this Schedule or, where a condition is that the defendant resides in a bail hostel or probation hostel, that it is necessary to impose it to assess his suitability for being dealt with for the offence in a way which would involve a period of residence in a probation hostel.

   (1A) No condition shall be imposed under section 3(6)(d) of this Act unless it appears to be necessary to do so for the purpose of enabling inquiries or a report to be made.

   (2) Sub-paragraphs (1) and (1A) above also apply on any application to the court to vary the conditions of bail or to impose conditions in respect of bail which has been granted unconditionally.

   (3) The restriction imposed by sub-paragraph (1A) above shall not apply to the conditions required to be imposed under section 3(6A) of this Act or operate to override the direction in section 30(2) of the Magistrates' Courts Act 1980

to a magistrates' court to impose conditions of bail under section 3(6)(d) of this Act of the description specified in the said section 30(2) in the circumstances so specified.

Decisions under paragraph 2

9   In taking the decisions required by paragraph 2 of this Part of this Schedule, the court shall have regard to such of the following considerations as appear to it to be relevant, that is to say –

(a) the nature and seriousness of the offence or default (and the probable method of dealing with the defendant for it),

(b) the character, antecedents, associations and community ties of the defendant,

(c) the defendant's record as respects the fulfilment of his obligations under previous grants of bail in criminal proceedings,

(d) except in the case of a defendant whose case is adjourned for inquiries or a report, the strength of the evidence of his having committed the offence or having defaulted,

as well as to any others which appear to be relevant.

9A (1) If –

(a) the defendant is charged with an offence to which this paragraph applies; and

(b) representations are made as to any of the matters mentioned in paragraph 2 of this Part of this Schedule; and

(c) the court decides to grant him bail,

the court shall state the reasons for its decision and shall cause those reasons to be included in the record of the proceedings.

(2) The offences to which this paragraph applies are –

(a) murder;

(b) manslaughter;

(c) rape;

(d) attempted murder; and

(e) attempted rape.

Cases under section 128A of Magistrates' Courts Act 1980

9B   Where the court is considering exercising the power conferred by section 128A of the Magistrates' Courts Act 1980 (power to remand in custody for more than 8 clear days), it shall have regard to the total length of time which the accused would spend in custody if it were to exercise the power.

PART II – DEFENDANTS ACCUSED OR CONVICTED OF NON-IMPRISONABLE OFFENCES

Defendants to whom Part II applies

1   Where the offence or every offence of which the defendant is accused or convicted in the proceedings is one which is not punishable with imprisonment the following provisions of this Part of this Schedule apply.

Exceptions to right to bail

2   The defendant need not be granted bail if –

(a) it appears to the court that, having been previously granted bail in criminal proceedings, he has failed to surrender to custody in accordance with his obligations under the grant of bail; and

(b) the court believes, in view of that failure, that the defendant, if released on bail (whether subject to conditions or not) would fail to surrender to custody.

3   The defendant need not be granted bail if the court is satisfied that the defendant should be kept in custody for his own protection or, if he is a child or young person, for his own welfare.

4   The defendant need not be granted bail if he is in custody in pursuance of the sentence of a court or of any authority acting under any of the Services Acts.

Magistrates' Courts Act 1980

Adjournment of trial

10 (1) A magistrates' court may at any time, whether before or after beginning to try an information, adjourn the trial, and may do so, notwithstanding anything in this Act, when composed of a single justice.

(2) The court may when adjourning either fix the time and place at which the trial is to be resumed, or, unless it remands the accused, leave the time and place to be determined later by the court; but the trial shall not be resumed at that time and place unless the court is satisfied that the parties have had adequate notice thereof.

(3) A magistrates' court may, for the purpose of enabling enquiries to be made or of determining the most suitable method of dealing with the case, exercise its power to adjourn after convicting the accused and before sentencing him or otherwise dealing with him; but it if does so, the adjournment shall not be for more than 4 weeks at a time unless the court remands the accused in custody and, where it so remands him, the adjournment shall not be for more than 3 weeks at a time.

(3A) A youth court shall not be required to adjourn any proceedings for an offence at any stage by reason only of the fact –

(a) that the court commits the accused for trial for another offence; or

(b) that the accused is charged with another offence.

(4) On adjourning the trial of an information, the court may remand the accused and, where the accused has attained the age of 17, shall do so if the offence is triable either way and –

(a) on the occasion on which the accused first appeared, or was brought, before the court to answer to the information he was in custody, or, having been released on bail, surrendered to the custody of the court; or

(b) the accused has been remanded at any time in the course of proceedings on information;

and, where the court remands the accused, the time fixed for the resumption of the trial shall be that at which he is required to appear or be brought before the court in pursuance of the remand or would be required to be brought before the court but for section 128(3A) below.

Summary trial of information against child or young person for indictable offence

24 (1) Where a person under the age of 18 years appears or is brought before a magistrates' court on an information charging him with an indictable offence other than homicide, he shall be tried summarily unless –

(a) the offence is such as is mentioned in subsection (2) of section 53 of the Children and Young Persons Act 1933 (under which young persons convicted on indictment of certain grave crimes may be sentenced to be detained for long periods) and the court considers that if he is found guilty of the offence it ought to be possible to sentence him in pursuance of subsection (3) of that section; or

(b) he is charged jointly with a person who has attained the age of 18 years and the court considers it necessary in the interests of justice to commit them both for trial;

and accordingly in a case falling within paragraph (a) or (b) of this subsection the court shall commit the accused for trial if either it is of opinion that there is sufficient evidence to put him on trial or it has power under section 6(2) above so to commit him without consideration of the evidence.

(1A) Where a magistrates' court –

(a) commits a person under the age of 18 for trial for an offence of homicide; or

(b) in a case falling within subsection (1)(a) above, commits such a person for trial for an offence,

the court may also commit him for trial for any other indictable offence with which he is charged at the same time if the charges for both offences could be joined in the same indictment.

(2) Where, in a case falling within subsection (1)(b) above, a magistrates' court commits a person under the age of 18 years for trial for an offence with which he is charged jointly with a person who has attained that age, the court may also commit him for trial for any other indictable offence with which he is charged at the same time (whether jointly with the person who has attained that age or not) if the charges for both offences could be joined in the same indictment.

(3) If on trying a person summarily in pursuance of subsection (1) above the court finds him guilty, it may impose a fine of an amount not exceeding £1,000 or may exercise the same powers as it could have exercised if he had been found guilty of an offence for which, but for section 1(1) of the Criminal Justice Act 1982, it could have sentenced him to imprisonment for a term not exceeding –

(a) the maximum term of imprisonment for the offence on conviction on indictment; or

(b) six months,
whichever is the less.

(4) In relation to a person under the age of 14 subsection (3) above shall have effect as if for the words '£1,000' there were substituted the words '£250'.

Power to change from summary trial to proceedings with a view to committal for trial, and vice versa

25 (1)–(4) [*Not reproduced.*]

(5) Where a person under the age of 18 appears or is brought before a magistrates' court on an information charging him with an indictable offence other than homicide, and the court –

(a) has begun to try the information summarily on the footing that the case does not fall within paragraph (a) or (b) of section 24(1) above and must therefore be tried summarily, as required by the said section 24(1); or

(b) has begun to consider the evidence and any representations permitted under section 6 above on an application for dismissal of a charge in a case in which, under paragraph (a) or (b) of section 24(1) above, the court is required to proceed with a view to transferring the proceedings to the Crown Court for trial,

subsection (6) or (7) below, as the case may be, shall have effect.

(6) If, in a case falling within subsection (5)(a) above, it appears to the court at any time before the conclusion of the evidence for the prosecution that the case is after all one which under the said section 24(1) ought not to be tried summarily, the court may discontinue the summary trial and proceed with a view to transfer for trial and, on doing so, shall adjourn the hearing.

(7) If, in a case falling within subsection (5)(b) above, it appears to the court at any time during its consideration of the evidence and any representations permitted under section 6 above that the case is after all one which under the said section 24(1) ought to be tried summarily, the court may proceed to try the information summarily.

(8) If the court adjourns the hearing under subsection (2) or (6) above it may (if it thinks fit) do so without remanding the accused.

Power of magistrates' court to remit a person under 18 for trial to youth court in certain circumstances

29 (1) Where –

(a) a person under the age of 18 years ('the juvenile') appears or is brought before a magistrates' court other than a youth court on an information jointly charging him and one or more other persons with an offence; and

(b) that other person, or any of those other persons, has attained that age,

subsection (2) below shall have effect notwithstanding proviso (a) in section 46(1) of the Children and Young Persons Act 1933 (which would otherwise require the charge against the juvenile to be heard by a magistrates' court other than a youth court).

In the following provisions of this section 'the older accused' means such one or more of the accused as have attained the age of 18 years.

(2) If –
    (a) the court proceeds to the summary trial of the information in the case of both or all of the accused, and the older accused or each of the older accused pleads guilty; or
    (b) the court –
        (i) in the case of the older accused or each of the older accused, proceeds to inquire into the information as examining justices and either commits him for trial or discharges him; and
        (ii) in the case of the juvenile, proceeds to the summary trial of the information,
then, if in either situation the juvenile pleads not guilty, the court may before any evidence is called in his case remit him for trial to a youth court acting for the same place as the remitting court or for the place where he habitually resides.

(3) A person remitted to a youth court under subsection (2) above shall be brought before and tried by a youth court accordingly.

(4) Where a person is so remitted to a youth court –
    (a) he shall have no right of appeal against the order of remission; and
    (b) the remitting court may, subject to section 25 of the Criminal Justice and Public Order Act 1994, give such directions as appear to be necessary with respect to his custody or for his release on bail until he can be brought before the youth court.

(5) The preceding provisions of this section shall apply in relation to a corporation as if it were an individual who has attained the age of 18 years.

37   [*Repealed.*]

Criminal Justice Act 1982

Detention in a young offender institution

1A (1) Subject to section 8 below and to section 53 of the Children and Young Persons Act 1933, where –
    (a) an offender under 21 but not less than 18 years of age is convicted of an offence which is punishable with imprisonment in the case of a person aged 21 or over; and
    (b) the court is of the opinion that either or both of paragraphs (a) and (b) of subsection (2) of section 1 of the Criminal Justice Act 1991 apply or the case falls within subsection (3) of that section,
the sentence that the court is to pass is a sentence of detention in a young offender institution.

(2) Subject to section 1B(2) below, the maximum term of detention in a young offender institution that a court may impose for an offence is the same as the maximum term of imprisonment that it may impose for that offence.

(3) Subject to subsection (4) below, a court shall not pass a sentence for an offender's detention in a young offender institution for less than 21 days.

(4) A court may pass a sentence of detention in a young offender institution for less than the minimum period applicable for an offence under section 17(1)

of the Crime (Sentences) Act 1997 as it has effect by virtue of section 19 of that Act.

(4A) [*Repealed.*]

(5) Subject to section 1B(4) below, where –

(a) an offender is convicted of more than one offence for which he is liable to a sentence of detention in a young offender institution; or

(b) an offender who is serving a sentence of detention in a young offender institution is convicted of one or more further offences for which he is liable to such a sentence,

the court shall have the same power to pass consecutive sentences of detention in a young offender institution as if they were sentences of imprisonment.

(6) Subject to section 102 of the Crime and Disorder Act 1998, where an offender who –

(a) is serving a sentence of detention in a young offender institution; and

(b) is aged over 21 years,

is convicted of one or more further offences for which he is liable to imprisonment, the court shall have the power to pass one or more sentences of imprisonment to run consecutively upon the sentence of detention in a young offender institution.

1B   [*Repealed.*]

Attendance centre orders

17 (1) Subject to subsections (3) and (4) below, where a court –

(a) would have power, but for section 1 above, to pass a sentence of imprisonment on a person who is under 21 years of age or to commit such a person to prison in default of payment of any sum of money or for failing to do or abstain from doing anything required to be done or left undone; or

(b) considers it appropriate to make an attendance centre order in respect of any person in pursuance of paragraph 3(2) of Schedule 5 to the Crime and Disorder Act 1998, or

(c) has power to commit to prison for default in payment of any sum of money a person who is under 25 but is not less than 21 years of age,

the court may, if it has been notified by the Secretary of State that an attendance centre is available for the reception of persons of his description, order him to attend at such a centre, to be specified in the order, for such number of hours as may be so specified.

(2) An order under this section is referred to in this Act as an 'attendance centre order'.

(3) [*Repealed.*]

(4) The aggregate number of hours for which an attendance centre order may require an offender to attend at an attendance centre shall not be less than 12 except where he is under 14 years of age and the court is of opinion that 12 hours would be excessive, having regard to his age or any other circumstances.

(5) The aggregate number of hours shall not exceed 12 except where the court is

of opinion, having regard to all the circumstances, that 12 hours would be inadequate, and in that case shall not exceed 24 where the offender is under 16 years of age, or 36 hours where the offender is under 21 or, as the case may be, 25 but not less than 16 years of age.

(6) A court may make an attendance centre order in respect of an offender before a previous attendance centre order made in respect of him has ceased to have effect, and may determine the number of hours to be specified in the order without regard –

    (a) to the number specified in the previous order; or

    (b) to the fact that that order is still in effect.

(7) An attendance centre order shall not be made unless the court is satisfied that the attendance centre to be specified in it is reasonably accessible to the person concerned, having regard to his age, the means of access available to him and any other circumstances.

(8) The times at which an offender is required to attend at an attendance centre shall be such as to avoid interference, so far as practicable, with his school hours or working hours.

(9) The first such time shall be a time at which the centre is available for the attendance of the offender in accordance with the notification of the Secretary of State and shall be specified in the order.

(10) The subsequent times shall be fixed by the officer in charge of the centre, having regard to the offender's circumstances.

(11) An offender shall not be required under this section to attend at an attendance centre on more than one occasion on any day, or for more than three hours on any occasion.

(12) Where a court makes an attendance centre order, the clerk of the court shall deliver or send a copy of the order to the officer in charge of the attendance centre specified in it, and shall also deliver a copy to the offender or send a copy by registered post or the recorded delivery service addressed to the offender's last or usual place of abode.

Discharge and variation of attendance centre orders

18 (1) An attendance centre order may be discharged on an application made by the offender or the officer in charge of the relevant attendance centre.

(2) An application under subsection (1) above shall be made to one of the courts specified in subsection (3) below or to the Crown Court under subsection (4) below, and the discharge of such an order shall be by order of the court.

(3) Subject to subsection (4) below, the power to discharge an attendance centre order shall be exercised –

    (a) by a magistrates' court acting for the petty sessions area in which the relevant attendance centre is situated; or

    (b) by the court which made the order.

(4) Where the court which made the order is the Crown Court and there is included in the order a direction that the power to discharge the order is reserved to that court, the power shall be exercised by that court.

(4A) Any power conferred by this section –

(a) on a magistrates' court to discharge an attendance centre order made by such a court, or

(b) on the Crown Court to discharge an attendance centre order made by the Crown Court,

includes any power to deal with the offender, for the offence in respect of which the order was made, in any manner which he could have been dealt with for that offence by the court which made the order if the order had not been made.

(4B) A person sentenced by a magistrates' court under subsection (4A) above for an offence may appeal to the Crown Court against the sentence.

(5) An attendance centre order may, on the application of the offender or of the officer in charge of the relevant attendance centre, be varied by a magistrates' court acting for the petty sessions area in which the relevant attendance centre is situated; and an attendance centre order made by a magistrates' court may also be varied, on such an application, by that court.

(6) The power to vary an attendance centre order is a power by order –

(a) to vary the day or hour specified in the order for the offender's first attendance at the relevant attendance centre; or

(b) to substitute for the relevant attendance centre an attendance centre which the court is satisfied is reasonably accessible to the offender, having regard to his age, the means of access available to him and any other circumstances.

(7) [*Repealed.*]

(8) It shall be the duty of the proper officer of a court which makes an order under this section –

(a) to deliver a copy to the offender or send a copy by registered post or the recorded delivery service addressed to the offender's last or usual place of abode; and

(b) to deliver or send a copy –

(i) if the order is made by virtue of subsection (1) or (6)(a) above, to the officer in charge of the relevant attendance centre; and

(ii) if it is made by virtue of subsection (6)(b) above, to the officer in charge of the attendance centre which the order as varied will require the offender to attend.

(9) In this section 'the relevant attendance centre', in relation to an attendance centre order, means the attendance centre specified in the order or substituted for the attendance centre so specified by an order made by virtue of subsection (6)(b) above.

(10) Where an offender has been ordered to attend at an attendance centre in default of the payment of a sum of money or for such a failure or abstention as is mentioned in section 17(1)(a) above, subsection (4A) above shall have effect in relation to the order as if the words 'for the offence in respect of which the order was made,' and 'for that offence' were omitted.

[*This subsection (10) inserted by Crime and Disorder Act 1998 s106 and Sch 7 para 37.*]

(10) In subsection (8) above 'proper officer' means –

(a) in relation to a magistrates' court, the justices' chief executive for the court; and

(b) in relation to the Crown Court, the appropriate officer.

[*This subsection (10) inserted by Access to Justice Act 1999 s90 and Sch 13 para 123.*]

(11) Where an attendance centre order has been made on appeal, for the purposes of this section it shall be deemed –

(a) if it was made on an appeal brought from the magistrates' court, to have been made by that magistrates' court;

(b) if it was made on an appeal brought from the Crown Court or from the criminal division of the Court of Appeal, to have been made by the Crown Court;

and subsection (4A) above shall have effect in relation to an attendance centre order made on appeal as if the words 'if the order had not been made' were omitted.

Breaches of attendance centre orders or attendance centre rules

19 (1) Where an attendance centre order is in force and it appears on information to a justice acting for a relevant petty sessions area that the offender –

(a) has failed to attend in accordance with the order; or

(b) while attending has committed a breach of rules made under section 16(3) above which cannot be adequately dealt with under those rules,

the justice may issue a summons requiring the offender to appear at the place and time specified in the summons before a magistrates' court acting for the area or, if the information is in writing and on oath, may issue a warrant for the offender's arrest requiring him to be brought before such a court.

(2) For the purposes of this section a petty sessions area is a relevant petty sessions area in relation to an attendance centre order –

(a) if the attendance centre which the offender is required to attend by an order made by virtue of section 17(1) or 18(6)(b) above is situated in it; or

(b) if the order was made by a magistrates' court acting for it.

(3) If it is proved to the satisfaction of the magistrates' court before which an offender appears or is brought under this section that he has failed without reasonable excuse to attend as mentioned in paragraph (a) of subsection (1) above or has committed such a breach of rules as is mentioned in paragraph (b) of that subsection, that court may, without prejudice to the continuation of the order, impose on him a fine not exceeding £1,000 or –

(a) if the attendance centre order was made by a magistrates' court, may revoke it and deal with him, for the offence in respect of which the order was made, in any manner in which he could have been dealt with for that offence by the court which made the order if the order had not been made;

(b) if the order was made by the Crown Court, may commit him in custody or release him on bail until he can be brought or appear before the Crown Court.

(3A) A fine imposed under subsection (3) above shall be deemed, for the purposes of any enactment, to be a sum adjudged to be paid by a conviction.

(4) A magistrates' court which deals with an offender's case under subsection (3)(b) above shall send to the Crown Court a certificate signed by a justice of the peace giving particulars of the offender's failure to attend or, as the case may be, the breach of the rules which he has committed, together with such other particulars of the case as may be desirable; and a certificate purporting to be so signed shall be admissible as evidence of the failure or the breach before the Crown Court.

(5) Where by virtue of subsection (3)(b) above the offender is brought or appears before the Crown Court and it is proved to the satisfaction of the court that he has failed without reasonable excuse to attend as mentioned in paragraph (a) of subsection (1) above or has committed such a breach of rules as is mentioned in paragraph (b) of that subsection, that court may revoke the attendance centre order and deal with him, for the offence in respect of which the order was made, in any manner in which it could have dealt with him for that offence if it had not made the order.

(5A) In dealing with an offender under subsection (3)(a) or (5) above, the court concerned –
   (a) shall take into account the extent to which the offender has complied with the requirements of the attendance centre order; and
   (b) may assume, in the case of an offender who has wilfully and persistently failed to comply with those requirements, that he has refused to give his consent to a community sentence which has been proposed by the court and requires that consent.

(6) A person sentenced under subsection (3)(a) above for an offence may appeal to the Crown Court against the sentence.

(7) In proceedings before the Crown Court under this section, any question whether there has been a failure to attend or a breach of the rules shall be determined by the court and not by the verdict of a jury.

(8) Where an offender has been ordered to attend at an attendance centre in default of the payment of a sum of money or for such a failure or abstention as is mentioned in section 17(1)(a) above, subsections (3) and (5) above shall have effect in relation to the order as if the words 'for the offence in respect of which the order was made' and 'for that offence' were omitted.

(9) Where an attendance centre order has been made on appeal, for the purposes of this section it shall be deemed –
   (a) if it was made on appeal brought from a magistrates' court, to have been made by that magistrates' court;
   (b) if it was made on an appeal brought from the Crown Court or from the criminal division of the Court of Appeal, to have been made by the Crown Court;

and, in relation to an attendance centre order made on appeal, subsection 3(a) above shall have effect as if the words 'if the order had not been made' were omitted and subsection (5) above shall have effect as if the words 'if it had not made the order' were omitted.

Prosecution of Offences Act 1985

PART III: MISCELLANEOUS

Power of Secretary of State to set time limits in relation to preliminary stages of criminal proceedings

22 (1) The Secretary of State may by regulations make provision, with respect to any specified preliminary stage of proceedings for an offence, as to the maximum period–

(a) to be allowed to the prosecution to complete that stage;

(b) during which the accused may, while awaiting completion of that stage, be –

   (i) in the custody of a magistrates' court; or

   (ii) in the custody of the Crown Court;

in relation to that offence.

(2) The regulations may, in particular–

(a) be made so as to apply only in relation to proceedings instituted in specified areas, or proceedings of, or against persons of, specified classes or descriptions;

(b) make different provision with respect to proceedings instituted in different areas, or different provision with respect to proceedings of, or against persons of, different classes or descriptions;

(c) make such provision with respect to the procedure to be followed in criminal proceedings as the Secretary of State considers appropriate in consequence of any other provision of the regulations;

(d) provide for the Magistrates' Courts Act 1980 and the Bail Act 1976 to apply in relation to cases to which custody or overall time limits apply subject to such modifications as may be specified (being modifications which the Secretary of State considers necessary in consequence of any provision made by the regulations); and

(e) make such transitional provision in relation to proceedings instituted before the commencement of any provision of the regulations as the Secretary of State considers appropriate.

(3) The appropriate court may, at any time before the expiry of a time limit imposed by the regulations, extend, or further extend, that limit; but the court shall not do so unless it is satisfied–

(a) that the need for the extension is due to–

   (i) the illness or absence of the accused, a necessary witness, a judge or a magistrate;

   (ii) a postponement which is occasioned by the ordering by the court of separate trials in the case of two or more accused or two or more offences; or

   (iii) some other good and sufficient cause; and

(b) that the prosecution has acted with all due diligence and expedition.

(4) Where, in relation to any proceedings for an offence, an overall time limit has expired before the completion of the stage of the proceedings to which the limit applies, the appropriate court shall stay the proceedings.

(5) Where –

    (a) a person escapes from the custody of a magistrates' court or the Crown Court before the expiry of a custody time limit which applies in his case; or

    (b) a person who has been released on bail in consequence of the expiry of a custody time limit–

        (i) fails to surrender himself into the custody of the court at the appointed time; or

        (ii) is arrested by a constable on a ground mentioned in section 7(3)(b) of the Bail Act 1976 (breach, or likely breach, of conditions of bail);

the regulations shall, so far as they provide for any custody time limit in relation to the preliminary stage in question, be disregarded.

(6) Subsection (6A) below applies where–

    (a) a person escapes from the custody of a magistrates' court or the Crown Court; or

    (b) a person who has been released on bail fails to surrender himself into the custody of the court at the appointed time;

and is accordingly unlawfully at large for any period.

(6A) The following, namely–

    (a) the period for which the person is unlawfully at large; and

    (b) such additional period (if any) as the appropriate court may direct, having regard to the disruption of the prosecution occasioned by–

        (i) the person's escape or failure to surrender; and

        (ii) the length of the period mentioned in paragraph (a) above,

shall be disregarded, so far as the offence in question is concerned, for the purposes of the overall time limit which applies in his case in relation to the stage which the proceedings have reached at the time of the escape or, as the case may be, at the appointed time.

(7) Where a magistrates' court decides to extend, or further extend, a custody or overall time limit, or to give a direction under subsection (6A) above, the accused may appeal against the decision to the Crown Court.

(8) Where a magistrates' court refuses to extend, or further extend, a custody or overall time limit, or to give a direction under subsection (6A) above, the prosecution may appeal against the refusal to the Crown Court.

(9) An appeal under subsection (8) above may not be commenced after the expiry of the limit in question; but where such an appeal is commenced before the expiry of the limit, the limit shall be deemed not to have expired before the determination or abandonment of the appeal.

(10) Where a person is convicted of an offence in any proceedings, the exercise, in relation to any preliminary stage of those proceedings of the power conferred by subsection (3) above shall not be called into question in any appeal against that conviction.

(11) In this section –

    'appropriate court' means –

    (a) where the proceedings against the accused are transferred for trial, sent for trial under section 51 of the Crime and Disorder Act 1998 or the accused has been indicted for the offence, the Crown Court; and

(b) in any other case, the magistrates' court specified in the summons or warrant in question or, where the accused has already appeared or been brought before a magistrates' court, a magistrates' court for the same area;

'custody' includes local authority accommodation to which a person is remanded or committed by virtue of section 23 of the Children and Young Persons Act 1969, and references to a person being committed to custody shall be construed accordingly;

'custody of the Crown Court' includes custody to which a person is committed in pursuance of –

(a) section 8(1) of the Magistrates' Courts Act 1980 (remand of accused where court is proceeding with a view to transfer for trial); or

(b) section 43A of that Act (magistrates' court dealing with a person brought before it following his arrest in pursuance of a warrant issued by the Crown Court); or

(c) section 5(3)(a) of the Criminal Justice Act 1987 (custody after transfer order in fraud case); or

(d) paragraph 2(1)(a) of Schedule 6 to the Criminal Justice Act 1991 (custody after transfer order in certain cases involving children);

'custody of a magistrates' court' means custody to which a person is committed in pursuance of section 128 of the Magistrates' Courts Act 1980 (remand);

'custody time limit' means a time limit imposed by regulations made under subsection (1)(b) above or, where any such limit has been extended by a court under subsection (3) above, the limit as so extended;

'preliminary stage', in relation to any proceedings, does not include any stage after the start of the trial (within the meaning given by subsections (11A) and (11B) below);

'overall time limit' means a time limit imposed by regulations made under subsection (1)(a) above or, where any such limit has been extended by a court under subsection (3) above, the limit as so extended; and

'specified' means specified in the regulations.

(11ZA) For the purposes of this section, proceedings for an offence shall be taken to begin when the accused is charged with the offence or, as the case may be, an information is laid charging him with the offence.

(11A) For the purposes of this section, the start of a trial on indictment shall be taken to occur when a jury is sworn to consider the issue of guilt or fitness to plead or, if the court accepts a plea of guilty before a jury is sworn, when that plea is accepted; but this is subject to section 8 of the Criminal Justice Act 1987 and section 30 of the Criminal Procedure and Investigations Act 1996 (preparatory hearings).

(11B) For the purposes of this section, the start of a summary trial shall be taken to occur–

(a) when the court begins to hear evidence for the prosecution at the trial or to consider whether to exercise its power under section 37(3) of the Mental Health Act 1983 (power to make hospital order without convicting the accused), or

(b) if the court accepts a plea of guilty without proceeding as mentioned above, when that plea is accepted.

(12) For the purposes of the application of any custody time limit in relation to a person who is in the custody of a magistrates' court or the Crown Court–

(a) all periods during which he is in the custody of a magistrates' court in respect of the same offence shall be aggregated and treated as a single continuous period; and

(b) all periods during which he is in the custody of the Crown Court in respect of the same offence shall be aggregated and treated similarly.

(13) For the purposes of section 29(3) of the Supreme Court Act 1981 (High Court to have power to make prerogative orders in relation to jurisdiction of Crown Court in matters which do not relate to trial on indictment) the jurisdiction conferred on the Crown Court by this section shall be taken to be part of its jurisdiction in matters other than those relating to trial on indictment.

Additional time limits for persons under 18

22A (1) The Secretary of State may by regulations make provision–

(a) with respect to a person under the age of 18 at the time of his arrest in connection with an offence, as to the maximum period to be allowed for the completion of the stage beginning with his arrest and ending with the date fixed for his first appearance in court in connection with the offence ('the initial stage');

(b) with respect to a person convicted of an offence who was under that age at the time of his arrest for the offence or (where he was not arrested for it) the laying of the information charging him with it, as to the period within which the stage between his conviction and his being sentenced for the offence should be completed.

(2) Subsection (2) of section 22 above applies for the purposes of regulations under subsection (1) above as if –

(a) the reference in paragraph (d) to custody or overall time limits were reference to time limits imposed by the regulations; and

(b) the reference in paragraph (e) to proceedings instituted before the commencement of any provisions of the regulations were a reference to a stage begun before that commencement.

(3) A magistrates' court may, at any time before the expiry of the time limit imposed by the regulations under subsection (1)(a) above ('the initial stage time limit'), extend, or further extend, that limit; but the court shall not do so unless it is satisfied–

(a) that the need for the extension is due to some good and sufficient cause; and

(b) that the investigation has been conducted, and (where applicable) the prosecution has acted, with all due diligence and expedition.

(4) Where the initial stage time limit (whether as originally imposed or as extended under subsection (3) above) expires before the person arrested is charged with the offence, he shall not be charged with it unless further evidence relating to it is obtained, and–

(a) if he is then under arrest, he shall be released;

    (b) if he is then on bail (and any duty or conditions to which it is subject) shall be discharged.

(5) Where the initial stage time limit (whether as originally imposed or as extended or further extended under subsection (3) above) expires after the person arrested is charged with the offence but before the date fixed for his first appearance in court in connection with it, the court shall stay the proceedings.

(6) Where –
    (a) a person escapes from arrest; or
    (b) a person who has been released on bail under Part IV of the Police and Criminal Evidence Act 1984 fails to surrender himself at the appointed time,

and is accordingly unlawfully at large for any period, that period shall be disregarded, so far as the offence in question is concerned, for the purposes of the initial stage time limit.

(7) Subsections (7) to (9) of section 22 above apply for the purposes of this section, at any time after the person arrested has been charged with the offence in question, as if any reference (however expressed) to a custody or overall time limit were a reference to the initial stage time limit.

(8) Where a person is convicted of an offence in any proceedings, the exercise of the power conferred by subsection (3) above shall not be called into question in any appeal against that conviction.

(9) Any reference in this section (however expressed) to a person being charged with an offence includes a reference to the laying of an information charging him with it.

Re-institution of proceedings stayed under section 22(4) or 22A(5)

22B (1) This section applies where proceedings for an offence ('the original proceedings') are stayed by a court under section 22(4) or 22A(5) of this Act.

(2) If–
    (a) in the case of proceedings conducted by the Director, the Director or a Chief Crown Prosecutor so directs;
    (b) in the case of proceedings conducted by the Director of the Serious Fraud Office, the Commissioners of Inland Revenue or the Commissioners of Customs and Excise, that Director or those Commissioners so direct; or
    (c) in the case of proceedings not conducted as mentioned in paragraph (a) or (b) above, a person designated for the purpose by the Secretary of State so directs,

fresh proceedings for the offence may be instituted within a period of three months (or such longer period as the court may allow) after the date on which the original proceedings were stayed by the court.

(3) Fresh proceedings shall be instituted as follows–
    (a) where the original proceedings were stayed by the Crown Court, by preferring a bill of indictment;

(b) where the original proceedings were stayed by a magistrates' court, by laying an information.

(4) Fresh proceedings may be instituted in accordance with subsections (2) and (3)(b) above notwithstanding anything in section 127(1) of the Magistrates' Courts Act 1980 (limitation of time).

(5) Where fresh proceedings are instituted, anything done in relation to the original proceedings shall be treated as done in relation to the fresh proceedings if the court so directs or it was done–

(a) by the prosecutor in compliance or purported compliance with section 3, 4, 7 or 9 of the Criminal Procedure and Investigations Act 1996; or

(b) by the accused in compliance or purported compliance with section 5 or 6 of that Act.

(6) Where a person is convicted of an offence in fresh proceedings under this section, the institution of those proceedings shall not be called into question in any appeal against that conviction.

Children Act 1989

Provision of services for children in need, their families and others

17 (1) It shall be the general duty of every local authority (in addition to the other duties imposed on them by this Part) –

(a) to safeguard and promote the welfare of children within their area who are in need; and

(b) so far as is consistent with that duty, to promote the upbringing of such children by their families,

by providing a range and level of services appropriate to those children's needs.

(2) For the purpose principally of facilitating the discharge of their general duty under this section, every local authority shall have the specific duties and powers set out in Part I of Schedule 2.

(3) Any service provided by an authority in the exercise of functions conferred on them by this section may be provided for the family of a particular child in need or for any member of his family, if it is provided with a view to safeguarding or promoting the child's welfare.

(4) The Secretary of State may by order amend any provision of Part I of Schedule 2 or add any further duty or power to those for the time being mentioned there.

(5) Every local authority –

(a) shall facilitate the provision by others (including in particular voluntary organisations) of services which the authority have power to provide by virtue of this section, or section 18, 20, 23 or 24; and

(b) may make such arrangements as they see fit for any person to act on their behalf in the provision of any such service.

(6) The services provided by a local authority in the exercise of functions conferred on them by this section may include giving assistance in kind or, in exceptional circumstances, in cash.

(7) Assistance may be unconditional or subject to conditions as to the repayment of the assistance or of its value (in whole or in part).

(8) Before giving any assistance or imposing any conditions, a local authority shall have regard to the means of the child concerned and of each of his parents.

(9) No person shall be liable to make any repayment of assistance or of its value at any time when he is in receipt of income support, working families' tax credit or disabled person's tax credit under Part VII of the Social Security Contributions and Benefits Act 1992 or of an income-based jobseeker's allowance.

(10) For the purposes of this Part a child shall be taken to be in need if –
   (a) he is unlikely to achieve or maintain, or to have the opportunity of achieving or maintaining, a reasonable standard of health or development without the provision for him of services by a local authority under this Part;
   (b) his health or development is likely to be significantly impaired, or further impaired, without the provision for him of such services; or
   (c) he is disabled,
   and 'family', in relation to such a child, includes any person who has parental responsibility for the child and any other person with whom he has been living.

(11) For the purposes of this Part, a child is disabled if he is blind, deaf or dumb or suffers from mental disorder of any kind or is substantially and permanently handicapped by illness, injury or congenital deformity or such other disability as may be prescribed; and in this Part –
   'development' means physical, intellectual, emotional, social or behavioural development; and
   'health' means physical or mental health.

Provision of accommodation for children: general

20 (1) Every local authority shall provide accommodation for any child in need within their area who appears to them to require accommodation as a result of –
   (a) there being no person who has parental responsibility for him;
   (b) his being lost or having been abandoned; or
   (c) the person who has been caring for him being prevented (whether or not permanently, and for whatever reason) from providing him with suitable accommodation or care.

(2) Where a local authority provide accommodation under subsection (1) for a child who is ordinarily resident in the area of another local authority, that other local authority may take over the provision of accommodation for the child within –
   (a) three months of being notified in writing that the child is being provided with accommodation; or
   (b) such other longer period as may be prescribed.

(3) Every local authority shall provide accommodation for any child in need within their area who has reached the age of sixteen and whose welfare the

authority consider is likely to be seriously prejudiced if they do not provide him with accommodation.

(4) A local authority may provide accommodation for any child within their area (even though a person who has parental responsibility for him is able to provide him with accommodation) if they consider that to do so would safeguard or promote the child's welfare.

(5) A local authority may provide accommodation for any person who has reached the age of sixteen but is under twenty-one in any community home which takes children who have reached the age of sixteen if they consider that to do so would safeguard or promote his welfare.

(6) Before providing accommodation under this section, a local authority shall, so far as is reasonably practicable and consistent with the child's welfare –
   (a) ascertain the child's wishes regarding the provision of accommodation; and
   (b) give due consideration (having regard to his age and understanding) to such wishes of the child as they have been able to ascertain.

(7) A local authority may not provide accommodation under this section for any child if any person who –
   (a) has parental responsibility for him; and
   (b) is willing and able to
      (i) provide accommodation for him; or
      (ii) arrange for accommodation to be provided for him, objects.

(8) Any person who has parental responsibility for a child may at any time remove the child from accommodation provided by or on behalf of the local authority under this section.

(9) Subsections (7) and (8) do not apply while any person –
   (a) in whose favour a residence order is in force with respect to the child; or
   (b) who has care of the child by virtue of an order made in the exercise of the High Court's inherent jurisdiction with respect to children,

agrees to the child being looked after in accommodation provided by or on behalf of the local authority.

(10) Where there is more than one such person as is mentioned in subsection (9), all of them must agree.

(11) Subsections (7) and (8) do not apply where a child who has reached the age of sixteen agrees to being provided with accommodation under this section.

Provision for accommodation for children in police protection or detention or on remand, etc

21 (1) Every local authority shall make provision for the reception and accommodation of children who are removed or kept away from home under Part V.

(2) Every local authority shall receive, and provide accommodation for, children –
   (a) in police protection whom they are requested to receive under section 46(3)(f);
   (b) whom they are requested to receive under section 38(6) of the Police and Criminal Evidence Act 1984;

(c) who are –
   (i) on remand under section 16(3A) or 23(1) of the Children and Young
      Persons Act 1969; or
   (ii) the subject of a supervision order imposing a residence requirement
      under section 12AA of that Act,

and with respect to whom they are the designated authority.

(3) Where a child has been –
   (a) removed under Part V; or
   (b) detained under section 38 of the Police and Criminal Evidence Act 1984,

and he is not being provided with accommodation by a local authority or
in a hospital vested in the Secretary of State or otherwise made available
pursuant to arrangements made by a Health Authority, any reasonable
expenses of accommodating him shall be recoverable from the local
authority in whose area he is ordinarily resident.

General duty of local authority in relation to children looked after by them

22 (1) In this Act, any reference to a child who is looked after by a local authority is
a reference to a child who is –
   (a) in their care; or
   (b) provided with accommodation by the authority in the exercise of any
      functions (in particular those under this Act) which stand referred to
      their social services committee under the Local Authority Social Services
      Act 1970.

(2) In subsection (1) 'accommodation' means accommodation which is provided for a continuous period of more than 24 hours.

(3) It shall be the duty of a local authority looking after any child –
   (a) to safeguard and promote his welfare; and
   (b) to make such use of services available for children cared for by their own
      parents as appears to the authority reasonable in his case.

(4) Before making any decision with respect to a child whom they are looking
after, or proposing to look after, a local authority shall, so far as is reasonably
practicable, ascertain the wishes and feelings of –
   (a) the child;
   (b) his parents;
   (c) any person who is not a parent of his but who has parental responsibility
      for him; and
   (d) any other person whose wishes and feelings the authority consider to be
      relevant,

regarding the matter to be decided.

(5) In making any such decision a local authority shall give due consideration –
   (a) having regard to his age and understanding, to such wishes and feelings
      of the child as they have been able to ascertain;
   (b) to such wishes and feelings of any person mentioned in subsection
      (4)(b) to (d) as they have been able to ascertain; and
   (c) to the child's religious persuasion, racial origin and cultural and lin-
      guistic background.

(6) If it appears to a local authority that it is necessary, for the purpose of protecting members of the public from serious injury, to exercise their powers with respect to a child whom they are looking after in a manner which may not be consistent with their duties under this section, they may do so.

(7) If the Secretary of State considers it necessary, for the purpose of protecting members of the public from serious injury, to give directions to a local authority with respect to the exercise of their powers with respect to a child whom they are looking after, he may give such directions to the authority.

(8) Where any such directions are given to an authority they shall comply with them even though doing so is inconsistent with their duties under this section.

Provision of accommodation and maintenance by local authority for children whom they are looking after

23 (1) It shall be the duty of any local authority looking after a child –
   (a) when he is in their care, to provide accommodation for him; and
   (b) to maintain him in other respects apart from providing accommodation for him.

(2) A local authority shall provide accommodation and maintenance for any child whom they are looking after by –
   (a) placing him (subject to subsection (5) and any regulations made by the Secretary of State) with –
      (i) a family;
      (ii) a relative of his; or
      (iii) any other suitable person,
   on such terms as to payment by the authority and otherwise as the authority may determine;
   (b) maintaining him in a community home;
   (c) maintaining him in a voluntary home;
   (d) maintaining him in a registered children's home;
   (e) maintaining him in a home provided in accordance with arrangements made by the Secretary of State under section 82(5) on such terms as the Secretary of State may from time to time determine; or
   (f) making such other arrangements as –
      (i) seem appropriate to them; and
      (ii) comply with any regulations made by the Secretary of State.

(3) Any person with whom a child has been placed under subsection (2)(a) is referred to in this Act as a local authority foster parent unless he falls within subsection (4).

(4) A person falls within this subsection if he is –
   (a) a parent of the child;
   (b) a person who is not a parent of the child but who has parental responsibility for him; or
   (c) where the child is in care and there was a residence order in force with respect to him immediately before the care order was made, a person in whose favour the residence order was made.

(5) Where a child is in the care of a local authority, the authority may only allow

him to live with a person who falls within subsection (4) in accordance with regulations made by the Secretary of State.

(5A) For the purposes of subsection (5) a child shall be regarded as living with a person if he stays with that person for a continuous period of more than 24 hours.

(6) Subject to any regulations made by the Secretary of State for the purposes of this subsection, any local authority looking after a child shall make arrangements to enable him to live with –
(a) a person falling within subsection (4); or
(b) a relative, friend or other person connected with him,
unless that would not be reasonably practicable or consistent with his welfare.

(7) Where a local authority provide accommodation for a child whom they are looking after, they shall, subject to the provisions of this Part and so far as is reasonably practicable and consistent with his welfare, secure that –
(a) the accommodation is near his home; and
(b) where the authority are also providing accommodation for a sibling of his, they are accommodated together.

(8) Where a local authority provide accommodation for a child whom they are looking after and who is disabled, they shall, so far as is reasonably practicable, secure that the accommodation is not unsuitable to his particular needs.

(9) Part II of Schedule 2 shall have effect for the purposes of making further provision as to children looked after by local authorities and in particular as to the regulations that may be made under subsections (2)(a) and (f) and (5).

Advice and assistance for certain children

24 (1) Where a child is being looked after by a local authority, it shall be the duty of the authority to advise, assist and befriend him with a view to promoting his welfare when he ceases to be looked after by them.

(2) In this Part 'a person qualifying for advice and assistance' means a person within the area of the authority who is under twenty-one and who was, at any time after reaching the age of sixteen but while still a child –
(a) looked after by a local authority;
(b) accommodated by or on behalf of a voluntary organisation;
(c) accommodated in a registered children's home;
(d) accommodated –
(i) by any Health Authority, Special Health Authority or local education authority; or
(ii) in any residential care home, nursing home or mental nursing home or in any accommodation provided by a National Health Service trust,
for a consecutive period of at least three months; or
(e) privately fostered,
but who is no longer so looked after, accommodated or fostered.

(3) Subsection (2)(d) applies even if the period of three months mentioned there began before the child reached the age of sixteen.

(4) Where –
  (a) a local authority know that there is within their area a person qualifying for advice and assistance;
  (b) the conditions in subsection (5) are satisfied; and
  (c) that person has asked them for help of a kind which they can give under this section,
  they shall (if he was being looked after by a local authority or was accommodated by or on behalf of a voluntary organisation) and may (in any other case) advise and befriend him.

(5) The conditions are that –
  (a) it appears to the authority that the person concerned is in need of advice and being befriended;
  (b) where that person was not being looked after by the authority, they are satisfied that the person by whom he was being looked after does not have the necessary facilities for advising or befriending him.

(6) Where as a result of this section a local authority are under a duty, or are empowered, to advise and befriend a person, they may also give him assistance.

(7) Assistance given under subsections (1) to (6) may be in kind or, in exceptional circumstances, in cash.

(8) A local authority may give assistance to any person who qualifies for advice and assistance by virtue of subsection (2)(a) by –
  (a) contributing to expenses incurred by him in living near the place where he is, or will be –
    (i) employed or seeking employment; or
    (ii) receiving education or training; or
  (b) making a grant to enable him to meet expenses connected with his education or training.

(9) Where a local authority are assisting the person under subsection (8) by making a contribution or grant with respect to a course of education or training, they may –
  (a) continue to do so even though he reaches the age of twenty-one before completing the course; and
  (b) disregard any interruption in his attendance on the course if he resumes it as soon as is reasonably practicable.

(10) Subsections (7) to (9) of section 17 shall apply in relation to assistance given under this section (otherwise than under subsection (8)) as they apply in relation to assistance given under that section.

(11) Where it appears to a local authority that a person whom they have been advising and befriending under this section, as a person qualifying for advice and assistance, proposes to live, or is living, in the area of another local authority, they shall inform that other local authority.

(12) Where a child who is accommodated –
  (a) by a voluntary organisation or in a registered children's home;
  (b) by any Health Authority, Special Health Authority or local education authority; or
  (c) in any residential care home, nursing home or mental nursing home or any accommodation provided by a National Health Service trust,

ceases to be so accommodated, after reaching the age of sixteen, the organisation, authority or (as the case may be) person carrying on the home shall inform the local authority within whose area the child proposes to live.

(13) Subsection (12) only applies, by virtue of paragraph (b) or (c), if the accommodation has been provided for a consecutive period of at least three months.

(14) Every local authority shall establish a procedure for considering any representations (including any complaint) made to them by a person qualifying for advice and assistance about the discharge of their functions under this Part in relation to him.

(15) In carrying out any consideration of representations under subsection (14), a local authority shall comply with any regulations made by the Secretary of State for the purposes of this subsection.

Use of accommodation for restricting liberty

25 (1) Subject to the following provisions of this section, a child who is being looked after by a local authority may not be placed, and, if placed, may not be kept, in accommodation provided for the purpose of restricting liberty ('secure accommodation') unless it appears –

    (a) that –

        (i) he has a history of absconding and is likely to abscond from any other description of accommodation; and

        (ii) if he absconds, he is likely to suffer significant harm; or

    (b) that if he is kept in any other description of accommodation he is likely to injure himself or other persons.

(2) The Secretary of State may by regulations –

    (a) specify a maximum period –

        (i) beyond which a child may not be kept in secure accommodation without the authority of the court; and

        (ii) for which the court may authorise a child to be kept in secure accommodation;

    (b) empower the court from time to time to authorise a child to be kept in secure accommodation for such further period as the regulations may specify; and

    (c) provide that applications to the court under this section shall be made only by local authorities.

(3) It shall be the duty of a court hearing an application under this section to determine whether any relevant criteria for keeping a child in secure accommodation are satisfied in his case.

(4) If a court determines that any such criteria are satisfied, it shall make an order authorising the child to be kept in secure accommodation and specifying the maximum period for which he may be so kept.

(5) On any adjournment of the hearing of an application under this section, a court may make an interim order permitting the child to be kept during the period of the adjournment in secure accommodation.

(6) No court shall exercise the powers conferred by this section in respect of a child who is not legally represented in that court unless, having been

informed of his right to apply for representation funded by the Legal Services Commission as part of the Community Legal Service or Criminal Defence Service and having had the opportunity to do so, he refused or failed to apply.

(7) The Secretary of State may by regulations provide that –

    (a) this section shall or shall not apply to any description of children specified in the regulations;

    (b) this section shall have effect in relation to children of a description specified in the regulations subject to such modifications as may be so specified;

    (c) such other provisions as may be so specified shall have effect for the purpose of determining whether a child of a description specified in the regulations may be placed or kept in secure accommodation.

(8) The giving of an authorisation under this section shall not prejudice any power of any court in England and Wales or Scotland to give directions relating to the child to whom the authorisation relates.

(9) This section is subject to section 20(8).

Criminal Justice Act 1991

Restrictions on imposing custodial sentences

1 (1) This section applies where a person is convicted of an offence punishable with a custodial sentence other than one fixed by law or falling to be imposed under section 2(2), 3(2) or 4(2) of the Crime (Sentences) Act 1997.

(2) Subject to subsection (3) below, the court shall not pass a custodial sentence on the offender unless it is of the opinion –

    (a) that the offence, or the combination of the offence and one or more offences associated with it, was so serious that only such a sentence can be justified for the offence; or

    (b) where the offence is a violent or sexual offence, that only such a sentence would be adequate to protect the public from serious harm from him.

(3) Nothing in subsection (2) above shall prevent the court from passing a custodial sentence on the offender if he fails to express his willingness to comply with –

    (a) a requirement which is proposed by the court to be included in a probation order or supervision order and which requires an expression of such willingness; or

    (b) a requirement which is proposed by the court to be included in a drug treatment and testing order or an order under section 61(6) of the Crime and Disorder Act 1998.

(4) Where a court passes a custodial sentence, it shall be its duty –

    (a) in a case not falling within subsection (3) above, to state in open court that it is of the opinion that either or both of paragraphs (a) and (b) of subsection (2) above apply and why it is of that opinion; and

    (b) in any case, to explain to the offender in open court and in ordinary language why it is passing a custodial sentence on him.

(5) A magistrates' court shall cause a reason stated by it under subsection (4) above to be specified in the warrant of commitment and to be entered in the register.

Length of custodial sentences

2 (1) This section applies where a court passes a custodial sentence other than one fixed by law or falling to be imposed under section 2(2) of the Crime (Sentences) Act 1997.

(2) Subject to sections 3(2) and 4(2) of that Act, the custodial sentence shall be –
   (a) for such term (not exceeding the permitted maximum) as in the opinion of the court is commensurate with the seriousness of the offence, or the combination of the offence and one or more offences associated with it; or
   (b) where the offence is a violent or sexual offence, for such longer term (not exceeding that maximum) as in the opinion of the court is necessary to protect the public from serious harm from the offender.

(3) Where the court passes a custodial sentence for a term longer than is commensurate with the seriousness of the offence, or the combination of the offence and one or more offences associated with it, the court shall –
   (a) state in open court that it is of the opinion that subsection (2)(b) above applies and why it is of that opinion; and
   (b) explain to the offender in open court and in ordinary language why the sentence is for such a term.

(4) A custodial sentence for an indeterminate period shall be regarded for the purposes of subsections (2) and (3) above as a custodial sentence for a term longer than any actual term.

(5) Subsection (3) above shall not apply in any case where the court passes a custodial sentence falling to be imposed under subsection (2) of section 3 or 4 of the Crime (Sentences) Act 1997 which is for the minimum term specified in that subsection.

Procedural requirements for custodial sentences

3 (1) Subject to subsection (2) below, a court shall obtain and consider a pre-sentence report before forming any such opinion as is mentioned in subsection (2) of section 1 or 2 above.

(2) Subsection (1) above does not apply if, in the circumstances of the case, the court is of the opinion that it is unnecessary to obtain a pre-sentence report.

(2A) In the case of an offender under the age of eighteen years, save where the offence or any other offence associated with it is triable only on indictment, the court shall not form such an opinion as is mentioned in subsection (2) or subsection (4A) below unless there exists a previous pre-sentence report obtained in respect of the offender and the court has had regard to the information contained in that report, or, if there is more than one report, the most recent report.

(3) In forming any such opinion as is mentioned in subsection (2) of section 1 or 2 above a court –
   (a) shall take into account all such information about the circumstances of

the offence or (as the case may be) of the offence and the offence or offences associated with it (including any aggravating or mitigating factors) as is available to it; and

(b) in the case of any such opinion as is mentioned in paragraph (b) of that subsection, may take into account any information about the offender which is before it.

(4) No custodial sentence shall be invalidated by the failure of a court to obtain and consider a pre-sentence report before forming an opinion referred to in subsection (1) above but any court on an appeal against such a sentence –

(a) shall, subject to subsection (4A) below, obtain a pre-sentence report if none was obtained by the court below; and

(b) shall consider any such report obtained by it or by that court.

(4A) Subsection (4)(a) above does not apply if the court is of the opinion –

(a) that the court below was justified in forming an opinion that it was unnecessary to obtain a pre-sentence report, or

(b) that, although the court below was not justified in forming that opinion, in the circumstances of the case at the time it is before the court, it is unnecessary to obtain a pre-sentence report.

(5) In this Part 'pre-sentence report' means a report in writing which –

(a) with a view to assisting the court in determining the most suitable method of dealing with an offender, is made or submitted by –

   (i) a probation officer;

   (ii) a social worker of a local authority social services department; or

   (iii) where the offender is under the age of 18 years, a member of a youth offending team; and

(b) contains information as to such matters, presented in such manner, as may be prescribed by rules made by the Secretary of State.

Additional requirements in the case of mentally disordered offenders

4 (1) Subject to subsection (2) below, in any case where the offender is or appears to be mentally disordered, the court shall obtain and consider a medical report before passing a custodial sentence other than one fixed by law or falling to be imposed under section 2(2) of the Crime (Sentences) Act 1997.

(2) Subsection (1) above does not apply if, in the circumstances of the case, the court is of the opinion that it is unnecessary to obtain a medical report.

(3) Before passing a custodial sentence other than one fixed by law or falling to be imposed under section 2(2) of the Crime (Sentences) Act 1997 on an offender who is or appears to be mentally disordered, a court shall consider –

(a) any information before it which relates to his mental condition (whether given in a medical report, a pre-sentence report or otherwise); and

(b) the likely effect of such a sentence on that condition and on any treatment which may be available for it.

(4) No custodial sentence which is passed in a case to which subsection (1) above applies shall be invalidated by the failure of a court to comply with that subsection, but any court on an appeal against such a sentence –

(a) shall obtain a medical report if none was obtained by the court below; and

(b) shall consider any such report obtained by it or by that court.

(5) In this section –

'duly approved', in relation to a registered medical practitioner, means approved for the purposes of section 12 of the Mental Health Act 1983 ('the 1983 Act') by the Secretary of State as having special experience in the diagnosis or treatment of mental disorder;

'medical report' means a report as to an offender's mental condition made or submitted orally or in writing by a registered medical practitioner who is duly approved.

(6) Nothing in this section shall be taken as prejudicing the generality of section 3 above.

Restrictions on imposing community sentences

6 (1) A court shall not pass on an offender a community sentence, that is to say, a sentence which consists of or includes one or more community orders, unless it is of the opinion that the offence, or the combination of the offence and one or more offences associated with it, was serious enough to warrant such a sentence.

(2) Subject to subsection (3) below, where a court passes a community sentence –

(a) the particular order or orders comprising or forming part of the sentence shall be such as in the opinion of the court is, or taken together are, the most suitable for the offender; and

(b) the restrictions on liberty imposed by the order or orders shall be such as in the opinion of the court are commensurate with the seriousness of the offence, or the combination of the offence and one or more offences associated with it.

(3) In consequence of the provision made by section 11 below with respect to combination orders, a community sentence shall not consist of or include both a probation order and a community service order.

(4) In this Part 'community order' means any of the following orders, namely –

(a) a probation order;

(aa) a drug treatment and testing order;

(b) a community service order;

(c) a combination order;

(d) a curfew order;

(e) a supervision order;

(f) an attendance centre order;

(g) an action plan order.

Procedural requirements for community sentences

7 (1) In forming any such opinion as is mentioned in subsection (1) or (2)(b) of section 6 above, a court shall take into account all such information about the circumstances of the offence or (as the case may be) of the offence and the offence or offences associated with it (including any aggravating or mitigating factors) as is available to it.

(2) In forming any such opinion as is mentioned in subsection (2)(a) of that section, a court may take into account any information about the offender which is before it.

(3) Subject to subsection (3A) below, a court shall obtain and consider a pre-sentence report before forming an opinion as to the suitability for the offender of one or more of the following orders, namely –

(a) a probation order which includes additional requirements authorised by Schedule 1A to the 1973 Act;

(aa) a drug treatment and testing order;

(b) a community service order;

(c) a combination order; and

(d) a supervision order which includes requirements imposed under section 12, 12A, 12AA, 12B or 12C of the Children and Young Persons Act 1969 ('the 1969 Act').

(3A) Subsection (3) above does not apply if, in the circumstances of the case, the court is of the opinion that it is unnecessary to obtain a pre-sentence report.

(3B) In the case of an offender under the age of eighteen years, save where the offence or any other offence associated with it is triable only on indictment, the court shall not form such an opinion as is mentioned in subsection (3A) above or subsection (5) below unless there exists a previous pre-sentence report obtained in respect of the offender and the court has had regard to the information contained in that report, or, if there is more than one such report, the most recent report.

(4) No community sentence which consists of or includes such an order as is mentioned in subsection (3) above shall be invalidated by the failure of a court to obtain and consider a pre-sentence report before forming an opinion referred to in that subsection, but any court on an appeal against such a sentence –

(a) shall, subject to subsection (5) below, obtain a pre-sentence report if none was obtained by the court below; and

(b) shall consider any such report obtained by it or by that court.

(5) Subsection (4)(a) above does not apply if the court is of the opinion –

(a) that the court below was justified in forming an opinion that it was unnecessary to obtain a pre-sentence report, or

(b) that, although the court below was not justified in forming that opinion, in the circumstances of the case at the time it is before the court, it is unnecessary to obtain a pre-sentence report.

Binding over of parent or guardian

58 (1) Where a child or young person ('the relevant minor') is convicted of an offence, the powers conferred by this section shall be exercisable by the court by which he is sentenced for that offence; and it shall be the duty of the court, in a case where the relevant minor has not attained the age of 16 years –

(a) to exercise those powers if it is satisfied, having regard to the circumstances of the case, that their exercise would be desirable in the interests of preventing the commission by him of further offences; and

(b) where it does not exercise them, to state in open court that it is not satisfied as mentioned in paragraph (a) above and why it is not so satisfied.

(1A) Subsection (1) has effect subject to section 4(5) of, and paragraph 13(5) of Schedule 1 to, the Youth Justice and Criminal Evidence Act 1999.

(2) The powers conferred by this section are as follows –

(a) with the consent of the relevant minor's parent or guardian, to order the parent or guardian to enter into a recognisance to take proper care of him and exercise proper control over him; and

(b) if the parent or guardian refuses consent and the court considers the refusal unreasonable, to order the parent or guardian to pay a fine not exceeding £1,000.

Where the court has passed on the relevant minor a community sentence (within the meaning of section 6 above) it may include in the recognisance a provision that the minor's parent or guardian ensure that the minor complies with the requirements of that sentence.

(3) An order under this section shall not require the parent or guardian to enter into a recognisance –

(a) for an amount exceeding £1,000; or

(b) for a period exceeding three years or, where the relevant minor will attain the age of 18 years in a period shorter than three years, for a period exceeding that shorter period;

and section 120 of the 1980 Act (which relates to the forfeiture of recognisances) shall apply in relation to a recognisance entered into in pursuance of such an order as it applies to a recognisance to keep the peace.

(4) A fine imposed under subsection (2)(b) above shall be deemed, for the purposes of any enactment, to be a sum adjudged to be paid by a conviction.

(5) In fixing the amount of a recognisance under this section, the court shall take into account among other things the means of the parent or guardian so far as they appear or are known to the court; and this subsection applies whether taking into account the means of the parent or guardian has the effect of increasing or reducing the amount of the recognisance.

(6) A parent or guardian may appeal to the Crown Court against an order under this section made by a magistrates' court.

(7) A parent or guardian may appeal to the Court of Appeal against an order under this section made by the Crown Court, as if he had been convicted on indictment and the order were a sentence passed on his conviction.

(8) A court may vary or revoke an order made by it under this section if, on the application of the parent or guardian, it appears to the court, having regard to any change in the circumstances since the order was made, to be in the interests of justice to do so.

(9) For the purposes of this section –

(a) 'guardian' has the same meaning as in the 1933 Act; and

(b) taking 'care' of a person includes giving him protection and guidance and 'control' includes 'discipline'.

SCHEDULE 2: ENFORCEMENT, ETC, OF COMMUNITY ORDERS

PART I – PRELIMINARY

1 (1) In this Schedule 'relevant order' means any of the following orders, namely, a probation order, a drug treatment and testing order, a community service order and a curfew order; and 'the petty sessions area concerned' means –

    (a) in relation to a probation, community service or drug treatment and testing order, the petty sessions area for the time being specified in the order; and

    (b) in relation to a curfew order, the petty sessions area in which the place for the time being specified in the order is situated.

    (2) Subject to sub-paragraph (3) below, this Schedule shall apply in relation to combination orders –

    (a) in so far as they impose such a requirement as is mentioned in paragraph (a) of subsection (1) of section 11 of this Act, as if they were probation orders; and

    (b) in so far as they impose such a requirement as is mentioned in paragraph (b) of that subsection, as if they were community service orders.

    (3) In its application to combination orders, paragraph 6(3) below shall have effect as if the reference to section 14(1A) of the 1973 Act were a reference to section 11(1) of this Act.

    (4) In this Schedule, references to the court responsible for a drug treatment and testing order shall be construed in accordance with section 62(9) of the Crime and Disorder Act 1998.

    (5) Where a probation order, community service order, combination order or curfew order has been made on appeal, for the purposes of this Schedule it shall be deemed–

    (a) if it was made on an appeal brought from a magistrates' court, to have been made by a magistrates' court;

    (b) if it was made on an appeal brought from the Crown Court or from the criminal division of the Court of Appeal, to have been made by the Crown Court.

    (6) Where a drug treatment and testing order has been made on an appeal brought from the Crown Court, or from the criminal division of the Court of Appeal, for the purposes of this Schedule it shall be deemed to have been made by the Crown Court.

PART II – BREACH OF REQUIREMENT OF ORDER

Issue of summons or warrant

2 (1) If at any time while a relevant order is in force in respect of an offender it appears on information to a justice of the peace acting for the petty sessions

area concerned that the offender has failed to comply with any of the requirements of the order, the justice may –

(a) issue a summons requiring the offender to appear at the place and time specified in it; or

(b) if the information is in writing and on oath, issue a warrant for his arrest.

(2) Any summons or warrant issued under this paragraph shall direct the offender to appear or be brought:

(a) in the case of any other relevant order which was made by the Crown Court and included a direction that any failure to comply with any of the requirements of the order be dealt with by the Crown Court, before the Crown Court; and

(b) in the case of any other relevant order which was made by the Crown Court and included in a direction that any failure to comply with any of the requirements of the order be dealt with by the Crown Court, before the Crown Court; and

(c) in the case of any other relevant order, before a magistrates' court acting for the petty sessions area concerned.

Powers of magistrates' court

3 (1) If it is proved to the satisfaction of a magistrates' court before which an offender appears or is brought under paragraph 2 above that he has failed without reasonable excuse to comply with any of the requirements of the relevant order, the court may deal with him in respect of the failure in any one of the following ways, namely –

(a) it may impose on him a fine not exceeding £1,000;

(b) subject to paragraph 6(3) to (5) below, it may make a community service order in respect of him;

(c) where –

   (i) the relevant order is a probation order and the offender is under the age of twenty-one years, or

   (ii) the relevant order is a curfew order and the offender is under the age of sixteen years,

and the court has been notified as required by subsection (1) of section 17 of the 1982 Act, it may (subject to paragraph 6(6) below) make in respect of him an order under that section (attendance centre orders); or

(d) where the relevant order was made by a magistrates' court, it may deal with him, for the offence in respect of which the order was made, in any manner in which it could deal with him if he had just been convicted by the court of the offence.

(2) In dealing with an offender under sub-paragraph (1)(d) above, a magistrates' court –

(a) shall take into account the extent to which the offender has complied with the requirements of the relevant order; and

(b) in the case of an offender who has wilfully and persistently failed to comply with those requirements, may impose a custodial sentence notwithstanding anything in section 1(2) of this Act.

(2A) Where a magistrates' court deals with an offender under sub-paragraph (1)(d) above, it shall revoke the relevant order if it is still in force.

(3) Where a relevant order was made by the Crown Court and a magistrates' court has power to deal with the offender under sub-paragraph (1)(a), (b) or (c) above, it may instead commit him to custody or release him on bail until he can be brought or appear before the Crown Court.

(4) A magistrates' court which deals with an offender's case under sub-paragraph (3) above shall send to the Crown Court –
   (a) a certificate signed by a justice of the peace certifying that the offender has failed to comply with the requirements of the relevant order in the respect specified in the certificate; and
   (b) such other particulars of the case as may be desirable;
   and a certificate purporting to be so signed shall be admissible as evidence of the failure before the Crown Court.

(5) A person sentenced under sub-paragraph (1)(d) above for an offence may appeal to the Crown Court against the sentence.

Powers of Crown Court

4 (1) Where under paragraph 2 or by virtue of paragraph 3(3) above an offender is brought or appears before the Crown Court and it is proved to the satisfaction of the court that he has failed without reasonable excuse to comply with any of the requirements of the relevant order, that court may deal with him in respect of the failure in any one of the following ways, namely –
   (a) it may impose on him a fine not exceeding £1,000;
   (b) in the case of an offender who has wilfully and persistently failed to comply with those requirements, may impose a custodial sentence notwithstanding anything in section 1(2) of this Act.
   (c) where –
      (i) the relevant order is a probation order and the offender is under the age of twenty-one years, or
      (ii) the relevant order is a curfew order and the offender is under the age of sixteen years,
      and the court has been notified as required by subsection (1) of section 17 of the 1982 Act, it may (subject to paragraph 6(6) below) make in respect of him an order under that section (attendance centre orders); or
   (d) it may deal with him, for the offence in respect of which the order was made, in any manner in which it could deal with him if he had just been convicted before the Crown Court of the offence.

   (2) In dealing with an offender under sub-paragraph (1)(d) above, the Crown Court –
   (a) shall take into account the extent to which the offender has complied with the requirements of the relevant order; and
   (b) may assume, in the case of an offender who has wilfully and persistently failed to comply with those requirements, that he has refused to give his consent to a community sentence which has been proposed by the court and requires that consent.

(2A) Where the Crown Court deals with an offender under sub-paragraph (1)(d) above, it shall revoke the relevant order if it is still in force.

(3) In proceedings before the Crown Court under this paragraph any question whether the offender has failed to comply with the requirements of the relevant order shall be determined by the court and not by the verdict of a jury.

Exclusions

5 (1) Without prejudice to paragraphs 7 and 8 below, an offender who is convicted of a further offence while a relevant order is in force in respect of him shall not on that account be liable to be dealt with under paragraph 3 or 4 above in respect of a failure to comply with any requirement of the order.

(2) An offender who:
  (a) is required by a probation order to submit to treatment for his mental condition, or his dependency on or propensity to misuse drugs or alcohol; or
  (b) is required by a drug treatment and testing order to submit to treatment for his dependency on or propensity to misuse drugs,

shall not be treated for the purposes of paragraph 3 or 4 above as having failed to comply with that requirement on the ground only that he has refused to undergo any surgical, electrical or other treatment if, in the opinion of the court, his refusal was reasonable having regard to all the circumstances.

Supplemental

6 (1) Any exercise by a court of its powers under paragraph 3(1)(a), (b) or (c) or 4(1)(a), (b) or (c) above shall be without prejudice to the continuance of the relevant order.

(2) A fine imposed under paragraph 3(1)(a) or 4(1)(a) above shall be deemed for the purposes of any enactment to be a sum adjudged to be paid by a conviction.

(3) The number of hours which an offender may be required to work under a community service order made under paragraph 3(1)(b) or 4(1)(b) above –
  (a) shall be specified in the order and shall not exceed 60 in the aggregate; and
  (b) where the relevant order is a community service order, shall not be such that the total number of hours under both orders exceeds the maximum specified in section 14(1A) of the 1973 Act.

(3A) A community service order shall not be made under paragraph 3(1)(b) or 4(1)(b) above in respect of a person who is under the age of sixteen years.

(4) Section 14(2) of the 1973 Act and, so far as applicable –
  (a) the following provisions of that Act relating to community service orders; and
  (b) the provisions of this Schedule so far as so relating,

shall have effect in relation to a community service order under paragraph

3(1)(b) or 4(1)(b) above as they have effect in relation to a community service order in respect of an offender.

(5) Where the provisions of this Schedule have effect as mentioned in sub-paragraph (4) above in relation to a community service order under paragraphs 3(1)(b) or 4(1)(b) above –

(a) the power conferred on the court by each of paragraphs 3(1)(d) and 4(1)(d) above and paragraph 7(2)(a)(ii) below to deal with the offender for the offence in respect of which the order was made shall be construed as a power to deal with the offender, for his failure to comply with the original order, in any manner in which the court could deal with him if that failure to comply had just been proved to the satisfaction of the court;

(b) the reference to paragraph 7(1)(b) below to the offence in respect of which the order was made shall be construed as a reference to the failure to comply in respect of which the order was made; and

(c) the power conferred on the court by paragraph 8(2)(b) below to deal with the offender for the offence in respect of which the order was made shall be construed as any manner in which the court which made the original order could deal with him if that failure had just been proved to the satisfaction of that court;

and in this sub-paragraph 'the original order' means the relevant order the failure to comply with whose requirements led to the making of the community service order under paragraph 3(1)(b) or 4(1)(b).

(6) The provisions of sections 17 to 19 of the 1982 Act (making, discharge, variation and breach of attendance centre order) shall apply for the purposes of paragraphs 3(1)(c) and 4(1)(c) above but as if there were omitted –

(a) subsection (13) of section 17;

(b) from subsection (4A) of section 18 and subsections (3) and (5) of section 19, the words ', for the offence in respect of which the order was made,' and 'for that offence'.

6A (1) Where a relevant order was made by a magistrates' court in the case of an offender under 18 years of age in respect of an offence triable only on indictment in the case of an adult, any powers exercisable under paragraph 3(1)(d) above by that or any other court in respect of the offender after he has attained the age of 18 years shall be powers to do either or both of the following –

(a) to impose a fine not exceeding £5,000 for the offence in respect of which the order was made;

(b) to deal with the offender for that offence in any way in which a magistrates' court could deal with him if it had just convicted him of an offence punishable with imprisonment for a term not exceeding six months.

(2) In sub-paragraph (1)(b) above any reference to an offence punishable with imprisonment shall be construed without regard to any prohibition or restriction imposed by or under any enactment on the imprisonment of young offenders.

PART III – REVOCATION OF ORDER

Revocation of order with or without re-sentencing

7 (1) This paragraph applies where a relevant order made by a magistrates' court is in force in respect of any offender and, on the application of the offender or the responsible officer, it appears to a magistrates' court acting for the petty sessions area concerned or, where the relevant order is a drug treatment and testing order, to the magistrates' court responsible for the order that, having regard to circumstances which have arisen since the order was made, it would be in the interests of justice –
    (a) that the order should be revoked; or
    (b) that the offender should be dealt with in some other manner for the offence in respect of which the order was made.

   (2) The court may –
    (a) revoke the order; or
    (b) revoke the order and deal with the offender, for the offence in respect of which the order was made, in any manner in which it could deal with him if he had just been convicted by the court of the offence.

   (3) The circumstances in which a probation order or drug treatment and testing order may be revoked under sub-paragraph (2)(a) above shall include the offender's making good progress or his responding satisfactorily to supervision or, as the case may be, treatment.

   (4) In dealing with an offender under sub-paragraph (2)(b) above, a magistrates' court shall take into account the extent to which the offender has complied with the requirements of the relevant order.

   (5) An offender sentenced under sub-paragraph (2)(b) above for an offence may appeal to the Crown Court against the sentence.

   [(6) *Repealed.*]

   (7) Where a magistrates' court proposes to exercise its powers under this paragraph otherwise than on the application of the offender it shall summon him to appear before the court and, if he does not appear in answer to the summons, may issue a warrant for his arrest.

   (8) No application may be made by the offender under sub-paragraph (1) above while an appeal against the relevant order is pending.

8 (1) This paragraph applies where –
    (a) a relevant order made by the Crown Court is in force in respect of an offender and the offender or the responsible officer applies to the Crown Court for the order to be revoked or for the offender to be dealt with in some other manner for the offence in respect of which the order was made; or
    (b) an offender in respect of whom a relevant order is in force is convicted of an offence before the Crown Court or, having been committed by a magistrates' court to the Crown Court for sentence, is brought or appears before the Crown Court.

   (2) If it appears to the Crown Court to be in the interests of justice to do so, having regard to circumstances which have arisen since the order was made, the Crown Court may–

(a) revoke the order; or

(b) revoke the order and deal with the offender, for the offence in respect of which the order was made, in any manner in which the court which made the order could deal with him if he had just been convicted of that offence by or before the court which made the order.

(3) The circumstances in which a probation order or drug treatment and testing order may be revoked under sub-paragraph (2)(a) above shall include the offender's making good progress or his responding satisfactorily to supervision or, as the case may be, treatment.

(4) In dealing with an offender under sub-paragraph (2)(b) above, the Crown Court shall take into account the extent to which the offender has complied with the requirements of the relevant order.

8A (1) This paragraph applies where a probation order is in force in respect of any offender and on the application of the offender or the responsible officer to a magistrates' court acting for the petty sessions area concerned (where the order was made by a magistrates' court) or the Crown Court (where the order was made by the Crown Court) it appears to the court that, having regard to circumstances which have arisen since the order was made, it would be in the interests of justice –

(a) for the probation order to be revoked; and

(b) for an order to be made under section 1A(1)(b) of the 1973 Act discharging the offender conditionally for the offence for which the probation order was made.

(2) No application may be made under paragraph 7 or 8 above for a probation order to be revoked and replaced with an order for conditional discharge under section 1A(1)(b) of the 1973 Act; but otherwise nothing in this paragraph shall affect the operation of paragraphs 7 and 8 above.

(3) Where this paragraph applies –

(a) the court dealing with the application may revoke the probation order and make an order under section 1A(1)(b) of the 1973 Act discharging the offender in respect of the offence for which the probation order was made, subject to the condition that he commits no offence during the period specified in the order under section 1A(1)(b); and

(b) the period specified in the order under section 1A(1)(b) shall be the period beginning with the making of that order and ending with the date when the probation period specified in the probation order would have ended.

[(4) and (5) *Repealed*.]

(6) For the purposes of sub-paragraph (3) above, subsection (1) of section 1A of the 1973 Act shall apply as if –

(a) for the words from the beginning to 'may make an order either' there were substituted the words 'where paragraph 8A of Schedule 2 to the Criminal Justice Act 1991 applies, the court which under sub-paragraph (3) of that paragraph has power to dispose of the application may (subject to the provisions of that sub-paragraph) make an order in respect of the offender'; and

(b) paragraph (a) of that subsection were omitted.

(7) An application under this paragraph may be heard in the offender's absence if –
  (a) the application is made by the responsible officer; and
  (b) the officer produces to the court a statement by the offender that he understands the effect of an order for conditional discharge and consents to the making of the application;
  and where the application is so heard section 1A(3) of the 1973 Act shall not apply.

(8) No application may be made under this paragraph while an appeal against the probation order is pending.

(9) Without prejudice to paragraph 11 below, on the making of an order under section 1A(1)(b) of the 1973 Act by virtue of this paragraph the court shall forthwith give copies of the order to the responsible officer, and the responsible officer shall give a copy to the offender.

(10) Each of sections 1(11), 2(9) and 66(4) of the Crime and Disorder Act 1998 (which prevent a court from making an order for conditional discharge in certain cases) shall have effect as if the reference to the court by or before which a person is convicted of an offence there mentioned included a reference to a court dealing with an application under this paragraph in respect of the offence.

Revocation of order following custodial sentence

9 (1) This paragraph applies where –
  (a) an offender in respect of whom a relevant order is in force is convicted of an offence –
    (i) by a magistrates' court other than a magistrates' court acting for the petty sessions area concerned; or
    (ii) where the relevant order is a drug treatment and testing order, by a magistrates' court which is not responsible for the order; and
  (b) the court imposes a custodial sentence on the offender.

(2) If it appears to the court, on the application of the offender or the responsible officer, that it would be in the interests of justice to do so having regard to circumstances which have arisen since the order was made, the court may –
  (a) if the order was made by a magistrates' court, revoke it; and
  (b) if the order was made by the Crown Court, commit the offender in custody or release him on bail until he can be brought or appear before the Crown Court.

(3) Where the court deals with an offender's case under sub-paragraph (2)(b) above, it shall send to the Crown Court such particulars of the case as may be desirable.

10 Where by virtue of paragraph 9(2)(b) above an offender is brought or appears before the Crown Court and it appears to the Crown Court to be in the interests of justice to do so, having regard to circumstances which have arisen since the relevant order was made, the Crown Court may revoke the order.

Supplemental

11 (1) On the making under this Part of this Schedule of an order revoking a relevant order, the proper officer of the court shall forthwith give copies of the revoking order to the responsible officer.

(1A) In sub-paragraph (1) above 'proper officer' means –

   (a) in relation to a magistrates'court, the justices' chief executive for the court, and

   (b) in relation to the Crown Court, the appropriate officer.

(2) A responsible officer to whom in accordance with sub-paragraph (1) above copies of a revoking order are given shall give a copy to the offender and to the person in charge of any institution in which the offender was required by the order to reside.

11A Paragraph 6A above shall apply for the purposes of paragraphs 7 and 8 above as it applies for the purposes of paragraph 3 above, but as if in paragraph 6A(1) for the words 'powers exercisable under paragraph 3(1)(d) above' there were substituted the words 'powers to deal with the offender which are exercisable under paragraph 7(2)(b) or 8(2)(b) below'.

11B Where under this Part of this Schedule a relevant order is revoked and replaced by an order for conditional discharge under section 1A(1)(b) of the 1973 Act and–

   (a) the order for conditional discharge is not made in the circumstances mentioned in section 1B(9) of the 1973 Act (order made by magistrates' court in the case of an offender under eighteen in respect of offence triable only on indictment in the case of an adult), but

   (b) the relevant order was made in those circumstances,

   section 1B(9) of the 1973 Act shall apply as if the order for conditional discharge has been made in those circumstances.

PART IV – AMENDMENT OF OTHER

Amendment by reason of change of residence

12 (1) This paragraph applies where, at any time while a relevant order (other than a drug treatment and testing order) is in force in respect of an offender, a magistrates' court acting for the petty sessions area concerned is satisfied that the offender proposes to change, or has changed, his residence from that petty sessions area to another petty sessions area.

(2) Subject to sub-paragraphs (3) and (4) below, the court may, and on the application of the responsible officer shall, amend the relevant order by substituting the other petty sessions area for the area specified in the order or, in the case of a curfew order, a place in that other area for the place so specified.

(3) The court shall not amend under this paragraph a probation or curfew order which contains requirements which, in the opinion of the court, cannot be complied with unless the offender continues to reside in the petty sessions area concerned unless, in accordance with paragraph 13 below, it either –

   (a) cancels those requirements; or

(b) substitutes for those requirements other requirements which can be complied with if the offender ceases to reside in that area.

(4) The court shall not amend a community service order under this paragraph unless it appears to the court that provision can be made for the offender to perform work under the order under the arrangements which exist for persons who reside in the other petty sessions area to perform work under such orders.

(5) Where –
(a) the court amends a probation order or community service order under this paragraph;
(b) a local authority is specified in the order in accordance with section 2(2)(b) or 14(4)(c) of the 1973 Act; and
(c) the change, or proposed change, of residence also is or would be a change of residence from the area of that authority to the area of another such authority,

the court shall further amend the order by substituting the other authority for the authority specified in the order.

(6) In sub-paragraph (5) above 'local authority' has the meaning given by section 42 of the Crime and Disorder Act 1998, and references to the area of a local authority shall be construed in accordance with that section.

Amendment of requirements of probation or curfew order

13 (1) Without prejudice to the provisions of paragraph 12 above, but subject to sub-paragraph (2) below, a magistrates' court for the petty sessions area concerned may, on the application of the offender or the responsible officer, by order amend a probation or curfew order –
(a) by cancelling any of the requirements of the order; or
(b) by inserting in the order (either in addition to or in substitution for any such requirement) any requirement which the court could include if it were then making the order.

(2) The power of a magistrates' court under sub-paragraph (1) above shall be subject to the following restrictions, namely –
(a) the court shall not amend a probation order –
(i) by reducing the probation period, or by extending that period beyond the end of three years from the date of the original order; or
(ii) by inserting in it a requirement that the offender shall submit to treatment for his mental condition, or his dependency on drugs or alcohol, unless the offender has expressed his willingness to comply with such a requirement and the amending order is made within three months after the date of the original order; and
(b) the court shall not amend a curfew order by extending the curfew periods beyond the end of six months from the date of the original order.

(3) In this paragraph and paragraph 14 below, references to the offender's dependency on drugs or alcohol include references to his propensity towards the misuse of drugs or alcohol.

Amendment of certain requirements of probation order

14 (1) Where the medical practitioner or other person by whom or under whose direction an offender is being treated for his mental condition, or his dependency on drugs or alcohol, in pursuance of any requirement of a probation order –

   (a) is of the opinion mentioned in sub-paragraph (2) below; or

   (b) is for any reason unwilling to continue to treat or direct the treatment of the offender,

he shall make a report in writing to that effect to the responsible officer and that officer shall apply under paragraph 13 above to a magistrates' court for the petty sessions area concerned for the variation or cancellation of the requirement.

  (2) The opinion referred to in sub-paragraph (1) above is –

   (a) that the treatment of the offender should be continued beyond the period specified in that behalf in the order;

   (b) that the offender needs different treatment;

   (c) that the offender is not susceptible to treatment; or

   (d) that the offender does not require further treatment.

14A (1) Without prejudice to the provisions of section 63(2), (7) and (9) of the Crime and Disorder Act 1998, the court responsible for a drug treatment and testing order may by order–

   (a) vary or cancel any of the requirements or provisions of the order on an application by the responsible officer under sub-paragraph (2) or (3)(a) or (b) below; or

   (b) amend the order on an application by that officer under sub-paragraph (3)(c) below.

  (2) Where the treatment provider is of the opinion that the treatment or testing requirement of the order should be varied or cancelled–

   (a) he shall make a report in writing to that effect to the responsible officer; and

   (b) that officer shall apply to the court for the variation or cancellation of the requirement.

  (3) Where the responsible officer is of the opinion–

   (a) that the treatment or testing requirement of the order should be so varied as to specify a different treatment provider;

   (b) that any other requirement of the order, or a provision of the order, should be varied or cancelled; or

   (c) that the order should be so amended as to provide for each subsequent review under section 63 of the Crime and Disorder Act 1998 to be made without a hearing instead of at a review hearing, or vice versa,

he shall apply to the court for the variation or cancellation of the requirement or provision or the amendment of the order.

  (4) The court–

   (a) shall not amend the treatment or testing requirement unless the offender expresses his willingness to comply with the requirement as amended; and

   (b) shall not amend any provision of the order so as to reduce the treatment and testing period below the minimum specified in section 61(2) of the Crime and Disorder Act 1998 or to increase it above the maximum so specified.

(5) If the offender fails to express his willingness to comply with the treatment or testing requirement as proposed to be amended by the Court, the court may–
(a) revoke the order; and
(b) deal with him, for the offence in respect of which the order was made, in any manner in which it could deal with him if he had just been convicted by the court of the offence.

(6) In dealing with the offender under sub-paragraph (5)(b) above, the court –
(a) shall take into account the extent to which the offender has complied with the requirements of the order; and
(b) may impose a custodial sentence notwithstanding anything in section 1(2) of this Act.

(7) Paragraph 6A above shall apply for the purposes of this paragraph as it applies for the purposes of paragraph 3 above, but as if for the words 'paragraph 3(1)(d) above' there were substituted the words 'paragraph 14A(5)(b) below'.

(8) In this paragraph–
'review hearing' has the same meaning as in section 63 of the Crime and Disorder Act 1998;
'the treatment requirement' and 'the testing requirement' have the same meanings as in Chapter I of Part IV of that Act.

Extension of community service order

15 Where –
(a) a community service order is in force in respect of any offender; and
(b) on the application of the offender or the responsible officer, it appears to a magistrates' court acting for the petty sessions area concerned that it would be in the interests of justice to do so having regard to circumstances which have arisen since the order was made,
the court may, in relation to the order, extend the period of twelve months specified in section 15(2) of the 1973 Act.

Supplemental

16 No order may be made under paragraph 12 above, and no application may be made under paragraph 13 or 15 above or, except with the consent of the offender, under paragraph 14A above, while an appeal against the relevant order is pending.

17 (1) Subject to sub-paragraph (2) below, where a court proposes to exercise its powers under this Part of this Schedule, otherwise than on the application of the offender, the court –
(a) shall summon him to appear before the court; and
(b) if he does not appear in answer to the summons, may issue a warrant for his arrest.

(2) This paragraph shall not apply to an order cancelling a requirement of a relevant order or reducing the period of any requirement, or substituting a new petty sessions area or a new place for the one specified in a relevant order.

18 (1) On the making under this Part of this Schedule of an order amending a relevant order (other than a drug treatment and testing order), the clerk to the court shall forthwith –

   (a) if the order amends the relevant order otherwise than by substituting a new petty sessions area or a new place for the one specified in the relevant order, give copies of the amending order to the responsible officer;

   (b) if the order amends the relevant order in the manner excepted by paragraph (a) above, send to the clerk to the justices for the new petty sessions area or, as the case may be, for the petty sessions area in which the new place is situated –

   (i) copies of the amending order; and

   (ii) such documents and information relating to the case as he considers likely to be of assistance to a court acting for that area in exercising its functions in relation to the order;

and in a case falling within paragraph (b) above the clerk to the justices for that area shall give copies of the amending order to the responsible officer.

   (1A) On the making under this Part of this Schedule of an order amending a drug treatment and testing order, the justices' chief executive for the court shall forthwith give copies of the amending order to the responsible officer.

   (2) A responsible officer to whom in accordance with sub-paragraph (1) or (1A) above copies of an order are given shall give a copy to the offender and to the person in charge of any institution in which the offender is or was required by the order to reside.

Crime and Disorder Act 1998

Anti-social behaviour orders

1 (1) An application for an order under this section may be made by a relevant authority if it appears to the authority that the following conditions are fulfilled with respect to any person aged 10 or over, namely –

   (a) that the person has acted, since the commencement date, in an anti-social manner, that is to say, in a manner that caused or was likely to cause harassment, alarm or distress to one or more persons not of the same household as himself; and

   (b) that such an order is necessary to protect persons in the local government area in which the harassment, alarm or distress was caused or was likely to be caused from further anti-social acts by him;

and in this section 'relevant authority' means the council for the local government area or any chief officer of police any part of whose police area lies within that area.

   (2) A relevant authority shall not make such an application without consulting each other relevant authority.

   (3) Such an application shall be made by complaint to the magistrates' court whose commission area includes the place where it is alleged that the harassment, alarm or distress was caused or was likely to be caused.

(4) If, on such an application, it is proved that the conditions mentioned in subsection (1) above are fulfilled, the magistrates' court may make an order under this section (an 'anti-social behaviour order') which prohibits the defendant from doing anything described in the order.

(5) For the purpose of determining whether the condition mentioned in subsection (1)(a) above is fulfilled, the court shall disregard any act of the defendant which he shows was reasonable in the circumstances.

(6) The prohibitions that may be imposed by an anti-social behaviour order are those necessary for the purpose of protecting from further anti-social acts by the defendant –

(a) persons in the local government area; and

(b) persons in any adjoining local government area specified in the application for the order; and a relevant authority shall not specify an adjoining local government area in the application without consulting the council for that area and each chief officer of police any part of whose police area lies within that area.

(7) An anti-social behaviour order shall have effect for a period (not less than two years) specified in the order or until further order.

(8) Subject to subsection (9) below, the applicant or the defendant may apply by complaint to the court which made an anti-social behaviour order for it to be varied or discharged by a further order.

(9) Except with the consent of both parties, no anti-social behaviour order shall be discharged before the end of the period of two years beginning with the date of service of the order.

(10) If without reasonable excuse a person does anything which he is prohibited from doing by an anti-social behaviour order, he shall be liable –

(a) on summary conviction, to imprisonment for a term not exceeding six months or to a fine not exceeding the statutory maximum, or to both; or

(b) on conviction on indictment, to imprisonment for a term not exceeding five years or to a fine, or to both.

(11) Where a person is convicted of an offence under subsection (10) above, it shall not be open to the court by or before which he is so convicted to make an order under subsection (1)(b) (conditional discharge) of section 1A of the Powers of Criminal Courts Act 1973 ('the 1973 Act') in respect of the offence.

(12) In this section –

'the commencement date' means the date of the commencement of this section;

'local government area' means –

(a) in relation to England, a district or London borough, the City of London, the Isle of Wight and the Isles of Scilly;

(b) in relation to Wales, a county or county borough.

Appeals against orders

4 (1) An appeal shall lie to the Crown Court against the making by a magistrates' court of an anti-social behaviour order or sex offender order.

(2) On such an appeal the Crown Court –

(a) may make such orders as may be necessary to give effect to its determination of the appeal; and

(b) may also make such incidental or consequential orders as appear to it to be just.

(3) Any order of the Crown Court made on an appeal under this section (other than one directing that an application be re-heard by a magistrates' court) shall, for the purposes of section 1(8) or 2(6) above, be treated as if it were an order of the magistrates' court from which the appeal was brought and not an order of the Crown Court.

Parenting orders

8 (1) This section applies where, in any court proceedings –

(a) a child safety order is made in respect of a child;

(b) an anti-social behaviour order or sex offender order is made in respect of a child or young person;

(c) a child or young person is convicted of an offence; or

(d) a person is convicted of an offence under section 443 (failure to comply with school attendance order) or section 444 (failure to secure regular attendance at school of registered pupil) of the Education Act 1996.

(2) Subject to subsection (3) and section 9(1) below, if in the proceedings the court is satisfied that the relevant condition is fulfilled, it may make a parenting order in respect of a person who is a parent or guardian of the child or young person or, as the case may be, the person convicted of the offence under section 443 or 444 ('the parent').

(3) A court shall not make a parenting order unless it has been notified by the Secretary of State that arrangements for implementing such orders are available in the area in which it appears to the court that the parent resides or will reside and the notice has not been withdrawn.

(4) A parenting order is an order which requires the parent –

(a) to comply, for a period not exceeding twelve months, with such requirements as are specified in the order; and

(b) subject to subsection (5) below, to attend, for a concurrent period not exceeding three months and not more than once in any week, such counselling or guidance sessions as may be specified in directions given by the responsible officer;

and in this subsection "week" means a period of seven days beginning with a Sunday.

(5) A parenting order may, but need not, include such a requirement as is mentioned in subsection (4)(b) above in any case where such an order has been made in respect of the parent on a previous occasion.

(6) The relevant condition is that the parenting order would be desirable in the interests of preventing –

(a) in a case falling within paragraph (a) or (b) of subsection (1) above, any repetition of the kind of behaviour which led to the child safety order, anti-social behaviour order or sex offender order being made;

(b) in a case falling within paragraph (c) of that subsection, the commission of any further offence by the child or young person;

(c) in a case falling within paragraph (d) of that subsection, the commission of any further offence under section 443 or 444 of the Education Act 1996.

(7) The requirements that may be specified under subsection (4)(a) above are those which the court considers desirable in the interests of preventing any such repetition or, as the case may be, the commission of any such further offence.

(8) In this section and section 9 below 'responsible officer', in relation to a parenting order, means one of the following who is specified in the order, namely –

(a) a probation officer;

(b) a social worker of a local authority social services department; and

(c) a member of a youth offending team.

Parenting orders: supplemental

9 (1) Where a person under the age of 16 is convicted of an offence, the court by or before which he is so convicted –

(a) if it is satisfied that the relevant condition is fulfilled, shall make a parenting order; and

(b) if it is not so satisfied, shall state in open court that it is not and why it is not.

(1A) Subsection (1) above has effect subject to section 4(5) of, and paragraph 13(5) of Schedule 1 to, the Youth Justice and Criminal Evidence Act 1999.

(2) Before making a parenting order –

(a) in a case falling within paragraph (a) of subsection (1) of section 8 above;

(b) in a case falling within paragraph (b) or (c) of that subsection, where the person concerned is under the age of 16; or

(c) in a case falling within paragraph (d) of that subsection, where the person to whom the offence related is under that age, a court shall obtain and consider information about the person's family circumstances and the likely effect of the order on those circumstances.

(3) Before making a parenting order, a court shall explain to the parent in ordinary language –

(a) the effect of the order and of the requirements proposed to be included in it;

the consequences which may follow (under subsection (7) below) if he fails to comply with any of those requirements; and

(c) that the court has power (under subsection (5) below) to review the order on the application either of the parent or of the responsible officer.

(4) Requirements specified in, and directions given under, a parenting order shall, as far as practicable, be such as to avoid –

(a) any conflict with the parent's religious beliefs; and

(b) any interference with the times, if any, at which he normally works or attends an educational establishment.

(5) If while a parenting order is in force it appears to the court which made it, on the application of the responsible officer or the parent, that is it

appropriate to make an order under this subsection, the court may make an order discharging the parenting order or varying it –

(a) by cancelling any provision included in it; or

(b) by inserting in it (either in addition to or in substitution for any of its provisions) any provision that could have been included in the order if the court had then had power to make and were exercising the power.

(6) Where an application under subsection (5) above for the discharge of a parenting order is dismissed, no further application for its discharge shall be made under that subsection by any person except with the consent of the court which made the order.

(7) If while a parenting order is in force the parent without reasonable excuse fails to comply with any requirement included in the order, or specified in directions given by the responsible officer, he shall be liable on summary conviction to a fine not exceeding level 3 on the standard scale.

Appeals against parenting orders

10 (1) An appeal shall lie –

(a) to the High Court against the making of a parenting order by virtue of paragraph (a) of subsection (1) of section 8 above; and

(b) to the Crown Court against the making of a parenting order by virtue of paragraph (b) of that subsection.

(2) On an appeal under subsection (1) above the High Court or the Crown Court –

(a) may make such orders as may be necessary to give effect to its determination of the appeal; and

(b) may also make such incidental or consequential orders as appear to it to be just.

(3) Any order of the High Court or the Crown Court made on an appeal under subsection (1) above (other than on directing that an application be reheard by a magistrates' court) shall, for the purposes of subsections (5) to (7) of section 9 above, be treated as if it were an order of the court from which the appeal was brought and not an order of the High Court or the Crown Court.

(4) A person in respect of whom a parenting order is made by virtue of section 8(1)(c) above shall have the same right of appeal against the making of the order as if –

(a) the offence that led to the making of the order were an offence committed by him; and

(b) the order were a sentence passed on him for the offence.

(5) A person in respect of whom a parenting order is made by virtue of section 8(1)(d) above shall have the same right of appeal against the making of the order as if the order were a sentence passed on him for the offence that led to the making of the order.

(6) The Lord Chancellor may by order make provision as to the circumstances in which appeals under subsection (1)(a) above may be made against decisions taken by courts on questions arising in connection with the transfer, or proposed transfer, of proceedings by virtue of any order under

paragraph 2 of Schedule 11 (jurisdiction) to the Children Act 1989 ('the 1989 Act').

(7) Except to the extent provided for in any order made under subsection (6) above, no appeal may be made against any decision of a kind mentioned in that subsection.

Child safety orders

11 (1) Subject to subsection (2) below, if a magistrates' court, on the application of a local authority, is satisfied that one or more of the conditions specified in subsection (3) below are fulfilled with respect to a child under the age of 10, it may make an order (a 'child safety order') which –

   (a) places the child, for a period (not exceeding the permitted maximum) specified in the order, under the supervision of the responsible officer; and

   (b) requires the child to comply with such requirements as are so specified.

(2) A court shall not make a child safety order unless it has been notified by the Secretary of State that arrangements for implementing such orders are available in the area in which it appears that the child resides or will reside and the notice has not been withdrawn.

(3) The conditions are –

   (a) that the child has committed an act which, if he had been aged 10 or over, would have constituted an offence;

   (b) that a child safety order is necessary for the purpose of preventing the commission by the child of such an act as is mentioned in paragraph (a) above;

   (c) that the child has contravened a ban imposed by a curfew notice; and

   (d) that the child has acted in a manner that caused or was likely to cause harassment, alarm or distress to one or more persons not of the same household as himself.

(4) The maximum period permitted for the purposes of subsection (1)(a) above is three months or, where the court is satisfied that the circumstances of the case are exceptional, 12 months.

(5) The requirements that may be specified under subsection (1)(b) above are those which the court considers desirable in the interests of –

   (a) securing that the child receives appropriate care, protection and support and is subject to proper control; or

   (b) preventing any repetition of the kind of behaviour which led to the child safety order being made.

(6) Proceedings under this section or section 12 below shall be family proceedings for the purposes of the 1989 Act or section 65 of the Magistrates' Courts Act 1980 ('the 1980 Act'); and the standard of proof applicable to such proceedings shall be that applicable to civil proceedings.

(7) In this section 'local authority' has the same meaning as in the 1989 Act.

(8) In this section and section 12 below, 'responsible officer', in relation to a child safety order, means one of the following who is specified in the order, namely –

(a) a social worker of a local authority social services department; and

(b) a member of a youth offending team.

Child safety orders: supplemental

12 (1) Before making a child safety order, a magistrates' court shall obtain and consider information about the child's family circumstances and the likely effect of the order on those circumstances.

(2) Before making a child safety order, a magistrates' court shall explain to the parent or guardian of the child in ordinary language –

(a) the effect of the order and of the requirements proposed to be included in it;

(b) the consequences which may follow (under subsection (6) below) if the child fails to comply with any of those requirements; and

(c) that the court has power (under subsection (4) below) to review the order on the application either of the parent or guardian or of the responsible officer.

(3) Requirements included in a child safety order shall, as far as practicable, be such as to avoid –

(a) any conflict with the parent's religious beliefs; and

(b) any interference with the times, if any, at which the child normally attends school.

(4) If while a child safety order is in force in respect of a child it appears to the court which made it, on the application of the responsible officer or a parent or guardian of the child, that it is appropriate to make an order under this subsection, the court may make an order discharging the child safety order or varying it –

(a) by cancelling any provision included in it; or

(b) by inserting in it (either in addition to or in substitution for any of its provisions) any provision that could have been included in the order if the court had then had power to make it and were exercising the power.

(5) Where an application under subsection (4) above for the discharge of a child safety order is dismissed, no further application for its discharge shall be made under that subsection by any person except with the consent of the court which made the order.

(6) Where a child safety order is in force and it is proved to the satisfaction of the court which made it or another magistrates' court acting for the same petty sessions area, on the application of the responsible officer, that the child has failed to comply with any requirement included in the order, the court –

(a) may discharge the order and make in respect of him a care order under subsection (1)(a) of section 31 of the 1989 Act; or

(b) may make an order varying the order –

(i) by cancelling any provision included in it; or

(ii) by inserting in it (either in addition to or in substitution for any of its provisions) any provision that could have been included in the order if the court had then had power to make it and were exercising the power.

(7) Subsection (6)(a) above applies whether or not the court is satisfied that the conditions mentioned in section 31(2) of the 1989 Act are fulfilled.

Appeals against child safety orders

13 (1) An appeal shall lie to the High Court against the making by a magistrates' court of a child safety order; and on such an appeal the High Court –

(a) may make such orders as may be necessary to give effect to its determination of the appeal; and

(b) may also make such incidental or consequential orders as appear to it to be just.

(2) Any order of the High Court made on an appeal under this section (other than one directing that an application be re-heard by a magistrates' court) shall, for the purposes of subsections (4) to (6) of section 12 above, be treated as if it were an order of the magistrates' court from which the appeal was brought and not an order of the High Court.

(3) Subsections (6) and (7) of section 10 above shall apply for the purposes of subsection (1) above as they apply for the purposes of subsection (1)(a) of that section.

Local child curfew schemes

14 (1) A local authority may make a scheme (a 'local child curfew scheme') for enabling the authority –

(a) subject to and in accordance with the provisions of the scheme; and

(b) if, after such consultation as is required by the scheme, the authority considers it necessary to do so for the purpose of maintaining order, to give a notice imposing, for a specified period (not exceeding 90 days), a ban to which subsection (2) below applies.

(2) This subsection applies to a ban on children of specified ages (under 10) being in a public place within a specified area –

(a) during specified hours (between 9 pm and 6 am); and

(b) otherwise than under the effective control of a parent or a responsible person aged 18 or over.

(3) Before making a local child curfew scheme, a local authority shall consult –

(a) every chief officer of police any part of whose police area lies within its area; and

(b) such other persons or bodies as it considers appropriate.

(4) A local child curfew scheme shall be made under the common seal of the local authority and shall not have effect until it is confirmed by the Secretary of State.

(5) The Secretary of State –

(a) may confirm, or refuse to confirm, a local child curfew scheme submitted under this section for confirmation; and

(b) may fix the date on which such a scheme is to come into operation;

and if no date is so fixed, the scheme shall come into operation at the end of the period of one month beginning with the date of its confirmation.

(6) A notice given under a local child curfew scheme (a 'curfew notice') may specify different hours in relation to children of different ages.

(7) A curfew notice shall be given –

(a) by posting the notice in some conspicuous place or places within the specified area; and

(b) in such other manner, if any, as appears to the local authority to be desirable for giving publicity to the notice.

(8) In this section –

'local authority' means –

(a) in relation to England, the council of a district or London borough, the Common Council of the City of London, the Council of the Isle of Wight and the Council of the Isles of Scilly;

(b) in relation to Wales, the council of a county or county borough;

'public place' has the same meaning as in Part II of the Public Order Act 1986.

Contravention of curfew notices

15 (1) Subsections (2) and (3) below apply where a constable has reasonable cause to believe that a child is in contravention of a ban imposed by a curfew notice.

(2) The constable shall, as soon as practicable, inform the local authority for the area that the child has contravened the ban.

(3) The constable may remove the child to the child's place of residence unless he has reasonable cause to believe that the child would, if removed to that place, be likely to suffer significant harm.

(4) In subsection (1) of section 47 of the 1989 Act (local authority's duty to investigate) –

(a) in paragraph (a), after sub-paragraph (ii) there shall be inserted the following sub-paragraph –

'(iii) has contravened a ban imposed by a curfew notice within the meaning of Chapter I of Part I of the Crime and Disorder Act 1998; or'; and

(b) at the end there shall be inserted the following paragraph –

In the case of a child falling within paragraph (a)(iii) above, the enquiries shall be commenced as soon as practicable and, in any event, within 48 hours of the authority receiving the information.'

Removal of truants to designated premises, etc

16 (1) This section applies where a local authority –

(a) designates premises in a police area ('designated premises') as premises to which children and young persons of compulsory school age may be removed under this section; and

(b) notifies the chief officer of police for that area of the designation.

(2) A police officer of or above the rank of superintendent may direct that the powers conferred on a constable by subsection (3) below –

(a) shall be exercisable as respects any area falling within the police area and specified in the direction; and

(b) shall be so exercisable during a period so specified;

and references in that subsection to a specified area and a specified period shall be construed accordingly.

(3) If a constable has reasonable cause to believe that a child or young person found by him in a public place in a specified area during a specified period –

(a) is of compulsory school age; and

(b) is absent from a school without lawful authority,

the constable may remove the child or young person to designated premises, or to the school from which he is so absent.

(4) A child's or young person's absence from a school shall be taken to be without lawful authority unless it falls within subsection (3) (leave, sickness, unavoidable cause or day set apart for religious observance) of section 444 of the Education Act 1996.

(5) In this section –

'local authority' means –

(a) in relation to England, a county council, a district council whose district does not form part of an area that has a county council, a London borough council or the Common Council of the City of London;

(b) in relation to Wales, a county council or a county borough council;

'public place' has the same meaning as in section 14 above;

'school' has the same meaning as in the Education Act 1996.

Powers of youth courts

47 (1) Where a person who appears or is brought before a youth court charged with an offence subsequently attains the age of 18, the youth court may, at any time –

(a) before the start of the trial; or

(b) after conviction and before sentence,

remit the person for trial or, as the case may be, for sentence to a magistrates' court (other than a youth court) acting for the same petty sessions area as the youth court.

In this subsection 'the start of the trial' shall be construed in accordance with section 22(11B) of the 1985 Act.

(2) Where a person is remitted under subsection (1) above –

(a) he shall have no right of appeal against the order of remission;

(b) the remitting court shall adjourn proceedings in relation to the offence; and

(c) subsections (3) and (4) below shall apply.

(3) The following, namely –

(a) section 128 of the 1980 Act; and

(b) all other enactments (whenever passed) relating to remand or the granting of bail in criminal proceedings,

shall have effect in relation to the remitting court's power or duty to remand the person on the adjournment as if any reference to the court to or before which the person remanded is to be brought or appear after remand were a reference to the court to which he is being remitted ('the other court').

(4) The other court may deal with the case in any way in which it would have power to deal with it if all proceedings relating to the offence which took place before the remitting court had taken place before the other court.

[*(5)–(7) Not reproduced.*]

Reprimands and warnings

65 (1) Subsections (2) to (5) below apply where –

(a) a constable has evidence that a child or young person ('the offender') has committed an offence;

(b) the constable considers that the evidence is such that, if the offender were prosecuted for the offence, there would be a realistic prospect of his being convicted;

(c) the offender admits to the constable that he committed the offence;

(d) the offender has not previously been convicted of an offence; and

(e) the constable is satisfied that it would not be in the public interest for the offender to be prosecuted.

(2) Subject to subsection (4) below, the constable may reprimand the offender if the offender has not previously been reprimanded or warned.

(3) The constable may warn the offender if –

(a) the offender has not previously been warned; or

(b) where the offender has previously been warned, the offence was committed more than two years after the date of the previous warning and the constable considers the offence to be not so serious as to require a charge to be brought;

but no person may be warned under paragraph (b) above more than once.

(4) Where the offender has not been previously reprimanded, the constable shall warn rather than reprimand the offender if he considers the offence to be so serious as to require a warning.

(5) The constable shall –

(a) give any reprimand or warning at a police station and, where the offender is under the age of 17, in the presence of an appropriate adult; and

(b) explain to the offender and, where he is under that age, the appropriate adult in ordinary language –

(i) in the case of a reprimand, the effect of subsection (5)(a) of section 66 below;

(ii) in the case of a warning, the effect of subsections (1), (2), (4) and (5)(b) and (c) of that section, and any guidance issued under subsection (3) of that section.

(6) The Secretary of State shall publish, in such manner as he considers appropriate, guidance as to –

(a) the circumstances in which it is appropriate to give reprimands or warnings, including criteria for determining –

(i) for the purposes of subsection (3)(b) above, whether an offence is not so serious as to require a charge to be brought; and

(ii) for the purposes of subsection (4) above, whether an offence is so serious as to require a warning;

(b) the category of constable by whom reprimands and warnings may be given; and

(c) the form which reprimands and warnings are to take and the manner in which they are to be given and recorded.

(7) In this section 'appropriate adult', in relation to a child or young person, means –

(a) his parent or guardian or, if he is in the care of a local authority or voluntary organisation, a person representing that authority or organisation;

(b) a social worker of a local authority social services department;

(c) if no person falling within paragraph (a) or (b) above is available, any responsible person aged 18 or over who is not a police officer or a person employed by the police.

(8) No caution shall be given to a child or young person after the commencement of this section.

(9) Any reference (however expressed) in any enactment passed before or in the same Session as this Act to a person being cautioned shall be construed, in relation to any time after that commencement, as including a reference to a child or young person being reprimanded or warned.

Effect of reprimands and warnings

66 (1) Where a constable warns a person under section 65 above, he shall as soon as practicable refer the person to a youth offending team.

(2) A youth offending team –

(a) shall assess any person referred to them under subsection (1) above; and

(b) unless they consider it inappropriate to do so, shall arrange for him to participate in a rehabilitation programme.

(3) The Secretary of State shall publish, in such manner as he considers appropriate, guidance as to –

(a) what should be included in a rehabilitation programme arranged for a person under subsection (2) above;

(b) the manner in which any failure by a person to participate in such a programme is to be recorded; and

(c) the persons to whom any such failure is to be notified.

(4) Where a person who has been warned under section 65 above is convicted of an offence committed within two years of the warning, the court by or before which he is so convicted –

(a) shall not make an order under subsection (1)(b) (conditional discharge) of section 1A of the 1973 Act in respect of the offence unless it is of the opinion that there are exceptional circumstances relating to the offence or the offender which justify its doing so; and

(b) where it does so, shall state in open court that it is of that opinion and why it is.

(5) The following, namely –

(a) any reprimand of a person under section 65 above;

(b) any warning of a person under that section; and

(c) any report on a failure by a person to participate in a rehabilitation programme arranged for him under subsection (2) above,

may be cited in criminal proceedings in the same circumstances as a conviction of the person may be cited.

(6) In this section 'rehabilitation programme' means a programme the purpose of which is to rehabilitate participants and to prevent them from re-offending.

Reparation orders

67 (1) This section applies where a child or young person is convicted of an offence other than one for which the sentence is fixed by law.

(2) Subject to the provisions of this section and section 68 below, the court by or before which the offender is convicted may make an order (a 'reparation order') which requires the offender to make reparation specified in the order –

(a) to a person or persons so specified; or

(b) to the community at large;

and any person so specified must be a person identified by the court as a victim of the offence or a person otherwise affected by it.

(3) The court shall not make a reparation order unless it has been notified by the Secretary of State that arrangements for implementing such orders are available in the area proposed to be named in the order and the notice has not been withdrawn.

(4) The court shall not make a reparation order in respect of the offender if it proposes –

(a) to pass on him a custodial sentence or a sentence under section 53(1) of the 1933 Act; or

(b) to make in respect of him a community service order, a combination order, a supervision order which includes requirements imposed in pursuance of sections 12 to 12C of the 1969 Act, an action plan order or a referral order under Part 1 of the Youth Justice and Criminal Evidence Act 1999.

(5) A reparation order shall not require the offender –

(a) to work for more than 24 hours in aggregate; or

(b) to make reparation to any person without the consent of that person.

(6) Subject to subsection (5) above, requirements specified in a reparation order shall be such as in the opinion of the court are commensurate with seriousness of the offence, or the combination of the offence and one or more offences associated with it.

(7) Requirements so specified shall, as far as practicable, be such as to avoid –

(a) any conflict with the offender's religious beliefs or with the requirements of any community order to which he may be subject; and

(b) any interference with the times, if any, at which the offender normally works or attends school or any other educational establishment.

(8) Any reparation required by a reparation order –

(a) shall be made under the supervision of the responsible officer; and

(b) shall be made within a period of three months from the date of the making of the order.

(9) A reparation order shall name the petty sessions area in which it appears to the court making the order, or to the court varying any provision included in the order in pursuance of this subsection, that the offender resides or will reside.

(10) In this section 'responsible officer', in relation to a reparation order, means one of the following who is specified in the order, namely –

(a) a probation officer;

(b) a social worker of a local authority social services department; and

(c) a member of a youth offending team.

(11) The court shall give reasons if it does not make a reparation order in a case where it has power to do so.

Reparation orders: supplemental

68 (1) Before making a reparation order, a court shall obtain and consider a written report by a probation officer, a social worker of a local authority social services department or a member of a youth offending team, indicating –

(a) the type of work that is suitable for the offender; and

(b) the attitude of the victim or victims to the requirements proposed to be included in the order.

(2) Before making a reparation order, a court shall explain to the offender in ordinary language –

(a) the effect of the order and of the requirements proposed to be included in it;

(b) the consequences which may follow (under Schedule 5 to this Act) if he fails to comply with any of those requirements; and

(c) that the court has power (under that Schedule) to review the order on the application either of the offender or of the responsible officer.

(3) Schedule 5 to this Act shall have effect for dealing with failure to comply with the requirements of reparation orders, for varying such orders and for discharging them with or without the substitution of other sentences.

Action plan orders

69 (1) This section applies where a child or young person is convicted of an offence other than one for which the sentence is fixed by law.

(2) Subject to the provisions of this section and section 70 below, the court by or before which the offender is convicted may, if it is of the opinion that it is desirable to do so in the interests of securing his rehabilitation, or of preventing the commission by him of further offences, make an order (an 'action plan order') which –

(a) requires the offender, for a period of three months beginning with the date of the order, to comply with an action plan, that is to say, a series of requirements with respect to his actions and whereabouts during that period;

(b) places the offender under the supervision for that period of the responsible officer; and

(c) requires the offender to comply with any directions given by that officer with a view to the implementation of that plan.

(3) The court shall not make an action plan order unless it has been notified by the Secretary of State that arrangements for implementing such orders are available in the area proposed to be named in the order and the notice has not been withdrawn.

(4) The court shall not make an action plan order in respect of the offender if –
   (a) he is already the subject of such an order; or
   (b) the court proposes to pass on him a custodial sentence or a sentence under section 53(1) of the 1933 Act, or to make in respect of him a probation order, a community service order, a combination order, a supervision order, an attendance centre order or a referral order under Part 1 of the Youth Justice and Criminal Evidence Act 1999.

(5) Requirements included in an action plan order, or directions given by a responsible officer, may require the offender to do all or any of the following things, namely –
   (a) to participate in activities specified in the requirements or directions at a time or times so specified;
   (b) to present himself to a person or persons specified in the requirements or directions at a place or places and at a time or times so specified;
   (c) to attend at an attendance centre specified in the requirements or directions for a number of hours so specified;
   (d) to stay away from a place or places specified in the requirements or directions;
   (e) to comply with any arrangements for his education specified in the requirements or directions;
   (f) to make reparation specified in the requirements or directions to a person or persons so specified or to the community at large; and
   (g) to attend any hearing fixed by the court under section 70(3) below.

(6) Such requirements and directions shall, as far as practicable, be such as to avoid –
   (a) any conflict with the offender's religious beliefs or with the requirements of any other community order to which he may be subject; and
   (b) any interference with the times, if any, at which he normally works or attends school or any other educational establishment.

(7) Subsection (5)(c) above does not apply unless the offence committed by the offender is punishable with imprisonment in the case of a person aged 21 or over.

(8) A person shall not be specified in requirements or directions under subsection (5)(f) above unless –
   (a) he is identified by the court or, as the case may be, the responsible officer as a victim of the offence or a person otherwise affected by it; and
   (b) he consents to the reparation being made.

(9) An action plan order shall name the petty sessions area in which it appears to the court making the order, or to the court varying any provision included in the order in pursuance of this subsection, that the offender resides or will reside.

(10) In this section 'responsible officer', in relation to an action plan order, means one of the following who is specified in the order, namely –
   (a) a probation officer;
   (b) a social worker of a local authority social services department; and
   (c) a member of a youth offending team.

(11) An action plan order shall be a community order for the purposes of Part I

of the 1991 Act; and the provisions of that Part, which include provisions with respect to restrictions on imposing, and procedural requirements for, community sentences (sections 6 and 7), shall apply accordingly.

Action plan orders: supplemental

70 (1) Before making an action plan order, a court shall obtain and consider –

    (a) a written report by a probation officer, a social worker of a local authority social services department or a member of a youth offending team, indicating –

        (i) the requirements proposed by that person to be included in the order;

        (ii) the benefits to the offender that the proposed requirements are designed to achieve; and

        (iii) the attitude of a parent or guardian of the offender to the proposed requirements; and

    (b) where the offender is under the age of 16, information about the offender's family circumstances and the likely effect of the order on those circumstances.

(2) Before making an action plan order, a court shall explain to the offender in ordinary language –

    (a) the effect of the order and of the requirements proposed to be included in it;

    (b) the consequences which may follow (under Schedule 5 to this Act) if he fails to comply with any of those requirements; and

    (c) that the court has power (under that Schedule) to review the order on the application either of the offender or of the responsible officer.

(3) Immediately after making an action plan order, a court may –

    (a) fix a further hearing for a date not more than 21 days after the making of the order; and

    (b) direct the responsible officer to make, at that hearing, a report as to the effectiveness of the order and the extent to which it has been implemented.

(4) At a hearing fixed under subsection (3) above, the court –

    (a) shall consider the responsible officer's report; and

    (b) may, on the application of the responsible officer or the offender, vary the order –

        (i) by cancelling any provision included in it; or

        (ii) by inserting in it (either in addition to or in substitution for any of its provisions) any provision that the court could originally have included in it.

(5) Schedule 5 to this Act shall have effect for dealing with failure to comply with the requirements of action plan orders, for varying such orders and for discharging them with or without the substitution of other sentences.

Detention and training orders

73 (1) Subject to section 53 of the 1933 Act, section 8 of the Criminal Justice Act 1982 ('the 1982 Act') and subsection (2) below, where –

    (a) a child or young person ("the offender") is convicted of an offence which is punishable with imprisonment in the case of a person aged 21 or over; and

(b) the court is of the opinion that either or both of paragraphs (a) or (b) of subsection (2) of section 1 of the 1991 Act apply or the case falls within subsection (3) of that section, the sentence that the court is to pass is a detention and training order.

(2) A court shall not make a detention and training order –

(a) in the case of an offender under the age of 15 at the time of the conviction, unless it is of the opinion that he is a persistent offender;

(b) in the case of an offender under the age of 12 at that time, unless –

(i) it is of the opinion that only a custodial sentence would be adequate to protect the public from further offending by him; and

(ii) the offence was committed on or after such date as the Secretary of State may by order appoint.

(3) A detention and training order is an order that the offender in respect of whom it is made shall be subject, for the term specified in the order, to a period of detention and training followed by a period of supervision.

(4) A detention and training order shall be a custodial sentence for the purposes of Part I of the 1991 Act; and the provisions of sections 1 to 4 of that Act shall apply accordingly.

(5) Subject to subsection (6) below, the term of a detention and training order shall be 4, 6, 8, 10, 12, 18 or 24 months.

(6) The term of a detention and training order may not exceed the maximum term of imprisonment that the Crown Court could (in the case of an offender aged 21 or over) impose for the offence.

(7) The following provisions, namely –

(a) section 1B of the 1982 Act (detention in young offender institutions: special provision for offenders under 18); and

(b) sections 1 to 4 of the 1994 Act (secure training orders), which are superseded by this section and sections 74 to 78 below, shall cease to have effect.

Duties and powers of court

74 (1) On making a detention and training order in a case where subsection (2) of section 73 above applies, it shall be the duty of the court (in addition to the duty imposed by section 1(4) of the 1991 Act) to state in open court that it is of the opinion mentioned in paragraph (a) or, as the case may be, paragraphs (a) and (b)(i) of that subsection.

(2) Subject to subsections (3) and (4A) below, a court making a detention and training order may order that its term shall commence on the expiration of the term of any other detention and training order made by that or any other court.

(3) A court shall not make in respect of an offender a detention and training order the effect of which would be that he would be subject to detention and training orders for a term which exceeds 24 months.

(4) Where the term of the detention and training orders to which an offender would otherwise be subject exceeds 24 months, the excess shall be treated as remitted.

(4A) A court making a detention and training order shall not order that its term shall commence on the expiration of the term of a detention and training order under which the period of supervision has already begun (under section 76(1) below).

(4B) Where a detention and training order ('the new order') is made in respect of an offender who is subject to a detention and training order under which the period of supervision has begun ('the old order'), the old order shall be disregarded in determining–

  (a) for the purposes of subsection (3) above whether the effect of the new order would be that the offender would be subject to detention and training orders for a term which exceeds 24 months; and

  (b) for the purposes of subsection (4) above whether the term of the detention and training orders to which the offender would (apart from that subsection) be subject exceeds 24 months.

(5) In determining the term of a detention and training order for an offence, the court shall take account of any period for which the offender has been remanded in custody in connection with the offence, or any other offence the charge for which was founded on the same facts or evidence.

(5A) Where a court proposes to make detention and training orders in respect of an offender for two or more offences–

  (a) subsection (5) above shall not apply, but

  (b) in determining the total term of the detention and training orders it proposes to make in respect of the offender, the court shall take account of the total period for which he has been remanded in custody in connection with any of those offences, or any other offence the charge for which was founded on the same facts or evidence.

(5B) Once a period of remand has, under subsection (5) or (5A) above, been taken account of in relation to a detention and training order made in respect of an offender for any offence or offences, it shall not subsequently be taken account of (under either of those subsections) in relation to such an order made in respect of the offender for any other offence or offences.

(6) Any reference in subsection (5) or (5A) above to an offender being remanded in custody is a reference to his being –

  (a) held in police detention;

  (b) remanded in or committed to custody by an order of a court;

  (c) remanded or committed to local authority accommodation under section 23 of the 1969 Act and placed and kept in secure accommodation; or

  (d) remanded, admitted or removed to hospital under section 35, 36, 38 or 48 of the Mental Health Act 1983.

(7) A person is in police detention for the purposes of subsection (6) above –

  (a) at any time when he is in police detention for the purposes of the 1984 Act; and

  (b) at any time when he is detained under section 14 of the Prevention of Terrorism (Temporary Provisions) Act 1989;

and in that subsection 'secure accommodation' has the same meaning as in section 23 of the 1969 Act.

(8) For the purpose of any reference in sections 75 to 78 below to the term of a detention and training order, consecutive terms of such orders and terms of such orders which are wholly or partly concurrent shall be treated as a single term if –

(a) the orders were made on the same occasion; or

(b) where they were made on different occasions, the offender has not been released (by virtue of subsection (2), (3), (4) or (5) of section 75 below) at any time during the period beginning with the first and ending with the last of those occasions.

The period of detention and training

75 (1) An offender shall serve the period of detention and training under a detention and training order in such secure accommodation as may be determined by the Secretary of State or by such other person as may be authorised by him for that purpose.

(2) Subject to subsections (3) to (5) below, the period of detention and training under a detention and training order shall be one-half of the term of the order.

(3) The Secretary of State may at any time release the offender if he is satisfied that exceptional circumstances exist which justify the offender's release on compassionate grounds.

(4) The Secretary of State may release the offender –

(a) in the case of an order for a term of 8 months or more but less than 18 months, one month before the half-way point of the term of the order; and

(b) in the case of an order for a term of 18 months or more, one month or two months before that point.

(5) If a youth court so orders on an application made by the Secretary of State for the purpose, the Secretary of State shall release the offender –

(a) in the case of an order for a term of 8 months or more but less than 18 months, one month after the half-way point of the term of the order; and

(b) in the case of an order for a term of 18 months or more, one month or two months after that point.

(6) An offender detained in pursuance of a detention and training order shall be deemed to be in legal custody.

(7) In this section and sections 77 and 78 below 'secure accommodation' means –

(a) a secure training centre;

(b) a young offender institution;

(c) accommodation provided by a local authority for the purpose of restricting the liberty of children and young persons;

(d) accommodation provided for that purpose under subsection (5) of section 82 of the 1989 Act (financial support by the Secretary of State); or

(e) such other accommodation provided for the purpose of restricting liberty as the Secretary of State may direct.

The period of supervision

76 (1) The period of supervision of an offender who is subject to a detention and training order –

(a) shall begin with the offender's release, whether at the half-way point of the term of the order or otherwise; and

(b) subject to subsection (2) below, shall end when the term of the order ends.

(2) The Secretary of State may by order provide that the period of supervision shall end at such point during the term of a detention and training order as may be specified in the order under this subsection.

(3) During the period of supervision, the offender shall be under the supervision of –

(a) a probation officer;

(b) a social worker of a local authority social services department; or

(c) a member of a youth offending team;

and the category of person to supervise the offender shall be determined from time to time by the Secretary of State.

(4) Where the supervision is to be provided by a probation officer, the probation officer shall be an officer appointed for or assigned to the petty sessions area within which the offender resides for the time being.

(5) Where the supervision is to be provided by –

(a) a social worker of a local authority social services department; or

(b) a member of a youth offending team,

the social worker or member shall be a social worker of, or a member of a youth offending team established by, the local authority within whose area the offender resides for the time being.

(6) The offender shall be given a notice from the Secretary of State specifying –

(a) the category of person for the time being responsible for his supervision; and

(b) any requirements with which he must for the time being comply.

(7) A notice under subsection (6) above shall be given to the offender –

(a) before the commencement of the period of supervision; and

(b) before any alteration in the matters specified in subsection (6)(a) or (b) above comes into effect.

Breaches of supervision requirements

77 (1) Where a detention and training order is in force in respect of an offender and it appears on information to a justice of the peace acting for a relevant petty sessions area that the offender has failed to comply with requirements under section 76(6)(b) above, the justice –

(a) may issue a summons requiring the offender to appear at the place and time specified in the summons before a youth court acting for the area; or

(b) if the information is in writing and on oath, may issue a warrant for the offender's arrest requiring him to be brought before such a court.

(2) For the purposes of this section a petty sessions area is a relevant petty sessions area in relation to a detention and training order if –

(a) the order was made by a youth court acting for it; or

(b) the offender resides in it for the time being.

(3) If it is proved to the satisfaction of the youth court before which an offender appears or is brought under this section that he has failed to comply with requirements under section 76(6)(b) above, that court may –

    (a) order the offender to be detained, in such secure accommodation as the Secretary of State may determine, for such period, not exceeding the shorter of three months or the remainder of the term of the detention and training order, as the court may specify; or

    (b) impose on the offender a fine not exceeding level 3 on the standard scale.

(4) An offender detained in pursuance of an order under subsection (3) above shall be deemed to be in legal custody; and a fine imposed under that subsection shall be deemed, for the purposes of any enactment, to be a sum adjudged to be paid by a conviction.

(5) An offender may appeal to the Crown Court against any order made under a subsection (3)(a) or (b) above.

Offences during currency of order

78 (1) This section applies to a person subject to a detention and training order if –

    (a) after his release and before the date on which the term of the order ends, he commits an offence punishable with imprisonment in the case of a person aged 21 or over; and

    (b) whether before or after that date, he is convicted of that offence ('the new offence').

(2) Subject to section 7(8) of the 1969 Act, the court by or before which a person to whom this section applies is convicted of the new offence may, whether or not it passes any other sentence on him, order him to be detained in such secure accommodation as the Secretary of State may determine for the whole or any part of the period which –

    (a) begins with the date of the court's order; and

    (b) is equal in length to the period between the date on which the new offence was committed and the date mentioned in subsection (1) above.

(3) The period for which a person to whom this section applies is ordered under subsection (2) above to be detained in secure accommodation –

    (a) shall, as the court may direct, either be served before and be followed by, or be served concurrently with, any sentence imposed for the new offence; and

    (b) in either case, shall be disregarded in determining the appropriate length of that sentence.

(4) Where the new offence is found to have been committed over a period of two or more days, or at some time during a period of two or more days, it shall be taken for the purposes of this section to have been committed on the last of those days.

(5) A person detained in pursuance of an order under subsection (2) above shall be deemed to be in legal custody.

Interaction with sentences of detention

79 (1) Where a court passes a sentence of detention in a young offender institution in the case of an offender who is subject to a detention and training order, the sentence shall take effect as follows –

(a) if the offender has been released by virtue of subsection (2), (3), (4) or (5) of section 75 above, at the beginning of the day on which it is passed;

(b) if not, either as mentioned in paragraph (a) above or, if the court so orders, at the time when the offender would otherwise be released by virtue of that subsection.

(2) Where a court makes a detention and training order in the case of an offender who is subject to a sentence of detention in a young offender institution, the order shall take effect as follows –

(a) if the offender has been released under Part II of the 1991 Act, at the beginning of the day on which it is made;

(b) if not, either as mentioned in paragraph (a) above or, if the court so orders, at the time when the offender would otherwise be released under that Part.

(2A) Subsection (1)(a) above has effect subject to section 78(3)(a) above and subsection (2)(a) above has effect subject to section 40(4)(b) of the 1991 Act.

(3) Subject to subsection (4) below, where at any time an offender is subject concurrently –

(a) to a detention and training order; and

(b) to a sentence of detention in a young offender institution,

he shall be treated for the purposes of sections 75 to 78 above, section 1C of the 1982 Act and Part II of the 1991 Act as if he were subject only to the one of them that was imposed on the later occasion.

(4) Nothing in subsection (3) above shall require the offender to be released in respect of either the order or the sentence unless and until he is required to be released in respect of each of them.

(5) Where, by virtue of any enactment giving a court power to deal with a person in a manner in which a court on a previous occasion could have dealt with him, a detention and training order for any term is made in the case of a person who has attained the age of 18, the person shall be treated as if he had been sentenced to detention in a young offender institution for the same term.

SCHEDULE 5: ENFORCEMENT, ETC OF REPARATION AND ACTION PLAN ORDERS

Preliminary

1   In this Schedule –

'the appropriate court', in relation to a reparation order or action plan order, means the youth court acting for the petty sessions area for the time being named in the order in pursuance of section 67(9) or, as the case may be, section 69(9) of this Act;

'local authority accommodation' means accommodation provided by or on behalf of a local authority (within the meaning of the 1989 Act).

General power to discharge or vary order

2 (1) If while a reparation order or action plan order is in force in respect of an offender it appears to the appropriate court, on the application of the responsible officer or the offender, that it is appropriate to make an order under this sub-paragraph, the court may make an order discharging the reparation order or action plan order or varying it –

(a) by cancelling any provision included in it; or

(b) by inserting in it (either in addition to or in substitution for any of its provisions) any provision that could have been included in the order if the court had then had power to make it and were exercising the power.

(2) Where an application under this paragraph for the discharge of a reparation order or action plan order is dismissed, no further application for its discharge shall be made under this paragraph by any person except with the consent of the appropriate court.

Failure to comply with order

3 (1) This paragraph applies where a reparation order or action plan order is in force and it is proved to the satisfaction of the appropriate court, on the application of the responsible officer, that the offender has failed to comply with any requirement included in the order.

(2) The court –

(a) whether or not it also makes an order under paragraph 2 above, may order the offender to pay a fine of an amount not exceeding £1,000, or make an attendance centre order or curfew order in respect of him; or

(b) if the reparation order or action plan order was made by a magistrates' court, may discharge the order and deal with him, for the offence in respect of which the order was made, in any manner in which he could have been dealt with for that offence by the court which made the order if the order had not been made; or

(c) if the reparation order or action plan order was made by the Crown Court, may commit him in custody or release him on bail until he can be brought or appear before the Crown Court.

(3) [*Repealed.*]

(4) Where a court deals with an offender under sub-paragraph (2)(c) above, it shall send to the Crown Court a certificate signed by a justice of the peace giving –

(a) particulars of the offender's failure to comply with the requirement in question; and

(b) such other particulars of the case as may be desirable;

and a certificate purporting to be so signed shall be admissible as evidence of the failure before the Crown Court.

(5) Where –

(a) by virtue of sub-paragraph (2)(c) above the offender is brought or appears before the Crown Court; and

(b) it is proved to the satisfaction of the court that he has failed to comply with the requirement in question, that court may deal with him, for the offence in respect of which the order was made, in any manner in which it could have dealt with him for that offence if it had not made the order.

(6) Where the Crown Court deals with an offender under sub-paragraph (5) above, it shall revoke the reparation order or action plan order if it is still in force.

(7) A fine imposed under this paragraph shall be deemed, for the purposes of any enactment, to be a sum adjudged to be paid by a conviction.

(8) In dealing with an offender under this paragraph, a court shall take into account the extent to which he has complied with the requirements of the reparation order or action plan order.

(9) Where a reparation order or action plan order has been made on appeal, for the purposes of this paragraph it shall be deemed –

(a) if it was made on an appeal brought from a magistrates' court, to have been made by that magistrates' court;

(b) if it was made on an appeal brought from the Crown Court or from the criminal division of the Court of Appeal, to have been made by the Crown Court;

and, in relation to a reparation order or action plan order made on appeal, sub-paragraph (2)(b) above shall have effect as if the words 'if the order had not been made' were omitted and sub-paragraph (5) above shall have effect as if the words 'if it had not made the order' were omitted.

Presence of offender in court, remands, etc

4 (1) Where the responsible officer makes an application under paragraph 2 or 3 above to the appropriate court, he may bring the offender before the court and, subject to sub-paragraph (9) below, the court shall not make an order under that paragraph unless the offender is present before it.

(2) Without prejudice to any power to issue a summons or warrant apart from this sub-paragraph, the court to which an application under paragraph 2 or 3 above is made may issue a summons or warrant for the purpose of securing the attendance of the offender before it.

(3) Subsections (3) and (4) of section 55 of the 1980 Act (which among other things restrict the circumstances in which a warrant may be issued) shall apply with the necessary modifications to a warrant under sub-paragraph (2) above as they apply to a warrant under that section and as if in subsection (3) after the word 'summons' there were inserted the words 'cannot be served or'.

(4) Where the offender is arrested in pursuance of a warrant under sub-paragraph (2) above and cannot be brought immediately before the appropriate court, the person in whose custody he is –

(a) may make arrangements for his detention in a place of safety for a period of not more than 72 hours from the time of the arrest (and it shall be lawful for him to be detained in pursuance of the arrangements); and

(b) shall within that period bring him before a youth court.

(5) Where an offender is, under sub-paragraph (4) above, brought before a youth court other than the appropriate court, that court may –

(a) direct that he be released forthwith; or

(b) subject to sub-paragraph (7A) below, remand him to local authority accommodation.

(6) [*Repealed.*]

(7) Subject to sub-paragraph (7A) below, where an application is made to a court under paragraph 2(1) above, the court may remand (or further remand) the offender to local authority accommodation if –

(a) a warrant has been issued under sub-paragraph (2) of this paragraph for the purpose of securing the attendance of the offender before the court; or

(b) the court considers that remanding (or further remanding) him will enable information to be obtained which is likely to assist the court in deciding whether and, if so, how to exercise its powers under paragraph 2(1) above.

(7A) Where the offender is aged 18 or over at the time when he is brought before a youth court other than the appropriate court under sub-paragraph (4) above, or is aged 18 or over at a time when (apart from this sub-paragraph) the appropriate court could exercise its powers under sub-paragraph (7) above in respect of him, he shall not be remanded to local authority accommodation but may instead be remanded–

(a) to a remand centre, if the court has been notified that such a centre is available for the reception of persons under this sub-paragraph; or

(b) to a prison, if it has not been so notified.

(8) A court remanding an offender to local authority accommodation under this paragraph shall designate, as the authority who are to receive him, the local authority for the area in which the offender resides or, where it appears to the court that he does not reside in the area of a local authority, the local authority –

(a) specified by the court; and

(b) in whose area the offence or an offence associated with it was committed.

(9) A court may make an order under paragraph 2 above in the absence of the offender if the effect of the order is one or more of the following, that is to say –

(a) discharging the reparation order or action plan order;

(b) cancelling a requirement included in the reparation order or action plan order;

(c) altering in the reparation order or action plan order the name of any area;

(d) changing the responsible officer.

Supplemental

5 (1) The provisions of section 17 of the 1982 Act (attendance centre orders) shall apply for the purposes of paragraph 3(2)(a) above but as if –

(a) in subsection (1), for the words from 'has power' to 'probation order' there were substituted the words 'considers it appropriate to make an attendance centre order in respect of any person in pursuance of paragraph 3(2) of Schedule 5 to the Crime and Disorder Act 1998'; and (b) subsection (13) were omitted.

(2) Sections 18 and 19 of the 1982 Act (discharge and variation of attendance centre order and breach of attendance centre orders or attendance centre rules) shall also apply for the purposes of that paragraph but as if there were omitted –

(a) from subsection (4A) of section 18 and subsections (3) and (5) of section 19, the words 'for the offence in respect of which the order was made,' and 'for that offence'; and

(b) from subsection (4B) of section 18 and subsection (6) of section 19, the words 'for an offence'.

(3) The provisions of section 12 of the 1991 Act (curfew orders) shall apply for the purposes of paragraph 3(2)(a) above but as if –

(a) in subsection (1), for the words from the beginning to 'before which he is convicted' there were substituted the words 'Where a court considers it appropriate to make a curfew order in respect of any person in pursuance of paragraph 3(2)(a) of Schedule 5 to the Crime and Disorder Act 1998, the court'; and

(b) in subsection (8), for the words 'on conviction' there were substituted the words 'on the date on which his failure to comply with a requirement included in the reparation order or action plan order was proved to the court'.

(4) Schedule 2 to the 1991 Act (enforcement etc. of community orders), so far as relating to curfew orders, shall also apply for the purposes of that paragraph but as if –

(a) the power conferred on the magistrates' court by each of paragraphs 3(1)(d) and 7(2)(a)(ii) to deal with the offender for the offence in respect of which the order was made were a power to deal with the offender, for his failure to comply with a requirement included in the reparation order or action plan order, in any manner in which the appropriate court could deal with him for that failure to comply if it had just been proved to the satisfaction of that court;

(b) the power conferred on the Crown Court by paragraph 4(1)(d) to deal with the offender for the offence in respect of which the order was made were a power to deal with the offender, for his failure to comply with such a requirement, in any manner in which that court could deal with him for that failure to comply if it had just been proved to its satisfaction;

(c) the reference in paragraph 7(1)(b) to the offence in respect of which the order was made were a reference to the failure to comply in respect of which the curfew order was made; and

(d) the power conferred on the Crown Court by paragraph 8(2)(b) to deal with the offender for the offence in respect of which the order was made were a power to deal with the offender, for his failure to comply with a requirement included in the reparation order or action plan order, in any manner in which the appropriate court (if that order was made by a magistrates' court) or the Crown Court (if that order was made by the Crown Court) could deal with him for that failure to comply if it had just been proved to the satisfaction of that court.

(5) For the purposes of the provisions mentioned in sub-paragraph (4)(a) and (d) above, as applied by that sub-paragraph, if the reparation order or action plan order is no longer in force the appropriate court's powers shall be determined on the assumption that it is still in force.

[(6) *Repealed.*]

(7) The offender may appeal to the Crown Court against –

(a) any order made under paragraphs 2 or 3 above, except an order made or which could have been made in his absence (by virtue of paragraph 4(9) above);

(b) the dismissal of an application under paragraph 2 above to discharge a reparation order or action plan order.

Youth Justice and Criminal Evidence Act 1999

PART I: REFERRALS TO YOUTH OFFENDER PANELS

REFERRAL ORDERS

Referral of young offenders to youth offender panels

1 (1) This section applies where a youth court or other magistrates' court is dealing with a person under the age of 18 for an offence and –

(a) neither the offence nor any associated offence is one for which the sentence is fixed by law;

(b) the court is not, in respect of the offence or any associated offence, proposing to impose a custodial sentence on the offender or make a hospital order in his case; and

(c) the court is not proposing to discharge him absolutely in respect of the offence.

(2) If –

(a) the compulsory referral conditions are satisfied in accordance with section 2, and

(b) referral is available to the court,

the court shall sentence the offender for the offence by ordering him to be referred to a youth offender panel.

(3) If –

(a) the discretionary referral conditions are satisfied in accordance with section 2, and

(b) referral is available to the court,

the court may sentence the offender for the offence by ordering him to be referred to a youth offender panel.

(4) For the purposes of this section referral is available to a court if –

(a) the court has been notified by the Secretary of State that arrangements for the implementation of referral orders are available in the area in which it appears to the court that the offender resides or will reside; and

(b) the notice has not been withdrawn.

(5) In this Part 'referral order' means an order under subsection (2) or (3).

The referral conditions

2 (1) For the purposes of section 1(2) the compulsory referral conditions are satisfied in relation to an offence if the offender –

(a) pleaded guilty to the offence and to any associated offence;

(b) has never been convicted by or before a court in the United Kingdom of any offence other than the offence and any associated offence; and

(c) has never been bound over in criminal proceedings in England and Wales or Northern Ireland to keep the peace or to be of good behaviour.

(2) For the purposes of section 1(3) the discretionary referral conditions are satisfied in relation to an offence if –

(a) the offender is being dealt with by the court for the offence and one or more associated offences;

(b) although he pleaded guilty to at least one of the offences mentioned in paragraph (a), he also pleaded not guilty to at least one of them;

(c) he has never been convicted by or before a court in the United Kingdom of any offence other than the offences mentioned in paragraph (a); and

(d) he has never been bound over in criminal proceedings in England and Wales or Northern Ireland to keep the peace or to be of good behaviour.

(3) The Secretary of State may by regulations make such amendments of this section as he considers appropriate for altering in any way the descriptions of offenders in the case of which the compulsory referral conditions or the discretionary referral conditions fall to be satisfied for the purposes of section 1(2) or (3) (as the case may be).

(4) Any description of offender having effect for those purposes by virtue of such regulations may be framed by reference to such matters as the Secretary of State considers appropriate, including (in particular) one or more of the following –

(a) the offender's age;

(b) how the offender has pleaded;

(c) the offence (or offences) of which the offender has been convicted;

(d) the offender's previous convictions (if any);

(e) how (if at all) the offender has been previously punished or otherwise dealt with by any court; and

(f) any characteristics or behaviour of, or circumstances relating to, any person who has at any time been charged in the same proceedings as the offender (whether or not in respect of the same offence).

(5) For the purposes of this section an offender who has been convicted of an offence in respect of which he was conditionally discharged (whether by a court in England and Wales or in Northern Ireland) shall be treated, despite –

(a) section 1C(1) of the Powers of Criminal Courts Act 1973 (conviction of offence for which offender so discharged deemed not a conviction), or

(b) Article 6(1) of the Criminal Justice (Northern Ireland) Order 1996 (corresponding provision for Northern Ireland), as having been convicted of that offence.

Making of referral orders: general

3 (1) A referral order shall –
   (a) specify the youth offending team responsible for implementing the order;
   (b) require the offender to attend each of the meetings of a youth offender panel to be established by the team for the offender; and
   (c) specify the period for which any youth offender contract taking effect between the offender and the panel under section 8 is to have effect (which must not be less than 3 nor more than 12 months).

   (2) The youth offending team specified under subsection (1)(a) shall be the team having the function of implementing referral orders in the area in which it appears to the court that the offender resides or will reside.

   (3) On making a referral order the court shall explain to the offender in ordinary language –
   (a) the effect of the order; and
   (b) the consequences which may follow –
      (i) if no youth offender contract takes effect between the offender and the panel under section 8, or
      (ii) if the offender breaches any of the terms of any such contract.

   (4) Subsections (5) to (7) apply where, in dealing with an offender for two or more associated offences, a court makes a referral order in respect of each, or each of two or more, of the offences.

   (5) The orders shall have the effect of referring the offender to a single youth offender panel; and the provision made by them under subsection (1) shall accordingly be the same in each case, except that the periods specified under subsection (1)(c) may be different.

   (6) The court may direct that the period so specified in either or any of the orders is to run concurrently with or be additional to that specified in the other or any of the others; but in exercising its power under this subsection the court must ensure that the total period for which such a contract as is mentioned in subsection (1)(c) is to have effect does not exceed 12 months.

   (7) Each of the orders mentioned in subsection (4) shall, for the purposes of this Part, be treated as associated with the other or each of the others.

   Making of referral orders: effect on court's other sentencing powers.

4 (1) Subsections (2) to (5) apply where a court makes a referral order in respect of an offence.

   (2) The court may not deal with the offender for the offence in any of the prohibited ways.

   (3) The court –
   (a) shall, in respect of any associated offence, either sentence the offender by making a referral order or make an order discharging him absolutely; and

    (b) may not deal with the offender for any such offence in any of the prohibited ways.

(4) For the purposes of subsections (2) and (3) the prohibited ways are –

    (a) imposing a community sentence (within the meaning of Part I of the Criminal Justice Act 1991) on the offender;

    (b) ordering him to pay a fine;

    (c) making a reparation order under section 67 of the Crime and Disorder Act 1998 in respect of him; and

    (d) making an order discharging him conditionally.

(5) The court may not make, in connection with the conviction of the offender for the offence or any associated offence –

    (a) an order binding him over to keep the peace or to be of good behaviour;

    (b) an order under section 58 of the Criminal Justice Act 1991 (binding over of parent or guardian); or

    (c) a parenting order under section 8 of the Crime and Disorder Act 1998.

(6) Subsections (2), (3) and (5) do not affect the exercise of any power to deal with the offender conferred by paragraph 5 (offender referred back to court by panel) or paragraph 14 (powers of a court where offender convicted while subject to referral) of Schedule 1.

(7) Where section 1(2) above requires a court to make a referral order, the court may not under section 1 of the Powers of Criminal Courts Act 1973 defer passing sentence on him, but section 1(2) and subsection (3)(a) above do not affect any power or duty of a magistrates' court under –

    (a) section 56 of the Children and Young Persons Act 1933 (remission to youth court, or another such court, for sentence),

    (b) section 7(8) of the Children and Young Persons Act 1969 (remission to youth court for sentence),

    (c) section 10(3) of the Magistrates' Courts Act 1980 (adjournment for inquiries),

    (d) section 37 of that Act (committal to Crown Court for sentence), or

    (e) section 35, 38, 43 or 44 of the Mental Health Act 1983 (remand for reports, interim hospital orders and committal to Crown Court for restriction order).

Making of referral orders: attendance of parents, etc

5 (1) A court making a referral order may make an order requiring –

    (a) the appropriate person, or

    (b) in a case where there are two or more appropriate persons, any one or more of them,

to attend the meetings of the youth offender panel.

(2) Where an offender is under the age of 16 when a court makes a referral order in his case –

    (a) the court shall exercise its power under subsection (1) so as to require at least one appropriate person to attend meetings of the youth offender panel; and

    (b) if the offender falls within subsection (6), the person or persons so required to attend those meetings shall be or include a representative of the local authority mentioned in that subsection.

(3) The court shall not under this section make an order requiring a person to attend meetings of the youth offender panel –
(a) if the court is satisfied that it would be unreasonable to do so, or
(b) to an extent which the court is satisfied would be unreasonable.

(4) Except where the offender falls within subsection (6), each person who is a parent or guardian of the offender is an 'appropriate person' for the purposes of this section.

(5) Where the offender falls within subsection (6), each of the following is an 'appropriate person' for the purposes of this section –
(a) a representative of the local authority mentioned in that subsection, and
(b) each person who is a parent or guardian of the offender with whom the offender is allowed to live.

(6) An offender falls within this subsection if he is (within the meaning of the Children Act 1989) a child who is looked after by a local authority.

(7) If, at the time when a court makes an order under this section –
(a) a person who is required by the order to attend meetings of a youth offender panel is not present in court, or
(b) a local authority whose representative is so required to attend such meetings is not represented in court, the court must send him or (as the case may be) the authority a copy of the order forthwith.

(8) In this section 'guardian' has the same meaning as in the Children and Young Persons Act 1933.

YOUTH OFFENDER PANELS

Establishment of panels

6 (1) Where a referral order has been made in respect of an offender (or two or more associated referral orders have been so made), it is the duty of the youth offending team specified in the order (or orders) –
(a) to establish a youth offender panel for the offender;
(b) to arrange for the first meeting of the panel to be held for the purposes of section 8; and
(c) subsequently to arrange for the holding of any further meetings of the panel required by virtue of section 10 (in addition to those required by virtue of any other provision of this Part).

(2) A youth offender panel shall –
(a) be constituted,
(b) conduct its proceedings, and
(c) discharge its functions under this Part (and in particular those arising under section 8), in accordance with guidance given from time to time by the Secretary of State.

(3) At each of its meetings a panel shall, however, consist of at least –
(a) one member appointed by the youth offending team from among its members; and
(b) two members so appointed who are not members of the team.

(4) The Secretary of State may by regulations make provision requiring persons appointed as members of a youth offender panel to have such qualifications, or satisfy such other criteria, as are specified in the regulations.

(5) Where it appears to the court which made a referral order that, by reason of either a change or a prospective change in the offender's place or intended place of residence, the youth offending team for the time being specified in the order ('the current team') either does not or will not have the function of implementing referral orders in the area in which the offender resides or will reside, the court may vary the order so that it instead specifies the team which has the function of implementing such orders in that area ('the new team').

(6) Where a court so varies a referral order –
  (a) subsection (1)(a) shall apply to the new team in any event;
  (b) subsection (1)(b) shall apply to the new team if no youth offender contract has (or has under paragraph (c) below been treated as having) taken effect under section 8 between the offender and a youth offender panel established by the current team;
  (c) if such a contract has (or has previously under this paragraph been treated as having) so taken effect, it shall (after the variation) be treated as if it were a contract which had taken effect under section 8 between the offender and the panel being established for the offender by the new team.

(7) References in this Part to the meetings of a youth offender panel (or any such meeting) are to the following meetings of the panel (or any of them) –
  (a) the first meeting held in pursuance of subsection (1)(b);
  (b) any further meetings held in pursuance of section 10;
  (c) any progress meeting held under section 11; and
  (d) the final meeting held under section 12.

Attendance at panel meetings

7 (1) The specified team shall, in the case of each meeting of the panel established for the offender, notify –
  (a) the offender, and
  (b) any person to whom an order under section 5 applies,
  of the time and place at which he is required to attend that meeting.

(2) If the offender fails to attend any part of such a meeting the panel may –
  (a) adjourn the meeting to such time and place as it may specify; or
  (b) end the meeting and refer the offender back to the appropriate court;
  and subsection (1) shall apply in relation to any such adjourned meeting.

(3) One person aged 18 or over chosen by the offender, with the agreement of the panel, shall be entitled to accompany the offender to any meeting of the panel (and it need not be the same person who accompanies him to every meeting).

(4) The panel may allow to attend any such meeting –
  (a) any person who appears to the panel to be a victim of, or otherwise affected by, the offence, or any of the offences, in respect of which the offender was referred to the panel;

(b) any person who appears to the panel to be someone capable of having a good influence on the offender.

(5) Where the panel allows any such person as is mentioned in subsection (4)(a) ('the victim') to attend a meeting of the panel, the panel may allow the victim to be accompanied to the meeting by one person chosen by the victim with the agreement of the panel.

YOUTH OFFENDER CONTRACTS

First meeting: agreement of contract with offender

8   (1) At the first meeting of the youth offender panel established for an offender the panel shall seek to reach agreement with the offender on a programme of behaviour the aim (or principal aim) of which is the prevention of re-offending by the offender.

(2) The terms of the programme may, in particular, include provision for any of the following –
(a) the offender to make financial or other reparation to any person who appears to the panel to be a victim of, or otherwise affected by, the offence, or any of the offences, for which the offender was referred to the panel;
(b) the offender to attend mediation sessions with any such victim or other person;
(c) the offender to carry out unpaid work or service in or for the community;
(d) the offender to be at home at times specified in or determined under the programme;
(e) attendance by the offender at a school or other educational establishment or at a place of work;
(f) the offender to participate in specified activities (such as those designed to address offending behaviour, those offering education or training or those assisting with the rehabilitation of persons dependent on, or having a propensity to misuse, alcohol or drugs);
(g) the offender to present himself to specified persons at times and places specified in or determined under the programme;
(h) the offender to stay away from specified places or persons (or both);
(i) enabling the offender's compliance with the programme to be supervised and recorded.

(3) The programme may not, however, provide –
(a) for the electronic monitoring of the offender's whereabouts; or
(b) for the offender to have imposed on him any physical restriction on his movements.

(4) No term which provides for anything to be done to or with any such victim or other affected person as is mentioned in subsection (2)(a) may be included in the programme without the consent of that person.

(5) Where a programme is agreed between the offender and the panel, the panel shall cause a written record of the programme to be produced forthwith –
(a) in language capable of being readily understood by, or explained to, the offender, and
(b) for signature by him.

(6) Once the record has been signed –
   (a) by the offender, and
   (b) by a member of the panel on behalf of the panel, the terms of the programme, as set out in the record, take effect as the terms of a 'youth offender contract' between the offender and the panel; and the panel shall cause a copy of the record to be given or sent to the offender.

First meeting: duration of contract

9 (1) This section applies where a youth offender contract has taken effect under section 8 between an offender and a youth offender panel.

(2) The day on which the contract so takes effect shall be the first day of the period for which it has effect.

(3) Where the panel was established in pursuance of a single referral order, the length of the period for which the contract has effect shall be that of the period specified under section 3(1)(c) in the referral order.

(4) Where the panel was established in pursuance of two or more associated referral orders, the length of the period for which the contract has effect shall be that resulting from the court's directions under section 3(6).

(5) Subsections (3) and (4) have effect subject to –
   (a) any order under paragraph 11 or 12 of Schedule 1 extending the length of the period for which the contract has effect; and
   (b) subsection (6).

(6) If the referral order, or each of the associated referral orders, is revoked (whether under paragraph 5(2) of Schedule 1 or by virtue of paragraph 14(2) of that Schedule), the period for which the contract has effect expires at the time when the order or orders is or are revoked unless it has already expired.

First meeting: failure to agree contract

10 (1) Where it appears to a youth offender panel to be appropriate to do so, the panel may –
   (a) end the first meeting (or any further meeting held in pursuance of paragraph (b)) without having reached agreement with the offender on a programme of behaviour of the kind mentioned in section 8(1), and
   (b) resume consideration of the offender's case at a further meeting of the panel.

(2) If, however, it appears to the panel at the first meeting or any such further meeting that there is no prospect of agreement being reached with the offender within a reasonable period after the making of the referral order (or orders) –
   (a) subsection (1)(b) shall not apply; and
   (b) instead the panel shall refer the offender back to the appropriate court.

(3) If at a meeting of the panel –
   (a) agreement is reached with the offender but he does not sign the record produced in pursuance of section 8(5), and
   (b) his failure to do so appears to the panel to be unreasonable,
the panel shall end the meeting and refer the offender back to the appropriate court.

Progress meetings

11 (1) At any time –

(a) after a youth offender contract has taken effect under section 8, but

(b) before the end of the period for which the contract has effect,

the specified team shall, if so requested by the panel, arrange for the holding of a meeting of the panel under this section ('a progress meeting').

(2) The panel may make a request under subsection (1) if it appears to the panel to be expedient to review –

(a) the offender's progress in implementing the programme of behaviour contained in the contract, or

(b) any other matter arising in connection with the contract.

(3) The panel shall make such a request if –

(a) the offender has notified the panel that –

(i) he wishes to seek the panel's agreement to a variation in the terms of the contract, or

(ii) he wishes the panel to refer him back to the appropriate court with a view to the referral order (or orders) being revoked on account of a significant change in his circumstances (such as his being taken to live abroad) making compliance with any youth offender contract impractical; or

(b) it appears to the panel that the offender is in breach of any of the terms of the contract.

(4) At a progress meeting the panel shall do such one or more of the following things as it considers appropriate in the circumstances, namely –

(a) review the offender's progress or any such other matter as is mentioned in subsection (2);

(b) discuss with the offender any breach of the terms of the contract which it appears to the panel that he has committed;

(c) consider any variation in the terms of the contract sought by the offender or which it appears to the panel to be expedient to make in the light of any such review or discussion;

(d) consider whether to accede to any request by the offender that he be referred back to the appropriate court.

(5) Where the panel has discussed with the offender such a breach as is mentioned in subsection (4)(b) –

(a) the panel and the offender may agree that the offender is to continue to be required to comply with the contract (either in its original form or with any agreed variation in its terms) without being referred back to the appropriate court; or

(b) the panel may decide to end the meeting and refer the offender back to that court.

(6) Where a variation in the terms of the contract is agreed between the offender and the panel, the panel shall cause a written record of the variation to be produced forthwith –

(a) in language capable of being readily understood by, or explained to, the offender; and

(b) for signature by him.

(7) Any such variation shall take effect once the record has been signed –
   (a) by the offender, and
   (b) by a member of the panel on behalf of the panel;
   and the panel shall cause a copy of the record to be given or sent to the offender.

(8) If at a progress meeting –
   (a) any such variation is agreed but the offender does not sign the record produced in pursuance of subsection (6), and
   (b) his failure to do so appears to the panel to be unreasonable,
   the panel may end the meeting and refer the offender back to the appropriate court.

(9) Section 8(2) to (4) shall apply in connection with what may be provided for by the terms of the contract as varied under this section as they apply in connection with what may be provided for by the terms of a programme of behaviour of the kind mentioned in section 8(1).

(10) Where the panel has discussed with the offender such a request as is mentioned in subsection (4)(d), the panel may, if it is satisfied that there is (or is soon to be) such a change in circumstances as is mentioned in subsection (3)(a)(ii), decide to end the meeting and refer the offender back to the appropriate court.

Final meeting

12 (1) Where the compliance period in the case of a youth offender contract is due to expire, the specified team shall arrange for the holding, before the end of that period, of a meeting of the panel under this section ('the final meeting').

(2) At the final meeting the panel shall –
   (a) review the extent of the offender's compliance to date with the terms of the contract; and
   (b) decide, in the light of that review, whether his compliance with those terms has been such as to justify the conclusion that, by the time the compliance period expires, he will have satisfactorily completed the contract;
   and the panel shall give the offender written confirmation of its decision.

(3) Where the panel decides that the offender's compliance with the terms of the contract has been such as to justify that conclusion, the panel's decision shall have the effect of discharging the referral order (or orders) as from the end of the compliance period.

(4) Otherwise the panel shall refer the offender back to the appropriate court.

(5) Nothing in section 7(2) prevents the panel from making the decision mentioned in subsection (3) in the offender's absence if it appears to the panel to be appropriate to do that instead of exercising either of its powers under section 7(2).

(6) Section 7(2)(a) does not permit the final meeting to be adjourned (or re-adjourned) to a time falling after the end of the compliance period.

(7) In this section 'the compliance period' in relation to a youth offender contract means the period for which the contract has effect in accordance with section 9.

FURTHER COURT PROCEEDINGS

Offender referred back to court or convicted while subject to referral order

13　Schedule 1, which –

(a) in Part I makes provision for what is to happen when a youth offender panel refers an offender back to the appropriate court, and

(b) in Part II makes provision for what is to happen when an offender is convicted of further offences while for the time being subject to a referral order, shall have effect.

SUPPLEMENTARY

Functions of youth offending teams

14 (1) The functions of a youth offending team responsible for implementing a referral order include, in particular, arranging for the provision of such administrative staff, accommodation or other facilities as are required by the youth offender panel established in pursuance of the order.

(2) During the period for which a youth offender contract between a youth offender panel and an offender has effect –

(a) the specified team shall make arrangements for supervising the offender's compliance with the terms of the contract; and

(b) the person who is the member of the panel referred to in section 6(3)(a) shall ensure that records are kept of the offender's compliance (or non-compliance) with those terms.

(3) In implementing referral orders a youth offending team shall have regard to any guidance given from time to time by the Secretary of State.

Interpretation of Part I

15 (1) In this Part –

'the appropriate court' shall be construed in accordance with paragraph 1(2) of Schedule 1;

'custodial sentence' means a sentence of detention in a young offender institution, a secure training order under section 1 of the Criminal Justice and Public Order Act 1994, a detention and training order within the meaning given by section 73(3) of the Crime and Disorder Act 1998 or a sentence of detention under section 53(3) of the Children and Young Persons Act 1933;

'hospital order' has the meaning given in section 37 of the Mental Health Act 1983;

'meeting', in relation to a youth offender panel, shall be construed in accordance with section 6(7);

'referral order' means (in accordance with section 1(5)) an order under section 1(2) or (3);

'the specified team', in relation to an offender to whom a referral order applies (or two or more associated referral orders apply), means the youth offending team for the time being specified in the order (or orders);

'youth offending team' means a team established under section 39 of the Crime and Disorder Act 1998.

(2) For the purposes of this Part an offence is associated with another if the offender falls to be dealt with for it at the same time as he is dealt with for the other offence (whether or not he is convicted of the offences at the same time or by or before the same court).

(3) References in this Part to a referral order being associated with another shall be construed in accordance with section 3(7).

16–17 [*Not reproduced.*]

SCHEDULE 1: YOUTH OFFENDER PANELS: FURTHER COURT PROCEEDINGS

PART I – REFERRAL BACK TO APPROPRIATE COURT

Introductory

1 (1) This Part of this Schedule applies where a youth offender panel refers an offender back to the appropriate court under section 7(2), 10(2) or (3), 11(5), (8) or (10) or 12(4).

(2) For the purposes of this Part of this Schedule and the provisions mentioned in sub-paragraph (1) the appropriate court is –

(a) in the case of an offender under the age of 18 at the time when (in pursuance of the referral back) he first appears before the court, a youth court acting for the petty sessions area in which it appears to the youth offender panel that the offender resides or will reside; and

(b) otherwise, a magistrates' court (other than a youth court) acting for that area.

Mode of referral back to court

2 The panel shall make the referral by sending a report to the appropriate court explaining why the offender is being referred back to it.

Bringing the offender before the court

3 (1) Where the appropriate court receives such a report, the court shall cause the offender to appear before it.

(2) For the purpose of securing the attendance of the offender before the court, a justice acting for the petty sessions area for which the court acts may –

(a) issue a summons requiring the offender to appear at the place and time specified in it, or

(b) if the report is substantiated on oath, issue a warrant for the offender's arrest.

(3) Any summons or warrant issued under sub-paragraph (2) shall direct the offender to appear or be brought before the appropriate court.

(4) Section 4 of the Summary Jurisdiction (Process) Act 1881 (execution of process of English courts in Scotland) shall apply to any process issued under sub-paragraph (2) as it applies to process issued under the Magistrates' Courts Act 1980.

Detention and remand of arrested offender

4 (1) Where the offender is arrested in pursuance of a warrant under paragraph 3(2) and cannot be brought immediately before the appropriate court –

   (a) the person in whose custody he is may make arrangements for his detention in a place of safety (within the meaning given by section 107(1) of the Children and Young Persons Act 1933) for a period of not more than 72 hours from the time of the arrest (and it shall be lawful for him to be detained in pursuance of the arrangements); and

   (b) that person shall within that period bring him before a court which –

   (i) if he is under the age of 18 when he is brought before the court, shall be a youth court, and

   (ii) if he has then attained that age, shall be a magistrates' court other than a youth court.

   (2) Sub-paragraphs (3) to (5) apply where the court before which the offender is brought under sub-paragraph (1)(b) ('the alternative court') is not the appropriate court.

   (3) The alternative court may direct that he is to be released forthwith or remand him.

   (4) Section 128 of the Magistrates' Courts Act 1980 (remand in custody or on bail) shall have effect where the alternative court has power under sub-paragraph (3) to remand the offender as if the court referred to in subsections (1)(a), (3), (4)(a) and (5) were the appropriate court.

   (5) That section shall have effect where the alternative court has power to so remand him, or the appropriate court has (by virtue of sub-paragraph (4)) power to further remand him, as if in subsection (1) there were inserted after paragraph (c) 'or

   (d) if he is under the age of 18, remand him to accommodation provided by or on behalf of a local authority (within the meaning of the Children Act 1989) and, if it does so, shall designate as the authority who are to receive him the local authority for the area in which it appears to the court that he resides or will reside'.

Power of court where it upholds panel's decision

5 (1) If it is proved to the satisfaction of the appropriate court as regards any decision of the panel which resulted in the offender being referred back to the court –

   (a) that, so far as the decision relied on any finding of fact by the panel, the panel was entitled to make that finding in the circumstances, and

   (b) that, so far as the decision involved any exercise of discretion by the panel, the panel reasonably exercised that discretion in the circumstances,

   the court may exercise the power conferred by sub-paragraph (2).

   (2) That power is a power to revoke the referral order (or each of the referral orders).

   (3) The revocation under sub-paragraph (2) of a referral order has the effect of revoking any related order under paragraph 11 or 12.

   (4) Where any order is revoked under sub-paragraph (2) or by virtue of sub-paragraph (3), the appropriate court may deal with the offender in accord-

ance with sub-paragraph (5) for the offence in respect of which the revoked order was made.

(5) In so dealing with the offender for such an offence, the appropriate court –

  (a) may deal with him in any manner in which (assuming section 1 had not applied) he could have been dealt with for that offence by the court which made the order; and

  (b) shall have regard to –

    (i) the circumstances of his referral back to the court; and

    (ii) where a contract has taken effect under section 8 between the offender and the panel, the extent of his compliance with the terms of the contract.

(6) The appropriate court may not exercise the powers conferred by sub-paragraph (2) or (4) unless the offender is present before it; but those powers are exercisable even if, in a case where a contract has taken effect under section 8, the period for which the contract has effect has expired (whether before or after the referral of the offender back to the court).

(7) Where, in exercise of the powers conferred by sub-paragraph (4), the appropriate court deals with the offender for an offence by committing him to the Crown Court for sentence, sub-paragraph (5) applies in relation to his being dealt with by the Crown Court, but as if –

  (a) the reference to the appropriate court were to the Crown Court; and

  (b) the reference in paragraph (b)(i) to the court were to the appropriate court.

Appeal

6 Where the court in exercise of the power conferred by paragraph 5(4) deals with the offender for an offence, the offender may appeal to the Crown Court against the sentence.

Court not revoking referral order or orders

7 (1) This paragraph applies –

  (a) where the appropriate court decides that the matters mentioned in paragraphs (a) and (b) of paragraph 5(1) have not been proved to its satisfaction; or

  (b) where, although by virtue of paragraph 5(1) the appropriate court –

    (i) is able to exercise the power conferred by paragraph 5(2), or

    (ii) would be able to do so if the offender were present before it, the court (for any reason) decides not to exercise that power.

(2) If either –

  (a) no contract has taken effect under section 8 between the offender and the panel, or

  (b) a contract has taken effect under that section but the period for which it has effect has not expired, the offender shall continue to remain subject to the referral order (or orders) in all respects as if he had not been referred back to the court.

(3) If –

  (a) a contract had taken effect under section 8, but

  (b) the period for which it has effect has expired (otherwise than by virtue of section 9(6)), the court shall make an order declaring that the referral order (or each of the referral orders) is discharged.

Exception where court satisfied as to completion of contract

8   If, in a case where the offender is referred back to the court under section 12(4), the court decides (contrary to the decision of the panel) that the offender's compliance with the terms of the contract has, or will have, been such as to justify the conclusion that he has satisfactorily completed the contract, the court shall make an order declaring that the referral order (or each of the referral orders) is discharged.

Discharge of extension orders

9   The discharge under paragraph 7(3) or 8 of a referral order has the effect of discharging any related order under paragraph 11 or 12.

PART II – FURTHER CONVICTIONS DURING REFERRAL

Extension of referral for further offences

10 (1) Paragraphs 11 and 12 apply where, at a time when an offender under the age of 18 is subject to referral, a youth court or other magistrates' court ('the relevant court') is dealing with him for an offence in relation to which paragraphs (a) to (c) of section 1(1) are applicable.

   (2) But paragraphs 11 and 12 do not apply unless the offender's compliance period is less than 12 months.

Extension where further offences committed pre-referral

11   If –
   (a) the occasion on which the offender was referred to the panel is the only other occasion on which it has fallen to a court in the United Kingdom to deal with the offender for any offence or offences, and
   (b) the offender committed the offence mentioned in paragraph 10, and any associated offence, before he was referred to the panel,
   the relevant court may sentence the offender for the offence by making an order extending his compliance period.

Extension where further offence committed after referral

12 (1) If –
   (a) paragraph 11(a) applies, but
   (b) the offender committed the offence mentioned in paragraph 10, or any associated offence, after he was referred to the panel,
   the relevant court may sentence the offender for the offence by making an order extending his compliance period, but only if the requirements of sub-paragraph (2) are complied with.

   (2) Those requirements are that the court must –
   (a) be satisfied, on the basis of a report made to it by the relevant body, that there are exceptional circumstances which indicate that, even though the offender has re-offended since being referred to the panel, extending his compliance period is likely to help prevent further re-offending by him; and
   (b) state in open court that it is so satisfied and why it is.

(3) In sub-paragraph (2) 'the relevant body' means the panel to which the offender has been referred or, if no contract has yet taken effect between the offender and the panel under section 8, the specified team.

Provisions supplementary to paragraphs 11 and 12

13 (1) An order under paragraph 11 or 12, or two or more orders under one or other of those paragraphs made in respect of associated offences, must not so extend the offender's compliance period as to cause it to exceed twelve months.

(2) Sub-paragraphs (3) to (5) apply where the relevant court makes an order under paragraph 11 or 12 in respect of the offence mentioned in paragraph 10; but sub-paragraphs (3) to (5) do not affect the exercise of any power to deal with the offender conferred by paragraph 5 or 14.

(3) The relevant court may not deal with the offender for that offence in any of the prohibited ways specified in section 4(4).

(4) The relevant court –
  (a) shall, in respect of any associated offence, either –
    (i) sentence the offender by making an order under the same paragraph, or
    (ii) make an order discharging him absolutely; and
  (b) may not deal with the offender for any associated offence in any of those prohibited ways.

(5) The relevant court may not, in connection with the conviction of the offender for the offence or any associated offence, make any such order as is mentioned in section 4(5).

(6) For the purposes of paragraphs 11 and 12 any occasion on which the offender was discharged absolutely in respect of the offence, or each of the offences, for which he was being dealt with shall be disregarded.

(7) Any occasion on which, in criminal proceedings in England and Wales or Northern Ireland, the offender was bound over to keep the peace or to be of good behaviour shall be regarded for those purposes as an occasion on which it fell to a court in the United Kingdom to deal with the offender for an offence.

(8) The Secretary of State may by regulations make such amendments of paragraphs 10 to 12 and this paragraph as he considers appropriate for altering in any way the descriptions of offenders in the case of which an order extending the compliance period may be made; and subsection (4) of section 2 shall apply in relation to regulations under this sub-paragraph as it applies in relation to regulations under subsection (3) of that section.

Further convictions which lead to revocation of referral

14 (1) This paragraph applies where, at a time when an offender is subject to referral, a court in England and Wales deals with him for an offence (whether committed before or after he was referred to the panel) by making an order other than –
  (a) an order under paragraph 11 or 12, or
  (b) an order discharging him absolutely.

(2) In such a case the order of the court shall have the effect of revoking –
   (a) the referral order (or orders), and
   (b) any related order or orders under paragraph 11 or 12.

(3) Where any order is revoked by virtue of sub-paragraph (2), the court may, if appears to the court that it would be in the interests of justice to do so, deal with the offender for the offence in respect of which the revoked order was made in any manner in which (assuming section 1 had not applied) he could have been dealt with for that offence by the court which made the order.

(4) When dealing with the offender under sub-paragraph (3) the court shall, where a contract has taken effect between the offender and the panel under section 8, have regard to the extent of his compliance with the terms of the contract.

(5) Where, in exercise of the powers conferred by sub-paragraph (3), a magistrates' court deals with the offender for an offence by committing him to the Crown Court for sentence, the Crown Court –
   (a) may deal with him for the offence in any manner in which (assuming section 1 had not applied) he could have been dealt with for that offence by the court which made the revoked order; and
   (b) shall, where a contract has taken effect as mentioned in sub-paragraph (4), have regard to the extent of his compliance with the terms of the contract.

Interpretation

15 (1) For the purposes of this Part of this Schedule an offender is for the time being subject to referral if –
   (a) a referral order has been made in respect of him and that order has not, or
   (b) two or more referral orders have been made in respect of him and any of those orders has not,

been discharged (whether by virtue of section 12(3) or under paragraph 7(3) or 8) or revoked (whether under paragraph 5(2) or by virtue of paragraph 14(2)).

(2) In this Part of this Schedule 'compliance period', in relation to an offender who is for the time being subject to referral, means the period for which (in accordance with section 9) any youth offender contract taking effect in his case under section 8 has (or would have) effect.

Statutory Instruments

Children (Secure Accommodation) Regulations 1991 SI No 1505

1   *[Citation and commencement: not reproduced.]*

Interpretation

2 (1) In these Regulations, unless the context otherwise requires –

'the Act' means the Children Act 1989;

'children's home' means a registered children's home, a community home or a voluntary home;

'independent visitor' means a person appointed under paragraph 17 of Schedule 2 to the Act;

'secure accommodation' means accommodation which is provided for the purpose of restricting the liberty of children to whom section 25 of the Act (use of accommodation for restricting liberty) applies.

  (2) Any reference in these regulations to a numbered regulation shall be construed as a reference to the regulation bearing that number in these Regulations, and any reference in a regulation to a numbered paragraph is a reference to the paragraph bearing that number in that regulation.

Approval by Secretary of State of secure accommodation in a children's home

3   Accommodation in a children's home shall not be used as secure accommodation unless it has been approved by the Secretary of State for such use and approval shall be subject to such terms and conditions as he sees fit.

Placement of a child aged under 13 in secure accommodation in a children's home

4   A child under the age of 13 years shall not be placed in secure accommodation in a children's home without the prior approval of the Secretary of State to the placement of that child and such approval shall be subject to such terms and conditions as he sees fit.

Children to whom section 25 of the Act shall not apply

5 (1) Section 25 of the Act shall not apply to a child who is detained (a) under any provision of the Mental Health Act 1983 or in respect of whom an order has been made under section 53 of the Children and Young Persons Act 1933 (punishment of certain grave crimes).

  (2) Section 25 of the Act shall not apply to a child –

(a) to whom section 20(5) of the Act (accommodation of persons over 16 but under 21) applies and who is being accommodated under that section,

(b) in respect of whom an order has been made under section 43 of the Act (child assessment order) and who is kept away from home pursuant to that order.

Detained and remanded children to whom section 25 of the Act shall have effect subject to modifications

6 (1) Subject to regulation 5, section 25 of the Act shall have effect subject to the modification specified in paragraph (2) in relation to children who are being looked after by a local authority and are of the following descriptions –

(a) children detained under section 38(6) of the Police and Criminal Evidence Act 1984 (detained children), and

(b) children remanded to local authority accommodation under section 23 of the Children and Young Persons Act 1969 (remand to local authority accommodation) but only if –

(i) the child is charged with or has been convicted of a violent or sexual offence, or of an offence punishable in the case of an adult with imprisonment for a term of 14 years or more, or

(ii) the child has a recent history of absconding while remanded to local authority accommodation, and is charged with or has been convicted of an imprisonable offence alleged or found to have been committed while he was so remanded.

(2) The modification referred to in paragraph (1) is that, for the words 'unless it appears' to the end of subsection (1), there shall be substituted the following words –

'unless it appears that any accommodation other than that provided for the purpose of restricting liberty is inappropriate because –

(a) the child is likely to abscond from such other accommodation, or

(b) the child is likely to injure himself or other people if he is kept in any such other accommodation'.

Children to whom section 25 of the Act shall apply and have effect subject to modifications

7 (1) Subject to regulation 5 and paragraphs (2) and (3) of this regulation section 25 of the Act shall apply (in addition to children looked after by a local authority) –

(a) to children, other than those looked after by a local authority, who are accommodated by health authorities, National Health Service trusts established under section 5 of the National Health Service and Community Care Act 1990 or local education authorities, and

(b) to children, other than those looked after by a local authority, who are accommodated in residential care homes, nursing homes or mental nursing homes.

(2) In relation to the children of a description specified in paragraph (1)(a) section 25 of the Act shall have effect subject to the following modifications –

(a) for the words 'who is being looked after by a local authority' in subsection (1) there shall be substituted the words 'who is being provided with accommodation by a health authority, a National Health Service trust established under section 5 of the National Health Service and Community Care Act 1990 or a local education authority'.

(b) for the words 'local authorities' in subsection (2)(c) there shall be substituted the words 'health authorities, National Health Service trusts or local education authorities'.

(3) In relation to the children of a description specified in paragraph (1)(b), section 25 of the Act shall have effect subject to the following modifications –

(a) for the words 'who is being looked after by a local authority' in subsection (1) there shall be substituted the words 'who is being provided with accommodation in a residential care home, a nursing home or a mental nursing home'; and

(b) for the words 'local authorities' in subsection (2)(c) there shall be substituted the words 'persons carrying on residential care homes, nursing homes or mental nursing homes'.

Applications to court

8   Subject to section 101 of the Local Government Act 1972, applications to a court under section 25 of the Act in respect of a child shall be made only by the local authority which are looking after that child.

Duty to give information of placement in children's homes

9   Where a child is placed in secure accommodation in a children's home which is managed by a person, organisation or authority other than the local authority which is looking after him, the person who, or the organisation or the authority which manages that accommodation shall inform the authority which are looking after him that he has been placed there, within 12 hours of his being placed there, with a view to obtaining their authority to continue to keep him there if necessary.

Maximum period in secure accommodation without court authority

10 (1) Subject to paragraphs (2) and (3), the maximum period beyond which a child to whom section 25 of the Act applies may not be kept in secure accommodation without the authority of a court is an aggregate of 72 hours (whether or not consecutive) in any period of 28 consecutive days.

(2) Where authority of a court to keep a child in secure accommodation has been given, any period during which the child has been kept in such accommodation before the giving of that authority shall be disregarded for the purposes of calculating the maximum period in relation to any subsequent occasion on which the child is placed in such accommodation after the period authorised by court has expired.

(3) Where a child is in secure accommodation at any time between 12 midday on the day before and 12 midday on the day after a public holiday or a Sunday, and

(a) during that period the maximum period specified in paragraph (1) expires, and

(b) the child had, in the 27 days before the day on which he was placed in secure accommodation, been placed and kept in such accommodation for an aggregate of more than 48 hours,

the maximum period does not expire until 12 midday on the first day, which is not itself a public holiday or a Sunday, after the public holiday or Sunday.

Maximum initial period of authorisation by a court

11   Subject to regulations 12 and 13 the maximum period for which a court may authorise a child to whom section 25 of the Act applies to be kept in secure accommodation is three months.

Further periods of authorisation by a court

12   Subject to regulation 13 a court may from time to time authorise a child to whom section 25 of the Act applies to be kept in secure accommodation for a further period not exceeding 6 months at any one time.

Maximum periods of authorisation by court for remanded children

13 (1) The maximum period for which a court, may from time to time authorise a child who has been remanded to local authority accommodation under section 23 of the Children and Young Persons Act 1969 to be kept in secure accommodation (whether the period is an initial period or a further period) is the period of the remand.

(2) Any period of authorisation in respect of such a child shall not exceed 28 days on any one occasion without further court authorisation.

Duty to inform parents and others in relation to children in secure accommodation in a children's home

14   Where a child to whom section 25 of the Act applies is kept in secure accommodation in a children's home and it is intended that an application will be made to a court to keep the child in that accommodation, the local authority which are looking after the child shall if practicable inform of that intention as soon as possible –

(a) his parent,
(b) any person who is not a parent of his but who has parental responsibility for him,
(c) the child's independent visitor, if one has been appointed, and
(d) any other person who that local authority consider should be informed.

Appointment of persons to review placement in secure accommodation in a children's home

15   Each local authority looking after a child in secure accommodation in a children's home shall appoint at least three persons, at least one of whom is neither a member nor an officer of the local authority by or on behalf of which the child is being looked after, who shall review the keeping of the child in such accommodation for the purposes of securing his welfare within one month of the inception of the placement and then at intervals not exceeding three months where the child continues to be kept in such accommodation.

Review of placement in secure accommodation in a children's home

16 (1) The persons appointed under regulation 15 to review the keeping of a child in secure accommodation shall satisfy themselves as to whether or not –

(a) the criteria for keeping the child in secure accommodation continue to apply;

(b) the placement in such accommodation in a children's home continues to be necessary; and

(c) any other description of accommodation would be appropriate for him,

and in doing so shall have regard to the welfare of the child whose case is being reviewed.

(2) In undertaking the review referred to in regulation 15 the persons appointed shall, if practicable, ascertain and take into account the wishes and feelings of –

(a) the child,

(b) any parent of his,

(c) any person not being a parent of his but who has parental responsibility for him,

(d) any other person who has had the care of the child, whose views the persons appointed consider should be taken into account,

(e) the child's independent visitor if one has been appointed, and

(f) the person, organisation or local authority managing the secure accommodation in which the child is placed if that accommodation is not managed by the authority which is looking after that child.

(3) The local authority shall, if practicable, inform all those whose views are required to be taken into account under paragraph (2) of the outcome of the review what action, if any, the local authority propose to take in relation to the child in the light of the review, and their reasons for taking or not taking such action.

17 [*Not reproduced.*]

18–19 [*Revoked.*]

Children (Secure Accommodation) (No 2) Regulations 1991 SI No 2034

1 [*Not reproduced.*]

Applications to court – special cases

2 (1) Applications to a court under section 25 of the Children Act 1989 in respect of a child provided with accommodation by a health authority, a National Health Service trust established under section 5 of the National Health Service and Community Care Act 1990 or a local education authority shall, unless the child is looked after by a local authority, be made only by the health authority, National Health Service trust or local education authority providing accommodation for the child.

(2) Applications to a court under section 25 of the Children Act 1989 in respect of a child provided with accommodation in a residential care home, nursing

home or mental nursing home shall, unless the child is looked after by a local authority, be made only by the person carrying on the home in which accommodation is provided for the child.

Magistrates' Courts (Children and Young Persons) Rules 1992 SI No 2071

PART I – GENERAL

Citation and commencement

1   [*Not reproduced.*]

Interpretation

2   (1) In these Rules –

'the Act of 1933' means the Children and Young Persons Act 1933;

'the Act of 1969' means the Children and Young Persons Act 1969;

'the Act of 1989' means the Children Act 1989;

'child' means a person under the age of fourteen;

'court' –

(a) in Parts II and IV and, subject to rule 13(2), in Part III, means a youth court, and

(b) in rules 26 to 29, means a magistrates' court whether a youth court or not;

'guardian' has the meaning given in section 107(1) of the Act of 1933;

'register' means the separate register kept for the youth court pursuant to rule 25 of these Rules; and

'young person' means a person who has attained the age of fourteen and is under the age of eighteen.

(2) In these Rules, unless the context otherwise requires, references to a parent in relation to a child or young person are references –

(a) where a local authority has parental responsibility for him under the Act of 1989, to the local authority, and

(b) in any other case, to a parent who has parental responsibility for him under that Act.

(3) In these Rules, unless the context otherwise requires, any reference to a rule, Part or Schedule shall be construed as a reference to a rule contained in these Rules, a Part thereof or a Schedule thereto, and any reference in a rule to a paragraph shall be construed as a reference to a paragraph of that rule.

Revocations and savings, etc

3   (1) Subject to paragraph (3), the Rules specified in Schedule 1 are hereby revoked to the extent specified.

(2) Subject to paragraph (3), the provisions of the Magistrates' Courts Rules 1981 shall have effect subject to these Rules.

(3) Nothing in these Rules shall apply in connection with any proceedings begun before the coming into force thereof.

PART II – PROCEEDINGS IN CRIMINAL MATTERS

Application of Part II

4 (1) This Part applies, subject to paragraph (3), where proceedings to which paragraph (2) applies are brought in a court in respect of a child or young person ('the relevant minor').

(2) This paragraph applies to proceedings in which the relevant minor is charged with an offence, and, where he appears or is brought before the court, to proceedings under –

(a) section 15 of the Act of 1969 (variation and discharge of supervision orders);

(b) Part II, III or IV of Schedule 2 to the Criminal Justice Act 1991 (breaches of requirements of, and revocation and amendment of, probation orders, community service orders, combination orders and curfew orders), or

(c) section 18 of the Criminal Justice Act 1982 (discharge and variation of attendance centre orders), or

(d) Schedule 5 to the Crime and Disorder Act 1998 (enforcement, etc, of reparation and action plan order).

(3) Where the court is inquiring into an offence as examining justices, only rules 5, 6 and 8(3) apply, and where the proceedings are of a kind mentioned in paragraph (2)(a), (b) or (c) rules 7 and 12 do not apply.

Assistance in conducting case

5 (1) Except where the relevant minor is legally represented, the court shall allow his parent or guardian to assist him in conducting his case.

(2) Where the parent or guardian cannot be found or cannot in the opinion of the court reasonably be required to attend, the court may allow any relative or other responsible person to take the place of the parent or guardian for the purposes of this Part.

Duty of court to explain nature of proceedings etc

6 (1) The court shall explain to the relevant minor the nature of the proceedings and, where he is charged with an offence, the substance of the charge.

(2) The explanation shall be given in simple language suitable to his age and understanding.

Duty of court to take plea to charge

7 Where the relevant minor is charged with an offence the court shall, after giving the explanation required by rule 6, ask him whether he pleads guilty or not guilty to the charge.

Evidence in support of charge or application

8 (1) Where –

(a) the relevant minor is charged with an offence and does not plead guilty, or

(b) the proceedings are of a kind mentioned in rule 4(2)(a), (b) or (c),

the court shall hear the witnesses in support of the charge or, as the case may be, the application.

(2) Except where –
   (a) the proceedings are of a kind mentioned in rule 4(2)(a), (b) or (c), and
   (b) the relevant minor is the applicant,
   each witness may at the close of his evidence-in-chief be cross-examined by or on behalf of the relevant minor.

(3) If in any case where the relevant minor is not legally represented or assisted as provided by rule 5, the relevant minor, instead of asking questions by way of cross-examination, makes assertions, the court shall then put to the witness such questions as it thinks necessary on behalf of the relevant minor and may for this purpose question the relevant minor in order to bring out or clear up any point arising out of any such assertions.

Evidence in reply

9   If it appears to the court after hearing the evidence in support of the charge or application that a prima facie case is made out, the relevant minor shall, if he is not the applicant and is not legally represented, be told that he may give evidence or address the court, and the evidence of any witnesses shall be heard.

Procedure after finding against minor

10 (1) This rule applies where –
   (a) the relevant minor is found guilty of an offence, whether after a plea of guilty or otherwise, or
   (b) in proceedings of a kind mentioned in rule 4(2)(a), (b) or (c) the court is satisfied that the case of the applicant –
      (i) if the relevant minor is not the applicant, has been made out, or
      (ii) if he is the applicant, has not been made out.

(2) Where this rule applies –
   (a) the relevant minor and his parent or guardian, if present, shall be given an opportunity of making a statement,
   (b) the court shall take into consideration all available information as to the general conduct, home surroundings, school record and medical history of the relevant minor and, in particular, shall take into consideration such information as aforesaid which is provided in pursuance of section 9 of the Act of 1969,
   (c) if such information as aforesaid is not fully available, the court shall consider the desirability of adjourning the proceedings for such inquiry as may be necessary,
   (d) any written report of a probation officer, local authority, local education authority, educational establishment or registered medical practitioner may be received and considered by the court without being read aloud, and
   (e) if the court considers it necessary in the interests of the relevant minor, it may require him or his parent or guardian, if present, to withdraw from the court.

(3) The court shall arrange for copies of any written report before the court to be made available to –
   (a) the legal representative, if any, of the relevant minor,

(b) any parent or guardian of the relevant minor who is present at the hearing, and

(c) the relevant minor, except where the court otherwise directs on the ground that it appears to it impracticable to disclose the report having regard to his age and understanding or undesirable to do so having regard to potential serious harm which might thereby be suffered by him.

(4) In any case in which the relevant minor is not legally represented and where a report which has not been made available to him in accordance with a direction under paragraph (3)(c) has been considered without being read aloud in pursuance of paragraph (2)(d) or where he or his parent or guardian has been required to withdraw from the court in pursuance of paragraph (2)(e), then –

(a) the relevant minor shall be told the substance of any part of the information given to the court bearing on his character or conduct which the court considers to be material to the manner in which the case should be dealt with unless it appears to it impracticable so to do having regard to his age and understanding, and

(b) the parent or guardian of the relevant minor, if present, shall be told the substance of any part of such information which the court considers to be material as aforesaid and which has reference to his character or conduct or to the character, conduct, home surroundings or health of the relevant minor, and if such a person, having been told the substance of any part of such information, desires to produce further evidence with reference thereto, the court, if it thinks the further evidence would be material, shall adjourn the proceedings for the production thereof and shall, if necessary in the case of a report, require the attendance at the adjourned hearing of the person who made the report.

Duty of court to explain manner in which it proposes to deal with case and effect of order

11 (1) Before finally disposing of the case or before remitting the case to another court in pursuance of section 56 of the Act of 1933, the court shall inform the relevant minor and his parent or guardian, if present, or any person assisting him in his case, of the manner in which it proposes to deal with the case and allow any of those persons so informed to make representations; but the relevant minor shall not be informed as aforesaid if the court considers it undesirable so to do.

(2) On making any order, the court shall explain to the relevant minor the general nature and effect of the order unless, in the case of an order requiring his parent or guardian to enter into a recognizance, it appears to it undesirable so to do.

Notice to be given where remand is extended in absence of child or young person

12 Where a child or young person has been remanded, and the period of remand is extended in his absence in accordance with section 48 of the Act of 1933, notice shall be given to him and his sureties (if any) of the date at which he will be required to appear before the court.

PART III – PROCEEDINGS IN CERTAIN OTHER MATTERS

Application and interpretation of Part III

13 (1) This Part applies in connection with proceedings in a court in the case of any child or young person in relation to whom proceedings are brought or proposed to be brought under –

(a) section 72 or 73 of the Social Work (Scotland) Act 1968 (persons subject to supervision requirements or orders moving from or to Scotland), or

(b) regulations made under section 25 of the Act of 1989 (authority to retain child in secure accommodation),

except that rules 14, 16(2), 20 and 21 do not apply in connection with proceedings under the enactments mentioned in sub-paragraph (a) above.

(2) In this Part –

'the applicant' means the person by whom proceedings are brought or proposed to be brought;

'court', in relation to proceedings of the kind mentioned in paragraph (1)(b), means a magistrates' court, whether a youth court or not, but does not include a family proceedings court; and

'the relevant minor' means the person in relation to whom proceedings are brought or proposed to be brought as mentioned in paragraph (1).

Notice by person proposing to bring proceedings

14 (1) The applicant shall send a notice to the clerk of the court specifying the grounds for the proceedings and the names and addresses of the persons to whom a copy of the notice is sent in pursuance of paragraph (2).

(2) Without prejudice to section 34(2) of the Act of 1969 and regulations made under section 25 of the Act of 1989, the applicant shall –

(a) send to each of the persons mentioned in paragraph (3) a copy of the said notice, and

(b) notify each of those persons of the date, time and place appointed for the hearing unless a summons is issued for the purpose of securing his attendance thereat.

(3) The persons referred to in paragraph (2) are –

(a) the relevant minor, unless it appears to the applicant inappropriate to notify him in pursuance of paragraph (2), having regard to his age and understanding,

(b) the parent or guardian of the relevant minor if the whereabouts of such parent or guardian is known to the applicant or can readily be ascertained by him, and

(c) where the father and mother of the relevant minor were not married to each other at the time of his birth, any person who is known to the applicant to have made an application for an order under section 4 of the Act of 1989 (acquisition of parental responsibility by father) which has not yet been determined.

Rights of parents and guardians

15   Without prejudice to any provision of these Rules which provides for a parent or guardian to take part in proceedings, the relevant minor's parent or guardian shall be entitled to make representations to the court at any such stage after the conclusion of the evidence in the hearing as the court considers appropriate.

Adjournment of proceedings and procedure at hearing

16 (1) The court may, at any time, whether before or after the beginning of the hearing, adjourn the hearing, and, when so doing, may either fix the date, time and place at which the hearing is to be resumed or leave the date, time and place to be determined later by the court; but the hearing shall not be resumed at that date, time and place unless the court is satisfied that the applicant, the respondent and any other party to the proceedings have had adequate notice thereof.

(2) Subject to the provisions of the Act of 1969, sections 56, 57 and 123 of the Magistrates' Courts Act 1980 (non-appearance of parties and defects in process) shall apply to the proceedings as if they were by way of complaint and as if any references therein to the complainant, to the defendant and to the defence were, respectively, references to the applicant, to the relevant minor and to his case.

(3) Rules 14 and 16(1) of the Magistrates' Courts Rules 1981 (order of evidence and speeches and form of order) shall apply to the proceedings as if they were by way of complaint and as if any references therein to the complainant, to the defendant and to the defence were, respectively, references to the applicant, to the relevant minor and to his case.

Duty of court to explain nature of proceedings

17   Except where, by virtue of any enactment, the court may proceed in the absence of the relevant minor, before proceeding with the hearing the court shall inform him of the general nature both of the proceedings and of the grounds on which they are brought, in terms suitable to his age and understanding, or if by reason of his age and understanding or his absence it is impracticable so to do, shall so inform any parent or guardian of his present at the hearing.

Conduct of case on behalf of relevant minor

18 (1) Except where the relevant minor or his parent or guardian is legally represented, the court shall, unless the relevant minor otherwise requests, allow his parent or guardian to conduct the case on his behalf, subject, however, to the provisions of rule 19(2).

(2) If the court thinks it appropriate to do so it may, unless the relevant minor otherwise requests, allow a relative of his or some other responsible person to conduct the case on his behalf.

Power of court to hear evidence in absence of relevant minor and to require parent or guardian to withdraw

19 (1) Where the evidence likely to be given is such that in the opinion of the court it is in the interests of the relevant minor that the whole, or any part, of the evidence should not be given in his presence, then, unless he is conducting his own case, the court may hear the whole or part of the evidence, as it thinks appropriate, in his absence; but any evidence relating to his character or conduct shall be heard in his presence.

(2) If the court is satisfied that it is appropriate so to do, it may require a parent or guardian of the relevant minor to withdraw from the court while the relevant minor gives evidence or makes a statement; but the court shall inform the person so excluded of the substance of any allegations made against him by the relevant minor.

Duty of court to explain procedure to relevant minor at end of applicant's case

20   If it appears to the court after hearing the evidence in support of the applicant's case that he has made out a prima facie case it shall tell the relevant minor or the person conducting the case on his behalf under rule 18 that he may give evidence or make a statement and call witnesses.

Consideration of reports: secure accommodation proceedings

21 (1) The court shall arrange for copies of any written report before the court to be made available, so far as practicable before the hearing to –

(a) the applicant,

(b) the legal representative, if any, of the relevant minor,

(c) the parent or guardian of the relevant minor, and

(d) the relevant minor, except where the court otherwise directs on the ground that it appears to it impracticable to disclose the report having regard to his age and understanding or undesirable to do so having regard to potential serious harm which might thereby be suffered by him.

(2) In any case in which the court has determined that the relevant criteria are satisfied, the court shall, for the purpose of determining the maximum period of authorisation to be specified in the order, take into consideration such information as it considers necessary for that purpose, including such information which is provided in pursuance of section 9 of the Act of 1969.

(3) Any written report may be received and considered by the court without being read aloud.

Duty of court to explain manner in which it proposes to deal with case and effect of order

22 (1) Before finally disposing of the case, the court shall in simple language inform the relevant minor, any person conducting the case on his behalf, and his parent or guardian, if present, of the manner in which it proposes to deal with the case and allow any of those persons so informed to make representations; but the relevant minor shall not be informed as aforesaid if the court considers it undesirable or, having regard to his age and understanding, impracticable so to inform him.

(2) On making any order, the court shall in simple language suitable to his age and understanding explain to the relevant minor the general nature and

effect of the order unless it appears to it impracticable so to do having regard to his age and understanding and shall give such an explanation to the relevant minor's parent or guardian, if present.

PART IV – EVIDENCE – TELEVISION LINKS AND VIDEO RECORDINGS

Evidence through television link where witness is a child or is to be cross-examined

23 (1) Any party may apply for leave under section 32(1)(b) of the Criminal Justice Act 1988 for evidence to be given through a live television link where –
   (a) the offence charged is one to which section 32(2) of that Act applies, and
   (b) the evidence is to be given by a witness who is either –
      (i) in the case of an offence falling within section 32(2)(a) or (b) of that Act, under the age of 14,
      (ii) in the case of an offence falling within section 32(2)(c) of that Act, under the age of 17, or
      (iii) a person who is to be cross-examined following the admission under section 32A of that Act of a video recording of testimony from him,
   and references in this Part to an offence include references to attempting or conspiring to commit, or aiding, abetting, counselling, procuring or inciting the commission of that offence.
   (2) An application under paragraph (1) above shall be made by giving notice in writing, which shall be in the form prescribed in Form 51 of Schedule 2 or a form to the like effect.
   (3) An application under paragraph (1) above shall be made within 28 days after the date on which the defendant first appears or is brought before the court on an information charging him with the offence.
   (4) The notice under paragraph (2) above shall be sent to the clerk to the court and at the same time a copy thereof shall be sent by the applicant to every other party to the proceedings.
   (5) A party who receives a copy of a notice under paragraph (2) above and who wishes to oppose the application shall within 14 days notify the applicant and the clerk to the court, in writing, of his opposition, giving the reasons therefor.
   (6) An application under paragraph (1) above shall be determined by a justice of the peace without a hearing, unless the justice otherwise directs, and the clerk to the court shall notify the parties of the time and place of any such hearing.
   (7) The clerk to the court shall notify all the parties and the person who is to accompany the witness (if known) of the decision of the court in relation to an application under paragraph (1) above. Where leave is granted, the notification shall state –
   (a) where the witness is to give evidence on behalf of the prosecutor, the name of the witness, and, if known, the name, occupation and relationship (if any) to the witness of the person who is to accompany the witness, and

(b) the location of the court at which the proceedings should take place.

(8) The period specified in paragraph (3) above may be extended, either before or after it expires, on an application made in writing, specifying the grounds of the application and sent to the clerk to the court and a copy of the application shall be sent by the applicant to every other party to the proceedings. The clerk to the court shall notify all the parties of the decision of the court.

(9) An application for extension of time under paragraph (8) above shall be determined by a justice of the peace without a hearing unless the justice otherwise directs.

(10) A witness giving evidence through a television link pursuant to leave granted under paragraph (7) above shall be accompanied by a person acceptable to a justice of the peace and, unless the justice of the peace directs, by no other person.

Video recordings of testimony from child witness

24 (1) Any party may apply for leave under section 32A of the Criminal Justice Act 1988 to tender in evidence a video recording of testimony from a witness where –

(a) the offence charged is one to which section 32(2) of that Act applies,

(b) in the case of an offence falling within section 32(2)(a) or (b) of that Act, the proposed witness is under the age of 14 or, if he was under 14 when the video recording was made, is under the age of 15,

(c) in the case of an offence falling within section 32(2)(c) of that Act, the proposed witness is under the age of 17 or, if he was under 17 when the video recording was made, is under the age of 18, and

(d) the video recording is of an interview conducted between an adult and a person coming within sub-paragraph (b) or (c) above (not being the accused or one of the accused) which relates to any matter in issue in the proceedings;

and references in this rule to an offence include references to attempting or conspiring to commit, or aiding, abetting, counselling, procuring or inciting the commission of, that offence.

(2) An application under paragraph (1) above shall be made by giving notice in writing, which shall be in the form prescribed in Form 52 of Schedule 2, or a form to the like effect. The application shall be accompanied by the video recording which it is proposed to tender in evidence and shall include the following, namely –

(a) the name of the defendant and the offence or offences charged,

(b) the name and date of birth of the witness in respect of whom the application is made,

(c) the date on which the video recording was made

(d) a statement that in the opinion of the applicant the witness is willing and able to attend the trial for cross-examination,

(e) a statement of the circumstances in which the video recording was made which complies with paragraph (4) below, and

(f) the date on which the video recording was disclosed to the other party or parties.

(3) Where it is proposed to tender part only of a video recording of an interview with the witness, an application under paragraph (1) above must specify that part and be accompanied by a video recording of the entire interview including those parts of the interview which it is not proposed to tender in evidence and by a statement of the circumstances in which the video recording of the entire interview was made which complies with paragraph (4) below.

(4) The statement of the circumstances in which the video recording was made referred to in paragraphs (2)(e) and (3) above shall include the following information, except in so far as it is contained in the recording itself, namely –

   (a) the times at which the recording commenced and finished, including details of any interruptions,

   (b) the location at which the recording was made and the usual function of the premises,

   (c) the name, age and occupation of any person present at any point during the recording, the time for which he was present and his relationship (if any) to the witness and to the defendant,

   (d) a description of the equipment used, including the number of the cameras used and whether they were fixed or mobile, the number and location of microphones and the video format used and whether there were single or multiple recording facilities, and

   (e) the location of the mastertape if the video recording is a copy and details of when and by whom the copy was made.

(5) An application under paragraph (1) above shall be made within 28 days after the date on which the defendant first appeared or was brought before a court on an information for the offence.

(6) The period of 28 days in paragraph (5) above may be extended by a justice of the peace, either before or after it expires, on an application made in writing, specifying the grounds of the application. The clerk to the court shall notify all the parties of the decision of the court.

(7) The notice under paragraph (2) or (6) above shall be sent to the clerk to the court and, at the same time, copies thereof shall be sent by the applicant to every other party to the proceedings. Copies of any video recording required by paragraph (2) or (3) above to accompany the notice shall at the same time be sent to the court and to any other party who has not already been served with a copy, or in the case of a defendant acting in person, shall be made available for viewing by him.

(8) A party who receives a copy of a notice under paragraph (2) above shall, within 14 days of service of the notice, notify the applicant and the clerk to the court in writing –

   (a) whether he objects to the admission of the video recording or recordings disclosed, giving his reasons why it would not be in the interests of justice for it to be admitted,

   (b) whether he would agree to the admission of part of the video recording or recording disclosed and if so, which part or parts, and

   (c) whether he wishes to be represented at any hearing of the application.

(9) After the expiry of the period referred to in paragraph (8) above, a justice of

the peace shall determine whether an application under paragraph (1) above is to be dealt with –

(a) without a hearing, or

(b) where any party notifies the clerk to the court pursuant to paragraph (8) that he objects to the admission of any part of the video recording and that he wishes to be represented at any hearing, or in any other case where the court so directs, at a hearing at which the applicant and such other party or parties as the court may direct may be represented,

and the clerk to the court shall notify the applicant and, where necessary, the other party or parties, of the time and place of any such hearing.

(10) The clerk to the court shall within 3 days (not counting Saturdays, Sundays, Good Friday, Christmas Day or Bank Holidays) of the decision of the court in relation to an application under paragraph (1) above being made, notify all the parties of it in the form prescribed in Form 53 of Schedule 2 or a form to the like effect, and, where leave is granted, the notification shall state whether the whole or specified parts only of the video recording or recordings disclosed are to be admitted in evidence.

PART V – MISCELLANEOUS

Register of proceedings in youth court

25   Such part of the register kept in pursuance of rules made under the Magistrates' Courts Act 1980 as relates to proceedings in a youth court shall be kept in a separate book.

Issue of summons or warrant to enforce attendance of parent or guardian

26   Where a child or young person is charged with an offence, or is for any other reason brought before a court, a summons or warrant may be issued by a court to enforce the attendance of a parent or guardian under section 34A of the Act of 1933, in the same manner as if an information were laid upon which a summons or warrant could be issued against a defendant under the Magistrates' Courts Act 1980 and a summons to the child or young person may include a summons to the parent or guardian to enforce his attendance for the said purpose.

Payment of money by person subject to attendance centre order

27 (1) Where a person under the age of eighteen is ordered, under section 17 of the Criminal Justice Act 1982, to attend at an attendance centre in default of payment of a sum of money, payment may thereafter be made –

(a) of the whole of the said sum, to the clerk of the court which made the order, or

(b) the whole or, subject to paragraph (2), any part of the said sum, to the officer in charge of the attendance centre specified in the order.

(2) The officer mentioned in paragraph (1)(b) may not accept a payment of part of the said sum unless it is an amount required to secure a reduction of one complete hour, or some multiple thereof, in the period of attendance specified in the order.

(3) The clerk of the court shall, on receiving a payment under paragraph (1), forthwith notify the officer mentioned in paragraph (1)(b).

(4) The officer mentioned in paragraph (1)(b) shall pay any money received by him under that paragraph to the clerk of the court which made the order and shall note the receipt of the money in the register maintained at the attendance centre.

Form of warrant where young person is committed to remand centre or prison

28 Where a young person is remanded or committed under subsection (4) of section 23 of the Act of 1969 (as modified by section 98 of the Crime and Disorder Act 1998) to –

(a) local authority accommodation with a requirement that he be placed and kept in secure accommodation;

(b) a remand centre; or

(c) a prison,

the court shall record in the warrant of commitment that it has declared as mentioned in that subsection.

Forms

29 (1) The forms in Schedule 2, or forms to the like effect, may be used with such variation as the circumstances may require, and may be so used in lieu of forms contained in the Schedule to the Magistrates' Courts (Forms) Rules 1981.

(2) For the purpose of facilitating the performance by supervisors of their functions under section 14 of the Act of 1969 of advising, assisting and befriending persons subject to supervision orders the following additional requirements to be complied with by the person subject to the order are prescribed for the purpose of inclusion (if the court considers it appropriate) in supervision orders made under section 7(7) of the Act of 1969, that is to say either or both of the requirements set out in paragraph (3).

(3) The requirements mentioned in paragraph (2) are –

(a) 'That he/she shall inform the supervisor at once of any change of his/her residence or employment';

(b) 'That he/she shall keep in touch with the supervisor in accordance with such instructions as may from time to time be given by the supervisor and, in particular, that he/she shall, if the supervisor so requires, receive visits from the supervisor at his/her home.'

Attendance Centre Rules 1995 SI No 3281

Citation and commencement

1 These Rules may be cited as the Attendance Centre Rules 1995 and shall come into force on the fourteenth day after the day on which they are made (ie, 30 December 1995).

Revocation

2   The Attendance Centre Rules 1958, the Attendance Centre (Amendment) Rules 1978 and the Attendance Centre (Amendment) Rules 1983 are hereby revoked.

Interpretation

3   In the Rules, the expression –

'centre' means an attendance centre provided by the Secretary of State under section 16(1) of the Criminal Justice Act 1982;

'member of the staff' means any person for the time being carrying out any instructional or supervisory duties at a centre;

'officer in charge' means the member of the staff for the time being in charge of a centre;

'order' means an order made by a court under section 17 of the Criminal Justice Act 1982, section 15(3)(a) of the Children and Young Persons Act 1969 or Part II of Schedule 2 to the Criminal Justice Act 1991, requiring an offender to attend at a centre.

Occupation and instruction

4 (1)   The occupation and instruction given at a centre shall include a programme of group activities designed to assist offenders to acquire or develop personal responsibility, self-discipline, skills and interests.

(2)   A female member of the staff shall, save in exceptional circumstances, always be in attendance at a centre which is available for the reception of female offenders; and female offenders attending at a centre shall, at any time when participating in physical training, so far as practicable be supervised by a female member of the staff.

Officer in charge

5 (1)   The officer in charge shall maintain a record in respect of each person required to attend showing –

(a) the number of hours specified in the order;

(b) every attendance or failure to attend;

(c) the duration of each attendance; and

(d) the commission by that person of any breach of these Rules and the manner in which it is dealt with.

(2)   Subject to the provisions of rules 6(3)(b) and 11(2)(b) of these Rules, it shall be the duty of the officer in charge to ensure that any person attending at the centre who has not completed the period of attendance specified in the order is, before leaving the centre, informed (both orally and in writing) of the day and time when he is next required to attend at the centre, unless in any particular case it is impracticable to give this information.

Attendance

6 (1)   Persons required to attend at a centre shall so attend –

(a) on the first occasion, at the time specified in the order; and

(b) on any subsequent occasion, at such time as may be notified to them in accordance with rule 5(2) above, or, if no such notification has been given, at such time as may be notified to them in writing by or on behalf of the officer in charge;

and on attending shall report to, and place themselves under the direction of, the officer in charge.

(2) The occasions of a person's attendance at a centre and the duration of each attendance shall, so far as practicable and subject to the provisions of rules 11 and 12 of these Rules, be so arranged by the officer in charge that the duration of attendance on any occasion is not less than one hour.

(3) Where a person without reasonable excuse attends at the centre later than the time at which he was required to attend, the officer in charge may refuse to admit him; in such a case the person shall be regarded as having failed to attend on that occasion and shall either –

(a) be instructed in accordance with rule 5(2) above as to his further attendance at the centre; or

(b) be informed (both orally and in writing) that he is not required to attend at the centre again and that it is intended in respect of the failure to attend at the required time to take steps to bring him before a court under section 19(1) of the Criminal Justice Act 1982.

Admission to centre

7 No person, other than a person on an occasion when he is required to attend in pursuance of an order, shall be admitted to, or remain in, a centre except with the permission of the Secretary of State or the officer in charge.

Unfitness for attendance

8 (1) The officer in charge may at any time require a person attending at the centre to leave it if, in the opinion of that officer, that person is –

(a) so unwell as to be unfit to remain at the centre on that occassion; or

(b) suffering from any infectious disease or otherwise in a condition likely to be detrimental to other persons attending at the centre.

(2) Where a person is so required to leave, he shall be instructed in accordance with the rule 5(2) above as to his further attendance at the centre.

Discipline

9 The discipline of a centre shall be maintained by the personal influence of the officer in charge and other members of the staff.

10 Persons shall while attending at a centre behave in an orderly manner and shall obey any instruction given by the officer in charge or any other member of the staff.

11 (1) The officer in charge may at any time require any person committing a breach of these Rules to leave the centre.

(2) Where a person is so required to leave, he shall either –

(a) be instructed in accordance with rule 5(2) above as to his further attendance at the centre; or

(b) be informed (both orally and in writing) that he is not required to attend at the centre again and that it is intended in respect of the said breach to take steps to bring him before a court under section 19(1) of the Criminal Justice Act 1982.

12   Without prejudice to rule 11 above, where a person is required to leave the centre in accordance with rule 8(1) or 11(1) above, the officer in charge shall not count towards the duration of his attendance on that occasion the period following the requirement to leave.

13   Without prejudice to rules 6(3), 11 and 12 above, the officer incharge or any other member of the staff may deal with a person committing a breach of these Rules in either or both of the following ways, that is to say –
(a) by separating him from other persons attending at the centre;
(b) by giving him an alternative form of occupation;
during the whole or any part of the period of attendance specified in the order then remaining uncompleted.

Prosecution of Offences (Youth Courts Time Limits) Regulations 1999 SI No 2743

Citation and commencement
1   These Regulations may be cited as the Prosecution of Offences (Youth Courts Time Limits) Regulations 1999 and shall come into force on 1st November 1999.

Interpretation
2 (1)   In these Regulations, 'the 1985 Act' means the Prosecution of Offences Act 1985.

   (2)   In these Regulations, references to a person's first appearance in a relevant court in connection with an offence include his first appearance in connection with the offence after any re-instituted proceedings.

   (3)   In these Regulations, 'a relevant area' means an area specified in the Schedule to these Regulations.

   (4)   In these Regulations, 'a relevant court' means a youth court in an area specified in the Schedule to these Regulations.

   (5)   A maximum period which would, apart from this paragraph, expire on any of the days to which this paragraph applies shall be treated as expiring on the first preceding day which is not one of those days.
   The days to which this paragraph applies are Saturday, Sunday, Christmas Day, Good Friday and any day which under the Banking and Financial Dealings Act 1971 is a bank holiday in England and Wales.

3   These Regulations shall apply only in relation to proceedings instituted in a relevant area.

Overall time limit
4   In any case where a person's first appearance in a relevant court in connection with an offence is fixed to take place on or after 1st November 1999, the maximum period to be allowed to the prosecution for the completion of the stage beginning with the date fixed for that appearance and ending with

the start of his trial in a relevant court in connection with the offence shall be 99 days.

Initial stage time limit

5   In any case where a person was arrested in connection with an offence –
(a) whilst under the age of 18;
(b) on or after 1st November 1999; and
(c) in a relevant area,
the maximum period to be allowed for the completion of the stage beginning with his arrest and ending with the date fixed for his first appearance in a relevant court in connection with that offence shall be 36 days.

Sentencing time limit

6   In any case relating to a person who –
(a) was under the age of 18 –
  (i) at the time of his arrest for an offence; or
  (ii) (where he was not arrested for the offence) at the time of the laying of an information charging him with an offence; and
(b) is convicted of the offence in a relevant court on or after 1st November 1999, the period within which the stage beginning with the date of his conviction and ending with the date of his being sentenced in a relevant court for the offence should be completed shall be 29 days.

Application for extension of overall or initial stage time limit by the prosecution

7 (1) An application by the prosecution unmder section 22(3) of the 1985 Act for an extension of the time limit prescribed in regulation 4 above shall be made before the expiry of the prescribed limit.

(2) An application by the prosecution under section 22A(3) of the 1985 Act for an extension of the time limit prescribed in regulation 5 above shall be made before the expiry of the prescribed limit.

(3) Any application referred to in paragraph (1) or (2) above shall be made orally.

(4) Subject to paragraphs (5) and (6) below, the prosecution shall, not less than 2 days before making such an application, give notice in writing to the person to whom the application relates or his representative and to the clerk of the court, stating that it intends to make such an application.

(5) it shall not be necessary for the prosecution to comply with paragraph (4) above if the person to whom the application relates or his representative has informed the prosecution that he does not require such notice.

(6) If the court is satisfied that it is not practicable in all the circumstances for the prosecution to comply with paragraph (4) above, the court may direct that the prosecution need not comply with that paragraph or that the minimum period of notice required by that paragraph shall be such lesser period as the court may specify.

SCHEDULE

Areas in which the Prosecution of Offences (Youth Court Time Limits) Regulations 1999 shall have effect

The petty sessions areas of: Aberconwy; Arfon; Blackburn, Darwen and Ribble Vallen; Bromley; Burnley and Pendle; Colwyn; Corby; Croydon; Daventry; Denbighshire; Dwyfor; Flintshire; Gateshead; Kettering; Meirionnydd; Newcastle-under-Lyme and Pirehill North; Newcastle-upon-Tyne; Northamption; Staffordshire Moorlands; Stoke-on-Trent; Towcester; Wellingborough; Wrexham Maelor; and Ynys Môn/Anglesey.

International standards

European Convention on Human Rights

Article 3[1] – Prohibition of torture

No one shall be subjected to torture or to inhuman or degrading treatment or punishment.

Article 5[1] – Right to liberty and security

(1) Everyone has the right to liberty and security of person. No one shall be deprived of his liberty save in the following cases and in accordance with a procedure prescribed by law:

(a) the lawful detention of a person after conviction by a competent court;

(b) the lawful arrest or detention of a person for non-compliance with the lawful order of a court or in order to secure the fulfilment of any obligation prescribed by law;

(c) the lawful arrest or detention of a person effected for the purpose of bringing him before the competent legal authority on reasonable suspicion of having committed an offence or when it is reasonably considered necessary to prevent his committing an offence or fleeing after having done so;

(d) the detention of a minor by lawful order for the purpose of educational supervision or his lawful detention for the purpose of bringing him before the competent legal authority;

(e) the lawful detention of persons for the prevention of the spreading of infectious diseases, of persons of unsound mind, alcoholics or drug addicts or vagrants;

(f) the lawful arrest or detention of a person to prevent his effecting an unauthorised entry into the country or of a person against whom action is being taken with a view to deportation or extradition.

(2) Everyone who is arrested shall be informed promptly, in a language which he understands, of the reasons for his arrest and of any charge against him.

(3) Everyone arrested or detained in accordance with the provisions of paragraph 1(c) of this article shall be brought promptly before a judge or other officer authorised by law to exercise judicial power and shall be entitled to

---

1   Text amended according to the provisions of Protocol No 11 (ETS No 155).

trial within a reasonable time or to release pending trial. Release may be conditioned by guarantees to appear for trial.

(4) Everyone who is deprived of his liberty by arrest or detention shall be entitled to take proceedings by which the lawfulness of his detention shall be decided speedily by a court and his release ordered if the detention is not lawful.

(5) Everyone who has been the victim of arrest or detention in contravention of the provisions of this article shall have an enforceable right to compensation.

Article 6¹ – Right to a fair trial

(1) In the determination of his civil rights and obligations or of any criminal charge against him, everyone is entitled to a fair and public hearing within a reasonable time by an independent and impartial tribunal established by law. Judgment shall be pronounced publicly but the press and public may be excluded from all or part of the trial in the interests of morals, public order or national security in a democratic society, where the interests of juveniles or the protection of the private life of the parties so require, or to the extent strictly necessary in the opinion of the court in special circumstances where publicity would prejudice the interests of justice.

(2) Everyone charged with a criminal offence shall be presumed innocent until proved guilty according to law.

(3) Everyone charged with a criminal offence has the following minimum rights:
(a) to be informed promptly, in a language which he understands and in detail, of the nature and cause of the accusation against him;
(b) to have adequate time and facilities for the preparation of his defence;
(c) to defend himself in person or through legal assistance of his own choosing or, if he has not sufficient means to pay for legal assistance, to be given it free when the interests of justice so require;
(d) to examine or have examined witnesses against him and to obtain the attendance and examination of witnesses on his behalf under the same conditions as witnesses against him;
(e) to have the free assistance of an interpreter if he cannot understand or speak the language used in court.

Article 8¹ – Right to respect for private and family life

(1) Everyone has the right to respect for his private and family life, his home and his correspondence.

(2) There shall be no interference by a public authority with the exercise of this right except such as is in accordance with the law and is necessary in a democratic society in the interests of national security, public safety or the economic well-being of the country, for the prevention of disorder or crime, for the protection of health or morals, or for the protection of the rights and freedoms of others.

UN Convention on the Rights of the Child

Article 3

(1) In all actions concerning children, whether undertaken by public or private social welfare institutions, courts of law, administrative authorities or legislative bodies, the best interests of the child shall be a primary consideration.

(2) States Parties undertake to ensure the child such protection and care as is necessary for his or her well-being, taking into account the rights and duties of his or her parents, legal guardians, or other individuals legally responsible for him or her, and, to this end, shall take all appropriate legislative and administrative measures.

(3) States Parties shall ensure that the institutions, services and facilities responsible for the care or protection of children shall conform with the standards established by competent authorities, particularly in the areas of safety, health, in the number and suitability of their staff, as well as competent supervision.

Article 12

(1) States Parties shall assure to the child who is capable of forming his or her own views the right to express those views freely in all matters affecting the child, the views of the child being given due weight in accordance with the age and maturity of the child.

(2) For this purpose, the child shall in particular be provided the opportunity to be heard in any judicial and administrative proceedings affecting the child, either directly, or through a representative or an appropriate body, in a manner consistent with the procedural rules of national law.

Article 37

States Parties shall ensure that:

(a) No child shall be subjected to torture or other cruel, inhuman or degrading treatment or punishment. Neither capital punishment nor life imprisonment without possibility of release shall be imposed for offences committed by persons below eighteen years of age;

(b) No child shall be deprived of his or her liberty unlawfully or arbitrarily. The arrest, detention or imprisonment of a child shall be in conformity with the law and shall be used only as a measure of last resort and for the shortest appropriate period of time;

(c) Every child deprived of liberty shall be treated with humanity and respect for the inherent dignity of the human person, and in a manner which takes into account the needs of persons of his or her age. In particular, every child deprived of liberty shall be separated from adults unless it is considered in the child's best interest not to do so and shall have the right to maintain contact with his or her family through correspondence and visits, save in exceptional circumstances;

(d) Every child deprived of his or her liberty shall have the right to prompt access to legal and other appropriate assistance, as well as the right to challenge the legality of the deprivation of his or her liberty before a court or other competent, independent and impartial authority, and to a prompt decision on any such action.

Article 40

(1) States Parties recognise the right of every child alleged as, accused of, or recognised as having infringed the penal law to be treated in a manner consistent with the promotion of the child's sense of dignity and worth, which reinforces the child's respect for the human rights and fundamental freedoms of others and which takes into account the child's age and the desirability of promoting the child's reintegration and the child's assuming a constructive role in society.

(2) To this end, and having regard to the relevant provisions of international instruments, States Parties shall, in particular, ensure that:
(a) No child shall be alleged as, be accused of, or recognised as having infringed the penal law by reason of acts or omissions that were not prohibited by national or international law at the time they were committed;
(b) Every child alleged as or accused of having infringed the penal law has at least the following guarantees:
　(i) To be presumed innocent until proven guilty according to law;
　(ii) To be informed promptly and directly of the charges against him or her, and, if appropriate, through his or her parents or legal guardians, and to have legal or other appropriate assistance in the preparation and presentation of his or her defence;
　(iii) To have the matter determined without delay by a competent, independent and impartial authority or judicial body in a fair hearing according to law, in the presence of legal or other appropriate assistance and, unless it is considered not to be in the best interest of the child, in particular, taking into account his or her age or situation, his or her parents or legal guardians;
　(iv) Not to be compelled to give testimony or to confess guilt; to examine or have examined adverse witnesses and to obtain the participation and examination of witnesses on his or her behalf under conditions of equality;
　(v) If considered to have infringed the penal law, to have this decision and any measures imposed in consequence thereof reviewed by a higher competent, independent and impartial authority or judicial body according to law;
　(vi) To have the free assistance of an interpreter if the child cannot understand or speak the language used;
　(vii) To have his or her privacy fully respected at all stages of the proceedings.

(3) States Parties shall seek to promote the establishment of laws, procedures, authorities and institutions specifically applicable to children alleged as, accused of, or recognised as having infringed the penal law, and, in particular:
(a) The establishment of a minimum age below which children shall be presumed not to have the capacity to infringe the penal law;

(b) Whenever appropriate and desirable, measures for dealing with such children without resorting to judicial proceedings, providing that human rights and legal safeguards are fully respected.

(4) A variety of dispositions, such as care, guidance and supervision orders; counselling; probation; foster care; education and vocational training programmes and other alternatives to institutional care shall be available to ensure that children are dealt with in a manner appropriate to their well-being and proportionate both to their circumstances and the offence.

United Nations Standard Minimum Rules for the Administration of Juvenile Justice ('Beijing Rules')

PART ONE – GENERAL PRINCIPLES

1 Fundamental perspectives

1.1 Member States shall seek, in conformity with their respective general interests, to further the well-being of the juvenile and her or his family.

1.2 Member States shall endeavour to develop conditions that will ensure for the juvenile a meaningful life in the community, which, during that period in life when she or he is most susceptible to deviant behaviour, will foster a process of personal development and education that is as free from crime and delinquency as possible.

1.3 Sufficient attention shall be given to positive measures that involve the full mobilisation of all possible resources, including the family, volunteers and other community groups, as well as schools and other community institutions, for the purpose of promoting the well-being of the juvenile, with a view to reducing the need for intervention under the law, and of effectively, fairly and humanely dealing with the juvenile in conflict with the law.

1.4 Juvenile justice shall be conceived as an integral part of the national development process of each country, within a comprehensive framework of social justice for all juveniles, thus, at the same time, contributing to the protection of the young and the maintenance of a peaceful order in society.

1.5 These Rules shall be implemented in the context of economic, social and cultural conditions prevailing in each Member State.

1.6 Juvenile justice services shall be systematically developed and co-ordinated with a view to improving and sustaining the competence of personnel involved in the services, including their methods, approaches and attitudes.

Commentary

These broad fundamental perspectives refer to comprehensive social policy in general and aim at promoting juvenile welfare to the greatest possible extent, which will minimise the necessity of intervention by the juvenile justice system, and in turn, will reduce the harm that may be caused by any intervention. Such care measures for the young, before the onset of delinquency, are basic policy requisites designed to obviate the need for the application of the Rules.

Rules 1.1 to 1.3 point to the important role that a constructive social policy for juveniles will play, inter alia, in the prevention of juvenile crime and delinquency. Rule 1.4 defines juvenile justice as an integral part of social justice for juveniles, while rule 1.6 refers to the necessity of constantly improving juvenile justice, without falling behind the development of progressive social policy for juveniles in general and bearing in mind the need for consistent improvement of staff services.

Rule 1.5 seeks to take account of existing conditions in Member States which would cause the manner of implementation of particular rules necessarily to be different from the manner adopted in other States.

2   Scope of the Rules and definitions used

2.1   The following Standard Minimum Rules shall be applied to juvenile offenders impartially, without distinction of any kind, for example as to race, colour, sex, language, religion, political or other opinions, national or social origin, property, birth or other status.

2.2   For purposes of these Rules, the following definitions shall be applied by Member States in a manner which is compatible with their respective legal systems and concepts:

(a) A juvenile is a child or young person who, under the respective legal systems, may be dealt with for an offence in a manner which is different from an adult;

(b) An offence is any behaviour (act or omission) that is punishable by law under the respective legal systems;

(c) A juvenile offender is a child or young person who is alleged to have committed or who has been found to have committed an offence.

2.3   Efforts shall be made to establish, in each national jurisdiction, a set of laws, rules and provisions specifically applicable to juvenile offenders and institutions and bodies entrusted with the functions of the administration of juvenile justice and designed:

(a) To meet the varying needs of juvenile offenders, while protecting their basic rights;

(b) To meet the needs of society;

(c) To implement the following rules thoroughly and fairly.

Commentary

The Standard Minimum Rules are deliberately formulated so as to be applicable within different legal systems and, at the same time, to set some minimum standards for the handling of juvenile offenders under any definition of a juvenile and under any system of dealing with juvenile offenders. The Rules are always to be applied impartially and without distinction of any kind.

Rule 2.1 therefore stresses the importance of the Rules always being applied impartially and without distinction of any kind. The rule follows the formulation of principle 2 of the Declaration of the Rights of the Child.

Rule 2.2 defines 'juvenile' and 'offence' as the components of the notion of the 'juvenile offender', who is the main subject of these Standard Minimum Rules (see, however, also rules 3 and 4). It should be noted that age limits will depend on, and are explicitly made dependent on, each respective legal system, thus fully respecting the economic, social, political, cultural and legal systems of Member States. This makes for a wide variety of ages coming under the definition of 'juvenile', ranging from 7 years to 18 years or above. Such a variety seems inevitable in view of the different national legal systems and does not diminish the impact of these Standard Minimum Rules.

Rule 2.3 is addressed to the necessity of specific national legislation for the optimal implementation of these Standard Minimum Rules, both legally and practically.

3 Extension of the Rules

3.1 The relevant provisions of the Rules shall be applied not only to juvenile offenders but also to juveniles who may be proceeded against for any specific behaviour that would not be punishable if committed by an adult.

3.2 Efforts shall be made to extend the principles embodied in the Rules to all juveniles who are dealt with in welfare and care proceedings.

3.3 Efforts shall also be made to extend the principles embodied in the Rules to young adult offenders.

Commentary

Rule 3 extends the protection afforded by the Standard Minimum Rules for the Administration of Juvenile Justice to cover:

(a) The so-called 'status offences' prescribed in various national legal systems where the range of behaviour considered to be an offence is wider for juveniles than it is for adults (for example, truancy, school and family disobedience, public drunkenness, etc) (rule 3.1);

(b) Juvenile welfare and care proceedings (rule 3.2);

(c) Proceedings dealing with young adult offenders, depending of course on each given age limit (rule 3.3).

The extension of the Rules to cover these three areas seems to be justified. Rule 3.1 provides minimum guarantees in those fields, and rule 3.2 is considered a desirable step in the direction of more fair, equitable and humane justice for all juveniles in conflict with the law.

4 Age of criminal responsibility

4.1 In those legal systems recognising the concept of the age of criminal responsibility for juveniles, the beginning of that age shall not be fixed at too low an age level, bearing in mind the facts of emotional, mental and intellectual maturity.

Commentary

The minimum age of criminal responsibility differs widely owing to history and culture. The modern approach would be to consider whether a child can live up to the moral and psychological components of criminal responsibility; that is, whether a child, by virtue of her or his individual discernment and understanding, can be held responsible for essentially antisocial behaviour. If the age of criminal responsibility is fixed too low or if there is no lower age limit at all, the notion of responsibility would become meaningless. In general, there is a close relationship between the notion of responsibility for delinquent or criminal behaviour and other social rights and responsibilities (such as marital status, civil majority, etc). Efforts should therefore be made to agree on a reasonable lowest age limit that is applicable internationally.

5   Aims of juvenile justice

5.1   The juvenile justice system shall emphasise the well-being of the juvenile and shall ensure that any reaction to juvenile offenders shall always be in proportion to the circumstances of both the offenders and the offence.

Commentary

Rule 5 refers to two of the most important objectives of juvenile justice. The first objective is the promotion of the well-being of the juvenile. This is the main focus of those legal systems in which juvenile offenders are dealt with by family courts or administrative authorities, but the well-being of the juvenile should also be emphasised in legal systems that follow the criminal court model, thus contributing to the avoidance of merely punitive sanctions. (See also rule 14.)

The second objective is 'the principle of proportionality'. This principle is well-known as an instrument for curbing punitive sanctions, mostly expressed in terms of just deserts in relation to the gravity of the offence. The response to young offenders should be based on the consideration not only of the gravity of the offence but also of personal circumstances. The individual circumstances of the offender (for example, social status, family situation, the harm caused by the offence or other factors affecting personal circumstances) should influence the proportionality of the reactions (for example, by having regard to the offender's endeavour to indemnify the victim or to her or his willingness to turn to wholesome and useful life). By the same token, reactions aiming to ensure the welfare of the young offender may go beyond necessity and therefore infringe upon the fundamental rights of the young individual, as has been observed in some juvenile justice systems. Here, too, the proportionality of the reaction to the circumstances of both the offender and the offence, including the victim, should be safeguarded.

In essence, rule 5 calls for no less and no more than a fair reaction in any given cases of juvenile delinquency and crime. The issues combined in the rule may help to stimulate development in both regards: new and innovative types of reactions are as desirable as precautions against any undue widening of the net of formal social control over juveniles.

6   Scope of discretion

6.1   In view of the varying special needs of juveniles as well as the variety of measures available, appropriate scope for discretion shall be allowed at all stages of proceedings and at the different levels of juvenile justice administration, including investigation, prosecution, adjudication and the follow-up of dispositions.

6.2 Efforts shall be made, however, to ensure sufficient accountability at all stages and levels in the exercise of any such discretion.

6.3 Those who exercise discretion shall be specially qualified or trained to exercise it judiciously and in accordance with their functions and mandates.

Commentary
Rules 6.1, 6.2 and 6.3 combine several important features of effective, fair and humane juvenile justice administration: the need to permit the exercise of discretionary power at all significant levels of processing so that those who make determinations can take the actions deemed to be most appropriate in each individual case; and the need to provide checks and balances in order to curb any abuses of discretionary power and to safeguard the rights of the young offender. Accountability and professionalism are instruments best apt to curb broad discretion. Thus, professional qualifications and expert training are emphasised here as a valuable means of ensuring the judicious exercise of discretion in matters of juvenile offenders. (See also rules 1.6 and 2.2.) The formulation of specific guidelines on the exercise of discretion and the provision of systems of review, appeal and the like in order to permit scrutiny of decisions and accountability are emphasised in this context. Such mechanisms are not specified here, as they do not easily lend themselves to incorporation into international standard minimum rules, which cannot possibly cover all differences in justice systems.

7   Rights of juveniles
7.1 Basic procedural safeguards such as the presumption of innocence, the right to be notified of the charges, the right to remain silent, the right to counsel, the right to the presence of a parent or guardian, the right to confront and cross-examine witnesses and the right to appeal to a higher authority shall be guaranteed at all stages of proceedings.

Commentary
Rule 7.1 emphasises some important points that represent essential elements for a fair and just trial and that are internationally recognised in existing human rights instruments. (See also rule 14.) The presumption of innocence, for instance, is also to be found in article 11 of the Universal Declaration of Human rights and in article 14, paragraph 2, of the International Covenant on Civil and Political Rights.
Rules 14 seq. of these Standard Minimum Rules specify issues that are important for proceedings in juvenile cases, in particular, while rule 7.1 affirms the most basic procedural safeguards in a general way.

8   Protection of privacy
8.1 The juvenile's right to privacy shall be respected at all stages in order to avoid harm being caused to her or him by undue publicity or by the process of labelling.

8.2 In principle, no information that may lead to the identification of a juvenile offender shall be published.

Commentary

Rule 8 stresses the importance of the protection of the juvenile's right to privacy. Young persons are particularly susceptible to stigmatisation. Criminological research into labelling processes has provided evidence of the detrimental effects (of different kinds) resulting from the permanent identification of young persons as 'delinquent' or 'criminal'.

Rule 8 stresses the importance of protecting the juvenile from the adverse effects that may result from the publication in the mass media of information about the case (for example the names of young offenders, alleged or convicted). The interest of the individual should be protected and upheld, at least in principle. (The general contents of rule 8 are further specified in rule 21.)

9   Saving clause

9.1   Nothing in these Rules shall be interpreted as precluding the application of the Standard Minimum Rules for the Treatment of Prisoners adopted by the United Nations and other human rights instruments and standards recognised by the international community that relate to the care and protection of the young.

Commentary

Rule 9 is meant to avoid any misunderstanding in interpreting and implementing the present Rules in conformity with principles contained in relevant existing or emerging international human rights instruments and standards – such as the Universal Declaration of Human Rights, the International Covenant on Economic, Social and Cultural Rights and the International Covenant on Civil and Political Rights, and the Declaration of the Rights of the Child and the draft convention on the rights of the child. It should be understood that the application of the present Rules is without prejudice to any such international instruments which may contain provisions of wider application. (See also rule 27.)

PART TWO – INVESTIGATION AND PROSECUTION

10   Initial contact

10.1   Upon the apprehension of a juvenile, her or his parents or guardian shall be immediately notified of such apprehension, and, where such immediate notification is not possible, the parents or guardian shall be notified within the shortest possible time thereafter.

10.2   A judge or other competent official or body shall, without delay, consider the issue of release.

10.3   Contacts between the law enforcement agencies and a juvenile offender shall be managed in such a way as to respect the legal status of the juvenile, promote the well-being of the juvenile and avoid harm to her or him, with due regard to the circumstances of the case.

Commentary

Rule 10.1 is in principle contained in rule 92 of the Standard Minimum Rules for the Treatment of Prisoners.

The question of release (rule 10.2) shall be considered without delay by a judge or other competent official. The latter refers to any person or institution in the broadest sense of the term, including community boards or police authorities having power to release an arrested person. (See also the International Covenant on Civil and Political Rights, article 9, paragraph 3.) Rule 10.3 deals with some fundamental aspects of the procedures and behaviour on the part of the police and other law enforcement officials in cases of juvenile crime. To 'avoid harm' admittedly is flexible wording and covers many features of possible interaction (for example the use of harsh language, physical violence or exposure to the environment). Involvement in juvenile justice processes in itself can be 'harmful' to juveniles; the term 'avoid harm' should be broadly interpreted, therefore, as doing the least harm possible to the juvenile in the first instance, as well as any additional or undue harm. This is especially important in the initial contact with law enforcement agencies, which might profoundly influence the juvenile's attitude towards the State and society. Moreover, the success of any further intervention is largely dependent on such initial contacts. Compassion and kind firmness are important in these situations.

11 Diversion

11.1 Consideration shall be given, wherever appropriate, to dealing with juvenile offenders without resorting to formal trial by the competent authority, referred to in rule 14.1 below.

11.2 The police, the prosecution or other agencies dealing with juvenile cases shall be empowered to dispose of such cases, at their discretion, without recourse to formal hearings, in accordance with the criteria laid down for that purpose in the respective legal system and also in accordance with the principles contained in these Rules.

11.3 Any diversion involving referral to appropriate community or other services shall require the consent of the juvenile, or her or his parents or guardian, provided that such decision to refer a case shall be subject to review by a competent authority, upon application.

11.4 In order to facilitate the discretionary disposition of juvenile cases, efforts shall be made to provide for community programmes, such as temporary supervision and guidance, restitution, and compensation of victims.

Commentary

Diversion, involving removal from criminal justice processing and, frequently, redirection to community support services, is commonly practised on a formal and informal basis in many legal systems. This practice serves to hinder the negative effects of subsequent proceedings in juvenile justice administration (for example, the stigma of conviction and sentence). In many cases, non-intervention would be the best response. Thus, diversion at the outset and without referral to alternative (social) services may be the optimal response. This is especially the case where the offence is of a non-serious nature and where the family, the school or other informal social control institutions have already reacted, or are likely to react, in an appropriate and constructive manner.

As stated in rule 11.2, diversion may be used at any point of decision-making by the police, the prosecution or other agencies such as the courts, tribunals, boards or councils. It may be exercised by one authority or several or all authorities, according to the rules and policies of the respective systems and in line with the present Rules. It need not necessarily be limited to petty cases, thus rendering diversion an important instrument.

Rule 11.3 stresses the important requirement of securing the consent of the young offender (or the parent or guardian) to the recommended diversionary measure(s). (Diversion to community service without such consent would contradict the Abolition of Forced Labour Convention.) However, this consent should not be left unchallengeable, since it might sometimes be given out of sheer desperation on the part of the juvenile. The rule underlines that care should be taken to minimise the potential for coercion and intimidation at all levels in the diversion process. Juveniles should not feel pressured (for example, in order to avoid court appearance) or be pressured into consenting to diversion programmes. Thus, it is advocated that provision should be made for an objective appraisal of the appropriateness of dispositions involving young offenders by a 'competent authority upon application'. (The 'competent authority' may be different from that referred to in rule 14.)

Rule 11.4 recommends the provision of viable alternatives to juvenile justice processing in the form of community-based diversion. Programmes that involve settlement by victim restitution and those that seek to avoid future conflict with the law through temporary supervision and guidance are especially commended. The merits of individual cases would make diversion appropriate, even when more serious offences have been committed (for example first offence, the act having been committed under peer pressure, etc).

12   Specialisation within the police

12.1 In order to best fulfil their functions, police officers who frequently or exclusively deal with juveniles or who are primarily engaged in the prevention of juvenile crime shall be specially instructed and trained. In large cities, special police units should be established for that purpose.

Commentary

Rule 12 draws attention to the need for specialised training for all law enforcement officials who are involved in the administration of juvenile justice. As police are the first point of contact with the juvenile justice system, it is most important that they act in an informed and appropriate manner.

While the relationship between urbanisation and crime is clearly complex, an increase in juvenile crime has been associated with the growth of large cities, particularly with rapid and unplanned growth. Specialised police units would therefore be indispensable, not only in the interest of implementing specific principles contained in the present instrument (such as rule 1.6) but more generally for improving the prevention and control of juvenile crime and the handling of juvenile offenders.

13 Detention pending trial

13.1 Detention pending trial shall be used only as a measure of last resort and for the shortest possible period of time.

13.2 Whenever possible, detention pending trial shall be replaced by alternative measures, such as close supervision, intensive care or placement with a family or in an educational setting or home.

13.3 Juveniles under detention pending trial shall be entitled to all rights and guarantees of the Standard Minimum Rules for the Treatment of Prisoners adopted by the United Nations.

13.4 Juveniles under detention pending trial shall be kept separate from adults and shall be detained in a separate institution or in a separate part of an institution also holding adults.

13.5 While in custody, juveniles shall receive care, protection and all necessary individual assistance – social, educational, vocational, psychological, medical and physical – that they may require in view of their age, sex and personality.

Commentary

The danger to juveniles of 'criminal contamination' while in detention pending trial must not be underestimated. It is therefore important to stress the need for alternative measures. By doing so, rule 13.1 encourages the devising of new and innovative measures to avoid such detention in the interest of the well-being of the juvenile.

Juveniles under detention pending trial are entitled to all the rights and guarantees of the Standard Minimum Rules for the Treatment of Prisoners as well as the International Covenant on Civil and Political Rights, especially article 9 and article 10, paragraphs 2 b) and 3.

Rule 13.4 does not prevent States from taking other measures against the negative influences of adult offenders which are at least as effective as the measures mentioned in the rule.

Different forms of assistance that may become necessary have been enumerated to draw attention to the broad range of particular needs of young detainees to be addressed (for example, females or males, drug addicts, alcoholics, mentally ill juveniles, young persons suffering from the trauma, for example, of arrest, etc).

Varying physical and psychological characteristics of young detainees may warrant classification measures by which some are kept separate while in detention pending trial, thus contributing to the avoidance of victimisation and rendering more appropriate assistance.

The Sixth United Nations Congress on the Prevention of Crime and the Treatment of Offenders, in its resolution 4 on juvenile justice standards, specified that the Rules, inter alia, should reflect the basic principle that pre-trial detention should be used only as a last resort, that no minors should be held in a facility where they are vulnerable to the negative influences of adult detainees and that account should always be taken of the needs particular to their stage of development.

PART THREE – ADJUDICATION AND DISPOSITION

14   Competent authority to adjudicate

14.1 Where the case of a juvenile offender has not been diverted (under rule 11), she or he shall be dealt with by the competent authority (court, tribunal, board, council, etc) according to the principles of a fair and just trial.

14.2 The proceedings shall be conducive to the best interests of the juvenile and shall be conducted in an atmosphere of understanding, which shall allow the juvenile to participate therein and to express herself or himself freely.

Commentary

It is difficult to formulate a definition of the competent body or person that would universally describe an adjudicating authority.

'Competent authority' is meant to include those who preside over courts or tribunals (composed of a single judge or of several members), including professional and lay magistrates as well as administrative boards (for example the Scottish and Scandinavian systems) or other more informal community and conflict resolution agencies of an adjudicatory nature.

The procedure for dealing with juvenile offenders shall in any case follow the minimum standards that are applied almost universally for any criminal defendant under the procedure known as 'due process of law'. In accordance with due process, a 'fair and just trial' includes such basic safeguards as the presumption of innocence, the presentation and examination of witnesses, the common legal defences, the right to remain silent, the right to have the last word in a hearing, the right to appeal, etc. (See also rule 7.1.)

15   Legal counsel, parents and guardians

15.1 Throughout the proceedings the juvenile shall have the right to be represented by a legal adviser or to apply for free legal aid where there is provision for such aid in the country.

15.2 The parents or the guardian shall be entitled to participate in the proceedings and may be required by the competent authority to attend them in the interest of the juvenile. They may, however, be denied participation by the competent authority if there are reasons to assume that such exclusion is necessary in the interest of the juvenile.

Commentary

Rule 15.1 uses terminology similar to that found in rule 93 of the Standard Minimum Rules for the Treatment of Prisoners. Whereas legal counsel and free legal aid are needed to assure the juvenile legal assistance, the right of the parents or guardian to participate as stated in rule 15.2 should be viewed as general psychological and emotional assistance to the juvenile – a function extending throughout the procedure.

The competent authority's search for an adequate disposition of the case may profit, in particular, from the co-operation of the legal representatives of the juvenile (or, for that matter, some other personal assistant who the juvenile can and does really trust). Such concern can be thwarted if the presence of parents or guardians at the hearings plays a negative role, for instance, if they display a hostile attitude towards the juvenile, hence, the possibility of their exclusion must be provided for.

16 Social inquiry reports

16.1 In all cases except those involving minor offences, before the competent authority renders a final disposition prior to sentencing, the background and circumstances in which the juvenile is living or the conditions under which the offence has been committed shall be properly investigated so as to facilitate judicious adjudication of the case by the competent authority.

Commentary

Social inquiry reports (social reports or pre-sentence reports) are an indispensable aid in most legal proceedings involving juveniles. The competent authority should be informed of relevant facts about the juvenile, such as social and family background, school career, educational experiences, etc. For this purpose, some jurisdictions use special social services or personnel attached to the court or board. Other personnel, including probation officers, may serve the same function. The rule therefore requires that adequate social-services should be available to deliver social inquiry reports of a qualified nature.

17 Guiding principles in adjudication and disposition

17.1 The disposition of the competent authority shall be guided by the following principles:
  (a) The reaction taken shall always be in proportion not only to the circumstances and the gravity of the offence but also to the circumstances and the needs of the juvenile as well as to the needs of the society;
  (b) Restrictions on the personal liberty of the juvenile shall be imposed only after careful consideration and shall be limited to the possible minimum;
  (c) Deprivation of personal liberty shall not be imposed unless the juvenile is adjudicated of a serious act involving violence against another person or of persistence in committing other serious offences and unless there is no other appropriate response;
  (d) The well-being of the juvenile shall be the guiding factor in the consideration of her or his case.

17.2 Capital punishment shall not be imposed for any crime committed by juveniles.

17.3 Juveniles shall not be subject to corporal punishment.

17.4 The competent authority shall have the power to discontinue the proceedings at any time.

Commentary

The main difficulty in formulating guidelines for the adjudication of young persons stems from the fact that there are unresolved conflicts of a philosophical nature, such as the following:
  (a) Rehabilitation versus just desert;

(b) Assistance versus repression and punishment;
(c) Reaction according to the singular merits of an individual case versus reaction according to the protection of society in general;
(d) General deterrence versus individual incapacitation.

The conflict between these approaches is more pronounced in juvenile cases than in adult cases. With the variety of causes and reactions characterising juvenile cases, these alternatives become intricately interwoven.

It is not the function of the Standard Minimum Rules for the Administration of Juvenile Justice to prescribe which approach is to be followed but rather to identify one that is most closely in consonance with internationally accepted principles. Therefore the essential elements as laid down in rule 17.1, in particular in subparagraphs (a) and (c), are mainly to be understood as practical guidelines that should ensure a common starting point; if heeded by the concerned authorities (see also rule 5), they could contribute considerably to ensuring that the fundamental rights of juvenile offenders are protected, especially the fundamental rights of personal development and education.

Rule 17.1(b) implies that strictly punitive approaches are not appropriate. Whereas in adult cases, and possibly also in cases of severe offences by juveniles, just desert and retributive sanctions might be considered to have some merit, in juvenile cases such considerations should always be outweighed by the interest of safeguarding the well-being and the future of the young person.

In line with resolution 8 of the Sixth United Nations Congress, rule 17.1(b) encourages the use of alternatives to institutionalisation to the maximum extent possible, bearing in mind the need to respond to the specific requirements of the young. Thus, full use should be made of the range of existing alternative sanctions and new alternative sanctions should be developed, bearing the public safety in mind. Probation should be granted to the greatest possible extent via suspended sentences, conditional sentences, board orders and other dispositions.

Rule 17.1(c) corresponds to one of the guiding principles in resolution 4 of the Sixth Congress which aims at avoiding incarceration in the case of juveniles unless there is no other appropriate response that will protect the public safety.

The provision prohibiting capital punishment in rule 17.2 is in accordance with article 6, paragraph 5, of the International Covenant on Civil and Political Rights.

The provision against corporal punishment is in line with article 7 of the International Covenant on Civil and Political Rights and the Declaration on the Protection of All Persons from Being Subjected to Torture and Other Cruel, Inhuman or Degrading Treatment or Punishment, as well as the Convention against Torture and Other Cruel, Inhuman or Degrading Treatment or Punishment and the draft convention on the rights of the child.

The power to discontinue the proceedings at any time (rule 17.4) is a characteristic inherent in the handling of juvenile offenders as opposed to adults. At any time, circumstances may become known to the competent authority which would make a complete cessation of the intervention appear to be the best disposition of the case.

18 Various disposition measures

18.1 A large variety of disposition measures shall be made available to the competent authority, allowing for flexibility so as to avoid institutionalisation to the greatest extent possible. Such measures, some of which may be combined, include:

(a) Care, guidance and supervision orders;
(b) Probation;
(c) Community service orders;
(d) Financial penalties, compensation and restitution;
(e) Intermediate treatment and other treatment orders;
(f) Orders to participate in group counselling and similar activities;
(g) Orders concerning foster care, living communities or other educational settings;
(h) Other relevant orders.

18.2 No juvenile shall be removed from parental supervision, whether partly or entirely, unless the circumstances of her or his case make this necessary.

Commentary

Rule 18.1 attempts to enumerate some of the important reactions and sanctions that have been practised and proved successful thus far, in different legal systems. On the whole they represent promising opinions that deserve replication and further development. The rule does not enumerate staffing requirements because of possible shortages of adequate staff in some regions; in those regions measures requiring less staff may be tried or developed.

The examples given in rule 18.1 have in common, above all, a reliance on and an appeal to the community for the effective implementation of alternative dispositions. Community-based correction is a traditional measure that has taken on many aspects. On that basis, relevant authorities should be encouraged to offer community-based services.

Rule 18.2 points to the importance of the family which, according to article 10, paragraph 1, of the International Covenant on Economic, Social and Cultural Rights, is 'the natural and fundamental group unit of society'. Within the family, the parents have not only the right but also the responsibility to care for and supervise their children. Rule 18.2, therefore, requires that the separation of children from their parents is a measure of last resort. It may be resorted to only when the facts of the case clearly warrant this grave step (for example, child abuse).

19 Least possible use of institutionalisation

19.1 The placement of a juvenile in an institution shall always be a disposition of last resort and for the minimum necessary period.

Commentary
Progressive criminology advocates the use of non-institutional over institutional treatment. Little or no difference has been found in terms of the success of institutionalisation as compared to non-institutionalisation. The many adverse influences on an individual that seem unavoidable within any institutional setting evidently cannot be outbalanced by treatment efforts. This is especially the case for juveniles, who are vulnerable to negative influences. Moreover, the negative effects, not only of loss of liberty but also of separation from the usual social environment, are certainly more acute for juveniles than for adults because of their early stage of development.

Rule 19 aims at restricting institutionalisation in two regards: in quantity ('last resort') and in time ('minimum necessary period').

Rule 19 reflects one of the basic guiding principles of resolution 4 of the Sixth United Nations Congress: a juvenile offender should not be incarcerated unless there is no other appropriate response. The rule, therefore, makes the appeal that if a juvenile must be institutionalised, the loss of liberty should be restricted to the least possible degree, with special institutional arrangements for confinement and bearing in mind the differences in kinds of offenders, offences and institutions. In fact, priority should be given to 'open' over 'closed' institutions. Furthermore, any facility should be of a correctional or educational rather than of a prison type.

20   Avoidance of unnecessary delay
20.1 Each case shall from the outset be handled expeditiously, without any unnecessary delay.

Commentary
The speedy conduct of formal procedures in juvenile cases is a paramount concern. Otherwise whatever good may be achieved by the procedure and the disposition is at risk. As time passes, the juvenile will find it increasingly difficult, if not impossible, to relate the procedure and disposition to the offence, both intellectually and psychologically.

21   Records
21.1 Records of juvenile offenders shall be kept strictly confidential and closed to third parties. Access to such records shall be limited to persons directly concerned with the disposition of the case at hand or other duly authorised persons.

21.2 Records of juvenile offenders shall not be used in adult proceedings in subsequent cases involving the same offender.

Commentary
The rule attempts to achieve a balance between conflicting interests connected with records or files: those of the police, prosecution and other authorities in improving control versus the interests of the juvenile offender. (See also rule 8.) 'Other duly authorised persons' would generally include, among others, researchers.

22 Need for professionalism and training

22.1 Professional education, in-service training, refresher courses and other appropriate modes of instruction shall be utilised to establish and maintain the necessary professional competence of all personnel dealing with juvenile cases.

22.2 Juvenile justice personnel shall reflect the diversity of juveniles who come into contact with the juvenile justice system. Efforts shall be made to ensure the fair representation of women and minorities in juvenile justice agencies.

Commentary

The authorities competent for disposition may be persons with very different backgrounds (magistrates in the United Kingdom of Great Britain and Northern Ireland and in regions influenced by the common law system; legally trained judges in countries using Roman law and in regions influenced by them; and elsewhere elected or appointed laymen or jurists, members of community-based boards, etc). For all these authorities, a minimum training in law, sociology, psychology, criminology and behavioural sciences would be required. This is considered as important as the organisational specialisation and independence of the competent authority.

For social workers and probation officers, it might not be feasible to require professional specialisation as a prerequisite for taking over any function dealing with juvenile offenders. Thus, professional on-the-job instruction would be minimum qualifications.

Professional qualifications are an essential element in ensuring the impartial and effective administration of juvenile justice. Accordingly, it is necessary to improve the recruitment, advancement and professional training of personnel and to provide them with the necessary means to enable them to properly fulfil their functions.

All political, social, sexual, racial, religious, cultural or any other kind of discrimination in the selection, appointment and advancement of juvenile justice personnel should be avoided in order to achieve impartiality in the administration of juvenile justice. This was recommended by the Sixth Congress. Furthermore, the Sixth Congress called on Member States to ensure the fair and equal treatment of women as criminal justice personnel and recommended that special measures should be taken to recruit, train and facilitate the advancement of female personnel in juvenile justice administration.

PART FOUR – NON-INSTITUTIONAL TREATMENT

23 Effective implementation of disposition

23.1 Appropriate provisions shall be made for the implementation of orders of the competent authority, as referred to in rule 14.1 above, by that authority itself or by some other authority as circumstances may require.

23.2 Such provisions shall include the power to modify the orders as the competent authority may deem necessary from time to time, provided that such modification shall be determined in accordance with the principles contained in these Rules.

Commentary

Disposition in juvenile cases, more so than in adult cases, tends to influence the offender's life for a long period of time. Thus, it is important that the competent authority or an independent body (parole board, probation office, youth welfare institutions or others) with qualifications equal to those of the competent authority that originally disposed of the case should monitor the implementation of the disposition. In some countries, a juge de l'exécution des peines has been installed for this purpose.

The composition, powers and functions of the authority must be flexible; they are described in general terms in rule 23 in order to ensure wide acceptability.

24 Provision of needed assistance

24.1 Efforts shall be made to provide juveniles, at all stages of the proceedings, with necessary assistance such as lodging, education or vocational training, employment or any other assistance, helpful and practical, in order to facilitate the rehabilitative process.

Commentary

The promotion of the well-being of the juvenile is of paramount consideration. Thus, rule 24 emphasises the importance of providing requisite facilities, services and other necessary assistance as may further the best interests of the juvenile throughout the rehabilitative process.

25 Mobilisation of volunteers and other community services

25.1 Volunteers, voluntary organisations, local institutions and other community resources shall be called upon to contribute effectively to the rehabilitation of the juvenile in a community setting and, as far as possible, within the family unit.

Commentary

This rule reflects the need for a rehabilitative orientation of all work with juvenile offenders. Co-operation with the community is indispensable if the directives of the competent authority are to be carried out effectively. Volunteers and voluntary services, in particular, have proved to be valuable resources but are at present under-utilised. In some instances, the co-operation of ex-offenders (including ex-addicts) can be of considerable assistance.

Rule 25 emanates from the principles laid down in rules 1.1 to 1.6 and follows the relevant provisions of the International Covenant on Civil and Political Rights.

PART FIVE – INSTITUTIONAL TREATMENT

26 Objectives of institutional treatment

26.1 The objective of training and treatment of juveniles placed in institutions is to provide care, protection, education and vocational skills, with a view to assisting them to assume socially constructive and productive roles in society.

26.2 Juveniles in institutions shall receive care, protection and all necessary assistance – social, educational, vocational, psychological, medical and physical – that they may require because of their age, sex, and personality and in the interest of their wholesome development.

26.3 Juveniles in institutions shall be kept separate from adults and shall be detained in a separate institution or in a separate part of an institution also holding adults.

26.4 Young female offenders placed in an institution deserve special attention as to their personal needs and problems. They shall by no means receive less care, protection, assistance, treatment and training than young male offenders. Their fair treatment shall be ensured.

26.5 In the interest and well-being of the institutionalised juvenile, the parents or guardians shall have a right of access.

26.6 Inter-ministerial and inter-departmental co-operation shall be fostered for the purpose of providing adequate academic or, as appropriate, vocational training to institutionalised juveniles, with a view to ensuring that they do not leave the institution at an educational disadvantage.

Commentary

The objectives of institutional treatment as stipulated in rules 26.1 and 26.2 would be acceptable to any system and culture. However, they have not yet been attained everywhere, and much more has to be done in this respect. Medical and psychological assistance, in particular, are extremely important for institutionalised drug addicts, violent and mentally ill young persons.

The avoidance of negative influences through adult offenders and the safeguarding of the well-being of juveniles in an institutional setting, as stipulated in rule 26.3, are in line with one of the basic guiding principles of the Rules, as set out by the Sixth Congress in its resolution 4. The rule does not prevent States from taking other measures against the negative influences of adult offenders, which are at least as effective as the measures mentioned in the rule. (See also rule 13.4.)

Rule 26.4 addresses the fact that female offenders normally receive less attention than their male counterparts, as pointed out by the Sixth Congress. In particular, resolution 9 of the Sixth Congress calls for the fair treatment of female offenders at every stage of criminal justice processes and for special attention to their particular problems and needs while in custody. Moreover, this rule should also be considered in the light of the Caracas Declaration of the Sixth Congress, which, inter alia, calls for equal treatment in criminal justice administration, and against the background of the Declaration on the Elimination of Discrimination against Women and the Convention on the Elimination of All Forms of Discrimination against Women.

The right of access (rule 26.5) follows from the provisions of rules 7.1, 10.1, 15.2 and 18.2. Inter-ministerial and inter-departmental co-operation (rule 26.6) are of particular importance in the interest of generally enhancing the quality of institutional treatment and training.

27 Application of the Standard Minimum Rules for the Treatment of Prisoners adopted by the United Nations

27.1 The Standard Minimum Rules for the Treatment of Prisoners and related recommendations shall be applicable as far as relevant to the treatment of juvenile offenders in institutions, including those in detention pending adjudication.

27.2 Efforts shall be made to implement the relevant principles laid down in the Standard Minimum Rules for the Treatment of Prisoners to the largest possible extent so as to meet the varying needs of juveniles specific to their age, sex and personality.

Commentary

The Standard Minimum Rules for the Treatment of Prisoners were among the first instruments of this kind to be promulgated by the United Nations. It is generally agreed that they have had a world-wide impact. Although there are still countries where implementation is more an aspiration than a fact, those Standard Minimum Rules continue to be an important influence in the humane and equitable administration of correctional institutions. Some essential protections covering juvenile offenders in institutions are contained in the Standard Minimum Rules for the Treatment of Prisoners (accommodation, architecture, bedding, clothing, complaints and requests, contact with the outside world, food, medical care, religious service, separation of ages, staffing, work, etc) as are provisions concerning punishment and discipline, and restraint for dangerous offenders. It would not be appropriate to modify those Standard Minimum Rules according to the particular characteristics of institutions for juvenile offenders within the scope of the Standard Minimum Rules for the Administration of Juvenile Justice.

Rule 27 focuses on the necessary requirements for juveniles in institutions (rule 27.1) as well as on the varying needs specific to their age, sex and personality (rule 27.2). Thus, the objectives and content of the rule inter-relate to the relevant provisions of the Standard Minimum Rules for the Treatment of Prisoners.

28 Frequent and early recourse to conditional release

28.1 Conditional release from an institution shall be used by the appropriate authority to the greatest possible extent, and shall be granted at the earliest possible time.

28.2 Juveniles released conditionally from an institution shall be assisted and supervised by an appropriate authority and shall receive full support by the community.

Commentary

The power to order conditional release may rest with the competent authority, as mentioned in rule 14.1 or with some other authority. In view of this, it is adequate to refer here to the 'appropriate' rather than to the 'competent' authority.

Circumstances permitting, conditional release shall be preferred to serving a full sentence. Upon evidence of satisfactory progress towards rehabilitation, even offenders who had been deemed dangerous at the time of their institutionalisation can be conditionally released whenever feasible. Like probation, such release may be conditional on the satisfactory fulfilment of the requirements specified by the relevant authorities for a period of time established in the decision, for example relating to 'good behaviour' of the offender, attendance in community programmes, residence in half-way houses, etc.

In the case of offenders conditionally released from an institution, assistance and supervision by a probation or other officer (particularly where probation has not yet been adopted) should be provided and community support should be encouraged.

29 Semi-institutional arrangements

29.1 Efforts shall be made to provide semi-institutional arrangements, such as half-way houses, educational homes, day-time training centres and other such appropriate arrangements that may assist juveniles in their proper reintegration into society.

Commentary

The importance of care following a period of institutionalisation should not be underestimated. This rule emphasises the necessity of forming a net of semi-institutional arrangements. This rule also emphasises the need for a diverse range of facilities and services designed to meet the different needs of young offenders re-entering the community and to provide guidance and structural support as an important step towards successful reintegration into society.

PART SIX – RESEARCH, PLANNING, POLICY FORMULATION AND EVALUATION

30 Research as a basis for planning, policy formulation and evaluation

30.1 Efforts shall be made to organise and promote necessary research as a basis for effective planning and policy formulation.

30.2 Efforts shall be made to review and appraise periodically the trends, problems and causes of juvenile delinquency and crime as well as the varying particular needs of juveniles in custody.

30.3 Efforts shall be made to establish a regular evaluative research mechanism built into the system of juvenile justice administration and to collect and analyse relevant data and information for appropriate assessment and future improvement and reform of the administration.

30.4 The delivery of services in juvenile justice administration shall be systematically planned and implemented as an integral part of national development efforts.

Commentary

The utilisation of research as a basis for an informed juvenile justice policy is widely acknowledged as an important mechanism for keeping practices abreast of advances in knowledge and the continuing development and improvement of the juvenile justice system. The mutual feedback between research and policy is especially important in juvenile justice. With rapid and often drastic changes in the life-styles of the young and in the forms and dimensions of juvenile crime, the societal and justice responses to juvenile crime and delinquency quickly become outmoded and inadequate.

Rule 30 thus establishes standards for integrating research into the process of policy formulation and application in juvenile justice administration. The rule draws particular attention to the need for regular review and evaluation of existing programmes and measures and for planning within the broader context of overall development objectives.

A constant appraisal of the needs of juveniles, as well as the trends and problems of delinquency, is a prerequisite for improving the methods of formulating appropriate policies and establishing adequate interventions, at both formal and informal levels. In this context, research by independent persons and bodies should be facilitated by responsible agencies, and it may be valuable to obtain and to take into account the views of juveniles themselves, not only those who come into contact with the system.

The process of planning must particularly emphasise a more effective and equitable system for the delivery of necessary services. Towards that end, there should be a comprehensive and regular assessment of the wide-ranging, particular needs and problems of juveniles and an identification of clear-cut priorities. In that connection, there should also be a co-ordination in the use of existing resources, including alternatives and community support that would be suitable in setting up specific procedures designed to implement and monitor established programmes.

Grave crimes

Detention under Children and Young Persons Act 1933 s53(2) and (3) is available for the following offences:

- Abduction of a woman by force or for the sake of her property (Sexual Offences Act 1956 s17 – 14 years).
- Aggravated burglary (Theft Act 1968 s10 – life).
- Aiding suicide (Suicide Act 1961 s2 – 14 years).
- Arson (Criminal Damage Act 1971 s1 – life).
- Assault with intent to rob (Theft Act 1968 s8 – life).
- Attempted murder (Criminal Attempts Act 1981 s4(1) – life).
- Attempting to strangle with intent to endanger life (Offences Against the Person Act 1861 s21 – life).
- Blackmail (Theft Act 1968 s21 – 14 years).
- Buggery with a person under the age of 16 or with an animal (Sexual Offences Act 1956 s12 – life).
- Burglary of dwelling (Theft Act 1968 s9(3)(a) – 14 years) (*nb: does not include non-dwelling burglaries*).
- Causing death by dangerous driving (Road Traffic Act 1988 s1 – 10 years).[1]
- Causing death by careless driving while under the influence of alcohol or drugs (Road Traffic Act 1988 s3 – 10 years).[2]
- Child destruction (Infant Life (Preservation) Act 1929 s1 – life).
- Demanding money with menaces (Theft Act 1968 s21 – 14 years).
- Destroying property with intent to endanger life (Criminal Damage Act 1971 s1 – life).
- Drugs:
  - production (Misuse of Drugs Act 1971 s4(2): class A – life; class B – 14 years);
  - supplying/offering to supply/being concerned in the supply (Misuse of Drugs Act 1971 s4(3): class A – life; class B – 14 years);
  - possession with intent to supply (Misuse of Drugs Act 1971 s5(3): class A – life; class B – 14 years);
  - cultivation of cannabis (s6(2) Misuse of Drugs Act 1971 s6(2) – 14 years).
- Endangering safety of aircraft (Aviation Security Act 1982 s3 – life).

1 Only applies to offenders who have attained the age of 14 by the date of conviction.
2 Ibid.

- Endangering safety of railway passengers (Offences Against the Person Act 1961 s32 – life).
- Explosives:
  - causing explosion likely to endanger life (Explosive Substances Act 1883 s1 – life);
  - attempting to cause explosion (Explosive Substances Act 1883 s2 – life);
  - possession of explosive substance with intent (Explosive Substances Act 1883 s2 – life);
  - making or possessing explosive substance (Explosive Substances Act 1883 s4 – 14 years).
- False imprisonment (common law).
- Firearms:
  - possession with intent to endanger life (Firearms Act 1968 s16 – life);
  - using a firearm with intent to resist arrest (Firearms Act 1968 s17(1) – life);
  - possession of a firearm during the commission of a scheduled offence (Firearms Act 1968 s17(2) – 14 years);
  - possession with intent to commit an indictable offence or to resist arrest (Firearms Act 1968 s18 – 14 years).
- GBH with intent (Offences Against the Person Act 1861 s18 – life).
- Handling stolen goods (Theft Act 1968 s22 – 14 years).
- Hijacking (Aviation Security Act 1982 s1 – life).
- Incest by man with girl under the age of 13 (Sexual Offences Act 1956 s10 – life).
- Indecent assault upon a female (Sexual Offences Act 1956 s14 – 10 years).[3]
- Indecent assault upon a male (Sexual Offences Act 1956 s15 – 10 years).[4] Grave crime by virtue of Crime (Sentences) Act 1997 s44 – only for offences committed on or after 1 October 1997.
- Infanticide (Infanticide Act 1938 s1 – life).
- Kidnapping (common law).
- Manslaughter (Offences Against the Person Act 1981 s5 – life).
- Perverting the course of justice (common law).
- Placing object on railway with intent to obstruct or overthrow any engine (Malicious Damage Act 1861 s35 – life).
- Rape (Sexual Offences Act 1956 s1 – life).
- Robbery (Theft Act 1968 s8 – life).
- Soliciting to murder (Offences Against the Person Act 1861 s4 – life).
- Throwing corrosive liquid with intent to endanger life (Offences Against the Person Act 1861 s29 – life).

---

3 Grave crime by virtue of Criminal Justice Act 1991 s64.
4 Grave crime by virtue of Crime (Sentences) Act 1997 s44 – only for offences committed on or after 1 October 1997.

- Throwing object with intent to endanger rail passenger (Offences Against the Person Act 1861 s33 – life).
- Torture (Criminal Justice Act 1988 s134 – life).
- Unlawful sexual intercourse with a girl under the age of 13 (Sexual Offences Act 1956 s5 – life).
- Wounding with intent (Offences Against the Person Act 1861 s18 – life).

Note that an attempt or conspiracy to commit any of the above offences will also be a grave crime (Criminal Attempts Act 1981 s1 and Criminal Law Act 1977 s1 respectively).

Sentencing options

Sentence	Age	Child				Young person				Young offender
		10	11	12	13	14	15	16	17	18–20
Discharges		•	•	•	•	•	•	•	•	•
Fine		•	•	•	•	•	•	•	•	•
Fine or one day										•
Compensation		•	•	•	•	•	•	•	•	•
Deprivation		P	P	P	P	P	P	P	P	
Attendance centre order		•	•	•	•	•	•	•	•	•
Supervision		•	•	•	•	•	•	•	•	
Action plan order		P	P	P	P	P	P	P	P	
Curfew		P	P	P	P	P	P	•	•	•
Probation								•	•	•
Community service order								•	•	•
Combination order								•	•	•
Drug treatment & testing order								P	P	P
Secure training order *				•	•	•				
YOI							•	•	•	•
Detention and training order ****				•	•	•	•	•	•	
s53(2)(a) detention		•	•	•	•	•	•	•	•	
s53(2)(b) detention (death by driving)						•	•	•	•	
Custody for life										•
s53(1) detention HMP **		•	•	•	•	•	•	•	•	
Hospital order		•	•	•	•	•	•	•	•	•
Guardianship order								•	•	•
Restriction order ***		•	•	•	•	•	•	•	•	•

*   Must have attained age of 12 at date of offence
**   Offence must have been committed while under the age of 18
***   Applies only in Crown Court. No power to commit until the age of 14
****   Not yet in force – implementation date planned for April 2000.
P   Pilot areas only – see appendix 8.

Further reading

Aggleton, P, Hurry, J, and Warwick, I (eds), *Young People and Mental Health* (Wiley, 2000)

Audit Commission, *Misspent Youth: Young People and Crime (National Report)* (1996).

Audit Commission, *Misspent Youth: The Challenge for Youth Justice* (1998).

Bedingfield, D, *The Child in Need: Children, the State and the Law* (Family Law, 1998).

Boswell, G, *Violent Victims: The prevalence of abuse and loss in the lives of section 53 offenders* (Prince's Trust, 1995).

Cape, E, with Luqmani, J, *Defending Suspects at Police Stations* (Legal Action Group, 3rd edn, 1999).

Cavadino, P (ed.), *Children Who Kill* (Waterside Press, 1996).

Coleman, J, and Hendry, L, The Nataure of Adolescence (Routledge, 2nd edn, 1990).

Dawson, P, and Stevens, R, *Secure Accommodation: A Labyrinthine Law* (Barry Rose, 1995).

Department of Health, *The Children Act 1989: Guidance and Regulations* (HMSO, 1991).

Department of Health and Welsh Office, *Mental Health Act 1983 Code of Practice* (HMSO, 1999).

Devlin, A, *Criminal Classes: Offenders at School* (Waterside Press, 1995).

Erooga, M, and Masson, H (eds), *Children and Young People Who Sexually Abuse Others* (Routledge, 1999).

Evans, R, *The Conduct of Police Interviews with Juveniles (Royal Commission on Criminal Justice Research Study No 8)* (HMSO, 1993).

Farrington, D, *Understanding and Preventing Youth Crime* (Joseph Rowntree Foundation, York, 1996).

Ford, J, Hughes, M, and Ruebain, D, *Education Law and Practice* (Legal Action Group, 1999).

Fortin, J, *Children's Rights and the Developing Law* (Butterworths, 1998).

Gordon, W, Watkins, M, and Cuddy, P, *Introduction to Youth Justice* (Waterside Press, 1999).

Graef, R, *Living Dangerously: Young Offenders in Their Own Words* (Harper Collins, 1992).

Graham, J, and Bowling, B, *Young People and Crime (Home Office Research Study 145)* (Home Office, 1995).

Grisso, T, *Forensic Evaluation of Juveniles* Professional Resource Press, Sarasota, USA, 1998).

Haines, K, and Drakeford, M, *Young People and Youth Justice* (Macmillan 1998).

Harris, R, and Timms, N, *Secure Accommodation in Child Care* (Routledge, 1993).

Harrison, J, and Cragg, S, *Police Misconduct: Legal Remedies* (Legal Action Group, 3rd edn, 1995).

HM Inspectorate of Prisons, *Young Prisoners: A Thematic Review* (Home Office, 1998).

Home Office, *No More Excuses – A New Approach to Tackling Crime in England and Wales*. Cm 3809 (1997).

Howard League for Penal Reform, *Banged Up, Beaten Up, Cutting Up* (1995).

JUSTICE, *Children and Homicide: Appropriate procedures for juveniles in murder and manslaughter cases* (1996).

Levenson, H, Fairweather, F, and Cape, E, *Police Powers* (Legal Action Group, 3rd edn, 1996).

McMillan, M (ed), *If I Could Fly: An anthology of writings from young men at Orchard Lodge Resource Centre* (London Borough of Southwark, 1998).

Martin, C (ed), *The ISTD Handbook of Community Programmes for Young and Juvenile Offenders* (Waterside Press, 2nd edn, 1998).

Nagell, A, and Newburn, T, *Persistent Young Offenders* (Policy Studies Institute, 1994).

Rutter, M, Giller, H, and Hagell, A, *Antisocial Behaviour by Young People* (Cambridge University Press, 1998).

Rutherford, A, *Growing out of Crime: The New Era* (Waterside Press, 1992).

Starmer, K, *European Human Rights Law* (Legal Action Group, 1999).

Van Bueren, G, *The International Law on the Rights of the Child* (Martinus Nijhoff Publishers, 1998).

White, R, Carr, P, and Lowe, N, *The Children Act in Practice* (Butterworths, 2nd edn, 1995).

Zander, M, *The Police and Criminal Evidence Act 1984* (Sweet & Maxwell, 3rd edn, 1995).

Useful contacts

Advisory Centre on Education
1B Aberdeen Studios
22–24 Highbury Grove
London N5 2DQ

Tel: 020 7354 8318
Advice line: 020 7354 8321 (open 2.00 to 5.00pm Monday to Friday)
Fax: 020 7354 9069
E-mail: ace-ed@easynet.co.uk
Website: www.ace-ed.org.uk

British Juvenile and Family Courts Society
44 Queen Anne Street
London W1M 9LA

Tel: 020 7224 3566
Fax: 020 7224 3577

Organises training courses and conferences. Affiliated to the International
Association of Juvenile and Family Court Magistrates.

Children's Legal Centre
University of Essex
Wivenhoe Park
Colchester
Essex CO4 3SQ

Advice line: 01206 873820 (open every afternoon Monday to Friday)
Website: www2.essex.ac.uk/clc/

Publishes information leaflets, handbooks and a monthly bulletin covering
all aspects of law and policy affecting children and young people in England
and Wales.

Department for Education and Employment
Sanctuary Building
Great Smith Street
London SW1 3BT

Tel: 020 7925 5000
Website: www.dfee.gov.uk

Department of Health
Richmond House
79 Whitehall
London SW1A 2NS

Tel: 020 7210 4850
Website: www.doh.gov.uk

Home Office
50 Queen Anne's Gate
London SW1H 9AT

Switchboard: 020 7273 4000
Webiste: www.homeoffice.gov.uk

NACRO

London office:
NACRO Youth Crime Section
169 Clapham Road
London SW9 0PU

Tel: 020 7582 6500
Fax: 020 7735 4666

Manchester office:
NACRO Youth Crime Section
First Floor
Princess House
105–107 Princess Street
Manchester M1 6DD

Tel: 0161 236 5271
Fax: 0161 236 5618

National Association of Youth Justice (NAYJ)
Ken Hunnybun
Membership Secretary
NAYJ
Bitter End
4 Spring Close
Ratby
Leicester LE6 0XD

E-mail: KenHunnybun@aol.com
Website: www.nayj.org.uk

National Remand Review Initiative
The Remand Review Initiative was established by the Children's Society. It
receives funding from the Youth Justice Board for England and Wales. The
regional projects provide a service to all children and young people between
the ages of 10 to 17 remanded to certain prisons and secure units and held
within the regional boundaries outlined below.

The Children's Society has a website at www.the-childrens-society.org.uk.

Central Unit
Sharon Moore, National Co-ordinator
Suite 2a and 2b, The Whitehouse
3a Chapel Street
Stafford ST16 2BX

Tel: 01785 250200
Fax: 01785 250300
E-mail: ncu@the-childrens-society.org.uk

London Project
(Inner London boroughs only)
Concetta Perôt, Project Leader
Suite 1, Charan House
18 Union Road
London SW4 6JP

Tel: 020 7622 1117
Fax: 020 7622 9488

North West Project
(Merseyside, Cheshire, Lancashire and Greater Manchester)
Liza Durkin, Project Leader
8 Midwood House
Midwood Street
Widnes WA8 6BE

Tel: 0151 424 7696
Fax: 0151 420 3404

West Midlands Project
(West Midlands, Shropshire, Staffordshire and Warwickshire)
Jan Chown, Project Leader
Suite 5, First Floor
St Johns House
St Johns Square
Wolverhampton WV2 4BH

Tel: 01902 422225
Fax: 01902 312905

Yorkshire and Humberside Project
Justine Ashton, Project Leader
George House
18 George Street
York YO1 1QB

Tel: 01904 634648
Fax: 01904 634684

Prison Service
Home Office
Abell House
John Islip Street
London SW1P 4LH

Switchboard: 020 7217 3000
Website: www.hmprisonservice.gov.uk

Address for both the Section 53 Casework Unit and the Tariff Unit
(detention during Her Majesty's pleasure).

Young Minds
102 Clerkenwell Road
London EC1M 5SA

Tel: 020 7336 8445
Fax: 020 7336 8446
Website: www.youngminds.org.uk

Works to promote the mental health of children and young
people.

Youth Justice Board of England and Wales
11 Carteret Street
London SW1H 9DL

Tel: 020 7273 2240
Fax: 020 7273 2256
Placements Clearinghouse 020 7271 3121
E-mail: yjb@gtnet.gov.uk
Website: www.youth-justice-board.gov.uk

Pilot areas

Action plan order
Hampshire, Southampton, Portsmouth and the Isle of Wight (jointly);
London Boroughs of Hammersmith and Fulham, Kensington and Chelsea
and the City of Westminster; Sheffield; Wolverhampton.

Child safety order
Devon; Hampshire, Southampton, Portsmouth and the Isle of Wight
(jointly); London Boroughs of Hammersmith and Fulham, Kensington and
Chelsea and the City of Westminster; London Borough of Lewisham; Luton
and Bedfordshire (jointly); St Helens; Sheffield; Sunderland;
Wolverhampton.

Curfew order (for 10- to 15-year olds)
Norfolk; Greater Manchester.

Drug treatment and testing order
Croydon; Liverpool; Gloucestershire

Parenting order
Devon; Hampshire, Southampton, Portsmouth and the Isle of Wight
(jointly); London Boroughs of Hammershmith and Fulham, Kensington
and Chelsea and the City of Westminster; London Borough of Lewisham;
Luton and Bedfordshire (jointly); St Helens; Sheffield; Sunderland;
Wolverhampton.

Referral orders and youth offender panels (to be piloted from June 2000)
Blackburn and Darwen; Cardiff; London Boroughs of Hammersmith
and Fulham, Kensington and Chelsea and the City of Westminster;
Nottinghamshire; Oxfordshire; Suffolk; Swindon and Wiltshire
(jointly).

Reparation order
Blackburn; Hampshire, Southampton, Portsmouth and the Isle of Wight
(jointly); London Boroughs of Hammersmith and Fulham, Kensington and
Chelsea and the City of Westminster; Sheffield; Wolverhampton.

Reprimands and warnings
Blackburn; London Boroughs of Hammersmith and Fulham, Kensington
and Chelsea and the City of Westminster; Hampshire, Southampton,
Portsmouth and the Isle of Wight (jointly); Sheffield; Wolverhampton.

Statutory time limits
The petty session areas of Aberconwy; Arfon; Blackburn, Darwen and Ribble Valley; Bromley; Burnley and Pendle; Colwyn; Corby; Croydon; Daventry; Denbighshire; Dwyfor; Flintshire; Gateshead; Kettering; Meironnyydd; Newcastle-under-Lyme and Pirehill North; Newcastle-upon-Tyne; Northampton; Staffordshire Moorlands; Stoke-on-Trent; Towcester; Wellingborough; Wrexham Maelor and Ynys Mon/Anglesey.

Youth offending teams
Blackburn; Devon, Hampshire, Southampton, Portsmouth and the Isle of Wight (jointly); London Boroughs of Hammersmith and Fulham, Kensington and Chelsea and the City of Westminster; London Borough of Lewisham; Luton and Bedfordshire (jointly); St Helens; Sheffield; Sunderland; Wolverhampton.

Practice Direction – Trial of Children and Young Persons in the Crown Court

1   This Practice Direction applies to trials of children and young persons in the Crown Court. Effect should be given to it forthwith. In it children and young persons are together called 'young defendants'. The singular includes the plural and the masculine the feminine.

2   The steps which should be taken to comply with this Practice Direction should be judged, in any given case, taking account of the age, maturity and development (intellectual and emotional) of the young defendant on trial and all other circumstances of the case.

The overriding principle

3   Some young defendants accused of committing serious crimes may be very young and very immature when standing trial in the Crown Court. The purpose of such trial is to determine guilt (if that is in issue) and decide the appropriate sentence if the young defendant pleads guilty or is convicted. The trial process should not itself expose the young defendant to avoidable intimidation, humiliation or distress. All possible steps should be taken to assist the young defendant to understand and participate in the proceedings. The ordinary trial process should so far as necessary be adapted to meet those ends. Regard should be had to the welfare of the young defendant as required by section 44 of the Children and Young Persons Act 1933.

Before trial

4   If a young defendant is indicted jointly with an adult defendant, the court should consider at the plea and directions hearing whether the young defendant should be tried on his own and should ordinarily so order unless of opinion that a joint trial would be in the interests of justice and would not be unduly prejudicial to the welfare of the young defendant. If a young defendant is tried jointly with an adult the ordinary procedures will apply subject to such modifications (if any) as the court may see fit to order.

5   At the plea and directions hearing before trial of a young defendant, the court should consider and so far as practicable give directions on the matters covered in paragraphs 9 to 15 below inclusive.

6   It may be appropriate to arrange that a young defendant should visit, out of court hours and before the trial, the courtroom in which the trial is to be held so that he can familiarise himself with it.

7   If any case against a young defendant has attracted or may attract widespread public or media interest, the assistance of the police should be enlisted to try and ensure that a young defendant is not, when attending for the trial, exposed to intimidation, vilification or abuse.

8   The court should be ready at this stage (if it has not already done so) to give a direction under section 39 of the Children and Young Persons Act 1933 or, as the case may be, section 45 of the Youth Justice and Criminal Evidence Act 1999. Any such order, once made, should be reduced to writing and copies should on request be made available to anyone affected or potentially affected by it.

The Trial

9   The trial should, if practicable, be held in a courtroom in which all the participants are on the same or almost the same level.

10   A young defendant should normally, if he wishes, be free to sit with members of his family or others in a like relationship and in a place which permits easy, informal communication with his legal representatives and others with whom he wants or needs to communicate.

11   The court should explain the course of proceedings to a young defendant in terms he can understand, should remind those representing a young defendant of their continuing duty to explain each step of the trial to him and should ensure, so far as practicable, that the trial is conducted in language which the young defendant can understand.

12   The trial should be conducted according to a timetable which takes full account of a young defendant's inability to concentrate for long periods. Frequent and regular breaks will often be appropriate.

13   Robes and wigs should not be worn unless the young defendant asks that they should or the court for good reason orders that they should. Any person responsible for the security of a young defendant who is in custody should not be in uniform. There should be no recognisable police presence in the courtroom save for good reason.

14   The court should be prepared to restrict attendance at the trial to a small number, perhaps limited to some of those with an immediate and direct interest in the outcome of the trial. The court should rule on any challenged claim to attend.

15   Facilities for reporting the trial (subject to any direction given under section 39 of the 1933 Act or section 45 of the 1999 Act) must be provided. But the court may restrict the number of those attending in the courtroom to report the trial to such number as is judged practicable and desirable. In ruling on any challenged claim to attend the courtroom for the purpose of reporting the trial the court should be mindful of the public's general right to be informed about the administration of justice in the Crown Court. Where access to the courtroom by reporters is restricted, arrangements should be made for the proceedings to be relayed, audibly and if possible visually, to another room in the same court complex to which the media have free access if it appears that there will be a need for such additional facilities.

16   Where the court is called upon to exercise its discretion in relation to any procedural matter falling within the scope of this Practice Direction but not the subject of specific reference, such discretion should be exercised having regard to the principles in paragraph 3 above.

Appeal and committals for sentence
17   This Practice Direction does not in terms apply to appeals and committals for sentence, but regard should be paid to the effect of it if the arrangements for hearing any appeal or committal might otherwise be prejudicial to the welfare of a young defendant.

The Lord Chief Justice of England and Wales
16 February 2000

Index